FOR GOD, KING, & PEOPLE

FOR GOD, KING, & PEOPLE

Forging Commonwealth Bonds in Renaissance Virginia

ALEXANDER B. HASKELL

Published by the
OMOHUNDRO INSTITUTE OF
EARLY AMERICAN HISTORY AND CULTURE,
Williamsburg, Virginia,
and the
UNIVERSITY OF NORTH CAROLINA PRESS,
Chapel Hill

*The Omohundro Institute of
Early American History and Culture
is sponsored by the College of William and Mary.
On November 15, 1996, the Institute
adopted the present name in honor of a bequest
from Malvern H. Omohundro, Jr.*

© 2017 The University of North Carolina Press
All rights reserved

Cover art: Title page illustration, *The History of the World,*
by Walter Ralegh (Sir Walter Raleigh), engraving. 283 mm x 179 mm.
Courtesy of the British Museum, London.

Library of Congress Cataloging-in-Publication Data
Names: Haskell, Alexander B., author. | Omohundro Institute of
Early American History & Culture.
Title: For God, king, and people : forging commonwealth bonds
in Renaissance Virginia / Alexander B. Haskell.
Description: Chapel Hill : Published for the Omohundro Institute of Early
American History and Culture, Williamsburg, Virginia, by the University of
North Carolina Press, [2017] | Includes bibliographical references and index.
Identifiers: LCCN 2016055624| ISBN 9781469618029 (cloth : alk. paper) |
ISBN 9781469684086 (pbk. : alk. paper) | ISBN 9781469618036 (ebook)
Subjects: LCSH: Virginia—Colonization—History—17th century. |
Virginia—Politics and government—17th century. | Philosophy, Renaissance. |
Providence and government of God—Christianity.
Classification: LCC F229 .H37 2017 | DDC 975.5/02—dc23
LC record available at https://lccn.loc.gov/2016055624

For my parents,
both historians, and humanists in the deepest sense,
DOROTHY *and* THOMAS HASKELL

ACKNOWLEDGMENTS

This book has roots that reach far back, leaving me indebted in ways that are a pleasure to reconstruct here, even if I am certain to render my thanks incompletely.

I have benefitted greatly from my teachers. In exploring the Renaissance world of early colonization and the biblicism that attended it, I reflected frequently on the happy fact that I was still working through ideas that had first excited me years earlier in undergraduate courses with Anthony Grafton and John Gager. In graduate school, Jack Greene was an endless fount of ingenious insights and helpful formulations, a number of which ideas provided rich springs for this study. I like to think that John Marshall's impact on the chapters that follow touch even more on the spirit of the age than its content. Michael Johnson's deceptively simple advice that teaching and writing are intimately conjoined activities remains one of my cherished touchstones.

A two-year National Endowment for the Humanities postdoctoral fellowship gave me the impetus to begin this study. The award is intended to shepherd newly minted dissertations into published monographs, but, as I plunged into sixteenth- and seventeenth-century records and became caught up in the joys of discovery, the project gradually evolved into a fundamentally new book I am profoundly grateful to Fredrika Teute for supporting me in this unexpected scholarly detour and for giving me critical advice along the way. The manuscript's two anonymous readers similarly steered me out of trouble more than once and helped me to see byways and vistas that I had initially rushed past. Kaylan Stevenson bore the brunt of my course correction and painstakingly copyedited multiple drafts with remarkable patience and seemingly unflappable cheerfulness. Paul Mapp expertly saw the project through to its conclusion.

Colleagues have also been of considerable help. My fellow department members, first at Southern Illinois University, Edwardsville, and then at University of California, Riverside, were vital sources of inspiration and reinforcement. Karen Ordahl Kupperman and David Harris Sacks offered useful feedback on the dissertation as well as some of the project's earliest iterations, and I have felt very fortunate in getting to know such brilliant and generous authorities in the field. At the Institute, Patrick Erben and Lisa Voigt were good friends, and Warren Billings, Rhys Isaac, and Thad Tate were dear lunchtime companions. Elizabeth Mancke and Peter Onuf have been longtime mentors and confidants, and their encouraging words seemed always to come at the right times. In a singular act of selflessness, Sharon Salinger lent me her office, a boon especially when I first began writing and revising the manuscript.

I am particularly pleased to thank those persons who have lived with the book intimately for the past decade. Dedicating the work to my parents is altogether fitting, for who else read chapters of it aloud over wine and tea in the evenings, working their way through even the earliest dense drafts? A devastating irony lurks in the fact that the study came together as my father's capacities diminished and Alzheimer's disease took its terrible toll. His lucidness, moral seriousness, and quiet warmth remain guiding lights for me, and I hope that the book captures something of the humane spirit he and my mother fostered at home and in life. My sister Susan Haskell Khan and her husband Rehan Khan, two of the smartest people I know, read chapters and encouraged my progress. My in-laws Hernan and Dolores Reyes have been the epitome of loving extended family members.

Closer to home, Isabela, Efren, and Gabriel Haskell have grown up with this project, and their eagerness to see the finished product was certainly one spur that brought about its conclusion. I am most thankful of all to Patricia Reyes. She is the reason the book exists in the first place, and her love and friendship have propelled it from the outset.

CONTENTS

Acknowledgments *vii*

Introduction *1*

CHAPTER ONE
Providence, the Renaissance Atlantic, and Law *25*

CHAPTER TWO
Conquerors, Governors, and Chroniclers:
The Persona of the "Captain" *82*

CHAPTER THREE
The Providential State and the Legitimizing
Fellowship of "Company" *137*

CHAPTER FOUR
Framing a New Public: Virginia's Commonwealth
and the Moral Case for the Planter *199*

CHAPTER FIVE
Sir William Berkeley, the Hobbists,
and the End of Renaissance-Era Colonization *272*

Epilogue *353*

Index *369*

FOR GOD, KING, & PEOPLE

INTRODUCTION

Sir Walter Ralegh published his monumental *History of the World* in 1614, two years after the untimely death of the young Prince Henry, heir apparent to James I, and seven years after the successful establishment of a Virginia colony at Jamestown, a fort situated along a grand river given the same sovereign-evoking name, the James. The three events were undoubtedly intertwined for Ralegh. Prince Henry was the darling of the Virginia colonizers. Embraced for his firm Protestant faith but also more broadly idealized as heaven-sent, Henry was eagerly courted by the adventurers, who wanted him to serve as the *"Protector of Virginia"* at a time when his father's sovereign commitment to American colonization seemed to waver in ways that suggested sinful irresolution. Ralegh's unsuccessful efforts to plant a Virginia colony in the 1580s did little to flag his dedication to securing the king's sovereignty in America and had even propelled his attempt to establish a colony closer to Spanish possessions at Guiana. He had written his *History* for the young prince, and he cited God's decision to remove Henry from the world as his reason for ending the work prematurely, with the founding of Rome and the Roman triumph against Perseus of Macedon, rather than proceeding with his planned second and third volumes. Moreover, the *History* was itself bound up in the colonizing enterprise. Although the book peers deeply into human history, beginning audaciously with Creation and devoting much of its thousand-odd pages to the ancient patriarchs and Israelites before turning to the rise of the Egyptians, Persians, Greeks, and Romans, at every moment Ralegh is also concerned with explaining the world that he and his contemporaries inhabited. At a certain level, the *History* is little more, or less, than an extended account of sovereign dominion, the planting of colonies, the noble exertions of "captains" acting both on behalf of kings and as kings in their own right, and the framing of new "commonwealths" that promised to wrestle fallen men into obedience to their callings — all taking place under the watchful eye of

Providence and all anticipating the same set of endeavors in which Ralegh saw himself as intensely and honorably engaged across the Atlantic.[1]

It would be wrong to say that Ralegh wrote his *History* to justify colonization, as though he were composing little more than a lawyerly brief. His concerns were too scholarly for that, too fundamental and ambitious in their Christian humanist aims. More than a thousand pages of painstaking history were not needed to provide colonization with a mere gloss of lawfulness. But a thousand pages might indeed be required to locate the law, to discern its glimmerings at the all-too-infrequent and often-obscure junctures where human actions and God's will converged. This was precisely how Ralegh perceived both history and law; both proceeded along pathways that, in certain unforeseeable circumstances and at certain moments easy to miss or to misjudge, brought human actions and God's Providence into the exquisite concordance that had been lost at the Fall. For Ralegh, the world was no longer wholly sinful. At important points, God's will converged happily with what Ralegh called human "invention," by which he meant not simply human contrivance but rather the noble exertion that arose when humans employed both "experience" (gained when necessity propelled risk-taking

---

1. [Walter Ralegh], *The History of the World* (London, 1614), 5.6.11., 776. Here and elsewhere, I deal with the mispagination in Ralegh's *History* by recording the book, chapter, section, and page number; the one exception to this format concerns references to the preface, which I cite with the Latin page numbers alone. Ralegh began writing his *History* in about 1607, while he was a prisoner in the Tower yet still held out hope of being recognized as a royal councillor. When two of James I's most influential councillors, the cryptopapist Henry Howard, earl of Northampton, and the moderate Protestant humanist Isaac Casauban died in 1614, Ralegh rushed his work into print. Disapproving of the book's strong judgments against particular historical monarchs, James initially had it suppressed, but his increasingly straitened financial circumstances ultimately led him to reconsider. In 1617, after granting Ralegh temporary freedom to seek gold in Guiana, the king allowed the *History* to be reprinted for crown profit. Nine more editions, a continuation, and a number of abridgements and excerpts appeared in the seventeenth century. On the immediate context in which Ralegh wrote the work and its publication history, see Nicholas Popper, *Walter Ralegh's History of the World and the Historical Culture of the Late Renaissance* (Chicago, 2012), 12–19; *Oxford Dictionary of National Biography*, online ed., s.v. "Ralegh, Sir Walter (1554–1618)," by Mark Nicholls and Penry Williams, accessed Nov. 15, 2013, http://www.oxforddnb.com/view/article/23039. On the colonizers' negotiations with Henry to accept his role as "*Protector of Virginia*," see Don Pedro de Zuñiga to Philip III, Mar. 5, 1609, in Alexander Brown, ed., *The Genesis of the United States: A Narrative of the Movement in England, 1605–1616 . . . in Two Volumes* (Boston, 1890), I, 246. For Prince Henry generally, see J. W. Williamson, *The Myth of the Conqueror: Prince Henry Stuart: A Study of 17th Century Personation* (New York, 1978).

actions that brought human judgment into alignment with divine knowledge) and "truth" (secured through the remnants of reason left to humans after the Fall) toward reconciling the world to God. Although much of the world remained a formidable wasteland of sinful error, human invention had established a few stable routes of lawfulness. These pathways needed to be walked with fierce resolution and maintained against any encroachments on their own integrity or any wayward misdirection on the part of the walkers. Part of the reason Prince Henry's death came as such a blow for the Virginia colonizers was that he seemed a king in the making, dutifully watchful of those lawful pathways and duly admiring of the valiant men who walked them. Long after Elizabeth I's death, Ralegh continued to chafe at her feminine weakness and her failure to honor properly the service he and other male adventuring courtiers had provided her. He similarly feared that James's wavering will, and his ear to Spanish ambassadors who insinuated false understandings of what was lawful, threatened to leave God's will and noble action alike terribly neglected.[2]

For Ralegh, the past and the present met at the crossroads of human exertion and divine will. He traced the law both through ancient chronicles and scripture and by way of his own ventures through a world he considered alive with signs of when human invention did or did not overlap with God's Providence. A richly eschatological view of time underlay this outlook. Just as the Bible could be read as a continuous narrative from humanity's fall from God's grace to the prophesied death of Jesus for humanity's sin, culminating in Jesus's promised Second Coming and the restoration of God's kingdom on Earth, so, too, could the law be seen as emerging at particular key moments along the way, propelling humans toward their own roles in readying the world for Judgment Day. In Ralegh's lifetime, this eschatologi-

---

2. One of Ralegh's most telling remarks about "invention" concerned the role the ancient Israelites played in preserving their experience in ways that defied the erasures of time, providing the present generation with unique insight into lawful worldly existence: "It was the story of the *Hebrewes*, of all before the *Olympiads*, that overcame the consuming disease of time; and preserved it selfe, from the very cradle and beginning to this day," he wrote. "To the same first Ages do belong the report of many Inventions therein found, and from them derived to us; though most of the Authors Names have perished in so long a Navigation. For those Ages had their Lawes; they had diversity of Government; they had Kingly rule; Nobility, Policy in war; Navigation; and all, or the most of needfull Trades." See Ralegh, *History of the World*, [C3]v–[C4]r. Ralegh's title page portrays Experience and Truth (Veritas) as the twin supports of the world under God's providential eye. On Ralegh's frustration with Elizabeth, see 5.6.2, 717–718.

cal perspective gave rise to a widely shared European conviction that the Last Days had begun and God's kingdom on Earth was either imminent or already coming into being. Lawfulness was inextricably tied to callings, or, as Ralegh and his contemporaries also referred to them, "offices," sets of duties that applied to particular personae as a result of God's ordination. Such callings gave to certain endeavors a fundamental lawfulness that stretched across millennia. That Ralegh's own much-touted persona as a colonizing captain had ancient, and biblical, counterpoints in "captains" like Moses and Joshua in their conquest of Canaan was itself an indication that he walked in a godly light (in the 1580s, Ralegh was explicitly analogized to Joshua, while Canaan was among the most common analogs for Virginia). Although the law created pathways along which humans could walk conscionably, even apparently divine routes through a still-fallen world were nevertheless studded with obstacles and vulnerable to hidden twists and turns. The law, therefore, was inevitably casuistic, requiring attention to those circumstances in which an office that was presumed lawful was rendered an offense to God and, vice versa, to those cases in which the seemingly immoral proved to be God's bidding.[3]

If Ralegh's *History* appears at times a strange blend of worldliness and

3. The eschatological context of early colonization has begun to receive the attention of twenty-first-century historians; see, for instance, David Harris Sacks, "Discourses of Western Planting: Richard Hakluyt and the Making of the Atlantic World," in Peter C. Mancall, ed., *The Atlantic World and Virginia, 1550–1624* (Chapel Hill, N.C., 2007), 410–453; Karen Ordahl Kupperman, *The Jamestown Project* (Cambridge, Mass., 2007), 12–16; Douglas Bradburn, "The Eschatological Origins of the English Empire," in Bradburn and John C. Coombs, eds., *Early Modern Virginia: Reconsidering the Old Dominion* (Charlottesville, Va., 2011), 15–56. Ralegh made clear that he viewed offices as callings. In his *History,* he referred to rulers as exercising "the Office or Magistracie to which they are called ... which in the Scriptures is called *walking with God,*" a reference to Genesis 5:22. By the same token, Ralegh defined the law of nature as the disposition that God imprinted in all the earth's inhabitants, whether animate or inanimate, that propelled them to perform their lawful offices. Even the earth, Ralegh explained, "performeth her office, according to the Law of God in nature: for it bringeth forth the bud of the hearbe which seedeth seede, etc. and the Beast, which liveth thereon." See Ralegh, *History of the World,* 1.2.2, 23 (the office of rulers), 2.4.6, 272 (the law of nature), and 2.4.6, 274 (the earth as fulfilling an office). For Ralegh's view of Moses as a "Captaine," an understanding he derived from Titus Flavius Josephus, see 2.3.9, 220. On Joshua as a colonizer, sending forth "Discoverers" and called by God to "possesse" Canaan, see 2.6.8, 324–326. My treatment of office here and elsewhere in the book owes a great deal to Conal Condren's valuable study of the theme in Condren, *Argument and Authority in Early Modern England: The Presuppositions of Oaths and Offices* (Cambridge, 2006).

providentialism, at once seeking out sovereign kingship and commonwealth in the age of Moses while no less earnestly insisting that God authorized present-day empires as though he were a monarch issuing letters patent, this was because the Renaissance had fully entered its Reformation and Counter-Reformation phase. Drawing on late medieval scholastic writers like Sir John Fortescue of England and John Mair of Scotland, Renaissance humanists had acquired an appreciation for both the heights to which God sometimes elevated earthly monarchs as well as the profoundly embedded nature of kingship. A few of the world's rulers might indeed enjoy what the scholastics called "imperium," or "empire" (a word increasingly defined as sovereignty in the sixteenth century), but they were also wrapped in reciprocal bonds of obligation, both on Earth and in heaven, that enmeshed even the loftiest king. Only God was free of all dependencies, for his office was to rule all others. Rejecting the methods of the "Schoole-men" as too centered on abstruse logic and too reliant on universalistic, hierarchical ideals that had little bearing on the real world, the humanists nevertheless sought to preserve the scholastics' insights on sovereignty and commonwealth by pushing them in newly hardheaded, even secular, directions. If life before Judgment Day was to be lived on Earth, the humanists deemed tangible experience and unblinking attention to the messy complexities of human nature preferable to an overly abstract metaphysics in pointing a polity and its rulers toward God. They adapted medieval Aristotelianism and scholastic theology centered on the eternal truths of nature or the perennial interplay between redemption and sin to more earthbound lessons, whether learned from experience or from the pagan Greek and Roman authorities. The philosophies of the latter enjoyed a great resurgence, in part because they spoke so richly of the material intricacies of governance and society. Universities focused on providing young men with a broader base of practical knowledge in history, rhetoric, and law that would equip them to serve their kings and commonwealths in a world of fragile and competing territorial polities. Of particular importance to the colonizing enterprise, princes were increasingly steered away from unattainable ideals like Dante's medieval vision of a universal empire and counseled instead in the more mundane realities of an earthly landscape characterized by an enormous multitude of small and delimited bodies politic, only sometimes and loosely held together under a single sovereign head. Of course, not all early modern Europeans took the same lessons from their late medieval predecessors. Of ominous significance to many sixteenth- and early-seventeenth-century Europeans, the Spanish Habsburg monarchy modeled itself instead on a prominent strand of scholastic thought that brought Dante's dream of universal monarchy rushing back to the fore. Yet, the Spaniards' claim to enjoy a rightful rule over all of humanity in anticipation of Judgment Day, an extraordinary ambition that fed much of the European determination to compete with Spanish kings over dominion in the New World, gave the broader humanist insistence on the multiplicity of the earth's polities an edge of defiance in addition to its already pronounced sense of realism.[4]

The Reformation did not so much challenge these humanist worldly impulses as resacralize them. Propelled by the Protestant directive to return to scripture for fundamental truths about God's plan, sixteenth- and seventeenth-century Europeans brought an intense biblicism to their contemplations of sovereignty and commonwealth. Civic humanism and Christian humanism merged into one in this determination to ground the world's civil institutions in histories and texts that spoke to when those human inventions did or did not enjoy God's approval. The Old Testament, especially the initial five books derived from the Hebrew Bible, attracted a wave of new interest, spurred by the perception that the narratives offered there of the earth in its infancy, especially when read in their original languages, provided singularly direct clues about God's will that princes and their advisers could not afford to ignore. Soon an outpouring of Hebraically informed scholarship, including works by English and Scottish authors like Edmund Bunny, Thomas Godwyn, John Weemes, and John Selden, scrutinized ancient Israel as a uniquely important, if not the prime, example of a common-

---

4. On the scholastic debates over monarchy and Fortescue's and Mair's significant contributions to these debates, see J. H. Burns, *Lordship, Kingship, and Empire: The Idea of Monarchy, 1400–1525*, The Carlyle Lectures 1988 (Oxford, 1992), esp. 58–70, 141, 143–145, 147–148, 155–156, 158–162. For Fortescue's use of "imperium" in relation to the medieval ideal of a power that enables a universal monarchy over the entire world, see [Sir John] Fortesecue, *A Learned Commendation of the Politique Lawes of England* . . . (London, 1567), Fo.35v. For an example of Ralegh's own criticism of the "Schoole-men" in which he condemns the late medieval theologian John Duns Scotus for his overly logical approach to scripture, see Ralegh, *History of the World*, 1.3.7, 44. For a useful analysis of the secularizing influence of humanism on politics, see William J. Bouwsma, *The Waning of the Renaissance, 1550–1640* (New Haven, Conn., 2000), 86–99. Also valuable on the adaptation of medieval scholastic categories to humanist concerns, with a special emphasis on civility, is John Hale, *The Civilization of Europe in the Renaissance* (London, 1994), 355–508. On the Spanish Habsburg revival of Dante's ideal of universal monarchy, see Anthony Pagden, *Lords of All the World: Ideologies of Empire in Spain, Britain, and France, c.1500–c.1800* (New Haven, Conn., 1995), 29–62; Frances A. Yates, *Astraea: The Imperial Theme in the Sixteenth Century* (London, 1975), 1–28.

wealth where God's blessings and curses could be delineated in exacting detail. Other writings also explored the often-obscure nexus between the human and the divine. Streams of translations and new editions of ancient and medieval texts on Providence made their way into private libraries, while an even greater flood of cheap print brought news of God's awful judgments and wondrous blessings to rural parishes and urban neighborhoods. The period also witnessed a florescence of so-called universal histories that similarly promised to shed light on humanity's earliest civil strivings under God. In his popular translation of the histories of the first-century Roman Jew Titus Flavius Josephus (first printed in 1602 before going through ten more seventeenth-century editions), Thomas Lodge offered readers an account of Canaan that, like Ralegh's own history, was not only indistinguishable from a colonization story but implicitly a glimpse of colonization's very beginnings — with God commanding Noah and his sons to "send certaine distinct Colonies to inhabite divers countries of the world" and calling Moses and Joshua to the conquest of Canaan as his colonizing "captaine[s]." In addition, Protestant efforts to adapt Catholic casuistry to the reformed faith stimulated the era's rich literature on callings and cases of conscience. The cleric William Crashawe, one of the most energetic defenders of Virginia colonization at the time Ralegh wrote his *History,* still recalled fondly his studies at Saint John's College, Cambridge, where he soaked up the radiance of one of the most celebrated of these authors, the Elizabethan divine William Perkins. "This holy man did spend him self like a Candle to give light unto others," Crashawe reminisced. John Donne, dean of Saint Paul's and another member of the Virginia Company that carried Virginia colonization forward in James's reign, was similarly known for his guidance in perplexing cases of conscience, a casuistic interest that seeped into not only his sermons and poetry but also his own avid advocacy for planting English settlements in North America.[5]

5. *The Famous and Memorable Workes of Josephus, a Man of Much Honour and Learning among the Jewes; Faithfully Translated Out of the Latin, and French, by Tho. Lodge, Doctor in Physicke* ([London], 1602), 9, 46. Crashawe's remark on Perkins appears in his published edition of one of his former teacher's works; see, *M. Perkins, His Exhortation to Repentance* . . . (London, 1605), [A6]v. On the resurgence of interest in the Hebrew Bible, see Eric Nelson, *The Hebrew Republic: Jewish Sources and the Transformation of European Political Thought* (Cambridge, Mass., 2010), 7–16. Something of the mingling of humanist and Reformation concerns can be observed in the concurrent creation of Regius professorships in Roman-derived civil law and in Hebrew at sixteenth- and seventeenth-century English and French universities; for example, Henry VIII

Driven by their humanism to pin the sovereign rulers and virtuous commonwealths of scholastic philosophy firmly to the earth and inspired by the Reformation to locate those worldly truths deep in sacred time and squarely within a broader providential order, early colonizers defended English colonization in the most fundamental terms possible. Like Ralegh, their impulse was not just to assert the lawfulness of colonization but rather to root that activity in a God-centered cosmos where law was always, albeit with the degree of latitude necessary to allow for human error, the equivalent of divine ordination. During the late sixteenth and early seventeenth centuries, these men transformed what had originally been an aspect of human history and society that impressed itself little on the contemporary imagination into a basic feature of civil and holy life. As late as the 1630s, writers were still not confident that their readers even knew the word "colony," a term only recently imported from the original Latin into the vernacular, so they still sometimes felt the need to define it. Yet, at the same time, these authors boldly projected the planting of colonies into a sanctified past and a righteous present that lent that enterprise an almost inviolable aura of naturalness.⁶

---

founded Regius chairs in civil law and Hebrew at both Oxford and Cambridge in 1540. On this point, compare Ken MacMillan, *Sovereignty and Possession in the English New World: The Legal Foundations of Empire, 1576–1640* (Cambridge, 2006), 25–29, and Nelson, *Hebrew Republic*, 9–10. On Providential writings in England, see Alexandra Walsham, *Providence in Early Modern England* (Oxford, 1999). For a brief survey of the publication of classical and medieval writings on the subject, see esp. 9n. On casuistry with a particular focus on Donne's poetry, see Meg Lota Brown, *Donne and the Politics of Conscience in Early Modern England* (Leiden, The Netherlands, 1995). On casuistry in this period more broadly, see Edmund Leites, ed., *Conscience and Casuistry in Early Modern Europe* (Cambridge, 1988).

6. One of the earliest published works in the British Isles to use the word "colony" in the vernacular appears to have been *The Complaynt of Scotland* [Paris, 1550], a pamphlet published during the "Rough Wooing," when Henry VIII sought to force a marriage between his young son, Edward, and Mary, Queen of Scots. In an argument that was infused by providentialism as well as the eschatological belief that the "warld is verray neir ane ende," Robert Wedderburn, the presumed author and a vicar in the Scottish Church, rebutted works penned by English authors to justify England's ensuing war against its northern neighbor and "to preve that Scotland was ane colone of ingland quhen it was first inabhit." Unimpressed by the English argument that such a colonial condition connoted God's favoritism, the author wrote that, although "god hes permittit the inglis men to scurge us, as he permittit sathan to scurge the holy man Job," it did not follow that "thai ar in the favoir of god." See *Complaynt of Scotland*, 21v, 29r, 45r. For a useful discussion of Wedderburn's text and its context in Anglo-Scottish relations, see David Armitage, *The Ideo-*

In other words, Christian humanists tied the colonizing venture to the world in the very act of similarly grounding sovereignty and commonwealth. Indeed, the three concepts acquired substance in tandem, becoming so intertwined that separating one from the others could seem well nigh impossible. Nowhere was this mutual dependence for meaning more explicit than in the way sovereignty, commonwealth, and plantation were folded into what quickly proved the era's most compelling and enduring formulation for grasping how colonies fit within God's plan. This theory, which underlay much of Ralegh's *History*, treated colonization as the mechanism by which God propelled humans in their essential duty to establish dominion over the earth. By planting new commonwealths and churches, thereby enabling their sovereign rulers to extend their awesome, divinely granted power over still-fallen communities and the earth's remaining unexploited bounty, colonizers fulfilled a calling that God first set in motion in the Garden of Eden and amid the tribes of ancient Palestine. For Ralegh, this archetypal understanding of colonization as commonwealth formation was so fundamental that it was the presupposition that quietly dictated his entire narrative of human history from Creation forward. A more succinct articulation of the same logic appeared in Captain John Smith's definition of planting in his pamphlet *Advertisements for the Unexperienced Planters of New-England, or Any Where; or, The Path-way to Experience to Erect a Plantation* (1631). As Smith wrote:

> Adam and Eve did first begin this innocent worke to plant the earth to remaine to posterity, but not without labour, trouble, and industry: Noah and his family began againe the second plantation, and their seed as it still increased, hath still planted new Countries, and one Coun-

---

logical Origins of the British Empire (Cambridge, 2000), 43–45. Richard Eden was sufficiently unsure of his readers' familiarity with the word "colony" in 1555 that he included it alongside other such exotic words as "Continente," "Caravel," "Hemispherium," and "Equinoctial," in a glossary. See Eden, trans., *The Decades of the Newe Worlde or West India, Conteynyng the Navigations and Conquestes of the Spanyardes, with the Particular Description of the Moste Ryche and Large Landes and Ilands Lately Founde in the West Ocean Perteynyng to the Inheritaunce of the Kinges of Spayne ... Wrytten in the Latine Tounge by Peter Martyr of Angleria, and Translated into Engiysshe by Rycharde Eden* (London, 1555), [biv]r. As late as 1630, the anonymous author of the pamphlet *The Planter's Plea; or, The Grounds of Plantations Examined, and Usuall Objections Answered...* (London, 1630) still felt the need to explain, "By a Colony we meane a societie of men drawne out of one state or people, and transplanted into another Countrey" (B[1]r).

try [after] another, and so the world to that estate it is; but not without much hazard, travell, mortalities, discontents, and many disasters.

Like Ralegh, Smith's impulse was to identify planting as a calling that stretched across the world and across time, linking the planter in the most direct way to God's overarching plan for restoring the world to its original wholeness before the Fall. Much the same logic informed Sir Francis Bacon's opening lines in "Of Plantations" (1625). "Plantations are amongst Ancient, Primitive, and Heroicall Workes," he explained. "When the World was young, it begat more Children; But now it is old, it begets fewer: For I may justly account new Plantations, to be the Children of former Kingdomes." For the anonymous author of *The Planter's Plea* (1630), colonization was likewise a primordial activity that originated in the very same divine ordination that brought kings and commonwealths into being: "Colonies (as other conditions and states in humane society) have their warrant from Gods direction and command; who as soone as men were, set them their taske, to replenish the earth, and to subdue it."[7]

This emphasis on the ancient and godly enterprise of planting colonies—equally concerned with substantiating sovereignty and commonwealth as justifying the act of colonization—worked in two directions at once. On the one hand, it strove to redefine English kingship as well as the English commonwealth in profoundly new terms, as connoting a hitherto unrecognized set of obligations to rule over and people a portion of the world not only seemingly larger than Christendom itself but separated from it by a vast and roiling ocean. This was a more daunting case to make than has sometimes been acknowledged, for it involved not only challenging preconceptions and arguments that discouraged such an enlarged view of English duties in the world but also bending the reluctant wills of monarchs and sub-

---

7. John Smith, *Advertisements for the Unexperienced Planters of New-England, or Any Where; or, The Path-way to Experience to Erect a Plantation* . . . (London, 1631), in Philip L. Barbour, ed., *The Complete Works of Captain John Smith (1580–1631)* . . . (Chapel Hill, N.C., 1986), III, 276; Francis [Bacon], "Of Plantations," in *The Essayes or Counsels, Civill and Morall, of Francis Lo. Verulam, Viscount St. Alban, Newly Written* (London, 1625), 198; *Planter's Plea*, B[1]r. In his essay, "Of Honor and Reputation" (1625), Bacon similarly identified, as the persons most deserving of "*Soveraign Honour,*" "*Conditores Imperiorum;* Founders of States, and *Common-Wealths:* Such as were *Romulus, Cyrus, Cesar, Ottoman, Ismael*" (*Essayes or Counsels, Civill and Morall*, 313–314). It is noteworthy that Bacon included Ishmael, Abraham's first son, among the founders of "*States* and *Common-Wealths.*"

jects toward an enterprise that was otherwise slow to win their full approval. On the other hand, the same argument also functioned to frame colonization as an undertaking that sought nothing less than to forge new commonwealths — or, as they were also initially called, kingdoms — on the other side of the Atlantic. Rather than merely settling a distant territory, colonization involved bringing into being the states that humanists now perceived as the key constituent elements of a world returning to God. This undertaking, in turn, invited much the same energetic considerations of what a lawful commonwealth entailed and how it came into being that already swirled through this late Renaissance and Reformation era as one of its principal preoccupations. Both of these aspects of the discourse surrounded the Virginia venture.

For Ralegh, as for most of his fellow early English colonizers, two realities fundamentally structured the late Tudor and early Stuart context he inhabited: the English commonwealth was poised to serve God and win his blessings, in no small part by extending English dominion to the other side of the Atlantic, and the primary obstacle to that desired end was the irresolution of English monarchs. Insecure kings were not just a persistent problem in realizing the dream of English sovereignty across the ocean; they were also a basic rationale for the colonizing endeavor itself. If English monarchs accepted that their kingly office included responsibilities of rule over not only familiar realms close to home but also a nascent Virginia kingdom that spanned, at least by the ambitious claims of James's 1606 letters patent, a massive North American territory from Florida to present-day Canada, then English sovereignty itself would gain much-needed strength. Or so the logic of the colonizing discourse itself strenuously and incessantly, if always circumspectly, implied. Although the colonizers usually kept prudently quiet about their frustration with their queens and kings (apart from occasional indirect jabs like Ralegh's remark about Elizabeth's stinginess, expressed safely from the other side of her grave), they left little doubt that the timidity of the English monarchy was a major concern. This anxiety was bound up, in turn, with the great promise that scholastic theories of sovereignty had bequeathed to early modern humanists of a power capable of restoring order to a still-fallen Earth. Conversely, it also contributed to the ongoing disappointments with English monarchs who continually failed to live up to their idealized persona as reforming emperors.[8]

8. The First Charter of Virginia, Apr. 10, 1606, The Avalon Project, Yale Law School, Lillian Goldman Law Library, http://avalon.law.yale.edu/17th_century/va01.asp.

Sovereign kingship had been asserted most authoritatively in England in 1533, when, in a bid to legitimize Henry VIII's divorce from Catherine, the king's ever busy Privy Councillor and soon-to-be chief minister Thomas Cromwell had pushed through Parliament the Act in Restraint of Appeals. Invoking the familiar medieval legal doctrine *rex est imperator in regno suo* (the king is emperor in his own realm), the act famously proclaimed, "This realm of England is an empire . . . governed by one supreme head and king having the dignity and royal estate of the imperial crown of the same." At the most basic level, such a claim to imperial rule was simply an assertion of independence from the shared exercise of authority over English subjects by the pope and Holy Roman emperor. It did not take a very great imaginative leap, however, to see in that imperial dignity, as well, what Fortescue a half century earlier had called *dominium regale*, a "royalle" power that he likened to God's own extraordinary capacity to purge sin through the exercise solely of his own will and that Fortescue associated, too, with Britain's legendary conqueror and founder, the Trojan Brutus. To be sure, Fortescue had insisted that England, like Scotland, was ruled, not by *dominium regale* alone, but rather by an intermingling of the royal will of the king and the civil (or "politike") wills of his subjects — an arrangement that he famously called *dominium politicum et regale* and that he considered an appropriate quality of rule for peoples who had already come far in forging commonwealths that sat right under God. Nevertheless, the assertion of the English king's imperium in Henry VIII's reign was an important step in the direction of establishing, for the realm's rulers, a degree, or amplitude, of power that, in an age newly alert to sovereignty as a vital element of civil dominion, was desirable in its own right. Ralegh himself referred admiringly to English monarchs' "absolute" power, a term that he undoubtedly drew from the scholastic argument that God enjoys *potestas absoluta* in the sense of a power complete unto itself. An absolute English king was one who could hold firm against carnal sin and human error, even when these existed on the far side of an ocean.[9]

9. An Act That the Appeals in Such Cases as Have Been Used to Be Pursued to the See of Rome Shall Not Be from Henceforth Had nor Used but Within This Realm (1533: 24 Henry VIII, c.12), in G. R. Elton, ed., *The Tudor Constitution: Documents and Commentary*, 2d ed. (Cambridge, 1982), 353 (An Act in Restraint of Appeals is the common name for the statute [24 Hen. VIII c.12]); John Fortescue, *The Governance of England: Otherwise Called the Difference between an Absolute and a Limited Monarchy*, ed. Charles Plummer (Oxford, 1885), 109, 111–112. The classic work on the legal and historical context of the 1533 act is Richard Koebner, "'The Imperial Crown of This Realm': Henry VIII, Constantine the Great, and Polydore Vergil," *Bulletin of the*

In fact, the determination of early modern colonizers to elevate sovereignty to the point where it could effectively secure dominion in distant climes — in effect, making England's monarchs the Brutuses of a latter age — led them to give the scholastic argument of *potestas absoluta* subtly new implications. Scholastic writers like Fortescue and Mair had been willing to accord enormous, even Christlike, powers to kings as the proper lawgivers and shepherds of their peoples, while also restraining such rulers by incorporating them into obligatory bonds predicated on laws considered even more fundamental than their own. Humanists adhered closely to this formulation; Ralegh's own elaborate treatment of the beginnings of government in his *History* lavished attention on both the rise of fierce and conquering kings and on their own gradual amelioration through obedience to divine, natural, and civil laws. But the colonizers now also saw the duties of sovereigns in newly adventurous terms, as having implications far beyond the limited territorial states within Christendom that were the scholastics' focus. Christopher Columbus's crossing of the Atlantic and his so-called discovery of a landmass apparently unknown to the ancients and not prophesied in scripture was an especially transformative influence in this regard, feeding the European sense that God's plans for humanity in the latter ages might require transcending local conventions of law and even of morality to perform his purposes abroad. A related interest in a more warlike kingship developed around the sixteenth- and early-seventeenth-century campaign to bind the multiple kingdoms of the British archipelago under a single Christlike sovereign head. This eagerness for imperial kings to have ample freedom of will to perform God's special bidding encouraged proponents of colonization like

---

Institute of Historical Research, XXVI (1953), 29–52. See also Dale Hoak, "The Iconography of the Crown Imperial," in Hoak, ed., *Tudor Political Culture* (Cambridge, 1995), 54–103. Ralegh's remarks about absolute power ranged in emphasis. He was contemptuous of Spanish monarchs' efforts to rule absolutely over the Netherlands, England, and France despite those states' own sovereignty (C[1]v) and he equated tyranny with "a sole and absolute rule" that is heedless of just laws (1.9.2, 180). Yet, he also associated absolute rule favorably with sovereign emperors like Augustus Caesar (1.10.2, 187). J. H Burns discusses Ralegh in relation to the earlier scholastic argument of *potestas absoluta* in Burns, *Lordship, Kingship, and Empire*, 156–157. For an analysis of Ralegh's *History* that similarly highlights his endorsement of absolute kingship in the context of James's own related arguments, see Popper, *Walter Ralegh's History of the World*, 33–36. The classic work on late medieval scholastics' revived interest in *potestas absoluta*, or *potentia absoluta*, is Heiko A. Oberman, "Some Notes on the Theology of Nominalism: With Attention to Its Relation to the Renaissance," *The Harvard Theological Review*, LIII (1960), 47–76.

Ralegh, Bacon, Smith, Crashawe, and Donne to call for a significantly expanded conception of the sovereign office. Part of the reason they burrowed so deep for colonization's lawfulness was to allow their monarchs to rise high above whatever narrow constraints they might encounter at home.¹⁰

Yet, rather than satisfying their allotted role as Renaissance versions of Brutus, England's new imperial monarchs proved meek and hesitant. Beset by succession crises and a religiously divided realm, and in Mary I's and Elizabeth's cases haunted by the added suspicion that God did not call female rulers to be emperors at all, England's late Tudor and early Stuart rulers were too insecure in their sovereignty to meet the heightened expectations the colonizers had for them. Even in those cases when they were convinced to issue letters patent authorizing colonizing voyages, these monarchs granted licenses that were recognized as so provisional and so lacking in other substantive signs of royal commitment that they rang hollow. To the colonizers, a great deal was at stake in this kingly irresolution. Threats loomed from both

---

10. As J. H. Burns describes the scholastic argument as it came to be adapted to early modern humanism, "In the late sixteenth and the early seventeenth century, there was, firmly established . . . , a concept of absolute monarchy which was not only compatible with but in fact inseparable from a framework of fundamental law." See Burns, *Lordship, Kingship, and Empire*, 157. For the alterations in understanding of sovereignty in the context of the American empire and Anglo-Scottish union, see Pagden, *Lords of All the World*, 11–28; Keechang Kim, *Aliens in Medieval Law: The Origins of Modern Citizenship* (Cambridge, 2000), 179–182; Armitage, *Ideological Origins of the British Empire*, 24–60; MacMillan, *Sovereignty and Possession*, 17–48; and Lauren Benton, *A Search for Sovereignty: Law and Geography in European Empires, 1400–1900* (Cambridge, 2010). Elaborations on sovereignty and polity are often discussed in relation to kingship and commonwealth or the related idea of England's monarchical republic; see Glenn Burgess, *British Political Thought, 1500–1660: The Politics of the Post-Reformation* (New York, 2009); Patrick Collinson, "The Monarchical Republic of Queen Elizabeth I," *Bulletin of the John Rylands University Library of Manchester*, LXIX (1987), 394–424; John F. McDiarmid, ed., *The Monarchical Republic of Early Modern England: Essays in Response to Patrick Collinson* (Burlington, Vt., 2007); Roger A. Mason, *Kingship and the Commonweal: Political Thought in Renaissance and Reformation Scotland* (East Lothian, Scotland, 1998); and D. Alan Orr, *Treason and the State: Law, Politics, and Ideology in the English Civil War* (Cambridge, 2002). The classic work on the ruler's mystical body and sovereign head as these ideas evolved from medieval scholasticism to Renaissance and Reformation thought is Ernst H. Kantorowicz, *The King's Two Bodies: A Study in Mediaeval Political Theology* (Princeton, 1957). At a certain level, Ralegh's discussion of the origins of kingship and commonwealth in his *History* extends to every page, but the discussion is particularly focused on 1.9.1–4, 178–185, and 2.4.3–16, 267–294.

the worldly and the spiritual extremes of their late Renaissance landscape. On the one hand were the Islamic Turks and Catholic Spaniards, by Ralegh's account the two most fearsome and recklessly secular powers since the fall of the Roman Empire. On the other were the Familists, Brownists, and Anabaptists, those Protestant sectaries and separatists who, in Ralegh's eyes, were prepared to dismantle the world entirely in their blind enthusiasm to meet their Maker. This perceived danger posed by forces that veered either too close to the world or too heedlessly of it underscores how readily the colonizing venture overlapped with other areas of concern that were similarly exacerbated by the problem of weak sovereignty, including not only the apprehensions over universal monarchy that divided Reformation-era Europe but also its bitter confessional politics. Vacillating monarchs who could not exercise their responsibilities solidly as Virginia's rightful kings were just as likely to seem poor ballast for England's dangerously listing church or insufficient guardians of its vulnerable commonwealth. Unsurprisingly, then, the writers who sought to elevate English sovereignty while coaxing it across the ocean were also often involved in the simultaneous efforts to convince their king to play his Christlike part in safeguarding England's ecclesiastical establishment or to improve its military capacities. By the same token, Virginia was never simply a commonwealth in the making; it was equally a church, standing as a beacon of the English king's persona not only as conqueror and emperor but also as shepherd and guide.[11]

To turn now from the problem of English royal sovereignty to the issue of Virginia commonwealth formation might suggest a case of moving from one topic to its opposite, especially in light of the very real tensions that soon

---

11. Helpful for thinking about not only female rule but also the complexities of sovereign kingship generally is A. N. McLaren, *Political Culture in the Reign of Elizabeth I: Queen and Commonwealth, 1558–1585* (Cambridge, 1999). For Ralegh's conflation of the Spanish and Turks as worldly tyrants, see Ralegh, *History of the World*, C[1]r, 5.6.12, 775. For his lament that rightful institutions, in this case the tabernacle, are "forgotten and cast away in this super-fine Age, by those of the *Familie*, by the *Anabaptist, Brownist*, and other *Sectaries*," see 2.5.1, 296–297. For scholarship that shares this study's approach to viewing Virginia's religious institutions and beliefs as integral aspects of its broader culture, see Edward L. Bond, *Damned Souls in a Tobacco Colony: Religion in Seventeenth-Century Virginia* (Macon, Ga., 2000); and Rebecca Anne Goetz, *The Baptism of Early Virginia: How Christianity Created Race* (Baltimore, 2012). For the colonies more generally, see Carla Gardina Pestana, *Protestant Empire: Religion and the Making of the British Atlantic World* (Philadelphia, 2009).

developed between English kings and their ostensible Virginia kingdom. But the two themes were more congruent than they might at first appear because of the particular way Ralegh and other colonizers framed colonization as a lawful undertaking. By defining the colonizing enterprise as an ages-old activity in the planting of new commonwealths under divinely favored sovereign kings, these writers made the realization of a Virginia commonwealth, no less than the summoning of English sovereigns to their American duties, a fundamental precondition for a just colonizing endeavor. The question that bedeviled colonization in these early years, therefore, was not whether colonies should be commonwealths in their own right but rather how they should achieve that end. Only with the rise of the theory of the sovereign state, a concept that was unavailable through most of the first century of colonization efforts in America until Thomas Hobbes's *Leviathan* (1651) offered it as a remedy for the horrors of England's Civil War, did the question around colonization suddenly and dramatically shift to whether colonies should be commonwealths at all or merely the provinces of the state that planted them. Once this question had been posed, the Renaissance era of colonization came to a quiet, indeterminate end. Before that time, however, colonial commonwealths and royal sovereignty remained in complex interrelationship, structuring both how colonizers envisioned that project and how they approached it.[12]

To see early English colonization as an exercise in commonwealth formation is to move beyond an anachronism introduced by the theory of state sovereignty itself: namely, that the planting of colonies like Virginia began right away as an exercise in settlement. The notion of settlement, which suggests a simple act of expanding the state's sovereign integrity into new provincial societies and frontier economic zones, does not capture how someone like Ralegh viewed the plantation enterprise. Instead of merely settling a distant province of the state, as would increasingly come to seem the nature of colonization in the late seventeenth and eighteenth centuries, the view that prevailed through the Tudor and early Stuart eras was that colonies were themselves newly planted commonwealths and churches. That is,

---

12. On the rise of the concept of the state, an essential part of the context of early modern European colonization in America that remains only sketchily incorporated into early American scholarship, see Quentin Skinner, "The State," in Terence Ball, James Farr, and Russell L. Hanson, eds., *Political Innovation and Conceptual Change* (Cambridge, 1989), 90–131; and Skinner, *The Foundations of Modern Political Thought*, 2 vols. (Cambridge, 1978), I, ix–x, xxiii, 11, II, 135, 287–290, 349, 351–352, 352–358.

they included from the outset the two constituent elements that leading humanist authorities on the subject, from Jean Bodin and Bacon to Ralegh himself, agreed were essential to all civil polities: a sovereign head and genuine bodies politic and spiritual. This was nothing more, of course, than a humanist adaptation of the scholastics' own such argument, a matter of Fortescue's *dominium politicum et regale* being recast as commonwealth and king. But it was also a vitally relevant formulation. In an era when colonies lacked a priori significance of their own (for the English Catholic humanist Richard Eden, writing in 1555, a colony was little more than "an habitacion"), the ideas of sovereign kingship and commonwealth formation were the conceptual building blocks from which colonization gradually acquired meaning.[13]

Tracing the justificatory efforts that surrounded the Tudor and early Stuart Virginia venture reveals how the colony slowly gained substance as a recognizable commonwealth. By the mid-seventeenth century, there was very little doubt that Virginia had realized itself as such a polity; in 1642, for instance, Governor Sir William Berkeley and the colony's assembly spoke unhesitatingly of the colony as a "commonwealth," a "republic" (as in res publica, or public thing), and one of the world's integral "states." But this confident assessment of the colony's basic progress in taking on the linea-

---

13. Eden, trans., *Decades of the Newe Worlde*, [biv]r. My concern to reframe early colorization as an endeavor in commonwealth formation arose originally from my interest in the language of commonwealth that was used in all the early-seventeenth-century colonies, most conspicuously Virginia and Massachusetts, and that dropped out of usage after the Restoration. I have also been influenced by scholarship that seeks to overcome the distortions in early American history introduced by the late-arriving theory of the sovereign state, in particular by paying closer attention to the distinctive logic and dynamics of early modern state formation. See, for instance, Jack P. Greene, "Negotiated Authorities: The Problem of Governance in the Extended Polities of the Early Modern Atlantic World," in Greene, *Negotiated Authorities: Essays in Colonial Political and Constitutional History* (Charlottesville, Va., 1994), 1–24; Elizabeth Mancke, "Polity Formation and Atlantic Political Narratives," in Nicholas Canny and Philip Morgan, eds., *Oxford Handbook of the Atlantic World, c.1450–c.1850* (Oxford, 2011), 382–399. By the time Adam Smith wrote his *Wealth of Nations*, the idea of colonization as settlement was largely taken for granted. See Smith, *An Inquiry into the Nature and Causes of the Wealth of Nations . . . in Two Volumes* (London, 1776), I, 113–114, II, 146–147, 156–157, 163–190. Drawing on Smith, Herman Merivale incorporated the same emphasis on settlement, which he associated with the colony's lower social "rank" than the state, into his influential nineteenth-century lectures on colonization. See Merivale, *Lectures on Colonization and Colonies, Delivered before the University of Oxford in 1839, 1840, and 1841* (London, 1861), xiii–xiv, 74–75.

ments of a genuine commonwealth neither overrode pronounced concerns about its success in meeting God's expectations nor reflected straightforward adherence to any preexisting blueprint for such a polity. Instead, fears of the colony's precarious position in the broader providential order remained acute through the seventeenth century. Meanwhile, the struggle to forge the colony's commonwealth took place in complex interaction with simultaneous efforts to grasp just what that process was meant to entail. Ralegh's *History* is itself an indication of how interwoven the justification of English colonization was with the search for plausible proof of how and when commonwealth formation satisfied divine will. Rather than a matter of neatly transferring or adapting English society to an American setting, colonial commonwealth formation involved ongoing inquiries and debate concerning when the inventions of this world did or did not overlap with Providence and how to bring about that earthly and divine correspondence.[14]

Such an intricate and open-ended process gave Virginia commonwealth building at once transatlantic dimensions and a sui generis sense of learning anew how dominion was to be achieved when a state was in its infancy, especially in a context as remote, strange, and filled with providential mystery as the New World. On the one hand, the positing of certain institutions or arrangements from England's commonwealth as essential to Virginia's own polity were never merely casual borrowings. They were, rather, active contributions to ongoing debates in England itself, or in Europe more generally, over what inventions were or were not lawful in the sense of pleasing God. The identification of Virginia as standing squarely under the liturgy and governance of the Church of England was scarcely a reflexive act innocent of any broader agenda but instead a bold intervention in that most vexed of issues: the legitimacy of England's ecclesiastical settlement as it evolved from Elizabeth's reign to James's and Charles I's. Likewise, the creation in 1618 of a representative assembly where Virginia's planters could participate in lawmaking was no simple afterthought. Instead, it self-consciously reinforced the foundational role that Parliament was asserting for itself within the English commonwealth. This was a role that the colonizers who were associated with the Virginia Company knew well because on a number of occasions they themselves sought to tie colonization more firmly to Parliament, an an-

---

14. The Declaration against the Company to Be Entered as the Twenty-First Act, Apr. 1, 1642, in William Waller Hening, *The Statutes at Large; Being a Collection of All the Laws of Virginia, from the First Session of the Legislature, in the Year 1619* . . . (New York, 1823), I, 233, "A Remonstrance of the Grand Assembly," July 1, 1642, I, 236.

choring move intended to overcome what they perceived as James's unpredictable vacillations. Similarly, the almost sacrosanct value that Virginians assigned to what they called their "public" was also a matter of taking sides in a European-wide controversy with English as well as colonial relevance. The public was that domain of communally shared land, buildings, institutions, and wealth that even those humanists like Bodin and Ralegh, who were insistent that their monarchs enjoyed absolute power to perform certain special, divinely established duties, nevertheless accepted needed to be preserved inviolable from even the most godlike king. What made this issue an especially tricky one in newly founded plantations like Virginia was that colonies themselves in this period began to be envisioned as an especially lucrative, and comparatively politically safe, way to augment the public revenues of the commonwealth that planted them. Such a metropolitan-oriented view, which came close to treating the colonies as an undistinguished marchland useful as both a dumping ground for undesirable subjects and a rich source of profitable commodities, obviously clashed with the colony's much-touted status as an integral commonwealth with its own sacred and inalienable public. That contradiction, in turn, generated much of the tensions of early Virginia politics and contributed in the long run to the rise of the Hobbesian argument that colonies should not be accepted as commonwealths but only as profit-making provinces of the commonwealth that sent them.[15]

In other respects, colonial commonwealth formation encouraged, not interventions in well-delineated debates over commonwealth and sovereignty on the other side of the Atlantic, but rather forays into distinctly unfamiliar terrain. Even this sui generis aspect of plantation building, however, was not undertaken in disregard of reassuring landmarks. The impulse was instead, as was manifest in Ralegh's *History*, to cast back to what was taken to be the very origin of colonization: the first nations planted by patriarchs, captains, and kings under God's direction as the world struggled back to order and obedience after the Fall. Here, in accounts of Canaan and in chronicles of the earliest polities and empires, writers with an eye toward what could seem a frighteningly uncharted experience of securing dominion in an altogether alien part of the world brought colonization within the

---

15. The use of the terms "publique" and "republique" to refer to the resources meant to contribute to the welfare of all the community's recognized members permeated early-seventeenth-century colonial documents. See, for instance, Hening, *Statutes*, I, 125 ("publique uses"), 128 ("publique debts"), 143 ("publique charges"), 196 ("publique service"), 240 ("the weale publique"), 297 ("the publique"), 327 ("publique taxes"), 343 ("the republique").

compass of the known and navigable. They frequently did so with a highly self-conscious, even brazen, sense of illuminating controversial pathways of behavior that were nonetheless, by their account, justifiable — conduct that the colonizers argued could credibly be linked to God's sanction even while risking offending conventional European norms of lawfulness and justice. Such claims were especially bold and capable of grounding highly questionable conduct in accepted law because they were commonly framed in terms of divine callings. Thus, it was because Virginia's planters "goe by Gods vocation," William Symonds wrote in *Virginia: A Sermon Preached at White-Chapel* (1609), his much-publicized defense of plantations, that their actions deserved wide latitude — as long, that is, as they remained God's "faithfull servants," as Abraham and other early planters of the gospel and new states did in their own performance of Adam's calling to "replenish the whole earth."[16]

This tendency to confront the novel uncertainties of colonization by turning again and again to the relatively solid basis of a world of scripture and callings was especially pronounced in the planters' conduct in relation to other peoples. Here, the argument that colonization enjoyed divine favor ran most abrasively against more sensitive consciences. Seizing lands held peacefully by native populations and reducing free persons to bondage struck many contemporary Europeans as flagrantly unjust. Fifteenth-century English scholastics like Fortescue as well as early-sixteenth-century Spaniards like Francisco de Vitoria and Bartolomé de Las Casas had questioned the very legitimacy of legal regimes that upheld such evident crimes in God's name. Yet, the Renaissance and Reformation return to a vigorous biblicism and heightened emphasis on archetypal commonwealths answered such doubts with an unyielding insistence that God's will sometimes trumps human morality, dramatically expanding the liberty of those within his chosen polities while justly curtailing the freedom of those without. This was the rationale that William Strachey, Virginia's early secretary of state, offered in response to the apprehension that hung persistently over the young colonial venture: whether it was "unhonest" because "injuryous to the Naturalls" (that is, the native inhabitants whose "naturalness" supposedly arose from their still-fallen condition). Strachey responded with the severe casuistry that as "true Christians" the English knew "that the world never was,

---

16. William Symonds, *Virginia: A Sermon Preached at White-Chappel, in the Presence of Many, Honourable and Worshipfull, the Adventurers and Planters for Virginia. 25. April. 1609* ... (London, 1609), 7, 41.

nor must be only and alone governed by morality." "Sometymes, and to the bettering of Mankynd," he went on, "the divyne pollitique lawe ytself (we see) doth put on chaung, and byndeth not *semper, et in omne;* as in the cases of *Theft,* and *Adultery,* etc." In other words, those Virginia colonizers who were really bent toward the performance of God's will, who were prepared, as Strachey put it, to "manly proceed" in their duties before Judgment Day, needed to recognize that they walked a rightful path at which the scrupulous might cavil. Such a knowingly contentious route through contemporary doubts and fears forged a commonwealth that rested, inevitably precariously, on norms of human bondage and territorial possession supposedly traceable to the Israelites' conquest of Canaan.[17]

There was, then, a fragile combination of self-righteousness and moral and legal ambiguity at the heart of Tudor and early Stuart colonization in America. Unsurprisingly, this fraught mixture of impulses gave not only Virginia but also the colonies that followed immediately in its wake a taut and mercurial atmosphere in which worldly and godly tendencies competed in complicated, rarely fully resolved struggles for primacy. Although these conflicts are most familiar for the Plymouth and Massachusetts Bay colonies as well as the other New England plantations that splintered off from them, Virginia's commonwealth also lurched uneasily between ever-insistent calls to bring the colony closer to God and the stout counter urge to hold fast to worldly arrangements and earthly hierarchies. These contending inclinations fostered in the colony much the same inflated antisectarian and antipapal rhetoric that structured and enflamed such contests elsewhere in the early English Atlantic world. At the same time, they also proved fertile ground for the volatile, and ultimately combustive, blend of providentialism and skepticism that sundered civil bonds during the English Civil War and that plunged Virginia into its own civil cataclysm in the conflict known as Bacon's Rebellion.[18]

---

17. William Strachey, *The Historie of Travell into Virginia Britania (1612) . . .* , ed. Louis B. Wright and Virginia Freund (London, 1953), xiv, 16–17. The literature on casuistry in this period is rich and growing; see, for instance, Leites, ed., *Conscience and Casuistry;* Brown, *Donne and the Politics of Conscience;* John Morrill, Paul Slack, and Daniel Woolf, eds., *Public Duty and Private Conscience in Seventeenth-Century England* (Oxford, 1993); Lowell Gallagher, *Medusa's Gaze: Casuistry and Conscience in the Renaissance* (Stanford, Calif., 1991); Camille Wells Slights, *The Casuistical Tradition in Shakespeare, Donne, Herbert, and Milton* (Princeton, 1981); and John M. Wallace, *Destiny His Choice: The Loyalism of Andrew Marvell* (Cambridge, 1968).

18. The classic study of the tension of living in the world while not being of it, as that problem

Amid these tensions lay the preconditions for a radical new theory of the relationship between the earthly and the divine, a dramatically secularized view of state sovereignty articulated most influentially in Hobbes's *Leviathan*. Although this study is concerned more with elucidating the world of colonization that preceded Hobbes's momentous argument than with exploring its development alongside, and sometimes in complex interrelationship with, colonization, nevertheless the close integration of colonies, commonwealth, and sovereignty in the previous century meant that *Leviathan* scarcely arose in a vacuum. It matters that Hobbes was a member of the Virginia Company during the early 1620s when tensions between the colony and its sovereign were growing worse. Likewise, *Leviathan*'s pointed discussions of colonies suggest that Hobbes was paying close attention to the colonizing rhetoric around him. His argument, in particular, that colonies can only be commonwealths if freed entirely from their originating sovereign state leaves little doubt that he was not only attentive to that language but also sharply disapproving of it. In the civil incompleteness of the colony, Hobbes seems to have found an especially useful conceptual counterpoint for envisioning the sovereign state's own civil integrity. This theorization of state sovereignty on the back of a still-struggling colonial endeavor would have profound long-term consequences, not least on an imperial crisis and eventual revolution that revolved incessantly around the question of what

---

was experienced specifically in early New England, is Edmund S. Morgan, *The Puritan Dilemma: The Story of John Winthrop* (Boston, 1958). For a richly updated version of the same story, see Michael P. Winship, *Making Heretics: Militant Protestantism and Free Grace in Massachusetts, 1636–1641* (Princeton, 2002). On anti-Calvinism, see Nicholas Tyacke, *Anti-Calvinists: The Rise of English Arminianism, c. 1590–1640* (Oxford, 1990); Peter Lake, "Anti-Puritanism: The Structure of a Prejudice," in Kenneth Fincham and Lake, eds., *Religious Politics in Post-Reformation England: Essays in Honour of Nicholas Tyacke* (Woodbridge, Suffolk, U.K., 2006), 80–97; and Patrick Collinson, "Antipuritanism," in John Coffey and Paul C. H. Lim, eds., *The Cambridge Companion to Puritanism* (Cambridge, 2008), 19–33. On antipopery, see Peter Lake, "Anti-Popery: The Structure of a Prejudice," in Richard Cust and Ann Hughes, eds., *Conflict in Early Stuart England: Studies in Religion and Politics, 1603–1642* (London, 1989), 72–106. For antipopery and anti-Calvinism in America, see Owen Stanwood, *The Empire Reformed: English America in the Age of the Glorious Revolution* (Philadelphia, 2011). The complex interrelationship between providential and skeptical thought deserves more attention. For a useful analysis of the rise of skepticism among late-sixteenth and early-seventeenth-century European intellectuals, see Richard Tuck, *Philosophy and Government, 1572–1651* (Cambridge, 1993).

kind of empire the first century of English colonization in America had wrought.¹⁹

Of even greater concern, however, is the problem of moving past the obscuring haze of the vocabulary and preconceptions of state sovereignty to see early English colonization in America on its own terms. The language colonizers used to justify their project not only drew from the most compelling discourse and conceptual frameworks that were available to them but also gave Renaissance-era colonization its own distinctive meanings. To focus on discourse, arguments, and concepts in this way is not solely an interpretive choice, however. It also flows out of the powerful persuasive as well as constitutive force that contemporaries themselves, trained in humanistic methods and alert to the linguistic nature of civil bonds and human thought, accorded to rhetoric. One reason the first century of English colonization in America generated such a rich outpouring of written materials as well as spoken sermons and speeches (the latter oral utterances available to the present day only in those few instances when they were committed to writing or print) was that language itself was regarded as an unusually effective means by which kings and subjects alike were steered toward their duties and commonwealths realized. In tracing the efforts to justify and bring into existence Virginia's polity, this book has tried to remain true to early modern usages and assumptions. It has not followed this approach puritanically; when concessions have seemed necessary for the argument's clarity and not overly misleading, modern usages have prevailed. Yet, the particular ways the colonizing project was defended and framed were instrumental in giving Virginia's polity its original integrity and shape. This was true even when

19. Hobbes was a regular attendee of Virginia Company meetings after June 19, 1622. On Hobbes's membership in the company and its possible influence on his ideas, see Noel Malcolm, "Hobbes, Sandys, and the Virginia Company," in Malcolm, *Aspects of Hobbes* (Oxford, 2002), 53–79. For Hobbes's argument that colonies are provinces and that they only become commonwealths if freed by their sovereigns, see Hobbes, *Leviathan*, ed. Richard Tuck, Cambridge Texts in the History of Political Thought (Cambridge, 1996), 176–177. The view that the American Revolution was at bottom a constitutional crisis over the makeup of the empire in an age still grappling with the meaning of state sovereignty has been the focus of a broad scholarly literature. See, for instance, Jack P. Greene, *The Constitutional Origins of the American Revolution* (Cambridge, 2011); J. G. A. Pocock, "Empire, State, and Confederation: The War of American Independence as a Crisis in Multiple Monarchy' in Pocock, *The Discovery of Islands: Essays in British History* (Cambridge, 2005), 134–163.

these aspects of the colony's commonwealth remained frighteningly open ended and contested, a harrowing fluidity between the earth's corruptions and Providence's mysteries that Renaissance-era colonization both invited and could never quite contain.[20]

20. Among the concessions that the book makes to modern rhetorical usages, two are apparent in this introduction. I have relied heavily on the words "colonization" and "colonizers," although these terms were not coined until late in the eighteenth century. At that time, both words carried implications of the Hobbesian state projecting its sovereign and commercial integrity outward. I have tried to use the terms more neutrally, to refer to the project of planting colonies and the persons promoting or actively carrying out that endeavor. For the words' late-eighteenth-century provenance, see *Oxford English Dictionary Online*, s.v. "colonization, n.," accessed June 24, 2014, http://www.oed.com/view/Entry/36538?redirectedFrom=colonization, and s.v. "colonizer, n.," accessed June 24, 2014, http://www.oed.com/view/Entry/36542?redirectedFrom=colonizer. My view of historical actors as reliant on the particular languages and concepts available to them to make credible moral claims, languages and concepts that, in turn, create the imaginative frameworks available to others is informed in part by Quentin Skinner, "Some Problems in the Analysis of Political Thought and Action," *Political Theory*, II (1974), 277–303. I have also found valuable Conal Condren's distinction between the early modern vocabulary and presuppositions of office and the modern quest for past ideologies. See Condren, *Argument and Authority*, 3–6, 276–281.

[I]
PROVIDENCE, THE RENAISSANCE ATLANTIC, AND LAW

In late 1583, England's young colonizing endeavor in America confronted its first minor crisis of legitimacy, a cloud of doubts and uncertainties blown in on the particularly confidence-shattering gusts of a violent Atlantic storm. The squall had struck on September 9, hitting Sir Humphrey Gilbert's convoy, en route home after boldly declaring Newfoundland to be Queen Elizabeth's lawful sovereign territory. Edward Hayes, one of the surviving captains, later described the swirling rains and sharply cresting waves as "breaking short and high Pyramid wise." In a moment, Gilbert's own small and overloaded frigate, the *Squirrel*, was gone, "devoured and swallowed up of the Sea." The critical issue at hand, however, lay less in Gilbert's actual drowning than in the questions that circulated afterward, once Hayes's own ship limped into Falmouth two weeks later with the venture's commanding officer conspicuously absent. Rumors about the stricken colonizing effort must have circulated quickly and with a palpable sense of unease. Few other eventualities in relation to American voyages spoke more vividly of God's will than the fierce storms that separated convoys and swallowed ships, except perhaps, violent attacks by indigenous peoples that contemporary English persons would be similarly quick to interpret in providential terms. No matter the assertive claims that Gilbert had just made in Newfoundland of the queen's rightful possession in America, storms that struck with a force that could only be God given pointed even more powerfully to what was and was not lawful.[1]

Key officials near the throne who, far more than the queen herself, were

---

1. "Edward Hayes' Narrative of Sir Humphrey Gilbert's Last Expedition," [October 1583?], in David Beers Quinn, ed., *The Voyages and Colonising Enterprises of Sir Humphrey Gilbert*, Works Issued by the Hakluyt Society, 2d Ser., no. 84 (London, 1940), II, 419–420.

the real partisans of her sovereignty across the ocean lost little time in trying to stem whatever damage might have been caused by Gilbert's drowning. Two justificatory writings quickly emerged, both almost certainly commissioned by some of Elizabeth's most powerful royal councillors. Hayes himself wrote one of the apologias, probably at the bidding of his patron, the Privy Councillor and sometime secretary of state William Cecil, first Baron Burghley. The document was explicit in its aim to head off anxieties about divine disapproval and most likely circulated in fairly close circles in and around Elizabeth's court in manuscript before it was eventually published in 1589 by the clergyman Richard Hakluyt as "A Report of the Voyage and Successe Thereof, Attempted in the Yeere of Our Lord, 1583; by Sir Humfrey Gilbert Knight..." in his *Principall Navigations, Voiages, and Discoveries of the English Nation*. Hakluyt, through his older cousin Richard Hakluyt the lawyer, had also been connected with Burghley and Sir Francis Walsingham before becoming the client of Burghley's son, Robert Cecil. In Hayes's words, he wrote the piece "least any man should be dismayd by example of other folks calamity, and misdeeme that God doth resist all attempts intended that way." In keeping with his emphasis on God's selectivity in resisting some but not all such attempts "intended that way," Hayes did not simply deny God's anger. Few of Elizabeth's courtiers, including the powerful faction of Catholic aristocrats who were in all likelihood the most ardent critics of English colonization in America, would have accepted that such a violent storm could be anything but a sign of the Almighty's wrath. Instead, he pointed to particular sins in Gilbert's voyage that must have led to the drowning. Various "misdemeanor[s]" committed by the crew, including horrific acts of piracy that involved torturing local fishermen, he argued, undoubtedly helped to explain the occasional sunken cockboats and other fatalities that could only be signs of "Gods justice." He even searched Gilbert's own soul for imperfections and found them in his "temeritie and presumption," qualities that stunk of the sin of pride. The "prodigall" way in which he spent both his own estate and the money of others and his impatience to embark before preparations for the voyage were truly complete made manifest his incapacity to be a leader. Grimly, Hayes concluded that Gilbert's venture was indeed preordained for a terrible end. The "issue of such actions," he surmised, is "always miserable" if they are "not guided by God, who abhorreth confusion and disorder."[2]

2. Ibid., II, 389, 399, 422–423. For biographical information on Hayes, see David Beers Quinn, *England and the Discovery of America, 1481–1620: From the Bristol Voyages of the Fifteenth Cen-*

On the other hand, Hayes also concluded that God's awful stroke against Gilbert contained a message. "God, who abhorreth confusion and disorder, hath left this for admonition," he wrote. Given that Gilbert's venture was "the first attempt by our nation to plant," God clearly intended to communicate "unto such as shall take the same cause in hand hereafter not to be discouraged from it: but to make men well advised how they handle his so high and excellent matters." In other words, prudent resolution, not weak-willed demoralization, was called for. As Hayes explained the moral juncture faced by any ocean-braving courtiers who might choose to follow in Gilbert's ill-destined footsteps:

> In the meane while, it behooveth every man of great calling, in whom is any instinct of inclination unto this attempt, to examine his owne motions: which if the same proceed of ambition or avarice, he may assure himselfe it commeth not of God, and therefore can not have confidence of Gods protection and assistance against the violence (els irresistible) both of sea, and infinite perils upon the land; whom God yet may use an instrument to further his cause and glory some way, but not to build upon so bad a foundation.

In short, the colonizing courtier was to undertake the enterprise with the utmost gravity, recognizing that, as God's instrument, he embarked on nothing less than a sacred trust.[3]

The second justificatory writing was intended for a somewhat broader audience. Appearing in the form of a pamphlet, it was offered for sale around November 12 in a decidedly more vulgar milieu — the bustling book mart at

---

tury to the Pilgrim Settlement at Plymouth: The Exploration, Exploitation, and Trial-and-Error Colonization of North America by the English (New York, 1973), 227–234. Richard Hakluyt the clergyman published Hayes's work in a collection of exploration accounts in 1589 dedicated to Walsingham. For a modern edition, see "A Report of the Voyage and Successe Thereof, Attempted in the Yeere of Our Lord, 1583; by Sir Humfrey Gilbert Knight . . . ," in Hakluyt, *The Principall Navigations, Voiages, and Discoveries of the English Nation by Richard Hakluyt, Imprinted at London, 1589*, Hakluyt Society Extra Series, no. 39, 2 vols. (Cambridge, 1965), [II], 679–697. The role of Catholic courtiers in objecting to the venture is difficult to confirm definitively, but for the perception in the later Sir Walter Ralegh expeditions of the 1580s that such actors were among the key adversaries of such voyages, see Chapters 2 and 3, below.

3. "Edward Hayes' Narrative," [October 1583?], in Quinn, ed., *Voyages and Colonising Enterprises of Sir Humphrey Gilbert*, II, 386–387, 389.

Saint Paul's Churchyard, where cheap books and newssheets were vended for a penny or two under such colorful booksellers' signs as the Golden Hind, the Swan, the Blue Bell, the Crane, and the Black Bear. Entitled *A True Reporte, of the Late Discoveries, and Possession, Taken in the Right of the Crowne of Englande, of the Newfound Landes: By That Valiaunt and Worthye Gentleman, Sir Humfrey Gilbert Knight* . . . (1583) and bearing the queen's own imprimatur "Seene and allowed," the pamphlet appears to have been commissioned by Secretary of State Walsingham, who was undoubtedly also responsible for the behind-the-scenes securing of Elizabeth's permission to issue the text. Although Walsingham, like Burghley, was a staunchly Protestant advocate for the queen's sovereignty, he entrusted the writing of the text to the Catholic Oxford scholar George Peckham. That a Catholic was assigned the delicate task of asserting the lawfulness of a colonizing endeavor already authorized by the queen almost certainly related to the councillors' perception that the most dire threat at this moment came from the combined forces of the Spanish monarchy, the pope, and English Catholic aristocrats. This formidable trio could be expected to seize the opportunity to interpret Gilbert's drowning as a vivid emblem of God's anger and Protestant England's broader heretical confusion about God's will. An apologia for Elizabeth's American imperium written by an adherent to the old faith at once undercut English Catholic opposition to that claim and spread the word at home and abroad that the queen would not be intimidated by Spanish or papal threats. Only the year before, Don Bernardino de Mendoza, Philip II's ambassador to England, had spread a warning to English subjects who chose to intrude on Philip's American lands. Not only could they expect to "immediately have their throats cut," a penalty already notoriously meted out to French settlers in Florida, but they would also imperil "their consciences by engaging in an enterprise prejudicial to His Holiness," Pope Gregory XIII. This threat to bodies as well as souls almost certainly informed Peckham's pamphlet. Addressing his work to English noblemen, gentlemen, and merchants, Peckham sought to assure them that Elizabeth's American title was sound. Investors and settlers alike could participate in the endeavor with little fear for either their consciences or their throats.[4]

4. The queen's authorization appeared on the title page of G[eorge] P[eckham], *A True Reporte, of the Late Discoveries, and Possession, Taken in the Right of the Crowne of Englande, of the Newfound Landes: By That Valiaunt and Worthye Gentleman, Sir Humfrey Gilbert Knight* . . . (London, 1583). For the attribution of the text to George Peckham, the scholarly son of the Catholic gentleman and investor in Gilbert's voyage, see Quinn, "The English Catholics and America,

Like Hayes, however, Peckham presumed to speak, not simply as a mouthpiece for the sovereign queen and her advisers, but rather as a person with unique insight into God's own intentions and desires. He conveyed this providential view with an anecdote drawn from Plutarch's life of Themistocles. Themistocles had just approached the citizens of Athens with a newly invented war tactic, a "devise for theyr common wealth very profitable." On his suggestion that the importance of the invention warranted its evaluation by some "prudent" person, the Athenians chose the philosopher Aristides as someone "indued with singuler wisedome and vertue." Aristides proceeded to contemplate the invention, which involved setting fire to the Athenians' enemy's navy, and determined, on the basis of his learned musings, that it "was a profitable practise for the common wealth but it was dishonest." Forming their own judgment on the basis of Aristides's reliable opinion, the Athenians, by "common consent," rejected the invention, "preferring honest and upright dealing before profite." The whole account spoke richly of a number of Christian humanist values: the commonwealth as grounded in wise counsel, a notion of profitability as necessarily tied to morality, and veneration for civic participation centered on the ideal of "common consent."[5]

But Peckham did not stop there. Treating this classical anecdote as Christian humanists so often did, as tantamount to a parable, he proceeded to relate how contemplating this story of commonwealth honesty gleaned by wise counsel led him on his own introspective search for truth, as though he were a latter-day Aristides who had the peculiar capacity to establish a truth that was nothing less than God's will:

1581–1633," in Quinn, *England and the Discovery of America*, 379n. For greater accessibility, all quotes to Peckham's text in this study are from the reprinted version "Sir George Peckham's *True Reporte*...," in Quinn, ed., *Voyages and Colonising Enterprises of Sir Humphrey Gilbert*, I, 435–482. For the threat to throats and consciences, see Don Bernardino de Mendoza to Philip II, July 11, 1582, in Quinn, ed., *Voyages and Colonising Enterprises of Sir Humphrey Gilbert*, II, 279. In the same letter, Mendoza also explained to the Spanish king that he had directed English Catholics who were still considering the trip to send their inquiries to the pope through the seminarian William Allen to "learn if they could justifiably make the voyage" (279). In 1565, the Spanish captain general Pedro Menéndez de Avilés attacked Fort Caroline, established on the Florida coast by the French Huguenot René Goulaine de Laudonnière, and killed most of the men inside. On Saint Paul's Churchyard in this period, see Joad Raymond, *Pamphlets and Pamphleteering in Early Modern Britain* (Cambridge, 2003), 1.

5. "Sir George Peckham's *True Reporte*," in Quinn, ed., *Voyages and Colonising Enterprises of Sir Humphrey Gilbert*, I, 446–447.

> By occasion of this historie, I drewe my selfe into a more deeper consideration, of thys late undertaken voyage, whether it were as well pleasing to almightie God, as profitable to men? as lawfull as it seemed honourable. As well gratefull to the Savages, as gainfull to the Christians. And upon mature deliberation, I founde the action to bee honest and profitable, and therefore allowable by the opinion of *Aristides* if he were nowe alive.

In other words, Peckham had arrived at a "deeper" truth, far more reliable than most of the rumors then circulating in and around the noisy environs of Saint Paul's Churchyard. He spoke of nothing less than what was "pleasing to almightie God." It was on the basis of that providential insight into God's intentions that Peckham asserted his queen's lawful title on the other side of the Atlantic, just as Hayes had similarly looked to the heavens when he advised the queen's courtiers to meditate on their colonizing intentions to determine if they truly came from God.[6]

These writings bring to the fore the providential presuppositions and the complex casuistic milieu that informed American colonization on the eve of the Virginia venture, an endeavor born to a great extent amid anxieties about divine disapproval that dramatic events like Gilbert's death repeatedly seemed to evidence. The period's intense providentialism insinuated itself into contemporary conceptions of law, sovereignty, and polity that, while supporting claims to paramount authority, did not yet constitute the sovereign states of a later age. By the time Gilbert made his voyage, Renaissance humanism had already reinforced and elaborated on the scholastic view that earthly monarchs might sometimes wield an imperium comparable to God's, a power perhaps nowhere more relevant than in the European quest for sound American dominion. Gilbert crossed the Atlantic under the "licence" of his queen, acting under the authority of Elizabeth's letters patent of June 11, 1578, which went a long way toward vouching for the legitimacy of his undertaking. Once in Newfoundland, he similarly relied on the law-giving power that he associated with the ideal of imperial monarchy. On August 5, 1583, he called together the sundry European fishermen who had historically exploited the area's cod-rich waters, informing them that the Church of England was now the region's official church, Elizabeth its queen, and anyone who vocally denied such claims a rebel warranting the loss of his ears and goods. Likewise, his reliance on civil law tenets and prescriptions

---

6. Ibid., II, 447.

under *ius gentium* (or the law of nations) to establish lawful "possession" also reflected the assumption that earthly sovereignty operated by identifiable norms. Rooted in ancient Roman law, this jurisprudence, which was available to early modern jurists in such works as Emperor Justinian's *Corpus Iuris Civilis (The Body of Civil Laws)* and Saint Thomas Aquinas's *Summa Theologiae,* provided Gilbert with legal tools that stood a chance at least of being accepted within Europe's own *ius commune,* a shared system of law that medieval canonists and civilians had gradually brought into being and that early modern kingdoms eager to assert their own imperium had similarly recognized. The perceived universality of these legal principles meant that for Gilbert they were the obvious instruments to deploy in attempting to override any comparatively private claims, such as those the Spanish or Portuguese fishermen might make in asserting the propriety of their own activities, or any erroneous claims, so understood by English Protestants in this era, such as the pope's exclusive grant of temporal dominion in America to the Castilian monarchy.[7]

Yet, earthly rule, no matter its heightened legitimizing power, was still dwarfed by the divine supremacy that stood momentously, and often terrifyingly, over the blackening skies, surging winds, and rolling waves that colonizers so often encountered in the tempestuous Atlantic. The law was not yet envisioned as solely human artifice, as Thomas Hobbes would insist must be

---

7. "The Letters Patents Graunted by Her Majestie to Sir Humfrey Gilbert Knight, for the Inhabiting and Planting of Our People in America," in Hakluyt, *Principall Navigations,* [II], 677–679; "Edward Hayes' Narrative," [October 1583?], in Quinn, ed., *Voyages and Colonising Enterprises of Sir Humphrey Gilbert,* II, 402–403. For the development in Europe from 1100 to 1600 of a *ius commune* forged from the combination of Roman, canon, and feudal law, see Kenneth Pennington, *The Prince and the Law, 1200–1600: Sovereignty and Rights in the Western Legal Tradition* (Berkeley, Calif., 1993), 6–7, 40–41, 77, 99, 103, 179, 185–201, 222–223, 271–272, 284–290. On the reception in Renaissance England of Roman law and its role in informing sixteenth- and seventeenth-century English claims to possession, see Ken MacMillan, *Sovereignty and Possession in the English New World: The Legal Foundations of Empire, 1576–1640* (Cambridge, 2006), 9–12, 25–31, 52, 61–62, 76, 84, 108–115. MacMillan's study helps to refute the once accepted view that early modern Europeans were limited by their local legal cultures in making substantive claims to New World title. Instead Roman law especially, and its derivatives, including civil law, natural law, and the law of nations, provided a common vocabulary and a loose set of procedures for asserting such claims in a manner that overcame national boundaries. For the useful observation that this legal lingua franca tended to be deployed creatively, rather than inflexibly, by travelers and colonizing actors themselves, see Lauren Benton, *A Search for Sovereignty: Law and Geography in European Empires, 1400–1900* (Cambridge, 2010), 23–30, 34, 113–116, 150, 211.

the case in a world still awaiting Judgment Day. Instead, in certain important respects, the period saw an intensified, not diminished, concern with the relationship of sovereignty and commonwealth to God's will. Inspired by the divine basis on which scholastics themselves had erected princely imperium and propelled by the era's renewed biblicism to give even greater significance to earthly power's foundations in God, contemporaries yoked royal imperium ever more firmly to the heavens. This invigorated providentialism is perhaps nowhere more revealingly indicated than by Hobbes's own explicit reliance on eschatology in *Leviathan* (1651). Until that prophesied moment when God's kingdom on Earth was actually restored, Hobbes argued, humans had little choice but to look to their earthbound rulers for final determinations on the law — a providential defense of a secularized commonwealth that seems paradoxical only in hindsight. Rather than moving inexorably from a deeply theological medieval scholasticism to an early modern humanistic culture that wrenched law and politics away from theology, no such straightforward secularization took place. Instead, humanism converged with the theological concerns and epistemological battles of the Reformation and Counter-Reformation, stimulating new waves of biblical scholarship, generating renewed interest in those Hebrew sources that promised to make the Old Testament a vital source of knowledge of God's will, and fostering a distinctively Christian humanist climate highly conducive, rather than hostile, to providential belief.[8]

Contributing greatly to the influence and spread of this vibrant sixteenth-

---

8. Hobbes's eschatological reasoning can be traced through several parts of *Leviathan*. For some key sections, see Thomas Hobbes, *Leviathan*, ed. Richard Tuck, Cambridge Texts in the History of Political Thought (Cambridge, 1996), 245–254, 280–320, 402–439. For a classic work on the eschatological dimensions of Hobbes's arguments, see J. G. A. Pocock, "Time, History, and Eschatology in the Thought of Thomas Hobbes," in Pocock, *Politics, Language, and Time* (London, 1972), 148–201. On the Protestant Reformation as encouraging an invigorated providentialism while also making Providence a central element of Christian faith, see Alexandra Walsham, *Providence in Early Modern England* (Oxford, 1999), 8–32. On the Hebrew revival, see Eric Nelson, *The Hebrew Republic: Jewish Sources and the Transformation of European Political Thought* (Cambridge, Mass., 2010), 7–16, 138–139. For the rise of Christian humanism in northern Europe that was tied to the biblical reformation of Christendom and thus distinct from the more "secularized philosophical inclinations" of the earlier Italian Renaissance, see Margo Todd, *Christian Humanism and the Puritan Social Order* (Cambridge, 1987), 17–26, 30n, 34, 37–41, 43–51, 56–67, 78, 80–82, 84–91. On the intertwined Christian notion of calling and the ancient Roman ideal of office, see Conal Condren, *Argument and Authority in Early Modern England: The Presuppositions of Oaths and Offices* (Cambridge, 2006), 25.

and seventeenth-century Christian humanist culture were the growth of print and the emergence of the kind of rhetorical activity evident in Hayes's and Peckham's writings: a politics of indirect, and self-consciously casuistic, efforts to define the contours of lawfulness, whether with or without the sovereign's authorization and often with the express purpose of bending the sovereign monarch's will in directions it seemed waywardly inclined to shun. Like Sir Walter Ralegh's *History of the World* (1614), which sought to provide Prince Henry with a chronicle of the world that was at once universal history and a mirror of past virtuous deeds and valorous men by which he was to understand his own kingly office, these writings took for granted the providential nature of the cosmos. Circulating either in print or in manuscript, they readily employed the era's widespread vocabulary of office, determining the rightful performance, or abuse, of duties on the basis of purported callings. And they concerned themselves with the traditional preoccupations of the casuist, presuming to speak to when the profitable was godly, the honorable lawful, and the beneficial redeeming. Thus consumed by the traditional Christian humanist problem of living in this world without becoming of it, these works always, at some level, addressed the ideal of commonwealth, exalting an archetypal union of lawful human relations that they took for granted was rooted as much in scripture as in history.[9]

9. Although this political culture of influence and pressure has sometimes been referred to as a post-Reformation "public sphere," I resist the term on the grounds that it suggests an understanding of sovereignty and its critique that, in my view, awaited Hobbes's secularizing arguments. As long as sovereign rule was grasped as a divinely ordained office in need of casuistic direction, it invited the kind of counsel, whether offered directly or indirectly, that these men were providing. The very idea of an autonomous arena of political criticism and opposition, which, in turn, presupposes a clearly defined and earthbound sovereign center, had little bearing on an era that regarded all power as subject to a higher authority over which nobody, not even monarchs, enjoyed an interpretive monopoly. On the idea of a post-Reformation public sphere, see Peter Lake and Steven Pincus, "Rethinking the Public Sphere in Early Modern England," in Lake and Pincus, eds., *The Politics of the Public Sphere in Early Modern England* (Manchester, U.K., 2007), 1–30. See also, Natalie Mears, *Queenship and Political Discourse in the Elizabethan Realms* (Cambridge, 2005), 1–32, 185–216. For a critical view that has contributed to my own sense of the inapplicability of the public sphere concept to this era, see Condren *Argument and Authority*, 34, 54, 77–79, 91, 94, 227. On universal history and the past as a mirror in this period, see Bart van Es, *Spenser's Forms of History* (Oxford, 2002), esp. 112–163. For these themes in relation to Ralegh's *History of the World* (1614) see Nicholas Popper, *Walter Ralegh's History of the World and the Historical Culture of the Late Renaissance* (Chicago, 2012), 6–7, 27–30, 34–36, 53–58, 69–74, 94–100, 254.

The justificatory campaigns around the colonizing endeavor both fed on and reinforced the era's providential milieu. This providential context elicited the frequent question, one that arose with particular pointedness in the aftermath of frightening storms or amid other portentous occurrences, whether God was perhaps less, or maybe more, immediately present in America than in England. Firsthand accounts of providential remorse powerfully shaped the colonizing discourse. Afflicted by a terrible famine during a voyage to Newfoundland in 1536 and resorting to cannibalism, the crew of Master Robert Hore purportedly felt terrible anguish after their captain furiously rebuked them "that the power of the Almightie was then no lesse, then in al former time it had bene." On his admonition, they supposedly fell to fretful prayer. Profound uncertainty must have beset many would-be voyagers to America, like the Londoners whom the Jacobean preacher William Symonds observed "will not goe abroad, for feare of loosing the blessing of God" if they choose to "liveth among barbarous people."[10]

Providential phenomena that steered even the sovereign will of kings were a commonplace in the Renaissance Atlantic. In 1572, Henry Hawkes, an English merchant who had lived and traveled for five years in New Spain, wrote to Hakluyt the lawyer to describe how Philip II changed law in response to unmistakable signs from God. Almost certainly writing with the assumption that his report would provide Walsingham or Burghley with relevant information about Spanish dominion overseas, Hawkes explained in detail the evident miracles that had influenced the Spanish king. In one instance, greedy local officials who sought to commandeer a mine from the poorer man who had discovered it found to their amazement that a moun-

---

10. "The Voyage of Master Hore and Divers Other Gentlemen, to Newfound Land, and Cape Breton, in the Yeere 1536. and in the 28. Yeere of King Henry the Eight," in Hakluyt, *Principall Navigations*, [II], 518; William Symonds, *Virginia: A Sermon Preached at White-Chappel, in the Presence of Many, Honourable and Worshipfull, the Adventurers and Planters for Virginia. 25. April. 1609* . . . (London, 1609), 30. The theme of Providence has been explored usefully in the American context, though largely in relation to New England rather than Virginia; see Michael P. Winship, *Seers of God: Puritan Providentialism in the Restoration and Early Enlightenment* (Baltimore, 1996); and David D. Hall, *Worlds of Wonder, Days of Judgment: Popular Religious Belief in Early New England* (New York, 1989). Providentialism has also attracted students of the justificatory literature around colonization; see Michael G. Moran, *Inventing Virginia: Sir Walter Raleigh and the Rhetoric of Colonization, 1584–1590* (New York, 2007), 82, 107, 234–235; and Alfred A. Cave, "Canaanites in a Promised Land: The American Indian and the Providential Theory of Empire," *American Indian Quarterly*, XII (1988), 277–297.

tain had mysteriously covered its entrance. In a similar dreadful portent, a mercury well vanished entirely when Spanish magistrates again attempted to exploit such God-given riches in disregard of the humble man to whom they had originally been revealed. According to Hawkes, as soon as the Spanish king learned of these miracles, he hastily wrote a law protecting all original discoverers of wealth, no matter the meanness of their station in life — a cringing acknowledgement, though probably for Walsingham and Burghley also a reassuring one, that even royal officialdom in the Spanish Indies sat under God's stern judgment.[11]

In addition to shifting mountains and disappearing wells, churning seas also had the potential to change human conceptions of what was or was not lawful. After the tempest that took Gilbert's life, the Atlantic's violent squalls remained a similarly suggestive force during his half-brother Ralegh's colonizing efforts at Roanoke. When a torrential storm struck on June 13, 1586, the colony's leader Ralph Lane used it controversially as an excuse to abandon the yearlong settlement, arguing "the very hand of God as it seemed, stretched out to take us from thence." Unimpressed by both Lane's interpretation and the colonists' craven departure, though not by the idea of Providence itself, Hakluyt the clergyman countered that "the hande of God came upon them for the crueltie, and outrages committed by some of them against the native inhabitances of that Countrie." During the Virginia Company's colonizing efforts in the Jacobean era, the most notorious storm was the one that separated the Virginia-bound convoy on July 24, 1609, marooning the *Sea Venture* under the command of Admiral Sir George Somers at Bermuda (for years afterward known in England as the Somers Islands). The event, which inspired Shakespeare's *Tempest*, stimulated numerous analyses of God's intentions for English colonists and their king. As one Virginia Company pamphleteer put it, "Who can withstand the counsell of God that sits in the stearne of all actions?"[12]

---

11. "Report from Henry Hawks to Richard Hakluyt, Lawyer," 1572, in E. G. R. Taylor, ed., *The Original Writings and Correspondence of the Two Richard Hakluyts,* Works Issued by the Hakluyt Society, 2d Ser., no. 76 (London, 1935), I, 102–103. Hakluyt the clergyman published Hawkes's report in 1589. See "A Relation of the Commodities of Nova Hispania, and the Maners of the Inhabitants, Written by Henry Hawkes Marchant . . . ," 1572, in Hakluyt, *Principall Navigations,* [II], 545–553.

12. "Ralph Lane's Discourse on the First Colony," Aug. 17, 1585–June 18, 1586, in David Beers Quinn, ed., *The Roanoke Voyages, 1584–1590: Documents to Illustrate the English Voyages to North America under the Patent Granted to Walter Raleigh in 1584,* Works Issued by the Hakluyt Society,

By the middle decades of the seventeenth century, skeptical currents were beginning to erode such vigorous providential interpretation, especially by questioning the capacity of humans to always comprehend God's omnipresent counsel with assurance. Yet, belief in the immediacy of divine judgment was itself slow to wane, tending to intermingle uneasily with the new skepticism rather than surrender to it. The resulting combination of impulses — lingering fearfulness about God's plan running alongside growing distrust of those persons most energetically professing it — had the effect of heightening confusion about the law rather than clarifying it. In England, these tensions contributed to the rapid escalation of mutual distrust between godly parliamentarians and royalists, each side convinced of the other's hypocrisy while no less assured of its own piety. In America, the same strains often appeared in relation to wars with native peoples, waves of bellicosity that repeatedly risked pitting fragile colonial governments against the bloodlust of frightened settlers — again, with connotations of righteousness that could quickly devolve into reciprocal accusations of angering God.

The massive attack on Virginia on March 22, 1622, led by the Powhatan warrior Opechancanough spurred just such a series of mutual recriminations across the ocean, as officials in England and those in the colony sought to identify whose sins were most to blame for an event that was clearly ordained by their Maker. "A *Flood*, a *Flood* of *bloud* have broken in upon them," cried John Donne, the dean of Saint Paul's, as if the violence of the attack was perfectly analogous to a divinely instigated storm. Opechancanough's even deadlier attack on the colony in 1644 similarly generated multipronged anxieties and complex allegations of responsibility. That the opening stages of the English Civil War had begun by this time gave the ensuing war with the natives a broader backdrop of significance, triggering an accompanying series of charges and countercharges between Governor Sir William Berkeley and local Puritans over whether Virginia's commonwealth displeased God because it was in the grip of sectarian madness or, in contrast, because it was threatened by quasi-papist tyranny. Bacon's Rebellion, too, emerged

---

2d Ser., no. 104 (London, 1955), I, 292, "The 1586 Voyages," 478; R[obert] J[ohnson], *The New Life of Virginea: Declaring the Former Successe and Present Estate of That Plantation, Being the Second Part of Nova Britannia; Published by the Authoritie of His Majesties Counsell of Virginea* (London, 1612), [B4]v. On the providential interpretations of the 1586 storm, see Moran, *Inventing Virginia*, 82, 234–235. For a useful discussion of some of the debates over Shakespeare's Virginia sources for *The Tempest*, see Alden T. Vaughan, "William Strachey's 'True Reportory' and Shakespeare: A Closer Look at the Evidence," *Shakespeare Quarterly*, LIX (2008), 245–273.

from fears of divine wrath that swirled around the growing violence between frontier settlers and local Doegs and Susquehannocks. As that event spiraled into a colony-wide civil war that pitted those counties that sided with Berkeley against those that sided with the alleged rebel, Nathaniel Bacon, Jr., God's severe will remained the most compelling explanation for such a profound civil conflagration, mirroring in various ways the righteous calls to arms that similarly rang out during the English Civil War. Thus, Berkeley could assert confidently, and with a bristling sense of vindication for what he regarded as England's own illicit takeover by the faux saint Oliver Cromwell, that Bacon's death by the "Bloody flux" was tangible proof that the "Justice and Judgement of God overtooke him."[13]

The law and Providence intertwined in this Renaissance era forming a set of complex issues. Three themes will be of especial significance. The Renaissance idea of the law as pathways of rightful conduct where God's will and human initiative intersected was nowhere more resonantly emblematized in this period than in Christopher Columbus's discovery. The contemporary mode of moral argument known as casuistry delineated and elaborated on such pathways while distinguishing them from the erroneous ways that too often determine human behavior. And the ideal of commonwealth as a constellation of rightly turned wills and lawfully performed offices served

---

13. John Donne, *A Sermon Preached to the Honourable Company of the Virginian Plantation* ... (London 1622), in George R. Potter and Evelyn M. Simpson, eds., *The Sermons of John Donne* (Berkeley, Calif., 1959), IV, 271; William Berkeley to Henry Coventry, Feb. 2, 1676/77, in Warren M. Billings, ed., with Maria Kimberly, *The Papers of Sir William Berkeley, 1605–1677* (Richmond, Va., 2007), 572–573. I treat the mutual recriminations that arose from the 1622 attack in Chapter 4, below. A Puritan writer of an article in the London newspaper *Mercurius Civicus* identified the 1644 attack as divine retribution for the unlawfulness of Governor Sir William Berkeley's treatment of the colony's Puritans. See Joseph Frank, ed., "News from Virginny, 1644," *Virginia Magazine of History and Biography*, LXV (1957), 85–86. The fear of papist rule that ran through the event and the Berkeleyites' own concern about Puritan zealousness are apparent in a contemporary letter by Richard Kemp, acting governor while Berkeley was in England purchasing weapons and ammunition. See Kemp to Berkeley, Feb. 27, 1644/45, in Billings, ed., *Papers of Sir William Berkeley*, 62–66. Berkeley's determination to deny Cromwell's divine favor can be traced through a number of writings. See, for instance, Berkeley, *A Discourse and View of Virginia* [January 1661/62], in Billings, ed., *Papers of Sir William Berkeley*, 167, Berkeley to Richard Nicolls, May 20, 1666, 280, and Berkeley, "Answers to the Inquiries from the Council for Foreign Plantations," June 20, 1671, 397. For Cromwell's providential view of the civil wars and his own rule, see, for instance, Blair Worden, *God's Instruments: Political Conduct in the England of Oliver Cromwell* (Oxford, 2012), 13–32.

to make even royal sovereignty an instrument in the performance of God's plan. Together, these themes helped to give the first century of English colonization efforts in America an important measure of coherence, buoying the colonizers even as they steered toward the darkening skies and gale-force winds that punished wayward souls.

Pathways of Lawful Conduct and Columbus's Discovery

The providential significance of storms rested on a view of the cosmos with ancient as well as medieval roots. In this conception of the universe, the world since the Fall had consisted of two sharply distinguished spheres, the "ethereal" heavens and the "elemental" Earth. Heavenly bodies moved predictably, as was consistent with God's power. The earth, in contrast, was a scene of relentless change and sublunary capriciousness. Though Calvinists grumbled that the vulgar continued to mistake such earthly vacillations for the pagan idea of Fortune, in fact, God's will and chance had long intertwined as ways of explaining the rise and fall of individuals, families, communities, and nations. The Church of England clergyman George Hakewill, who shared Ralegh's humanistic optimism that such worldly mutability could eventually be overcome, was characteristic of many of those involved in the colonizing venture in regarding the never-certain condition of "*Monarchies* and *Kingdomes* . . . much lesse petty states and private families" as itself a spur to virtuous industry, the ups and downs of civil life motivating the truly energetic actor both to resist despair and to shrug off complacency.[14]

To adventure, as the planting of new colonies overseas or the engagement

14. [John Rastell], *A New Iuterlude and a Mery of the Nature of the .iiii. Element Declarynge Many Proper Poynt of Phylosophy Naturall, and of Dyvers Straunge Landys, and of Dyvers Straunge Effects [and] Causis* . . . [London, 1520?], [A.v.]r; G[eorge] H[akewill], *An Apologie of the Power and Providence of God in the Government of the World; or, An Examination and Censure of the Common Errour Touching Natures Perpetuall and Universall Decay* . . . (Oxford, 1627), C[1]v. On the ancient and medieval views that provided the long-term backdrop for such a two-part conception of the cosmos as well as the slowness of Copernican and Galilean arguments in changing it, see William J. Bouwsma, *The Waning of the Renaissance, 1550–1640* (New Haven, Conn., 2000), 20, 67–85. On the often-complex interrelationship between Fortune and Providence in this era, see Walsham, *Providence in Early Modern England*, 20–22; R. A. D. Grant, "Providence, Authority, and the Moral Life in *The Tempest*," *Shakespeare Studies*, XVI (1983), 235–263.

in long-distance trade was often called, was to hazard chance — a meaning that, when conjoined with providential thought, enjoyed connotations of a tough and resolute piety. Constancy was necessary because God ordinarily relied on earthly instruments to perform his will, binding to himself not only persons but also other parts of the elemental world — beasts, plants, minerals — through callings, or offices, that marked out a set of duties that were lawful by the very fact of their divine ordination. Though conducted by earthly beings, the performance of such offices functioned as a form of mediated divine intervention, becoming the "second causes, and subalterne meanes" by which God, as primary mover, realized his will on Earth. Nor need such offices be in any obvious sense moral or good. That even seemingly evil actions took place in accordance with God's plan (thus rendering them at a certain fundamental level good despite their infliction of harm and misery) was one of the age's great paradoxes, a mystery that English Protestants at this time often invoked when contemplating in dismay the blessings in power and wealth that God manifestly heaped on the Spaniards and Turks.[15]

In the idea of Providence, the humanists' interest in people's active role in returning a fallen world to obedience intersected with the medieval scholastics' fascination with God's power and humanity's free will. From the late fifteenth century onward, frequent translations and reprinting of Boethius's sixth-century work *Consolation of Philosophy* spoke to this dualistic interest in divine sovereignty and human autonomy. Although Boethius himself wrote in a broadly Platonic language shorn of explicit Christian references, his later Christian commentators, including Aquinas, read his notion of Providence in Christian terms. Philosophy counsels Boethius as part of her "consolation" of his worldly uncertainty that all human action requires "two things . . . will and power, of which if either be wanting, there can

---

15. The quotation "second causes" comes from Philemon Holland's preface to Plutarch, "Of Fortune," in *The Philosophie, Commonlie Called, the Morals Written by the Learned Philosopher Plutarch of Chaeronea* . . . (London, 1603), 229. The emphasis on the need for human constancy helps to explain the contemporary fascination with ancient Stoicism. See, for instance, Gerhard Oestreich, *Neostoicism and the Early Modern State* (Cambridge, 2008); Adriana McCrea, *Constant Minds: Political Virtue and the Lipsian Paradigm in England, 1584–1650* (Toronto, 1997). For an example of an English author seeking to reconcile Turkish prosperity with God's mysterious Providence, see Richard Knolles, *The Generall Historie of the Turkes from the First Beginning of That Nation to the Rising of the Ottoman Familie: With All the Notable Expeditions of the Christian Princes against Them* . . . (London, 1603), [A.iv.]v.

nothing be performed." Power comes from Providence, the "Creatour" who "sittes on high, / Whose hand the raines [that is, reins] of the whole world doth bend." But, although Providence provides the power that underlies all rightful human action, the will to follow such providential courses derives in great part from humans as an outgrowth of reason—"for there can be no resonable nature," Boethius wrote, "unlesse it be endewed with freewill." By Philosophy's account, humans naturally pursue their happiness, and they retain enough virtue to desire "that, which is truely good." Too often such worldly routes to happiness as earthly riches, dignities, power, glory, and pleasure become the mistaken "by-pathes" by which humans seek their common good when the true "waies to happinesse" lie elsewhere, especially in what Boethius's Renaissance translators (though not Boethius himself) called "the Soveraigne God."[16]

Despite the high degree of determinism at the heart of the idea of Providence, then, there was also a certain circumscribed freedom imagined for the exercise of human wills. To be sure, such an idea of human agency generated controversy, especially as confessional divisions heightened both between Protestants and Catholics and within England's own established church. Yet, even the Protestant doctrine of predestination, which emphasized divine sovereignty over human will, nevertheless still operated from within this same general providential framework. Jean Calvin himself allowed that the Holy Spirit permits a certain freedom of cooperation and willing compliance in the saved even if the influence of the Holy Spirit itself cannot be resisted. Most important to the relation of providential thought to colonization is that Protestants and Catholics alike were prepared to regard God as acting on the earth through human instruments, persons called to act on his behalf and whose exerted wills in the pursuit of such callings are necessary for their fulfillment. Even if Protestants, especially those of a Calvinist persuasion, tended to emphasize humanity's reliance on God's grace over mere works as the key to salvation, satisfying God's will through the performance of callings was nevertheless a traditional conception of the moral order that

---

16. Boethius's text was published in English a number of times in the sixteenth and early seventeenth centuries. Geoffrey Chaucer's *Boecius de consolacione philosophie*, printed at Westminster by William Caxton in 1478, led the way. Here I quote from a 1609 edition: see I. T. [Michael Walpole], *Five Bookes, of Philosophicall Comfort Full of Christian Consolation, Written a 1000. Yeeres Since; By Anitius, Manlius, Torquatus, Severinus, Boetius; A Christian Consul of Rome; Newly Translated Out of Latine, Together with Marginall Notes, Explaining the Obscurest Places* (London, 1609), 52r, 64v, 72v, 90v–91r, 116v, 123r.

very few Renaissance Christians, Protestant or Catholic, were prepared to dispute entirely. No one wished to risk the dreaded label of "antinomian," a rejecter of all law, including the *nomos* of God.[17]

Indeed, far from abandoning the scholastic emphasis on human free will, Renaissance and Reformation writers injected into it a new energy and vigor. They did so by incorporating the scholastics' ideal of human free will into their own newly revitalized sense that world history since the Fall had consisted of a long, uneven, and still-incomplete civilizing process. Enthralled by accounts like Publius Tacitus's description of how his father-in-law, the Roman captain Gnaeus Julius Agricola, brought civility to dark corners of the earth including Britain itself, humanists reimagined the scholastics' ideal of a free-willed humanity acting in concert with God and gave it new muscle and dynamism. Not simply "participators in Providence itself," as Aquinas had called such free-willed human beings, the humanists envisioned them also as warriors against sin, conquerors of barbarism, guides to fellow humans still blinded by the Fall If it had not been for civilizing colonizers like Agricola, William Strachey wrote, "We might yet have lyved overgrowne Satyrs, rude, and untutred, wandring in the woodes, dwelling in Caves, and hunting for our dynners, (as the wyld beasts in the forrests for their prey,) prostetuting our daughters to straungers, sacrificing our Children to our Idolls, nay eating our owne Children, as did the Scots in those dayes." Thomas Wilson, whose popular guide *The Arte of Rhetorique* (1553) argued that eloquence itself was effective in moving the minds (or "witte") of men to their duties, asked hypothetically how commonwealths could even have come into being without the extraordinary exertions of will needed to coax humans from the sensual liberty of their fallen condition to the unquestionably onerous demands of their civil and divine callings:

---

17. The Elizabethan divine William Perkins makes clear that the Protestant emphasis on God's will did not entirely override the traditional providential emphasis on the human will. The "Heathenish opinion" that he was determined to overthrow, and that he associated with Catholicism, was "that the particular condition and state of man in this life comes by chance: or by the bare will and pleasure of man himselfe." Few contemporary Christians, whether Catholic or Protestant, would have seen Providence any differently. See Perkins, "A Treatise of the Vocations, or Callings of Men: With the Sorts and Kindes of Them, and the Right Use Thereof," in *The Workes of That Famous and Worthy Minister of Christ in the Universite of Cambridge, Mr. William Perkins . . .* (London, 1635), 750. On the willingness of even Calvinists to see Providence as entailing human free will, see Walsham, *Providence in Early Modern England*, 8–15.

Who woulde digge and delve, from morne till evening? Who would travaile and toyle with the sweate of his browes? Yea, who woulde for his kynges pleasure adventure and hasarde his life, if witte hadde not so wonne men, that they thought nothing more nedefull in this world, nor anye thing wherunto they were more bounden: then here to live in their duty, and to traine their whole lyfe, accordynge to their ... callynge[?]

In the humanists' hands, the free will of the scholastics was transformed into the great moving force that, in tandem with God's will, brought the rebellious world back to order and obedience.[18]

This was a view of the civilizing process that imagined human exertion and Providence as mutually involved in the world's redemption. It was in the industrious and resolute pursuit of lawful (because godly) endeavors that the woeful divide between the ethereal and the elemental spheres grew narrower, the world's sinful mutability more and more reduced to its original godly order. This thinking could explain any number of causal relationships, including what would prove one enduring truism of colonizing rhetoric: the purported providential link between America's abundant riches and God's desire for European Christians to cross the Atlantic fearlessly and with conviction. In an encomium to Martin Frobisher's search for the Northwest Passage and the Arctic's ever-elusive gold mines, George Best, for instance, could extoll in 1578 "the greate industrie of oure present age, and the invincible mindes of oure Englishe nation, who have never lefte anye worthy thing unattempted." Such an upsurge in humans' industriousness at their callings was, by Best's account, directly reciprocated by God's generosity. New discoveries in the form of American gold and silver could only be a "blessing of

---

18. Saint Thomas Aquinas, *Summa Theologiae; Latin Text and English Translation, Introduction, Notes, Appendices, and Glossaries*, ed. Thomas Gilby O.P. (New York, 1966), XXVIII, 23 (Ia.IIae, q.91 a.2); William Strachey, *The Historie of Travell into Virginia Britania (1612) ...*, ed. Louis B. Wright and Virginia Freund (London, 1953), 24; Thomas Wilson, *The Arte of Rhetorique, for the Use of All Suche as Are Studious of Eloquence ...* ([London], 1553), A.iii.r [A.iv.r]. For the revival of the ancient categories of civility and barbarism as a major, even defining, feature of Renaissance culture, see John Hale, *The Civilization of Europe in the Renaissance* (New York, 1994), 355–463. For an early publication of Tacitus's *Life of Julius Agricola* in English, see Henry Savile, [trans.], *The Ende of Nero and Beginnning of Galba; Fower Bookes of the Histories of Cornelius Tacitus; The Life of Agricola* (Oxford, 1591), 237–267. The translation does not, however, do justice to Strachey's own far more imaginative reading of Tacitus.

God to Mankind," making the era a uniquely "liberall and flourishing age." Best was not saying that humans could multiply wealth solely by their own devices. He held to the conventional medieval and early Renaissance view, which remained largely unchallenged until the rise of seventeenth-century theories of the dynamic interplay between production and consumption, that the world's riches are static because composed, like all earthly things, of the selfsame, fixed elements from Creation. Instead, he envisioned a juncture between God's will and human wills that made previously inaccessible goods newly available by divine ordination, such that, as Best put it, "the whole world increaseth in common wealth, and not only of gold and silver is such great encrease, but also of all other things."[19]

The law, too, carried connotations of the converging of human wills and God's will, a view that lent considerable moral force to the common contemporary assertion that God gave newfound territories to those peoples who effectively possessed them. Ralegh spoke in just such providential terms about his long-sought-after 'Empyre of *Guiana*." When his initial efforts at conquering the region failed, he wrote, "It pleased not God so much to favour me at this time." Yet, this early disappointment was no reason to succumb to fainthearted irresolution. Ample evidence existed of the failures of various Spanish captains to make "discovery and conquest" there. Surely God's interference in this regard was a sign of his intention for an eventual English possession: "It seemeth to me that this Empyre is reserved for her Majestie and the *English* nation, by reason of the hard successe which all these and other *Spaniards* found in attempting the same." Matthew Sutcliffe, the legally trained and intensely anti-Catholic dean of Exeter, who became a member of the council for Virginia on March 9, 1607, and of the New England Council on November 3, 1620, similarly took the limited success of the Spanish conquest in the New World as evidence that God had no in-

---

19. George Best, "The Epistle Dedicatorie," in Best, *A True Discourse of the Late Voyages of Discoverie* . . . (London, 1578), a.iij.r [a.iv.r], Best, "The Fyrst Booke of the First Voyage of *Martin Frobisher* . . . ," May 15, 1576, c[i].v. On the rise of an English discourse of trade from the 1620s to the Restoration era that reenvisioned commerce in more generative terms as a morally sanctioned cycle of production and consumption, see Blair Hoxby, *Mammon's Music: Literature and Economics in the Age of Milton* (New Haven, Conn., 2002), 3, 20–22, 88, 115, 205–232. On the actual considerable growth of the sixteenth-century English economy and the overwhelming contemporary impulse to interpret such economic change in relation to the reciprocal bonds and mutual fellowship of commonwealth, see Craig Muldrew, *The Economy of Obligation: The Culture of Credit and Social Relations in Early Modern England* (New York, 1998), esp. 15–59, 123–172.

tention of allowing either Philip II or the pope an absolute lordship over the Indies. Was it unlawful to assert dominion over a newfound territory? Not if it was "waste [that is, a region whose God-given abundance remained unexploited], and dispeopled; which countrey God giveth to these that can possesse it." Here, the emphasis was as much on the capacity of the possessors to transform a still-idle part of the earth to its lawful offices of habitability and productivity as it was on the purported misuse of the land in the first place. Thus, Sutcliffe eagerly used the doctrine (sometimes known as res nullius from Roman law) as a claim to undercut Spanish universalist pretensions to rightful rule over all new discoveries: "The Spaniards have no reason by force and lawe to keepe other nations out of the Indies, which notwithstanding themselves are not able to people." In promoting his New England venture, Captain John Smith echoed this same providential argument for lawful possession, his own eye cast on the feebleness of native Americans in relation to British heartiness. He wrote in 1631, "There is vast [that is, waste] land enough for all the people in England, Scotland, and Ireland: and it seemes God hath provided this Country for our Nation, destroying the natives by the plague, it not touching one Englishman, though many traded and were conversant amongst them."[20]

20. W[alter] Ralegh, *The Discoverie of the Large, Rich, and Bewtiful Empire of Guiana* . . . (London, 1596), 9, 14, 17; Matthew Sutcliffe, *The Practice, Proceedings, and Lawes of Armes, Described Out of the Doings of Most Valiant and Expert Captaines, and Confirmed Both by Ancient, and Modern Examples, and Praecedents* . . . (London, 1593), 9; John Smith, *Advertisements for the Unexperienced Planters of New-England, or Any Where; or, The Path-way to Experience to Erect a Plantation* (London, 1631), in Philip L. Barbour, ed., *The Complete Works of Captain John Smith (1580–1631)* (Chapel Hill, N.C., 1986), III, 275. For Sutcliffe and his involvement in both colonization and religious polemics, see *Oxford Dictionary of National Biography*, online ed., s.v. "Sutcliffe, Matthew (1549/50–1629)," by Nicholas W. S. Cranfield, accessed Nov. 30, 2013, http://www.oxforddnb.com/view/article/26792. Legal historians have begun to modify the once-accepted view that res nullius was a definitive element of English claims to American title. The emphasis on possession offered here is in keeping with Lauren Benton and Benjamin Straumann's argument that the Roman law doctrine of res nullius in the early modern era was often crudely understood, that it made up only part of a repertoire of strategies that colonizers used to establish their claims against other Europeans, and that what colonizing agents themselves, as opposed to metropolitan theorists, usually emphasized was not the actual vacancy of land but rather simple tangible proof of possession. See Benton and Straumann, "Acquiring Empire by Law: From Roman Doctrine to Early Modern European Practice," *Law and History Review*, XXVIII (2010), 1–38. Civil law and *ius gentium* in this period are sometimes mistaken for their highly secular eighteenth- and nineteenth-century counterparts; yet, as Peter Goodrich notes, the civilians in this era who turned

This is not to say that Renaissance-era persons regarded all law as directly God given, apart from the truism that human law was a pale reflection of either natural law, the law of humans in their innocence, or divine law, the law for fallen man. Rather, the assumption was that earthly law, like all human efforts to accord with God's commandments, was a fumbling approximation of divine judgment. Accordingly, lawfulness was inevitably a proposition, a claim to have mirrored God's will despite its profound elusiveness. It was a claim, moreover, made unavoidably in counterposition to other such claims. Just as the earth was a scene of restless mutability, so, too, did the law reflect a confused cacophony of rival assertions about the truth, their myriad errors a basic outgrowth of humanity's fallen condition. The law was readily imagined, therefore, as a conflicting array of asserted passages, or pathways, of godly conduct — a view that also placed a great deal of emphasis on those actions or ventures, also known as "projects," that propelled (or projected) a given set of human wills along those lawful passages and toward commonwealth, ideally with the resolution needed to traverse such paths without falling prey to worldly error and vacillation.[21]

The logic of the legitimizing effort behind American colonization flowed directly out of the idea that, at certain moments and inevitably with God's active assistance, pathways of lawful conduct become clear, beckoning to humans to follow them. To be sure, the very identification of particular routes through sin and error as conscionable (literally, where the conscience can proceed with assurance of doing God's will) aroused indignant denials by some that they were lawful pathways at all. Yet, few ideas were more familiar at this time than the scriptural requirement, associated especially with the teachings of the apostle Paul, that humans must overcome the sinful course presented to them by a carnal world and walk instead in obedience to divinely ordained vocations. What transformed such biblical language from merely rich figurative speech to a substantive starting point for determina-

---

to the Roman emperor Justinian's *Digest* for much of their understanding of civil law would scarcely have missed that its opening section was titled "Deo auctore" ("By God") and that the work as a whole claimed to offer "knowledge of things divine and human." See Goodrich, "The New Casuistry," *Critical Inquiry*, XXXIII (2007), 677n.

21. I regard this providential view that pathways of lawful conduct led to lawful commonwealths as corresponding closely with Lauren Benton's argument that sovereignty in the early modern era "was exercised mainly over narrow bands, or corridors, and over enclaves and irregular zones around them," rather than in highly integrated territorial empires. See Benton, *Search for Sovereignty*, 2, 10–23.

tions of lawful conduct was the corresponding tradition of casuistry. Derived from medieval confessional manuals designed to assist priests during the sacrament of penance, casuistry lent early modern law an abiding concern with how human norms and God's judgment coincided. Weighing cases in response to anxious questions or strenuous objections about the lawfulness of given actions, the casuist was in the remarkable position of distinguishing the solid ground of godly life from the morass of human error. As a result, even controversial claims about lawful pathways proved eminently exploitable, establishing corridors of godly conduct broad enough to permit a whole range of interlopers to scramble onto the same legal thoroughfares, even while disagreeing about the particular twists and turns of the road. In the latter regard, no pathway proved more significant in relation to American colonization than the singularly broad one marked out by Columbus's discovery.[22]

The idea that God effected Columbus's western voyage and his discovery, or revealing, of a new world was of paramount importance to virtually all subsequent claims about the lawfulness of American colonization. As early as the late 1490s and early 1500s, when John Cabot and his sons were making their own ventures across the Atlantic under English patronage, Henry VII's court was apparently filled with solemn speculation about God's likely role in inspiring Columbus's voyage. It seemed "a thing rather divine than human to have found that way never before known to go to the East where the spices are produced." But such thinking was simply an outgrowth of the theories that revolved around Columbus's American landfall both in Spain and more broadly in Europe. Probably the first materials to spread word of, and seek interpretive control over, the discovery were letters dated February 15, 1493. Though ascribed to Columbus, they were most likely a carefully tailored, politically sanitized, and vigorously circulated version of a letter he sent on March 4 to the Spanish and Portuguese sovereigns. As he put it in this letter, God "favors and gives victory to all those who walk in His path." The providential framework in which Columbus placed his discovery was not itself controversial, but the conclusion he drew from that truism, namely that Ferdinand and Isabela should ready themselves for their evident eschatological duty to retake Jerusalem from the Turks, was a more ambitious interpretation of those monarchs' office than they were prepared to accept. In

---

22. A helpful introduction to casuistry's origins in medieval penitential manuals can be found in Meg Lota Brown, *Donne and the Politics of Conscience in Early Modern England* (Leiden, The Netherlands, 1995), 42–50.

the sanitized letter, Columbus's counsel to bring the war against the infidels all the way to the Holy Land was prudentially suppressed.[23]

After returning from his third voyage in late November 1500, Columbus was briefly arrested in the course of a royal investigation into whether he had fostered disorder on Hispaniola. To defend his actions, he threw himself into an even more elaborate theory of the providential significance of his discovery. This took the form of a remarkable manuscript compilation known as his *Book of Prophecies,* a collection of texts, consisting mainly of passages from scripture (with a heavy emphasis on the prophecies of Isaiah) but also of excerpts of a number of writings by ancient and modern writers, ranging from Seneca and Augustine to the millenarian theorist Pierre d'Ailly. He used these to demonstrate that his discovery was both ordained by God and filled with eschatological import, pointing toward the duties humans must take in hand before Judgment Day. Again, the work appears to have been quietly set aside and was perhaps never given to the king and queen. Yet, here, too, Columbus linked his evidently God-given role in ushering in the prophesied conversion of the earth's peoples in the Last Age to Ferdinand and Isabela's corresponding duty to lead the Church Militant, taking the helm of the Christian army that, with the assistance of the many Asians whom Columbus was confident would quickly be converted, would retake the Holy Land.[24]

Undoubtedly, the most significant interpretation of Columbus's discovery emerged from Rome. There, the newly elevated Spanish pope Alexander VI made the first concerted attempt to establish an interpretive monopoly over Columbus's divine "way." In a series of five bulls issued in 1493, he granted, or donated, to Ferdinand and Isabela and their heirs all islands and mainlands "discovered and to be discovered" one hundred miles west

---

23. Giovanni Battista Ramusio, *Primo volume delle navigationi et viaggi* (Venice, 1550), in James A. Williamson, ed., *The Cabot Voyages and Bristol Discovery under Henry VII,* Works Issued by the Hakluyt Society, 2d Ser., no. 120 (Cambridge, 1962), 272. On the February 15 letter, see Margarita Zamora, *Reading Columbus* (Berkeley, Calif., 1993), 9–21. The quotation is from the transcription of the March 4 letter that Zamora provides as an appendix (194).

24. Roberto Rusconi, ed., *The Book of Prophecies Edited by Christopher Columbus,* trans., Blair Sullivan, Repertorium Columbianum, III (Berkeley, Calif., 1997). For Columbus's millenarian theory about Ferdinand and Isabela's duties, some of which appeared in the words of Gaspar Gorricio, the Italian monk who served as Columbus's religious counselor and guardian of the Columbus family's archives, see esp., 54–59, 66–77. On the history of the manuscript, see Rusconi's helpful introduction, esp. 3–35.

from the Azores and Cape Verde islands. Such a donation, which harked back to the much-contested legend of Emperor Constantine's donation of his own imperium to the papacy, was not a straightforward act of sovereign delegation. Reliant on a fundamentally providential set of presuppositions, Alexander's bulls were a matter of interpreting the pathway revealed by Columbus with "divine aid" *(divino auxilio)* as pertaining to two callings in particular: the pope's "vicarship of Jesus Christ" and the kingly office of the Spanish monarchs as the rulers who, in assisting Columbus's voyage, showed themselves to be the monarchs most favored by God to rule over the new discoveries. It was their temporal duties in relation to the newly found lands and their office as the secular helpmeets of the pope in his own spiritual authority over the earth that had been enacted by Columbus's Atlantic crossing. In keeping with this providential logic, the pope warned that any violation of the decree would "incur the wrath of Almighty God" *(indignationem Omnipotentis Dei)* as well as the apostles Peter and Paul.[25]

As the initial excitement of discovery gave way to the messier realities of securing dominion, the nature of such providential argumentation shifted. Although the miraculous import of Columbus's achievement remained a dominant theme, it now sat alongside or acted in service of more complicated polemical agendas. Ferdinand Columbus's history of his father (published in 1571, several decades after Ferdinand's death) grappled with a number of changed circumstances during his lifetime, including his father's investigation in 1500 for governmental abuses on Hispaniola as well as criticism that had arisen about Columbus's modest origins. The Genoese physician Baliano de Fornari who first published Ferdinand's book as *Historie ... della vita, e de' fatti dell'Ammiraglio D. Christoforo Colombo (History ... of the Life and Deeds of the Admiral Christopher Columbus)* in 1571 recognized the work's overall providential orientation. Hence, Fornari's dedication limned the commonplace view of Columbus's discovery as simultaneously a revela-

---

25. "Letter of Columbus, Describing the Result of His First Voyage," in L. A. Vigneras, ed., *Journal of Christopher Columbus,* trans. Cecil Jane (London, 1960), 201. According to Vigneras, Columbus's letter was printed in Barcelona as early as April 1493 and published in Rome a month later (xxi). Quotations relating to the papal bulls are from the Bull Inter Caetera, May 4, 1493, in Frances Gardiner Davenport, ed., *European Treaties Bearing on the History of the United States and Its Dependencies* (Washington, D.C., 1917), 73, 75, 76–78. On the contemporary debate about Constantine's donation, see Richard Koebner, "'The Imperial Crown of This Realm': Henry VIII, Constantine the Great, and Polydore Vergil," *Bulletin of the Institute of Historical Research,* XXVI (1953), 29–52.

tion and an invention. In the same sense as found in Ralegh's *History*, a profound human exertion brings God's will to light: "Certainly the inventor of a useful thing is much favored of God, the true source of all things good, Who frequently deigns to reveal through a single man what had been hidden for long centuries." Yet, Ferdinand wrote his history not only to celebrate his father but also to defend him. Therefore, the book lingered over such stories as the storm that, supposedly in divine retribution, destroyed the fleet carrying the officials whom Ferdinand blamed for his father's arrest. Likewise, Ferdinand fenced off reports of his father's artisanal origins by stressing his martial valor, bodily strength, and great learning, a decided shift from Columbus's own willingness in his "Libro de las profecías" to describe himself as God's meek instrument. Evidently, the Renaissance ideal of a more robust human actor in carrying out divine providence had begun to leave its mark, and Ferdinand adapted his father's story accordingly.[26]

Among the shepherds of Columbus's pathway who were as insistent that it attract resolute walkers as scornful of those who walked it wrongly, few were as devoted as Bartolome de Las Casas. A Spanish encomendero turned Dominican friar, he proved one of the fiercest critics of the wayward followers of Columbus's divinely ordained discovery. The English eagerly drew on Las Casas's excoriating accounts of Spanish captains and planters abusing their own godly offices by failing to lead the Indians humanely, or effectually, to theirs. But the so-called Black Legend that the English constructed from such accounts was more complicated than has sometimes been recognized. The challenge that Spanish cruelties in America posed was not simply to chronicle untold murders and tortures of Indians as so many signs of the extent to which Spanish carnality overrode justice but to parse where Spanish "invention" did, and equally where it did not, deviate from God's will. Such intricate casuistry is vividly on display in *The Spanish Colonie* (1583), an English translation, by one M. M. S., of Las Casas's *Brevísima relación de la destrucción de las Indias (Very brief account of the destruction of the Indies)*, first published in Spain in 1552. There the many parts of the Hebrew Bible where God seems to allow the destruction of heathens were considered at some length, particularly the passage in which God commands that the Canaanites and Amalekites be "rooted out." In this instance, God's will was seem-

---

26. Ferdinand Columbus, *The Life of the Admiral Christopher Columbus by His Son Ferdinand*, ed. and trans. Benjamin Keen, 2d ed (New Brunswick, N.J., 1992), lxxiii, 228. For the differences between Ferdinand's and Columbus's own depictions of his character, compare ibid., 3–9, and Rusconi, ed., *Book of Prophecies*, trans. Sullivan, 67–71.

ingly unambiguous. When did God's will give way to human error? Remarkably, the translator acknowledged that, at bottom, the Spaniards' "murder of 12. 15. or 20. millions of poore reasonable creatures," however cruel it might have been, was just, for how could God have allowed it otherwise? "Sith [Since] he hath done it, it is justly done." Nevertheless, God sometimes used instruments for his vengeance who were themselves wicked and whose own "abominable cruelties" he would eventually punish. Such was the case with the Spaniards, whose evil course the author was confident God would ultimately stem, just as he was throwing up embankments against overflowing Spanish pride in the Low Countries.[27]

The circumstance that most influenced both Spanish and English anxieties about the possible overreach of American conquest was the Spanish monarch's enhanced claim in the sixteenth century to universal monarchy. Because Columbus's "way" was regarded as divinely ordained, and thus as illuminating godly callings rather than merely temporal legal jurisdiction, it provided powerful reinforcement when Ferdinand and Isabela's offspring, especially their grandson Charles V and great-grandson Philip II, theorized their own imperial kingship in the most robust terms imaginable. Through a strategic Habsburg marriage, Charles V became not only the Spanish king but also the Holy Roman emperor, and he claimed powers far beyond those historically associated with the latter title. Remarkably, he promoted his rule as nothing less than the fulfillment of Dante's dream of a Last Reforming Emperor, called by God to bring all the earth's peoples to order in anticipation of Judgment Day. Philip II of Spain did not inherit his father's imperial title but nevertheless still referred to himself as emperor, also presenting himself as a universal monarch, the rightful lord of all Christians and redeemable souls in the Last Age. That these claims to universal rule owed something to Columbus's providential pathway seems almost certain. Their logic centered on Charles's and Philip's alleged divine calling, not simply an assertion of sovereign jurisdiction. That calling, in turn, was closely, though not exclusively, associated with Charles's and Philips's particular lordship in the Indies.[28]

---

27. Bartolomé de las Casas, *The Spanish Colonie; or, Briefe Chronicle of the Acts and Gestes of the Spaniardes in the West Indies, Called the Newe World, for the Space of xl. Yeeres: Written in the Castilian Tongue by the Reverend Bishop Bartholomew de las Cases or Casaus, a Friar of the Order of S. Dominicke; and Nowe First Translated into English*, by M. M. S. (London, 1583), ¶3v–¶¶r.

28. Anthony Pagden, *Lords of All the World: Ideologies of Empire in Spain, Britain, and France, c. 1500–c. 1800* (New Haven, Conn., 1995), 29–62. See also Frances A. Yates, *Astraea: The Imperial Theme in the Sixteenth Century* (London, 1975), 1–28.

Indeed, the Spanish crown's assertion of universal monarchy could seem frighteningly realized by Charles's and Philip's impressive sixteenth-century rule over much of Europe, America, and even parts of Asia and Africa, and it elicited a persistent shrill counterclaim. The accusation regularly made against the Spanish-Habsburg monarchs was not only that they had succumbed to pride, a sinful overreach in their imperial office, but also that their abuse of God's calling in this regard was most vividly manifest in their cruel government in America. This crucial underlying logic of the Black Legend effectively turned the Columbian discovery that undergirded the Spaniards' professed worldwide imperium into its most powerful source of critique. For instance, Philip II in 1580 issued his notorious proscription against William the Silent permitting any Christian to "hurt him and to kill him" on the grounds that he defied Philip's own "absolute and soveraigne" rule over the Netherlands — a licensed execution that did ultimately lead to William's assassination. In response, the targeted Dutch prince, in a widely republished treatise, pointed to "the Indies and . . . other places, where they commaunded absolutely" as "proofe" of the Spanish monarchs' "perverse, naturall disposition, and tyrannous affection and will." In warning against excessive Spanish influence at the English court and insinuating that the Spanish ambassador Diego Sarmiento de Acuña, first count of Gondomar, had so much influence over James I that the latter "esteemes his speeches Oracles and Scripture," *Vox Coeli; or, Newes from Heaven* (1624) made even more explicit the relationship between Spanish claims to universal monarchy and the Columbian discovery. In the pamphlet, a deceased Henry VIII looks down from heaven, where his access to the truth is greater than on Earth. He observes that, when "*Columbus . . . Cortez,* and *Pizarro* (with as much judgement as fortunacy) discovered to *Castile* the rich *America,* and in it the Gold and Silver Mines," such a providential occurrence gave "wings" to the Spanish king's "Ambition to fly to the height of this earthly Greatnesse, wherein we see *Spaine* seated and founded." As England's other historic monarchs, sharing Henry VIII's heavenly perch, similarly ponder the link between Spanish sovereign overreach and the American discovery, the suggestion is even made that the Spaniards' greed for empire has confused them about the source of their power, as if it originated in their own persons rather than God. Edward VI argues, "The Kings of Spaine make this the tenth Article of their Creede, that the Rules of Empire and State ought to give Lawes, but not to receive any." Elizabeth responds, "But this is contrary to the Lawes of the KING of Kings." Mary concludes the thought: "But in the Councell of *Spaine,* the Rules of State are always too sublime and powerfull for those of Religion." Spanish sovereignty was condemned as absolutist, not on the grounds that it was divine, but just the opposite: it had become sinfully worldly.[29]

Proponents for English colonization in America similarly regarded the Columbian discovery as the most compelling starting point for their own efforts to legitimize such an undertaking. In 1555, the Catholic Englishman Richard Eden published *The Decades of the New Worlde or West India*, his translation of Peter Martyr's *De Orbe Novo* and several other accounts of the Spanish experience in America. He thus made available to English readers rich iterations of the providential theory of Columbus's way, including an English translation of one of the bulls that constituted Pope Alexander's donation. Among the principal truisms underlying the volume were that "god of his singular providence and infinite goodnesse" was the force behind the winds that blew Columbus's caravel across the Atlantic and that Columbus had "this matter reveled unto hym not withowte goddes providence." In an extended preface to the reader, Eden developed at length the idea that the Spanish colonization endeavors following Columbus's discovery were an extension of that same divine calling. He argued that such "entreprises have taken good effect to the great glory of god who cauleth men unto hym by dyvers meanes and at dyvers ages of the declinynge worlde." Given that Philip sat on England's own throne as Mary's husband and thus the realm's consort king, much of Eden's piece was devoted to answering those criticisms that Charles V and Philip II abused their calling, a view that Eden vehemently refuted. Yet, Eden's overall premise was that Columbus's discovery opened up a pathway of lawful behavior that the English could ignore only at the risk of proving themselves persons of less "manhodde and pollicie" — that is, of weaker personal and civil will — than the Spaniards. The need for such a resolute will was, for Eden, predicated precisely on the eschatological promise that Columbus had outlined. Eden characterized this promise in terms that make clear the duties of the godly in the Last Age could potentially involve righteous and unapologetic violence against native Americans. He envisioned, "Partely by the slaughter of suche as coulde by no meanes be brought to civilitie, and partly by reservynge such as were

---

29. *A Treatise against the Proclamation Published by the King of Spayne, by Which He Proscribed the Late Prince of Orange*... (Delft [London], 1584), F2r, P3r, Q4v; [John Reynolds], *Vox Coeli; or, Newes from Heaven, of a Consultation There Held by the High and Mighty Princes, King Hen. 8. King Edw. 6. Prince Henry. Queene Mary. Queene Elizabeth, and Queene Anne*... (Elesium [London], 1624), 6, 44, 45.

overcome in the warres, and convertynge them to a better mynde, ... the prophecie may herein bee fulfylled that the woolfe and the lambe shall feed together, and the wylde fieldes with the vale of Achor, shalbe the folde of the heard of gods people." For Eden, as for Columbus, this millenarian promise would bring not only mass conversions but also a vigorous strike against Islam. He anticipated a combined force of European Christians and converted Chinese and Persians attacking the Turks, thereby aiding Christ in his battle against Antichrist.[30]

In the century after Eden's *Decades* appeared, the pathway marked out by Columbus's discovery remained the core avenue from which most English claims to lawful title in America branched off. This was implicitly the case even in those instances when some predecessor to Columbus was put forward as the true first discoverer of America. The legendary sixth-century British king Arthur allegedly conquered Greenland, "Estotiland" (Baffin Island), and "Friseland" (probably the Faroe Islands) as well as many kingdoms in Europe and the British Isles, and the twelfth-century Welsh prince Madoc ap Owen Gwynedd supposedly arrived somewhere on the Atlantic side of America in 1170 in search of an "apt region to plant hym selfe in with soveraignty." When Elizabethan proponents of English colonization like John Dee and Richard Hakluyt promoted these pre-Columbian discoverers in the 1570s and 1580s, however, they were not making a legal claim but a historical claim with expressly providential implications. If Arthur or Madoc preceded Columbus to the New World, then God graced these Britons in the same way he graced Columbus — indeed, he blessed them even more by showing them the pathway first. For both Elizabethan writers, Providence — what Dee called the world's "Cosmopoliticall Government ... under the King Almighty: passing on, very swiftly, toward the most Dreadful, and most Cumfortable Term prefixed" — was the natural starting point for any consideration of lawful title on the other side of the Atlantic.[31]

---

30. Richar[d] Eden, trans., *The Decades of the Newe Worlde or West India, Conteynyng the Navigations and Conquestes of the Spanyardes, with the Particular Description of the Moste Ryche and Large Landes and Ilands Lately Founde in the West Ocean Perteynyng to the Inheritaunce of the Kinges of Spayne... Wrytten in the Latine Tounge by Peter Martyr of Angleria...* (London, 1555), A2v, C2v, D3r, 313r.

31. John Dee, "Unto Your Majesties Tytle Royall to These Forene Regions and Ilandes Do Appertayne 4 Poyntes," in Ken MacMillan, ed., with Jennifer Abeles, *John Dee: The Limits of the British Empire* (Westport, Conn., 2004), 44, 46; Hakluyt, *Principall Navigations*, [I], 245, [II], 507; John D[ee], *General and Rare Memorials Pertayning to the Perfect Arte of Navigation*...

Columbus's discovery continued to attract English interlopers throughout the Tudor and early Stuart eras. In Peckham's *True Reporte*, he dutifully trotted out Madoc's alleged anticipatory voyage, but his impulse was still to give Columbus the greater billing. By Peckham's account, Columbus was "the firste instrument to manifest the great glorie of almightie God in planting the Christian Faith" in America, the person whom "God... first sturred uppe... to that enterprise." In *The Haven of Health* (1584), an immensely popular work on physic that Strachey, for instance, cited approvingly, Thomas Cogan echoed this providential interpretation: "Whereas now through the providence of God, and travaile of men there is found further in the West, as it were a new world, a goodly countrey named *America*, or newe *India*, for largenesse, plentie, wholesome and temperate ayer, comparable with *Affrike, Europe*, or *Asia*." Samuel Purchas remarked similarly, "Yea, this Indian Trade set Columbus, and after him Cabot on worke to find the way to the Indies by the West; which their industrious simplicitie God rewarded with a New World by them discovered." No less an authority than George Abbot, elevated to archbishop of Canterbury in 1611, placed this presupposition right at the beginning of his discussion of America in his highly popular cosmography *A Briefe Description of the Whole Worlde Wherein Are Particularly Described All the Monarchies, Empires, and Kingdomes of the Same: With Their Severall Titles and Situations Thereunto Adjoyning*, first published in 1599, with several reprintings and updated versions before and after his death in 1633. By the time of the 1605 edition, Abbot was flatly dismissive of Dee's Arthurian arguments about Elizabeth's American sovereignty, calling them "fabulous foundations" unworthy of further acceptance. Yet, throughout the life of his book, Abbot held to the providential view of Columbus's path-

---

(London, 1577), 54. For Dee's civil law training, see MacMillan, *Sovereignty and Possession*, 49–78. For the reminder that Dee's legal outlook was inextricably tied to his eschatological theories and magical practices, see Glyn Parry, *The Arch-Conjuror of England: John Dee* (New Haven, Conn., 2011), 94–145; Parry, "John Dee and the Elizabethan British Empire in Its European Context," *Historical Journal*, XLIX (2006), 643–675. In his study of John Dee's marginalia in Ferdinand Columbus's *Historie... della vita, e de' fatti dell' Ammiraglio D. Christoforo Colombo (History... of the Life and Deeds of the Admiral Christopher Columbus)*, William Sherman concludes that Dee's concerns appear to be more "pragmatic" than centered on "prophecy or the supernatural." But Dee's many notations relating to the Spaniards' injustice and even his prevalent concern with their "pollicie," a word suggesting civil exertions, arguably should be seen as fitting within his providentialism, not standing apart from it. See William H. Sherman, *Used Books: Marking Readers in Renaissance England* (Philadelphia, 2008), 113–126.

way. According to Abbot, not only did God, "remembring the prophecie of his sonne, that the Gospell of the kingdome should before the daie of judgement, be preached in all coastes and quarters of the worlde," raise up "the spirit" of Columbus and "set his minde to the discoverie of a new worlde," God also "move[d] the minde" of Isabela, convincing her to furnish Columbus with ships for the voyage.[32]

As late as 1635, the idea that the Eschaton was intimately linked to the American discovery was still vibrant. In that year, the English theologian William Twisse wrote to the learned millenarian theorist Joseph Mede of his own "thoughts at the providence of God concerning that [new] world, not discovered till this old world of ours is almost at an end." Given the "opinion of many grave Divines concerning the Gospel's fleeting Westward," he had sometimes let his mind drift to "our *English* Plantations" and wondered, "Why may not that be the place of New Jerusalem?" Although Mede was unsure whether America would prove to be the New Jerusalem or perhaps its apocalyptic opposite, the source of the armies of Gog and Magog, both men were alike in assuming that the cosmos had arrived at a particular juncture, the circling heavenly bodies and the imperfect pathways of earthly existence meeting in a broad corridor of lawfulness that sliced reassuringly across the Atlantic.[33]

---

32. "Sir George Peckham's *True Reporte*," in Quinn, ed., *Voyages and Colonising Enterprises of Sir Humphrey Gilbert*, II, 448; Thomas Cog[an], *The Haven of Health: Chiefely Gathered for the Comfort of Students, and Consequently of All Those That Have a Care of Their Health* . . . (London, 1584), ¶¶2r; Samuel Purchas, *Hakluytus Posthumus; or, Purchas His Pilgrimes: Contayning a History of the World in Sea Voyages and Lande Travells by Englishmen and Others* (New York, 1965), I, 119–120; George Abbot, *A Briefe Description of the Whole Worlde Wherein Are Particularly Described All the Monarchies, Empires, and Kingdomes of the Same: With Their Severall Titles and Situations Thereunto Adjoyning* (London, 1599), [G4]r–[G4]v; [George Abbot], *A Briefe Description of the Whole Worlde; Wherein Is Particularly Described All the Monarchies, Empires, and Kingdomes of the Same: Newly Augmented and Enlarged* . . . (London, 1605), Q[1]r–Q2r; *Oxford Dictionary of National Biography*, online ed., s.v. "Abbot, George (1562–1633)," by Kenneth Fincham, accessed July 17, 2014, http://www.oxforddnb.com/view/article/4.

33. "Dr. *Twisse* His Fourth Letter to Mr. *Mede*, Approving His Conjectures Touching *Gog* and *Magog*, and Desiring His Opinion of the *English* Plantations in *America*," in *The Works of the Pious and Profoundly-Learned Joseph Mede, B.D. Sometime Fellow of Christ's Colledge in Cambridge* (London, 1672), 799, "Mr. *Mede's* Answer to Dr. *Twisse* His Fourth Letter, Touching the First Gentile Inhabitants and the Late Christian Plantations, in *America* . . . ," 800.

The Casuistry of Colonization

If law proceeded ideally along pathways in which humans had greater than normal assurance of following God's will, then the language for negotiating, defending, and disputing those lawful thoroughfares was necessarily casuistic. Often narrowly associated with highly formal manuals of cases, such as those produced by the Spanish theologian Francisco de Vitoria or the Elizabethan divine William Perkins, casuistry is arguably more properly understood in general terms as simply the art of aligning human behavior with Providence in light of the difficulty of knowing God's will with assurance. Casuistry, therefore, was a mode of moral argument that permeated contemporary discourse. It could reach rarefied and uniquely authoritative forms in the hands of brilliant and learned casuists like Vitoria and Perkins, which is one reason why sovereign monarchs in this era often turned to such sage men for advice in the conduct of their rule. On the other hand, casuistry was also, at a much less exclusive or systematized level, the basic language for navigating a providential world understood as tying humans to one another and to their Maker through callings. Contemporaries ranging from commoners to gentlemen, from good wives to queens, relied implicitly on the general logic and presuppositions of casuistry virtually any time they made claims about the powers, or liberties, they derived from those offices, or, by extension, whenever they accused one another of a lapse in duty, that is, of an abused office. Casuistry was not only a means of evaluating conduct. It was also a starting point for asserting the lawfulness of previously unacknowledged duties or formerly untried areas of endeavor on the contestable grounds that they were rooted in God's will. Unsurprisingly, therefore, colonization itself was fundamentally reliant on casuistic discourse for its own legitimacy.[34]

---

34. I follow Conal Condren in wanting to use a more general definition of casuistry that does not limit it to its most formal applications or doctrines. See Condren, *Argument and Authority*, 172–173. On Charles V's reliance on Vitoria's casuistry, see Albert R. Jonsen and Stephen Toulmin, eds., *The Abuse of Casuistry: A History of Moral Reasoning* (Berkeley, Calif., 1988), 144–145. Other works on casuistry that I have found helpful include Edmund Leites, ed., *Conscience and Casuistry in Early Modern Europe* (Cambridge, 1988); Brown, *Donne and the Politics of Conscience*; John Morrill, Paul Slack, and Daniel Woolf, eds., *Public Duty and Private Conscience in Seventeenth-Century England* (Oxford, 1993); Lowell Gallagher, *Medusa's Gaze: Casuistry and Conscience in the Renaissance* (Stanford, Calif., 1991); Camille Wells Slights, *The Casuistical Tradi-*

To see this vital dimension to colonization requires taking a new look at the literature that surrounded colonizing ventures. This literature took a variety of forms. Some of it appeared as manuscripts or expensive bound volumes that probably circulated closely in and around the royal court, the universities, and other similarly socially exclusive venues. Other works consisted of published pamphlets or broadsides that were intended for a broader audience and offered for sale at Saint Paul's Churchyard or one of the other increasingly bustling book marts of the era. Contextualizing of this literature as humanistic and attuned to Roman law arguments as well as the views of writers associated with the Salamanca School in Spain restores to the pamphlets, broadsides, and sermons of the early colonizing endeavor much of their original significance and gravity. But this humanism intermingled with an intensely providential culture; the Salamanca School itself, after all, was a group of theologians, none more famous than Vitoria himself. Associated with the university's theological seminary, these men were primarily known for their learned casuistry. The titles of some of the justificatory pamphlets for English colonization suggest their own concern with elucidating lawful pathways that originated in God's will, such as Robert Gray's *Good Speed to Virginia* (1609), Richard Eburne's *Plaine Path-Way to Plantations* ... (1624), and Samuel Purchas's *Hakluytus Posthumus or Purchas His Pilgrimes* ... (1625). Even works that did not advertise their concern with divine pathways, or pilgrim ways, quite so directly, however, still spoke in a distinctly casuistic idiom.[35]

Casuistry partook in the providential language of divine callings, upright consciences, and lawful pathways — in short, in a vocabulary that took for granted that law originated primarily in God's will and only secondarily in the dictates of earthly sovereigns. Accordingly, casuistry also often concerned itself with "ventures," "attempts," "assays," "actions," and "projects" — that is, with the understanding that following God's pathways is always something of a gamble, a risk that one pursues with faith though rarely with unassailable proof that one's actions accord perfectly with God's providence. The

---

tion in Shakespeare, Donne, Herbert, and Milton (Princeton, 1981); and John M. Wallace, *Destiny His Choice: The Loyalism of Andrew Marvell* (Cambridge, 1968).

35. David Armitage, *The Ideological Origins of the British Empire* (Cambridge, 2000); Andrew Fitzmaurice, *Humanism and America: An Intellectual History of English Colonization, 1500–1625* (Cambridge, 2003); Fitzmaurice, "Moral Uncertainty in the Dispossession of Native Americans," in Peter C. Mancall, ed., *Atlantic World and Virginia, 1550–1624* (Chapel Hill, N.C., 2007), 383–409; and MacMillan, *Sovereignty and Possession*.

notion of "project," which was a commonplace way to describe the colonial endeavor, suggested the bold exertion of wills in a direction deemed likely to win God's approval but always susceptible to false interpretation or sinful mishandling. "Man purposeth and god disposeth," as Gilbert stated the familiar maxim in a discourse to the queen in 1577. Historians have made much of the "projectors" in this era, whose interest in the colonial enterprise often ran alongside other such projects that similarly sought to direct the sovereign will and the commonwealth down particular paths. Gilbert, for instance, was a projector, his Newfoundland endeavor coinciding with an iron mining and smelting operation that centered on the alchemical promise that iron could be transformed into copper and quicksilver. The project, which attracted the patronage of Privy Councillors Sir Thomas Smith, Burghley, and Robert Dudley, first earl of Leicester, was a royal monopoly, operating under a patent that the queen issued on December 4, 1571, incorporating the group as "the Governour and Societye of the newe arte." Hayes, too, was a projector. He busily devised various schemes for reforming the commonwealth, including a copper coinage plan he called "The Bee Hive" and "The complaint of the poor" on the grounds that it would elevate the poor by making them more industrious. To see these endeavors as overlapping with colonization is in itself accurate and highly useful, for they were indeed all projects. But what gave these ventures both their great sense of promise as well as their lurking hint of danger was less the later conception of state functions being farmed out to private undertakers than the Renaissance idea of sovereign power being yoked to arcane knowledge.[36]

Often associated with prophetical insight and linked to processes like alchemy that sought to overcome worldly inferiority by channeling divine wisdom, projects identified lawful action for the sovereign queen and the commonwealth alike to follow. They located pathways that promised to accord with God's will and that therefore demanded bold action in recognition that their legitimacy was likely to become clearer only through experience. This association of projects with the resolute pursuit of a divinely ordained corridor clearly emerges in a 1587 epistolary dedication to Sir Walter Ralegh. There, Richard Hakluyt the clergyman could "exhort" and "admonish" Ralegh "to persist in your project" of colonizing Virginia on the grounds that,

---

36. [Humphrey Gilbert], "A Discourse How Hir Majestie May Meete with and Annoy the King of Spayne," [Nov. 6, 1577], in David Beers Quinn, ed., *The Voyages and Colonising Enterprises of Sir Humphrey Gilbert,* Works Issued by the Hakluyt Society, 2d Ser., no. 83 (London, 1940), I, 177, "Introduction," I, 20–21; Quinn, *England and the Discovery of America,* 232–234.

despite what certain "published ill reports" had alleged, experience thus far vouched for the project's divine approval:

> That God will be with you, you have no reason to doubt, for his glory, the salvation of countless souls, and the increase of the Kingdom of Christ is at stake. Up then, go on as you have begun, leave to posterity an imperishable monument of your name and fame, such as age will never obliterate. For to posterity no greater glory can be handed down than to conquer the barbarian, to recall the savage and the pagan to civility, to draw the ignorant within the orbit of reason, and to fill with reverence for divinity the godless and the ungodly.

Ralegh's "project" had every appearance of being sound, and Hakluyt, in true casuistic fashion, encouraged him to proceed with unflagging resolve.[37]

Also known as case divinity, casuistry reflected a medieval and early modern truism that law and moral principles can never be cut and dried in a world in which God's will remains imperfectly known. Predicated on the assumption that the moral status of an act—whether it is sinful and deserving of penance (or just how sinful it is and what kind of penance should be exacted)—might vary in different circumstances. casuistry was a mode of moral reasoning that assumed the circumstantial basis of moral and immoral conduct: stealing might be wrong, but some cases might justify it. The persona of the person engaged in the conduct was also relevant: what was permissible in a king was inexcusable in a blacksmith; while a mother might steal bread for her starving children, a neighbor was to avoid such roguish behavior; a master's liberties were inevitably different from a servant's. The pervasive idea that callings, or offices, defined one's proper duties placed considerable weight on the persona, or personae, of the person claiming to execute them. In a pre-Kantian world in which the morally autonomous individual was scarcely conceivable, except perhaps as the most woefully de-

---

37. "Epistle Dedicatory to Sir Walter Ralegh by Richard Hakluyt," 1587, in E. G. R Taylor, ed., *The Original Writings and Correspondence of the Two Richard Hakluyts,* Works Issued by the Hakluyt Society, 2d Ser., no. 77 (London, 1935), II, 367–368. Even before the rise of the New Science gave new emphasis to empiricism as a route to truth, "experience" also figured large in earlier humanist views of how providential knowledge is best grounded; see, for instance, Best, "The Fyrst Booke of the First Voyage of *Martin Frobisher . . . ,*" May 15, 1576, in Best, *A True Discourse of the Late Voyages of Discoverie,* 45. For an earlier example, see [Rastell], *A New Iuterlude and a Mery of the Nature of the .iiii. Element,* B7v–C1r.

generate of fallen men, such personae were not envisioned as merely masks one wore over the true self. They were instead archetypal moral types — king, mother, nobleman, slave — that could be traced readily through time and space. That early modern Europeans often looked for such types — kings and emperors, gentlemen and priests, the better sort and the base — in native American societies reflected this presupposition of the universality of personae. Their fundamentality rested in the fact of a God-centered world that called people into service by way of offices.[38]

Because casuistry assumed a two-part cosmos, the earth and the heavens at once divided and yet also ideally brought back into harmonious convergence, the moral order it delineated was similarly two-tiered. William Perkins accordingly distinguished between people's general calling, the duties they owed to God, and their particular callings, the duties they exercised as members of earthly bodies. Perkins identified these bodies as the family, the commonwealth, and the church. The general calling was an office everyone performs (or should perform) as part of their shared persona as fellow children of God. Particular callings, in contrast, varied in accordance with peoples' more specific personae on this earth and gave rise to a range of offices, such as, Perkins stated, "the calling of a Magistrate, the calling of a Minister, the calling of a Master, of a father, of a childe, of a servant, of a subject." If one's particular calling interfered with one's general duties to God, then the latter naturally prevailed.[39]

This readiness to perceive morality as two-tiered, linking cosmic and earthly duties into a single frame, made casuistry itself continually Janus-faced, at once emphasizing that the faithful were perfect equals in their persona as fellow brothers and sisters in Christ while also insisting that people's particular callings on Earth were contingent on their qualitatively different places in the family, commonwealth, and church. At one moment, the logic might be used to insist on Christian solidarity. As John Donne declared to the Virginia Company during a time of growing divisiveness within its

---

38. On personae in a pre-Kantian world, see Condren, *Argument and Authority*, 15–35, 138–146, 184–185, 346–349. For examples of European interest in finding recognizable types in Indian societies, see Karen Ordahl Kupperman, *Indians and English: Facing Off in Early America* (Ithaca, N.Y., 2000), 92–97; Peter Cook, "Kings, Captains, and Kin: French Views of Native American Political Cultures in the Sixteenth and Early Seventeenth Centuries," in Mancall, ed., *Atlantic World and Virginia*, 307–341.

39. Perkins, "A Treatise of the Vocations, or Callings of Men," in *Workes of That Famous and Worthy Minister of Christ*, 752, 757.

ranks: "*Yeoman,* and *Labourer,* and *Spinster,* are distinctions upon Earth . . . in the Grave there is no distinction. The *Angell* that shall call us out of that dust, will not stand to survay, who lyes naked, who in a Coffin, who in Wood, who in Lead; who in a fine, who in a courser Sheet." At another moment, the logic might be used to insist on the necessity for earthly inequality. Thus, John Winthrop, preaching en route to the new Massachusetts Bay Colony and undoubtedly eager to remind the zealous Puritans on board the *Arbella* that they had not arrived at the spiritual equality of the New Jerusalem quite yet, asserted, "God Almightie in his most holy and wise providence hath soe disposed of the Condicion of mankinde, as in all times some must be rich some poore, some highe and eminent in power and dignitie; others meane and in subjeccion." Modern efforts to locate hard-and-fast ideological divisions between these diverging emphases between earthly hierarchy and spiritual equality regularly founder on the shoals of Renaissance casuistry's own more fluid and circumstantial reasoning; the era's moral argumentation lent itself to, not clear-cut ideological positioning, but rather what Conal Condren has aptly called the "liquid empire of office."[40]

Against this fluid backdrop, the casuistry of colonization, which is the label most appropriately applied to Tudor and early Stuart colonization literature, was intended to reassure various constituencies, or various personae, that they were walking lawful pathways in their particular involvement in the colonizing project. One conscience that needed reassuring in this regard, undoubtedly the most important one in this context, was the sovereign monarch's. Thus, the Catholic humanist and magus John Dee met with Elizabeth in a number of private audiences in November 1577 and on August 5, 1578. The meetings appear to have been arranged by Walsingham as an effort to bring Dee's uniquely prodigious knowledge and its singularly forceful casuistic implications to the queen at a moment when her sovereign office needed reinforcing. Among the problems at hand, the matter of America and the colonizing projects that Frobisher and Gilbert had been promoting at court over the past decade were only of secondary importance. Rather, a number of more-pressing issues were brewing, including the recent negotiations over whether Elizabeth would accept sovereignty over the Dutch states in rebellion against the Spanish king as well as the related question of

---

40. Donne, *Sermon Preached to the Honourable Company of the Virginian Plantation,* in Potter and Simpson, eds., *Sermons of John Donne,* IV, 277; John Winthrop, "A Modell of Christian Charity," in *Winthrop Papers,* II, *1623–1630* (Boston, 1931), 282–295; Condren, *Argument and Authority,* 13.

her proposed marriage to Francis, duke of Anjou. Yet, it was in the nature of casuistic considerations of office that duties that were perceived as neglected in one area had implications for duties in other domains.[41]

One result of the failed deliberations over the Low Countries, and undoubtedly, too, an outgrowth of the queen's near match to a Catholic prince, was a revival of the question that periodically rose to the surface during periods of crisis in both Mary's and Elizabeth's reigns: whether God reserved sovereign kingship for men. "I am assured that God hath revealed to some in this our age that it is more than a monster in nature that a woman shall reign and have empire above man," the Calvinist Protestant John Knox had thundered on the eve of Elizabeth's accession. It was presumably to tamp down the same anxiety about female rule both in the aftermath of the Dutch negotiations and amid the controversy over whether the queen required a husband to fulfill her sovereign obligations fully that James Sandford, a Protestant scholar and translator, published a dedication to Sir Christopher Hatton in 1576 that expressly denied that nature had "condemned that sexe of slowenesse or dulnesse." Undoubtedly writing at the behest of his

---

41. For the timing of these meetings and their relationship to both the drawing up of Gilbert's letters patent as well as Dee's writings on empire, see MacMillan, ed., *John Dee*, 1-29. For the argument that Dee's writings also arose in relation to the negotiations over the Low Countries and Elizabeth's proposed match to Anjou, see Parry, *Arch-Conjuror of England*, 103-137. Parry further observes that Elizabeth had little need of legal justification for American colonization. Not only did she see such justification as arising from her inherent prerogative, the rationale for colonization had also already been provided by Philip and Mary's letters patent of 1555 to the Muscovy Company. This charter granted the company powers of territorial possession and dominion that pertained to all areas touched by northern seas, a license that Parliament confirmed in 1566 (96-97). A similar indication that Dee's civil law arguments had already been articulated by the time of his 1577 meetings can be seen in the March 1573 document that states: "Beside that not only traffic, but also possession, planting of people, and habitation, hath been already judged lawful for other nations in such places as the Spaniards and Portugals have not already added to their possessions. As is proved by your Majesties most honourable and lawful grant to Thomas Stuclee and his company for Terra Florida [that is, in 1563]. Also the French mens inhabiting in Florida and Bresil, who albeit they acknowledge the Pope's authority in such things as they graunt to pertain to him, yet in this *universal right* of traffic and temporal dominion they have not holden them bound by his power." A portion of the document appears as "Extracts from Camden's *Annals*," 1571, in E. G. R. Taylor, ed., *Original Writings and Correspondence of the Two Richard Hakluyts*, I, 89. For the argument that female imperium was a major concern in the late Tudor era, see A. N. McLaren, *Political Culture in the Reign of Elizabeth I: Queen and Commonwealth, 1558-1585* (Cambridge, 1999).

patron, Leicester, who had taken a lead role in pushing the queen and other timid souls like Hatton both to accept her sovereign responsibilities over the breakaway Dutch provinces and to shun her Catholic suitor, Sandford insisted that a female ruler could be "a mightie piller of Gods Church" and "waxe mightier in power and spirite, to the utter confusion of Antichrist." Observing that even one of Philip II's most warlike ambassadors had quaked at Elizabeth's feet, he argued, "There must needes be some diviner thing in hir Majestie, than in the Kings and Queens of other countries." He then tied this remarkable judgment about Elizabeth's robust sovereignty to an even loftier claim: the world's end would occur as early as 1588, and England's queen was evidently one of the earthly rulers whom God intended to secure order in anticipation of that momentous event.[42]

Dee's own casuistry about Elizabeth's imperial duties was of a piece with this kind of exuberant prophesying. His meetings with the queen and the several writings he composed to accompany them, all of which arose from the same context of tensions over Elizabeth's sovereignty in which Sandford wrote, were manifestly casuistic in intent. Their "chefe purpose," as he put it, was "to stire upp your Majesties most noble hart and to directe your godlie conscience"—that is, to point the queen toward the lawful pathways that God had prepared for her. These pathways met in a set of responsibilities that were every bit as exalted as the ones Sandford envisioned for her, for Dee's own point of departure in limning her sovereign office was similarly the approaching apocalypse. A decade earlier he had begun to develop his eschatological theory of imperial rule, though initially not with Elizabeth in mind but rather in regards to the new Holy Roman emperor, the Habsburg-descended Hungarian king and Charles V's nephew, Maximilian II. Dee's ecumenical approach to religion had encouraged him to see Maximilian as a Last Reforming Emperor who could transcend Christendom's divisions in anticipation of Judgment Day. Yet, even before Maximilian's death in October 1576, Dee had begun to view Elizabeth as more probably ordained for the role. A wide range of knowledge-seeking pursuits had led him to this conclusion. These included not only such humanistic studies as history and law but also more occult inquiries into millenarianism and the Hebrew Kabbalah

---

42. John Knox, *The First Blast of the Trumpet against the Monstrous Regiment of Women* (1558) in Marvin A. Breslow, ed., *The Political Writings of John Knox* (Washington, D.C., 1985), 38; [Lodovico Guicciardini], *Houres of Recreation; or, Afterdinners, Which May Aptly Be Called the Garden of Pleasure . . . Done Firste Out of Italian into Englishe by James Sandford Gent. . . .* (London, 1576), a.iiij.r–a.vi.r.

as well as outright magical practices like angelic communication through crystals, alchemy, and his persistent quest for the philosopher's stone. Given the cosmic scope of these investigations, Dee's message to Elizabeth that she was "our true, lawfull, and undoubted Brytish Empresse" meant a good deal more than that her title over her terrestrial kingdoms was sound. It suggested, too, that God had called her to duties far in excess of what she and many of her advisers currently recognized.[43]

The queen's duties were, as Dee put it, "cosmopoliticall" in significance, by which he meant not only that they contributed to the world's greater peace and prosperity for anyone fortunate enough to live under a sovereign as "Puissant" as Elizabeth but also that, in the very extent and magnitude of her power, she furthered God's own imminent kingdom. Puissance mattered in Dee's eschatological understanding of the queen's office. It did so for much the same reason that it concerned Leicester, Gilbert, and other militant Protestants who called for greater belligerence against Spain in these years. Dee enjoyed a complex marriage of convenience with these men based on a reciprocity of favors: they offered him protection and influence at a time when he was hounded by rumors that he had participated in the interrogation of Protestants under Mary and when the magical arts he practiced were increasingly targeted as dark remnants of Catholicism, while he, in turn, tutored them in those same arts, read the queen's future, and stood on hand when his sorcery was needed to counter other, more sinister witchcraft.[44]

Like his Protestant bedfellows, Dee held to the humanist conviction that only a soaring, God-like sovereign monarch could, in combination with a similarly robust and virtuous commonwealth, effectively do God's bidding.

---

43. John Dee, "The Limits of the British Empire," in MacMillan, ed., *John Dee*, 56. On Dee's ecumenical Christianity and his initial hopefulness for Maximilian II, see Parry, *Arch-Conjuror of England*, 19, 47, 51–53, 56, 59–60, 79, 107, 110, 179.

44. D[ee], *General and Rare Memorials*, 54–55; Dee, "Limits of the British Empire," in MacMillan, ed., *John Dee*, 56. For a vivid example of the anti-Spanish sentiment of these men, see Humphrey Gilbert's memorandum to Elizabeth that he offered her at the same time Dee was dispensing his casuistry about her British Empire. In no uncertain terms, Gilbert wrote that, as the queen "owght undoubtedly to seeke the kingdome of heaven," so "upon that fowndacion" she was to understand "that there can never be constant, and firme league of amytie betwene those princes, whose division is planted by the woorme of thier consciences." See [Gilbert], "Discourse How Hir Majestie," Nov. 6, 1577, in Quinn, ed., *Voyages and Colonising Enterprises of Sir Humphrey Gilbert*, I, 170–171.

Hence, the central importance that Dee's theory of Elizabeth's rule assigned to King Arthur. At this time, the legendary Arthur figured more as a paragon of Habsburg rule than as a founder of British sovereignty. Charles V had celebrated him as an archetype of his own valorous emperorship, and he also appeared in the eschatological theories that Johannes Trithemius had dedicated to Maximilian I. Dee was an admirer of Trithemius's view that the world was proceeding toward Judgment Day in successive ages, each of which was 354 years and four months long and ruled by an angel associated with one of the seven planets. In these stages, angels ruled in tandem with particular earthly rulers, and Trithemius had identified one of these ordained rulers as the great conqueror, King Arthur. Adapting Trithemius's scheme to his own theories about the End Time, Dee determined that the world must currently be governed by Anael, the angel of Venus, a conclusion he tied explicitly to the preponderance of female rulers in sixteenth-century Europe. Furthermore, he greatly enlarged the emphasis Trithemius had given to Arthur. In addition to identifying him as Elizabeth's ancestor, Dee argued that Arthur's triumphs over thirty heathen kingdoms on both sides of the Atlantic comprised a "Brytish Impire" that was her lawful and ancient inheritance. These inherited royal demesnes were not only in America but also scattered over the entirety of the British Isles and large portions of Europe, including Castile itself—a detail that undoubtedly explains why Dee now reversed his former opposition to the legitimacy of Alexander's donation and accepted it as further reinforcement of Elizabeth's grand imperium. In short, Dee had revealed an imperial calling for Elizabeth that far surpassed how she, or anyone else for that matter, had previously conceived it. This remarkably expansive sovereign office did not just permit the queen to authorize colonizing expeditions. They placed her under great obligation to serve God in a project that, by Dee's account, involved not only seeking new discoveries but also restoring a centuries-old Arthurian composite kingdom. When Elizabeth authorized Gilbert's colonizing voyage on June 11, 1578, she was taking one small step—as it turned out, a characteristically tentative one—in the direction of fulfilling that vision of her duties.[45]

In presenting his cosmopolitical arguments for Elizabeth's empire, Dee

---

45. On the sometimes tepid and often mutually benefiting alliance between Dee and the Protestants, see Parry, *Arch-Conjurer of England*, 22, 84–88, 122–123, 132–136, 148–149, 152–160. On Dee's use of Trithemius, see ibid., 50, 58, 106–107, 110, 112, 152, 209. Dee had denied the pope's authority to grant New World territories to Castile in his annotations in Ferdinand Columbus's *History* and in Oviedo's *Navigations*; see, ibid., 130–131.

prepared a map for one of their meetings, a northern projection on which her own portrait, equipped with angel-like wings, was dramatically superimposed over much of North America and Asia. The map was Dee's handiwork, reflecting a knowledge of the northern hemisphere and especially the American Arctic that, in Dee's own proud boast, surpassed even that of his friend Gerard Mercator. But the point of the presentation was, not to show Elizabeth the unrivaled accuracies of his cartography, but to demonstrate the wondrous, indeed miraculous, way his rendering of the New World corresponded with the contours of her own portrait. By a "wonderful chance," he said, the queen's portrait corresponded almost perfectly with the waterways and landmasses surrounding the Northwest Passage. Directly under her crown was Japan. On the left side of her throne sat the Chinese capital, Cambalu. Under the "middle joint of the index finger which encircles the hilt of your sword" lay Quinsay, the "City of Heaven." Moving down her body and eastward, the queen could see the American coastline, neatly positioned "almost opposite Quinsay," as though it were a natural gateway to that wealthy city. And, finally, at her feet lay the passage itself, an area, Dee told Elizabeth, that "your British subjects" were "the first to visit, and to sail through, to the honor of yourself and to the benefit of the commonweal." It was "as if by Divine will," Dee said, that there could be such an astonishing overlap between the queen's regal body and the earth's geography in this particular part of the world.[46]

Such casuistry did more than simply allege the queen's American title in relation to other European sovereigns; it presumed to locate her empire in a broader, God-centered cosmos. It suggested that Elizabeth's sovereignty on the other side of the Atlantic was divinely ordained, tying her rule in providentially meaningful ways to America as well as Asia, as securely to an Arthurian past as to an eschatological future. It therefore defended her American rule as a set of divinely ordained duties that she, in effect, already possessed—indeed, that she neglected at the risk of abusing her sovereign office.

---

46. Dee, "Concerning This Example of Geographic Reform," in MacMillan, ed., *John Dee*, 41. The map with Elizabeth's image on it is evidently no longer extant. On the other hand, Dee prepared a northern projection for Gilbert in 1582 that might resemble the one he presented to the queen; for a reproduction of this image, see MacMillan, ed., *John Dee*, 36.

Sovereignty and Commonwealth in Renaissance Colonization

In 1604, George Waymouth used the term "royall frontire" to refer to James I's sovereign possession in America. Something of a self-proclaimed expert in frontier pacification, he had set off two years earlier in quest of the fabled Northwest Passage to Asia with thirty-five battle-ready men at his side, a learned minister in tow, and a tin box conveying a delicately illuminated letter from Queen Elizabeth to the emperor of China. The work in which his phrase appeared, a treatise entitled "The Jewel of Artes" that he presented to the king on two separate occasions, outlined the technologies, ordnances, and town plans required to fortify those American areas that were in the "possession of our English nation" but that remained too "weakly planted" with English subjects to "defend" them from the "invasions of the heathen." The image, which reverberated with much the same Canaan-like undertones of Ralegh's own remarks on planting, presumed that America already fell under the king's lawful sovereignty and that the so-called heathen who resisted were invaders of the king's domain. Crucially, then, the frontier was less a territorial border than a point at which the king's own rights and power arising from his sovereign office required extraordinary defense. It was a distinctly royal frontier, and as such it imagined the persons who resisted the king's authority as not only barbarians but also rebels.[47]

This conception of a royal frontier, which is also apparent in Dee's remarkable delineation of Elizabeth's angel-like body hovering over North America, derived from the providential logic that sovereignty was first and foremost a power, originating ultimately in God, that enabled a king to perform his unique office as divinely ordained "Ruler and Conductor" (to quote Ralegh's two-part view of the sovereign's prime role in bending rebellious wills back to God). Much the same idea of America as a royal frontier appeared in a proclamation that James I issued in 1617. It identified Virginia as one location — the others being areas in which England was at war — to banish persons in England's historic march areas of Northumberland, Cumberland,

---

47. George Waymouth, Preface to "The Jewel of Artes," in David B. Quinn and Alison M. Quinn, eds., *The English New England Voyages, 1602–1608*, Works Issued by the Hakluyt Society, 2d Ser., no. 161 (London, 1983), 232–235; *Oxford Dictionary of National Biography*, online ed., s.v. "Waymouth, George (*fl.* 1587–1611)," by David R. Ransome, accessed Nov. 15, 2013, http://www.oxforddnb.com/view/article/29155.

and Westmoreland Counties who were judged to be incorrigibly "lewd" and "wicked" so "they may no more infect the places where they abide within this our Realme." The king effectively designated Virginia as a marchland in its own right, an even more "remote" one than his traditional northern marches and hence an appropriate dumping ground for that region's most "notorious ill livers, and misbehaved persons." Such a status as marchland related to the king's sovereignty, an area where his will and prerogative perhaps necessitated a certain extraordinary license to bring stubborn evil to heel but likewise where the imperative of establishing godly order gave considerable, even greater, weight to the realization of commonwealth.[48]

48. [Walter Ralegh], *The History of the World* (London, 1614), 1.9.1, 180; "A Proclamation for the Better and More Peaceable Government of the Middle Shires of Northumberland, Cumberland, and Westmerland," Dec. 23, 1617, in Clarence S. Brigham, *British Royal Proclamations Relating to America: 1603–1783* (New York, 1968), 7. Waymouth and James I's assumption that the royal frontier was most understandable in relation to the sin-purging power of sovereign kingship offers a corrective to two views that strongly influenced early American scholarship during the late twentieth century. According to the first view, the colonies in the seventeenth century were a marchland world in the sense of a wild outer edge of European civilization, a scene of regressive violence that disrupted not only English ideas of civility but also native American and African ones. For this view, see Bernard Bailyn, *Atlantic History: Concept and Contours* (Cambridge, Mass., 2005), 62–63; Bailyn, *The Barbarous Years: The Peopling of British North America: The Conflict of Civilizations, 1600–1675* (New York, 2012), xiii–xv, 284, 298, 425. Such an interpretation does not capture the Renaissance view of the civilizing process as intensely dynamic, often dependent on violence, and far from complete even in Europe. It is helpful in this regard to recognize that as late as 1772 Dr. Samuel Johnson was still reluctant to include the word "civilization" in his dictionary, evidently because he did not think such a settled state of civility had yet been achieved; see Hale, *Civilization of Europe in the Renaissance*, 355. Similarly, the second view, which approaches early modern empires using the rubric of center and peripheries, also risks projecting back into the period assumptions that only became meaningful later. In particular, the notion of a center arguably arose in large part as an outgrowth of Hobbes's conception that the secular state required a single sovereign that could be readily identified and located. For this second view, see, for instance, Jack P. Greene, *Peripheries and Center: Constitutional Development in the Extended Polities of the British Empire and the United States, 1607–1788* (Athens, Ga., 1986); Ken MacMillan, *The Atlantic Imperial Constitution: Center and Periphery in the English Atlantic World* (New York, 2011); Christine Daniels and Michael V. Kennedy, eds., *Negotiated Empires: Centers and Peripheries in the Americas, 1500–1820* (New York, 2002). Given that the idea of a center probably did not catch hold until after *Leviathan* exerted its influence, it is notable that Greene's book, which was largely responsible for introducing the center-periphery theme to early American history, begins its analysis in the 1670s.

The legitimizing force of commonwealth in this era cannot be overemphasized. The complex relationship of commonwealths with imperial kingship, and the related idea of the royal frontier, gave Renaissance colonization much of its distinctive logic. Although this era is associated with the rise of theories of sovereignty like those by Jean Bodin and Hobbes, both of those writers' most famous treatments of sovereignty suggestively appeared in studies that were at heart treatises on commonwealth, or what Bodin called "la Republique." The commonwealth was the starting point for any contemplation of law and governance because of its perceived archetypal status. A hint of this fundamentality appears in Richard Knolles's 1606 translation of Bodin's work, *The Six Bookes of a Commonweale,* the first line of which reads, "A Commonweale is a lawfull government of many families, and of that which unto them in common belongeth, with a puissant soveraigntie." Strikingly, in this formulation, the commonwealth seems to be lawful in its own right, whereas sovereignty contributes, not law per se, but puissance, the strength to hold that lawfulness in place. A few lines down, the rationale becomes somewhat clearer. A commonwealth needed to be seen as "a lawfull or rightfull government" not only to distinguish it from unlawful communities, like bands of pirates or thieves, but also because "the name of a Commonweale is holy."[49]

Of course, the name of a commonwealth was holy, because it appeared in the Bible. It appeared most significantly in the apostle Paul's second epistle to the Ephesians, where membership in the mystical body of Christ is described as transforming gentiles from their original fallen condition as the "children of wrath" who walk in the rebellious ways of the world, into godly persons who, "quickned" by the blood and love of Christ, possess the renewed capacity to walk true to their lawful vocations. Some of the key verses, taken from the King James Bible (1611), appear below:

> 12. That at that time yee were without Christ, being aliens from the common wealth of Israel, and strangers from the covenants of promise, having no hope, and without God in the world.
>
> 13. But now in Christ Jesus, ye who sometimes were far off, are made nigh by the blood of Christ. . . .

---

49. [Jean] Bodin, *The Six Bookes of a Commonweale; A Facsimile Reprint of the English Translation of 1606 Corrected and Supplemented in the Light of a New Comparison with the French and Latin Texts,* ed. Kenneth Douglas McRae (Cambridge, Mass., 1962), 1; J[ean] Bodin, *Les six livres de la republique . . .* (Paris, 1576).

19. Now therefore yee are no more strangers and forreiners; but fellow citizens with the Saints, and of the houshold of God,

20. And are built upon the foundation of the Apostles and Prophets, Jesus Christ himselfe being the chiefe corner stone.

The notion of the "common wealth of Israel," which began to appear in vernacular Bibles in the sixteenth century, still connoted the miraculous conversion suggested by the Latin Vulgate's term "conversatione Israel," or John Wycliffe's fourteenth-century usage, "lyvyng of Israel," but it was also clearly different. The change appears to reflect the Christian humanists' fresh appreciation for Israel as not simply a covenanted relationship with God but also a *politeia*. The return to Greek and Hebrew sources enabled them to better grasp the Bible's meanings before its Latin corruptions. The change also derived from the broader Renaissance fascination with finding God's truth in the world while also locating the world in scripture.[50]

Israel, then, was the archetypal commonwealth, and it was most richly imagined in relation to Paul's conception of membership in Christ's body as the ultimate path to worldly redemption. These premises gave a certain basic uniformity to Renaissance ideas of commonwealth and sovereignty, albeit with plenty of room, of course, for often profound disagreement about particulars. Focusing here on the broad common ground allowed by these basic presuppositions of the commonwealth's archetypal status permits the identification of a few connotations to this outlook that were of special significance in the colonizing context.

The first was the importance attached to the ideal of incorporation. The redeeming bonds of commonwealth incorporated with a proper head allowed for the transformative experience from fallen man to faithful servant of godly offices. Even Christ in this formulation was intriguingly both the

---

50. Eph. 2:1, 3, 12–13, 19–20, in *The Holy Bible, Conteyning the Old Testament, and the New: Newly Translated Out of the Originall Tongues: And with the Former Translations Diligently Compared and Revised, by His Majesties Speciall Co[m]mandement* (London, 1611). For the Latin Vulgate's term "conversatione Israel," see Eph. 2, in *Sacrae Bibliae tomus primus in quo continentur, quinque libri Moysi, libri Josue, et Judicum, liber Psalmorum, Proverbia Salomonis, liber Sapientie, et nouum testamentum Iesu Christi* (London, 1535). Compare with Eph. 2:12, in Josiah Forshall and Frederic Madden, eds., *The Holy Bible, Containing the Old and New Testaments, with the Apocryphal Books, in the Earliest English Versions Made from the Latin Vulgate by John Wycliffe and His Followers* (Oxford, 1850). Eric Nelson's study of Renaissance Hebraism helps to make sense of why this view of Israel as a polity became so resonant at this time. See Nelson, *Hebrew Republic*, 16–22.

body itself and a member; as the body's head, according to Paul, Christ's role in the body was analogous to a husband's own two-part office, joined to his wife through ties of love but also acting as head in their sanctified relationship. Contemporary efforts to explain the relationship between kingship and commonwealth often resorted to this complex Pauline reasoning, striving to explain how kings could be simultaneously ordained by God as heads of their people while also incorporated within the commonwealth's own sanctifying bonds.[51]

The highly choreographed symbology of coronation pageants was an occasion for the enactment and reinforcement of such a subtle logic. During his coronation pageant in 1604, for instance, James I's symbolic incorporation into the English commonwealth, the anointed head becoming one with its body, was expressed through a set of highly nuanced iterations on love. In his speech to his first Parliament, which was itself part of the occasion's imagery of the sovereign becoming one with the body politic, James referred to his English subjects' affectionate reception of their new sovereign king in terms meant to suggest the faithful becoming rapturously reunited with their Maker: "their eyes flaming nothing but sparkles of affection, their mouths and tongues uttering nothing but soundes of joy, their hands, feete, and all the rest of their members in their gestures discovering a passionate longing, and earnestnesse to meete and embrace their new Soveraigne." The theme figured prominently, too, in the coronation pageant through London that preceded the meeting. There, love appeared as Agape, the personification of Christian love. In keeping with the Renaissance ideal that rule inevitably involves the interplay between love and fear, she accompanied her father Genius Urbis, who was identified as the protector of London's citizens. His appearance alongside the London Council and "warrelike Force of the City" emblematized his manly wisdom and martial vigor. The interrelationship between Agape and her father Genius Urbis was carefully explained as mutual, for "no watch or guard could be so safe to the estate, or person of a Prince, as the love and naturall affection of his Subjects." This blend of fear and love, force and consent formed the vital underpinning of the relationship between the will of the sovereign monarch and the collective will of his people and conveyed the ideal of the commonwealth as a consensual though

---

51. Eph. 1:22, 4:15, 5:23, in *The Holy Bible* (1611). The classic work on the *corpus mysticum*, on which this ideal of incorporation is based, is Ernst H. Kantorowicz, *The King's Two Bodies: A Study in Mediaeval Political Theology* (Princeton, 1957).

unreservedly binding union of wills that allowed everyone, from the king to the humblest subject, to perform his offices properly.[52]

Thus, in Ben Jonson's description of the procession, he identified the people's love as a two-way force, transforming king and people simultaneously. The king, according to Jonson, proceeded "with his peoples hearts / Breath'd in his way," as though their love was an essence through which he must pass. At the same time, their love was what drew them to him, their "Soules (their better Parts) / Hasting to follow forth in shouts, and cries. / Upon his face all threw their covetous eyes, / As on a Wonder." Jonson called this rapturous exchange a "concent / Of Hearts, and Voices," by which he meant, not a narrow legal notion of consent, as though king and people were entering into a provisional contract, but rather a transformative enactment of wills and consciences, the people's loving "concent" being the essential force that brought the king's conscience and the collective conscience of his people into one sanctified whole.[53]

The explosion of petitions for grants of legal incorporation in the century after Parliament confirmed Henry VIII's imperium in the Act in Restraint of Appeals (1533) was an outgrowth of this ideal of incorporation. As boroughs, cities, universities, and other communities sought royal corporate charters that preserved their local privileges, they were acting on the idea that kingly sovereignty was both a potential benefit for their own commonwealths' well-being as well as a likely threat if left unabsorbed. Exalting themselves as commonwealths in their own right, these communities were in effect establishing that their own corporate integrity under the king's sovereign head was as substantive as that of the body politic of the realm. Colonizing endeavors followed this same premise when they sought corporate franchises for their own members. In 1587, Ralegh was awarded a patent that identified Virginia's governor and his twelve assistants as forming "one Bodye pollitique and Corporate." A similar patent was granted to the Virginia Company in 1609, ensuring that the colony's "Planters" (those persons actually transplanting themselves across the ocean) and its "Adven-

---

52. *The Kings Majesties Speech, as It Was Delivered by Him in the Upper House of the Parliament to the Lords Spirituall and Temporall, and to the Knights, Citizens, and Burgesses There Assembled; on Munday the 19. Day of March 1603; Being the First Day of This Present Parliament, and the First Parliament of His Majesties Raigne* (Edinburgh, 1604), A2v; Ben Jonson, *B. Jon: His Part of King James His Royall and Magnificent Entertainement through His Honorable Cittie of London, Thurseday the 15. of March. 1603* . . . (London, 1604), A3r-v, B1r-v, C2r.

53. Jonson, *B. Jon: His Part of King James His Royall and Magnificent Entertainement*, E3v, E4r.

turers" (those persons venturing their purses in the enterprise) constituted "one Body or Commonalty perpetual."[54]

Closely related to the ideal of incorporation was a second connotation of the Renaissance outlook on sovereignty and commonwealth — namely, their inherent distinguishability. This is an aspect of contemporary thought that is perhaps clearest in light of Hobbes's own determination to banish it to the realm of the absurd. When, in *Leviathan,* he insisted that sovereignty was to the commonwealth as the soul is to the body, he was making a claim about the indistinguishable nature of commonwealth and sovereignty that is so taken for granted today that it is hard to imagine a time when it did not seem commonsensical. But in his own lifetime they were distinguishable, perhaps nowhere more vividly, or literally, displayed than with the decapitation of Charles I in 1649 on the grounds that he had proven himself an "enemy to the Commonwealth" and a violator of the "public interest." This act not only severed the sovereign head from its commonwealth body (or bodies, given that many commonwealths, including Virginia, lost their sovereign that day) but also suggested (appallingly to Hobbes) that such a safeguarding of the commonwealth from its own sovereign was lawful. By arguing that sovereignty was a thoroughly human-made power, arising simply

---

54. On the rush for incorporation patents, see Phil Withington, *The Politics of Commonwealth: Citizens and Freemen in Early Modern England* (Cambridge, 2005), 18–25. On the ideals behind corporation, see, in addition to Withington, Paul D. Halliday, *Dismembering the Body Politic: Partisan Politics in England's Towns, 1650–1730* (Cambridge, 1998) For Ralegh's corporation, see "Grant of Arms for the City of Raleigh in Virginia, and for Its Governor and Assistants," [Jan. 7, 1587], in David Beers Quinn, ed., *The Roanoke Voyages, 1584–1590; Documents to Illustrate the English Voyages to North America under the Patent Granted to Walter Raleigh in 1584,* Works Issued by the Hakluyt Society, 2d Ser., no. [105], (London, 1955), II, 506–512. For the incorporated planters and adventurers of the Virginia Company, see The Second Charter of Virginia, May 23, 1609, The Avalon Project: Documents in Law, History, and Diplomacy, Yale Law School, Lillian Goldman Law Library, http://avalon.law.yale.edu/17th_century/va02.asp. In outlawing the pope's authority in England, the Act in Restraint of Appeals also led the way to the dissolution of the monasteries and the plundering of monastic properties. These very terrestrial acts of sovereign power, which helped to desacralize the Catholic Church in part by inviting lay people to indulge in the spoils, undoubtedly contributed to the sense by communities that seeking corporate protection under royal imperium was prudent, even if the greatest threat lay in royal power itself. On community involvement in the plundering of monastic properties and the implications of such popular participation for the progress of the Reformation, see Ethan H. Shagan, *Popular Politics and the English Reformation* (Cambridge, 2003), 24, 30, 163–164, 193–196, 235–236, 241, 243, 268.

from the accumulation of the bonds that people formed as they entered the commonwealth, Hobbes sought to make impossible any further confusion about the two concepts' inherent distinguishability.[55]

In the late Tudor and early Stuart eras, colonizers themselves contributed to the narrowing of this gap between the sovereign and commonwealth. They did so both by envisioning these concepts in newly exalted terms that allowed for the remarkable extension of English dominion across the ocean and by experimenting with the word "state" to suggest the enlarged potential for fulfilling God's will that such a magnified power entailed. Dee, for instance, in his *General and Rare Memorials Pertayning to the Perfect Arte of Navigation* (1577), wrote that he looked forward to the time when the queen and her subjects "can atteyne to the excellent Scope, and perfection of Civill State: unto which, both, by the Law of God and Nature: and also by Humaine Policy, all sound Common-Wealths, and Bodies Politike, ought to direct all their Actions Civill." Where Dee emphasized the cosmic scope and apocalyptic perfection of such an entity, Ralegh stressed its capacity to tie in place those human inventions that already accorded with God's will, lashing them down against the world's own capriciousness. In *The Prince; or, Maxims of State* (published posthumously in 1642) that was originally composed for Prince Henry, he wrote, "*State,* is the frame or set order of a Commonwealth, or of the Governours that rule the same, specially of the chiefe and Soveraigne Governour that commands the rest." In "Of the Greatnesse of Kingdomes" (first published in 1612 and reprinted under the expanded name "Of the True Greatnesse of Kingdomes and Estates" in 1625), Francis Bacon argued that even territorially small kingdoms like England had the capacity to become great states, a latent ability he analogized to the kingdom of heaven sprouting from even the tiniest mustard seed (Matthew 13:31). The key to such growth in power from small beginnings, he suggested, was a resolute and valorous people, a battle-ready populace that he associated in part with the Romans' planting of colonies in new territories and absorbing hardy new members. In 1622, Ferdinand Gorges called his proposed New England colony a state in order to suggest the strength it would derive from sitting squarely under God and king while calling on the commonwealth's own elite members to participate actively in government through the making and enforcing of laws. "By this Head, and these Members, united

---

55. "The Sentence of the High Court of Justice upon the King," [Jan. 27, 1648–1649], in Samuel Rawson Gardiner, ed., *The Constitutional Documents of the Puritan Revolution, 1625–1660* (Oxford, 1906), 378–379.

together, the great affaires of the whole State is to be managed, according to their severall authorities, given them from their Superiours," he asserted.[56]

As with Dee, Ralegh, and Bacon, what is striking about Gorges's description is that the state referred as much to the body politic, or commonwealth, as to the royal (and divine) head that sat atop it. This locution allowed him to speak of the colony as though it comprised multiple states, not only the state constituted by a body of officers who would remain resident in England but also the civil and ecclesiastical states in New England itself. Here, for instance, is how he spoke of the process by which the colony's laws would be established:

> And for that all men by nature are best pleased to be their owne carvers, and doe most willingly submit to those Ordinances, or Orders whereof themselves are authors: it is therefore resolved, that the generall lawes whereby that State is to be governed, shall be first framed and agreed upon by the generall assembly of the States of those parts, both Spirituall and Temporall.

The laws would then go to the president and council in England for final authorization because "under God, and his Sacred *Highnesse,* they are the principall Authors of that foundation." In effect, the state existed anywhere the king's sovereign power and the active wills of the people blended into one.[57]

It is easy to see from these examples that, even before Hobbes offered his own theory of the state, there were already rich antecedents for imagining such an entity not only in terms of the fundamental mutuality between sov-

---

56. D[ee], *General and Rare Memorials*, 79; Walter Ra[legh], *The Prince; or, Maxims of State; Written by Sir Walter Rawley, and Presented to Prince Henry* . . . (London, 1642), 1; Sir Francis Bacon, "Of the Greatnesse of Kingdomes," *The Essaies of S[i]r Francis Bacon Knight, the Kings Solliciter Generall* (London, 1612), 231; Francis Bacon, "Of the True Greatnesse of Kingdomes and Estates," *The Essayes or Counsels, Civill and Morall, of Francis Lo[rd] Verulam, Viscount St. Alban. Newly Written* (London, 1625), 167; *A Briefe Relation of the Discovery and Plantation of New England* . . . (London, 1622), E[1]r–E[1]v. Although the pamphlet appeared under the auspices of the New England Council, Gorges was its likely author as he was both the most active member of the council and the author of a number of other works associated with the colony; see James Phinney Baxter, ed., *Sir Ferdinando Gorges and His Province of Maine* . . . , Prince Society, Publications, XVIII (Boston, 1890), I, 122–124.

57. *Briefe Relation of the Discovery and Plantation of New England*, E[1]r–E[1]v.

ereign and commonwealth but also as a source of extraordinary power and dynamism in its own right. Clearly, too, the colonizing enterprise had contributed to that novel conceptualizing of the state as marrying the sovereign and commonwealth in a newly potent and lively amalgamation, a factor that perhaps lends added historical significance to Hobbes's own brief involvement in the Virginia endeavor. Yet, what is equally evident is that Dee, Ralegh, Bacon, and Gorges, no matter their enhanced sense of the commonwealth's potential, remained rooted in the providential assumptions of their age. Their innovations were still self-consciously built on the scholastic edifice of Sir John Fortescue's *dominium politicum et regale,* which remained the intellectual starting point bar none for envisioning the incorporation of the royal will and the people's civil wills into a single body politic.

Yet, the ways these authors adapted Fortescue's ideal were not insignificant. Bacon, for instance, quietly abandoned Fortescue's view that the common laws of the realm should bind the king to his royal duties. Instead, in order to liberate his king and to unleash the potential of England's valorous subjects, Bacon located the tie of allegiance not narrowly in local laws but rather in the wide-ranging imperatives of natural law. This less place-bound legal basis was appropriate, he argued, for "a warlike and magnanimous nation fit for empire." Freed by the endless expanse of nature, allegiance could stretch indefinitely to wherever barbarism and sin might dwell. Ralegh similarly modified Fortescue's argument to make it fit a Christian humanist age more concerned with taking the civilizing process to the far corners of the earth than simply safeguarding humanity's free will in relation to royal power. In his *History,* Ralegh called Fortescue "that notable Bulwarke of our Lawes." Ralegh's own characterization of law, however, was subtly different from his scholastic predecessor's. Fortescue had treated law as the sinews that bound a fierce and conquering monarch to a people already rendered gentle by faith, thereby creating the conditions for a greater reciprocity of wills between them. Ralegh wanted it both ways: the people's virtue mollifies the monarch's conquering ferocity, while his power lends them a certain fierceness in carrying out God's will. He identified law, in familiar Fortescuian terms, as fundamental to civil polity, saying "There can be neither foundation, building, nor continuance of any Common-wealth, without the rule, levell, and square of Lawes." Yet, the historical moment he identified with this truism was no simple scene of Arcadian civil order; it was rather when God gave Moses "the powerfullest meane (his miraculous grace excepted) to governe that multitude which he conducted, to make them victorious in their passage, and to establish them assuredly in their conquest." Law bolstered the righteousness of sovereign and commonwealth alike in undertaking a conquest with distinct echoes in how Ralegh imagined his own civilizing exertions: the forging of a virtuous polity amid heathen nations in a wild and alien land.[58]

Even in adjusting scholastic theory to fit the new Christian humanist fascination with the brute vigor involved in restoring a fallen world to order and obedience, however, Ralegh and Bacon had not yet so collapsed sovereignty and commonwealth to the point of equivalence where Hobbes sought to bring them. Instead, they continued to assume that polities aspiring to do right by God were ultimately two-part composites, bringing a sovereign head into reciprocal relationship with commonwealth bodies in order to contribute to the world's ever-greater redemption. This leads to the third point to make about sovereignty and commonwealth: namely, the transformative power that contemporaries associated with reciprocity itself. Just as offices in general were envisioned as relational, and as tying two or more personae together in bonds that held them mutually to their duties while also endowing them both with the benefits, or blessings, that arose from such "naturall obedience" (as such reciprocity was often called), so, too, did the sovereign monarch and the commonwealths he governed stand in reciprocal relationship to one another. The Latin Vulgate term *"conversatione"* for the Israelites' relationship with God is suggestive of this two-way bond imagined

---

58. "The Case of the Postnati, or of the Union of the Realm of Scotland with England; Triu. 6 James I. A.D. 1608," in *Cobbett's Complete Collection of State Trials and Proceedings for High Treason and Other Crimes and Misdemeanors from the Earliest Period to the Present Time* (London, 1809), II, 595; [Ralegh], *History of the World*, 2.4.3, 268, 2.4.16, 294. Bacon made his arguments in the famous *Calvin's Case* (1608), which sought to settle the question of the legal status of Scotsmen in England after the accession of James I. The plaintiff Robert Calvin was a child born in Scotland after the king's accession. Lawyers who argued against his claim to naturalization asserted that allegiance was based on laws and the particular realm within which those laws had bearing. Those who argued for him, like Bacon and Sir Edward Coke made the case that the bond of allegiance transcended place. For a useful discussion of Bacon's and Coke's arguments in this case and how they parted ways with Fortescue, see Keechang Kim, *Aliens in Medieval Law: The Origins of Modern Citizenship* (Cambridge, 2000), 179–188. Fortescue argued that royal power entered England through the conqueror Brutus and only mingled with the political wills of the people once they were more "mansuete [that is, gentle], and bettir disposid to vertu"; see John Fortescue, *The Governance of England: Otherwise Called the Difference between an Absolute and a Limited Monarchy*, ed. Charles Plummer (Oxford, 1885), 112.

as the most "natural" of ties. Contemporaries loved to locate these natural reciprocal relationships at every level of the commonwealth: husbands and wives, parents and children, masters and servants, magistrates and neighbors, ministers and parishioners, kings and subjects. In the Pauline view as interpreted by scholastics and humanists alike, power arises from such reciprocal bonds themselves. For denizens of the early modern Euro-American world, capacity — the capacity for liberty and obedience, the capacity for meaningful invention and progress, the capacity to do good in the world — materialized through the simple fact of being bound together with one's fellows and God in the redeeming fellowship of commonwealth.[59]

This view lay at the heart of one of the most remarkable contemporary depictions of Virginia's commonwealth, an elaborate word picture that John Donne presented in 1622 to Virginia Company members on the occasion of their second annual Michaelmas feast in London. Donne, who in a 1620 sermon had defined commonwealth simply as "where God hath given thee thy station," spoke to the company at a bleak moment when God's purpose for the colonizers seemed especially uncertain and equivocal. Opechancanough's attack had forcefully reawakened doubts about God's design in Virginia, and James I's recent revocation of the public lotteries similarly cast a pall on the colonizing endeavor. Donne's message to the colonizers, however, was that they possessed power. This was a power they acquired not simply from the king's letters patent but also from standing right with God.[60]

In making this case, Donne encouraged the members to see themselves as part, perhaps even as peculiarly representative, of England's own status as an elect people. His meaning in this regard was simply the fairly standard Anglican viewpoint, a commonplace since the Tudor era, that, as members of the English king's church and commonwealth, all English subjects enjoyed a special relationship with God. Their subjecthood alone signaled their elect status as godly persons, tying them to God through a king whose own sovereignty evidenced as well as permitted such an infusion of divine grace. On the other hand, Donne was also insistent that, in addition to "our Election,"

59. T. H. Breen, "George Donne's 'Virginia Reviewed': A 1638 Plan to Reform Colonial Society," *William and Mary Quarterly*, 3d Ser., XXX (1973), 456.

60. Donne, *Sermon Preached to the Honourable Company of the Virginian Plantation*, in Potter and Simpson, eds., *Sermons of John Donne*, IV, 264–282; "A Sermon Preached at Whitehall, April 2. 1620," III, 65. On the dissolution of the lotteries, see Emily Rose, "The End of the Gamble: The Termination of the Virginia Lotteries in March 1621," *Parliamentary History*, XXVII, pt. 2 (2008), 175–197.

the company members enjoyed another "beame of Sanctification." It was this "present beame of Sanctification," a special blessing by God, that Donne wanted to demonstrate touched all the persons involved in the Virginia venture, no matter how great or small.[61]

All the venture's members, a group whom Donne identified as including everyone from the sovereign king and the company's gentleman and merchant leadership all the way down to free planters and bound laborers, received this further sanctification, he argued, by a special calling, a calling they had collectively inherited from the apostles. The calling appeared in the New Testament passage Acts 1:8 on which Donne based his homily: "But ye shall receive power after that the holy Ghost is come upon you, and ye shall be witnesses unto me, both in Hierusalem, and in all Judea, and in Samaria, and unto the uttermost part of the earth." In the Bible, this calling functions as divine reassurance in the face of great uncertainty. The apostles, told by God that it is not for them to know when the yearned-for restoration of his kingdom will occur, are nevertheless promised that they will receive power, in the sense of an extraordinary infusion of human capacity that only God's righteousness could provide. His gift of the Holy Spirit will keep them exquisitely in his service and thus comfortingly yoked to him as they preach the gospel in a perilous world far removed from the holy commonwealth of Israel's sanctifying bonds. Accordingly, Donne's treatment of power equated it with a redeemed conscience so bent to God's service that it added weight even to the king's own God-given sovereignty. A conscience thus "rectified," Donne said, "Seales the great Seale," "justifies Justice it selfe," "authorises Authoritie, and gives power to strength it selfe." To the gentlemen and merchant shareholders in the pews, such a message undoubtedly reverberated with their own sense of themselves as royal subjects who were simultaneously among the most active citizens not only of London's commonwealth but also of the commonwealth of the realm.[62]

---

61. Donne, *Sermon Preached to the Honourable Company of the Virginian Plantation*, in Potter and Simpson, eds., *Sermons of John Donne*, IV, 281. For a brilliant study of the development of the legal category of subjecthood around the notion of the bond of "faith and alliance," a conceptualization of subjecthood filled with implications for not only the civil personalities of subjects but also their personae as children of God, see Kim, *Aliens in Medieval Law*, 142.

62. Donne, *Sermon Preached to the Honourable Company of the Virginian Plantation*, in Potter and Simpson, eds., *Sermons of John Donne*, IV, 265, 269, 274–275, 276–277; Acts 1:8, in *The Holy Bible* (1611). On the persona of the citizen and his relationship to corporate life in cities as well as other so-called commonwealths, see Withington, *Politics of Commonwealth*, 10–15, 51–84.

But the real thrust of Donne's treatment of godly "power" and its miraculous edification of human consciences appeared in his sermon's dramatic finale. Encouraging his listeners to imagine the colony as the culmination of all the rightly turned wills and, hence, lawfully performed offices that could only come about through such a redeeming power, he portrayed Virginia as a mystical body that spectacularly spanned the Atlantic, binding within itself the various personae whose respective vocations created the colony's lawful bodies political and spiritual, or what Donne called the "beginning of that Common Wealth, and of that Church." Because God's blessing, the "present beame of Sanctification," was what made such a polity possible, Donne did not hesitate to identify this mystical body as one built and "compacted" by God himself. Indeed, his word picture of Virginia's commonwealth took the form of a prayer, imploring God for the blessings that would hold everyone to his or her offices:

> Looke gratiously, and looke powerfully upon this body, which thou hast bene now some yeares in building and compacting together, this Plantation. Looke gratiously upon the Head of this Body, our *Soveraigne* and blesse him with a good disposition to this work, and blesse him for that disposition: Looke gratiously upon them, who are as the *braine* of this body, those who by his power, counsell and advise, and assist in the Government thereof: blesse them with [a] disposition to unity and concord, and blesse them for that disposition. Looke gratiously upon them who are as *Eyes* of this Body, those of the *Clergy*, who have any interest therein: blesse them with a disposition to preach there, to pray heere, to exhort every where for the advancement thereof, and bless them for that disposition. Blesse them who are the *Feete* of this body, who goe thither, and the *Hands* of this body, who labour there, and them who are the *Heart* of this bodie, all that are heartily affected, and declare actually that heartinesse to this action, bless them all with a cheerefull disposition to that, and bless them for that disposition. . . . Bless it so in this calme, that when the tempest comes, it may ride it out safely; blesse it so with friends now, that it may stand against Enemies hereafter; prepare thy selfe a glorious harvest there, and give us leave to be thy Labourers, That so the number of thy *Saints* being fulfilled, wee may with better assurance joyne in that prayer, *Come Lord Jesus come quickly,* and so meet all in that kingdome which the Sonne of GOD hath purchased for us with the inestimable price of his incorruptible bloud.

In other words, at the end of Virginia commonwealth formation lay the ultimate reward, the fulfillment of Jesus's eschatological promise.[63]

In Donne's rendering, the colony becomes little more, or less, than the collective obliging wills, or "cheerefull disposition[s]," that permit a constellation of reciprocal offices to be performed as a way of furthering the Eschaton. Everyone from the sovereign king (head) to his Virginia council (brain) to the clergy (eyes) to free planters (feet) to laborers (hands) to the company's own investors (heart) gives the colony's commonwealth and church their essence, and thus everyone encourages Jesus's saving return. Or at least they do so as long as everyone's "disposition" is, indeed, rightly turned in the realization of such a body of lawful offices. There was, then, a warning as well as reassurance in Donne's message. The colony remained lawful, in the most fundamental sense of resting on a power granted by God, if the various offices that composed it were properly performed and its corporate unity preserved. Otherwise, even James's sovereign kingship, itself not quite yet envisioned as the state's center but still imagined as one of the offices that made up the colony's commonwealth, was not enough on its own to sustain it.

---

63. Donne, *Sermon Preached to the Honourable Company of the Virginian Plantation*, in Potter and Simpson, eds., *Sermons of John Donne*, IV, 280, 282.

[2]
CONQUERORS, GOVERNORS, AND CHRONICLERS
THE PERSONA OF THE "CAPTAIN"

In October 1586, John Hooker, a student of civil law and theology known for his antiquarianism and brief member of both the Irish and English parliaments, composed a lengthy preface for the Irish section of the second edition of Raphael Holinshed's *Chronicles* (1587). Addressed to Sir Walter Ralegh, the preface mirrored Ralegh's own concern with situating colonization firmly in providential time and law. At this juncture, Ralegh's Virginia venture rested precariously on a few tangible successes tinged by a broader aura of uncertainty. An expedition in 1585 led by Sir Richard Grenville, Ralegh's cousin, and governed for a number of months by the military captain Ralph Lane had managed to plant itself securely for an entire year, an achievement that was itself bound to elicit providential connotations. Grenville's own survival of an Atlantic tempest was widely reported as divine delivery, and Sir Francis Drake's more or less contemporaneous victories against the Spanish at Cartagena and Saint Domingo were also promoted as godly triumphs. That Hooker regarded the persistence of Ralegh's young Virginia colony as similarly suggestive of God's will is indicated by his related interpretation of the continuing English conquest of Ireland. There the terrible defeats suffered by the Irish and the simultaneous peace and prosperity of the planters within the English pale were not just accidents of history but providential signs: "Two notable examples (I saie) and woorthie to be throughlie observed; the one of Gods just judgement against the rebels and traitors, and the other of mercie and love towards the obedient and dutifull subject." Nevertheless, nagging problems of human frailty and inconstancy already haunted the nascent Virginia colony. Reports of divisions among the officers and hints of perceived infractions by particular leaders and planters circled relentlessly, and returning settlers voiced even more vocal complaints of harsh discipline and the region's failure to live up to its much-touted promise of miraculous bounty. Ralegh's supporters sharply denounced these rumors as base lies and slander, and Hooker himself explained them on the grounds that "the more noble enterprises a man shall take in hand, the more adversaries he shall have to deprave and hinder the same." Hooker did not proceed, however, simply by defending the "noble enterpris[e]" of colonization.[1]

Hooker devoted much of his preface to identifying the various ways in which Ralegh's evident favor in God's eyes, and the connection between him and other divinely ordained "capteins" and governors, leaders martial and civil, both past and present, conferred authority on his project. Hooker's logic flowed directly out of the Renaissance presuppositions that God grants offices to individual personae, moral types that transcend space and time, and those personae accordingly have a profound obligation to fulfill their distinctive duties faithfully. Reminding Ralegh that, like all "sonnes of Adam," he was "borne to walke in a vocation, and therein to be a profitable member in the church of God, and in maintenance of the common societie," Hooker launched into an extended account both of Ralegh's ancestors and of the "course" of his own life. In so doing, he sought out a distinctly Renaissance conception of self as a persona walking a particular "course" for God and commonwealth. In an age that took for granted that law proceeds along pathways navigated by God's instruments, such a persona was a powerful legitimating conceit in its own right. It explains why so much of the early defense of colonization in Elizabeth's reign took the form not only of casuistic treatises like George Peckham's *True Reporte, of the Late Discoveries, and Possession, Taken in the Right of the Crowne of Englande, of the Newfound Landes: By That Valiaunt and Worthye Gentleman, Sir Humfrey*

---

1. John Hooker, "To the Right Worthie and Honorable Gentleman Sir Walter Raleigh Knight...," in Hooker, *The First and Second Volumes of Chronicles, Comprising 1 the Description and Historie of England, 2 the Description and Historie of Ireland, 3 the Description and Historie of Scotland: First Collected and Published by Raphaell Holinshed*... [London, 1587], A.iii.r–A.iii.v; *Oxford Dictionary of National Biography*, online ed., s.v. "Hooker, John (c. 1527–1601)," by S. Mendyk, accessed Nov. 18, 2013, http://www.oxforddnb.com/view/article/13695. For Hooker's own favorable report on Drake's victories in the West Indies, see "John Hooker on the Results of Drake's Voyage," 1586, in David Beers Quinn, ed., *The Roanoke Voyages, 1584–1590; Documents to Illustrate the English Voyages to North America under the Patent Granted to Walter Raleigh in 1584*, Works Issued by the Hakluyt Society, 2d Ser., no. 104 (London, 1955), I, 312–313.

Gilbert Knight ... (1583) but also of a diverse array of dedicatory epistles, poetic commendations, and panegyrical recommendations whose primary end was to vouch for the persona of specific colonizing captains.[2]

Hooker related Ralegh's life and virtues with a clarity of purpose and design that betrayed how well he already knew the template into which Ralegh's persona needed to fit. Ralegh's ancestors not only possessed "great honour and nobilitie" but they also produced an especially impressive line of men recognized for their singular civil and martial capacities, "some greatlie commended for their wisedomes and deepe judgements in matters of counsell, some likewise much praised for their prowesse and valiantnesse in martiall affaires, and manie of them honored for both." An impressive patrilineal legacy, however, did not alone determine Ralegh's virtues. The world's sinful imperfections and carnal impermanence ("all things" being "variable under the sunne," as Hooker put it) had allowed even Ralegh's own noble ancestry to fall into decay and almost disappear from view — until, that is, it "pleased God to raise the same even as it were from the dead" by calling Ralegh back to his service and inclining Elizabeth's "princelie hart" to favor him with honors and rewards.[3]

Hooker turned from the variability of family lineages to the constancy that he discerned in the "course" of Ralegh's life, including, especially, the "knowledge and experience" he had gained in the wars in France and in maritime travels in quest of undiscovered countries with his half brother Sir Humphrey Gilbert. Their search for discoveries was itself an indication of godly virtue, for, "if they had beene then discovered, infinit commodities in sundrie respects would have insued." In this light, even Gilbert's death at sea was not a sign of God's disfavor. Instead, it provided yet another opportunity for Ralegh to show his own extraordinary captain-like resolution. Although Gilbert's loss was "a matter sufficient to have discouraged a man of a right good stomach and value from anie like seas attempts," Hooker advised Ralegh, "yet you, more respecting the good ends, whereunto you levelled your line for the good of your countrie, did not give over, untill you had recovered

---

2. Hooker, "To the Right Worthie and Honorable Gentleman Sir Walter Raleigh Knight," in Hooker, *First and Second Volumes of Chronicles*, A.ij.v, A.iii.r–v. On the importance of not conflating post-Kantian notions of autonomous selfhood with early modern conceptions of persona and office, see Conal Condren, *Argument and Authority in Early Modern England: The Presuppositions of Oaths and Offices* (Cambridge, 2006), 6–10.

3. Hooker, "To the Right Worthie and Honorable Gentleman Sir Walter Raleigh Knight," in Hooker, *First and Second Volumes of Chronicles*, A.ij.r–A.iii.v.

a land, and had made a plantation of the people of your owne English nation in *Virginia,* the first English colonie that ever was there planted, to the no little derogation of the glorie of the Spaniards, and an impeach to their vaunts." Even Ralegh's role in encouraging the chronicles of colonization that his subordinate captains wrote for him — and that he would later pen for his own Guiana voyage, before turning, in his *History of the World* (1614) to such supposed plantation chronicles as Titus Flavius Josephus's accounts of the Israelites — also fit into this persona. As Hooker explained at great length, the chronicling of virtuous deeds began as soon as humans dispersed "through out the world" and "divided into severall nations." It was a gift that God gave men to make them "more apt, readie, and willing to applie themselves to vertue and to a commendable course of life, both concerning God how he was to be honored, the magistrate how he was to be obeied, and the common societie how it was to be conserved." That Julius Caesar himself did not regard as "prejudiciall to his imperiall estate and majestie" either a reliance on histories to "draw a paterne for his owne direction, both for his civill and his martiall affaires," or a willingness to provide to "posteritie" a "historie of his owne age and dooings" indicated the worthiness of such chronicling for a world continually seeking to bring human governance into alignment with Providence.[4]

Hooker knew precisely how to delineate Ralegh's character and history because there was already a rich discourse around the figure of the captain, a role that had become so associated in the past quarter century with various royal frontiers, including Ireland as well as America, little question existed that it best captured Ralegh's calling. In his 1555 paean to Philip II in the preface of *Decades of the Newe Worlde,* Richard Eden even associated Philip himself with the peculiar virtues of the captain, an office that Eden regarded as first instantiated in the Spanish king's great-grandfather, Ferdinand. Not only did Ferdinand's valorous defeat of the Moors and his expulsion of the Jews mark him out as a holy warrior "whom God raysed for a Capitayne of his people as an other Gedion under whose banner they myght overcome theyr enemies and pourge his vineyarde from suche wycked weedes." So, too, did his fierce captaincy appear in his victories across the Atlantic, which by Eden's effusive account outdid even Abraham's own achievements in subduing the earth after the Fall. "Dyd he or his posteritie see Israell increase to such multitudes and nations as kyng Ferdinandos posteritie may see?" Eden asked. When John Dee in the 1570s valorized King Arthur for his conquest

4. Ibid.

of thirty heathen kingdoms, he likewise hailed him as one "of the nyne most valiant captains that ever have byn since the world began." Here, Dee was referring to the medieval tradition of the Nine Worthies, a mix of biblical, ancient, and medieval warriors including David, Joshua, Judah Maccabee, Alexander, Julius Caesar, Hector, Charlemagne, Godfrey of Bouillon, and King Arthur—an almost unassailable roster of godly nobility and intrepid bellicosity. Gilbert had also been exalted as a captain because of his valorous service to God and queen not only in America but also in Ireland. In defending Gilbert's American colonizing endeavor, Dee proclaimed that he was a "Courragious Capitaine,... as the Irish Rebels have tasted." In his Irish *Chronicles,* Hooker similarly wrote that, in "service upon the [Irish] enimie," Gilbert "was as valiant and couragious as no man more."⁵

The persona of the captain, therefore, not only possessed a great deal of legitimating weight by the time Hooker identified its particular virtues in Ralegh but also made up part of the discourse defending the queen's sovereignty in outward dominions like America and Ireland. To execute the office of captain was to perform a distinctly sovereign duty, bringing rule to a distant and disordered frontier that the monarch either chose not to pacify herself or, far more troublingly, might be incapable of subduing in her own person. It was this latter concern, far more than the commonplace acceptance that sovereigns must delegate their power to subordinate magistrates in order to satisfy certain official obligations, that gave captains their uniquely exalted standing in Elizabeth's reign. One of the most remarkable aspects of

5. Richar[d] Eden, trans., *The Decades of the Newe Worlde or West India, Conteynyng the Navigations and Conquestes of the Spanyardes, with the Particular Description of the Moste Ryche and Large Landes and Ilands Lately Founde in the West Ocean Perteynyng to the Inheritaunce of the Kinges of Spayne . . . Wrytten in the Latine Tounge by Peter Martyr of Angleria, and Translated into Englysshe by Richarde Eden* (London, 1555), [a.iii.]v, [a.iv.]v; John Dee, "The Limits of the British Empire," in Ken MacMillan, ed., with Jennifer Abeles, *John Dee: The Limits of the British Empire* (Westport, Conn., 2004), 52; "John Dee on Gilbert's Project of 1567," Feb. 9, 1571, in David Beers Quinn, ed., *The Voyages and Colonising Enterprises of Sir Humphrey Gilbert,* Works Issued by the Hakluyt Society, 2d Ser., no. 83 (London, 1940), I, 116; Hooker, *The First and Second Volumes of Chronicles,* 132–133. Scholars have often noted the involvement of Virginia leaders and settlers in the Irish reconquest; for an investigation of this theme that refutes the idea of the English experience in Ireland as a precursor, or model, for Virginia colonization and approaches the two domains instead as contemporaneous fields of action that sometimes drew on, and just as often ignored, lessons from one another, a view that fits the concept of disparate royal frontiers offered here, see Audrey Horning, *Ireland in the Virginian Sea: Colonialism in the British Atlantic* (Chapel Hill, N.C., 2013), 76–91, 272–275, 279, 342.

Hooker's delineation of Ralegh's persona as captain was the way it presumed a certain corresponding set of responsibilities on the part of the queen that basically amounted to rewarding his service with almost unbounded generosity while also allowing him extraordinary license to exert his captain-like virtues largely unhindered. This view of the queen's obligations, too, had become a familiar dimension of the captain's persona by the time Hooker wrote, for Gilbert's captaincy had also been promoted as entailing a unique relationship with Elizabeth that made him effectively the vital complement to her own sovereign authority in still-untamed dominions.[6]

George Gascoigne, a poet at Elizabeth's court who lauded a number of captains in these years, including his kinsman Sir Martin Frobisher, expressed the reciprocal bonds between sovereigns and their captains with remarkable forthrightness in his preface to Gilbert's *Discourse of a Discoverie for a New Passage to Cataia* (1576). Drawing on a maxim often invoked in relation to the commonwealth, that the "industrie of the diligent" deserved encouragement and praise no less than the "slouth or abuse of the negligent" warranted condemnation and punishment, he stressed the honor the queen should shower on a subject as "well deserving" as Gilbert:

> For if princes doe not aswell rewarde and cherish the well deserving subjecte, as their Judges and Magistrates are readie to correct the offendour, the Common Wealth might then quickly be deprived both of the one and the other: I meane that as fast as the sword of Justice should weede out the one, so fast the scourg of ingratituce woulde chase out the other. And so thereby their dominions might (in the end) become naked and altogether unfurnished.

Here, Gascoigne managed deftly to call attention to the "sword of Justice" that captains like Gilbert promised to wield unflinchingly in the queen's most rebellious frontiers and, simultaneously, to the "ingratitude" that would drive those valiant men away. Astonishingly, the ingrate who threatened to make the queen's dominions a wasteland if that generosity was not forthcoming was none other than the queen herself.[7]

---

6. For Elizabethan martial men and colonizers in relation to their broader Christian humanist backdrop, including the contemporary preoccupation with imperium, see Rory Rapple, *Martial Power and Elizabethan Political Culture: Military Men in England and Ireland, 1558–1594* (Cambridge, 2009); and Nicholas Canny, *Making Ireland British, 1580–1650* (Oxford, 2003), esp. 1–58.

7. George Gascoigne, Preface to the Reader, in "Sir Humphrey Gilbert, *A Discourse of a Dis-*

This brand of bold rhetoric, which gave the persona of the captain a veneer of potential menace even as it elevated him above most subjects, was, in part, simply an outgrowth of the rise of sovereign monarchy in an age that associated imperium especially with divinely ordained outward conquests, both across the ocean and in Europe. It is telling in this regard that Henry VIII's reign was remembered as much for restoring martial virtue to England as for ushering in the historic imperial kingship announced in the Act in Restraint of Appeals (1533). "All Chevalrie was cherished," wrote Thomas Churchyard in *A Generall Rehearsall of Warres* (1579), "Soldiours" were respected and "manhood so muche esteemed, that he was thought happie and moste valiaunt, that sought credite by the exercises of Armes, and discipline of warre." Like Hooker, Churchyard did not associate such captainly virtues narrowly with birth. As he stated, "when Adam was created, and a long while after, men were all a like." Rather, he associated these captainly virtues with manly exertion that "shines to the heavens," naturally winning favor in the eyes of God and the world.[8]

Such an emphasis on virtuous action over birth undoubtedly had particular resonance for comparatively humble soldiers like Churchyard. At a time when many martial men were second sons of noblemen and gentlemen, forced by the dictates of primogeniture to seek their fortunes away from their families' landed estates, military performance gave additional luster to Henry VIII's ideal of imperium. Moreover, it was during the reign of the Tudors and especially under Henry VIII that the ideal of service to the monarch was cultivated as the ultimate source of nobility. The king's new role as the premier fount of honor, the elaboration of the herald's office, and the granting of seized monastic lands to worthy military men all contributed to burnishing the captain's reputation. Eden similarly looked back on Henry's reign as a period when the English did not remain "in soft beddes at home, among the teares and weping of women" but ventured forth in "manlye courage." Not only did Eden's longing for more valorous days hark back to the reign of "our sovereigne Lord of noble memorie Kinge Henry the. viii," but it centered specifically on his American colonizing efforts. Henry had

---

coverie for a New Passage to Cataia" (London, 1576), in Quinn, ed., *Voyages and Colonising Enterprises of Sir Humphrey Gilbert*, I, 129–130. On Gascoigne in the context of Elizabeth's court, see Gillian Austen, *George Gascoigne* (Cambridge, 2008).

8. Thomas Churchyard, *A Generall Rehearsall of Warres, Wherein Is Five Hundred Severall Services of Land and Sea: As Sieges, Battailles, Skirmiches, and Encounters . . .* (London, 1579), A.i.r, N.ii.r.

"furnished and sent forth ce=ten shippes under the governaunce of Sebastian Cabot," although Cabot's own voyage ran against the moral shoals of "one syr Thomas Perte, whose faynt heart was the cause that that viage toke none effect." This fate merely underscored that manly action was what brought vacillating human endeavors in line with God's own constancy.[9]

Yet, as these examples suggest, the persona of the captain, even if associated with virtually all Renaissance quests for sovereign possession and dominion, was certain to take on particular connotations in a context of female rule. Nostalgia for Henry VIII's reign like that expressed by Hooker and Churchyard reflected the simmering fear in Mary's and Elizabeth's reigns that female sovereignty really did involve a gross mismatch between persona and office. Perhaps stern Calvinists like John Knox were right that God really did not deign to raise up a woman to the imperial office, except perhaps as a punishment for the kingdom's sins. That Eden singled out Ferdinand and Philip as God-favored captains, leaving both Isabela and Mary almost completely out of his narrative of manly imperium, suggested the problems that female rulers in this period could pose when wielding the imperial crown on their own. Unless, for instance, they subordinated themselves to a proper king through marriage, a route that Mary took but that Elizabeth did not. Captains like Gilbert and Ralegh also offered a solution to this dilemma. Although Elizabeth could not easily—certainly not as straightforwardly as her father, or perhaps even Philip—perform the persona of a captain of her people, she might nevertheless be called by God to the role of the platonic, even celestial, center of attraction around which her own chivalrous captain-subjects orbited. In a providential era accustomed to creatively safeguarding divine pathways, and under no circumstance more than when God's anger seemed directed at the unfit personae walking them, presuming that some of the queen's more valiant subjects might bear the mantle of captain for her required only a minor imaginative leap. They could help to anchor her rule to the firmament precisely by offsetting the variability and irresolution associated with her sex that made her an implausible captain-sovereign in the first place. In other words, the colonizing captain and the sovereign queen

---

9. Richard Eden, trans., *A Treatyse of the Newe India, with Other New Founde Landes and Islandes*... [London, 1553], aa.iiii.r. Rapple observes that many of the captains in arenas like Ireland, including Gilbert, were second sons; see Rapple, *Martial Power and Elizabethan Political Culture*, 58, 234. On the Tudor ideal of the monarch as the fount of honor, see Melvyn James, "English Politics and the Concept of Honour," in James, *Society, Politics, and Culture: Studies in Early Modern England* (Cambridge, 1986), 327–339.

would be complementary personae, the one reinforcing the moral integrity of the other.[10]

This rationale gave long-term significance to the persona of the captain. From the sixteenth century to at least the last decades of the seventeenth, the idea that captains brought singular capacities for martial and civil affairs, as well as a felt obligation to chronicle those experiences as lessons for others, gave English colonization much of its original logic and flavor. The many captains who led colonizing ventures and put pen to paper are a testament to the sheer legitimizing weight this persona attained in the Tudor era, especially in Elizabeth's reign. The basic continuities in logic tied together a Sir Humphrey Gilbert, a Sir Thomas Gates, a Captain John Smith, or, for that matter, a Samuel Mathews and a William Claiborne into the single broadly recognized contemporary persona of captain that brimmed with connotations of righteous conduct under God and king. Rather than being sui generis, Virginia captains like Mathews and Claiborne were performing according to the norms of contemporary society. Thus, even as late as the 1660s and 1670s, Sir William Berkeley could still be judged according to this Rennaissance ideal. His dual role as governor and captain general of Virginia provided both the most substantive grounds for justifying his office and for criticizing him as a once-trusted guide for the Virginia commonwealth who had gone wickedly off course.[11]

At the same time, however, the particular travails of Elizabeth's own captains did give the justification of colonization in her reign certain distinctive qualities. Navigating the complexities of sovereign queenship and colonization, whether in Ireland or in America, proved immensely difficult. The period is lined with unsuccessful captains: Gilbert at Newfoundland; Walter Devereux, first earl of Essex, at Ulster; Robert Devereux, second earl of Essex, at Tyrone's Rebellion in Ireland; Ralegh at Roanoke and Guiana. In a period when captaincy was exalted as bringing much-needed resolution and valor to an English sovereign monarchy that ever since Henry VIII's

---

10. My thinking on the theme of female sovereignty and its influence on the legitimizing of American colonization owes a great deal to Anne McLaren's interpretation of Elizabeth's reign as posing particular problems both in relation to Henry VIII's asserted imperium and the Reformation. See A. N. McLaren, *Political Culture in the Reign of Elizabeth I: Queen and Commonwealth, 1558–1585* (Cambridge, 1999).

11. On John Smith as chronicler and analog of the valiant ancient Briton, see David S. Shields, "The Genius of Ancient Britain," in Peter C. Mancall, ed., *The Atlantic World and Virginia, 1550–1624* (Chapel Hill, N.C., 2007), 489–509.

death had been unable to place an adult male king on the throne, the inability to establish order in outward dominions or to bring rebels to heel was not just a political debacle but also a deeply felt moral and providential one. That both the second earl of Essex and Ralegh fell out of favor and ultimately met ignominious ends on charges of treason reflected how high the stakes could be when an office as momentous as that of the captain was unsatisfactorily handled. In the wake of such failures, colonizers themselves had to scramble for new justificatory strategies, a quest for new legitimizing personae that, without eclipsing the persona of the captain entirely, placed him in subtly new configurations, including most significantly the Virginia Company. Great expectations focused on the captain, and consequently his shortcomings could arouse much disdain.[12]

Under God and Queen:
The Captain as Complement to Elizabeth's Sovereignty

The appeal of the captain as a persona who boasted a unique heartiness of body and soul derived to a great extent from the Renaissance association of sovereignty with puissance. Like the revival of annual accession day tilts in this period and other revitalizations of a past eagerly romanticized as chivalric, the persona of the captain reflected in part a nostalgia for the increasingly obsolete medieval ideal of the Three Estates of Christendom, a nod especially to the image of the valiant warriors and stout kings of the Second Estate who dutifully protected both the praying men of the First Estate and the laboring commonalty of the Third. But the captain's persona was also a way of conceptualizing sovereign kingship in its particular Renaissance promise of bringing the world into civil and Christian alignment with God's will. The idealization of the captain as singularly tied, both in mind and body, to the steadiness of the heavens, standing strong against the caprices and confusions of a fallen world, made him, at the same time, a paragon of sovereignty itself.[13]

---

12. Reinterpretations of the second earl of Essex and his so-called rebellion have influenced my thinking about the captains in this era. See Janet Dickinson, *Court Politics and the Earl of Essex, 1589–1601* (London, 2012); and Alexandra Gajda, *The Earl of Essex and Late Elizabethan Political Culture* (Oxford, 2012).

13. The adaptation of the medieval ideal of the Three Estates to new humanist concerns is discussed helpfully in John Hale, *The Civilization of Europe in the Renaissance* (New York, 1994),

At once powerful and civilizing, the captain was associated readily with the conqueror, in turn giving a kind of mythical quality to the endeavors he led on royal frontiers like the New World. Conquest had been the unapologetic description for English colonization in America ever since Henry VII issued his first letters patent to John Cabot and his sons on March 5, 1496. The license authorized the Cabots and their company to discover any territories that were inhabited by heathens and infidels but still unknown to Christians and to "conquer, occupy, and possess" those regions under the king's banner. Humanists sometimes argued on behalf of gentle, rather than warlike, methods of subduing the unfaithful and rebellious. As Thomas Wilson put it in 1553, "What greater gayne can we have, then withoute bloudshed to achive a conquest?" Nevertheless, the goals of conquering barbarous lands and subordinating whatever heathen peoples could be brought within the fold were themselves never in question. Not necessarily violent, conquest was ineluctably subjugating; rebellious wills needed to be bent back in the direction of virtue.[14]

When John Rastell published his versified *New Interlude and a Mery of the Nature of the .iii. Element* (circa 1520), the first publication in English to use the name America to describe the newfound lands, he stressed that his own aborted voyage to the New World in 1517 had intended to do its part in taming American lands by gathering a wide range of useful and marketable

---

355–419. On the accession day tilts, see Frances A. Yates, *Astraea: The Imperial Theme in the Sixteenth Century* (London, 1975), 88–111.

14. "The First Letters Patent Granted to John Cabot and His Sons," Mar. 5, 1496, in James A. Williamson, ed., *The Voyages of the Cabots and the English Discovery of North America under Henry VII and Henry VIII* (London, 1929), 25–27; Thomas Wilson, *The Arte of Rhetorique, for the Use of All Suche as Are Studious of Eloquence, Sette Forth in English, by Thomas Wilson* ([London], 1553), A.i.v. For the argument that the era's humanism encouraged a nonbellicose understanding of American conquest, see Ken MacMillan, "Benign and Benevolent Conquest? The Ideology of Elizabethan Atlantic Expansion Revisited," *Early American Studies*, IX (2011), 32–72. Although MacMillan is surely right to recognize that conquest had a great deal of Christian humanist idealism attached to it in this period, that same humanism could also justify extraordinary violence against persons deemed irremediably sinful. For an illuminating discussion of this violent side of humanism, see Nicholas Canny, *Making Ireland British, 1580–1650* (Oxford, 2003), 1–58. Again, the crucial point is that even Elizabethan English protestations of proceeding more gently than their Spanish counterparts in American conquest revolved around the casuistic premise that circumstance always outweighs principle. Hence, loving conquest could become belligerent conquest in the blink of an eye, if circumstance so dictated.

goods, including copper, fir and pine timber, tar and pitch, soap ashes, and fish. But what more broadly gave the attempted venture honor and merit was its effort to bring Henry VIII's authority to bear on a region his father had discovered through the Cabots' voyages. "What an honorable thynge," he wrote, to have the king's "domynyon extendynge / There into so farre a grounde." As a direct result of that proper kingly rule, colonizers like Rastell could enact the same intensive commonwealth reforms that concerned them at home. Summing up this humanistic agenda, Rastell wrote, "That man occupied is / For a comyn wealth whiche is ever labcrynge / To releve pore people with temporall goodys / . . . to brynge / People from vyce and to use good lyvynge / . . . [and] bryngyth them to knowlege the yngnora[n]t be." Once those civilizing exertions crossed the ocean, the native people would likewise be "instructed / To lyve more vertuously / And to lerne to knowe of men the maner / And also to knowe god theyr maker / whiche as yet lyve all bestly."[15]

When the early English humanist Thomas More, Rastell's brother-in-law, described the origins of his own imaginary polity in *Utopia* (1516), he similarly identified it as the result of conquest. Evidently unconcerned whether Utopus, the founder of Utopia, was a king (only later, in the more tumultuous mid-sixteenth century would the English translators of More's Latin insist on his monarchical status), More was nevertheless emphatic that he was a leader or captain *(duce)*. Utopus's victory over the region and its inhabitants set in motion certain civilizing tendencies. Above all, he lured the natives away from their sinful idleness and back to industriousness. Putting these rude and uncultivated *(rudem atque agrestem)* persons to work on digging a channel that separated the country from the mainland, he even set his soldiers to the task in order to demonstrate the dignity in labor. Long after More wrote, this humanistic ideal of captains laboring with their own hands as an example of virtuous industry for others would remain resonant in colonial discourse, figuring prominently in descriptions of Frobisher's expedition in 1578 as well as in Jacobean-era relations of Virginia leaders like Sir Thomas Gates and Captain John Smith.[15]

---

15. [John Rastell], *A New Iuterlude and a Mery of the Nature of the .iiii. Element Declarynge Many Proper Poynt of Phylosophy Naturall, and of Dyvers Straunge Landys, and of Dyvers Straunge Effects [and] Causis* . . . [London, 1520?], A.iij.v, C.i.v, C.ii.r.

16. Thomas More, *Utopia: Latin Text and English Translation*, ed George M. Logan, Robert M. Adams, and Clarence H. Miller (Cambridge, 1995), 110 (the reference to Utopus as *"duce"* is in the marginalia.) On the different contexts that contributed to More's relative indifference to Uto-

Associated with king-like potency and standing in symbolically for the ruler whose dominion he was securing, the colonizing captain engaged in an endeavor whose success or failure inevitably had significant implications for his master's sovereignty. Eden had recognized this intimate relationship between distant colonizing endeavors and rule closer to home when, in 1555, he fended off the diverse fears that revolved around Philip II's consort kingship. Was England's new king a tyrant? Protestants strenuously pointed to the realm's sudden rash of monstrous births as proof that he was, every deformed baby speaking to God's wrath at the unnatural head now atop the body politic. Lashing out at these allegations, Eden condemned the "phantastical opinions, dissolute lyuynge, licentious talke, and such other vicious behavoures" that currently corrupted the English body politic and demanded another, closer look at the misshapen infants to see that the true source of God's anger was, not the king, but some of his more froward subjects: "Marke well that in them al, the headde is perfect, so that the monstrositie groweth owt of the body, although not owt of the hole body but certeyne partes therof." Meanwhile, a similar objection centered on the claim that, rather than dutifully leading the native Americans to their rightful callings, the Spanish "possesse and inhabyte theyr regions and use theym as bondemen and tributaries, where before they were free." Eden's response to this argument, which probably owed a great deal to criticism directed against Spain's own colonizing captains by casuists like Bartolomé de Las Casas, was that Spanish rule was beneficial both in bridling the most wayward natives (those "cruell Canibales" whose freedom was "rather a horrible licenciousnesse then a libertie") and in freeing the more "innocent" Americans from their terrible "bondage" to such "manhuntynge wolves."

---

pus's monarchical status and the later insistence that he was a king, see David Harris Sacks, "Introduction," in *Utopia: By Sir Thomas More, Translated by Ralph Robynson, 1556*, ed. Sacks (Boston, 1999), 67–68. For examples of the topos of the captain who labors as an example for his inferiors, see George Best, "The Thirde Voyage of Captayne Frobisher...," in Best, *A True Discourse of the Late Voyages of Discoverie, for the Finding of a Passage to Cathaya, by the Northwest, under the Conduct of Martin Frobisher Generall: Devided into Three Bookes...* (London, 1578), 36; William Strach[e]y, "A True Reportory of the Wracke, and Redemption of Sir Thomas Gates Knight...," July 15, 1610, in Samuel Purchas, *Hakluytus Posthumus; or, Purchas His Pilgrimes: Contayning a History of the World in Sea Voyages and Lande Travells by Englishmen and Others* (New York, 1965), XIX, 28; John Smith, *The Generall Historie of Virginia, New-England, and the Summer Isles...* (1624), in Philip L. Barbour, ed., *The Complete Works of Captain John Smith (1580–1631)* (Chapel Hill, N.C., 1986), II, 144.

This Manichean distinction between worthy innocents and savage rebels was a logic Eden was prepared to direct as well, with only slight modification, at England's own recalcitrant subjects: "Stoope Englande stoope, and learne to knowe thy lorde and master, as horses and other brute beastes are taught to doo," he admonished.[17]

Yet, Eden also encountered another set of fears, which were directed, not at the supposedly tyrannical proclivities of a Spanish Catholic monarch, but rather at the opposite apprehension: the possibility that Philip was not as potent as his reputation as a God-favored captain might suggest. Perhaps expressed by English Catholics as well as less zealous Protestants, these caveats centered on the concern that Philip was not as blessed by God with divine capacities and rewards as he promised: "Spayne is a beggerly countrey sayth one: Themperour is but poore sayth an other: He is deade sayth an other: The Indies have rebelled sayth an other, and eyther there commeth no more golde from thense, or there is no more founde nowe." In listing these concerns, Eden gave voice to the darker side of the otherwise sunny idealization of "catholyke and puissaunt" kingship that he sought to identify with Philip's rule. What if the king was not, in fact, resolute and blessed enough to bring the sinful to heel and to reap the material rewards of godly rule and conquest? What if God did not favor him with the extraordinary manly disposition for captaincy at all? In these worrisome possibilities, the colonizers' perceived failures in taming a royal frontier could reflect back on a monarch, suggesting a weakness that was itself threatening to the commonwealth.[18]

Female sovereignty exacerbated these fears of monarchical impotence. To be sure, God had been known to favor female rulers. Elizabeth was often analogized with Deborah, one of the judges who governed ancient Israel while it remained under God's immediate rule. Yet, the captain-like qualities of the sovereign office were closely associated with male capacities. One of the few references Eden made to Mary in his preface was about the weakness of the Protestants, so disfavored by God that they could be "miraculously overthrowne by a woman." On the other hand, the Bible indicated how the imperfections of female imperium could be overcome in the Pentateuch story of Deborah. Although a judge and thus divinely favored to rule godly men, Deborah is identified in the Old Testament as enacting God's will specifically through a man, and not just any man. A frontier-purifying captain, the military leader Barak was responsible for vanquishing the Canaanites.

17. Eden, trans., *Decades of the Newe Worlde,* a.ii.v, b.i.v–b.ii.r.
18. Ibid., a.ii.r, b.ii.v.

That the second earl of Essex was often analogized to Barak during Essex's Rebellion, when his effort to force his way back into Elizabeth's favor after his Irish defeat left him vulnerable to charges of treason, indicates how powerfully this image of England's Deborah surrounded by various Barak-like captains captured the contemporary imagination.[19]

Although Elizabeth's American colonizers do not appear to have been compared with Barak directly (no doubt out of prudential concern lest Elizabeth's dependence on them be asserted too forcefully), they were regularly analogized with other captains who executed God's will in Canaan and Israel. Hooker likened Ralegh to Joseph, son of Jacob, and to Daniel, both of whom appear in the Old Testament as men graced with special knowledge and wisdom in the form of visions and dreams that link them to God. Richard Hakluyt the clergyman urged Ralegh to exhibit "valiant courage and faint not," remembering God's exhortation to Joshua "to proceede on forwarde in the conquest of the lande of promise." In the preface to Virginia's published early legal code, *For the Colony in Virginea Britannia: Lawes Divine, Morall, and Martiall, etc.* (1612), William Strachey likewise called Sir Thomas Dale and Sir Thomas Gates, the colony's governors and leading captains, "Ethnarches," a reference to the judges who led ancient Israel under God's direction. In doing so, he implied Virginia's leaders were ordained to institute the godly order for "this new *Sion*."[20]

Even as Virginia's colonizers invited parallels with the conquerors of Canaan and leaders of Israel, contemporary histories of the Israelites and providential treatises, whether or not they were explicitly concerned with colonization, reinforced the aura of legitimacy that swirled around the era's colonizing captains. In reading these texts, which epitomize the era's concern with finding conjunctions between the world and scripture, it is hard not to draw the conclusion that their authors always had at least one eye on the colonizing voyages taking place around them, even if their primary objective was not to legitimize those endeavors per se. When Edmund Bunny turned

---

19. Ibid., b.ii.r. On the analogizing of Essex to Barak, see McClaren, *Political Culture in the Reign of Elizabeth I*, 24, 56; and Gajda, *Earl of Essex*, 77.

20. Hooker, "To the Right Worthie and Honorable Gentleman Sir Walter Raleigh Knight," in Hooker, *First and Second Volumes of Chronicles*, A.iii.r–A.iii.v; R[ichard] H[akluyt], "To the Right Worthie and Honorable Gentleman, Sir Walter Ralegh Knight . . . ," in [René Goulaine de Laudonnière], *A Notable Historie Containing Foure Voyages Made by Certayne French Captaynes unto Florida . . .*, trans. H[akluyt] (London, 1587), dedicatory epistle; William Strachey, *For the Colony in Virginea Britannia: Lawes Divine, Morall, and Martiall, etc.* (London, 1612), [A3]v.

to the nature of the Israelite commonwealth in *The Scepter of Judah; or, What Maner of Government It Was, That unto the Common-Wealth or Church of Israel Was by the Law of God Appointed* (1584), he spoke of the Israelites entering Canaan as if they were analogous to England's colonizers eyeing the New World and its own heathen nations: "The land therfore that was appointed for their possession, was at this time in the possession of others, and those not under any one prince, but under many." Bunny even offered a rationale for colonization that made Moses's followers seem straightforward precursors to Renaissance casuists, painstakingly sifting through the conditions under which captain-led colonization was lawful: "The maner of their entrie and getting the land into their hands, was not to challenge it by discent, or any such title; but by a kind of purchase: and yet not with monie, or monie worth; but only by the dint of the sword, I mean by conquest." Again and again, Bunny's emphasis was on the legitimacy of colonial conquest because it was rooted in God's will. "It was the Lord, and he alone, that gave unto them that good land," Bunny wrote, "and that by his goodnes they now had the same in quiet and peaceable possession."[21]

Captains often appeared in these texts as some of God's most active instruments, even as direct offshoots of his own power, itself always defined as sovereignty. In his translation of Seneca's *De Providentia,* Thomas Lodge called God himself the "soveraigne Captaine and Lord of our lives." He rejected Seneca's own mistaken valorization of Cato's suicide, which he believed a characteristic Stoic failure to acknowledge that only God has the right to call men to death. Lodge's translation of Josephus's histories of the Israelites, *The Famous and Memorable Workes of Josephus* (1602), similarly interwove God's power, sovereignty, colonization, and captaincy, suggesting a timeless and universal arrangement. Noah's children did not just disperse themselves over the earth, they "planted colonies in all places." Jacob's children were not only granted Canaan by God; he gave them "the soveraigntie over this countrey." Moses, with God's assistance, was not just the Israelites' leader; he was "captaine and guide of the Hebrew nation." In perhaps the

---

21. Edmund Bunny, *The Scepter of Judah; or, What Maner of Government It Was, That unto the Common-Wealth or Church of Israel Was by the Law of God Appointed* (London, 1584), 13, 21–22, 46; *Oxford Dictionary of National Biography,* online ed., s.v. "Bunny, Edmund (1540–1618)," by William Joseph Sheils, accessed Nov 19, 2013, http://www.oxforddnb.com/view/article/3943. Bunny would become best known for his massively popular Protestant apologetic *A Booke of Christian Exercise, Appertaining to Resolution . . .* (first printed in 1534, with a stunning thirty more editions published before the end of the century).

most indicative passage of all, at a time when the aged Elizabeth remained on the throne, her days numbered, Lodge returned to the familiar story of Deborah and Barak. In Lodge's rendering, Deborah asks Barak a pregnant question that undoubtedly also loomed over Elizabeth's own captain-led conquests: "Wilt though (said she) surrender the dignitie which God hath given thee to a woman?" The question functioned in part as an assertion of female capacity; in Lodge's account, Barak and his men were fearful, and it was only when Deborah bravely agreed to join them that they eventually triumphed. Perhaps Lodge intended such an image of queenly resolution to refer indirectly, and no doubt ironically, to the starkly different experience of English colonization, in which captains incessantly grumbled about Elizabeth's inadequate support. The question also pointed up another issue. By stressing that God gave Barak his power directly, Lodge gestured toward another anxiety that had become associated with Elizabethan colonization: as men carrying out the queen's sovereign duties on frontiers she herself neglected, her captains really did risk appearing to be king-like, conquerors who might or might not surrender their sovereignty willingly.[22]

The justificatory literature around the colonizing endeavor echoed this exalted view of captains as unique human actors who were unusually capable of wielding sovereign powers that had their origin in God, an interpretation that took on special significance under a sovereign queen. In his dedicatory epistle to Ralegh in his 1587 edition of Peter Martyr's *Decades of the New Worlde or West India* (a work that he, like Eden, sought to bring to an English audience), Hakluyt remarked that, although Henry VIII had wanted to send Sebastian Cabot back to America to secure English discoveries there, God had other plans: "This task it seems, most honoured Knight, divine Providence has reserved for you." Conscious of the abundance of "Elizabeth's Virginia," which Hakluyt analogized to a maidenhead and fertile womb not yet "probed" for their "hidden resources and wealth," Ralegh would not be like those "foolish drones, mindful only of their bellies and gullets, who fresh from that place, like those whom Moses sent to spy out the promised land

---

22. "Lucius Annaeus Seneca His Discourse of Providence; or, Why Good Men Are Afflicted, Since There Is a Divine Providence," in *The Workes of Lucius Annaeus Seneca, Both Morrall and Naturall... Translated by Tho. Lodge, D. in Physicke* (London, 1614), 500; *The Famous and Memorable Workes of Josephus, A Man of Much Honour and Learning among the Jews; Faithfully Translated Out of the Latin, and French, by Tho. Lodge, Doctor in Physicke* ([London], 1602), 9, 22, 46, 115.

flowing with milk and honey, have treacherously published ill reports about it." This creative merging of Elizabeth's sovereignty and God's sovereignty harked back to the cherished Christian miracle of virgin birth and envisioned Ralegh in the role of a singularly important intermediary, hovering between God's will and the fulfillment of his queen's own sovereign duty of bringing forth Virginia's fruits. In a similar metaphor, Hakluyt posited Elizabeth's imperial role as that of matchmaker and Ralegh's knightly role as that of a suitor responsible for providing loving authority over a young wife in the sanctified relationship of marriage. In this formulation, Elizabeth granted Virginia to Ralegh in the same way that she might encourage him to wed one of her prime maidens at court, the colony being that "fairest of nymphs . . . whom our most generous sovereign has given you to be your bride." Such an image allowed the queen a role largely limited to the liberality and moral oversight of the godmother; Ralegh, in contrast, would be the true governor, coaxing Virginia to order much as a patriarchal husband tempers his wife's untoward affections. "There yet remain for you new lands, ample realms, unknown peoples," Hakluyt wrote in spurring Ralegh to secure the queen's imperium across the Atlantic, a duty that he was convinced even the Spanish monarchy recognized as lawful. "They wait yet, I say, to be discovered and subdued, quickly and easily, under the happy auspices of your arms and enterprise, and the sceptre of our most serene Elizabeth, Empress—as even the Spaniard himself admits—of the Ocean." In other words, Ralegh's "arms and enterprise," his own manly exertion, formed the perfect, and lawful, complement to Elizabeth's sovereignty.[23]

To be sure, the martial expertise and leadership capabilities of experienced captains were valued in all colonizing ventures in this period. Here, as in so many other respects, the English found not only worthy models for emulation in other nations' colonizing endeavors but also mirrors of archetypal moral personae and lawful conduct in their chronicles. The history of Hernán Cortés by his most hagiographic chronicler, Francisco López de Gómara, at-

23. "Epistle Dedicatory to Sir Walter Ralegh by Richard Hakluyt," 1587, in E. G. R. Taylor, ed., *The Original Writings and Correspondence of the Two Richard Hakluyts,* Works Issued by the Hakluyt Society, 2d Ser., no. 77 (London, 1935), II, 366–368. Hakluyt referred to Elizabeth explicitly as a godmother, in the context of an expressed wish that she honor Ralegh's exertions with generous monetary support. See H[akluyt], "To the Right Worthie and Honorable Gentleman, Sir Walter Ralegh Knight . . . ," in [Laudonnière], *Notable Historie,* trans. H[akluyt], dedicatory epistle.

tracted the pen of the English Protestant merchant Thomas Nicholas, who procured and translated a number of valuable texts relating to Spanish colonization for Sir Francis Walsingham. In his dedication to Walsingham at the outset of *The Pleasant Historie of the Conquest of the Weast India, Now Called New Spayne* (1578), Nicholas wrote that the work could serve as "a Mirrour and an excellent president, for all such as shall take in hande to governe newe Discoveries." And how was this "Mirrour" to work?

> For here they shall behold, how Glorie, Renowne, and perfite Felicitie, is not gotten but with greate paines, travaile, perill and daunger of life: here shall they see the wisedome, curtesie, valour and pollicie of worthy Captaynes, yea and the faithfull hartes whiche they ought to beare unto their Princes service: here also is described, how to use and correct the stubbern and mutinous persons, and in what order to exalt the good, stoute and virtuous Souldiers, and chiefly, how to preserve and keepe that beutifull Dame Lady Victorie when she is obtayned.

In particular, the mirror would provide a reflection of the ideal captain that English colonizers themselves could imitate.[24]

Hakluyt similarly found in René Goulaine de Laudonnière's *Notable Historie Containing Foure Voyages Made by Certayne French Captaynes unto Florida* (which Hakluyt published in English in 1587) a useful guide for Ralegh's exertions. As Hakluyt put it, "No historie hetherto set foorth hath more affinitie, resemblance or conformitie with yours of Virginea, then this of Florida." By Hakluyt's reckoning, the French Protestant colony initially planted by John Ribault followed a favorable course that distinguished it subtly from many historical colonial endeavors, even though it ultimately failed. Hakluyt contrasted their comparatively more upright attempt with

---

24. [Francisco López de Gómara], *The Pleasant Historie of the Conquest of the Weast India, Now Called New Spayne*, trans. T[homas] N[icholas] (London, 1578), a.ii.r–a.ii.v. On the shared providential premises of Spanish and English colonizing endeavors, see David A. Boruchoff, "Piety, Patriotism, and Empire: Lessons for England, Spain, and the New World in the Works of Richard Hakluyt," *Renaissance Quarterly*, LXII (2009), 809–858; Boruchoff, "New Spain, New England, and the New Jerusalem: The 'Translation' of Empire, Faith, and Learning *(translatio imperii, fidei ac scientiae)* in the Colonial Missionary Project," *Early American Literature*, XLIII (2008), 5–34; and Boruchoff, "The Politics of Providence: History and Empire in the Writings of Pietro Martire, Richard Eden, and Richard Hakluyt," in Anne J. Cruz, ed., *Material and Symbolic Circulation between England and Spain, 1554–1604* (Aldershot, England, 2008), 103–122.

mere profit seeking through trade, the unloading of surplus population, and the pursuit of what Hakluyt took to be the ancient Roman approach whereby colonies aimed at little more than the transplantation of their own "lawes, customes, and religion" into new "provinces" won by "force of armes." This last method Hakluyt deemed erroneous and ultimately ineffectual, chalking it up to the "Romane and tirannicall ambition" of "universall monarchie." The French Huguenot way involved industrious captains, "men of good activitie," creating plantations that revolved around honest work at callings that at once drew profits, brought the land to civility, and, less assuredly though admirably if it happened, allured the natives to Christian life. "For this cause," Hakluyt reasoned, "princes have sent foorth out of their dominions certaine men of good activitie, to plante themselves in strang countries, there to make their profite to bring the countrie to civilitie, and, if it might be, to reduce the inhabitantes to the true knowledg of our God." In short, the French Protestants offered a vision of colonization as commonwealth formation that focused more on drawing people to their lawful offices than the merely temporal ambition of augmenting imperial power.[25]

Captains took center stage in these colonizing visions because their valor, combined with a nobility predicated more on godly virtue than birth, suggested the capacities necessary to reduce barbarous lands and subdue the rebellion left by sin. Even Eden's mid-sixteenth-century paean to the Spanish king Ferdinand was intended to spur Englishmen to look for such capacities within themselves, for "thexemple of this woorthy capitayne kynge Ferdinando" could hardly help but "encourage al other to theyr poure [power] to attempte the lyke vyages." Eden did not envision Ferdinand as traveling across the ocean to enact his captain-like duties on his own. Instead, he delegated the offices of venturing across the Atlantic and chronicling dangerous feats to certain worthy male subjects, "as Governours, Lieuetenauntes, Capitaynes, Admirals, and Pylottes, who by theyr paineful travayles and prowes, have not onely subdued these landes and seas, but have also with lyke diligence commytted thorder therof to wrytinge." No colonizing vision in these years, no matter how much it rested on the value of gentle engagement with

---

25. [Laudonnière], *Notable Historie*, trans. H[akluyt], dedicatory epistle, A[1]r–A[1]v. On the flow of knowledge among European colonizers, often through captives taken for the express purpose of garnering otherwise closely protected information about the New World, see Lisa Voigt, *Writing Captivity in the Early Modern Atlantic: Circulations of Knowledge and Authority in the Iberian and English Imperial Worlds* (Chapel Hill, N. C., 2009). For the English involvement in this interchange, see esp. 254–319.

the natives, was conceivable without the sword-toting, gun-bearing, and armored captains, marshals, and other soldiers whose fort building and patrols, as well as clashes with various enemies and disciplining of planters, made up such a large part of the planting of new commonwealths. Thousands of veterans, hardened men returning from fronts like the Low Countries with few prospects other than to "go idle up and downe in swarmes for lacke of honest intertainment," could be spared for the colonizing project.[26]

In a dedicatory epistle to Ralegh at the beginning of his 1587 translation of Laudonnière's text, Hakluyt explained: "I see no fitter place to employ some part of the better sort of them traynedup thus long in service, then inward parts of the firme of Virginea against such stubborne Savages as shall refuse obedience to her Majestie." Hakluyt reiterated this theme in 1609, in a dedicatory epistle to the Virginia council under James I. He made clear that even under a suitably adult male king he still regarded captains as necessary for managing resistant natives who did not succumb to their rightful sovereign by milder methods: "To handle them gently, while gentle courses may be found to serve, it will be without comparison the best; but if gentle polishing will not serve, then we shall not want hammerours and rough masons enow, I meane our old soldiours trained up in the Netherlands, to square and prepare them to our Preacher's hands." Even when English writers insisted on the preferability of a "gentle course without crueltie and tyrannie" as best for drawing the natives "into love with our nation," a view that significantly did not rule out the widespread casuistic assertion that a violent approach was in some circumstances wholly lawful, the need for captains was still emphasized.[27]

Richard Hakluyt the lawyer shared his younger cousin's interest in promoting a vision of English colonization centered on the planting of industrious commonwealths that would trade with the Indians and across the Atlantic, but he, too, took for granted the need for the governance of captains, the proper persons to make the English effective lords of the region. As he put it:

26. Eden, trans., *Decades of the Newe Worlde*, a.ii.r, [b.iv.]v; [Laudonnière], *Notable Historie*, trans. H[akluyt], dedicatory epistle.

27. [Laudonnière], *Notable Historie*, trans. H[akluyt], dedicatory epistle; "Epistle Dedicatory to the Council of Virginia by Richard Hakluyt," 1609, in Taylor, ed., *Original Writings and Correspondence of the Two Richard Hakluyts*, II, 503, "Pamphlet for the Virginia Enterprise by Richard Hakluyt, Lawyer," 1585, II, 334. For Ribault's own speech to his men lauding valor over good birth, see [Laudonnière], *Notable Historie*, trans. H[akluyt], 9r–10r.

For the more quiet exercise of our manurance [tillage]of the soiles where we shall seat, and of our manuall occupations, it is to be wished that some ancient captaines of milde disposition and great judgement be sent thither with men most skilfull in the arte of fortification; and that direction be taken that the mouthes of great rivers, and the Islands in the same (as things of great moment) be taken, manned, and fortified; and that havens be cut out for safetie of the Navie, that we may be lords of the gates and entries.

As long as colonization was envisioned as an exercise in the securing of dominion in a still-rebellious land, an assumption that prevailed whether a sovereign queen or a sovereign king sat on the throne, captains would be valued.[28]

Nevertheless, queenship added the complicating variable of a sovereign whose own natural body was widely regarded as more corrupted by the Fall, and thus weaker in withstanding worldly caprice, than a man's. Therefore, queens posed a corresponding risk of fatally weakening the bodies politic with which they were incorporated. That Elizabeth's captains were idealized, then, as not only tied to her by bonds of mutual and platonic love but also uniquely hearty in body and soul was significant. It suggested that the impressive integration of sovereignty and captaincy that Eden saw in Ferdinand, or that Dee imagined in King Arthur, or that Hooker found in Julius Caesar, or that Churchyard glorified in Henry VIII could be realized even in the reign of a female head of state.

This reasoning helps to explain the otherwise strange logic of Churchyard's poem, "A Matter Touching the Journey of Sir Humfrey Gilbarte Knight" (1578), which considered in a distinctly casuistic fashion the lawfulness of Gilbert's first voyage of 1578–1579. Perhaps because the voyage was in fact shrouded in secrecy and at one point hinted by Gilbert to be an intended, though ultimately unrealized, strike against the Spanish in the Caribbean, Churchyard reassured his audience, almost certainly an elite body of courtiers, that the shadowy venture taking place under the queen's sovereignty was acceptable to God. Cloistering himself in his "study," the humanist-casuist Churchyard pondered the news of Gilbert's departure, "musing" on Gilbert's potential dereliction in his duties at home while venturing abroad:

---

28. "Pamphlet for the Virginia Enterprise by Richard Hakluyt, Lawyer," 1585, in Taylor. ed., *Original Writings and Correspondence of the Two Richard Hakluyts*, II, 334.

> I marveld howe this Knight,
>   could leave his Lady heere,
> His friends, and prettie tender babes,
>   that he did hold so deere,
> And take him to the Seas,
>   where dayly dangers are.

Having underscored Gilbert's office as patriarch in a way that echoed the common contemporaneous assertion that the captain was robust and hearty even in comparison with Elizabeth's own delicate courtiers, Churchyard acknowledged the probable objection that leaving the realm, like leaving his family, was an abuse of Gilbert's calling. But Churchyard's conscience was satisfied when he considered that the immortal needs of God, impressed on those special mortals whom he "appoyntes" for the carrying out of his will, outstripped mere "worldly care":

> Then wayd I how, immortall Fame,
>   was more than worldly care,
> And where great mind remaynes,
>   the bodyes rest is small,
> For Countreys wealth, for private gayne,
>   or glory seeke we all.
> And such as markes this world,
>   and notes the course of things,
> The weake and tickle stay of states,
>   and great affayres of Kings,
> Desires to be abroade,
>   for causes more than one,
> Content to live as God appoyntes,
>   And let the world alone.

Here, remarkably, was a defense of Gilbert's voyage that rested, not on its authorization by the queen, but rather on Gilbert's own special relationship with Providence. He was one of those prophetically alert persons who "markes this world, / and notes the course of things." The political tumult of the era ("the weake and tickle stay of states") and the rivalry over sovereignty (the "great affayres of Kings") did not distract him. He rose above "the world" even in helping to save it. While the "world doth last" (a reference to the Last Age), those persons assigned as God's instruments needed to perform special duties, including ones not evident to the ignoble.[29]

Accordingly, Churchyard's roll call of Gilbert and his fellow godly adventurers, which he was now prepared to announce to the "World" as a result of his satisfied conscience, carried more than a whiff of the Knights Templar marching to the Crusades:

> O Gilbert noble Knight,
>   God send thee thy desire,
> O manly Knolles, and worthy Wight,
>   whose heart doth still aspire,
> I wish thee great renowne,
>   and noble Carie too,
> And noble North, with Wigmore wise,
>   I wish you well to do.
> O Rawley ripe of sprite,
>   and rare right many wayes,
> And lively Nowell, God you guide,
>   to purchase endlesse prayse.
> Goe comely Cotten too,
>   and march amide the rancke,
> And honest Dennie with the best,
>   must needes deserve some thanke.
> George Carie forth I call,
>   and sure John Roberts heere,
> A speciall sparke with present witte,
>   in person shall appeare.
> Miles Morgan gayness good Fame,
>   and Whetstone steps in place,
> And seekes by travell, and by toyle,

---

29. Thomas Churchyard, "A Matter touching the Journey of Sir Humfrey Gilbarte Knight," 1578, in Quinn, ed., *Voyages and Colonising Enterprises of Sir Humphrey Gilbert*, I, 216–219; *Oxford Dictionary of National Biography*, online ed., s.v. "Churchyard, Thomas (1523?–1604)," by Raphael Lyne, accessed July 14, 2013, http://www.oxforddnb.com/view/article/5407. Churchyard's intended elite audience is suggested by the poem's appearance in *A Discourse of the Queenes Majesties Entertainement in Suffolk and Norffolk* . . . (London, 1578), a work probably directed at courtiers and would-be courtiers.

> to winne him double grace.
> John Udall is not hidde
> 　nor Rowles I do forgette,
> The rest I vow to publish out,
> 　and so dwell in their dette.

About all of these figures it could be said, "God you guide," for, like the captain who led them, they were all purportedly men under the immediate direction of their Maker.[30]

The Perils of "Private Men"

In Elizabeth's reign, another term in addition to captain became so closely associated with the colonizer as almost to define him: "private man." The label referred to the captain's lamentable need in the face of the queen's parsimony to fund his ventures largely by his own devices; he was private in the sense of having to shoulder royal responsibilities while Elizabeth offered little concrete assistance of her own apart from her authorizing patents. Over and over again in these years, Elizabeth's captains, whether in America or while pursuing her sovereign duties in Ireland or the Low Countries, complained of proceeding under her impressive public authority while at the same time suffering the diminished private condition of supplying their own provisions or personnel. But the colonizers' private status was not solely a pragmatic problem; more was at stake than simply the financial challenge of funding expensive overseas voyages. Rather, the real issue here, as was true of American colonization generally in this providential era that took for granted the flightiness of the human grasp of God's will, was the difficulty of pinning down lawful corridors without the corresponding puissance of a robust ruler. The queen's stinginess betokened her wariness about the activities taking place in her name; her tightfistedness highlighted her uncertainty about where her conscience was most safely aligned. To be sure, the limited means of early modern kingdoms undoubtedly played a role in the queen's failure to grant her most forward subjects the support they considered necessary for carrying out endeavors they took to be God's will; meager resources could only be stretched so far. But, in late Renaissance England,

---

30. Churchyard, "A Matter touching the Journey of Sir Humfrey Gilbarte Knight," in Quinn, ed., *Voyages and Colonising Enterprises of Sir Humphrey Gilbert*, I, 218.

governance concerned itself less with the modern administrative state's preoccupation with always-strained revenue streams than with identifying and holding firm to worldly arrangements that enjoyed God's blessing. In this intensely casuistic atmosphere, the queen's illiberality had connotations that went well beyond the economic or budgetary, conjuring instead questions about how divinely sanctioned institutions could be secured if the sovereign herself was only halfheartedly committed to them.[31]

What gave this ambiguous status of private colonization much of its contemporary relevance and sense of tension was the sharply politicized confessional environment of the last decades of Elizabeth's reign. Beginning especially around the time of the Anjou affair in the late 1570s and growing more intense and complex in the 1580s and 1590s, multiple voices competed to locate the proper uses for Elizabeth's sovereignty. Rather than clear-cut ideological positions, these rival voices articulated highly fluid and dialogical casuistic claims about what courses of action were lawful under God; they thus tugged this way and that on the queen's conscience, striving to convince her of the sanctity of one civil policy over another. On one side of this debate were the realm's most zealous Protestants, reformers who insisted that Elizabeth employ her awesome imperium to purge the remaining corruptions in her church and commonwealth. In the 1570s, these persons often flocked to the open-air sermons known as prophesyings, local venues for scriptural interpretation that attracted mixed multitudes, clerics as well as laity, elite

---

31. Twentieth-century scholarship tended to focus on the pragmatic rather than casuistic dimensions of Tudor and early Stuart monarchs' reluctance to fund colonizing voyages. In Charles M. Andrews's histories, for instance, the colonizers were motivated above all by commercial profit and their private risk taking was more or less perfectly analogous to Progressive Era entrepreneurs operating in relative autonomy from state regulation. See, for instance, Charles McLean Andrews, *The Colonial Period* (New York, 1912), 9–10; Andrews, *The Colonial Period of American History*, I, *The Settlements* (New Haven, Conn., 1934), xiii. Less anachronistic, though similarly focused on the problem of financing colonization rather than legitimating it, was the valuable work of David Beers Quinn. His acute attention to the distinction between, in his words, private colonization and state-sponsored colonization has been of great help in this study, though I am more interested than he was in scrutinizing "private" and "state" as terms with a particular bearing in a broader contemporary discourse about Providence and law. See, for instance, David Beers Quinn, *England and the Discovery of America, 1481–1620: From the Bristol Voyages of the Fifteenth Century to the Pilgrim Settlement at Plymouth: The Exploration, Exploitation, and Trial-and-Error Colonization of North America by the English* (New York, 1973), 291–299, 483–484. For a helpful discussion of the meaning of "private" and "public" at this time that relates the concepts to contemporary conceptions of office, see Condren, *Argument and Authority*, 71–79.

magistrates as well as more ordinary men and women. Increasingly derided as Puritans in these years because of their vigorous denunciations of institutions other Protestants accepted as lawful, these godly sermon goers worried the queen because of the sheer cacophony of their assertions about the law—a motley casuistry that, in the eyes of Elizabeth and some of her more conformist-minded advisers like John Aylmer and Sir Christopher Hatton, reflected menacingly the vulgar heterogeneity of the persons pronouncing it. Archbishop of Canterbury Edmund Grindal found himself sequestered in 1577 for taking the side of these ragtag remonstrators of divine truth; in a bold moment he had written to Elizabeth that such communal sermonizing enjoyed the sanction of the "law of God" and that he chose rather "to offend your earthly majesty, than to offend the heavenly majesty of God." His successor John Whitgift held instead to a less tolerant casuistry that favored a firmly hierarchical episcopal establishment as well as imprisonment and even the gallows for nonconforming saints, arousing the Puritans' own shrill retort that the bishopric itself was a wholly worldly office rather than a truly divine calling.[32]

Colonizers often took an active stand in these intra-Protestant debates, treating them as basically an extension of their efforts to locate colonization itself in the broader providential order. Hakluyt the clergyman, for instance, proposed to the queen in 1584 that a stint in America might help to restore Puritan preachers to their true vocation. By turning such "contentious" clergymen to the "frutefull labor" of converting the Indians, they could be diverted from their ever-busy "coyning of newe opynions" and rendered more "contented with the truthe in Relligion alreadie established by aucthoritie." Similarly, Ralegh was in favor of expelling all Brownists from the realm. Making this argument in the House of Commons in 1593, he went on to suggest that some accommodation should be provided for the thousands of households he estimated would be left destitute by the separatists' departure overseas. Almost certainly, the plea was an effort to coax the queen

---

32. Edmund Grindal to Elizabeth I, Dec. 20, 1576, in William Nicholson, ed., *The Remains of Edmund Grindal, D.D., Successively Bishop of London, and Archbishop of York and Canterbury* (Cambridge, 1843), 383, 387. On the prophesyings and the anti-Puritanism surrounding Grindal's downfall, see Peter Lake, "A Tale of Two Episcopal Surveys: The Strange Fates of Edmund Grindal and Cuthbert Mayne Revisited (The Prothero Lecture)," *Transactions of the Royal Historical Society*, 6th Ser., XVIII (2008), 129–163. Puritan arguments against the lawfulness of bishops in this period appeared in a number of works, including the satirical Marprelate tracts and the anti-prelacy writings by the separatists Henry Barrows, John Greenwood, and John Penry.

toward the extensive royal support for colonization that he and Hakluyt had been bruiting for since the mid-1580s.[33]

If the struggles among Protestants pulled in various directions on Elizabeth's authority, so, too, did intensified tensions between Protestants and Catholics. The torture and execution of the English Jesuit Edmund Campion for his mission to England in 1580–1581, one of several controversies that brought the Reformation and Counter-Reformation into collision in these years, sparked an explosive paper war, providing yet another instance in which the era's confessional politics and the justificatory efforts around colonization subtly intersected. Widely interpreted by Protestants as a subversive popish plot, Campion's tour quickly became in the hands of his Catholic defenders a peaceful spiritual journey cut short tragically by his brutal martyrdom. The anonymous pamphlet that Elizabeth's Protestant Privy Councillors issued as their own entry into this casuistic debate left little doubt about where they stood on the matter; penned by William Cecil, first Baron Burghley, the pamphlet was entitled *The Execution of Justice in England for Maintenance of Publique and Christian Peace, against Certeine Stirrers of Sedition, and Adherents to the Traytors and Enemies of the Realm* (1584). The anticipated Catholic response, which Hakluyt monitored closely for Walsingham while serving as chaplain to the English ambassador in Paris, came from the nearby college at Douai where the seminarian William Allen served as something of an English Catholic casuist in exile. In addition to responding to Burghley's apologia, Allen had also written the 1582 pamphlet that originally condemned Campion's execution. There he had observed slyly that more Englishmen seemed predisposed to banish Puritans than Catholics to the Indies, surely a sign of which "humor ... our commonwealth had more need to be purged of."[34]

---

33. "Discourse of Western Planting by Richard Hakluyt," 1584, in Taylor, ed., *Original Writings and Correspondence of the Two Richard Hakluyts*, II, 217. For a useful account of the relationship between anti-Puritanism in 1570s England and various schemes to send separatists to America, including the short-lived 1597 expedition led by the Brownist Francis Johnson, see Quinn, *England and the Discovery of America*, 337–363 Ralegh endorsed the banishment of Brownists during the debates in the House of Commons over An Act to Retain the Queen's Subjects in Obedience (1593: 35 Eliz. I, c. I), which sought to enforce conformity to the Elizabethan church. For the act, see G. R. Elton, *The Tudor Constitution: Documents and Commentary*, 2d ed. (Cambridge, 1982), 458–461. For Ralegh's contribution to the debate, see Simonds D'Ewes, *The Journals of All the Parliaments during the Reign of Queen Elizabeth* ... (London, 1682), 517.

34. [William Allen], *A Briefe Historie of the Glorious Martyrdom of XII. Reverend Priests, Exe-*

For Allen, American colonization was more than an idle reference. He recognized the extent to which the Protestants' effort to give that controversial endeavor the full backing of royal authority was a key wedge in the era's broader struggles over interpreting God's will in relation to sovereign dominion. In characterizing this casuistic line drawing in his 1584 response to the Privy Councillors, he wrote that the realm's current "disorder" resulted not from true religious differences but rather from the merely political "partialitie of a few powerable persons" who took advantage of the queen's "clemencie and credulitie" to steer the realm away from its Maker. There was more than a hint here of the familiar lament about the queen's feminine weakness in her failure to stand up against worldly men who threatened to lead her astray. Thus, Allen remarked at one point that Elizabeth, "being a woman," was a "monstrous and unnatural" persona to uphold the English church; indeed, she was "the verie gappe to bring anie Realme to the thraldome of al sectes, Heresie, Paganisme, Turcisime or Atheisme." From Allen's perspective, the "private men" who stood at the most troublesome remove from Elizabeth's imperium, rendering them incapable of giving her the direction she needed to abide by God's will, were not the Protestants but rather out-of-favor Catholics like himself. Protestant statesmen like Burghley and Walsingham were, in contrast, "publique persons" who took advantage of their proximity to the queen to pressure her into following "injust actions." One of these unlawful endeavors was colonization.[35]

In his 1582 treatise, Allen held up colonization as a Protestant plot that cast doubt on the reformed church itself. "By the law of God and good conscience," he wrote, the English could not justly "possesse those partes which by former composition and by decree of Alexander the vi, pertaineth to an other Prince." Remarkably, his very next sentence shifted abruptly from the question of lawful possession in America to the matter of rightful dominion in England, as if the two issues were perfectly conjoined. "It is the Catholikes that have justly possessed England these thousand yeres," he asserted; thus,

---

cuted within These Twelvemonethes for Confession and Defence of the Catholike Faith; But under the False Pretence of Treason . . . ([Rheins?], 1582), 41. For Hakluyt's attention to rumors about Allen's pamphlet, see Richard Hakluyt to F[rancis] Walsingham, Apr. 1, 1584, in Taylor, ed., *Original Writings and Correspondence of the Two Richard Hakluyts,* Works Issued by the Hakluyt Society, 2d Ser., no. 76 (London, 1935), I, 209–210.

35. [William Allen], *A True, Sincere, and Modest Defence, of English Catholiques That Suffer for Their Faith Both at Home and Abrode* . . . ([Rouen, 1584]), *3r, [*4]r–v, 7.

there "is no reason they should be thrust into the Indes for their dwelling." The comment evoked, in part, the contemporary view that effective possession was proof in itself of divinely favored rule: that is, the sheer duration of Catholic dominion in England over the centuries evidenced the lawfulness of the old faith. At the same time, Allen's portrayal of Protestants as a worldly minded faction who had artfully duped a gullible queen into following their wayward will provided a ready rationale for why truly godly subjects like himself were momentarily on the sidelines, reduced to the status of private men.[36]

From a Protestant perspective, Allen's talk of lawful Catholic possession in England must have carried ominous undertones, especially in view of the very real fears of invasion that haunted the era. In the early 1580s, the idea of Catholic reconquest in England was no mere paranoid fantasy. In short succession, a shocking series of conspiracies came to light, including a number of small uprisings in Ireland, an assassination attempt against the queen in 1583 known as the Throckmorton plot, and an even more elaborate scheme that sought to convince the young James VI, later James I of England, to permit the use of Scotland as a staging ground for an English invasion. Investigations into these plots uncovered considerable evidence that papal nuncios, the Spanish crown, and English, Scottish, and Irish Catholics had colluded to reinstate the old faith by force. In light of such dangers, Elizabeth's notoriously careful navigation between her Protestant and Catholic constituencies could seem a sign not of political prudence but of wayward complacency. Much of the anxiety around the private status of Elizabeth's captains swirled around this context of fears about the risks the queen's timidity posed to the commonwealth if she did not more resolutely take the side of the godly men around her. A powerful impulse in these years was to bind the queen more substantively to the broader commonwealth, especially insofar as that entity could be defined as the collective wills of her Protestant subjects. Among the most notable efforts in this regard was the Bond of Association, an oath instituted in 1584 by Walsingham and Burghley in the wake of both the Throckmorton plot and the assassination of William the Silent. Ostensibly issued to preserve the queen's safety against enemies that the language of the oath left little doubt were meant to be Catholics, the bond also worked the other way around, pressuring Elizabeth to abide by the subscribers' own sense of what was needed for her preservation. The queen felt the sting of

36. [Allen], *Briefe Historie of the Glorious Martyrdom of XII. Reverend Priests*, 41–42.

this co-optation to her great resentment when the association's rationale of safeguarding her from her adversaries was eventually used as legal justification for the execution of her cousin Mary Stuart, Queen of Scots.[37]

It was against this broader backdrop of confessional division and intensive casuistry over God's will that Elizabeth's captains navigated the challenging persona of the private man. Their sense of acting at a worrying remove from the queen's own legitimizing authority arose on various royal frontiers. The first earl of Essex, for instance, acknowledged the trickiness of proceeding with only the shadow of the queen's authority from his vantage point in the Irish reconquest. Writing from Ulster in 1573, he explained to the queen the challenges of being "the instrument, under your Majesty" to "compel" her most "obstinate" subjects to "confess the greatness of your Highness and your sovereignty here." First, his less-stalwart comrades, would-be knightly "adventurers" who were actually too devoted to the "delicacies of England . . . to endure the travail of a year or two in this waste country," deserted him and spread damaging rumors about the "enterprise" at home. Second, the "common hired soldiers" did not consider themselves obliged to the crown at all; by their understanding they "were not pressed" into service "by commission but by persuasion" and thus could leave at any time. Finally, the native inhabitants, observing Essex's inability to preserve the loyalties even of his own men, became similarly convinced that the crown played little part in the endeavor but that instead "this war is altogether mine; alleging, that if it were your Majesty's, it should be executed by the Lord Deputy, being your chief General here." In other words, Essex, as a private man, simply did not have the public bearing to persuade all the necessary persons that he acted under the aegis of a true sovereign. As he put it, "I must acknowledge the weakness of myself, and so, consequently, of any subject that shall attempt any great service." The circumstance was so bad that he wondered if there was some way simply to improve the appearance of his status, that "this war may seem

---

37. Expelled from England for his participation in the Throckmorton plot, the Spanish ambassador to London Don Bernardino de Mendoza was also involved in and kept Philip II abreast of the Irish and Scottish conspiracies. On the relationship of these conspiracies to English royal policy, especially vis-à-vis the Low Countries, see Simon Adams, "The Decision to Intervene: England and the United Provinces, 1584–1585," in José Martínez Millán, ed., *Felipe II (1527–1598): Europa y la Monarquía Católica*, 5 vols. (Madrid, 1999), I, 19–31. For a compelling reading of the politics of the Bond of Association in light of Walsingham and Burghley's effort to bring the Protestant nation to bear on Elizabeth's inconstancy as a female sovereign, see McLaren, *Political Culture in the Reign of Elizabeth I*, 42–43, 48, 163, 194–195, 227, 229, 238.

to be your Majesty's; the war yours, and the reformation [of Ireland] your Majesty's, and I only the instrument and executor of this service."[38]

Sir Philip Sidney similarly gave voice to the plight of the private man in relation to the expedition of Robert Dudley, first earl of Leicester, in 1585–1586 to the Low Countries. Complaining to his father-in-law, Walsingham, that the queen had failed to fund adequately the troops that Leicester led to support the breakaway Dutch provinces against their ostensible overlord Philip II, Sidney mused that when the conductors of a lawful cause were hindered by the irresolution of their own ruler they perhaps had little choice but to commit themselves directly to God:

If her Majesty wear the fowntain I woold fear considring what I daily fynd that we shold wax dry, but she is but a means whom God useth and I know not whether I am deceaved but I am faithfully persuaded that if she shold withdraw her self other springes woold ryse to help this action.

More apprehensive than blustery, Sidney's proclamation of fidelity to his Maker conveyed Christian resignation. The same stoical attitude infused his advice to beleaguered captains like Leicester. Acting on their sovereign's behalf but without her full support, such godly men should seek solace in the demands of their office rather than give in to the frustrations of serving a woefully vacillating queen. Or as Sidney put it: "I think a wyse and constant man ought never to greev whyle he doth plai . . . his own part truly."[39]

American colonization was another endeavor that suffered this disjuncture between Elizabeth's lukewarm commitment and the far greater zeal of

---

38. Walter Devereux, first earl of Essex, to Elizabeth I, Nov. 2, 1573, in Walter Bourchier Devereux, ed., *Lives and Letters of the Devereux, Earls of Essex, in the Reigns of Elizabeth, James I., and Charles I., 1540–1646* (London, 1853), I, 45–46. Rapple observes the occasional use of the intriguing term "*Imperium precarium*," or "*precarii imperium*," in the Irish context, a term that underscored the weakness of the "private man" in his assertion of Elizabeth's sovereignty when she herself seemed uncommitted to the cause. See Rapple, *Martial Power and Elizabethan Political Culture*, 182–184.

39. Sir Philip Sidney to Francis Walsingham, Mar. 24, 1586, Albert Feuillerat, ed., *The Complete Works of Sir Philip Sidney* (Cambridge, 1923), III, 166. On the frustrations with Elizabeth's inconstancy by Sidney and other forward Protestants in the Leicester-Walsingham circles, see Blair Worden, *The Sound of Virtue: Philip Sidney's Arcadia and Elizabethan Politics* (New Haven, Conn., 1996), 77–78, 120–123, 127, 134, 136, 138, 154–155, 177–178, 204, 252, 337, 357.

certain forward subjects. Even when the queen offered concrete support, her patronage was understood to be equivocal rather than wholehearted. For instance, in Sir Martin Frobisher's 1578 voyage, Elizabeth was initially quite generous, providing a gift of £1350 as well as the use of one of her naval vessels, the *Ayde,* which Frobisher captained as the venture's flagship. Yet, as doubts set in about whether the black ore Frobisher had brought back after his 1577 voyage truly contained gold, he and his merchant backers found themselves increasingly marooned from the crown and the various Privy Councillors who had promised money but had thus far failed to pay. The sheer parade of assayers whom the councillors brought in to evaluate the ore suggests that, for the queen, the presence of gold in the rock would have been a legitimating sign in its own right, proof even that the enterprise enjoyed God's blessing. When the ore proved worthless, her declining commitment to the venture more or less quashed its viability. One of the most significant merchant investors, the London mercer Michael Lok, ended up in debtors' prison after he and Frobisher clashed over who was responsible for all outstanding expenses. In his testimony, written perhaps around late 1579 and probably in support of his several suits with creditors, Lok attacked Frobisher in a manner that suggests the ease with which the private man's distance from his queen could be rendered into proof that he sought nothing more than to seize her power. Not altogether different from Allen's allegation that Elizabethan Protestants were politically motivated men who masqueraded as the godly, Lok lashed out at "Captaine Furbushers great pride," the sinful origins of his desire "to advaunce his owne kingdome" and "Empier." Suggestive of the degree to which American colonization had become a key context for imagining such sovereign desires, he even denounced Frobisher as the English equivalent of a Spanish conquistador lasciviously bent on world dominion: "And nowe Captaine Furbysher havinge the thinge that he so mutch hunted for, grewe into such a monsterous minde, that a whole Kingdome coold not conteyne it, but as alredy by discoverye of a new worlde, he was become another Columbus so allso nowe by conquest of a new world he woold become another Cortes." Here, the divinely ordained sovereignty associated with Columbus's discovery and Cortés's conquest received a menacing gloss, envisioned not as the rightful capacity of a true ruler but as the frightening power of a usurper.[40]

40. James McDermott, ed., *The Third Voyage of Martin Frobisher to Baffin Island, 1578,* Works Issued by the Hakluyt Society, 3d Ser., no. 6 (London, 2001), 84n, 85. For the queen's assistance

The queen's uncertain commitment also affected Gilbert's voyages. For instance, Elizabeth's patent of 1578 is striking in granting Gilbert extraordinary sovereign powers, on the one hand, while, on the other, warning him stringently against any infringement of that sovereign grant. Any act of piracy or of "unjust and unlawfull hostilitie" against English subjects, or against foreign subjects in league and amity with England, would lead to the ultimate penalty, the loss of subjecthood. If Gilbert or his heirs went astray on the other side of the Atlantic, they and "the inhabitants" under their charge would forthwith be deemed "out of our allegiance and protection" and "free for all princes and others to pursue with hostilitie as being not our Subjects." Such provisional authorization, which left the queen plenty of room to deny that Gilbert's voyages enjoyed her endorsement if circumstances so warranted, went hand in hand with her parsimonious support of his voyages. After his drowning in 1583, one lesson attached to Gilbert's venture was "that it is a difficulter thing to carry over Colonies into remote Countries upon private mens Purses, that he and others in an erroneous Credulity had perswaded themselves, to their own Cost and Detriment."[41]

The queen's divided will in relation to American colonization was sufficiently conspicuous that it became a prominent theme in the justificatory literature. Evidently deciding that confronting her ambivalence head-on was more productive than wishing it away, writers like the clergyman Hakluyt embraced the lament of the private, divinely directed man expressed by Protestants like Sidney (to whom Hakluyt dedicated his first book) and turned it into a legitimating motif. Peckham's *True Reporte of the Late Discoveries* (1583), which devoted a whole section to the theme, used language so similar to Hakluyt's that one suspects this part of Peckham's casuistry came

---

to the voyage, the ever-changing mood (by turns hopeful and anxious) that orbited for months around the assaying of the ore, and Lok's eventual disproportionate financial burdens, see esp. 4-11, 46-48.

41. "Letters Patent to Sir Humfrey Gylberte," June 11, 1578, The Avalon Project: Documents in Law, History, and Diplomacy, Yale Law School, Lillian Goldman Law Library, http://avalon.law.yale.edu/16th_century/humfrey.asp; "Extract from Camden's *Annals*," in Quinn, ed., *Voyages and Colonising Enterprises of Sir Humphrey Gilbert*, II, 428. As a counterpoint to Elizabeth's provisional license, consider, for instance, the much less cautious one issued by Henry VII in 1501 to a number of English and Portuguese merchants in "Letters Patent Granted to Richard Warde, Thomas Asshehurst, John Thomas, João Fernandez, Francisco Fernandez, and João Gonsalvez...," Mar. 19, 1501, in Williamson, ed., *Voyages of the Cabots*, 46-54.

from Hakluyt's pen. In Peckham's pamphlet, the reader was reassured by a list of impressive historic conquerors, all invariably described as "private" and "noble," who were credited with securing territories and peoples on behalf of faraway princes. Had not Richard fitz Gilbert de Clare, earl of Chepstow in South Wales (also known as Strongbow), "beeing but a subjecte in this Realme" in the era of Henry II, ventured "by himself and his Alleis and assistaunts" into Ireland and "at their own proper charges... made conquest of the... kingdom of Lympster, at which time it was verie populous and strong"? And what about the Spaniards in America? Was not Vasco Núñez de Balboa "a private Gentleman of Spayne, who with the number of 70. Spaniardes at Tichiri, gave an overthrow unto that mightie King Chemacchus, having an Armie of an hundred Canoas and 5000. men"? Did not Cortés, "beeing also but a private Gentleman of Spayne," likewise have "many most victorious and triumphant conquests"? Portuguese subjects, too, despite the country's small size had established dominions around the world on behalf of their kings, even managing in southern India to "compell all the Mores, the subjectes of the mighty Emperor of the Turks to pay tribute unto them" whenever "they passed the Gulfe of Arabia" — a show of robust and godly dominion that had enabled their neighbors, the Persians, to check Turkish power "to the great quiet of all Christendome."[42]

Hakluyt developed the same theme in relation to Ralegh's voyages. In his edition of Laudonnière's *Notable Historie,* he brought up not only many of the historic conquerors cited by Peckham but also, suggestively, Joshua, called by God to lead the Israelites into Canaan and "to proceede forwarde in the conquest of the lande of promise." In effect, Joshua was the ultimate private man, a dwarf in comparison with God and yet ordained to fulfill godlike duties. Hakluyt drew the point succinctly: "Remember that private men have happily wilded and waded through as great enterprises as this, with lesser meanes then those which God in his mercie hath bountifully bestowed upon you, to the singular good, as I assure my selfe, of this our commonwealth wherein you live." Hakluyt's advice was basically the same as that which Sidney had offered the year before in relation to Leicester's campaign: in the absence of the queen's more direct support, captains like

42. "To the Right Worshipfull and Most Vertuous Gentleman Master Phillip Sidney Esquire," in R[ichard] H[akluyt], *Divers Voyages touching the Discoverie of America...* (London, 1582), ¶[1]r–[¶4r]; "Sir George Peckham's *True Reporte...,*" in Quinn, ed., *Voyages and Colonising Enterprises of Sir Humphrey Gilbert,* II, 471, 474–476.

Ralegh had little choice but to proceed as though they were the immediate instruments of their Maker."[43]

Of course, Hakluyt's broader goal was to secure Elizabeth's more active commitment to the colonizing endeavor. This was the principal aim of the treatise he presented to the queen on October 5, 1584, that is now known as his "Discourse of Western Planting." In that manuscript intended for the queen's eyes rather than a broader audience of domestic and foreign readers, he expressed far greater reservations about the capacities of private men than appeared in his published works. For instance, at one point he questioned the adventuring captain's ability to instill the kind of order that a sovereign prince could command. "Men are more apte to make themselves subjecte in obedience to prescribed lawes sett downe and signed by a prince, then to the changeable will of any Capitaine be he never so wise or temperate, never so free from desire or revenge," he candidly wrote. More generally, however, he organized the discourse as an ambitious casuistry, designed, as he put it, "to induce her Majestie and the state to take in hande the westerne voyadge and the plantinge there." Here, "state" conveyed the same meaning that other colonizers like Dee were beginning to attach to it. Rather than the queen's personal estate or status, as the term had commonly meant in the Middle Ages, Hakluyt used "state" to suggest the commonwealth in its particular role in holding all its members, not least the queen, to their respective, divinely ordained duties. As the anchor that held firm against earthly vacillations and errors, the state promised to steer even the most hesitant will in a godly direction. For Hakluyt, the state was undoubtedly the Protestant nation writ large, almost certainly as embodied by Parliament. Indeed, very likely the "Discourse" was meant in part to prepare the queen for the colonizers' plan to approach Parliament for its own endorsement of Ralegh's voyages. Such an intention fit the period's search for strategies to more effectively bind the queen to controversial actions; accordingly, it risked provoking Elizabeth's ire and perhaps her resistance.[44]

As it happens, Ralegh's effort to augment his private status by securing Parliament's acceptance of Elizabeth's letters patent ultimately failed. The House of Commons approved Ralegh's bill on December 18 under the title An Act for the Confermacion of the Quenes Maiesties Lettres Patentes

---

43. [Laudonnière], *Notable Historie*, trans. H[akluyt], dedicatory epistle.

44. "Discourse of Western Planting," 1584, in Taylor ed., *Original Writings and Correspondence of the Two Richard Hakluyts*, II, 313, 325.

Graunted to Walter Ralegh Esquire touchinge the Discoverie and Inhabitinge of Certeyn Foreynge Landes and Cuntries. The House's approval was not without conditions; certain provisos were added to the bill intended to tie Ralegh's hands in specific ways. In particular, he was prohibited from culling would-be settlers from debtor's prison or other jails; infringing on the powers of a head of household by taking his wife, ward, or apprentice; or commandeering ships or supplies by force. But the bill died in the House of Lords. Undoubtedly, opposition came in part from the "mightie faction of the papistes" whom Hakluyt identified as the greatest obstacle to the venture. But, maybe Elizabeth, too, had a hand in the act's dismissal. Indirect evidence for her role in this regard comes from her striking volte-face on the matter of supplies in the months following the bill's downfall. In early 1585, she authorized Ralegh to take up and impress from the counties of Devon and Cornwall and from Bristol whatever ships, personnel, and provisions he needed. This sudden burst of royal generosity, deriving from her prerogative rather than any parliamentary involvement, perhaps functioned in part as a symbolic assertion of queenly sovereignty, a refusal to cede her powers over newfound discoveries to Parliament. If so, the gesture was short-lived. Two years later, Hakluyt was once again remarking, this time in print, that Virginia required an actively committed queen. As he put it in a 1587 dedication to Ralegh, "the speedie and effectuall pursuing of your action . . . woulde demaunde a princes purse to have it throughly followed without lingring." Noting the comparative success of the recent voyage that Ralegh had sent under Grenville and Lane, Hakluyt commented lamely that he hoped the queen's "forwardness and bountie" would soon follow.[45]

The fleeting nature of Elizabeth's support heightened the aura of autonomy that already revolved around her adventuring captains. This was, again, a danger built into the relationship, for the captain really was expected

---

45. "Bill to Confirm Raleigh's Patent, as Passed by the House of Commons," December 1584, in David Beers Quinn, ed., *Roanoke Voyages*, I, 126–129; "Discourse of Western Planting," 1584, in Taylor, ed., *Original Writings and Correspondence of the Two Richard Hakluyts*, II, 280; [Laudonnière], *Notable Historie*, trans. H[akluyt], dedicatory epistle. For the queen's requisition order, see "Signet Letter for Sir Walter Raleigh," June 10, 1585, in Quinn, ed., *Roanoke Voyages*, I, 156–157. For a draft of the commission that might have been drawn up as early as January, see "Draft Commission to Sir Walter Raleigh to Take up Shipping and Mariners," [circa January 1585], ibid., 144–145. For Elizabeth's letters patent to Ralegh, which she issued about nine months before Ralegh sought Parliament's confirmation of her license, see "Letters Patent to Walter Raleigh," Mar. 25, 1584, ibid., 82–89.

to act more or less like a king in conquering and establishing dominion over the queen's own sovereign territories. Both Gilbert and Ralegh referred to the commonwealths they were establishing in America as effectively their own kingdoms. A grant of authority by Gilbert to three of his associates, his brother Sir John Gilbert, Sir George Peckham, and William Aucher, that was entered onto the queen's rolls on July 8, 1582, suggests this mindset. The grant was a matter of deputing some of the "estate righte title power and aucthoritie" that Gilbert himself had received from "our said soveraign ladie the Quene" in her 1578 letters patent. He extended those same sovereign powers to the persons he deemed most suitable for carrying out his office in the event of his death. Sovereignty, therefore, remained the queen's, but it passed down to Gilbert as "chief lord and governor of those Countries under the crowne of England" and was then transferable to his own deputies.[46]

As "chief lord and governor," Gilbert was clearly not king, but one could be forgiven for thinking he was. Within his "remote landes and countries" as well as along the "waye by the seas thether and from thence," he possessed, according to this legal document, "full and mere power and aucthority to correcte punyshe pardone governe and rule" by his own "good discretions and pollicies" in virtually any cause, whether civil, criminal, capital, marine, or "other." His wife and children similarly possessed power to dispense their own justice in special seigniories that they would govern semi-autonomously. He and his heirs could grant land, dispense offices, and raise rents and revenues. They would receive a certain proportion of all gold, silver, pearl, and other precious stones found in the region. They would manage wars and oversee the planning and formation of towns, forts, common lands, and pastures. They would regulate the maintenance of the poor. In an era when the imperial monarch's own relationship to the church was a matter of continuing and intense debate, one wonders what the queen's lawyers must have thought as they wrote up the lengthy details establishing Gilbert's "Church" — of course meant to conform to the Church of England as it was "nowe professed" under a queen who was "ymediate soveraigne under God." A network of "Countrie parishe[s]," each three "Englishe myles square" and encompassing glebe lands, a centrally located church, and a vaguely identified "lorde of the parishe," would extend outward and upward to accommodate a phalanx of bishops, each allotted ten thousand acres of land, and even

---

46. "Grant of Authority by Sir Humphrey Gilbert, regarding His Rights in America, to Sir John Gilbert, Sir George Peckham, and William Aucher," July 8, 1582, in Quinn, ed., *Voyages and Colonising Enterprises of Sir Humphrey Gilbert*, II, 266, 270–272.

archbishops, who were to receive twenty thousand acres apiece. No wonder that, in describing this new polity, the natural inclination was to call it, as it appeared in one official document, "the common Wealth of the said Sir Humfry his heyres or Successors."[47]

The American territory that Gilbert discovered and ruled in the queen's name might rest under her impressive sovereign crown, but it would, to a very great extent, be his commonwealth. In much the same spirit, the private indenture that Ralegh entered into in 1587 with his appointed governor Captain John White and his twelve assistants incorporated them as "one Bodye pollitique and Corporate, by the name Tytle and Aucthoritye of The GOVERNOUR AND ASSISTANTS OF THE CITTIE OF RALEGH IN VIRGINEA WITH THE APPERTENANCES," a name that similarly conveyed the sense of Virginia as Ralegh's own personal dominion. The intriguing title that Ralegh gave to coats of arms he had prepared for the colony also suggested the colony's status as his own personal commonwealth: "Raleigh Civitas in Virginia."[48]

The sense, at once fearful and realistic, that Elizabeth's captains were forging American commonwealths under their own auspices, rather than directly under the will of their sovereign queen, surely helps to explain the political isolation of the "CITTIE OF RALEGH" that contributed to its miserable fate as the "Lost Colony." At this direst of low points in Ralegh's colonizing endeavor, the planters whom White left behind when he made his return to England for supplies in August 1587 probably moved into the North Carolina interior. They likely lived with the Tuscaroras and Chowanocs for nearly two decades before becoming caught up in the Powhatans' violent conquests in the region to obtain control over prestige goods like copper as well as European commodities. The circumstance could not have turned more fully on its head the colonizing captain's vaunted claim of vigorously bringing American peoples and territory under his own firm dominion; one

---

47. Ibid., 270, 277–278; "Additional Articles of Agreement between Sir Humphrey Gilbert and the Adventurers, with His Instructions for the Voyage," [Dec. 12, 1582], in Quinn, ed., *Voyages and Colonising Enterprises of Sir Humphrey Gilbert*, II, 328. See also "Agreement between Sir Humphrey Gilbert and Philip Sidney," July 7, 1582, ibid., 266.

48. "Grant of Arms for the City of Raleigh in Virginia, and for Its Governor and Assistants," [Jan. 7, 1587], in David Beers Quinn, ed., *The Roanoke Voyages, 1584–1590: Documents to Illustrate the English Voyages to North America under the Patent Granted to Walter Raleigh in 1584*, Works Issued by the Hakluyt Society, 2d Ser., no. 105 (London, 1955), II, 506n, 508–509.

chief Eyanoco reportedly "preserved" one group of seven former inhabitants of Ralegh's "CITTIE" to beat his copper.⁴⁹

But the colony's political isolation is most apparent in the remarkable legitimizing ceremony that the planter population enacted as Governor White prepared for his departure. White wrote a detailed narrative of the ceremony, undoubtedly regarding it not only as a valuable defense of his choice to return home while the planters themselves remained in America but also as manifest evidence that the bonds of commonwealth really were in existence on the other side of the ocean, marking out a firm English dominion in Virginia. According to his narrative, expanding circles of the "CITTIE OF RALEGH'S" members gave their consent to his departure: first, his assistants; then "the whole companie, both of the Assistants, and planters"; and, finally, "divers others, as well women, as men, beganne to renewe their requests to the Governour againe, to take uppon him to returne into England for the supplie, and dispatch of all other thinges, as there were to be done." The inclusion of the women suggested an especially plaintive moral petition to tend to the commonweal's most basic needs.⁵⁰

This remarkable collective appeal to the governor by the polity as a whole was followed up by the writing of a formal agreement. Evidently signed by the male "planters" only, "which bonde, with a testimonie under their handes, and seales, they foorthwith made, and delivered into his hands." The "bonde," which White recorded in his manuscript report verbatim, is worth quoting in full here as well to capture the pains taken to ground White's departure as a lawful act arising from an exquisite harmony of wills between the governor and the governed:

> May it please you, her Majesties Subjects of England, wee your friendes and Countrey men, the planters in Virginia, doe by these presents let you, and every of you to understande, that for the present and speedie supplie of certaine our knowen, and apparent lackes, and needes, most requisite and necessarie for the good and happie planting of us, or any

---

49. James Horn, *A Kingdom Strange: The Brief and Tragic History of the Lost Colony of Roanoke* (New York, 2010), 217, 224–232

50. "John White's Narrative of His Voyage," 1587, in Quinn, ed., *Roanoke Voyages*, II, 532–535. Quinn speculates the piece was compiled "before 25 March 1588, using his journal as a basis" (515n). It evidently remained in manuscript until Hakluyt printed it in Hakluyt, *Principall Navigations, Voiages, and Discoveries of the English Nation* ... (London, 1589).

other in this lande of Virginia, wee all of one minde, and consent, have most earnestly intreated, and uncessantly requested John White, Governour of the planters in Virginia, to passe into England, for the better and more assured helpe, and setting forward of the foresayde supplies: and knowing assuredly that he both can best, and will labour, and take paines in that behalfe for us all, and hee not once, but often refusing it, for our sakes, and for the honour, and maintenance of the action, hath at last, though much against his will, through our importunacie, yeelded to leave his government, and all his goods among us, and himselfe in all our behalfes to passe into Englande, of whose knowledge, and fidelitie in handling this matter, as all others, wee doe assure our selves by these presents, and will you to give all credite thereunto. the five and twentieth of August.

Reminiscent of the Privy Councillor Sir Thomas Smith's definition of commonwealth as "a society or common doing of a multitude of free men collected together and united by common accord and covenauntes among themselves for the conservation of themselves aswell in peace as in warre," this articulation of a unity of wills directed at the preservation of Virginia was a self-conscious expression of commonwealth.[51]

The Virginia planters' agreement mirrored a number of other such expressions of commonwealth in local English communities and in the realm at large in these decades, haunted as they often were by economic dislocation and religious conflict as well as the ever-present possibility of Elizabeth dying without an heir or with only an uncertain succession behind her. In 1596 the southern English manorial community of Swallowfield, facing a period of pronounced economic hardship, would adopt a set of articles for governing some of its own basic affairs on the grounds that "non of us is ruler of hym selfe, but the whole companye or the moste parte is ruler of us all." As a "companye" — or commonwealth of godly persons — Swallowfield was, like Ralegh's "CITTIE," concerned for its self-perpetuation and had taken appropriate measures to uphold the lawful order, by no means disregarding the queen's supremacy (which was held up repeatedly as placing extraordinary obligations on the community's residents) yet at the same time acknowledging the need to keep obedient wills trained on the locality's wellbeing in light

---

51. "John White's Narrative of His Voyage," 1587, in Quinn, ed., *Roanoke Voyages,* II, 534–535; Mary Dewar, ed., *De Republica Anglorum by Sir Thomas Smith* (Cambridge, 1982), 57.

of the world's ever-unpredictable variability. The Swallowfield articles' caveat that the "companye" was not entirely inclusive — for only "the moste parte" of its body was imagined as involved in its self-governing fellowship of "good love and Amyte" — might have reflected a determination to uphold its Protestant membership against either insufficiently zealous inhabitants or perhaps even committed Catholics. Certainly many of the articles concerned safeguarding the church and religious community, for instance by empowering church wardens against Sabbath breakers and tipplers as well as by seeing to the "edifycation" of all residents, including servants. The Bond of Association similarly forged its vision of "one fyrme and loyall societie" in very deliberate exclusion of those "myschevous persons" who were understood to be Catholics and hence to pose a risk to queen and commonwealth alike.[52]

Likewise, in his narrative of Virginia's own "companie" and "bonde," White also went out of his way to portray that body as poised against Catholic opposition. As he put it, he worried about returning home in person for fear that "some enemies to him, and the action," probably a reference to Ralegh's Catholic rivals at court, would "at his returne into England . . . not spare to slander falsely both him, and the action, by saying he went to Virginia, but politikely, and to no other ende, but to leade so many into a Countrey, in which he never meant to stay himselfe, and there to leave them behind him." White's allusion to the familiar Catholic charge, expressed for instance by Allen, that the Protestants proceeded only "politikely" evoked succinctly the wider casuistic context in which Ralegh's commonwealth sought to anchor itself. As a concatenation of wills joined consensually into one, the "CITTIE OF RALEGH" stood, like all of the commonwealths that bound themselves under God and queen in these years, as a body set force-

---

52. Steve Hindle, "Hierarchy and Community in the Elizabethan Parish: The Swallowfield Articles of 1596," *The Historical Journal*, XLII (1999), 848–849, 851 (Hindle's useful discussion of the context of economic dearth and expensive military campaigns in which the articles were written appears on 838–840); "Associations for Defence of the Queen," in J. Payne Collier, ed., *The Egerton Papers: A Collection of Public and Private Documents, Chiefly Illustrative of the Times of Elizabeth and James I . . .* (London, 1840), 109. The classic discussion of both the Swallowfield Articles and the Bond of Association in their relation to Elizabethan political culture is Patrick Collinson, "The Monarchical Republic of Queen Elizabeth I," *Bulletin of the John Rylands Library*, LXIX (1987), 394–424. For the Bond of Association, see also, David Cressy, "Binding the Nation: The Bonds of Association, 1584 and 1696," in DeLloyd J. Guth and John W. McKenna, eds., *Tudor Rule and Revolution: Essays for G. R. Elton from His American Friends* (Cambridge, 1982), 217–234.

fully against those erroneous voices that could be expected to question its legitimacy.[53]

There was nothing unusual then in self-proclaiming commonwealths that asserted their lawfulness but were in fact highly cognizant of their own vulnerability; in this regard, the "CITTIE OF RALEGH," with its elaborate expression of consensual wills set against the expected hostility of Catholic courtiers, was of a piece with other English communities that sought at this time to safeguard themselves in relation to the various vicissitudes of fortune. But Virginia's bond was arguably more fragile and isolated than most. As if acknowledging that the colony remained Ralegh's dominion while enjoying only nominal support from the queen, the planters addressed their show of fidelity, not to Elizabeth herself, but rather to "her Majesties Subjects of England." Identified as the planters' "friendes and Countrey men," these fellow subjects evidently seemed the proper addressees of a community that had not yet succeeded in transcending its status as a private undertaking. As the still-controversial project of a private man, Virginia had little choice but to seek aid from other private individuals rather than a queen whose own recognition of the colony's legitimacy was neither a sure thing nor likely to win out if other more-pressing obligations presented themselves. This highly ambivalent state of affairs was realized dramatically in the profoundly transformed atmosphere of the first half of 1588, when preparations for the anticipated attack of the Spanish Armada suddenly dominated all other royal priorities. In these months, when ships were officially restrained for the queen's military uses, Ralegh and White's highly improvisatory and repeatedly stymied efforts to secure vessels and supplies for the colony underscored pathetically—and, as it turned out, tragically—the dangers of colonization when it was envisioned as a merely private endeavor.[54]

In the scores of lives lost as the planters, women, and children of Ralegh's city vainly awaited relief from England, the allegation that such colonies were intended only "politikely" could acquire a sickening sense of realism. By the end of the century, Virginia colonization had become a convenient shorthand for selfish behavior that wickedly violated the commonwealth at the expense of its most vulnerable members. Thus, in "Sit paean merenti," one of the poetical "byting satyres" that Joseph Hall, later bishop of Exeter,

---

53. "John White's Narrative," 1587, in Quinn, ed., *Roanoke Voyages*, II, 533.

54. Ibid., 533–535. For a useful discussion and documents relating to the difficulties of mustering ships and supplies for the colony in the period of the Spanish Armada, see Quinn, ed., *Roanoke Voyages, 1584–1590*, II, 553–578. See also Horn, *Kingdom Strange*, 166–184.

published in 1598, the colonizer willing to dump subjects' bodies on Virginia's barbarous shores served as an apt analogy for the enclosing landlord. The landlord's greedy disregard for the welfare of his tenants made him tantamount to the colonizer who would cruelly "dislodge whole Collonyes of poore," giving their "bagge and baggage to his Citizens" and shipping them "to the new-nam'd *Virgin-land,* / Or wilder wales, where never wight yet wound."[55]

Pillorying Elizabeth's Feeble Captains

If the captain suffered in part under a reputation for misusing power usurped from a reluctant American empress, his greater problem lay in his basic ineffectuality against the wildness of the "*Virgin-land.*" Meant to exert an extraordinary vigor and resolution of will in the pursuit of a divinely ordained frontier-taming project that the queen was deemed incapable of pursuing herself, Elizabeth's captains instead came up disgracefully short. By the end of Elizabeth's reign, the sinful impotence of the captain, not his king-like virtues, most captured the contemporary imagination. In turn, the queen's own incapacities as a sovereign monarch seemed worryingly evident, rekindling desires for a more manly emperor. These interrelated views appear in two especially harsh censures of the colonizing endeavor, Hall's *Mundus alter et idem* and George Chapman, Ben Jonson, and John Marston's *Eastward Hoe*. Because few works more fully anatomized the Elizabethan captain's decline in relation to contemporary anxieties about sovereign kingship and commonwealth, they merit detailed examination here.

Hall published *Mundus alter et idem* (translated into English in 1609 as *A Discovery of a New World*) in 1605, a prudent two years after Elizabeth's death. As a committed Anglican and one of his era's great casuists, Hall's own desires for a male sovereign appear to have related especially to his eagerness to steer the church between the twin dangers of Catholic error and Protestant sectarianism. One consequence of the wavering will of a female sovereign was a similarly vacillating church. Although the Scottish king James VI's succession to the English throne was controversial on many grounds, Hall himself evidently welcomed his new monarch, almost wholly on the basis of his status as an adult male. In his poetic encomium to the newly ascended

55. [Joseph Hall], *Virgidemiarum; The Three Last Bookes; Of Byting Satyres* (London, 1598), V, 53, 59.

English sovereign, *The Kings Prophesie; or, Weeping Joy; Expressed in a Poeme, to the Honor of Englands Too Great Solemnities* (1603), Hall located James's legitimacy quite straightforwardly in his noble lion-like visage, an aspect of his masculinity that Hall suggested was evidence of the presence in him of God's own sovereign grace:

> His lively Image, in whose awfull face
> Appeare deepe stamps of dreadfull majestie,
> Whose glorious beames from his diviner grace
> Dazle the weake, and dim the bolder eye.
> Mercie sits on his brow; and in his brest
> Under his Lions paw, doth courage rest.

Bravery and mercifulness, awe and glory, dreadfulness and grace: James combined within his very body, a reassuringly male one, the attributes that made his own sovereignty a credible extension of God's.[56]

Hall injected these same assumptions about female incapacity and the need for a more vigorous, world-ordering sovereignty into *Mundus alter et idem*. Like More's *Utopia*, Hall's deeply moralistic work used America as a starting point for offering a more general criticism of Christendom's vices, though Hall's topsy-turvy New World was the very inversion of More's utopian one. Rather than a region brought effectively to order and virtue through Christian sovereign rule, the America that Hall depicted was a scene of deplorable licentiousness, an immorality exacerbated, not bridled, by European colonizers. Vice-filled locales shamelessly announced their sins in their names: Eat-allia, Drink-allia, Idle-bergh, Fooliana, and Robbers-waldt. Other places trumpeted the confusions introduced there by their Catholic and separatist Protestant inhabitants: Leger-dumayne was where Spanish Jesuits had taken up residence ever since "*Spaine* got the conquest of those *Indies*"; Trust-fablia was another Catholic home; Sectariona was the confusing and much-divided colony of Protestant Dissenters.[57]

But the single greatest focus of Hall's mockery, serving at once as the key emblem of, and chief explanation for, his New World's persistent dis-

---

56. Jos[eph] Hall, *The Kings Prophecie; or, Weeping Joy; Expressed in a Poeme, to the Honor of Englands Too Great Solemnities* (London, 1603), B[1]r. On Hall as a casuist, see Meg Lota Brown, *Donne and the Politics of Conscience in Early Modern England* (Leiden, The Netherlands, 1995), 10, 26–34.

57. Joseph Hall, *The Discovery of a New World . . .* ([London, 1609]) (New York, 1969), 234.

order was female rule. The region was governed by women. They lived in Gossipingoa, a city in Shee-landt, also called Womandeçoia. And the men who served them were strangely neutered by their queenly superiors. As the women rulers themselves shouldered the burden of taming their surrounding frontiers, their male "captaines" became little more than feminized domestics. Strapping on swords and bucklers, Gossipingoa's women rushed out, as "cruell conqueresses," to subdue rebellious borders, while their male counterparts busied themselves with knitting needles and spinning wheels. Stupefied, Hall's narrator laments, "O how many noble captaines did I see here wearing out their lives in spinning, carding woll and knitting?" If anyone missed that these emasculated captains were to be associated directly with Elizabethan colonization, Hall made the connection explicit. He remarked that Womandeçoia was sometimes mistakenly called Wingandecoia, the name Ralegh had promoted as the original native American designation for the region he hoped to plant, and therefore should be regarded as "a part of Virginia." In short, Elizabeth's colonizing efforts, the frontier-taming endeavors of her godly captains, had become the very symbol of the inefficacy of her rule. Sin and disorder were all that were left in the wake of her godless governance, and bobbing shamefully in the surf were her listless captains, impotent lumps in an Atlantic still teeming in vice.[58]

Eastward Hoe, which appeared in print in 1605 and was performed by the Children of the Queen's Revels that year and by other companies shortly thereafter, including at James's court, similarly took aim at the persona of the Elizabethan colonizing captain. Although the play also functioned as a Jacobean city comedy, satirizing various perceived vices in contemporary London society and for a brief time landing Jonson and Chapman in prison for a subtle jab at the king's Scottish favorites, a reference to Sir Francis Drake at one point in the play makes clear that its satirical punches were also directed at the previous reign. Perhaps because signs had begun to appear suggesting a renewed interest in the American colonizing endeavor, including a canoe demonstration on the Thames in 1603 by a small group of native

---

58. Ibid., 96, 98, 101. The bill to confirm Ralegh's patent, passed by the House of Commons in December 1584, called the region Ralegh was to plant "A Land called Wyngandacoia." See "Bill to Confirm Raleigh's Patent," December 1584, in Quinn, ed., *Roanoke Voyages,* I, 127. Likewise, the armigerial documents by which arms were granted to the "CITTIE OF RALEGH" and to John White identified Virginia as a "barbarous and heathen Land or Contry fownde owt and discovered, called or now termed OSSOMOCOMUCK al*ias* WYNGANDACOIA al*ias* VIRGINEA"; see "Grant of Arms for the City of Ralegh," [Jan. 7, 1587], in Quinn, ed., *Roanoke Voyages,* II, 508.

Virginians residing at the home of Burghley's son Sir Robert Cecil, the subject felt timely and relevant. Probably, too, Ralegh's imprisonment that year under murky charges of involvement in a planned Spanish invasion left such onetime-heralded captains open for criticism. Likewise, Elizabethan colonization might have seemed like too rich a cautionary tale about unrighteous sovereignty to let pass when a new king sat on the throne, similarly requiring counsel in how to exercise his awesome imperial power.[59]

The playwrights were not critics either of sovereign kingship itself or of colonization. Like Hall, their sympathies lay with a well-grounded English commonwealth and Anglican Church. Puritan Dissenters repeatedly appear in their works as fantastical idealists and as disturbers of kingdoms. Both the commonwealth and the church were to be brought to order under a genuine sovereign monarch whose reforming efforts ought to be devoted also to rooting out sinfulness in the broader world. Thus, Jonson wrote a panegyric in honor of James's first session of Parliament on March 19, 1604, that treated his sovereignty as a God-given edifying force that not only purged sin but also safeguarded the imperial crown itself from the evil forces that threatened it and that therefore "offend all good mens Eies." The passage is far closer to Hall's treatment of James as a lion-like embodiment of God's own virtues than the ambivalence that surrounded Elizabeth's persona as an imperial queen:

From his Eies are hoorl'd,
(To day) a thousand radiant lights, that streame
To every nooke, and angle of his realme.
His former raies, did only cleare the skie;
But these his searching beames are cast, to prie
Into those darke, and deepe concealed vaults,
Where men commit black incest with their faults;
And snore supinely in the stall of Sinne:
Where *Murder, Rapine, Lust,* do sit within

---

59. On the "Virginians," who could have originated almost anywhere on North America's east coast at a time when Virginia referred to most of that region, see Quinn, *England and the Discovery of America*, 419–431; Alden T. Vaughan, *Transatlantic Encounters: American Indians in Britain, 1500–1776* (Cambridge, 2006), 42–44. On the ambiguous circumstances behind Ralegh's imprisonment, see *Oxford Dictionary of National Biography*, online ed., s.v. "Ralegh, Sir Walter (1554–1618)," by Mark Nicholls and Penry Williams, accessed Aug. 17, 2014, http://www.oxforddnb.com/view/article/23039.

Carowsing humane blood, in iron bowles,
And make their Den the slaughter house of soules:
From whose foule reeking cavernes first arise
Those dampes, that so offend all good mens eies;
And would (if not dispers'd) infect the Crowne,
And in their vapor her bright Mettall drowne.

James's imperium penetrated even the darkest of immoral lairs and thereby preserved his diadem against Earth's corruptions.[60]

A masque that Chapman wrote for Princess Elizabeth's marriage to Frederick V, count Palatine of the Rhine, which was performed at Whitehall on February 14, 1614, similarly treated the king's sovereignty as bringing order to a fallen world, in this case with explicit reference to Virginia. American barbarism and heathenism were alluded to right away in the form of a "mock-Masque," or inversion of true nobility, featuring a procession of figures intended to simultaneously entertain and repulse: baboons bedecked in Italian fashion and mounted on donkeys, English musicians dressed as "Virginean Priests" with turbans and feathers, "Virginian Princes" with feathers, gold, and silver, and "Moores, attir'd like *Indian* slaves." The whole scene drew on a logic not unlike the keeping of dwarves and other oddities of nature at this time at the Habsburg and Spanish courts. Such monstrosities were a fit emblem of the need for sovereignty, showcasing the emperor's rightful dominion over a still-sinful world.[61]

Various other references made clear that James was to be seen as one of God's instruments for bringing such worldly disorder to heel. For instance, one allegorized figure, the aptly named Capriccio, alleges Britain to be one of the few places in the world anchored to the circular and steady heavens rather than cast adrift on the ever-moving Earth, and he ties this providential boon to James's related miraculous discovery of American wealth. As Capriccio puts it, "This Ile stands fixt on her owne feete, and defies the Worlds mutability, which this rare accident of the arrival of Riches, in one of his

---

60. Ben Jonson, *B. Jon: His Part of King James His Royall and Magnificent Entertainement through His Honorable Cittie of London Thurseday the 15. of March 1603* . . . (London, 1604), E3r.

61. Geo[rge] Chapman, *The Memorable Masque of the Two Honourable Houses or Innes of Court* . . . (London, [1614?]), [A4]r–B[1]v; Janet Ravenscroft, "Invisible Friends: Questioning the Representation of the Court Dwarf in Habsburg Spain," in Waltraud Ernst, ed., *Histories of the Normal and the Abnormal: Social and Cultural Histories of Norms and Normativity* (London, 2006), 26–52.

furthest-off-scituate dominions, most demonstratively proves." Meanwhile, another allegorized figure, Eunomia, represents the "sacred power of Lawe," that is, God's laws. Evoking James's sovereign role as Phoebus, the British sovereign "Sun," an image also evident in Jonson's depiction of James's light-streaming eyes, Eunomia calls the Virginians to their true master, understood to be simultaneously God and James:

> Virginian Princes, ye must now renounce
> Your superstitious worship of these Sunnes
> Subject to cloudy darknings and descents,
> And of your sweet devotions, turne the events
> To this our Britan *Phoebus,* whose bright skie
> (Enlightned with a Christian Piety)
> Is never subject to black Errors night,
> And hath already offer'd heavens true light,
> To your dark Region, which acknowledge now;
> Descend, and to him all your homage vow.

Here, the dominion of a true sovereign king is a force of almost unparalleled virtue, and notably Chapman felt no need to identify James's sovereignty in Virginia as mediated by male captains. Whatever oceangoing captains might actually be required to turn Virginia's sun-worshipping princes toward their true sovereign and God are quietly hidden from view. He identifies James's "bright skie" as enough to scatter America's "darknings" on its own.[62]

Indeed, in *Eastward Hoe,* colonizing captains appear as the very opposite of kingly virtue. Thrusting mercilessly at the "brave Captaines" who were "bound for Virginia," the play brought to the relatively mixed audience of the Blackfriars, as well as whatever readers might have encountered the play in print, a sidesplitting view of America-bound captains, not as virtuous gentlemen or as stalwart Britons, but as louche braggadocios, unworthy titleholders who boasted of their overseas conquests yet who longed mainly to be free of the civilizing restraints of the commonwealth in order to indulge their base appetites. The two recognizable colonizers in *Eastward Hoe,* Francis Quick-Silver and Sir Petronell Flash, both of whom sign on for an ill-fated voyage to Virginia, are effectively the mirror opposite of the moral character that had been devised for the Elizabethan captain. Rather than noble and prophetical, they are the epitome of sinful ambition and pride-

---

62. Chapman, *Memorable Masque,* D2r, [E4]v, F2v, F3v.

ful self-love. Quick-Silver is Master Touchstone the goldsmith's disappointing apprentice, a "prodigall coxcombe" who, in an empty show of gallantry, parades around town in hat, pumps, short sword, and dagger and throws borrowed money at meat, drink, and women. The foil to the "drunke whore-hunting rake-hell" Quick-Silver is temperate and hardworking Goulding, his fellow apprentice at Touchstone's shop, who is also, tellingly, more manly than Quick-Silver. Despite the latter's knightly blustering, Goulding easily bests him in an impromptu scuffle. Sir Petronell Flash is just as insubstantial and predatory as Quick-Silver. A suitor to Touchstone's impulsive and socially ambitious daughter Gertrude whose inheritance he seeks, Flash seduces her with both his knightly title, which is eventually revealed to have been bought rather than earned, as well as promise of life in a castle, which similarly turns out to be nothing but air. Again the antithesis to such insubstantiality is the responsible Goulding, who marries Touchstone's far more respectable daughter, the modest and dutiful Mildred. For his hard work and honesty, as opposed to the illicit social climbing of so many of the play's other characters, Goulding earns his freedom, secures a modest income, and attracts the favorable attention of London civic leaders. In an act of patronage that the play clearly seeks to identify as the one true way in which virtue rises up in the polity, these men, in turn, appoint him deputy alderman. Like Quick-Silver, Flash does not enjoy any such respectable office but rather inevitably falls into a galling dependence by having to rely on rogues for his livelihood, especially the archfiend of the play, Security the usurer. Of course, even Goulding does not emerge from the play wholly unscathed but in a final send-up is teased for being altogether too good, probably a gibe at Puritan perfectionism.[63]

A central theme of the play was the conventional Christian humanist notion that the commonwealth is composed of bonds, whether good or ill, that people enter into with one another. A matrix of reciprocal ties makes Flash's and Quick-Silver's trust in the usurer a stand-in for the entire mishmash of misbegotten civil attachments that such would-be colonizers were likely to forge on the other side of the ocean. It was here where the play thrust most uncompromisingly at the Virginia venture. The colonizing cap-

---

63. Geo[rge] Chapman, Ben Jonson, and Joh[n] Marston, *Eastward Hoe* . . . (London, 1605), [A3]v, B3r, C2v, C3r, F[1]v. I owe this latter observation of the subtle anti-Puritan jab at Goulding to the analysis of the play offered in Peter Lake with Michael Questier, *The Antichrist's Lewd Hat: Protestants, Papists, and Players in Post-Reformation England* (New Haven, Conn., 2002), 394–407.

tain was meant to be, more than anything else, a forger of civil bonds. He was the agent who was both unusually willing and unusually able to withstand the barbarism of a distant frontier, to eschew the comforts of court life for the frontier's own sinful outer reaches, in order to bring about the conditions of commonwealth. But it was precisely this core element of the adventuring captain's persona that the play singled out for scorn. A quarter century of failed colonizing efforts—the continuing Irish reconquest and efforts at internal colonization along the English-Scottish border perhaps figuring quietly in the scorn alongside Virginia—had left the entire enterprise open for disdain.

The delight with which the playwrights skewered the pretensions of the colonizer as the essential forger of commonwealth ties indicates the significance of this dimension of his persona. Both Quick-Silver and Flash are appalling judges of the social and moral relationships of civil life. Quick-Silver welcomes Security as a friend just after spurning the one true, mutually beneficial bond in which he was engaged. Burning the sheepskin vellum on which his indenture to the good master Touchstone was printed, he declares: "Come old *Securitie,* thou father of destruction: th'indented Sheepe-skinne is burn'd wherein I was wrapt, and I am now loose, to get more children of perdition into thy usurous Bonds. Thou feed'st my Lecherie, and I thy Covetousnes." His freedom from an indentured apprenticeship is not beneficially liberating, but destructively so. Loosed from his covenant with the good Touchstone, Quick-Silver falls instead into the "usurous Bonds" of the greedy moneylender Security. This vicious trap of a relationship scarcely speaks favorably to the good service that, as a knight, Quick-Silver is meant to perform, let alone the sanctified commonwealth that he is supposed to forge across the ocean. In a similarly wayward fashion, Flash, who appeals to Security to ensnare for him the wife of a lawyer to take as his lover, agrees to become the godfather of the usurer's first child, normally a bond of the most sacred variety. Indeed, from the point at which they enter into this cherished, trusting relationship, the two men, sealing their bond with a kiss, henceforth call one another "Gossip," connoting the spiritual tie that now binds them. Yet, the perversity of such an arrangement is so twisted as to nauseate. Neither the usurer nor the shifty knight enters into the pact save for a crude calculation of self-interest.[64]

But what of the captain's much-vaunted nobility? In *Eastward Hoe*'s irreverent treatment, such nobility is at best an archaism and at worst the stuff

---

64. Chapman, Jonson, and Marston, *Eastward Hoe*, [B4]v, D2r.

of fiction. After Flash's promises to Gertrude are revealed to be nothing but empty lies, she complains to the aptly named Syndefy (Syn for short), the usurer's wife, who herself has had an affair with the lustful Quick-Silver, that their knightly lovers have ill-used them. "Would the Knight o' the *Sunne*, or *Palmerin* of England, have usd their Ladies so, *Syn.*? or sir *Lancelot?* or sir *Tristram?*" The joke here was in part that these were the figures in popular chivalrous tales, like Diego Ortúñez de Calahorra's *Mirrour of Princely Deedes and Knighthood* and *Palmerin of England*, often attributed to the Portuguese writer Francisco de Morais, that increasingly attracted ridicule in London theater circles as fantastical stories aimed at the vulgar. But Gertrude goes on, suggesting even more fully that the persona of the knight had fallen from grace, no longer living up to his once-noble reputation:

> The Knighthood now a daies, are nothing like the Knighthood of old time. They rid a horseback Ours goe afoote. They were attended by their Squires, Ours by their Lacquaies. They went buckled in their Armor, Ours muffled in their Cloaks. They travaild wildernesses, and desarts, Ours dare scarce walke the streets. They were stil prest to engage their Honour, Ours stil ready to paune their cloaths. They would gallop on at sight of a Monster, Ours run away at sight of a Serjeant. They would helpe poore Ladies, Ours make poore Ladies.

In Gertrude's cynical cataloging of all the ways the knight has become the very opposite of the noble knight of yore — fearing the law rather than chasing down evil, preying on women rather than saving them from danger, and cringing fearfully on the way to the pawnshop rather than boldly seeking adventure — whatever moral authority had once clothed the colonizing captain by the very essence of his knightly persona now stood on distinctly shaky grounds. Indeed, the persona itself threatened to become a liability, a source of suspicion and contempt rather than automatic legitimacy.[65]

65. Ibid., H2r; [Diego Ortúñez de Calahorra], *The Mirrour of Princely Deedes and Knighthood... Now Newly Translated Out of Spanish into Our Vulgar English Tongue*, by M. T. (London, [1578]); [Francisco de Morais], *[The (First) Seconde Part, of the No Lesse Rare, Historie of Palmerin of England.]*, trans. Anthony Munday [London, 1596]. In addition to *Eastward Hoe*, another Jacobean play that ridiculed such Elizabethan chivalries was Francis Beaumont's *The Knight of the Burning Pestle* (performed in 1607–1608 and published in 1613). See *The Oxford Companion to English Literature*, online ed., s.v. "The Knight of the Burning Pestle," by Dinah Birch, accessed Nov. 19, 2013, http://oxfordreference.com/view/10.1093/acref/9780192806871.001.0001/acref

Eastward Hoe built its critique so gleefully on the familiar tropes of the casuistry of colonization that its associations with that enterprise are largely unmistakable. Take the drunken acclamations of Virginia's virtues by Quick-Silver and Flash's disreputable crew, Captain Seagull and his shady associates Scapethrift and Spendall. "Come boyes," the leering Seagull says, "*Virginia* longs till we share the rest of her Maiden-head." If this remark harked back lasciviously to the conceit of Virginia as a virgin wife in need of subduing—perhaps even drawing directly, if crudely, on Hakluyt's far more modest rendering of the region as a gift from the queen that Ralegh was to treat with the respect due to one of her ladies-in-waiting—other comments by the sailors dug even more ferociously into memories of the botched Gilbert and Ralegh enterprises. To Seagull's titillating remark about Virginia's awaiting her next conqueror, Spendthrift replies, "Why is she inhabited alreadie with any *English?*" That question spoke more than any other to the failure of England's knights to establish the dominion that they were meant to forge in America. It prompts Seagull to wax enthusiastically about the likely result of Ralegh's famous "lost" colony, its male inhabitants necessarily dispersed not only into the villages of local Indians but also into their beds. "A whole Country of English is there man, bred of those that were left there in 79. They have married with the Indians, and make 'hem bring forth as beautifull faces as any we have in England: and therefore the Indians are so in love with 'hem, that all the treasure they have, they lay at their feete." Predictably, talk of treasure arouses as much excitement as does talk of sex in the dissolute sailors. They fantasize about the gold that must line every Indian tool and creature comfort, from their "dripping Pans" to "their Chamber pottes." Finally, they gush about the prospect of lax laws and easy social advancement.

> You shall live freely there, without Sargeants, or Courtiers, or Lawyers, or Intelligencers [informants]. Then for your meanes to advancement, there, it is simple, and not preposterously mixt: You may be an Alderman there, and never be Scavinger, you may be any other officer, and never be a Slave. You may come to preferment enough, and never be a *Pandar* [procurer of women for illicit affairs]. To Riches and Fortune inough and have never the more Villany, nor the lesse witte. Besides, there we shall have no more Law then Conscience, and not too much

---

-9780192806871-e-4228, s.v. "Palmerin of England (Palmeirim de Inglaterra)," by Birch, accessed Nov. 19, 2013, http://www.oxfordreference.com/view/10.1093/acref/9780192806871.001.0001/acref-9780192806871-e-5710.

of either; serve God inough, eate and drinke inough, and *inough is as good as a Feast.*

That latter quip, the idea that America was a space in which the Englishman could expect to find "no more Law then Conscience, and not too much of either," was perhaps the play's most damning thrust of all. It evoked the casuistry of colonization in the very act of sending it up.[66]

Conscience was indeed meant to be the anchor that grounded the lawfulness of the Virginia enterprise. But neither law nor conscience had much bearing on the American frontier that *Eastward Hoe* depicts. Rather than a frontier brought to order, Virginia has been made even more licentious by its would-be conquerors. The joke receives extended treatment in a scene that revolves around a tempest, the providential culture of the era remaining the key backdrop against which the play's events were imagined. The storm has swept up the Thames, scuttling Flash's idle fantasy that he and Quick-Silver will soon dine aboard none other than "Sir *Frances Drakes* Ship" and throwing the men helter-skelter, marooning them, not on a desert island, but in one of London's most notorious dens of vice, Cuckhold's Haven. Quick-Silver, fetched up on the notorious gallows at Wapping, offers a lament that could serve as a summation of the play's overall assessment of the adventuring captain in his relation to the moral order:

> How fatall is my sad arivall here?
> As if the *Starres,* and *Providence* spake to mee,
> And sayd, the drift of all unlawful courses.
> (What ever ende they dare propose themselves,
> In frame of their licentious policyes.)
> In the firme order of just *Destinie,*
> They are the ready high wayes to our Ruines.

Rather than a prophet confidently discerning the rightful path in a world of sin and error, Quick-Silver could scarcely fathom what "unlawful courses" had brought him to his current state of infamy. It was not a reassuring condition for the sovereign's noble captains, and it suggested that a very different persona would be needed to legitimize American colonization in the future.[67]

66. Chapman, Jonson, and Marston, *Eastward Hoe,* E3v-[E4]v.
67. Ibid., [E4]r, F[1]r, F3v.

The end of Elizabeth's reign did not, however, dramatically transform the context in which that legitimizing process would take place. As much as figures like Hall, Jonson, and Chapman—or, for that matter, Ralegh and Hakluyt—longed for a resolute masculine king to leave Elizabeth's feminine inconstancy in the past, in fact the circumstances that had produced her hesitancy were not settled by the Stuart succession. Instead, the considerable uncertainties that bedeviled James's ascension, the realm's continuing confessional divisions, and the king's own determination to uphold his prerogative with as much fervor as Elizabeth clung to hers virtually guaranteed that the colonizers would need to rely on legitimizing strategies not altogether different from those utilized in the previous reign. While certainly a self-conscious departure from the Elizabethan private man, the Virginia Company harked back to several decades of experimentation with how to keep a lawful action on course when the sovereign ostensibly piloting it veered unpredictably in stormy weather.

[3]
THE PROVIDENTIAL STATE AND THE LEGITIMIZING FELLOWSHIP OF "COMPANY"

On February 23, 1609, Don Pedro de Zúñiga, Philip III's special ambassador to England, enclosed a pamphlet from Samuel Meacham's bookshop in a carefully encrypted letter to Spain. The Spanish king had sent Zúñiga, his chief huntsman and the son of a former ambassador to France, to England in 1605 for the delicate task of pursuing a dynastic union of the Spanish and English crowns through the marriage of Princess Anne and Prince Henry. Expected to win over James I in part by playing to his and Philip's shared love of the hunt, Zúñiga was also an astute observer of the intricate politics surrounding sovereign kingship and Europe's confessional divisions. His instructions directed him to pay particular attention to the continuing issue of the Low Countries, taking special pains to ward off English Protestant efforts to lure James into supporting the Dutch rebels against Philip's sovereign claims there. The pamphlet, however, spoke to another intensifying front in the contest over imperium: Virginia, an area that Zúñiga considered indisputably a part of the Indies and thus Philip's lawful dominion as established by Pope Alexander's Bulls of Donation. Commissioned by the soon-to-be incorporated London Company of Virginia (also known as the Virginia Company), the publication, entitled *Nova Britannia: Offering Most Excellent Fruites by Planting in Virginia,* had been registered at Stationers' Hall a mere five days earlier. Bundling the book with a *"placarte,"* probably a handbill, that by Zúñiga's account was "issued to all [Virginia-bound] officials" indicating "what they are given to go," he sent the texts to Philip and his council. Joseph Creswell, the onetime Jesuit rector of the English College at Rome who, a quarter of a century earlier, had assisted Edmund Campion and Robert Persons on their ill-fated English tour, translated large sections of the works into Spanish — a small token of the continuing collusion between English Catholic exiles and Spanish royal officials in these years when a new monarch sat on the English throne.[1]

Zúñiga had good reason to take *Nova Britannia* seriously. The pamphlet effectively announced the colonizer's adoption of a bold new legitimating strategy—an assertion of the state, embodied by the collective wills of individuals, as the agent active in colonization. This shift toward state-directed colonization efforts, rather than those advanced by individual captains, held considerable implications for the broader politics over sovereignty and Christian truth in which Zúñiga saw himself engaged. Virginia Company officials had acknowledged this movement toward state-driven exploration and settlement in private when they first debated whether publishing such a justificatory booklet was prudent. The argument for issuing it rested on two casuistic considerations. First, such a pamphlet, it was hoped, would spur what amounted to a contagion of assurance. By giving adventurers in the enterprise "a clearnes and satisfaction, for the Justice of the action," it would "encourage, them and draw on others." Second, a statement of the colonizers' lawful conduct would also serve as a rebuke to challengers. In particular, "the Spaniard might out of this intimation reasonably collect, that wee understood our owne case to be such, that the state would neyther feare, nor be ashamed to proceed in that persecution ther of, if any Course should be held agaynst it." The two rationales were in fact intertwined. An ever-growing body of participants, all of them stirred by the argument that their involvement in the colonizing endeavor was conscionable, would forge in their very collectivity of wills the state, now deemed the colonizing agent enabling them to proceed without fear or shame. *Nova Britannia*'s author

---

1. Don Pedro de Zúñiga to Philip III, [Feb. 23/] Mar. 15, 1609, in Philip L. Barbour, ed., *The Jamestown Voyages under the First Charter, 1606–1609*, 2 vols. (Cambridge, 1969), II, 256; R[obert] J[ohnson], *Nova Britannia: Offering Most Excellent Fruites by Planting in Virginia . . .* (London, 1609). On Zúñiga and his secret instructions regarding the Low Countries, see Paul C. Allen, *Philip III and the Pax Hispanica, 1598–1621: The Failure of Grand Strategy* (New Haven, Conn., 2000), 149; see also, Charles Carter, *The Western European Powers, 1500–1700* (Ithaca, N.Y., 1971), 48–63. Philip III reported seeing Creswell's translation, endorsed *La poblacion de la Virginia*, on April 10 (Barbour, ed., *Jamestown Voyages*, II, 256–257n). Zúñiga's letters concerning Virginia also appear, with slightly different translations, in Alexander Brown, ed., *The Genesis of the United States: A Narrative of the Movement in England, 1605–1616 . . .* , 2 vols. (Boston, 1890). On the timing of *Nova Britannia*'s publication and Zúñiga's speed in obtaining it, see ibid., I, 242. On Creswell, see Barbour, ed., *Jamestown Voyages*, II, 256–257; *Oxford Dictionary of National Biography*, online ed., s.v. "Creswell, Joseph (1556–1623)," by A. J. Loomie, accessed Aug. 22, 2014, http://www.oxforddnb.com/view/article/6675.

"R. J.," who was probably the London alderman and merchant Robert Johnson, asserted this logic succinctly and with explicit reference to the ignominious reputation of Elizabethan colonizers that had propelled this newfound emphasis on state-led colonization in the first place. "I conceive with joy," he wrote, "that howsoever the businesse of this plantation hath beene formerly miscaried, yet it is now going on in better way, not enterprised by one or two private subjects, who in their greatnesse of minde, sought to compasse that, which rather beseemed a mighty Prince, (such as ours) or the whole State to take in hand." The remark summed up the thinking behind the revitalized colonizing endeavor under James perfectly, while also quietly introducing the Virginia Company's own adopted persona as the state in microcosm.²

Behind the new state-led colonizing endeavor were the busy exertions of Robert Cecil, earl of Salisbury. Secretary of state since the last years of Elizabeth I's reign, Salisbury had also played a vital behind-the-scenes role in bringing about James's accession and quickly made himself so indispensable that the king relied on him in multiple arenas. Like his father, William Cecil, Lord Burghley, Salisbury regarded American colonization as vital to giving the imperial crown the strength it needed to pin down lawfulness in a world filled with sin and error. He played a quiet role as the Virginia Company's most active leader, a part that involved especially putting his large network of clients to work in realizing the newly revitalized Virginia venture.

2. "A Justification for Planting Virginia," before 1609, in Susan Myra Kingsbury, ed., *The Records of the Virginia Company of London*, 4 vols. (Washington, D.C., 1906–1935), III, 1; J[ohnson], *Nova Britannia*, B3v. Historians have long identified Alderman Johnson as the "R. J." who authored *Nova Britannia*, no doubt because Johnson was close to Sir Thomas Smythe, eventually becoming his son-in-law, and defended his treasurership in the company's factional battles of the early 1620s. Yet, the attribution is not altogether certain. Other persons who might plausibly have authored the work include Sir Robert Johnson, a parliamentarian who was also a Virginia Company member; Robert Johnson, the archdeacon of Leicester; and Richard Johnson, the prolific writer and author of the popular romance *The Most Famous History of the Seaven Champions of Christendome* (published in two parts in 1596 and 1597). At the death of Secretary of State Robert Cecil, the earl of Salisbury, Richard Johnson was one of the few persons to come out in print defending the secretary from his libelers. In this chapter, I cautiously follow the usual attribution of *Nova Britannia* to the alderman Robert Johnson. I do so because several other works in which the author signed his name "R. J." or alternatively "Rob. Johnson, Gent." have strong thematic links with *Nova Britannia*. These works, which promoted a distinctively statist philosophy, are discussed in this chapter. Likewise, Robert Johnson's involvement in projects, like the East India Company, that attracted Cecil's attention fits chronologically the publication history of these other writings and suggests an ongoing patron-client relationship between the two men.

It was Salisbury's man, the bishop of London Thomas Ravis, who submitted *Nova Britannia* to Stationer's Hall, and Johnson also looked to Salisbury as a patron. Richard Hakluyt, the clergyman, who once served as a client to Burghley, now acted on behalf of Burghley's son, and the Reverend William Crashawe, another of the Virginia Company's strenuous defenders, was similarly in Salisbury's clientele. An especially dedicated aid was Sir Walter Cope. He wrote to the secretary sometime in 1605 or early 1606 with news that Lord Chief Justice Sir John Popham was similarly "bent to the plantation of Virginia," a communication that probably accounts for the Salisbury-Popham connection that so greatly characterized the early Jacobean colonizing effort. Salisbury's interests centered on the "first" colony at Jamestown and Popham's on the "second" colony in present-day Maine. In addition to his clients, Salisbury was also joined in the Virginia enterprise by a number of higher-ranking friends and allies, including men like Solicitor-General John Doddridge, Henry Wriothesley, earl of Southampton, William Herbert, third earl of Pembroke, Sir Edwin Sandys, and Lord Chamberlain Thomas Howard, earl of Suffolk. Until his death in 1612, Salisbury's mark on the revitalized Virginia project was profound, and the changes he wrought had a lasting impact on the English colonizing experience in America generally.[3]

Of particular importance to the transition Salisbury was so instrumental in bringing about was his determination to wrench the colonizing endeavor out of its ignoble condition as a private enterprise that enjoyed only the ambivalent support of the queen, grounding it instead in what he championed

---

3. Sir Walter Cope to the earl of Salisbury, 1605 [or circa January 1606], in David B. Quinn, ed., *New American World: A Documentary History of North America to 1612*, V, *The Extension of Settlement in Florida, Virginia, and the Spanish Southwest* (New York, 1979), 166; The First Charter of Virginia, Apr. 10, 1606, The Avalon Project, Yale Law School, Lillian Goldman Law Library, http://avalon.law.yale.edu/17th_century/va01.asp. On Ravis's submission of *Nova Britannia* to Stationers' Hall, see Brown, *Genesis of the United States*, I, 242. Cecil's patronage or friendship is a common feature in many biographies of Virginia Company members or persons otherwise affiliated with the company. See, for instance, *Oxford Dictionary of National Biography*, online ed., s.v. "Ravis, Thomas (b. in or before 1560, d. 1609)," by C. S. Knighton, accessed Oct. 5, 2014, http://www.oxforddnb.com/view/article/23175, s.v. "Cope, Sir Walter (1553?–1614)," by Elizabeth Allen, accessed Oct. 5, 2014, http://www.oxforddnb.com/view/article/6257, s.v. "Crashawe [Crashaw], William (bap. 1572, d. 1625/6)," by W. H. Kelliher, accessed Oct. 5, 2014, http://www.oxforddnb.com/view/article/6623, s.v. "Hakluyt, Richard (1552?–1616)," by Anthony Payne, accessed Oct. 5, 2014, http://www.oxforddnb.com/view/article/11892?docPos=1, s.v. "Sandys, Sir Edwin (1561–1629)," by Theodore K. Rabb, accessed Oct. 5, 2014, http://www.oxforddnb.com/view/article/24650?docPos=3.

as the more solid basis of the state. Undoubtedly, lessons learned during his father Burghley's involvement in the colonizing endeavor helped propel the younger Cecil toward such a deliberate turn from the valorous exertions of the captain, surely in part because these ventures had so often resulted in disappointments that suggested God's disfavor. Probably, too, the arrival of an adult male king to the throne heightened expectations of kingly resolution, a hopefulness suggested by the Virginia Company's frequent reference to Virginia as a new Britain, alluding to James's desire to unite England and his native Scotland into a single, powerful kingdom. Salisbury was clearly also motivated by a new literature on statecraft that was just beginning to gain currency in England in the last decades of Elizabeth's reign and the first years of James's. Imparting a body of knowledge that Salisbury's client Edward Forset called "politicall science," in optimism that the polity could be approached with the same moral seriousness and intellectual rigor as other sciences like natural philosophy, this literature promised innovative solutions to some of the concerns about American colonization, subtly altering the very categories by which that endeavor was imagined and defended.[4]

In turning to the new scholarship on state politics, the Salisbury circle no doubt thought of itself as relying on the most solid knowledge then available for navigating a still-fallen world. Written by late-sixteenth-century continental authors like Justus Lipsius, Louis LeRoy, Jean Bodin, and Giovanni Botero, this work on "Civil pollicie," as it was also called, was no secularizing departure from earlier worries about aligning human action and God's will. On the contrary, it was a direct outgrowth of Renaissance providential thought, a matter of identifying the state as an indispensable instrument in its own right in grounding ever-inconstant human affairs in accordance with divine judgment. Based on an eclectic mix of scholarship in ancient texts, studies of history, and experiences gained from service to European rulers, the new books on statecraft approached the state much in the same way as Sir Walter Ralegh would do in his *History of the World* (1614), a natural overlap given that Ralegh himself was clearly drawn to these new studies of civil polity and constructed his ambitious providential history self-consciously

---

4. Edward Forset, *A Comparative Discourse of the Bodies Natural and Politique* ... (London, 1606), 85. On Forset and his reliance on the Cecils' patronage, see *Oxford Dictionary of National Biography*, online ed., s.v. "Forsett, Edward (1553/4–1629/30)," by Sean Kelsey, accessed Oct. 5, 2014, http://www.oxforddnb.com/view/article/9900; *The History of Parliament: British Political, Social, and Local History*, online ed., s.v. "Edward Carr," accessed Oct. 5, 2014, http://www.historyofparliamentonline.org/volume/1604-1629/member/carr-edward.

on their model. As in Ralegh's *History,* the state figured in these works as a historical product of human invention, an innovation that arose as fallen persons became more obedient to God and grew more knowledgeable about what was necessary to preserve themselves against sin. Rather than a novel entity, the state connoted an ancient and vigorous institution that had risen and fallen over the ages. Convinced of the antiquity of much that was lawful in the world, these authors nonetheless regarded the knowledge of those lawful civil arrangements as still dimly understood, necessitating the political science that they themselves made available.[5]

Although their studies were directed in part at rulers, it is suggestive of the growing emphasis these writers gave to the authority of councillors, ministers, and other servants to kings that their books also provided guidance on the office of the statesman, a newly appreciated calling that LeRoy described as "the charge and managing of matters of State." As if acknowledging his own allegiance to this vocation, Cecil wrote a tract for his new king entitled "The State and Dignitie of a Secretarie of Estates Place, with the Care and Perill Thereof." Referring to "this calling and office, in the managing of publick businesses" as Salisbury's greatest legacy, one admiring writer identified him first and foremost as a "well governed Statist," someone who not only dedicated himself to the state with singular devotion but did so with stoic

---

5. Justus Lipsius, *Sixe Bookes of Politickes or Civil Doctrine . . . Done into English by William Jones Gentleman* (London, 1594), 13. Some of this statecraft literature had begun to circulate in the universities as early as 1579, as is indicated by Gabriel Harvey's report from Cambridge to Edmund Spenser: "You can not stepp into a schollars studye but (ten to on) you shall litely finde open ether Bodin de Republica or Le Royes Exposition upon Aristotles Politiques." See Edward John Long Scott, ed., *Letter-Book of Gabriel Harvey, A.D. 1573–1580* (London, 1884), 79. A current of excitement ran through this statesman's literature, as is suggested by LeRoy's enthusiastic portrait of what could be gained by greater attention to what he called the "science which teacheth how to govern mankind aright": "By this Science we know the dutie of Princes towards their Subjects, of Magistrates towards their Princes, and also towards private persons: What Offices are most necessarie and most honourable: what obedience, honor, and reverence the inferiours owe to their superiors: how men ought to behave themselves in buying, in selling, in exchanging, in prizing, in giving, in receiving, in promising, in bargaining, and in pleading. In great disorder should wee be, if it had not knit us together by marriages, kinreds, alliances, and households, devided inheritances, stablished successions, and ordained seates of Justice. For otherwise we could not have knowne our own from other men, or kinsman from a stranger, or the servant from the maister. To bee short, without this science it were not possible to live either publickly or privately, nor in anie wise to deale wel with men or mens matters" (L[oui]s LeRoy, *Aristotles Politiques; or, Discourses of Government . . .* [London, 1598], B[i]v, Bijr).

self-mastery. This tempering loyalty to the state could even moderate Salisbury's otherwise unflagging service to kingship. At one point in his description of the secretary's vocation to James, Salisbury offered the stern admonition, "The place of a secretary is dreadful, if he serve not a constant Prince." The state's great providential promise of bringing everyone to his or her divine duties required that not only secretaries but also kings do their part.[6]

Salisbury and his clients had begun laying the groundwork for their state-centered vision in the last years of Elizabeth's reign. Cecil, not yet awarded his earldom, contended with the queen's favorite, Robert Devereux, second earl of Essex, over the most effective way to deal with the Spanish and papal threats. Johnson himself appears to have served Cecil in these early struggles over defining the English regime. In the 1590s, Johnson was associated with the newly organized East India Company, a body that evidently enjoyed Cecil's own support as a means of strengthening the English state by opening the door to Asian wealth. Overshadowing that project and putting it briefly on hold was Cecil's effort to establish a negotiated peace with Spain. Essex, who remained wedded to the old ideal of striking out against the Spanish with manly vigor, opposed the idea of a Spanish peace as a foolhardy exercise in allying with an untrustworthy enemy. Yet, he also evidently recognized in Cecil's initiative something more: a fundamental transformation of the Elizabethan polity, one that placed the political exertions of commoner statesmen like Cecil over the valorous deeds of aristocratic captains like himself.[7]

Recently returned from his failed attack on the Spanish in the Azores in 1597 with Ralegh, Essex lashed out at Cecil's plan with a fierce *Apologie* (written in 1598 and published in 1600). There he uttered the familiar

6. LeRoy, *Aristotles Politiques,* B[i]v; Robert Cecil, *The State and Dignitie of a Secretarie of Estates Place, with the Care and Perill Thereof* (London, 1642), 3; Richard J[oh]nson, *A Remembrance of the Honors Due to the Life and Death of Robert Earle of Salisbury, Lord Treasurer of England, etc.* (London, 1612), [A3v], B2r.

7. For Essex's early interest in the East India Company, see, for instance, Foulke Grevil [Fulke Greville] to [Sir Robert Cecil], Mar. 10, 1600, in W. Noel Sainsbury, ed., *Calendar of State Papers, Colonial Series, East Indies, China, and Japan, 1513–1616* (London, 1862), 104–105. Robert Johnson and Sir Thomas Smythe's involvement in the early East India Company can be traced in John Shaw, *Charters relating to the East India Company from 1600 to 1761: Reprinted from a Former Collection with Some Additions and a Preface* (Madras, 1887). 1–3, 13, 17–18, 20. For Cecil's early interest in a peace with Spain, see Pauline Croft, "Rex Pacificus, Robert Cecil, and the 1604 Peace with Spain," in Glenn Burgess, Rowland Wymer, and Jason Lawrence, eds., *The Accession of James I: Historical and Cultural Consequences* (New York, 2006), 140–154.

lament of Elizabeth's captains, acknowledging that his burdensome journeys for the commonweal often turned out to be "no allowed action of her Majesties, but a mere adventure of private men." Then, in a probable jab at nonaristocratic court politicians like Cecil, he asserted that what propelled him and his fellow "men of action" in spite of their uncertain support by the queen was the "greatnesse of minde" that "God in his providence" gave them to uphold their constancy, allowing them to transcend those worldly interests that the "little mindes" of "soft loping men" hungered after, like "love[,] ease[,] pleasure[,] and profit."[8]

Johnson responded to Essex in 1601 with what could only have been Cecil's retort, a published collection of essays whose very first entry considered the theme "Of Greatnes of Mind." Acknowledging that greatness of mind was a distinctive, God-given capacity that endowed its possessors with "a puissant resolution to enter uppon the bravest enterprises," Johnson also observed that it could be "abused." Just as "the best wine becometh the egrest [that is, most acrid] vinegar," so, too, "this greatnesse of mind, if it be not accompanied with vertue, maketh men daungerouslie bad and terrible." Presumably, with Cecil's direction, Johnson was slyly reconfiguring the celebrated virtue of Elizabeth's captains, suggesting that it was dependent, not on their asserted nobility that secured their obedience to God, but rather on their compliance with state measures. When in *Nova Britannia* he pointed to greatness of mind as the singular failing of Elizabeth's colonizers, he was similarly implying that they had misunderstood virtuous conduct. Notably, it was a critique he was just as prepared to make against the Spaniards: "Their greatnes of minde arising together with their money and meanes, hath turmoiled all Christendome these fourtie yeares and more." In contrast, it was the honorable minds and good dispositions of the company's members, not their greatness of mind, that he emphasized in his introduction of the Virginia Company to the realm. "It is not unknown to you all," he wrote, "how many Noble men of honourable mindes, how many worthy Knights, Merchants, and others of the best disposition, are now joyned together in one Charter, to receive equall priviledges, according to their severall adventures." An assemblage of distinguished members like the Virginia Company, made up of noble and nonnoble elements, was in its very collectivity of impressive

---

8. [Robert Devereux, earl of Essex], *An Apologie of the Earle of Essex, against Those Which Fasly and Maliciously Taxe Him to Be the Onely Hinderer of the Peace, and Quiet of His Countrey* [London?, 1600?], A3r, B2r–v, B3r–v.

wills able to provide a more tempered, and thus more reliable and steady, pursuit of godly ends than any individual actors could do on their own.⁹

In *Nova Britannia*, Johnson very clearly echoed one of the great preoccupations of the new writers on the state—the vicissitudes of the self-aggrandizing will, or what LeRoy called the "disquietnesse and perturbations of the minde." Such a concern about the ease with which inflated dispositions gave rise to dangerous pride reflected, on the one hand, these authors' keen interest in allowing sovereignty free rein to perform its divine functions on Earth. On the other hand, their determination to stifle dangerously independent wills also grew out of their recognition of the severe disruptions that sovereignty could produce when mishandled, a view shaped in large part by their horror at the era's civil and religious divisions. Kings needed the spur of ambition in first leading humans out of sin, Lipsius reasoned, but they eventually became susceptible to the world's own inconstancy if they did not incorporate their own glory-seeking minds into the broader framework of laws and mutual relations that gave the commonwealth its godly firmness. When Johnson suggested that greatness of mind originated as a special power God imparted to conquering captains but over time risked devolving into something worldly and wicked, he was making a similar case for the need to encompass private wills into the state's own constellation of reciprocal bonds.¹⁰

Stressing the inconstancy of private wills, these authors made a case for the steadying influence of law and of what they had begun to refer to as the "forme of pollicy." A key phrase in this literature that only gradually yielded to the word "constitution," "forme of pollicy" connoted a stabilizing frame-

---

9. Rob[ert] Johnson, *Essaies; or, Rather Imperfect Offers* (London 1601), B[1]r, B4r; J[ohnson], *Nova Britannia*, B3r–B3v. Cecil's argument for a negotiated peace over belligerent strikes against the enemy was an important theme in the statecraft literature. LeRoy's dedication to Henry III, written in July 1596, stressed with a notably providential emphasis, "Many Kings and Emperours set their whole felicitie on warre, and in conquering new countries, but if they looke well hereinto, they shall find it better for a Prince to governe wisely, and to order their estate conveniently, than to invade and conquer another Princes realme; considering that the chiefe cause why he is set up of God, and why God is so gracious to him, as to put innumerable persons in subjection to him, is that hee should holde them together in the knowledge and observation of the true Religion, rule them with good lawes, defende them by force of armes, and in all cases be so carefull of their welfare, as they may regarde him as their father and Sheapheard" (LeRoy, *Aristotles Politiques*, [Av]v).

10. LeRoy, *Aristotles Politiques*, 173, 177.

work capable of withstanding the gusts of worldly vicissitude and keeping everyone to his duties. Less constitutionalists than apologists for the providential state, these writers were quick to laud strong, even absolute, kingship for its effectiveness in securing obedience over still-fallen humans. Nevertheless, their concern to insulate a sinful humanity against its own capriciousness also made them instrumental in giving added legitimacy to a set of concepts — the public weal, parliaments, the law, the constitution — that further promised to hold all people, including even the king himself, to their godly duties. LeRoy anticipated the reverential treatment of the law that Ralegh would develop in his *History* by explaining that God's providence itself allowed for the "invention of good Lawes" so "that some thing more divine then man, sitteth at the sterne of humane societies to guide and direct them in the right course." The collectivity of wills and laws that constituted the bonds between the polity's diverse members came to supplement the once-lauded resolution of the conquering captain and even, by extension, the private will of the absolute king as forces deemed even more important in holding a fallen humanity to godly pathways.[11]

In the same year that his essays appeared, Johnson also published another work that similarly gestured toward this ideal of the state as a steadying agent. This was a loose translation and adaptation of Botero's *Delle relationi universali* (1591). Originally written while Botero was secretary to the archbishop of Milan, one of the many satellite dominions of the Spanish crown, the *Relationi* offered lessons in statecraft in the same tradition as Lipsius, LeRoy, and Bodin but with a particular emphasis on the Counter-Reformation ideal of a reunified Christendom brought back to Roman Catholicism by Spanish universal monarchy. In Johnson's hands, Botero's survey of the world's "greatest Princes and States" and his proem on how states could best enhance themselves through an "enlarging of Dominion" became, not an apology for Spanish power, but rather a blueprint for how England, too, could participate like other honorable states in the "uniting and establishing of divers ter-

---

11. Ibid., 148, 177–178. Defining "forme of pollicy," LeRoy wrote: "Policy therefore is the order and description, as of other offices in a city, so of that which hath the greatest and most soveraine authority: for the rule and administration of a Commonweale, hath evermore power and authority joined with it: which administration is called policie in Greeke, and in English a Commonweale: for example sake, as in a Democratie the authority is in the hands of the people, in an Ologarchie in the hands of a few. . . . Policy is the order and disposition of the city in regard of Magistrats, and specially in regard of him that hath the soverain authority over al, in whose government the whole comonweale consisteth" (148–149).

ritories under one soveraigntie and government." Reminiscent of Johnson's refutation of the Elizabethan captains' greatness of mind, Botero considered at length what made up the "true valour" needed for "any project of woorthie consideration." His answer was basically that the qualities of the statesman and the soldier needed to be merged: "For wisedome without courage, may rather be termed subtiltie, then judicious cariage: and courage without discretion is rather furious rashnesse, then true valour." Here, too, was a shrewd moratorium on the age of conquering captains, for Botero's broader point was that the true strength of a kingdom came not only from the brave exploits of kings and their noble warriors but also from the quieter, more banal concerns of the statesman. Matters like population size, the wealth of the polity, the industriousness of citizens, and relations between prince and people all must factor in the governance that allowed a polity to do right by God. These statesmanlike concerns, which the writers on the state typically referred to under the category of civil prudence to insist on their equal importance with martial prudence, practically necessitated a ruler's reliance on wise councils, assemblies, and even corporations like the Virginia Company, bodies that brought a collectivity of honorable minds and good dispositions to work on a matter of concern to the state.[12]

In *Nova Britannia*, Johnson quietly worked a number of Botero's key themes and insights into his own account of the reinvigorated Virginia endeavor. Botero's repeated praise for the skills of navigation and merchandising as key civil exertions that accounted for the strength of the Spanish and Portuguese states became in Johnson's pamphlet a subtle reinterpretation of the biblical story of King Solomon's riches; such lucre, according to Johnson, "did not raine from heaven upon the heads of his subjects" but rather arose from their own divinely blessed "Navigations and publike affayres, the chiefe meanes of their wealth." This emphasis on state affairs

12. Giovanni Botero, *The Worlde: or, An Historicall Description of the Most Famous Kingdomes and Common-Weales Therein* ... (London, 1601), B[1]r, 2–3. On prudence as a kingly virtue that also involves the help of wise counsel and ministers, see Lipsius, *Sixe Bookes of Politickes or Civil Doctrine*, 39–58. On military prudence, see ibid., 124–186. On Johnson's translation of Botero's work, see Andrew Fitzmaurice, "The Commercial Ideology of Colonization in Jacobean England: Robert Johnson, Giovanni Botero, and the Pursuit of Greatness," *William and Mary Quarterly*, 3d Ser., LXIV (2007), 791–820. Although Fitzmaurice credits Botero's reception in late Elizabethan England with ushering in a commercial ideology to colonization, the argument made here is that Botero's concern, like that of the other statecraft writers, was principally with the providential state, only one implication of which was greater attention to trade.

as the way a king and his subjects enriched themselves while also satisfying God's providence also underlay Botero's argument that large population sizes were a virtue rather than a bane, allowing a commonwealth to grow and prosper rather than merely eating away at its meager resources. Johnson likewise identified England's large population as a reason the English "neede not doubt" their capacity as colonizers, for "our land abounding with swarmes of idle persons, which having no meanes of labour to releeve their misery" practically begged for "forreine employment." In his own work, Botero hailed colonies as the means by which an already populous state might create "branches" of itself to serve as "nurseries" of people and wealth, thereby adding further to its strength. Johnson utilized both of these metaphors, similarly treating Virginia as an extended branch of the ever-growing English state and as a nursery-like incubator of its subjects and wealth. Identifying England's strength as better secured than ever before, he wrote, "Our plant, we trust, is firmly rooted, our armes and limmes are strong, our branches faire, and much desire to spread themselves abroad." Elsewhere, he asserted that Virginia would soon "become a most royall addition to the Crowne of England, and a very nursery and fountaine of much wealth and strength to this kingdome."[13]

Another major theme that Johnson borrowed from Botero was that of "opportunity," or "occasion." Probably drawing on Niccolò Machiavelli, whose earlier writings on the state were an important foundation for Botero and his fellow sixteenth-century writers, Botero defined opportunity as "a meeting and concurring of divers circumstances, which at one instant do make a matter very easie" and "at another time ... impossible, or very hard, to bring to effect." In essence an updating of the notion of a lawful pathway that God makes available for resolute human actors, opportunity figured for Botero as a consideration especially for statesmen, persons with the wisdom and experience necessary for judging divinely granted opportunity well and seizing on it before time wrought its inevitable alterations. In *Nova Britannia,* Johnson repeatedly invoked occasion as a key factor in the success or failure of the Virginia venture, even attributing the tragedy of Ralegh's lost colony to the "corruption of time" that allowed the captains returning to the

13. J[ohnson], *Nova Britannia,* B2r ("Our plant"), B3r ("become a most,"), [C4]r ("did not raine," "Navigations"), D[1]r ("neede not," "our land," "forreine"); Botero, *Worlde,* 2 ("branches," "nursery"). For Botero's emphasis on the strength derived from Spanish and Portuguese navigations, see ibid., 11; for his identification of England's abundant population as a benefit, see ibid., 24.

colony with supplies to become greedily diverted by the thought of raiding the Spanish coast, so "by this occasion" an "honourable enterprise so happily begunne" was "most unhappily ended."[14]

For Salisbury and his circle, a major Botero-like opportunity opened up in the form of the Anglo-Spanish treaty of 1604 that finally realized Salisbury's more-than-a-decade-long striving for a statesmanlike peace. James made only a brief, largely ceremonial appearance at the negotiations, which lasted several days, and departed for a hunting expedition, happily leaving the negotiations in Salisbury's capable hands. In the meetings, Salisbury managed to shepherd the English and Spanish delegates' often-heated debates about the Indies in such a way as to ensure that no mention of the subject appeared in the final treaty. The resulting silence on the Indies, which the Spaniards preferred to interpret as preserving Philip's exclusive title in the New World, was for Salisbury a classic case of divers circumstances wondrously intersecting, eliciting state action almost as a moral imperative. As one 1610 pamphlet put it, "this opportune and generall Summer of peace" was the impetus behind the company's determination "to provide and build up for the publike *Honour* and *safety* of our *gratious King* and his *Estates* . . . some small Rampier of our owne . . . by trans-planting the ranckness and multitude of increase in our people." Or, as Johnson put it, "The honour of our nation is now very great by his Majesties meanes . . . if we sitte still and let slip occasions, we shall gather rust, and doe unfeather our owne wings." Virginia colonization, then, appeared to Salisbury and his circle as uniquely suited for their time and for their own distinctive capacities. Reorganized as a state venture, the enterprise would successfully transcend the problems that had befallen it in the past.[15]

Yet, the ignobility of Elizabethan colonization did not prove so easy to

14. Botero, *Worlde*, 9 ("opportunity," "occasion," "meeting," "at another time"); J[ohnson], *Nova Britannia*, B2v ("corruption of time"), B3r ("by this occasion," "honourable," "most unhappily"). On Machiavelli's use of the concept of occasion, especially as complexly antithetical to and interwoven with fortune, see J. G. A. Pocock, *The Machiavellian Moment: Florentine Political Thought and the Atlantic Republican Tradition* (Princeton, 1975), 168, 170, 172, 174, 181, 139, 190, 193, 206, 301, 318–319, 453.

15. [Counseil for Virginia], *A True and Sincere Declaration of the Purpose and Ends of the Plantation Begun in Virginia . . .* (London, 1610), 3; J[ohnson], *Nova Britannia*, E2v. On Salisbury's central role in the negotiations and James's comparative noninvolvement, see Croft, "Rex Pacificus, Robert Cecil, and the 1604 Peace with Spain," in Burgess, Wymer, and Lawrence, eds., *Accession of James I*, 140–154.

overcome for the simple reason that what the Jacobeans strenuously put forward as an honorable public endeavor perpetually risked appearing as still private in the sense of not really reflecting a unity of upstanding wills after all. A number of factors contributed to this tension, but the most important was the king's own wary attitude toward the state-building efforts of his busiest servant. James's priorities did not always align neatly with his secretary's, and the problems of legitimacy that haunted the new king's reign encouraged a cautious approach to governance not unlike Elizabeth's. Under such circumstances, James was unlikely to satisfy Salisbury's call for constancy. But Salisbury's own methods for securing that kingly resolution were similarly bound to contribute to the king's wariness. Like Elizabeth, James viewed with suspicion efforts to coopt his sovereignty by pressuring his conscience with aggressive shows of the purportedly united wills of his subjects—a tactic he referred to ruefully as appeals to "popularity." In other words, the very strategies that the colonizers employed to uphold the public stature of their endeavor also had the unintended effect of bolstering the king's own determination to treat the colony as he saw fit.[16]

Especially in the years after Salisbury's death in 1612, when the popularizing methods he had inaugurated fell to less well-placed company members, James increasingly felt justified in looking on the company as simply one of several private pots of money available to him, an extra-parliamentary source of funds that were rightfully his as the granter of the Virginia Company's corporate charter. This view, which treated the company effectively as a royally patented monopoly, turned on its head the colonizers' own vigorous claim to have left the years of private colonization mercifully behind. The king's refusal to adopt the colonizers' vision of state-led colonization was a constant source of tension for the company and eventually produced the circumstances that led to its dissolution in 1624.

16. James's perception that popularity held alarming sway in England related closely to his strained relations with his parliaments. After he dissolved the 1610 parliament, he asserted that his English subjects' stubbornness in relation to his agendas could only be motivated by "a desiring to lay the foundations of a popular state"; see PRO State Papers, 14/58/26, quoted in Conrad Russell, *The Addled Parliament of 1614: The Limits of Revision*, The Stenton Lecture 1991 (Reading, U.K., 1992), 18. Growing concerns about popularity in early Stuart England probably owed something to the literature of statecraft, which was wary about popular, as opposed to aristocratic or monarchical, government and convinced that England had an excess of the former. For instance, LeRoy wrote, "In England the populacy is stronger then the nobility, and easier to bee stirred up, being armed by a publick decree" (LeRoy, *Aristotles Politiques*, 154).

Even in the face of these disappointments, however, the Salisbury group's efforts remained highly significant. In particular, their ideal of the providential state as a force that holds lawful arrangements in place fundamentally insinuated itself into the colonizing endeavor. Powerfully informing the makeup of the new Virginia colony as well as the colonies that followed in its wake, the ideal of the state also created a set of lingering expectations, perhaps the most important of which was that colonies that were truly honorable must enjoy the same civil integrity as the state from which they branched off.

Toward a Colony "Fownded for a Publique-well"

Salisbury's vision of state-led colonization was driven by a pronounced sense of the infamy of Elizabethan colonizers and the indignity that consequently attached itself to the English commonwealth. Of course, the eagerness to clothe colonizers in a greater aura of honor was not new to the Jacobeans; rather, the same impulse had propelled Burghley and Sir Francis Walsingham's clients to begin their own tentative groping toward state-led colonization. Hakluyt, for instance, had argued in his "Discourse of Western Planting" (1584) that the full commitment of the queen and the state to the venture was the key to warding off the shame that any struggling colony faced, a disgrace that he attributed especially to the eagerness with which the Catholics at Elizabeth's court "maliced" it. Providing sufficient backing for a colony early on, he wrote, was essential so that "the burden may leste tyme reste on the backe of the bearer of the same, that he sincke not under the same, but that he maye stande upp in full strengthe, and goe throughe with ease, fame, and profitt withoute shame of all the bymedlers and fauters of the same." In continuing to look for ways to allow the colonizer to stand up in full strength and with the dignity becoming a righteous agent of God's will, the Salisbury circle made the state into an even more elaborated providential actor. At the heart of that vision was the Virginia Company. Possessing one point of origin in the trading companies of the Elizabethan era like the Company of Merchant Adventurers, the Muscovy Company, and the Levant Company, the Virginia Company was also meant to transcend those organizations' reputations for narrow commercial pursuits. The Virginia Company's public essence was its real focus, as its own literature repeatedly underscored by emphasizing that merchants made up only one of its constituent elements. Borne out of the disgrace associated with Elizabeth's private men, the Virginia Company arose in a Jacobean climate intensely concerned with appearance and increasingly sensitive to the problem of giving an air of honor, majesty, and public interestedness to particular enterprises to distinguish them as matters of state rather than merely private ventures.[17]

Of especial importance in this reputation-conscious atmosphere was warding off any hints that the company's carefully cultivated image of public integrity simply masked private-oriented behaviors little different from those associated with the previous generation of colonizers. Salisbury was as alert to this problem of the colonizers' fame as anyone. On June 7, 1607, he spoke before the English parliament on the highly inflammatory subject of the Spanish seizure of the English ship *Richard*, which had been captured the previous November off the Florida Strait and taken back to Spain where its crew were imprisoned and, in some cases, sent to the galleys. Salisbury was eager to allay the members' fury, perhaps in part because of James's desire for a conciliatory atmosphere with Spain to pursue his own pet project, an ecumenical European religious council that would ease Christendom's divisions by resolving otherwise irresolvable questions of heterodoxy and orthodoxy.[18]

Salisbury proceeded carefully and with more than normal candidness about the thin line he perceived between the honorableness of the colonizing venture and its indignity. The *Richard*'s Virginia-bound voyage had been "intended for trade and plantation where the Spaniard hath no people nor possession," he asserted, echoing what had become the standard English line on the 1604 treaty in its relation to the Indies. Yet, he acknowledged that the "offences and scandals of some" had complicated this otherwise lawful purpose, such that the voyage "is already become infamed for piracy." By this time, the notoriety of piracy was already a well-established way of speaking of the excesses of Elizabethan colonization, whether or not the plundering

---

17. "Discourse of Western Planting by Richard Hakluyt," 1584, in E. G. R. Taylor, ed., *The Original Writings and Correspondence of the Two Richard Hakluyts*, Works Issued by the Hakluyt Society, 2d Ser., no. 77 (London, 1935), II, 280. For an analysis that focuses more on the city merchants' perspective on the colonizing companies than the leadership role of the Salisbury circle but that arrives at a similar conclusion that "the project of the Virginia Company" was distinguished "from those of the purely trading ventures of this era" and thus followed a "deviant line of development," see Robert Brenner, *Merchants and Revolution: Commercial Change, Political Conflict, and London's Overseas Traders, 1550–1653* (Princeton, 1993), 92–95.

18. For James's ardent quest to establish an ecumenical religious council, see W. B. Patterson, *King James VI and I and the Reunion of Christendom* (Cambridge, 1997).

of ships was the main issue at hand. Hakluyt had invoked the same bogeyman in his "Discourse of Western Planting." Remarking that the English and French were "moste infamous" for incidents of "outeragious, common, and daily piracies," Hakluyt proposed that the English more faithfully follow the Spanish and Portuguese example of planting colonies of subjects that provide "many honest wayes to sett them on worke." The real issue for both men was less piracy per se than the worrying reputation that hovered over the colonizing venture — that it was pursued by maverick souls who, because of their very independence from the commonwealth's bonds, were imagined as slipping unpredictably from honesty to villainy. Colonization performed by the state was meant to be the honorable alternative to this scene of moral licentiousness, eschewing mere belligerence and profit seeking for the godly end of putting people to industrious work at their callings.[19]

Besides piracy, colonization also veered perilously near the tricky moral territory of monopoly. The issue of monopolies had become controversial in the last decades of Elizabeth's reign in no small part because these exclusionary arrangements under the queen so powerfully exposed the uncertainties still associated with royal imperium and its relationship to the broader commonwealth. A monopoly was authorization that the queen gave to an individual or group, the latter often called a privileged society, to perform some action, such as vending a particular commodity or initiating a certain art or industry, with the power to exclude others from the same activity. Colonizers were from an early date apologists for monopolies because the costs and difficulties of managing ambitious foreign conquests for the queen seemed to practically dictate such a protected status. Yet, these men also recognized the distrust that monopolies engendered, a suspicion related both to the unnatural intimacy to sovereign power entailed by such a relationship

---

19. "Sir Francis Bacon's Report to the Commons of the Earl of Salisbury's Speech to the Conference of Lords and Commons on the Merchants' Petition for Redress against Spain," June 15, 1607, in David B. Quinn, Alison M. Quinn, and Susan Hillier, eds., *New American World: A Documentary History of North America to 1612*, III, *English Plans for North America; The Roanoke Voyages; New England Ventures* (New York, 1979), 417; "Discourse of Western Planting," 1584, in Taylor, ed., *Original Writings and Correspondence of the Two Richard Hakluyts*, II, 233–234. Salisbury expressed more sympathy for the captured merchants in private correspondence with the English ambassador to Spain, Sir Charles Cornwallis, while also disavowing "that it is any parte of myne adventure," that is, related to his Virginia project; see [Robert Cecil], earl of Salisbury, to Sir Charles Cornwallis, Apr. 12, 1607, in [Edmund Sawyer, ed.], *Memorials of Affairs of State in the Reigns of Q. Elizabeth and K. James I . . .* , 3 vols. (London, 1725), II, 303.

and to worries about what this special protection accorded to a few subjects meant for the welfare of the rest.[20]

John Dee addressed the issue of monopolies as early as 1577 in a proposal for a "Pety-Navy-Royall" to serve as a safeguard to the queen's ancient "Brytish Impire." Such a naval force, he argued, would prove "faithfull, servisable, Comfortable, and profitable to the Political Body of this Brytish Common-wealth: Whereof, we all, be Members, by God his mercifull Ordinance." To fund such an entity, he called for a small tax levied on subjects as well as a larger duty to be imposed on foreign fishermen trolling British waters. The amount drawn from the latter in particular would be sufficient, Dee believed, to generate a surplus, which could then be put to work not only augmenting the queen's customs but also, significantly, recompensing the "Partners of Privileged voyages," or, as he also described them, the "Societies" set up to further "Forreyn Discoveries." Recognizing that such exclusive liberties contributed to the trading companies' ambiguous reputation, Dee argued that the "Benefit Publik" that would arise from the entire arrangement would sweep the merchants themselves into its legitimizing orbit: "And all the Commons, and Body of the Realm, will grow in greater love, with the Marchants Dooings: and better like of the Princes establishing of such Privileged Societies: When, the wary and carefull Diligence of the Merchant, and the gracious Privilege of the Prince, shall (PROPORTIONALLY) be beneficiall to ONE, A FEW, and ALL." In other words, monopolies need not generate misgivings as long as they ultimately benefited everybody. Once the merchant companies' reputation improved—that is, when they became associated with the "Benefit Publik" of the realm as a whole; when their "Dooings" came to be seen "asmuch avaylable to the Commonwealth, then, as, now they are to the Private Lucre of a Few"; and when the "things, which they Bring in, or Deale with," no longer seemed "deerer bought than they were, before any such New Trade or Society, therin Privi-

---

20. Useful studies that tie contemporary concerns about monopoly to broader patterns of thought and argument include David Harris Sacks, "The Countervailing of Benefits: Monopoly, Liberty, and Benevolence in Elizabethan England," in Dale Hoak, ed., *Tudor Political Culture* (Cambridge, 1995), 272–291; Sacks, "Parliament, Liberty, and the Commonweal," in J. H. Hexter, ed., *Parliament and Liberty from the Reign of Elizabeth to the English Civil War* (Stanford, Calif., 1992), 93–101; Sacks, "The Greed of Judas: Avarice, Monopoly, and the Moral Economy in England, ca. 1350–ca. 1600," *Journal of Medieval and Early Modern Studies*, XXVIII (1998), 263–307. See also Blair Hoxby, *Mammon's Music: Literature and Economics in the Age of Milton* (New Haven, Conn., 2002), 25–61.

leged" was formed—then the realm as a whole would be ready to embrace the merchants as one of their own, no longer scorning them for the "decaying and weakening of the wealth and hability of the Commons."[21]

The new writers on statecraft also addressed the issue of monopolies, acknowledging their ill repute while also seeking to create room for sovereign-protected enterprises that fulfilled particular public uses. Notably, Bodin wrote on this theme in relation to corporations, or as he called them companies—a treatment that is suggestive of the Virginia Company's own careful self-presentation as an assembly that shunned the monopolistic impulses of the merchant for a public mindedness and service to God and king more associated with Parliament than with the merchant societies of Dee's day. Like Dee, Bodin, too, acknowledged the tendency of protected companies to devolve into hated monopolies that sought "to sell their marchandize and wares the dearer" or that fostered "jealousies and quarels." Corporations when "evill governed," he wrote, "draw after them many factions, seditions, part-takings, monopolies, yea and sometimes the ruine of the whole Commonweale also." Yet, he disagreed with those critics who proposed that such privileged societies should be removed altogether, or that "the Commonweale may well be without them." Instead, he argued that corporations were little different from any authorized popular assemblies, including colleges and even parliaments. After all, what were such communities but the very flowering of the ages-old process whereby humans associated with one another in their emergence from the Fall? It took only the barest understanding of the human civilizing instinct to see

> men every where to be, and alwaies to have bene desirous of the societie and companie of men: and so out of a familiar and natural societie by little and little to have growne into a colledge, into a corporation, into a communitie, and so at length into a citie: and so to have made these empires and kingdomes, which we here in the world see, having no surer foundation wherupon to rest (next unto God) than the love and amitie of one of them towards another.

In other words, the company was no less natural than the commonwealth; it composed one of its essential building blocks.[22]

21. [John Dee], *General and Rare Memorials Pertayning to the Perfect Arte of Navigation* . . . [London, 1577], 3, 6, 11, 28, 29, 30.
22. Jean Bodin, *The Six Bookes of a Commonweale; A Facsimile Reprint of the English Trans-*

Salisbury and his associates eagerly grasped at this reasoning that a company was both a civil entity analogous to the state and a public-oriented community capable of rising above the indignity of a mere monopoly. Cecil himself had taken part in the debates that roiled Elizabeth's parliament in 1601 when monopolists were accused of restraining what was rightly "Publick, in a City, or Common-Wealth, to a Private Use"; or of funneling "the General Profit into a Private Hand"; or even of being "Blood-Suckers of the Common-Wealth." In his speech to Parliament on November 23, Cecil had advanced the far more cautious position that a monopoly fell ambiguously between the "Prince's Power" and the "Freedom of *English*-men," neither of which key elements of the commonwealth should be trifled with. Allowing that some monopolies were bad in that they took away the livelihoods of subjects or otherwise impinged on their welfare, he insisted that others were beneficial and deserved continuance. Cecil's cousin Francis Bacon had taken much the same line in the debates, arguing that when such a privilege was "good for the Common-Wealth" the queen's judges permitted it and, when "otherwise," either they disallowed it or the queen herself repealed it, whether through her quo warranto power or by her "Express Command."[23]

In a much subtler argument, Bacon shrewdly pointed out that, while many of the ministers were prepared to "cry out" when the queen granted such a patent to an individual courtier or favorite, "If She grants it to a Number of Burgesses, or Corporation, that must stand; and that, forsooth, is no Monopoly." Bacon was mischievously playing on the presupposition by the many gentry members who were themselves investors in the great trading companies that these gentry-supported corporations somehow fell outside the realm of monopoly, nobly rising above the abuses the members were prepared to see in the individual monopolies of courtiers or favorites. Siding with the gentleman MPs' view, Cecil himself preferred to think of corporations as a category apart from monopolies. This sentiment appears in a colonizing tract from about the 1590s that was probably written by Edward Hayes, the onetime casuist for Lord Burghley who was now in Cecil's service, and Christopher Carleill, Walsingham's son-in-law. Corporations received special emphasis as unusually suitable for the "honorable worke" of

---

lation of 1606 Corrected and Supplemented in the Light of a New Comparison with the French and Latin Texts, ed. Kenneth Douglas McRae (Cambridge, Mass., 1962), 379, 380, 383, 386.

23. Hayward Townshend, *Historical Collections; or, An Exact Account of the Proceedings of the Four Last Parliaments of Q. Elizabeth of Famous Memory* (London, 1680), 230, 231–232, 233, 234, 242.

founding a new commonwealth for Elizabeth on the other side of the Atlantic. Such an enterprise needed the firm and upright governance that a "boddy pollitike and incorporat" could provide because otherwise the "comon sort," overly excited by quick gains, might "goe to[o] fast over into those parts, inflamed with the comon bruite of the pleasures and proffytts of the same contries as it happened in Spayn after the discovery of the West Indies." The corporate model, being the most "indifferent and requysit above other fourmes of goverment, to the erection and advancement of thys new state and comon weal," provided just the right blend of disinterestedness and elite leadership to undertake such a weighty sovereign endeavor. Such a rationale no doubt underlay the Virginia Company's claim to embody in its sheer assemblage of honorable men a dramatic departure from Elizabeth's private colonizers. At the same time, Bacon's wry observation that a company was not so different from a monopoly after all reflected the precariousness of that claim to a distinctively public stature.[24]

James's first parliaments shed somewhat greater light on the ambiguous question of the identity of companies in relation to monopolies, especially in the sessions of 1604 and 1605–1606 where considerable debate took place over when companies were or were not monopolistic. A subtle distinction emerged from those debates that treated joint-stock companies, which made membership available to anyone willing to pay for a share, as qualitatively more honorable than regulated companies, which limited membership to a select number of shareholders. Again, such categories were murky rather than hard-and-fast, but the idea that joint-stock companies were more inclusive and thus more compatible with the commonwealth than a regulated company provided yet another basis for the Virginia Company's gradually evolving assertion that the company mirrored the kingdom as a whole in its diverse membership.[25]

---

24. Ibid., 232; [Edward Hayes and Christopher Carleill], "A Discourse concerning a Voyage Intended for the Planting of Chrystyan Religion and People in the North West Regions of America in Places Most Apt for the Constitution of Our Bodies, and the Spedy Advauncement of a State," n.d., in Quinn, Quinn, and Hillier, ed., *New American World,* III, 165. On the growing role of the gentry in trading companies, see Theodore K. Rabb, *Enterprise and Empire: Merchant and Gentry Investment in the Expansion of England, 1575–1630* (Cambridge, 1967); on the Virginia Company's stunning success in attracting gentlemen involved in Parliament, see ibid., 93.

25. On the murky line drawn between joint-stock companies and regulated companies in parliamentary debates, see Theodore K. Rabb, *Jacobean Gentleman: Sir Edwin Sandys, 1561–1629* (Princeton, 1998), 88–95.

This conflation of joint-stock companies and the commonwealth became especially prominent to the colonizers' message as they began to announce the changes authorized by James's second Virginia-related patent of May 23, 1609. Johnson in *Nova Britannia* emphasized the Virginia Company's "joynt stock" toward which anyone could contribute for the initial share price of twelve pounds ten shillings as a major reason the company stood to benefit the commonwealth as a whole. At the same time, he strenuously insisted that the company would shun any persons who "seeke by lying suggestions, under colour of good pretence to the Common-wealth to infringe our aunciant liberties, and... make a monopoly to themselves, of each thing after other, belonging to the freedome of every mans possession." Calling such monopolists "the very wrack of merchandizing," Johnson sought to distance the Virginia Company from any imputations of monopoly, an impulse no doubt spurred in part by the fact that the king's grant of exclusive power over trade and dominion could in reality make the company appear monopolistic. Behind Johnson's painstaking definition of the company as the virtuous other of the monopolist lay Bacon's still relevant quip about the actual blurriness of that distinction. Bacon's own preference was to pin the lawfulness of monopolies instead more or less entirely on the basis of what the king in his sovereign judgment deemed most necessary for the public weal. This position would increasingly characterize James's own approach to the Virginia Company. For the time being, the colonizers themselves sought mainly to avoid the infamy of monopoly, a focus that encouraged a succession of innovative experiments in giving the colonizing endeavor as public a face as possible.[26]

Salisbury's first significant effort to put his ideal of state-centered colonization into practice appears to have occurred sometime in early 1606 when he was the quiet mover behind a proposal that Parliament raise and maintain a "publique stocke" for the Virginia endeavor. Possibly his proposal circulated in advance of the March 11 meeting in which a number of members' projects were discussed as solutions to the increasingly contentious issue of supply, the grant of money that Parliament provided toward the costs of government. The problem of supply was one of Salisbury's major concerns in the new reign, and his impulse in dealing with it was consistently in line with the statecraft literature's own emphasis on finding a prudent mean between a kingdom's financial needs and the consent of the people in order to strengthen the state while avoiding undue discord. This balance would prove

---

26. J[ohnson], *Nova Britannia*, D[1]v–D2r, [D4]v.

difficult to establish in a realm still adjusting to the new Stuart monarchy. Over the years, Salisbury's conciliations to the Commons in return for their compliance on various funding initiatives repeatedly irked James, while the secretary's efforts to secure predictable and substantial revenue for the king in Parliament similarly aroused the members' distrust. Salisbury's decision to turn to Parliament for aid in the colonizing endeavor even before James had issued his first Virginia-related patent of April 10, 1606, was almost certainly a tactic intended in part to bring about that royal compliance. The maneuver also had the effect of inserting Virginia colonization itself into this growing tension between king and Parliament. Like the ambiguities surrounding monopolies, the Virginia Company's hazy identification with both Parliament and king placed it in a nebulous position. Standing somewhere between the commonwealth and the king's imperium, the company tried to straddle a divide that was increasingly fraught, harboring considerable perils for an enterprise still struggling for legitimacy.[27]

Although Salisbury's proposal evidently did not attract enough support among the MPs to become a bill or even to receive mention in the House's journal, the ideas it advanced convey strongly the state-centered thinking that drove the Virginia venture at this early moment in James's reign. Edward Hayes and his kinsman Thomas Hayes apparently circulated the proposal under their own names; a letter addressed to Salisbury that was probably originally appended to the tract announced that the "project" was theirs and that they looked to his patronage as someone "whom God hathe extraordinarily indued and made Cumpleat in all abilities which may extend to thadvauncement of most high and honest Causis." As that encomium suggests, however, the Hayeses probably had not devised the proposal themselves but were rather playing the familiar role of casuists for a project expected to raise objections and thus best associated with its true author, the secretary of state, only at a dignified remove. Their offer to explain and defend the plan so as "to leave as little scruple as may be in mens myndes and Consciences" was reminiscent of the similar casuistic part Edward Hayes had played a quarter century earlier for Burghley after Sir Humphrey Gilbert's drowning at sea. Whether for father or son, Hayes's purpose was to defend as godly the

---

27. "Reasons to Move the High Court of Parlament to Raise a Stocke for the Maintaining of a Collonie in Virgenia," 1606, in Quinn ed., *New American World*, V. 168. For evidence of proposals for projects being bruited on March 11, see "House of Commons Journal Volume 1: 11 March 1606," in *Journal of the House of Commons*, I, *1547–1629* (London, 1802), 282–283, accessed Oct. 6, 2014, http://www.british-history.ac.uk/report.aspx?compid=8105.

schemes of his masters. What had changed was not that broader providential backdrop of earnest defenses of divine pathways by trusted clients but rather the striking new primacy of the state in Salisbury's explanation of how English colonizers might best accommodate themselves to God's will.[28]

Salisbury's proposal entitled "Reasons to Move the High Court of Parlament to Raise a Stocke for the Maintaining of a Collonie in Virgenia" was explicit in its turn from Elizabethan private colonization to a state-led enterprise. As the Hayeses wrote in their letter to Salisbury, colonization "by private means" was a "Course som of us have many yeares past ventred both life and substance without Fruite." In the face of such disappointment, they had "devised another waye without offence to publike or private," a "meanes" that "requyreth the Consent of Parliament." The proposal itself offered a number of "motives" for this shift, several of which probably derived from the new literature on the state. For instance, trade was recommended as especially suitable for maritime nations that were also islands, a theme that Botero had expressed with particular reference to England. Likewise, the proposal's more general emphasis on a public stock reflected the great attention that Bodin and others paid to carefully managed public treasuries as "holy, sacred, and inalienable," untouchable for private purposes even by the king. The Salisbury group's concern with the ignominy of Elizabethan colonization received expression in a statement that intriguingly also sought to distance the Virginia Company from the hint of monopoly: "It is honorable for a state rather to backe an exploite by a publique consent, then by a private monopoly." Using the label "Collonies . . . fownded for a publique-well" to describe their state-oriented venture, they explained that such an approach was by its very nature more conducive to noble action than the private ventures of the past:

> Where Collonies are fownded for a publique-well [being? They?] maye continewe in better obedience, and become more industrious, then where private men are absolute signors of a voyage, for as much as better men of haviour and qualitie will ingage themselves in a publique service, which carrieth more reputacion with it, then a private, which is for the most parte ignominious in the end, as being presumed to ayme at a lucre and is subject to emulacon, fraude and invie, and when it is

---

28. Edward and Thomas Hayes to the earl of Salisbury, [Between Mar. 25 and Apr. 9, 1606], in Quinn, ed., *New American World*, V, 167.

at the greatest hight of fortune, can hardly be tolerated, by reason of the Jelosie of state.

The statement neatly summed up the spectrum of concerns that had once orbited around Elizabethan captains. On the one hand, their distance from the queen had weakened the captains' moral authority over their followers. On the other hand, their successes made them appear too king-like, threatening the state from which they came.[29]

Some of the rationales Salisbury gave for pursuing colonization as a state action were directed as much at James as Parliament, suggesting that the proposal either expressed arguments that Salisbury was then using with the king to secure a colonizing patent or was itself meant to be instrumental toward that end. James had not yet issued his first Virginia-related patent of April 20, and Salisbury's message to the king was that a "publique" plantation attempt befitted a realm now sitting squarely under a sovereign with James's own manifestly king-like capacities. At one point, the proposal lamented "discoveries in strange coastes" that were left neglected or prematurely abandoned in Elizabeth's reign in such a way as to suggest that the realm was finally returning to the manly virtue and nobility of "our Ancestors." Halfhearted conquests, like that at Roanoke, betrayed "our own Idelnes and want of Counsell to mannage our enterprices, as if the glorious state of ours, rather broched by the vertue of our Ancestors, then of our owne worthines." Likewise, there was the legal danger that an unmanly idleness in relation to royal frontiers posed to the king's sovereign integrity. The realm's failure to supply colonies adequately and thus to maintain their viability, the proposal stated, "hath in manner taken awaye the title which the Lawe of nacions giveth us unto the Coast first fownde out by our industrie, forasmuch as whatsoever a man relinquiseth mayebe claymed by the next findor as his just property." The prescriptions of *ius gentium* required a would-be sovereign to do more than merely "set foot in a Countrie"; he needed also "to possesse and howld it." Such manly pursuit of possession, moreover, was at no time more pertinent than the present. Even now, the Hayeses warned — again, no doubt ventriloquizing Salisbury's own counsel to James — "the King of Denmarke intendeth into northwest passage (as it is reported) and it is also reported

29. Ibid., "Reasons to Move the High Court of Parliament," 168, 170; Bodin, *Six Bookes of a Commonweale,* ed. McRae, 651. For the argument that islands are peculiarly dependent on commerce, see Botero, *Worlde,* 26–27.

that the French intendeth to inhabit Virginia." The occasion was nigh for James to fulfill the sovereign duty that opportunity demanded, authorizing the colonizers' state-led enterprise as a means of returning to the former robustness of the ancient British state.[30]

With the "whole state . . . ingaged in theise adventures," Salisbury envisioned a feedback loop in which the state was both the principal mover and the prime beneficiary of the colonizing project. Parliament's "publique purse" would allow the venture to proceed without fear of the "disreputacon" of poor supplies, while the colony in turn would provide the realm with natural commodities it was currently forced to purchase from "adversaries, or cowld frendes," a reference to Catholic rivals. Freed from their dependence on such enemies, the king's subjects could limit their trade to "frendes and naturall kinsmen," an arrangement that Salisbury appears to have envisioned as a constellation of Protestant nations who together formed what amounted to a supranational commonwealth, its mutual callings and reciprocity of benefits little different from the bonds of commonwealth at home but only extended farther in space. A vital moral component underlay this shift of trade from enemies to friends, again almost certainly because Salisbury thought of these categories in confessional terms. Evidently imagining trade with adversaries as the equivalent of a perversely friendly intercourse with God's own opponents, Salisbury celebrated the fact that the realm would now be freed from paying hundreds of thousands of pounds to such devilish foes, consumption from whom incurred "the displeasure of God and hurte of the people."[31]

Meanwhile, Parliament's own gathering of funds for the colony was similarly meant to be virtuous. No levies that might "hinder the Comon wealth to injoye the necessaries of victualls and aparell" would be tolerated, nor would they "be raised upon the sweat of the poore, or industrie of the husbandman Artificer, or tradisman." The funds would come from a variety of sources, both involuntary and voluntary. On the involuntary side were fees levied against the "emoderate gaines of those that contrary to lawe abuse the

---

30. "Reasons to Move the High Court of Parlament," in Quinn, ed., *New American World*, V, 169. On the *ius gentium* emphasis on establishing dominion as an essential complement to asserting sovereignty, see Ken MacMillan, *Sovereignty and Possession in the English New World: The Legal Foundations of Empire, 1576–1640* (Cambridge, 2006), 8, 9–10, 11, 12, 14, 15, 18, 25, 47, 48, 62, 63, 69, 72, 80, 87, 105–106, 122, 159–160, 181, 186, 188, 202, 204.

31. "Reasons to Move the High Court of Parlament," in Quinn, ed., *New American World*, V, 169, 170.

poore" — probably a reference to exploitative landlords and masters who violated the Poor Laws. On the voluntary side were the ventures of shareholders whose generosity would be awarded by making no demands on them "without presente aparence of gaine and hope of fwtwre profit." Suggestive of Salisbury's insistence that no single private will would dominate the project, one provision held that "merchant adventuors" were not to be "greater gainers" than other investors, a specification that was probably meant to ensure that the Virginia Company neither became associated solely with the merchant nor risked being tarred by his reputation for self-interested profit making. Instead, the merchant would be simply one of the personae who composed the company's diverse ranks, his role subordinated to the even more honorable part played by the nobility and gentry.[32]

Finally, the entire arrangement was intended also to benefit the king. Perpetually concerned with reconciling the commonwealth with the king's financial needs, Salisbury also recognized that James would more likely authorize the colonizing venture if convinced that Virginia would contribute substantively to his income. Promising James a share of whatever imposts and customs were raised by the scheme, Salisbury framed his appeal in terms designed to cater to the king's own high view of his monarchy. "It would savior to much of affectacion of a populor State to levie monies without imparting some convenient porcion to his Majestie," he asserted, and "That porcion [granted to James] ought not to be so smale, that it showld seame to undervalue the kings greatnes and favour." These rationales, too, undoubtedly sought to sweeten for James the prospect of becoming a true Virginia king. By pandering to his self-perception as a powerful British sovereign, Salisbury strove to reassure James that state-led colonization posed no threat to his kingship, no matter how much the commonwealth also figured in the scheme.[33]

Although it failed to convince Parliament to play the role of Virginia's permanent treasurer, Salisbury's proposal was a powerful statement of his vision for reconstituting colonization on new, more publicly oriented grounds. In his list of reasons why the commonwealth as a whole should "backe a Collony sent owt" from the realm, he had commented succinctly on why a state-centered effort was the natural next step after the disappointments of captain-led colonization. "As fewe are most apt to make a conquest, so are publique weales fitter to howld what is gotton and skilfullor by indus-

32. Ibid., 169.
33. Ibid., 167, 170.

trie to inrich it," he wrote. That is, while captains might excel in making a beachhead, the state was the stabilizing agent that gave a colony true civil bearing. But an even more telling indication of Salisbury's mindset appeared in the very first of his reasons for why a colony should proceed from the public weal: namely, the "reputacion and opinion of thinterprice." In other words, the problem of legitimacy remained as pertinent an issue for the colonizing endeavor in James's reign as in Elizabeth's, and Salisbury clearly saw in the honorableness of the state a way to finally insulate the colonizing venture from the doubts and indignity that so often dogged it. A colony "fownded for a publique-well" was meant to bind such an impressive collectivity of wills behind the venture as to preserve it against all naysayers. Yet, keeping those wills unified would prove difficult — perhaps no less difficult than Salisbury's more general efforts to bring king and commonwealth around to his ideal of a powerful British state.[34]

The Virginia Kingdom and Its Reluctant King

When Zúñiga sent *Nova Britannia* to Spain in early 1609, he perceived the pamphlet with dismay as simply one small part of a broader and rapidly mounting scheme to pressure James into making Virginia colonization a larger sovereign commitment. By surrounding the cause with a greater and greater mass of zealous participants, the colonizers would, in Zúñiga's words, "put the King in the position of taking it in his own hands." Zúñiga likely overestimated the colonizers' perspicacity; even the shrewd Salisbury struggled to steer his various programs, only one of which was the Virginia project, through the gauntlet of an often-suspicious king, a rarely compliant parliament, and ever-plotting ambassadors. Yet, Zúñiga had a point. Even if the colonizers were not actively conspiring to win the king's commitment by going, as he put it, ever "deeper into this business," their impulse to wrap the enterprise increasingly in the mantle of the public weal despite the king's own cautious remove from that endeavor nevertheless had the effect of defining Virginia as a state affair well in advance of James's active involvement. The colonizers' evident gamble was that this rather brazen mobilizing effort would render obsolete the nagging question of Virginia's lawfulness. By forging a colony quickly and building on whatever growing tide of support from the realm they could muster through a redefinition of colonization as an effort undertaken by the

34. Ibid., 168, 169.

commonwealth as a whole, they sought to give Virginia enough substance as an overseas dominion that the king could not easily forgo his responsibilities there. The strategy might yield unexpected results, especially if the king saw such popularizing methods as an excuse in themselves for asserting his own understanding of the company's proper role: as little more than an extra-parliamentary means of augmenting his royal revenue.[35]

Serving king and commonwealth alike, Salisbury walked a precarious tightrope in relation to the rapidly mobilizing Virginia venture. On the one hand, he regularly mouthed the king's own cautious stance "that those who went, went at their own risk, and if they were caught there, there could be no complaint if they were punished." This conciliatory position had first been floated during the Anglo-Spanish peace talks of 1604, and Salisbury had clearly latched onto it as a way to pacify Philip while also accommodating James's own natural timidity in relation to sovereign actions as bold and contentious as the Virginia venture. He articulated this view of the colonizers' private status in his June 15, 1607, speech to Parliament over the *Richard* fiasco, and he even reiterated it with Zúñiga shortly after the ambassador met with James on September 27 to first discuss the Virginia issue. On the other hand, Salisbury's repetition of this ameliorating stance was disingenuous, an example of the prudent statesmanship that his rivals characterized less flatteringly as his "Machivillian skill." Even as he was echoing the king's sentiment in public that the colonizers were on their own, he was acting quietly as their most powerful patron.[36]

Immediately after returning on July 29 from his first voyage to Jamestown, Captain Christopher Newport reported directly to Salisbury, clearly seeing the secretary of state as the enterprise's main mover. Likewise, Sir Thomas Smythe, the prominent London merchant who served as the first

---

35. Pedro de Zúñiga to Philip III, Sept. [12/]22, 1607, in Barbour, ed., *Jamestown Voyages*, I, 115, Zúñiga to Philip III, [Feb. 23/] Mar. 15, 1609, II, 256.

36. Pedro de Zúñiga to Philip III, [Sept. 28/] Oct. 8, 1607, in Barbour, ed., *Jamestown Voyages*, I, 118. The libel about Cecil's "Machivillian skill" was directed at both Cecils and reflected the angry view of Essex and his aristocratic circle that powerful commoners like the secretaries used their influence to curb the nobility; see Pauline Croft, "The Reputation of Robert Cecil: Libels, Political Opinion, and Popular Awareness in the Early Seventeenth Century," *Transactions of the Royal Historical Society*, 6th Ser., I (1991), 47. The 1604 negotiations appear in the journal printed in "Manuscripts of the Right Honourable the Earl of Jersey, at Osterley Park, in the County of Middlesex," in *Eighth Report of the Royal Commission on Historical Manuscripts: Report and Appendix (Part One)* (London, 1881), Appendix 1, 95–98.

treasurer of the Virginia Company, similarly looked to Salisbury for direction. In common with Johnson, who would eventually become his son-in-law, Smythe had long been involved in trading corporations that had also attracted the secretary's interest, and no doubt his office as governor of the East India and Muscovy Companies had helped recommend him to the post of Virginia's treasurer. In regards to Virginia, however, he recognized Salisbury as the final authority. Smythe made his reliance on the secretary clear in a cringing letter to Salisbury on August 17 excusing Newport for his error in reporting too hastily that the ore he had brought back from Virginia contained gold. Newport "resolves never to see your Lordshippe before he bringe that with hym which he confidentlie beleeved he had broughte before," Smythe wrote. All that was needed for the "speedye dispatche" of Newport's second expedition to the colony in search of more promising ore was for "your Lordshipp to approove" it. A little more than a month later, Salisbury would reassure Zúñiga that the king viewed any punishment the colonizers received as their fault, yet at this time he was authorizing their voyages as if they flowed directly from his office as secretary of state.[37]

Salisbury probably had a hand in one of the first significant innovations of the Jacobean venture: the institution of a number of governing councils. These conciliar bodies, which had no precedent in Elizabethan colonization, were the main focus of James's patent of April 10, 1606, that Salibury almost certainly helped to prepare. The patent licensed two royal councils of Virginia, one to be based in London and the other in Plymouth. The first was to oversee the "first" colony based at Jamestown, the other to govern the more northerly "second" colony in which Popham played a major organizing role until his unexpected death on June 10, 1607. In addition to these two England-based councils, each colony would have its own subordinate council that would govern over all immediate matters in the colonies themselves under the authority of the king's privy seal.[38]

The conciliar form no doubt appealed to Salisbury's state-centered sensibilities. Councils had long been used on royal frontiers like the marches,

---

37. Sir Thomas Smythe to Lord Salisbury, Aug. 17, 1607, in Barbour, ed., *Jamestown Voyages*, I, 112. Newport's letter to Salisbury appears in ibid., 76–77. On Smythe's governance of several powerful corporations and his general civic leadership at this time, see *Oxford Dictionary of National Biography*, online ed., s.v. "Smythe, Sir Thomas (c.1558–1625)," by Basil Morgan, accessed Oct. 6, 2014, http://www.oxforddnb.com/view/article/25908?docPos=2.

38. The First Charter of Virginia, Apr. 10, 1606, The Avalon Project, Yale Law School, Lillian Goldman Law Library, http://avalon.law.yale.edu/17th_century/va01.asp.

where since the late Middle Ages they had functioned as administrative and judiciary bodies on which local magnates sat under the authority of the distant king. The new literature of statecraft likewise extolled councils as the natural and vital complement of sovereignty. As Bodin put it, "There is nothing that giveth greater credit and authoritie unto the lawes and commandements of a prince, a people, or state, or in any manner of Commonweale, than to cause them to passe by the advise of a grave and wise Senat or Councell." But what probably most recommended the creation of the Council of Virginia was the Council of the Indies that Charles V had established in the early sixteenth century to help him govern over his Habsburg American empire. By reproducing that familiar governing structure, Salisbury very quickly communicated both at home and abroad the seriousness of the Jacobean colonizing effort. Certainly Zúñiga took note. In January 1607, he observed that the colonies had their own councils and that the "Supreme" one based in London was still "being chosen." The councillors whom Zúñiga singled out for mention were nonaristocratic, Protestant, petty officials who all to one degree or another were connected to Salisbury. They included Sir William Waad, lieutenant of the Tower and a longstanding terror to English recusants and foreign Jesuits; Walter Cope's brother Sir Anthony Cope; Sir John Popham's son Sir Francis; and Doddridge. To Zúñiga, such common and zealous men confirmed that "more insolent councillors than these they could not find in the world." Although Virginia's new council mirrored an admirable form of governance that Zúñiga knew well, the Protestant cast of the councillors themselves spoke to him more darkly of their sinister intentions.[39]

Until it was quietly abandoned at the time of the Virginia Company's dissolution, the Council of Virginia provided a vital layer in the ongoing

---

39. Bodin, *Six Bookes of a Commonweale*, ed. McRae, 254; Pedro de Zúñiga to Philip III, Jan. [14/] 24, 1607, in Barbour, ed., *Jamestown Voyages*, I, 68, 70. On the precedent of marchland councils for the Virginia councils, see David Thomas Konig, "'Dale's Laws' and the Non-Common Law Origins of Criminal Justice in Virginia," *The American Journal of Legal History*, XXVI (1982), 354–375. For biographical information on the councillors, see *Oxford Dictionary of National Biography*, online ed., s.v. "Waad, Sir William (1546–1623)," by Gary M. Bell, accessed Oct. 5, 2014, http://www.oxforddnb.com/view/article/28364, s.v. "Cope, Sir Anthony, first baronet (1548x50–1614)," by Elizabeth Allen, accessed Oct. 5, 2014, http://www.oxforddnb.com/view/article/6251?docPos=2, s.v. "Popham, Sir Francis (1572/3–1644)," by Henry Lancaster, accessed Oct. 5, 2014, http://www.oxforddnb.com/view/article/22540?docPos=1, s.v. "Dodderidge, Sir John (1555–1628)," by David Ibbetson, accessed Oct. 5, 2014, http://www.oxforddnb.com/view/article/7745?docPos=1.

effort to improve the colonizing venture's aura of legitimacy. The council's essence as a royally established entity was its most important feature in this regard. Although James probably deferred to Salisbury the actual responsibilities of appointing the council's members and approving its decisions, the Council of Virginia was emphatically "his Majesties Counsell for that kingdome." Especially beginning in 1609 when rapidly circulating rumors about the miseries of the initial Jamestown settlement led the Salisbury group to devote ever-greater attention to improving the public face of the colonizing effort, most of the publications relating to the enterprise issued forth from the council rather than the company, a simple gesture that conveyed the colonizers' own vigorous insistence that their actions were in perfect accord with the king's will. Likewise, correspondence between the London-based and Virginia-based councils quickly became ensconced as a routine formality, as if proof in its own right that a regular government was taking shape on both sides of the ocean. The first such letter of June 22, 1607, written by the council in "James towne in virginia" to satisfy "your wisedomes" in the London-based council, was self-conscious in its statesmanlike tone and finished with a flourish that appropriately referenced the king: "Wee moste humblie praie the heavenly Kings hand to blesse *our* labours with such counsailes and helps, as wee may further and stronger proceede in this our Kinges and Contries service." This bold declaration of the colony's service to the state was a far cry from the decidedly more plaintive appeal that the "CITTIE OF RALEGH" had uttered in 1587, when it painfully acknowledged its status as the private project of an individual courtier by addressing not the queen but her subjects. It was just this additional symbolic link between the monarch and public weal that councils provided. Missing from the Elizabethan colonizing projects, the Jacobean councils were a first step in signaling the Virginia colony's new, more state-like bearing.[40]

The councils, however, quickly proved insufficient. Confronted by reports

---

40. W[illiam] Crashaw[e], *A Sermon Preached in London before the Right Honorable the Lord Lawarre, Lord Governour and Captaine Generall of Virginea, and Others of His Majesties Counsell for That Kingdome, and the Rest of the Adventurers in That Plantation, at the Said Lord Generall His Leave Taking of England His Native Countrey, and Departure for Virginea, Febr. 21, 1609* (London, 1610), titlepage; "Letter from the Council in Virginia," June 22, 1607, in Barbour, ed., *Jamestown Voyages*, I, 79, 80; "Grant of Arms for the City of Raleigh in Virginia, and for Its Governor and Assistants," [Jan. 7, 1587], in David Beers Quinn, ed., *The Roanoke Voyages, 1584–1590; Documents to Illustrate the English Voyages to North America under the Patent Granted to Walter Raleigh in 1584*, Works Issued by the Hakluyt Society, 2d Ser., no. [105] (London, 1955), II, 508.

of young Jamestown's miserable descent into licentiousness and starvation, the company was prepared to adjust when its first efforts at state-led colonization came up short. This is indicated by its willingness to publish, albeit with subtle editorial interventions, Captain John Smith's deeply unflattering view of Jamestown's 1607–1608 experience in *A True Relation* (1608). Smith was uncompromising in his scorn for Virginia's first local council, which he viewed as riven by factions driven by the self-interestedness of some of his fellow councillors. The editing of the pamphlet provided by one "J. H.," probably the prolific translator John Healey, upheld the institution of councils while accepting that Virginia's residential council had failed to live up to the high expectations surrounding it. According to Smith, the original local council had fallen almost immediately into factionalism, a sinful "disorder" that explained why "God (being angrie with us) plagued us with such famin and sicknes, that the living were scarce able to bury the dead." Healey's emendations left this providential interpretation untouched while nevertheless underscoring the worthiness of the colonizing councils generally. In his preface to the reader, he noted that Smith was "one of the Counsell there in Virginia" and offered the reassurances that "the worst" was "already past" and the action remained under the direction of the "grave Senators, and worthy adventurors" in England. In addition, he carefully deleted some of Smith's narrative, including an account of his own temporary exclusion from the council by some of his fellow councillors, thereby giving greater emphasis to Smith's description of the ritual inauguration of Virginia's first council of state. In the ceremony, a sealed box containing the names of the councillors was solemnly opened, the council sworn in, and its first president elected by the councillors from within their ranks. By preserving this description and cutting away Smith's extraneous account of his poor treatment by his fellow councillors, Healey placed the focus on the council's ceremonial origins, suggesting that the institution held firm even if its personnel had succumbed to sinful division.[41]

The reforms authorized by James's second Virginia-related patent of May 23, 1609, sought to make up for the council's inadequacies by surrounding the existing conciliar structure with yet more elements that spoke to the venture's public integrity. The patent, which was in the works for several months before it finally passed the royal seal, dovetailed with Salisbury's in-

---

41. John Smith, *A True Relation of Such Occurrences and Accidents of Noate as Hath Hapned in Virginia* . . . (London, 1608), in Philip L. Barbour, ed., *The Complete Works of Captain John Smith (1580–1631)* (Chapel Hill, N.C., 1986), I, 24, 25, 33.

creasingly open role in the venture as well as with efforts to secure Prince Henry's patronage. There was a general buildup of momentum even before the patent took effect. A major change introduced by the patent was the incorporation of the company as "one Body or Commonalty perpetual," an elevated legal status that reinforced the colonizers' claim to represent a distinguished group of subjects who mirrored the realm itself in their diversity of callings and public substance. Another significant change concerned the colony's "fourme of government." This preoccupation with the Virginia commonwealth's form evoked the statecraft literature's emphasis on an anchoring structure that held everyone to his or her duties. In recognition that the original council had failed in that end, the new arrangement included, in addition to the local council members who were still to be called to give "advise and graver *proceedinge*," a governor invested with considerable discretionary power.[42]

Ambassador Marc'Antonio Correr, keeping abreast of these changes to Virginia's governing institutions for the Spanish satellite Venice, paid particular attention to what the newly configured Virginia Company might mean regarding the English king's own relationship to the endeavor. On February 17, he wrote to the doge and senate, remarking that James continued to tell Zúñiga "that the undertaking is a private one, and that he cannot interfere." "All the same," Correr continued, "I hear that not only are many great personages in the scheme — Lord Salisbury sending a number of stallions and other animals on his own account — but the Prince [Henry] has put some money in it, so that he may, some day, when he comes to the crown, have a claim over the Colony." On March 26, Correr wrote with news that a governor had been posted to the colony, again tying this development to James's evidently bending will in the face of the colonizers' pressure. "The King although he has frequently told the Spanish ambassador that he would take no steps in this business, yet has this time made up his mind to confer the title of viceroy on the commander, and has given him patents for the distribution of lands subject to his Majesty's authority." For Correr, a governor carried worrying implications of the embodiment of royal authority in Virginia, further proof that the colony was taking on a degree of political coherence beyond James's repeated assertion of the colonizers' private status.[43]

42. The Second Charter of Virginia, May 23, 1609, The Avalon Project, Yale Law School, Lillian Goldman Law Library, http://avalon.law.yale.edu/17th_century/va02.asp; Instructions to Sir Thomas Gates, before May 15, 1609, in Barbour, ed., *Jamestown Voyages*, II, 263.

43. Marc'Antonio Correr to the doge and senate, Feb. 17/27, 1609, quoted in "Events in En-

Zúñiga, too, followed these developments with an eye toward their broader political implications. In his February 23 letter to Philip, he emphasized that a "Governor General" had been selected for the colony: Thomas West, third Baron De La Warr, a onetime officer in Ireland under Essex, a Privy Councillor to Elizabeth as well as James, and a member of the Council of Virginia. Another captain, Sir Thomas Gates, "a very remarkable soldier who has served the [Dutch] Rebels," would precede De La Warr to the colony as the interim governor. Each man would bring hundreds of men and smaller numbers of women to settle Virginia. Called planters in the 1609 patent to distinguish them from the adventurers who would support the colony through their investments in England, these persons were all to swear the Oath of Supremacy to establish their loyalty to James's Protestant rule. The hasty dispatch of settlers was assuredly an effort to render his own negotiations with the king moot, he conjectured, for "These [busybodies] will plant a vast number of people there, because they have too many, and they do not know what to do with them." Evidently the kingdom's supernumerary population had become a tactical advantage, a conclusion that Zúñiga confirmed several weeks later when a confidant shared the sentiment of Lord Chancellor Thomas Egerton, Lord Ellesmere, that "at first we always thought of sending people little by little, but now we see that what we should do is establish ourselves [on a large scale] all at once, because [then] when they open their eyes in Spain they will not be able to do anything about it." Zúñiga was certain that these machinations were meant to break down James's will until he "openly takes a hand in this business." Zúñiga perceived a similar intent in the linking of colonization to the Protestant cause. The Gunpowder Plot of November 1605 in which a small group of Catholics sought to blow up Parliament and kill the king continued to cast a shadow at this time, helping to give the colonizers' Protestant appeal an especially infectious tone of righteousness.[44]

---

gland, 1608," in Barbour, ed., *Jamestown Voyages*, I, 212, Correr to the doge and senate, [Mar. 26, 1609], II, 252 (the date is identified in Horatio F. Browne, ed., *Calendar of State Papers Relating to English Affairs in the Archives of Venice* [London, 1904], XI, 249).

44. Zúñiga to Philip III, [Feb 23/] Mar. 15, 1609, in Barbour, ed., *Jamestown Voyages*, II, 254–257, Zúñiga to Philip III, Apr. [2/]12, 1609, II, 259–260. For the distinction between planters and adventurers, see The Second Charter of Virginia, May 23, 1609, Avalon Project, http://avalon.law.yale.edu/17th_century/va02.asp. Johnson's *Nova Britannia* explained this two-tiered arrangement for membership. "Planters" were those persons "that goe in their persons to dwell there." Any "ordinary man or woman," or child more than ten years of age—almost certainly en-

In describing *Nova Britannia* to Philip, Zúñiga especially noted the recasting of the Virginia venture as a larger Protestant project. He wrote, "They have printed *a book,* which I also send to Your Majesty, in which they call that [country] Great Britain, which, for the exaltation of their religion and its extension throughout the world, all should come to support with their persons and their property." Several weeks later, he evidently heard Bishop Ravis's chaplain, Richard Crakanthorpe, preach at Paul's Cross on March 24. The sermon echoed many of the same Salisbury-ian themes, including that Protestants could rejoice in seeing "a new BRITAINE in another world" and that they should contribute actively to the "honourable expedition now happily intended for *Virginea.*" On April 2, Zúñiga reported that his previous accounts of the "determination of these [people] to go to Virginia . . . always fall short, . . . for they have seen to it that the ministers, in their sermons, stress the importance of filling the world with their religion, and of everyone exerting themselves to give what they have to so great an undertaking." Repugnant to Zúñiga for both its Protestant zeal and its broad-based communication to those both high and low, such an appeal was also alarming in its effectiveness. "They have collected in 20 days an amount of money for this voyage that frightens me," he noted on February 23. "Between fourteen of them, the earls and barons have given 40,000 ducats; the merchants give much more; and there is no fellow or woman who does not go offering [something] for this enterprise." Both the numbers of planters being sent to the colony and the requirement that they be Protestant struck Zúñiga as suggestive of the colonizers' changing tactics.⁴⁵

---

visioned by the company as household units — who went over received "for each of their persons a single share, as if they had adventured twelve pound ten shillings in money." Any "extraordinarie man, as Divines, Governors, Ministers of state and Justice, Knights, Gentlemen, Physitions, and such as be men of worth for speciall services" would similarly go "as planters" and would receive special benefits on the basis of the respective quality of their persons (which would be "rated" by the royal Virginia Council and "set downe and Registred in a booke, that it may alwaies appeare what people have gone to the Plantation, at what time they went, and how their persons were valued"). The "adventurers" were those persons who did not go but who paid the twelve pound, ten shilling cost per share. See J[ohnson], *Nova Britannia,* [D4]r-[D4]v. On De La Warr, see *Oxford Dictionary of National Biography,* online ed., s.v. "West, Thomas, third Baron De La Warr (1577–1618)," by J. Frederick Fausz, accessed Sept. 25, 2014, http://www.oxforddnb.com/view/article/2911.

45. Zúñiga to Philip III, [Feb. 23/] Mar. 15, 1609, in Barbour, ed., *Jamestown Voyages,* II, 254–257, Zúñiga to Philip III, Apr. [2/]12, 1609, II, 259; Richard Crakanthorpe, *A Sermon at the Sol-*

In encouraging this sudden burst of enthusiasm at all levels of English society for an endeavor that the king himself viewed warily, the colonizers were conscious that they were entering uncharted political territory. In the meeting in which they deliberated over whether to publish *Nova Britannia*, much of the discussion centered on the continuing uncertainty of the enterprise's legitimacy and especially the unpredictable factor of the king's commitment. Although they agreed that "justification of our plantation might be conceived" and distributed "into many handes," some of the members advised that the writing proceed under the company's own auspices and "not by publique authorytye," a provision that almost certainly related to perceptions of the king's still-ambiguous support for the project. When some members objected that "this was a lowe and impotent way to convey" the company's case, others answered that "example" could be cited "of other things carried in that manner" that had "wrought the same effect, as a more publique declaration of the state could doe." Hovering over these questions of how the colonizers should present themselves was the still-unsettled casuistic question of the endeavor's lawfulness.[46]

Defending the venture, some of the company's members pointed out, could actually weaken its fragile legitimacy. "Already some of best Judgement," they reasoned, "startle upon the first noyse of it." A pamphlet might disrupt waters that were better left undisturbed: "Ther is much of a Confession, in every unnessary Apology" and "to move scruple, especially of Conscience, wher ther is afore quiettnes and no doubting rather shakes and deterrs, then settles, or confirmes." But the king's will was perhaps the most precarious element of all. A pamphlet could do little to add to the support he had already given, for "the Spaniard hath already seene more publique, and authentique testemonyes, of the States good affection to the Journy, by establishing it under the great seale [in the king's letters patent]: and by seconding, and Iterating supplyes." And, worse, a pamphlet might force his hand in ways that nobody could predict and, indeed, that would undoubtedly attract the machinations of the Spanish king as carried out especially by

---

emnizing of the Happie Inauguration of Our Most Gracious and Religious Soveraigne King James . . . Preached at Paules Crosse, the 24. of March Last. 1608 (London, 1609), D2r–D2v. On Crakanthorpe, see *Oxford Dictionary of National Biography,* online ed , s.v. "Crakanthorpe, Richard (bap. 1568, d. 1624)," by A. P. Cambers, accessed Oct. 14, 2016, http://www.oxforddnb.com /view/article/6587.

46. "Justification for Planting Virginia," before 1609, in Kingsbury, ed., *Records of the Virginia Company,* III, 1–2.

Zúñiga. "It is more then probable," the members warned, "that his Ambassador will forthwith expostulate with his Majestie about this writing, and then it is not conceav'd how far his Majestie wilbe pleasd to avow it [the Virginia colony], which may intimate disavowing." Aware that the king kept the venture at arm's length and might even disavow their enterprise, the colonizers proceeded with a keen sense of the novelty of what they were doing, buoyed by the conviction that their action was godly.[47]

The sheer unanimity of the Virginia venturers' message to the realm suggests the power with which Salisbury's state-centered vision propelled the colonizers in these early years surrounding the issuing of the 1609 patent. Over and over again, the company presented itself as a corporate body that deserved to be seen as an analog of the state. For its remarkably energized justificatory campaign that involved reaching out to men and women, highborn and lowborn, in pamphlets, sermons, broadsides, and other media, the company leaned on a number of writers, many of them learned clergymen accustomed to the casuistic logic of defending lawful conduct from its naysayers. Or, at least clergymen figured prominently among the authors who carried their own names into this sudden flurry of justificatory writings. Though an array of Protestant ministers like Crakanthorpe, Daniel Price, Robert Gray, William Symonds, Crashawe, Alexander Whitaker, Patrick Copland, Samuel Purchas, and John Donne wrote on the endeavor's behalf as recognizable godly advocates, other writers retained their anonymity when speaking either for the Council of Virginia or for the company itself. Johnson, who preserved his own anonymity in both *Nova Britannia* and a follow-up pamphlet entitled *The New Life of Virginea* (1612), conveyed the rationale behind this anonymity in the opening pages of *Nova Britannia*, making clear that the work was to be seen as an outgrowth of the company's own generalized chorus of grave and godly voices. In effect, Johnson framed the entire pamphlet as the casuistical conclusion that an unidentified author reached after weighing his own doubts against the convincing speeches of other company members. During "our last meeting and conference the other day, observing your sufficient reasons answering all objections, and your constant resolution to go on in our Plantation, they gave me so good content and satisfaction, that I am driven against my selfe, to confesse mine own error in standing out so long," the speaker says. One "wise and prudent speech," in particular, given by "a most painful manager of such publike affayres within this Cittie," was the deciding factor: It "moved so effectu-

47. Ibid., 2.

ally, touching the publike utilitie of this noble enterprise, that withholding no longer, I yeelded my money and endevours as others did to advance the same." Here was a glimpse into the company's idealized civic fellowship that left little room for individual wills. Only the collective judgment reached through the sage speeches of members, their own identity irrelevant except insofar as it vouched for the weight of their casuistic counsel, allowed for the resolution to proceed unwaveringly in a truly righteous cause for the commonweal.[48]

In their writings, the Virginia Company's apologists consistently treated its corporate identity as a prerequisite for satisfactorily following God's will. Crakanthorpe referred to the Virginia Company's members as the "many honorable and worthy personages in this State and kingdome" who, led "by the most wise and religious direction and protection of our chiefest Pilot," should give "encouragement" to others "to further so noble and so religious an attempt." In *Sauls Prohibition Staide*, a sermon preached at Paul's Cross on May 28 that was later sold (like most of these works) as a cheap print at Saint Paul's Churchyard, Price asserted that the Virginia endeavor could only amount to greatness because it was "countenanced by our gracious King, consulted on by the Oracles of the Councel, adventured in by our wisest and greatest Nobles, and undertaken ... by many other parties of this Land, both Cleargy and Laity." Gray identified the biblical story of Joshua giving leave to Joseph's "great people" to conquer the Canaanites as a "precept" underscoring the lawfulness of the Virginia Company's own action. He argued that the English were effectively reenacting that scriptural colonizing story when "many of our Noble men of honorable minds, worthy knights, rich marchants, and diverse other of the best disposition, solicited our Joshua, and mightie Monarch, that most religious and renowned King James, that by his Majesties leave, they might undertake the plantation of Virginia." Crashawe conveyed much the same message in a 1610 sermon before De La Warr's departure. "It is more honourable in regard of the undertakers," he declared:

> Where was there ever voiage that had such a King and such a Prince to bee the Patrons and protectors of it? the one to begin, the other to second it. What voiage ever was there which had so many honourable undertakers, and of so many sorts and callings, both of the *Clergie* and *Laitie*, *Nobilitie*, *Gentrie*, and *Commonaltie*, *Citie* and *Countrie*,

48. J[ohnson,] *Nova Britannia*, [A4]r.

Merchants and *Tradesmen, Private persons* and *Corporations?* as though every kinde and calling of men desired to have their hands in so happie a worke.

Indeed, such a remarkable array of supporters suggested that more than human intervention alone was involved. "This I say was done by Gods perswasion," Crashawe asserted, "for what man can be perswaded by a man to undertake a matter of such a nature as this is? "Nay," he concluded, "we dare say, that all who are gone thither ... have gone onely upon the powerfull perswasion of Gods spirit to their consciences."[49]

Despite the stirring nature of this rhetoric of the colonizers' corporate unity, its vigor reflected less righteous optimism than a defensiveness borne from the continually pestering recognition of the venture's frail legitimacy. Major setbacks across the ocean were especially threatening to the venture's shaky reputation. The stranding of the *Sea Venture* in Bermuda in the summer of 1609 stimulated rumors in England that the ship and all of the colony's newly appointed officers, including Lieutenant Governor Gates, had been lost to a violent storm. The stream of providential interpretations that the company put forth to explain the accident were in direct response to the "mocking spirit" of some and the conscience-nagging *"doubt of lawfulnes of the action"* in others that continued to circle around the endeavor, especially when it showed signs of ineffectualness in wrestling Virginia into a genuine civil dominion. God undoubtedly had his own reasons for the colony's many misfortunes, Crashawe observed, but it was the Devil who set in motion any resulting doubtfulness or irresolution. "Satan is now so busie to sift us by all discouragements," he lamented. "By slanders, false reports, backwardnesse of some, basenesse of others, by raising objections and devising doubts, [he] endeavours to da[u]nt us, and so to betray the businesse that God himselfe hath put into our hands." Unsurprisingly given the ongoing concerns about James's commitment to the endeavor, the Devil worked his main mischief by keeping alive doubts that the king was one of the colonizers at all. The project remains "subject to the mockes and floutes of many,

---

49. Crakanthorpe, *Sermon*, D2r; Daniel Price, *Sauls Prohibition Staide; or, The Apprehension, and Examination of Saule; and the Inditement of All That Persecute Christ, with a Reproofe of Those That Traduce the Honourable Plantation of Virginia; Preached in a Sermon Commaunded at Pauls Crosse, upon Rogation Sunday, Being the 28. of May. 1609* (London, 1609), F2v; R[obert] G[ray], *A Good Speed to Virginia* (London, 1609), B2v, B3r; Crashaw[e], *A Sermon Preached in London before the Right Honorable the Lord Lawarre*, I[1]r, I2v.

who say it is but the action of a few private persons," Crashawe complained ruefully. To the critics' jeering question whether a colony that had "so poore and small a beginning" was really intended as one of the king's genuine kingdoms, Crashawe could only answer, "Many greater States (then this is like to prove) had as little or lesse beginnings then this hath." After all, Israel itself began as a mere "*seventie soules*" and yet grew "to six hundred thousand men, beside children, and soone after to one of the greatest kingdomes of the earth." Similar unpromising origins had afflicted Rome: "How poore, how meane, how despised it was; and yet on that base beginning grew to be the *Mistresse of the world*." Virginia might one day stand tall among the world's great kingdoms, but even the most hopeful colonizer could not deny that it was now poor, mean, and despised.[50]

To defend the Virginia endeavor's embattled reputation, the company leaned on its own carefully cultivated persona as an assemblage of the realm's gravest and most substantial members. Issuing pamphlets whose contents were attributed to the "advise and direction of the Councell of VIRGINIA" and whose anonymous authorship reinforced the impression of a disinterested and rightful pursuit of godly intentions, the company presented itself as possessing a capacity for judging the enterprise's worthiness that was simply unavailable to most of the king's subjects. In *A True Declaration of the Estate of the Colonie of Virginia, With a Confutation of Such Scandalous Reports as Have Tended to the Disgrace of So Worthy an Enterprise* (1610), the anonymous author began:

> There is a great distance, betwixt the vulgar opinion of men, and the judicious apprehension of wise men. Opinion is as blind *Oedipus*, who could see nothing, but would heare all things. . . . But judgement, is as *Salomon* in his throne, able by the spirit of wisedome, to discerne betwixt *contesting* truth, and falshood: neither depending on the popular breath of fame, which is ever partiall, nor upon the event of good designes, which are ever casuall. These two commanders of our affections, have divided the universall spirits of our land, whilst (in the honorable

---

50. Crashaw[e], *A Sermon Preached in London before the Right Honorable the Lord Lawarre*, [A4]r, D3r, E2r–E2v, E3v. For an early report in England of the *Sea Venture*'s separation from the fleet, see John More to William Trumbull, Nov. 9, 1609, in Barbour, ed., *Jamestown Voyages*, II, 285. John Ratcliffe, a Virginia councillor and one of the original council's short-term presidents, wrote to Salisbury directly concerning the *Sea Venture*'s disappearance on October 4; see Ratcliffe to Lord Salisbury, Oct. 4, 1609, in ibid., 283–284.

enterprise for plantation in *Virginia*) some, are caried away with the tide of vulgar opinion, and others, are encouraged, by the principles of religion, and reason.

In *A True and Sincere Declaration of the Purpose and Ends of the Plantation Begun in Virginia* (1610), itself purportedly set forth by the "authority of the Governors and Councellors established for that Plantation," the anonymous authors started with a similar nod to the divine origins of all truth about lawful conduct: "It is reserved, and onely proper to *Divine wisedome* to fore-see and ordaine, both the *Endes* and *Wayes* of every action." An enterprise as exalted as the planting of Virginia particularly required special insight, for "the higher the quality, and nature, and more removed from ordinary action (such as this is, of which we discourse) the more perplexed and misty are the pathes there-unto." Therefore, in setting out "roundly and clearely, our *endes* and *Wayes* to the hopefull Plantations begun in *Virginia*," the company intended "to redeeme our selves and so Noble an action, from the imputations and aspertions, with which ignorant rumor, virulent envy, or impious subtilty, daily callumniateth our industries, and the successe of it."[51]

In addition to confronting its critics by asserting a singularly weighty judgment in godly actions, the company also continued its efforts to spread the responsibility for funding the enterprise as expansively throughout the realm as possible. A third royal patent for the colony issued on March 12, 1612, authorized the company to hold lotteries as a way of ensuring a steady stream of revenue when the commitment of the company's own members proved disappointingly capricious. In a broadside published that same year, the company promoted this funding mechanism by offering verses designed to appeal to every man, indeed to be sung to the tune of the "Lusty Gallant." Addressing all "farmers" and "Country men whom God hath blest with store," calling on "Tradesmen" and "Gentlemen" to "venture there your chaunce," the song reinforced the idea of Virginia colonization as an undertaking in which the realm as a whole was engaged. Probably because the lottery was openly acknowledged to be their purview, the "London Merchants" and the "Merchants of Virginia" were highlighted to a degree that was un-

---

51. *A True Declaration of the Estate of the Colonie in Virginia, with a Confutation of Such Scandalous Reports as Have Tended to the Disgrace of So Worthy an Enterprise; Published by Advice and Direction of the Councell of Virginia* (London, 1610), titlepage, 1–2; *True and Sincere Declaration of the Purpose and Ends of the Plantation Begun in Virginia*, 1–2.

usual in the company's broader justificatory campaign. But, once again, the focus was only secondarily on trade and primarily on a statewide venture in commonwealth formation. As a result, participation in the lottery was not a straightforward matter of enjoying a share of the commercial spoils. It was rather an opportunity to engage in a broader virtuous endeavor that had received both divine and royal affirmation:

> It pleaseth God, contentes the King,
>   in venturing thus your store:
> To plant that Land in government,
>   which never was before.

Reminding readers (and presumably foot-stomping listeners) that England was once a "Wildernesse and savage place / Till government and use of men, that wildnesse did deface," the song listed the impressive personages who already purportedly stood behind the cause, cajoling participation through their own unanimity of wills:

> The King, the Queene, and noble Prince,
>   gives courage to perswade:
> The Peeres and Barrons of the Land,
>   hath not their loves dellayde:
> Court and Citie doth the like,
>   where willingly each man,
> To builde up fast Virginias state,
>   performes the best he can.

In short, the project to "builde up fast Virginias state" was already so universally endorsed that contributing to it through the lottery was not a matter of selfish prodigality but the very height of "Countries good."[52]

Although the company's efforts to overcome vulgar opinion and secure a broader funding base centered on galvanizing support at home, other initia-

---

52. *Londons Lotterie: With an Incouragement to the Furtherance Thereof, for the Good of Virginia, and the Benefite of This Our Native Countrie, Wishing Good Fortune to All That Venture in the Same; to the Tune of Lusty Gallant* (London, 1612); The Third Charter of Virginia, Mar. 12, 1611 [that is, 1612], The Avalon Project, Yale Law School, Lillian Goldman Law Library, http://avalon.law.yale.edu/17th_century/va03.asp.

tives undertaken in these years focused on the colony itself. The statist orientation of Salisbury's circle practically demanded that Virginia take form as a genuine polity; as a result, the company's exertions in relation to the young settlement focused on addressing those problems that seemed to hinder Virginia's foundation as a recognizable state. Overwhelmingly, the company approached this task as one of remedying the young colony's tender and ailing body politic.

A commonplace in contemporary discourse, the metaphor of the body politic held particular attraction for Salisbury. He used it, for instance, in explaining to James the so-called Great Contract of 1610. A vivid example of his statist philosophy of marrying sovereignty and popular consent into a stronger whole, the Great Contract was Salisbury's ultimately unsuccessful effort to create a permanent, parliamentary-funded revenue for the king in exchange for James's relinquishing of certain widely despised royal powers, such as the purveyances by which Elizabeth had authorized Ralegh to seize ships and supplies for his voyages. Arguing that measures that "generate greatest love, and cherish greatest hopes" are best for remedying the "disease of want" (a reference to James's meager revenues), Salisbury observed the strongest medicine was of no avail "unless the body be otherwise carefully governed with temperance and moderation." Perhaps Salisbury's own condition as a hunchback, which his rivals seized on as proof of his incapacities and evil designs, helped nourish his interest in how careful governance could strengthen even "a body much spent with a long and lingering sickness." Certainly, Salisbury cultivated in his work and in his remarkably expansive circle a view of the commonwealth as effectively a body on the physician's table, requiring statesmen like himself and the many magistrates and ministers at his call to ward off destabilizing distempers and heal dangerous rifts between the king and his subjects.[53]

Salisbury's client Edward Forset's book *A Comparative Discourse of the Bodies Natural and Politique* (1606), published the same year as the Virginia Company's founding, set forth the "true forme of a Commonweale, with the dutie of Subjects, and the right of the Soveraigne" in medical terms that mirrored closely Salisbury's ideal of a well-governed and carefully tempered body. By Forset's account, the sovereign was to be recognized as "the principall Phisicion for the redressing or remedying the maladies of the bodie politique," but most of the actual work of healing would go to "undergovernours

---

53. Pauline Croft, *A Collection of Several Speeches and Treatises of the Late Lord Treasurer Cecil*, Camden 4th Ser., Miscellany xxix (1987), 299–300, 302–303.

or subphisicions of the commonweale, having under their charge so worthy a subject as the states happinesse, and enabled by their Soveraigne with a portion of his power, to reforme disorders, and rectifie what is perverted." Although Forset was prepared to include all but the meanest magistrates like constables, bailiffs, and jurors under this category of under governors, his envisioned subphysiciar in chief was surely Salisbury himself.[54]

Almost as if taking a page from Forset's book, the Virginia colonizers filled their descriptions of the colony's changing circumstances with references to the evolving condition and health of Virginia's body politic. In early 1610, the Council of Virginia issued an advertisement for settlers that insisted that they exhibit the industriousness and neighborliness necessary for "the foundation of a Common-wealth." Any "idle and wicked persons" were not welcome, for being the "surfet, of an able, healthy, and composed body," they "must needes bee the poison of one so tender, feeble, and yet unformed." Possibly this eagerness to pin blame for the colony's problems on idle settlers followed news arriving from across the Atlantic of the wretched condition of Virginia after the stranding of the *Sea Venture* in Bermuda. Captain John Smith had returned to England by this time, recovering from a severe burn, and maybe it was his description of the colony's disorder that spurred the repeated insistence in these months on Virginia's consumption by sin. William Strachey, evidently approaching his own role as the colony's secretary of state as not unlike Salisbury's office of caring for England's body politic, described Virginia in just such terms, as wasted by an excess idleness that amounted to a disease-like over sensuality. "In this neglect and sensuall Surfet, all things suffered to runne on, to lie sicke and languish," could "it be expected" that the colony would exhibit the "health, plentie, and all the goodnesse of a well ordered State?" he asked. Denying that the colonists' malaise related to the climate or to the country's capacity to support life, Strachey instead blamed their problems on their own sinfulness as well as the misgovernment that set in when their newly appointed governors were marooned in Bermuda.[55]

---

54. Forset, *Comparative Discourse of the Bodies Natural and Politique*, 73–74.

55. *True and Sincere Declaration of the Purpose and Ends of the Plantation Begun in Virginia*, 25; William Strach[e]y, "A True Reportory of the Wracke, and Redemption of Sir Thomas Gates Knight . . . ," July 15, 1610, in Samuel Purchas, *Hakluytus Posthumus; or, Purchas His Pilgrimes: Contayning a History of the World in Sea Voyages and Lande Travells by Englishmen and Others* (New York, 1965), XIX, 47. On the relationship between climate and early modern moral discourse, see Michael R. Hill, "Temperateness, Temperance, and the Tropics: Climate and Morality

This theme of the "headlesse multitude" that naturally fell into squalid disorder when not restrained by the firm hand of governance became central to the Virginia Company's own interpretation of the colony's maladies. "The ground of all those miseries," explained one work published by the Council of Virginia, "was the permissive providence of God, who, in the fore-mentioned violent storme, seperated the head from the bodie, all the vitall powers of regiment being exiled with *Sir Thomas Gates*" in Bermuda. In his *New Life of Virginea,* Johnson similarly described the effect of the storm as not only leaving Virginia's young state acephalous but also as filling the colony with a large number of new undisciplined settlers who rendered the body politic itself unusually disordered: "By which meanes the body of the plantation, was now augmented with such numbers of irregular persons, that it soone became as so many members without a head." The resulting "distemper," Johnson continued, "grew to such speedie confusion, that in few monethes, Ambition, sloth and idlenes had devoured the fruits of former labours, planting and sowing were cleane given over, the houses decaied, the Church fell to ruine, the store was spent, the cattell consumed, our people starved, and the poore Indians by wrongs and injuries were made our enemies." Without a sound governing head, Virginia's fragile commonwealth gave way to sinful abandon.[56]

The idea of the colony as a body politic so badly afflicted by sin that only the sharpest governance might save it provided the rationale for the company's draconian legal regimen known as the "Lawes Divine, Morall, and Martiall." Instituted and implemented between 1610 and 1611 by Gates, De La Warr, and the colony's marshal and onetime deputy governor Sir Thomas Dale, the harsh laws were an unapologetic remedy for those ailments — idleness, disunity, disobedience — that seemed to the company and its colonial leaders as the obvious source of God's anger and thus as the most formidable obstacle to the colony's florescence as a viable commonwealth. Strachey published the laws in London in early 1612 with the explanation

---

in the English Atlantic World, 1555–1705" (Ph.D. diss., Georgetown University, 2013). On the timing of these publications in relation to Smith's return home, see the helpful "Chronology of Events in Virginia, 1608–1612," in Barbour, ed., *Complete Works of Captain John Smith,* I, 127–130.

56. Strach[e]y, "A True Reportory of the Wracke, and Redemption of Sir Thomas Gates Knight . . . ," July 15, 1610, in Purchas, *Hakluytus Posthumus,* XIX, 47; *True Declaration of the Estate of the Colonie of Virginia,* 34; R[obert] J[ohnson], *The New Life of Virginea: Declaring the Former Successe and Present Estate of That Plantation, Being the Second Part of Nova Britannia; Published by the Authoritie of His Majesties Counsell of Virginea* (London, 1612), C[1]r–C[1]v.

that their publication aimed in part to disprove the rumors then in circulation that the colony was little more than a scene of licentiousness, "as if we lived there lawlesse, without obedience to our Countrey, or observancie of Religion to God." Amid the publication's detailed instructions to officers and the long list of capital punishments it prescribed for even small infractions, a succinct statement of the commonwealth ideal that drove this introduction of martial law also appeared. Evidently penned by Dale as part of his instructions to the captain of the watch, the statement captured the corporal logic and the concern with turning all members of the polity to their rightful callings that more broadly characterized the Salisbury group's approach to Virginia commonwealth formation:

> Sithence, as in every living creature, there be many and sundry members, and those distinct in place and office, and all yet under the regiment of the soule, and heart, so in every army, commonwealth, or Colonie (all bodies a like compounded) it cannot be otherwise for the establishment of the same in perfect order and vertue, but that there should be many differing parts, which directed by the chiefe, should helpe to governe and administer Justice under him.

Dale went on to argue that this corporate hierarchy of mutual offices had a vital historical precedent in Moses, "that first and great commander over the Colony of the children of Israel," who in arriving at Canaan similarly "appointed Captains over Tribes and hundreds for the wars, and Elders to sit upon the bench." Thus grounded in holy writ, Virginia's beginnings in a disciplined martial and legal regime were unquestionably lawful and a proven starting point for transforming a disordered colony into a "well setled State."[57]

Although the Virginia Company was remarkably nimble and coherent in responding to the crises of these early years, it encountered a far more devastating downturn in late 1612 when the deaths of Salisbury and then Prince Henry left it without its principal patrons. The Spanish court did not take long after Salisbury succumbed to illness on May 24 to see Virginia as more fatherless than ever before. At least that seems the most plausible way to interpret how Antonio de Aróstegui, Philip's secretary of state, described the Spanish council's take on Virginia to Sir John Digby, James's ambassador to

---

57. William Strachey, *For the Colony in Virginea Britannia; Lawes Divine, Morall, and Martiall, etc.* (London, 1612), A2v, 47.

Spain, that October. As Digby reported Aróstegui's statement to Sir Dudley Carleton, James's ambassador to Venice: "This [Council] helde that very unfitt, that a Companie of Voluntarye and loose people (as hee tearmed them) without the commaunde or interposition of their King, should goe forward with that which mighte in tyme prove of so muche inconvenience to the King of Spaine." The statement was a sly insinuation that, without Salisbury, the colonizers really did amount to little more than a voluntary body of colonizers seeking their fortunes with only provisional promises of James's sovereign protection. Digby was himself a Virginia Company member, and he had kept Salisbury abreast of the evolving Spanish plans in relation to Virginia until just a few weeks before the secretary's death. Digby's own awareness that the Virginia venture had suddenly lost its prime mover must have been acute, given that he was now compelled to report the Spaniards' machinations toward the colony to two new superiors, neither of whom had played a very active part in the colonizing endeavor before, including Carleton and, increasingly, James himself. Among the many adjustments that must have taken place in the wake of Salisbury's death, Digby's alertness to the Spaniards' change in tone on Virginia and his turn to superiors other than the secretary were harbingers of a period of uncertainty for the colonizers.[58]

58. [Sir John] Digby to [Sir Dudley] Carleton, Oct. 10, 1612, in Brown, ed., *Genesis of the United States*, II, 593. For Digby's membership in the Virginia Company, see his inclusion in the list of names included in The Second Charter of Virginia, May 23, 1609, Avalon Project, http://avalon.law.yale.edu/17th_century/va02.asp. Digby's voluminous correspondence with Salisbury about Virginia and his subsequent turn to Carleton and James after the secretary's death can be followed in Brown, ed., *Genesis of the United States*, I, 524, II, 530, 536, 539, 556, 561, 577, 588, 590, 592, 598, 602, 606, 609, 632, 634–636, 656–658, 660, 662, 667–669, 683, 697. Another ambassador who followed Virginia-related news for Salisbury was Sir Henry Wotton, who in 1608 wrote enthusiastically to the secretary while at the embassy in Venice. "There is here much discoursing of his Majesty's footings and foundations in Virginia, which I pray the God of Heaven to prosper," Wotton wrote, "for never to my poor understanding did anything sound more beneficial for us, both for the diversion and amusement of Spain, and venting of our own people, and the commodities that may be hoped from thence, besides the enlargement of the Christian faith, which is the supremest end. And who knoweth but that in time it may come to be a good portion for some sixth or eighth son of his Majesty's? For which considerations I protest unto your Lordship that, if I had anything of mine own (for that which my gracious master doth now allow me is his), I would, out of my zeal to my country, contribute my part unto those colonies"; see Henry Wotton to the earl of Salisbury, Aug. 1, 1608, in Logan Pearsall Smith, ed., *The Life and Letters of Sir Henry Wotton* (Oxford, 1907), I, 431–432.

Strachey provides a sense of the pall that must have set in among many of the colonizers as they contemplated a Virginia endeavor without its most powerful advocate. Hurrying together a manuscript now known under its abbreviated title as "The Historie of Travell into Virginia Britania," he dedicated a copy of it in late 1612 to Henry Percy, ninth earl of Northumberland. Perhaps Strachey considered Northumberland as a prospective new protector for the colony. Imprisoned in the Tower under suspicion of complicity in the Gunpowder Plot, Northumberland nevertheless retained his influence as the scion of a venerable noble family. His political power is suggested by the fact that years earlier, working alongside Salisbury in the secret negotiations to bring James to the throne, he had been recommended as the realm's interim protector. A scholar whose interest in alchemical experiments earned him a reputation as the Wizard Earl, he was also an intimate friend of Ralegh at a time when the Virginia colonizers continued to regard the imprisoned nobleman as a wellspring of useful knowledge about Virginia. In addition, Northumberland's younger brother George Percy had long been involved in the Virginia venture as one of the colony's early leaders. Strachey noted this family connection, observing that the younger Percy had been one of the original sufferers "in all those fatall miseries which of necessity must attend the foundation and structure of new states in so remote and barbarous Corners of an unknown world." As if acknowledging that the principal architect of the colony's infant state had now passed, Strachey turned from the language of statecraft to that of religion, characterizing the Virginia venture as an initially zealous enterprise that had suffered a decline in ardor. "Virginia was a thing once so full of expectaunce (and not above 3 years since) as not a Pilgrimage to a romain yeare of Jubile, could have been followed with more heat or zeale," he wrote.

> The discourse and Visitation of that tooke up all meetings, tymes, termes, all degrees, all purses, and such thronges and concourse of personall Undertakers, as the aire seemed not to have more lightes, then that holie Cause inflamed Spiritts to partake with that: in so much as that might appeare somwhat in wonder to see how manie brought their Free-will-offringes and professed then to throwe their bread upon those waters.

But now the colony's flagging support was evidence of the "repining eye," "falce freindes," and "petulant feares" of a community fallen out of communion. For Strachey, the post-Salisbury era posed the troubling likelihood of a Virginia enterprise with no true friends and a sharp decline in enthusiasm.[59]

Salisbury's death was tricky for the colonizers in part because his name soon became tainted by allegations of corruption and ambition. Old enemies who had quietly nourished their bitterness toward the powerful secretary of state during his lifetime gleefully wrote and circulated vicious libels about him at his death. An inner circle of devoted friends and admirers, including Cope, Pembroke, Johnson, and Samuel Daniel quickly took up their pens to defend him. Yet, his suddenly darkened reputation probably helps to explain why his conspicuous involvement in the Virginia Company up until that time now went more or less unmentioned. A quiet hint that the colonizers nevertheless felt his absence appears in the flurry of rebukes the company's writers directed in these years at the backsliders, those persons "whose unconstancie and irresolution" led them to withdraw from the project in droves. These false friends, as Strachey had called them, probably regarded the deaths of Salisbury and Prince Henry as bringing an end to the Virginia project with much the same certainty that Popham's passing had killed off the short-lived northern colony. Arguing that "Gods secret purpose" was evidently bent on "stirring up the mindes and undaunted spirits of a very small remnant of constant Adventurers," the company's writers all but acknowledged that a major force that had once held the enterprise together

59. William Strachey, *The Historie of Travell into Virginia Britania (1612)* . . . , ed. Louis B. Wright and Virginia Freund (London, 1953), 3–4; *Oxford Dictionary of National Biography*, online ed., s.v. "Percy, Henry, ninth earl of Northumberland (1564–1632)," by Mark Nicholls, accessed Oct. 5, 2014, http://www.oxforddnb.com/view/article/21939?docPos=1; Strachey, *The Historie of Travaile into Virginia Britannia* . . . , ed. R. H. Major (London, 1849), unpaginated dedication. On the Virginia Company's continuing interest in knowledge gained from Ralegh's Roanoke venture, see James Horn, *A Kingdom Strange: The Brief and Tragic History of the Lost Colony of Roanoke* (Philadelphia, 2010), 201–215. Six years after Salisbury's death, Strachey was still courting would-be patrons for the colony, this time approaching Salisbury's cousin Francis Bacon, now Baron Verulam, Lord High Chancellor of England. In his 1618 dedication of his "Historie" to Bacon, Strachey even cast back subtly to Salisbury's era, as if acknowledging discreetly the colony's once-hopeful beginnings. Praising Bacon as someone "who in all vertuous and religious endeavours have ever bene, as a supreame encourager, so an inimitable patterne and perfecter," Strachey reminded the chancellor that he, too, had been a "most noble fautor [that is, patron] of the Virginian Plantation, being from the beginning (with other lords and earles) of the principal counsell applyed to propogate and guide it." Strachey's remark sounded a wistful note about the Virginia Company's continuing inability to attract a powerful patron comparable to its founder.

was gone. If Salisbury had become a persona non grata, Prince Henry was an easier patron to mourn out loud. For Dale, "He was the great Captain of our Israell, the hope to have builded up this heavenly new Jerusalem." Fearing that "the whole frame of this businesse, fell into his grave," Dale warned that "Virginia stands in desperate hazard" unless everyone on both sides of the ocean did their "duties." The life of the venture now rested more critically than ever on its under governors and subphysicians.[60]

One significant source of hope in this period of uncertainty was the sheer endurance of Salisbury's state-centered vision of colonization. A devoted core of his old clients and allies took in hand the task of keeping the momentum behind the Virginia venture going, including Smythe, Johnson, Southampton, Crashawe, and Sandys in England as well as leaders in the colony like Gates, Dale, and Strachey's successor as Virginia's secretary of state, Ralph Hamor. These persons clung to the Salisbury-ian ideal of colonization as a state-led enterprise. A pamphlet issued by the Council of Virginia in 1616 harked back to the incorporating patent of 1609 with its "many hundred Names, both Honourable, and others of all sorts" as continuing proof that Virginia was a "charge" of such "waight" as "beseemed a whole State and Commonwealth to take in hand."[61]

The company also trumpeted successes in the colony itself, especially the peace settlements that were established between 1612 and 1614 with native peoples including the Patawomeck, Powhatan, and Chickahominy. Even this achievement evoked Salisbury's patrimony, for his statesmanlike emphasis on the prudence of negotiated settlements was almost certainly one factor behind the Jamestown colonists' regular insistence that their dealings with natives adhered closely to the legal prescriptions and ceremonies associated with treaty making. Some early leaders like Captain John Smith, who occasionally bristled at the statist directives coming from the company, had scoffed at such formalities, deeming them an insult to James's imperial office because they implicitly treated the native rulers' heathen sovereignty as comparable to that of a Christian king. But the statists responded with their own

60. [Counseil for Virginia], *A Briefe Declaration of the Present State of Things in Virginia* . . . (London, 1616), 3; "Thomas Dale to the R[everend] and My Most Esteemed Friend Mr. D. M. at His House at F. Ch. in London," June 18, 1614, in Ra[l]phe Hamor, *A True Discourse of the Present Estate of Virginia* (London, 1615), 51–52. On the libelous attacks on the recently deceased Cecil and his defenders, see Croft, "Reputation of Robert Cecil," *Transactions of the Royal Historical Society*, 6th Ser., I (1991), 43–69.

61. [Counseil for Virginia], *A Briefe Declaration of the Present State of Things in Virginia*, 1–2.

defense of the steadying power of treaties to hold otherwise fallen men to their duties.[62]

Hamor placed this theme of the moral, as opposed to merely practical, benefits to be derived from a negotiated peace with the natives at the heart of his self-consciously statesmanlike report *A True Discourse of the Present Estate of Virginia* (1615). Crediting Captain Samuel Argall with forging a loose alliance with "our neighbours," Hamor argued that even these barbarous peoples still emerging from the corruptions of the Fall nevertheless possessed the sociable instincts for civil life that drew them to Argall's leadership. They "trust upon what he promiseth, and are as carefull in performing their mutuall promises, as though they contended to make that *Maxim*, that there is no faith to be held with Infidels, a meere and absurd *Paradox*," Hamor wrote. Reminiscent of Salisbury's old disagreement with Essex over whether Spanish Catholics could be trusted to commit to a peace, Hamor's view of the reciprocal bonds possible between natives and planters was in keeping with the emphasis by Lipsius and other writers on statecraft on the strength a state derived from alliances. This dream of a sustainable peace among multiple nations, a view communicated in part by the frequent comparisons of Virginia to ancient Israel and its neighboring Canaanite tribes, also fit closely Botero's argument that colonies might serve as productive nurseries, generating new loyal subjects for kings and God alike. Hence Hamor's great interest in the numbers of warriors each allied nation brought with it, every group of several hundred "fighting men" bringing "tribute of their obedience to his Majestie, and to his deputy there," serving the divine end of making Virginia "a Sanctum Sanctorum an holy house, a Santuary to him, the God of the Sprits, [and] of all flesh." Built on such sturdy foundations, the Virginian kingdom would project itself indefinitely into the future. The baptism of the Indian ruler Powhatan's daughter Pocahontas and her marriage to the Virginia planter John Rolfe figured especially promi-

---

62. Smith heaped particular scorn on the coronation ceremony that Christopher Newport staged with Powhatan on the grounds that it would cause Powhatan to "overvalue himselfe," as though any "heathen king" could possess the same infusion of God's grace that blessed England's own sovereign. See John Smith, *The Proceedings of the English Colonie in Virgini*, [1606–1612], in Barbour, ed., *Complete Works of Captain John Smith*, I, 234, 237. Or, as Samuel Purchas described Smith's position a few years later, it was Newport who "disgraced" himself "in seeking to grace with offices of humanity, those which are gracelesse" ("The Proceedings of the English Colony in Virginia," in Samuel Purchas, *Hakluytus Posthumus; or, Purchas His Pilgrimes* . . . [Glasgow, 1906], XVIII, 497).

nently in Hamor's discourse as tangible proof that the two peoples would now be united in "a firme peace forever."[63]

Despite these hopeful efforts to keep state-led colonization alive, the loss of Salisbury's leadership left a critical weakness in one area in particular. Without Salisbury's busy exertions in making Virginia the viable addendum of a newly strengthened British state, the king's own grudging participation in that endeavor was left with little to sustain it. From the outset, James had clearly supported Virginia as a way to refute the universalistic pretensions of the pope and Spanish king, a point he had expressed unreservedly with Zúñiga even while denying personal responsibility for the colonizers' actions. He also clearly looked favorably on plantations as a means of plucking out peoples hardened in sin and replacing them with loyal subjects. This had been his philosophy, for instance, in relation to the Scottish Highlanders. "Planting Colonies among them of answerable In-lands subjects," he argued in *Basilicon Doron*, his tract on the kingly office for Prince Henry, was the most effective means to "reforme and civilize the best inclined among them" while "rooting out or transporting the barbarous and stubborne sort." Yet, James's determination to subordinate Highland rebels and pacify "Border oppressions" close to home evidently always outweighed his interest in founding a new polity in America. Ardent in his desire to forge a single empire out of his multiple realms, he did not place the American colonies on the same plane as his kingdoms on the British archipelago despite the colonizers' own regular insistence that Virginia Britannia stood firmly alongside those other dominions. Highly symbolic of James's slighting attitude toward the colony was his 1617 "Proclamation for the Better and More Peaceable Government of the Middle Shires of Northumberland, Cumberland, and Westmerland," which sought to banish "notorious ill livers" from England's northern marches to Virginia. Issued at a time when colonial leaders like Hamor were announcing they had successfully subdued their own "bordering" peoples, destroyed the colony's own "incurable members," and brought the colony "to such perfection" that it needed only more upright and industrious people to transform it into a genuine commonwealth, the king's proclamation made clear that he still thought of the colony less as an emergent and honorable state than as a remote and wild territory under his imperium over which he could assert his will as he pleased.[64]

63. Hamor, *True Discourse of the Present Estate of Virginia*, [A4]r, 3, 10, 13.
64. "Basilicon Doron; or, His Majesties Instructions to His Dearest Sonne, Henry the Prince," (1603), in Neil Rhodes, Jennifer Richards, and Joseph Marshall, eds., *King James VI and I: Selected*

Where James's priorities were most likely to clash with the colonists', however, related to his ongoing problems with revenue. Notoriously profligate in an era when the income of the English crown was steadily losing ground to inflation, James had lost not only his busy secretary of state but also a devoted servant to his dwindling finances, a duty that Salisbury had taken on in full in 1608 when he was promoted to lord treasurer. Pinched by his insolvency, facing a recession, and pressured after 1618 to support the military engagements of his new Calvinist son-in-law the elector Palatine Frederick V, James had also become more and more reluctant to call Parliament into session after the bruising collapse of the Great Contract in 1610 and the equally maddening so-called Addled Parliament of 1614. Complaining of the latter's intransigence in satisfying his need for supply, James groused candidly to the new Spanish ambassador Diego Sarmiento de Acuña that the House of Commons was like "a body without a head" and he was "surprised that my ancestors should ever have permitted such an institution to come into existence." Sarmiento, who had arrived in the kingdom in 1613 and who was ennobled as the count of Gondomar in 1617, was in England on yet another quest to establish an Anglo-Spanish dynastic union, this time through the proposed wedding of Prince Charles and the infanta Maria Anna. Set in motion by the powerful English Catholic Howard family, including Salisbury's old nemesis Henry Howard, earl of Northampton, the marriage promised not only a large dowry but also the opportunity for James to play his favored role as Christendom's peacemaker, balancing Frederick's zealous Protestantism and the infanta's Catholicism under his own moderating influence. In relation to the weighty issue of the Spanish match, Virginia was decidedly of secondary importance. Yet, the continuing problem of supply gave the colony a newfound significance for the king, encouraging him to see Virginia in a light that would prove to be the Virginia Company's undoing. In effect, James increasingly saw the colony as one of several sources of revenue that he could exploit lawfully on the basis of his royal prerogative and without having to call a potentially contentious parliament into session.[65]

Writings (Burlington, Vt., 2003), 222; "A Proclamation for the Better and More Peaceable Government of the Middle Shires of Northumberland, Cumberland, and Westmerland," Dec. 23, 1617, in Clarence S. Brigham, *British Royal Proclamations Relating to America, 1603–1783* (New York, 1968), 7; Hamor, *True Discourse of the Present Estate of Virginia*, 2, 27, 34. For James's eager refutation of the papal and Spanish claims to universal monarchy, see Zúñiga to Philip III, [Sept. 28/] Oct. 8, 1607, in Barbour, ed., *Jamestown Voyages*, I, 118.

65. Stephen Clucas and Rosalind Davies, "Introduction," in Clucas and Davies, eds., *The*

A major shift in the king's closest advisers helped to bring about James's changing outlook on Virginia. The rise of George Villiers, the duke of Buckingham, as James's new favorite helped ensconce Bacon as lord keeper in 1617 and lord chancellor early the next year, which explains why colonizers like Strachey and Captain John Smith, seeking patronage for his New England project, reached out to Bacon at this time to protect the colonizing enterprise in Salisbury's absence. An adherent of the same statist philosophy that had energized Salisbury, Bacon had often felt overlooked for positions acquired by his cousin, and he now pursued issues of state, especially the problem of the king's finances, with particular assiduousness. Ultimately these exertions were his undoing. In the parliament of 1620, grievances once again centered on monopolies. When revelations emerged that Bacon had been involved in certifying a number of monopoly patents, James let him take the fall, permitting his impeachment to mollify the members and deflect anger at Buckingham for his own lucrative monopolies. The move anticipated the expedience with which James also increasingly approached the Virginia Company. On the one hand, his growing impulse was to treat the company as a monopoly in its own right, a privileged society operating under his protection and therefore obliged to reimburse him substantially for its continuing life. On the other hand, he was prepared to condemn the company on the same grounds if such an antimonopoly stance proved politically advantageous.[66]

The man who orchestrated much of the king's new machinations in relation to the company was Lionel Cranfield, a London merchant brought in to help the Treasury in its ongoing efforts to solve the king's revenue problems. Bringing an energy to the Treasury once associated with Salisbury,

---

Crisis of 1614 and The Addled Parliament: Literary and Historical Perspectives (Burlington, Vt., 2003), 3. On James's growing hostility to English parliaments and the context of the Spanish match, see Andrew Thrush, "The Personal Rule of James I, 1611–1620," in Thomas Cogswell, Richard Cust, and Peter Lake, eds., *Politics, Religion, and Popularity: Early Stuart Britain, Essays in Honour of Conrad Russell* (Cambridge, 2002), 84–102; Thrush, "The French Marriage and the Origins of the 1614 Parliament," in Clucas and Davies, eds., *Crisis of 1614*, 25–35; and Cogswell, *The Blessed Revolution: English Politics and the Coming of War, 1621–1624* (Cambridge, 1989), 12–20.

66. John Smith to Sir Francis Bacon, 1618, in Barbour, ed., *Complete Works of Captain John Smith*, I, 373–383; *Oxford Dictionary of National Biography*, online ed., s.v. "Bacon, Francis, Viscount St Alban (1561–1626)," by Markku Peltonen, accessed Oct. 6, 2014, http://www.oxforddnb.com/view/article/990

Cranfield became indispensable in increasing both James's and Buckingham's incomes through a series of innovative measures, including cutting costs in the royal household and navy, raising rents on the customs farms, and devising various projects that similarly promised crown profits. One of his enacted proposals was an unprecedented duty on Virginia tobacco that James authorized in proclamations on May 25 and November 10, 1619. An effort to take advantage of the lucrative tobacco trade that had taken off in Virginia during the previous half decade, the tax was a naked attempt to generate extra-parliamentary revenue for the crown.[67]

The rationale that James offered for the tobacco duty spoke to his emerging view of Virginia as a distinctive part of his dominions whose function was narrowly commercial and profit generating, a view that stood at odds with the Salisbury-ian approach to Virginia as an aspiring state. In his *Counterblaste to Tobacco* (1604), James had argued that the weed was a sinful outgrowth of native American society that the English consumed only at great risk to not only their own bodies and souls but also the broader "Body-politicke." In his May 1619 proclamation, he gave a new twist to this view of tobacco's harmfulness to bodies natural and politic. Ordering that the planting of tobacco in England and Wales be ceased on the grounds that it was little more than a "nourishment of vice," he permitted tobacco growing in Virginia and the Somer Islands given that their warmer climates were better suited to the crop and that colonists received "much comfort" from the commodity and therefore should be allowed to grow it "at least in the Interim, untill Our said Colonies may grow to yeeld better and more solide commodities." In other words, a crop that was to be discouraged as a possible corruption to the realm was to be tolerated across the ocean as long as it paid into the royal coffers, the implicit message being that Virginia was valuable mainly as a contributor to the king's wealth.[68]

Cranfield took this logic of Virginia's frontier status and corresponding suitability for profit making one step further. In 1621, James called a parliament after studiously avoiding one for more than half a decade. It was early on in the 1621 parliament, on February 24, that Cranfield (soon to be

---

67. By the king, *A Proclamation to Restraine the Planting of Tobacco in England and Wales* (London, 1619); By the king, *A Proclamation concerning the Viewing and Distinguishing of Tobacco in England and Ireland, the Dominion of Wales, and Towne of Barwicke* (London, 1619).

68. James I, *A Counterblaste to Tobacco* (London, 1604), A3r; By the king, *A Proclamation to Restraine the Planting of Tobacco*.

awarded the title earl of Middlesex for his role in the affair) seized the opportunity of a thinly attended session for a strategic attack on the Virginia public lottery. Sandys, the Virginia Company's treasurer since April 1619, had taken advantage of the assembly to seek a parliamentary-endorsed royal charter for the colony, and Cranfield's move was probably intended to pressure the company into giving up the customary seven-year tax exemption awarded with new patents. In making this strong-arm move, he offered the rationale "let Virginia lose rather than England," a seemingly patriotic concern for the English commonwealth that made the attack on the lottery appear congruent with the parallel complaints in the same assembly over monopolies. Making clear that James himself stood behind this antilottery campaign, Cranfield announced two days later that the king would be willing to suspend the lotteries. Although James had originally approved the company's new patent and even initially accepted the provision of parliamentary approval, he now was convinced that the Virginia leaders deserved to be stymied. Almost certainly it was the intervention of Gondomar that brought about this change of course. Already predisposed to despise Sandys because of his active role in the parliaments of 1604 and 1610 where he had argued forcefully against the proposed British union and the Great Contract as dangerous to the English commonwealth, James was also swayed by the Spanish ambassador to regard the new Virginia leaders as the "roots of sedition." The attack on the lottery, therefore, took on constitutional overtones.[69]

Preventing Sandys and his principal ally in the Virginia Company, Salisbury's old friend Southampton, from prevailing in their quest to protect Virginia over the king's will became a matter of defending the kingly office itself. Another royal favorite Sir George Calvert (soon to become the first Baron Baltimore) explained James's position in this regard in relation to another matter at the 1621 session that aroused the Virginia Company's alarm, a royal

---

69. Wallace Notestein, Frances Helen Relf, and Hartly Simpson, eds., *Commons Debates, 1621*, 7 vols. (New Haven, Conn., 1935), II, 135, IV, 256; Charles Howard Carter, *The Secret Diplomacy of the Habsburgs, 1598–1625* (New York, 1964), 291n. The description here of Cranfield's maneuver and its context in James's pursuit of extra-parliamentary revenue derives from Emily Rose, "The End of the Gamble The Termination of the Virginia Lotteries in March 1621," *Parliamentary History*, XXVII, pt. 2 (2008), 175–197. James called the parliament of 1621 in light of recent Spanish assaults on the Palatinate and Bohemia after Frederick V boldly accepted the Bohemian throne, putting him in line for the Holy Roman emperorship and creating considerable Protestant enthusiasm for England to support him against Spanish aggression.

monopoly on North American fishing granted to Sir Ferdinando Gorges's New England colony: "If Regall Prerogative have power in any thinge it is in this. Newe Conquests are to be ordered by the Will of the Conquerour. Virginia is not anex't to the Crowne of England And therefore not subject to the Lawes of this Howse." In other words, the king was prepared to see America as first and foremost his own royal frontier, a territory over which his sovereign will reigned supreme and whose rule did not require the sanctifying consent of wills and consciences that might more properly moderate his sovereignty in relation to the commonwealth of the realm. Although this derogatory view of the colony clashed with the Salisbury-ian vision of state formation that had motivated the Virginia Company from the beginning, James was also unlikely to suffer any political backlash from a campaign that seemed to benefit English subjects while simultaneously punishing stingy colonizers by removing their principal funding source.[70]

The cancellation of the Virginia lotteries in the 1621 parliament plunged the Virginia Company into several years of factional infighting as that body's once-touted unity of multiple constituencies came undone under the pressure of the king's unwelcome intervention. Once Cranfield prodded James to see Virginia as an almost limitless source of royal income as long as additional commodities were encouraged and domestic tobacco production was suitably cut back, the king became a disruptive force in the company's affairs. In particular, his effort to redefine Virginia colonization as a narrowly commercial undertaking had the effect of setting the merchants and the company's gentry leaders against one another. During the company's 1620 elections, James had lashed out mainly at the hated treasurer, reputedly saying the company could "choose the Devil if you will but not Sir Edwin Sandys." But, in 1622, when the treasurership went to Southampton and the deputy treasurership to another Sandys ally, Nicholas Ferrar, the king made even clearer that he preferred the merchants in the company's leadership.[71]

Southampton acknowledged James's clear preference for merchant ascendancy and responded to it with a defensive appeal that captures not only the growing infighting in the company but also the degree to which both planters and merchants in the company now felt compelled to frame their actions in relation to the king's own demand for profits:

70. Notestein, Relf, and Simpson, eds., *Commons Debates,* IV, 256; Charles Howard Carter, *The Secret Diplomacy of the Habsburgs, 1598–1625* (New York, 1964), 291n; Rose, "End of the Gamble," *Parliamentary History,* XXVII, pt. 2 (2008), 175–197.

71. Alexander Brown, *The First Republic in America* (Boston, 1898), 367.

His Majestie conceavinge that Merchants were fittest for the government of that Plantation in respect of their skill and habilities for raising of Staple Comodities, and instancinge Sir Tho: Smith in whose times many Staple Comodities were sett upp which were nowe laid downe and onely Tobacco followed to which his l[ordshi]p: made Answer that in this pointe as likewise in many other perticulers touchinge the Companie and their proceedings his Majestie had bin much misinformed, the followinge of Tobacco onely and the neglectinge of all staple Comodities have bin the fruits of Sir Thomas Smiths and Alderman Johnsons times but on the contrary ever since it hath bin laboured with all industrie care and diligence to erect Iron-Mills, plant Vineyards nourish Silke and other like, of some whereof they hoped very shortly to give his Majestie good proufe, and that since the time of Sir Thomas Smith, the Colony had growne almost to as many Thousands of people as he left hundreds, good encrease hath bin also of the Cattle: And that with ten thousand pounds expence there had bin more pformed for the advancement of the Plantacon then by Sir Thomas Smith with fowerscore Thousands.

In short, Southampton lauded the gentry as the company's true thrifty leaders, promising profits that the merchants had proven incapable of producing. Smythe and Johnson, who were at one time joined to Sandys and Southampton through their shared attachment to Salisbury, were now clearcut adversaries, the ignoble leaders of the colony's earliest struggling years that the Southampton-Sandys circle now claimed to have left happily behind, forgotten in the sheer numbers of settlers, cattle, and productive industries that the gentry leaders had set in motion.[72]

Yet, James's clearly articulated stance that merchants themselves were best for governing over a colony whose sole purpose was, by the king's own reckoning, to generate staple commodities offered a sharp counterposition to the gentry's claim. The irreconcilability of those two positions led gradually to quo warranto proceedings against the company. On May 24, 1624, the King's Bench decreed that the Virginia Company was guilty of usurping liberties, privileges, and franchises given them by the king and therefore no longer deserved corporate recognition.[73]

---

72. "At A Generall Court Held For Virginia 5 Junii 1622," in Kingsbury, ed., *Records of the Virginia Company of London*, II, 35.

73. For a description of the King's Bench decision, see Kingsbury, ed., *Records of the Vir-*

Even as the dissolution of the Virginia Company brought Salisbury's colonizing enterprise effectively to a close in England, another dynamic taking shape on the other side of the Atlantic suggested that the Salisburyian dream of state-led colonization would perhaps exert its most enduring impact in the colony itself. In 1618, the Virginia Company, not yet divided into factions and still hopeful that it could sustain Salisbury's state-building vision after his death, provided George Yeardley, the colony's recently appointed governor, with instructions authorizing not only the passage of a new land policy and a reform of existing Virginia laws but also the creation of the colony's own representative assembly. Drawing on the language of the providential state that had persisted in the colony since its earliest years, they explained that this "greate Charter, or commission of privileges, orders, and lawes" was required "to lay a foundation whereon A flourishing State might in process of time by the blessing of Almighty God be raised." This move was highly in keeping with the Salisbury circle's broader strategy of steering the king's own will through the greater instantiation of a "flourishing State" awaiting his legitimating authority. Just as the Virginia Company had promoted its own public status under the king through its justificatory campaign in England, so, too, was the company more firmly wrapping the colony itself in the mantle of commonwealth. The highly symbolic creation of a Virginia parliament established the *corpus mysticum* in which the king's own sovereign will was theoretically bound.[74]

Virginia's leading planters knew more or less exactly how to play their own parts in this ritual enactment of the colony's commonwealth. In "A Reporte of the Manner of Proceeding in the General Assembly Convented at James City in Virginia," July 30, 1619, a carefully chronicled testimony of the assembly's first meeting that John Pory, the secretary and speaker, pre-

---

ginia Company, I, 103. The fullest account of the company's dissolution remains Wesley Frank Craven, *Dissolution of the Virginia Company: The Failure of a Colonial Experiment* (Gloucester, Mass., 1964).

74. "Virginia Company; Instructions to George Yeardley," Nov. 18, 1618, in Kingsbury, ed., *Records of the Virginia Company*, III, 98–109, esp. 98–99. The reference to the "greate charter" was made several times during the first meeting of the General Assembly as recorded in John Pory, "A Reporte of the Manner of Proceeding in the General Assembly Convented at James City," July 30–31, Aug. 2–4, 1619, in Kingsbury, ed., *Records of the Virginia Company*, III, 156, 158. For an assessment of the Virginia assembly's rise, evolution, and importance, see Warren M. Billings, *A Little Parliament: The Virginia General Assembly in the Seventeenth Century* (Richmond, Va., 2004).

pared for the Virginia Company in England, the proceedings followed what amounted to a loose script. There were plenty of deviations that arose simply from the difficulties inherent in coming to agreement over what everyone present recognized was a significant founding moment. But the widely accepted ritual elements of the occasion, rather than the hiccups along the way, stand out.

Summoned by Yeardley as "Governor and Captaine general of Virginia," the assembly symbolically convened in the "Quire" of the church, which was held to be the "most convenient place we could finde to sitt in." The members sat as a recognizable state assembly, complete with secretary, speaker, clerk, and sergeant. Acknowledging that it was necessary to "please God to guide and sanctifie all our proceedings to his owne glory and the good of this Plantation," Reverend Richard Buck opened with a prayer. But, as the colony's newly gathered assembly was quick to recognize, not only a heavenly king, but an earthly sovereign sat atop Virginia's body politic. The bonds of communion that the members had just celebrated readily called to mind their obligations of allegiance:

> Prayer being ended, to the intente that as we had begun at God Almighty, so we might proceed with awful and due respecte towards the Lieutenant, our most gratious and dread Soveraigne, all the Burgesses were intreatted to retyre themselves into the body of the Churche, which being done, before they were fully admitted, they were called in order and by name, and so every man (none staggering at it) tooke the oathe of Supremacy, and entred the Assembly.

Pory's description of the opening prayer and oath of supremacy exhibited in striking delineation the assembly's enactment of the sanctifying union of wills that the commonwealth was meant to entail.[75]

Characterizing this unity of wills between planters and king as a "body" in evident allusion to the familiar Pauline metaphor of Christ's redeeming body, Pory proceeded to make a case for the legitimacy of the planters as a body assembled to review and enact laws for the colony. After he read the "greate Charter" aloud, he explained, two of its "books" (the assembly divided it into four books total) were "referred to the perusall of twoe Co-

75. Pory, "Reporte of the Manner of Proceeding in the General Assembly Convented at James City," July 30–31, Aug. 2–4, 1619, in Kingsbury, ed., *Records of the Virginia Company*, III, 153–155.

mitties, which did reciprocally consider of either, and accordingly brought in their opinions." Pory acknowledged that the company might cavil at this step. Would "some may here objecte to what ende we should presume to referre that to the examination of Comitties which the Counsell and Company in England had already resolved to be perfect, and did expect nothing but our assente thereunto"? he queried. Pory answered this possible objection in classic casuistic fashion: Laws rarely accord perfectly with all circumstances, and the assembly proceeded with their inquiry "in case we should finde ought not perfectly squaring with the state of this Colony or any lawe which did presse or binde too harde, that we might by waye of humble petition, seeke to have it redressed, especially because this great Charter is to binde us and our heyers for ever." That notion of reciprocal bonds meant to last "for ever" conveyed much of the great charter's promise. Just as the peace with the Powhatans was envisioned as projecting the polity into eternity, so, too, was the 1618 patent meant to lay the foundations for a Virginia state that would endure through the ages.[76]

Pory's description could not have more succinctly or vividly captured the Renaissance philosophy of state behind Virginia's transatlantic commonwealth. With its sovereign located in England, its God in the heavens, and, for the time being, a body of additional leaders in the company, Virginia's commonwealth would nevertheless be constituted by laws that arose from the particular blending of consciences and judgments embodied by the General Assembly. Here was the "public" with which even the king's will needed to be harmoniously conjoined.

76. Ibid., III, 155, 158.

[4]
FRAMING A NEW PUBLIC
VIRGINIA'S COMMONWEALTH AND THE MORAL CASE FOR THE PLANTER

Between February 16 and March 5, 1624, Virginia's General Assembly met with great intensity, their sense of foreboding captured in the members' utterance that leaving the colony's "sufferinge" unaddressed would be nothing less than a "sinne against God." Hovering at the fringe of the assembly and contributing significantly to its unease was a recently appointed investigative commission, four men authorized by James I's Privy Council to inquire into the colony's conditions as part of the quo warranto proceedings against the Virginia Company. The commissioners, Captain John Harvey, John Pory, Abraham Piercy, and Captain Samuel Mathews, were all known in the colony. Each had arrived or had had dealings in Virginia within the last decade, and they had quickly assumed various leadership positions there. They were threatening, therefore, not because they were outsiders or nameless officials of the king, but rather because they embodied the sudden profound uncertainty facing the colony as the Virginia Company's own legitimacy was thrown into question. The commission's purpose, as Harvey understood it, was to "extract such Maximes and conclusions as whearby that Collony in a fewe yeares may bee brought to the flourishing estate of a kingdome, and may yeeld bothe honnor, and Revenue to his Royall Ma[jes]tie." But that rationale itself captured the indeterminacy haunting this newest phase in Virginia commonwealth formation.[1]

---

1. "The Answere of the Generall Assembly in *Virginia* to a Declaration of the State of the Colonie in the 12 Yeeres of S[i]r *Thomas Smiths* Goverment, Exhibited by Alderman *Johnson* and Others," n.d., in H. R. McIlwaine, ed., *Journals of the House of Burgesses of Virginia, 1619–1658/59* (Richmond, Va., 1915), 21; "Heads of Inquiry in Virginia by the Com[missione]rs There,"

Ever since revoking the Virginia Company's lottery, the king had made clear that he viewed the colony more as a producer of revenue than as a genuine kingdom in the making. The intensifying continental conflict between his son-in-law, the Calvinist elector Palatine Frederick V, and the Austrian and Spanish Habsburgs that eventually would develop into the Thirty Years War gave the king plenty of leeway to justify this newly commercial take on the colony as state necessity, a rationale that the colonizers learned to anticipate with dread. In addition to hinting that he favored merchants like Sir Thomas Smythe as the colony's fittest governors simply on the basis of their merchant status, he had also begun to articulate a new conception of colonies as mere helpmeets of the state. His most recent iteration of this view appeared in a Privy Council act of October 24, 1621, in which the explanation was given that the king's own "princely judgement" had determined that all tobacco and other commodities from Virginia must pass through England before being marketed elsewhere. Such a measure, the Privy Councillors went on, was just recompense for the king's original gift of "verie large immunities and priviledges" to the colonizers. The aim of colonization all along had been for planters to "apply themselves unto such courses as might most firmly incorporate that plantation unto this Commonwealth and be most beneficiall to the same." Not only would the fruits of their labor contribute rightly to the king's income but their direct assistance to his monetary needs also comported with "the honor of the state," Virginia "being but a Colonie derived from hence." Here was a conception of the colony as a stunted polity, or a mere appendage of the mother state, that anticipated Thomas Hobbes's own such argument three decades later. No wonder the assemblymen were apprehensive. The once-touted providential argument that colonies would satisfy God only if they realized themselves as true states or commonwealths lay newly open to question, the king himself raising doubts about whether a colony could amount to a fully realized polity at all.[2]

Faced with the prospect that Virginia might be redefined narrowly as a private source of income for the king as well as a windfall for whichever canny merchants, noblemen, or gentlemen projectors won the right to farm the customs generated by the colony's commodities, the assemblymen pushed back with their own understanding of Virginia's essence. Perceiving

---

April (?), 1623, in Susan Myra Kingsbury, ed., *The Records of the Virginia Company of London*, 4 vols. (Washington, D.C., 1906–1935), IV, 88.

2. W. L. Grant and James Munro, eds., *Acts of the Privy Council of England; Colonial Series*, I, *A.D. 1613–1680* (Hereford, England, 1908), 48–49.

their interests as lying fundamentally in Virginia's continuing status as an ascendant commonwealth, they invoked a moral persona meant to replace the drooping legitimacy of the company. This figure was the planter, whom the colonists now identified as the natural partner to God and king in the planting of a viable civil and ecclesiastical polity. The assemblymen made clear their new reliance on the planter as a legitimating figure in the flurry of writings they sent to England as the product of their 1624 deliberations. One of these works, entitled "A Breife Declaration of the Plantation of *Virginia* during the First Twelve Yeares, When Sir *Thomas Smith* Was Governor of the Companie, and Downe to This Present Tyme," purported to be by the "Ancient Planters nowe remaining alive in *Virginia*." The latter reference was to settlers who had arrived in the colony's founding years and who had miraculously "through the blessinge of God uppon our willinge labors" survived the conditions that had early on given Virginia a reputation for pervasive and gruesome mortality. The implication in attributing the work to these survivors drew from a familiar providential logic: their very endurance against local afflictions and the long-term experience they had gained across the ocean gave their relation of the colony's conditions a weight and trustworthiness based on nothing less than God's own manifest regard for their efforts.[3]

A further hint of the moral significance that was now claimed for the planter appeared in the answers that Governor Francis Wyatt and the rest of the assembly provided in response to the commissioners' questions, especially their last two queries: "What hopes may truly and really bee conceived of this Plantation[?]" and "Which bee the directest meanes to attaine to these hopes[?]" In answer to the first question, the assemblymen declared Virginia to be fruitful beyond compare. In a shrewd gesture to James's responsibilities, they asserted, there was no "country more worthie of a Princes care and supportance," suggesting a far more significant role for the king than simply welcoming in tax receipts. But it was in response to the latter question about how Virginia's promise was to be realized that the planters' own office took center stage, as though the actualizing of their duties was the fundamental reason for the king to fulfill his. The company went conspicuously unmentioned, its role ambiguous except perhaps as the unnamed

3. "A Breife Declaration of the Plantation of *Virginia* duringe the First Twelve Yeares, When Sir *Thomas Smith* Was Governor of the Companie, and Downe to This Present Tyme; By the Ancient Planters Nowe Remaining Alive in *Virginia*," n.d., in McIlwaine, ed., *Journals of the House of Burgesses of Virginia, 1619–1658/59*, 36.

supplier of the ships that Wyatt and the company now depicted in a very particular way: as brimming with healthy, well-provisioned, highly skilled, industrious, and war-ready persons. These were the planters: the people whose hard work at their vocations, whose regular marches and raids as a "runninge armye" to "keepe the Indians from settlinge on any place that is neere us," whose "blessed" relationship with God as evidenced by their growing numbers and enhanced ability to sustain themselves, and whose eventual movement toward the "mountaines" and "Seas" in pursuit of further sources of sustenance and wealth would gradually convert Virginia into "a riche and flowrishinge Kingedome." In short, the planter was asserting his place as Virginia's providential actor of greatest consequence, a position that ostensibly guided how even the king should understand his American obligations.[4]

The circumstances that inspired this robust brandishing of the planter's moral office had been developing for almost a decade and lay in particular in the machinations of two especially assiduous projectors. Lionel Cranfield, the merchant who would soon serve the king in challenging the Virginia Company's public lottery, and Abraham Jacob, a merchant who along with his son was appointed in 1618 collector of tobacco customs for life, epitomized the creative financiering and subtle moral argumentation that dramatically transformed the reputation of projectors in these years. Whereas projects in the Tudor era had conveyed resolute actions in pursuit of godly ends, they acquired almost wholly worldly connotations in James's reign. A mounting tidal wave of proposals that promised to solve the king's financial woes while personally advancing the projectors themselves stimulated dark thoughts of the commonwealth sinking under the schemes of unscrupulous men. Perhaps with Cranfield or his similarly busy mentor Sir Arthur Ingram in mind, Ben Jonson satirized these arrangements in *The Divell Is an Asse* (1616), a send-up of modern vices in which projects were defined quite simply as "Waies to enrich men, or to make 'hem great." One of the play's main characters, a projector named Meer-craft, wheedles a gentleman with the promise that "I have a Project to make you a Duke, now," and reassures his anxious conscience with the soothing pledge that the scheme comports with the "true reason of state." The troubling joke behind his statist rationalization was that the projectors' proposals inevitably were justified on the

---

4. The Commissioners to Sir Francis Wyatt and the General Assembly, n.d., in McIlwaine, ed., *Journals of the House of Burgesses of Virginia, 1619–1658/59*, 37, "The Generall Assemblies Replie to Those Foure Propositions Made unto Them by the Com[m]ission[e]rs to Bee Presented to the Lordes of His Ma[jes]ties Most Hono[ra]ble Privie Counsell," Mar. 2, 1623, 38–39.

basis of such newly resonant principles as the state's necessities or the king's interest.[5]

The latter basis for projects had particular significance for the projectors. Building on the medieval Latin usage that distinguished *interesse* from *usura* as just recompense for a lawful debt rather than heinous sin, the idea that the king's own private interest needed to be taken into account any time God's blessings rained down on the commonwealth had an air of almost indisputable propriety. Yet, the projector was often seen as pushing this casuistic reasoning dangerously far into the realm of self-serving sophistry, losing sight of the close marriage between the state and commonwealth that Robert Cecil, earl of Salisbury, for instance had promoted earlier. One minister reportedly pointed incriminatingly at Cranfield while giving a sermon before the king that treated the Devil as the very incarnation of the overly worldly monarch surrounded by grasping officers. Although James was allegedly amused by the scolding directed at his treasurer, Cranfield sat with his hat pulled down low as the preacher railed "That man — that man that makes himself rich and his master poor, he is a fit treasurer for the devil." Notably the minister did not condemn the king for expecting to be rich himself. Instead, the opprobrium here was directed at the projector who cynically twisted the sovereign's acceptable measure of self-interest into a profit-making scheme that threatened the entire commonwealth. That same message would underlie the Virginians' argument for a planter commonwealth for decades to come.[6]

As a result of associations with sin, tobacco was an easy target for the projectors' claim that they were merely righting a moral balance by ensuring that the king received his due as his subjects profited from the crop. As one Virginia Company official conceded, conscionable men could scarcely object

5. Ben Johnson, *The Divell Is an Asse; A Comedie Acted in the Yeare, 1616* . . . (London, 1641), 14, 16. On Cranfield and Jacob, see *Oxford Dictionary of National Biography*, online ed., s.v. "Cranfield, Lionel, first earl of Middlesex (1575–1645)," by Michael J. Braddick, accessed Jan. 23, 2015, http://www.oxforddnb.com/view/article/6609, s.v. "Jacob, Sir John, first baronet (*bap.* 1597, d. 1666)," by J. T. Peacey, accessed Jan. 23, 2015, http://www.oxforddnb.com/view/article/58113.

6. Godfrey Goodman, *The Court of King James the First* . . . , ed. John S. Brewer (London, 1839), II, 203n. On the changing conception of interest at this time, see Craig Muldrew, *The Economy of Obligation: The Culture of Credit and Social Relations in Early Modern England* (New York, 1998), 114. In describing the growing emphasis on interest, Louis LeRoy offered the wry explanation, "Men have now invented interest in steed of usury, which is of divers sorts, according to divers places: for they limite in some places five for a hundred, in other places tenne or twelve upon the hundred. The banquers or Marchants set it as high as they can" (LeRoy, *Aristotles Politiques; or, Discourses of Government* . . . [London, 1598], 52).

if the king chose to render a "superfluous weede" that was "fit to be regulated" to "good, just, honorable and publique endes." Cranfield knew this moral logic well. He undoubtedly played a significant role in bringing about James's proclamation of December 30, 1619, that forbade domestic tobacco production on the grounds of the crop's vicious character. His intense preoccupation with his fellow subjects' tobacco profits strongly suggests that he saw them as so many untoward rewards whose impropriety should in a justly ordered world be put in service to lessening the king's financial difficulties. That helps to explain the otherwise obscure reasoning by which Cranfield somehow convinced a group of customs farmers who had been awarded a three-year tobacco contract in 1615 to give up some of their lucrative profits of £4,000 a year as "Interest" to the king despite their patent's original silence on the issue. Much the same rationale probably underlay the remarkable boldness with which Jacob in July 1619 seized a large shipment of tobacco arriving from Virginia and refused to give it up unless the Virginia Company paid a substantial twelve pence per pound in royal customs. As if anticipating this assertive move, Cranfield had carefully calculated the amount the king had sacrificed as a result of the seven-year exemption from taxes that the company enjoyed as one of the privileges awarded in its 1612 patent. Reckoning that between 1616 and 1618 tobacco production in the colony had surged from twenty-three hundred pounds to almost fifty thousand pounds, he estimated that the abatement approached the not inconsiderable sum of £2,000. Such a deficit was again one that he and Jacob evidently viewed in moral and not just financial terms, as more or less unscrupulous wealth that would be better put to aiding the king than merely lining the pockets of subjects who persisted in encouraging what James's 1619 proclamation had labeled the "spreading evill" of tobacco.[7]

The political conflict between the Virginia Company and the Treasury instigated by "mr Jacobbs deteyninge a wholl years harvest" would not be resolved until December, when Attorney General Sir Henry Yelverton finally

---

7. "Proposals of Sir Nathaniel Rich," [circa 1623], in "Lord Sackville's Papers Respecting Virginia, 1613–1631, II," *American Historical Review,* XXVII (1922), 754; "Notes of Cranfield, December 25, 1616 (?)," in "Lord Sackville's Papers Respecting Virginia, 1613–1631, I," *American Historical Review,* XXVII (1922), 522; By the king, *A Proclamation to Restrain the Planting of Tobacco in England and Wales* (London, 1619). For Cranfield's calculations of Virginia tobacco production, see "Allowance for Customs Duties Not Levied, December 24, 1611–1618," in "Lord Sackville's Papers Respecting Virginia, 1613–1631, I," *American Historical Review,* XVII (1922), 497–498.

rendered his opinion that, even in light of the expiration of the company's original tax-exempt status, its patent freed it from all but a six pence a pound subsidy. But, by that time, Jacob, with Cranfield's advice, had devised a new scheme: a tobacco contract that promised the king not only a regular impost of eighteen pence per pound but also a steady rent of £8,000 per year, a momentous fee that the tobacco cultivators would need to pay down before they could begin to profit from the crop themselves. Cranfield endorsed the plan succinctly as "Tobacko: Mr. Jacobs new offer of 8000 *l.* per annum," perhaps already imagining the proposal's career over the next two decades as the blueprint for a dizzying array of future attempts to secure such a lucrative agreement. Even more satisfying than customs for profiting the king through his subjects' ill-gotten income, tobacco contracts would become the preferred arrangement for redeeming them both.[8]

For company officials and planters, the proposed tobacco contracts were invitations to enter into a distinctly sinister bond. Years later, after the convulsions introduced by Cranfield and Jacob's innovations had contributed to the company's demise, Sir Edwin Sandys and his allies would refer to the two men and certain unspecified "other[s]" as the malicious instigators of "severall projects concerning Tobacco" who, "under colour of advancing proffitt to his Ma[jes]tie," nearly "ruyned the Plantation" if "Gods assistance and the constancy of the Companie" had not intervened. Likewise, when in 1621 Jacob sought to clarify the terms of his proposed tobacco monopoly with the company, Sandys and his colleagues wrote to the Privy Council that they "could not from him understand any possible means of accomodacon butt such as would breed the utter ruyne and overthrowe of ye Plantacon to w[i]ch out of their bounden duety to god and his Ma[jes]ty they may not agree." Leaders in the colony were no less disconcerted. Writing in early 1623, when for a brief mistaken moment they believed the king had abandoned his quest for a tobacco contract and was "pleased to extend his princely care for the establishm[en]t of this Colony," they referred back to their encounter with the projectors as though they had just wrangled with

---

8. "At a Great and Generall Quarter Court Houlden for Virginia on Wedensday the 17th of Novemb[er] 1619," in Kingsbury, ed., *Records of the Virginia Company*, I, 272; "Offer of Abraham Jacob for the Farm of the Tobacco Duties, December (?), 1619," in "Lord Sackville's Papers Respecting Virginia, 1613–1631, I," *American Historical Review*, XVII (1922), 524. For the company's struggle with Jacob over the seized tobacco, see Kingsbury, ed., *Records of the Virginia Company*, I, 245, 258–259, 272, 275, 276–277, 281–284; Grant and Munro, eds., *Acts of the Privy Council of England*, I, 27–28.

demons. Attesting to the "great prejudice that this colony hath receaved by divers contracts made wholy w[i]thout our consents or pryvity, and sett on foote by avaritious and unconscionable men intendinge their owne private lucre and gaine," they bemoaned "the snares whereof wee have continually for these six yeares ben intangled and misirabley p[er]plexed to the generall discouragm[en]t of all men, and hinderance of the proceedings of this Plantation." However, the truly insidious character of the tobacco contracts lay in their co-optive nature. Even while threatening the vision of a godly commonwealth on which the colony had thus far rested, they presented themselves as the only viable solution for the colony's persistent problem of meager resources.[9]

This perilous choice between holding true to Virginia's ascendancy as a kingdom and giving in to a more mundane view of the colony as a producer of wealth became especially pressing after Cranfield took advantage of the 1621 parliament to dissolve the company's public lotteries. Sandys, who had replaced Smythe as treasurer in April 1619, spent the months when Jacob held Virginia's tobacco hostage reminding everyone who would listen that the company's purpose had never been to cultivate a marketable commodity but was always focused on the nobler end of a "foundation Laid for a future great state." In a general court that met on June 5, 1622, however, Sandys himself was the reluctant messenger of a striking new proposal by Lord Treasurer Cranfield, now earl of Middlesex, that the Virginia Company and the Somers Island Company enter into their own contract with the king, an arrangement that offered them the tantalizing privilege of enjoying the "sole Importation of Tobacco" into England and Ireland in return for a substantial "advanceinge of his Ma[jes]t[ie]s proffitt and Revenue." With the smooth-tongued Ingram at his side, Sandys lamented the "uncertainty of this deceaveable weede Tobacco w[hi]ch served neither for necessity nor for ornament to the life of man, but was founded onely upon an humor w[hi]ch might soone vanish into smoake and come to nothing." He then conceded that he had settled for reaching the most favorable deal he could with the crown, implicitly acknowledging that the king was prepared to contract with private men if the company itself did not enter into this devil's bargain.[10]

---

9. "Discourse of the Old Company, April (?), 1625," in Kingsbury, ed., *Records of the Virginia Company*, IV, 532, "At a Courte Helde the 24th: October 1621," I, 531, Council in Virginia to Henry Viscount Mandevil[l]e, Mar. 30, 1623, IV, 69.

10. "At a Great and Generall Quarter Court Houlden for Virginia on Wednesday the 17th

The battles that erupted over Sandys's prudentiary move to preserve the colony by relenting to the king's projectors were ferocious, dividing the company into warring factions. On one side were Sandys and powerful allies like Henry Wriothesley, earl of Southampton, who regarded the contract as the only way to save the plantation; on the other, the merchants Smythe and Alderman Robert Johnson who, together with their new allies Robert Rich, second earl of Warwick, and his cousin Sir Nathaniel Rich, viewed the contract as so detrimental that they instigated the investigation into the colony's conditions as a means of regaining control over a once-noble colonizing cause now suddenly adrift. Reminding one commentator of the "Guelfs and Gebelines" who divided Italy into warring camps between supporters of the Holy Roman emperor and the pope's clientele, the factions gave James plenty of grounds for entering into the quo warranto proceedings that would dissolve the company on May 24, 1624. But the damage had already been done. From defending the colony as a true commonwealth to acquiescing to its status as a mere contract, Sandys had played his own grudging part in diluting the Renaissance vision of colonization as an ages-old project in building new states.[11]

Yet, Sandys also knew that vision intimately, and one of his preoccupations during these years points toward why the persona of the planter would figure so prominently in the colonists' own efforts to cling to the colony's civil integrity. In his speeches after becoming the company's treasurer, he

---

of Novemb[er] 1619," in Kingsbury, ed., *Records of the Virginia Company*, I, 269, "At a Generall Court Held for Virginia 5° Junij 1622," II, 36. Although Sandys's motives are murky, perhaps his about-face related in part to the intensification of political and religious tensions in 1622. The confessional atmosphere that summer was especially fraught, as militant Protestants and James I faced off over the Palatine crisis and as negotiations over the Spanish match stimulated fears of empowered Catholics and Spaniards in the realm. By the parliament of 1624, Sandys had entered into the strange political partnership with Prince Charles and George Villiers, first duke of Buckingham, known as the "patriot" coalition, and maybe Sandys at this point was already factoring the continental war into his calculus about how best to meet the king's demands in relation to the Virginia Company. On the charged atmosphere of 1622–1623 and Sandys's peculiar partnership with Charles and Buckingham, see Thomas Cogswell, *The Blessed Revolution: English Politics and the Coming of War, 1621–1624* (Cambridge, 1989), 20–36, 137–165.

11. John Chamberlain to Sir Dudley Carleton, July 26, 1623, in Norman Egbert McClure, ed., *The Letters of John Chamberlain* (Philadelphia, 1939), II, 509. On the Virginia Company's factionalism and dissolution, see Wesley Frank Craven, *Dissolution of the Virginia Company: The Failure of a Colonial Experiment* (Gloucester, Mass., 1964), 220–250; and Theodore K. Rabb, *Jacobean Gentleman: Sir Edwin Sandys, 1561–1629* (Princeton, 1998), 356–371.

insisted regularly on the need for the colony to have a firmer "Publique." This theme of a solid public captured Sandys's sense of what primarily distinguished the projectors' false view of Virginia from the true one that the king himself should embrace. Using the term much as his old patron Salisbury had done in his 1606 proposal to Parliament, Sandys deemed the public a precondition for any civil polity. It was that honorable repository of wealth that should be held sacred from any mere private interest, including the king's. At the same time, by its very essence as a nutritive foundation for the commonwealth as a whole, the public would ultimately benefit all its divers members. Such reasoning no doubt resonated all the more easily in relation to colonies because of how vexed the issue had become in the realm itself, where the king's quest for extra-parliamentary revenue placed the public's fragility in sharp relief. As Sandys stated in one speech to the Virginia Company's general court, "The maintayning of the publiq in all estates [that is, states]" is "of noe lesse importance, even for the benefitt of the Private, then the roote and body of a Tree are to the perticuler branches." Given that Sandys was also writing to Cranfield at this time about the importance of tending to "the Publick" for "that Commonwealth," it seems reasonable to infer that his arboreal analogy for Virginia's public was directed at least in part to the king and his most ardent treasurer, a hint in effect that a well-nurtured tree yielded better fruits than a roughly treated sapling.[12]

The colonists' ideal of the planter operated in close tandem with this notion of the colony's public. The very existence of a public, with its promise of supporting the exertions of one generation of inhabitants after the next, conveyed a community's determination to exist as an autonomous polity, or what one Virginia planter described as "a commonwealth able to maintaine it selfe by itselfe." Of course, a public was not irrelevant to trading companies, which also relied on public stocks to preserve their own investments. However, the vehemence with which Virginia's leaders would later use the term "factorie for trade" to denounce the new Maryland colony for its encroachment on Virginia's historical borders suggests their sensitivity to the

12. "At a Great and Generall Quarter Court Houlden for Virginia on Wedensday the 17th of Novemb[er] 1619," in Kingsbury, ed., *Records of the Virginia Company*, I, 267–268; Sir Edwin Sandys to Sir Lionel Cranfield, Sept. 9, 1619, in "Lord Sackville's Papers Respecting Virginia, 1613–1631, I," *American Historical Review*, XXVII (1922), 498. On Sandys's initially close reliance on and growing independence from Salisbury's patronage both before and after his elevation to the peerage, see Rabb, *Jacobean Gentleman*, 17–19, 41, 46, 52, 53, 61, 63, 65, 78, 98, 100, 101, 111–113, 128–129, 140–173.

connotations of purely commercial activity that the king's tobacco contracts had so expediently applied to them. To the colonists' dismay, English monarchs showed no immediate interest in desisting from such contracts, which, after James's unexpected death in March 1625, Charles I sought just as ardently as his father had done. The colonists remained acutely defensive about their civil status, unsure of what the future would hold.[13]

The challenge faced by Virginians in the 1620s and 1630s lay in establishing compellingly that the moral bonds that tied the king to the Virginia plantation obliged him to play the part of the colony's monarch and not simply its prime merchant. Herein lay the value of the planter. Associated broadly with the planting of new commonwealths and not yet narrowly with the cultivation of marketable goods, the planter carried a moral weight that was not easily dismissed. This is not to say that he was immune from the desacralizing accusations that so characterized politics in this age of endless efforts to pin down lawfulness and expose error. On the contrary, the very emphasis given to his role in complementing the king's sovereignty in America made him a target for such charges. He attracted especially the contempt of nonconforming Protestants and wary Catholics who saw in his dishonor a bracing field for defending their own claims to godliness. Such confessional tilting made the persona of the planter itself highly contested, especially as English sectarians and Catholics donned the planter's mantle in their own colonizing expeditions. But these skirmishes over who properly fulfilled the planter's duties were but the backdrop to the larger engagement over the problem of defending the planter commonwealth as a genuine polity. That goal dominated Virginia's politics in these decades, often pitting planters against their king though with the rather paradoxical objective of establishing that their interests were, far from separable, the mutually constitutive parts of a divinely favored bond.

The Renaissance history of justifying English colonization in Virginia had entered into a third and final phase. The tie between planter and king had become the key focus of contestation. Although both the Elizabethan ideal of providentially attuned captains and Salisbury's conception of colonization as a state-centered project continued to make their respective influences felt,

13. John Bargrave, "A Forme of Polisie to Plante and Governe Many Families in Virginea, Soe as It Shall Naturally Depend one the Soveraignetye of England," before Dec. 7, 1623, in Kingsbury, ed., *Records of the Virginia Company*, IV, 418; "A Declaration Shewing the Illegality and Unlawfull Proceedings of the Patent of Maryland," in William Hand Browne, ed., *Archives of Maryland*, V, *Proceedings of the Council of Maryland, 1667–1687/8* (Baltimore, 1887), 180.

the planter now stood at the heart of the struggle over the meaning of colonization. His place there was not merely coincidental but rather the result of deliberate moral argumentation as well as often-forceful political actions that intensified over time. Already by the mid-1620s, the colonists upheld their office as planters with a brash sense of the expansive liberties that such a weighty calling entailed. But, the challenge still seemed a fairly straightforward one of convincing the king to see his office and that of planters, not as adversarial, but as exquisitely conjoined. By the late 1620s and early 1630s, as Virginia's troubles increasingly seemed to reflect England's own fracturing political environment in the aftermath of Charles's Forced Loan of 1626–1627, a new factor crept in to this already tense relationship. Planters grew fearful that the king's will was no longer the obliging one necessary for commonwealth but an absolute one hardened against true complaisance. Eager for their king to commit to his role as Virginia's imperial monarch, they were nevertheless insistent that his sovereignty be wedded to their own exertions as planters. An imperial king made for the commonwealth's very best husband, but only if he steered clear of the absolute will that was the hallmark of papalism and separatism. The 1630s brought the politics of commonwealth to an even more fraught level, culminating in the arrest of Sir John Harvey for treason. For the leading planters who impeached him, the actions of the onetime investigative commissioner, now governor, became a symbol of the era's worrying drift toward absolute wills of all sorts.[14]

Envisioning the Bond between Planter and King

To grasp why clarifying the planters' true bond with their king became such an important feature of Virginia's politics, it helps to recognize that the 1624 assembly itself began by considering, and quickly rejecting, an unsigned "forme of Subscription." Amounting to a highly open-ended agreement between king and planters, the document had arrived with Harvey and his fellow commissioners, whose primary charge was to secure the colonists' assent to the subscription's several ambiguous promises. A contract in appearance, though in reality more like a testimonial that the commissioners were urging the planters to sign, it indicated their "thankfullness"

14. On the Forced Loan controversy, see Richard Cust, *The Forced Loan and English Politics, 1626–1628* (Oxford, 1987).

and humble submission to James's own kingly will. The only reassurances it offered them for such heartfelt compliance were vague assertions of "his Majesty's Royal resolution" to preserve the "Lands and priviledgs" that already accorded with "each mans adventure, and proper interests" and of his "gratious pleasure . . . to institute another forme of Government, whereby this worke may be upheld and better prosper in time to come." Such indefinite promises exposed the subscription to be little more than an overture to the intricate commercial arrangements that Middlesex had already begun floating in the company. Envisioning the colony as the realm's largest granary, or its most valuable tobacco fields, or, as James himself preferred to imagine, its most luxuriant silk factory, the contract was premised on the logic that planters needed to be brought around to their own mundane duties of pushing plows, hoeing rows, and tending mulberries. Fundamentally lost in such a cold economic calculus was the richness of the planter's office as it had been delineated in much-reprinted works like Sir Walter Ralegh's *History of the World,* or Thomas Lodge's popular translation of Titus Flavius Josephus's relations of first-century Judaism and early Christianity. In these works, planters were associated admiringly with the leaders of the Israelites, the patriarchs, and other ancient state builders and assumed to be following God's calling to restore the earth to order through the planting of peoples and the faith.[15]

Not surprisingly, Virginians were hardly alone in clinging to that exalted understanding of their calling of planters. When in 1622 Middlesex dispatched an investigative commission across the Irish Sea not unlike the one he would send two years later to Virginia, local leaders reacted viscerally to his narrow view of their enterprise as simply another endeavor to be converted from a drain on the exchequer into a profit maker for the king. In particular, they responded with a stream of writings with titles like "Reasons for the Plantations in Ireland" (1622) and "There Have Been Six Plantations in Ireland Since the Memory of Man" (undated). In the Irish settlements, no less than Virginia, the fear of being diminished to the status of

---

15. Public Record Office, CO 1/3/3 quoted in full in William S. Powell, *John Pory, 1572–1636: The Life and Letters of a Man of Many Parts* (Chapel Hill, N.C., 1977), 114–115. By this time, both Ralegh's and Lodge's books had gone through multiple reprintings: Ralegh's *The History of the World* had appeared in 1614, 1617, and 1621; Lodge's *The Famous and Memorable Workes of Josephus, A Man of Much Honour and Learning among the Jewes* . . . had been published in 1602 and 1609.

remote marketplaces stimulated planters to invoke their archetypal condition, stressing the primitive and godly roots of plantations that no treasurer with newfangled contracts should be allowed to disrupt.[16]

A similar impulse to pin down the true relationship between king and people through recourse to the past also prevailed in England. One other important context for the colonizers' defenses of the planter-kingly bond was the unease that state innovations were producing in the realm itself, especially in the midst of a war that allowed for considerable experimentation with the very idea of the state. "I feare, as I doe Stabbing," the poet Michael Drayton confessed privately,

> this word, State,
> I dare not speake of the *Palatinate*,
> Although some men make it their hourely theame
> And talke what's done in Austria, and in *Beame* [that is, Bohemia].

Drayton shared this confidence sometime in the early 1620s in a poem addressed to George Sandys, Sir Edwin's brother, who at that moment happened to be in Virginia as the colony's treasurer. The verse captured, in part, how prominently the Bohemian crisis loomed in the background of the teetering Virginia enterprise. In an era when clashing sovereign rulers and confessional conflict played out on both sides of the ocean, America and the Thirty Years War could readily seem intertwined. One author in 1626 expressed his fear that Philip IV "will quickly lead all Europe in triumph, make the Pope himselfe become his Chaplaine, turne all Kingdoms into his Provinces, and Plant them with colonies of Moores or Indians, all Princes to be petty Officers of his House, and send the meane people to dig in his Mines, or to fish Him some Pearles in America." This nightmarish image of European kingdoms being transformed into something comparable to the Spanish ruler's American colonies was also suggestive of the limits of antistatism, for what few persons on either side of the English Atlantic wanted was a weak king. The challenge was rather to hold the early Stuarts to their exalted responsibilities while arguing against statist rationales that diminished the offices of everyone else. By 1628, during the debates over the Petition of Right, Sir John Coke, one of Charles's secretaries of state, could argue quite simply, "We are in the government of a state," as a preliminary to arguing

---

16. The Irish documents are discussed in relation to Cranfield's commission of 1622 in Nicholas Canny, *Making Ireland British, 1580–1650* (Oxford, 2003), 243–258.

that kings sometimes needed to stand above the commonwealth's laws. As "God's captains and leaders of His people," they could not be limited by common law alone but needed also, for the performance of their own kingly callings, free exercise over martial law and the law of equity. It was in the face of such open-ended statism that the antiquarians and common lawyers who were so busy in these years, men like Sir Robert Bruce Cotton, John Selden, and Sir Edward Coke, sought to do their own part in grounding the offices and relationships of commonwealth more firmly in history and immemorial custom, thereby delineating an ancient constitution that preceded any royal will.[17]

Nor was this effort to ground commonwealth in history merely a matter of preserving secular liberties. Few institutions seemed as vulnerable to statist interventions as the church. As part of his negotiations over the Spanish match, James felt compelled to ease historical restrictions on English Catholics, an exceedingly controversial move that for most Protestants was every bit as alarming as the new, nonconsensual taxes. He had a ready ally, however, in his new lord keeper, John Williams, bishop of Lincoln. A prominent Hispanophile on the issue of the Spanish match, Williams was part of a new generation of clerics who took a high view of the sanctity of the king's sovereignty. He was also the first clerical appointment to the lord keeper since the mid-sixteenth century. By placing a churchman in the office, James sought to elevate the chancery above the common law courts, reserving the law of equity as that special domain where God's law and the king's conscience were given ample room in the pursuit of a sovereign's most sacred duty of dispensing justice. One of Williams's early tasks involved delivering the startling news to circuit judges that they were to free all imprisoned Catholics. In an August 2, 1622, communication, he explained that the judges were

---

17. "To Master George Sandys Treasurer for the English Colony in Virginia," in J. William Hebel, ed., *The Works of Michael Drayton* (Oxford, 1961), III, 206; [Paolo Sarpi], *The History of the Quarrels of Pope Paul V* . . . (London, 1626), [¶¶3]r; Robert C. Johnson et al., eds., *Commons Debates 1628*, III, *21 April–27 May 1628* (Rochester, N.Y., 1977), 24. On the concept of the ancient constitution, see Glenn Burgess, *British Political Thought, 1500–1660: The Politics of the Post-Reformation* (New York, 2009), 152–169, 193–203, 225–245. See also J. G. A. Pocock, *The Ancient Constitution and the Feudal Law: A Study of English Historical Thought in the Seventeenth Century: A Reissue with a Retrospect* (Cambridge, 1987); Burgess, *The Politics of the Ancient Constitution: An Introduction to English Political Thought, 1603–1642* (London, 1992); David Underdown, *A Freeborn People: Politics and the Nation in Seventeenth-Century England* (Oxford, 1996), 14, 23–27, 31, 40, 48–49, 52, 55–56, 62, 67, 87, 105, 129, 129–132.

to make no lawyerly "niceness or difficulty" of the matter but were to take the king's "princely favour to all such papists" as the product of his "deep reasons of state," the *arcana imperii* into which no subject should pry too far. Such cautions against resistance were appropriate given the dark millenarian thoughts the newly enlarged liberties of Catholics produced in some Protestants. One alarmed clergyman expressed such concerns in a dedicatory epistle addressed to the wife and sisters-in-law of the Virginia adventurer and warden of the Cinque Ports Edward la Zouche, eleventh Baron Zouche. As this writer put it, Satan had already "entred the field" and was flanked by the "Pope and his Cardinals, with their chiefe Agents the Jesuites, and other Seminarie Priests." Again, however, the remedy for such a fearsome opponent was not an enfeebled king but rather a monarch who recognized that his own power was magnified when truly incorporated within the collectivity of callings that made up the broader commonwealth. While antiquarians like Cotton and Selden emphasized England's freeborn people as the natural counterpart of the king's prerogative, Virginia's colonizers placed that burden squarely on the colony's free planters. In a number of writings in the 1620s, the colony's supporters elaborated on the sheer heights to which the planters' polity could reach—as long, that is, as the king followed sound counsel and recognized the worth of the planter population.[18]

An early example of such discourse that vaunted the planters' bond with their king emerged in the wake of Opechancanough's March 1622 attack. Entitled *A Declaration of the State of the Colony and Affaires in Virginia . . .* (1622), the anonymous pamphlet, by the company's secretary Edward Waterhouse, sought to frame that "fatall Friday morning" in compelling providential terms. Undoubtedly Waterhouse saw his purpose in large part as providing a plausible alternative to the interpretation on which the king and his councillors had settled: namely, that the catastrophe was proof that a moral imbalance really did exist between the colonizers and their sovereign. At a July 17 court, Sir Edward Sackville conveyed this withering view of the planters' licentiousness. The king "with great indignacion apprehended the cause thereof to be the same that their lordships did," Sackville reported, "vizt that the Planters in Virginia attended more their present proffitt rather then their safety and pleasing their humors and fancies by Lyvinge so scat-

---

18. The Lord Keeper to the Judges, Aug. 2, 1622, in M. A. Tierney, *Dodd's Church History of England*, V, *From the Commencement of the Sixteenth Century to the Revolution in 1688* (London, 1843), ccxcv–ccxcvi; John Brinsley, *The Fourth Part of the True Watch . . .* (London, 1624), [A9]v–[A10]v.

teringly and dispersedly." Implicit in such a judgment was James's acceptance of Middlesex's reasoning that the planters' gross self-interestedness deserved to be reined in for the state's greater welfare. Writing on behalf of the company's Sandys-Southampton leadership, Waterhouse offered a sharply different explanation that stressed the attack's significance in illuminating the true scope of the planters' office.[19]

God had directed the Indians' attack on the colony primarily not to punish it but rather to liberate it, Waterhouse argued. Although planting had originally seemed an activity requiring a delicate circumnavigation around natives' God-given rights, Providence had suddenly revealed through the natives' "more then unnaturall bruitishnesse" that planters were freer than they had once supposed. The Indians' violation of the treaties the planters had established with them was nothing less than a divine sign. It relieved the colonists of the duties of converting and civilizing their barbarous neighbors while also giving them greater latitude in carrying out their other planter obligations. "God Almighty making way for severitie there, where a fayre gentlenesse would not take place," Englishmen no longer need settle for Indian's "waste" but could partake also of their "cultivated places" and "cleared grounds"; indeed, they could move forward with an untroubled conscience in "possessing the fruits of others labours." Moreover, the native peoples had proven themselves so far outside of God's grace that they "may now most justly be compelled to servitude and drudgery." Indian slavery would benefit the commonwealth in multiple respects at once by allowing "even the meanest" planters to employ themselves "more entirely in their Arts and Occupations, which are more generous, whilest Savages performe their inferiour workes of digging in mynes, and the like."[20]

Freed to concentrate on the more generous, or noble, vocations suitable to a godly people, the planters were also liberated in another respect. By overriding the critics who had once stayed the planters' hand, Opechancanough's

---

19. [Edward Waterhouse], *A Declaration of the State of the Colony and Affaires in Virginia; With a Relation of the Barbarous Massacre in the Time of Peace and League, Treacherously Executed by the Native Infidels upon the English, the 22 of March Last* . . . (London, 1622), 14; "At a Court Held for Virginia on Wednesday the 17th Julij 1622," in Kingsbury, ed., *Records of the Virginia Company*, II, 96.

20. [Waterhouse], *Declaration of the State of the Colony and Affaires in Virginia*, 12, 15, 23, 25–26. Waterhouse's casuistry here contributed significantly to the notion of "hereditary heathenism" that Rebecca Anne Goetz has charted; see, Goetz, *The Baptism of Early Virginia: How Christianity Created Race* (Baltimore 2012), 3.

attack excused the toughness they really needed to protect themselves: "Thus upon this Anvile shall wee now beate out to our selves an armour of proofe, which shall for ever after defend us from barbarous Incursions, and from greater dangers that otherwise might happen." Here, Waterhouse was probably suggesting the planters' immunity from the barbs especially of grave Puritans, precisians who caviled at the Virginia enterprise as falling into the Spanish Catholic error of mistaking worldly for religious ends. In light of God's own endorsement of the planters' righteousness, Waterhouse implied, even the godly must concede Virginia's lawful path.[21]

The message of the *Declaration* was not only concerned with the planter, for the planting of Virginia's "growing State" also necessitated an obliging king. Waterhouse addressed James I's duties by playing on the anti-Spanish concerns that had recently enflamed the 1621 parliament. Still eager to pursue a strategic marriage for Prince Charles to the infanta Maria, James had courted the Protestants in the Commons with promises of readying an army. By sending a show of force into the continental war, James hoped to have a stronger hand at the negotiating table, pressuring the Spaniards into accepting not only a lucrative dowry but also a politically favorable one that included restoring the Palatinate to Frederick V and Elizabeth. Leaping at the king's welcome overture to bellicosity, Waterhouse made clear that Virginia's commonwealth deserved to be seen in the same light as any other military or diplomatic effort to limit Spanish imperium. In particular, he observed the Spaniards' own dedication to kingdom building abroad, a commitment that went well beyond a meager commercial outlook on colonies. Noting the "ample and rich Kingdomes" the Spanish kings now enjoyed both "in their Indies East and West" as a result of their aggressive acquisition of the Portuguese throne, he stressed that the American plantations most flourished once their king had agreed "to annexe and unite the West Indies inseparably for ever to the Crowne of Spaine." Rather than stand idly by while the ravenous Spanish monarchy consumed his dominions as it had Portugal's historical holdings, James should apply his own energies to "the Plantation of this his lawfull and rightfull Kingdome of VIRGINIA, which by the blessing of Almighty God is growne to good perfection." Waterhouse hinted, too, that the same militant Protestants who were pushing for a hard-line anti-Spanish policy on the grounds that they were the realm's true patriots would also favor the king's firmer commitment to Virginia. He addressed his

---

21. [Waterhouse], *Declaration of the State of the Colony and Affaires in Virginia*, 26.

pamphlet to "every good Patriot" who "will take these things seriously into his thoughts, and consider how deeply the prosecution of this noble Enterprise concerneth the honor of his *Majestie* and the whole Nation." Waterhouse acknowledged that James had every right to profit from Virginia, but he insisted that this end was best served by supporting, not thwarting, the colony's commonwealth-building efforts. Situated in a country that was "spatious and fruitful," "very temperate and healthfull to the Inhabitants," and "abounding" with "naturall blessings," the colony simply awaited time and the combined energies of planters and king to bring about "the rich augmenting of his Revennues." Toward that end, James needed merely to think of Virginia in much the same robustly sovereign terms that already made him "absolute King of three of the most populous Kingdomes." By acting as Virginia's true king, James could count on the colony to flourish as his fourth realm.[22]

The argument that Virginia might become not only one of the king's affluent kingdoms but also one of his most populous ones was a recurring theme in the colonial writings of the 1620s, a point that related closely to Sir Edwin Sandys's insistence that a well-tended public was ultimately more lucrative than an over-hasty pruning. Waterhouse observed that the Habsburg emperor Charles V himself had called the British kingdoms "*Officina gentium,* the shop or forge of men." The statement echoed the arguments by statecraft authors like Giovanni Botero that large populations were the true source of a kingdom's wealth, and writers on Virginia's commonwealth were quick to emphasize in the same humanist spirit the colony's promise as a shop for men and not just goods. Captain John Smith made this theme central to many of his own works, including his monumental *The Generall Historie of Virginia, New-England, and the Summer Isles* . . . (1624). Smith assembled the lengthy volume hurriedly in the months after the Privy Council approved an initial investigative commission in May 1623 headed by Sir William Jones, justice of the Court of Common Pleas, to inquire into the colony's reorganization. Entered for publication on July 12, 1624, a few short weeks after the company's dissolution, the *Generall Historie* urged the king to devote "his Princely wisedome and powerfull hand, renowned through

---

22. Ibid., 2, 3, 27, 29, 34. For James's grudging strategy of relenting to an armed force in order to pursue a diplomatic solution to the Palatine crisis, see Thomas Cogswell, "War and the Liberties of the Subject," in J. H. Hexter, ed., *Parliament and Liberty from the Reign of Elizabeth to the English Civil War* (Stanford, Calif., 1992), 228–229; Cogswell, *Blessed Revolution,* 18–19 27, 58–59, 72.

the world for admirable government, ... to set these new Estates into order," for "nothing but the touch of the Kings sacred hand can erect a Monarchy."[23]

Appearing in the work's fourth book were answers Smith had provided Jones's commission on how he thought Virginia's circumstances could be "rectified," and, here, he reiterated his advice of the colony's need for royal commitment. The only sure route for the colony, Smith asserted, was if "his Majestie would please to intitle it to his Crowne." But then he quickly added the necessary caveat. The job could not be undertaken by just any "workmen," certainly not by "such delinquents as here cannot be ruled by all the lawes in England." "To rectifie a common-wealth with debaushed people is impossible," he continued, "and no wise man would throw himselfe into such a society, that intends honestly." Certainly "when the foundation is laid ... and a common-wealth established," then even the most vicious person could be reformed by the work that the colony would make available. Until then, the colony needed honest planters. To underscore the point, he stated, as though it were a maxim, the key to commonwealth building in America: "There is no Country to pillage as the Romans found: all you expect from thence must be by labour." In other words, if the king wanted his American states to generate wealth like the colonies that elevated Rome, he needed to treat his planters, not as mean scavengers of the region's wealth, but rather as honorable subjects working hard for their bread.[24]

Other authors similarly stressed the need for planters to be virtuous, making clear that commonwealth building was a holy and venerable enterprise that should not be approached only with a treasurer's mercantile eye for quick yields. For instance, Francis Bacon, Viscount Saint Alban, included in the 1625 edition of his *Essayes* a piece entitled "Of Plantations" that was clearly a direct response to Middlesex's meddling. Bacon opened the essay with a strong emphasis on planting's sheer anquity:

Plantations are amongst Ancient, Primitive, and Heroicall Workes. When the World was young, it begate more Children; But now it is

23. [Waterhouse], *Declaration of the State of the Colony and Affaires in Virginia*, 3, 9; John Smith, *The Generall Historie of Virginia, New-England, and the Summer Isles* ... (1624), in Philip L. Barbour, ed., *The Complete Works of Captain John Smith (1580–1631)*, 3 vols. (Chapel Hill, N.C., 1986), II, 43, 330. A useful discussion of the circumstances behind the writing and publication of the *Generall Historie* appears in ibid., 27–30.

24. Smith, *Generall Historie* (1624), in Barbour, ed., *Complete Works of Captain John Smith*, II, 330.

old, it begets fewer: For I may justly account new *Plantations,* to be the Children of former Kingdomes.

As the offspring of kingdoms rather than a project of merchants, plantations required a different mindset than simply a counting house's concern with commodities:

> *Planting* of Countries, is like *Planting* of Woods; For you must make account, to leese almost Twenty yeeres Profit, and expect your Recompense, in the end. For the Principall Thing, that hath beene the Destruction of most *Plantations,* hath beene the Base, and Hastie drawing of Profit, in the first Yeeres. It is true, Speedie Profit is not to be neglected, as farre as may stand, with the Good of the *Plantation,* but no further.

Having established that plantations were part of an ages-old process in kingdom formation that required at least a generation to produce reliable profits, Bacon offered the natural follow-up observation that the quality of the people mattered more than the quantity of their goods. "It is a Shamefull and Unblessed Thing," he concluded, "to take the Scumme of People, and Wicked Condemned Men, to be the People with whom you *Plant.*"[25]

Undoubtedly, part of what was stimulating these vigorous complaints about the morality of planters was the king's own continuing eagerness to see the colony as a repository for the realm's least desirable subjects. On October 20, 1619, the company deliberated uncomfortably over a letter James had sent requiring that "divers dissolute persons" imprisoned at Bridewell be sent to the colony. Not until the next court in November did the company agree to "send them over to be servants." In the face of such indications that James was content to see the colony as an undifferentiated royal frontier, the colonizers could do little more than remain insistent that planting was not a mere expedient solution to problems at hand. Samuel Purchas, chaplain to the archbishop of Canterbury, George Abbot, made the point particularly vividly. "God almighty, the great Founder of Colonies," did not intend for Virginia to be "made a Port Exquiline for such as by ordure or vomit were by good order and physicke worthy to be evacuated from This Body," he wrote. Richard Eburne did not employ quite such graphic metaphors, but he placed

---

25. Francis Bacon, "Of Plantations," in *The Essayes or Counsels, Civill and Morall, of Francis Lo. Verulam, Viscount St. Alban. Newly Written* (London, 1625), 198–199.

much the same emphasis on planter virtue in his 1624 advice to Secretary of State George Calvert, first Baron Baltimore, in relation to Baltimore's proposed Newfoundland venture. Writing that criminals, maimed soldiers, and the idle poor could play a part in new plantations, Eburne nevertheless argued, "But withal, and above all, speciall regard ought to be had, to draw thither . . . men of speciall and present employment, that is, men of such Trades, Faculties, Sciences, Handicrafts, Occupations and Employments, as are most necessary for a present and uprising common wealth." Without such upright persons, he went on, "there can be no commodious or good dwelling or living at all for men . . . of our breed and manner of Living any where. For mans life you know is such as cannot stand in any good sort without the helpe and supply of many very other men besides himselfe." A commonwealth was composed of the people who formed it, and a man of Baltimore's breeding needed comparably fine fellows.[26]

One reason men mattered as much as goods, of course, was that a kingdom needed to defend itself. Since the Elizabethan era, authors like Richard Hakluyt the clergyman had identified fort building as one of the most important early activities of the planter. It was that labor-intensive undertaking essential to the commonwealth's foundation that explained why London-based provisioning by merchants and other adventurers was indispensable early on until the planters could establish commercial ties and other rudiments of society on their own. In the 1617 edition of his *Briefe Description of the Whole Worlde*, Archbishop Abbot had accordingly summed up Virginian's achievements as twofold: their sheer continuance on the spot and their construction of "three Townes and forts" as "sure retreats for them against the force of the natives, and reasonable secured places against any power that may come against them by Sea." Writers were quick to emphasize that the martial qualities of a young colony were consistent with what the Bible indicated about the ancient origins of states. "Examples of Planta-

26. "October the 20th 1619," in Kingsbury, ed., *Records of the Virginia Company*, I, 253, "November the Third 1619," I, 259; Samuel Purchas, *Hakluytus Posthumus; or, Purchas His Pilgrimes: Contayning a History of the World in Sea Voyages and Lande Travells by Englishmen and Others* (New York, 1906), XIX, 236, 237; Richard Eburne, *A Plaine Path-Way to Plantations; That Is, a Discourse in Generall, concerning the Plantation of Our English People in Other Countries . . .* ([London], 1624), 62–63. Ancient Rome's Port Esquiline, where the lowest social orders were buried and criminals executed, became in this period a metaphor for the venting of sin and filth out of the body politic. See, for instance, Maurice Hunt, "The Backward Voice of Coriol-anus," *Shakespeare Studies*, XXXII (2004), 220–221.

tion are best taken out of the Scriptuers," Governor Wyatt's father George Wyatt counseled him sometime around June 1624. Like Captain Smith, the senior Wyatt was convinced that "Adam was first set on Worke in Plantation of the world" and that "Noah and his posteritie" carried on the same task. The "most perfect Idea of the best Plantation," Wyatt went on, came from "Canticles" (or the Song of Solomon), which "describes the Churches Plantation by the Husbandry of Christ and his Spouse raisinge it to the hight of a kingdome." Husbandry clearly meant more for Wyatt than cultivating crops. It also involved all the skills, or "Sciences," necessary for civil life, not only the economical but also the martial. He envisioned the "invention of Sciences" as having arisen among humans gradually: "Spade workes, useful in al, Navigation, Carpentership, Ieronworkes, Musicke, vineyardinge, refreshments in their werie travels, with Noah and his posteritie grew, and Husbandlife and Soldgership with the Patriarks in Tents were bred and nurished." The same broad range of sciences would need to be nurtured in Virginia; hence, Wyatt devoted the majority of his letter to elaborating on the "artes of Peace and War," giving roughly equal attention to both.[27]

Another writer who tied the martial dimensions of Virginia to a deep and sacred past was Captain John Martin. An original member of the colony's 1607 residential council, Martin had been granted one of the private, or particular, plantations with which the company had briefly experimented as a way to pass on some of the costs and responsibilities of planting settlers to individual adventurers. Martin had powerful connections in England, initially to Salisbury who undoubtedly was behind Martin's appointment to the council because of his father's role as master of the mint, and later to his brother-in-law, the Privy Councillor and master of the rolls Sir Julius Caesar. Probably as a result of these valuable contacts, Martin managed to secure a patent giving him extraordinarily large privileges that permitted his community's almost complete autonomy from the rest of the colony apart from shared military service. Accordingly, the vision for Virginia that Martin out-

27. [George Abbot], *A Briefe Description of the Whole Worlde; Wherein Is Particularly Described All the Monarchies, Empires, and Kingdomes of the Same* . . . , 4th ed. (London, 1617), V[1]r–V[1]v; J. Frederick Fausz and John Kukla, eds., "A Letter of Advice to the Governor of Virginia, 1624," *William and Mary Quarterly*, 3d Ser., XXXIV (1977), 113–114. For Hakluyt's emphasis on the importance of fort building as a vital first step in planting, see "Discourse of Western Planting by Richard Hakluyt," 1584, in E. G. R. Taylor, ed., *The Original Writings and Correspondence of the Two Richard Hakluyts,* Works Issued by the Hakluyt Society, 2d Ser., no. 77 (London, 1935), II, 274–279.

lined in two manuscripts that he submitted to Caesar on December 15, 1622, was singular in its emphasis on a highly decentralized settlement. In one of these works, he drew on scripture as well as his own experience to refute those writers like Waterhouse who maintained the natives could and should be extirpated. Martin argued instead that the colony needed many native friends like the ones whom he intended to enlist as trading partners and workers on his own domain. "Holy writt sayeth," Martin wrote, that God admonished "the Children of Israell though they were of farr greater numb[e]rs, then wee are yet in many ages like to be, and came into a Countrie where weare walled townes, not to utterly distroy the heathen, least the woods and wilde beasts should over runn them." In the second manuscript, Martin developed his ideal of Virginia as a localized, multiethnic Israel even further, averring that the best way to make the colony a truly "Royall plantation" was to take advantage of the "32 Kingdoms" that Opechancanough had forfeited through his treason, allotting each one to a different commanding officer. This officer would be modeled on England's own deputy lieutenants, and, accordingly, Martin believed that the English shires where such men traditionally held sway should play the lead part in sending men and supplies to convert Virginia's native kingdoms into an English one. In Martin's Virginia, multiple communities would provide mutual defense while also hosting an extensive arena of ironworks, tanneries, shipbuilders, weavers, and other trades. Natives would supply both armed assistance and labor, and veteran captains like Martin himself—a "Noble Generall fitt for so Royall a plantacion," as he put it—would preserve military-style discipline over the colony's many discrete neighborhoods.[28]

An even more breathtaking vision of the colony's military potential emerged several years later in a tract by Purchas. Appearing in his *Hakluytus Posthumus; or, Purchas His Pilgrimes* (1625), the treatise considered, alongside other questions of Virginia's "lawfulnesse," the "case of Warre." In keeping with his patron Abbot's own pro-war stance, Purchas eagerly contributed to the era's Elizabethan cult, hailing the sixteenth-century colonizers

---

28. John Martin, "The Manner Howe to Bringe the Indians into Subjection," Dec. 15, 1622, in Kingsbury, ed., *Records of the Virginia Company*, III, 706, Martin, "How Virginia May Be Made a Royal Plantation," Dec. 15, 1622, III, 707–708. For a still useful biographical sketch of Martin, see James P. C. Southall, "Captain John Martin of Brandon on the James," *Virginia Magazine of History and Biography*, LIV (1946), 21–67. On Martin's father, Sir Richard Martin, see *Oxford Dictionary of National Biography*, online ed., s.v. "Martin, Sir Richard (1533/4–1617)," by C. E. Challis, accessed Mar. 18, 2015, http://www.oxforddnb.com/view/article/18205.

like Hakluyt and Ralegh as models of anti-Spanish vigor who should shame the current generation into taking a firmer stand in the looming continental conflict. Avowing that Bellona, the goddess of war, was visibly "pregnant," her issue "alreadie conceived," and "abortion" (while no doubt "wished" by many) overridden by "necessitie," Purchas self-consciously tied Virginia to the expectant Palatinate confrontation. He entitled his piece "Virginias Verger," referring to the official who leads church dignitaries forward while holding their symbol of office aloft. Almost certainly a statement of his intention of guiding none other than the church's supreme head in his Virginia duties, the title indicated that Purchas would approach James's longing for neutrality in the familiar role of the casuist, weighing whether war was or was not justified. Purchas's verdict was that, though "honorable" and "beauteous," James's peaceful inclinations did not disallow the prudence of "forewarning and forearming men by the Sword drawne to prevent the drawing of Swords." And in identifying "fit Watch-towers and Arsenals to maintaine right against all wrong-doers," Purchas singled out Virginia and its fellow American colonies as the necessary complements to England's own martial pursuits.[29]

Purchas proceeded to offer a sweeping vision of England's full capacities in which the colonies were vital sentinels that contributed to the realm's larger battle against the papal Antichrist and his strongest secular defenders. Still hopeful that Virginia's planters would discover in their backcountry a South Sea that led to Asia, Purchas imagined the colony as one among a constellation of English states extending East and West that posed a genuine challenge to the Spanish Catholic threat. Though still but a "small thing, as the Map sheweth, to Spaine," England could be transformed over time, he suggested, into an elaborate phalanx of kingdoms that linked the Atlantic to the Pacific while providing numerous waystations for ships carrying goods and soldiers. This dream of the globe-straddling dominion that would proceed from James's sovereignty and his subjects' industry in America rested on Purchas's assumption that Waterhouse was perfectly correct in his assessment of the enormous latitude of the planters' God-given rights in the wake of the 1622 attack. As Purchas put it, Opechancanough's "disloyall treason" really had "confiscated whatsoever remainders of right the unnaturall Naturalls had, and made both them and their Countrey wholly English." Insisting that the time was ripe for James to make good on Solomon's proverb, "The honour of a King is in the multitude of his Subjects," Purchas called

29. Purchas, *Hakluytus Posthumus*, XIX, 218, 254, 256.

on him to see that the "honour" of his "Kingdome" required its own procreative "growing and multiplying into Kingdomes." Just "as Scotland and England seeme sisters, so Virginia, New England, New found Land ... together with Bermuda, and other Ilands" deserved to "be the adopted and legall Daughters of England." In a war-ready age that had little choice but to prepare Christian soldiers for a fundamental showdown, young kingdoms were needed to reinforce the struggles of the old.[30]

Though many of these works were scanty on details about the governmental structures that would accompany such ambitious kingdom building, one proposal was downright labyrinthine in its complexities. This was a treatise by Captain John Bargrave entitled "A Forme of Polisie to Plante and Governe Many Families in Virginea, Soe as It Shall Naturally Depend one the Soveraignetye of England." Bargrave does not appear to have visited the colony personally, though his younger brother George Bargrave lived there, collaborating for a time with Captain Martin whose daughter he had married, and another brother Thomas died in the colony in 1621. Nevertheless, Bargrave evidently still thought of himself as a planter owing to his considerable investments in shipping other English subjects across the ocean. He seems to have been especially active in peopling the colony's so-called particular plantations, including one funded by Zouche as well as Martin's Brandon plantation. Though he sought an audience for his proposal in the company and at Whitehall off and on through the early 1620s, he managed mainly to anger both sides in the factious company by spending much of that same time also issuing rancorous complaints against company officials for his alleged losses. Bargrave perceived the colony as still woefully short of realizing itself as a commonwealth, and he placed most of the blame for Virginia's stalled promise on the company itself. The title of his piece reflects the contemporary fascination with the idea of a form of polisy, or governing frame, that could pin down godly duties that otherwise risked being neglected by still-sinful leaders and subjects. Such a focus reveals Bargrave's close familiarity with the era's statecraft literature by the likes of Jean Bodin, Louis LeRoy, and Botero. Bargrave's additional hint that he offered a means of naturally binding the sovereign and his planters was a deliberate nod to the Anglican ideal of the natural obedience that tied subjects to their king on the same instinctual basis that bound the faithful to their Maker.[31]

30. Ibid., 229, 238–239, 258.

31. Bargrave, "Forme of Polisie," before Dec. 7, 1623, in Kingsbury, ed., *Records of the Virginia Company*, IV, 408–434. The document is also printed in Arthur Percival Newton, "A New Plan to

The staunch conformism at the heart of Bargrave's tract probably captures best the otherwise obscure attachments of this outspoken man. A longtime soldier who likely fought mainly in the Low Countries, Bargrave enjoyed ties to the church hierarchy through his brother Isaac Bargrave, who served for a time as chaplain to Sir Henry Wotton, the English ambassador to Venice, and, after 1622, to Prince Charles. Both brothers were evidently attracted to that idealized view of the righteousness of the king's sovereignty that was also winning favor in those quarters that opposed the increasingly overt resistance being shown to royal impositions. Perhaps Bargrave's ability to bend the ear of Middlesex and his similar success in winning Lord Keeper Williams's sympathy for a petition he had made against the company in chancery reflected this high-church ideological affinity. Maybe, too, the preservation of Bargrave's proposal in the personal papers of Sir Caesar suggests Bargrave's loose ties to those royalist-inclined civil lawyers like Caesar who tended to fret over perceived encroachments on the king's prerogative. Bargrave was well educated, having apparently matriculated as a fellow commoner from Clare College Cambridge in 1588, and he also had legal training, having been admitted to the bar at Lincoln's Inn on November 7, 1590. These experiences and his time in the Low Country evidently hardened him in his royalism.[32]

Govern Virginia, 1623," *American Historical Review*, XIX (1914), 559–578. Although Bargrave's biography remains sketchy, useful insights can be found in Stephen Bann, *Under the Sign. John Bargrave as Collector, Traveler, and Witness* (Ann Arbor, Mich., 1994), 28–45; Southall, "Captain John Martin of Brandon," *VMHB*, LIV (1946), 42–44, 48–50, 54, 61–62. Bargrave's stay-at-home status is suggested in Governor Sir George Yeardley's remark in 1619 that Bargrave was "a man as I conceave that wicheth [that is, wishes] well to the plantation and doth entend himselfe to come over" (Yeardley to [Sir Edwin Sandys], [1619], in Kingsbury ed., *Records of the Virginia Company*, III, 125). Given Bargrave's busy dealings over the next few years in pursuing his various lawsuits, it seems unlikely that he ever made the journey. Zouche's hiring of Bargrave's ship in 1618 to transport planters and Bargrave's later involvement with his brother George Bargrave in relation to Martin's plantation can be traced in Kingsbury. ed., *Records of the Virginia Company*, I, 37, 69, 129, IV, 95, 511, 512, 517.

32. John Bargrave, "Petition to the Privy Council," Apr. 12, 1622, Kingsbury, ed., *Records of the Virginia Company*, II, 608–609 Bargrave's ten years as a soldier is mentioned in his letter to [Cranfield], the Lord Treasurer Middlesex, early December 1623 (Kingsburg, ed., *Records of the Virginia Company*, IV, 435), where he also discusses the Spanish kings' overly costly empire (IV, 436). For Isaac Bargrave, see *Oxford Dictionary of National Biography*, online ed., s.v. "Bargrave, Isaac (*bap.* 1586, *d.* 1643)," by Sidney Lee, rev. Stephen Bann, accessed Mar. 18, 2015, http://www.oxforddnb.com/view/article/1370. Bargrave's victory in chancery appears in "Lord Keeper

Bargrave lost no opportunity to rail against any forces that undermined monarchy, and these he perceived just about everywhere. For instance, reacting against the company's organizational structure in which decisions were rendered by stockholders' individual votes, he scoffed that "adventurours here . . . give lawes and government by popular voyces to the planters in Virginia as if they were their tenantes or servantes." Likewise, he rued the Sandys administration for their "profuse throwinge out libertie, amongst the planters, whereby they have made them forsake their former discipline, strength and vertue to defend themselves against the domestick enemie." Such licentiousness was especially inexcusable, Bargrave believed, because "populer goverment doth directlie take away the power of the monarchie . . . extreame libertie beinge worse then extreame Tirranie, as it appeared by *the troubles in Rome after Neroes death.*" Where Bargrave particularly drew the line, however, was with Protestant separatism. Thus, in his proposal he made clear that dissent would simply not be tolerated. Expressing the point as though the king himself was asserting it as part of his new letters patent to planters, Bargrave wrote:

> Where Moses and Aaron agree not there religion will not onely bee scandalled but the soveraignetye must needes goe to wracke, therefore wee doe ordayne that whoesoever hee shall bee that shall refuse to bee governed by our eclesiasticall government established, he shall be heald and esteemed as a resister of our soveraigne power, commaundeing all our administers of justice, whome it shall concerne, not to suffer any person or persons to remaine or abide within our sayde plantacions, whoe shall professe any doctrine contrarie to oures.

For Bargrave, divergence of religious opinion was ineluctably dangerous to the king's sovereign office.[33]

[John] Williams. Decree in Chancery, Bargrave versus Sir Thomas Smythe et al.," Feb. 19, 1622, in Kingsbury, ed., *Records of the Virginia Company*, III, 598–602. The preservation of Bargrave's and Martin's proposals in Sir Julius Caesar's papers is noted in Kingsbury, ed., *Records of the Virginia Company*, I, 69. On Caesar's concern for the king's prerogative, a royalist proclivity that contributed to his betrayal of his patron Robert Cecil, earl of Salisbury, on the issue of the Great Contract, see *Oxford Dictionary of National Biography*, online ed., s.v. "Caesar [*formerly* Adelmare], Sir Julius (*bap.* 1558, *d.* 1636)," by Alain Wijffels, accessed Mar. 19, 2015, http://oxforddnb.com/view/article/4328. Bargrave's education is noted in Bann, *Under the Sign*, 29.

33. Bargrave, "Forme of Polisie," before Dec. 7, 1623, in Kingsbury, ed., *Records of the Virginia*

This conflation of loyalty to the church and unbending obedience to the king's sovereignty was a view that Bargrave associated eagerly with Archbishop Abbot, though Abbot's own comparatively broad toleration for nonseparatist dissenters was probably markedly removed from Bargrave's stricter conformity. Bargrave claimed that Abbot confided in him his aversion to Sandys's recent permission to the Pilgrims to settle in Virginia's northern regions, it serving to endorse "those Brownistes" despite "their Doctrine clayminge a libertie to disagreeing to the Goverm[en]t of Monarches." Yet, Bargrave's real loyalties seem to have leaned more to Hispanophiles like Middlesex and Williams than to Abbot's fierce anti-Catholicism. Most of Bargrave's remarks about Spain took the form, not of the patriot belligerence of a true Abbot protégé like Purchas, but rather of admiration for the might of Habsburg sovereignty. Charles V and Philip II did not earn opprobrium in his eyes for their papalism or universal monarchy; they did so for the exorbitant amounts those Spanish kings paid to garrison an empire predicated on force rather than the natural and loving obedience of planters. Bargrave's Virginia would be different, and notably he did not shrink from the era's statism, remarking to Middlesex his greatest hope was to "bragg that I have helped the state" by showing how to profit from Virginia while also building it up into "as great an Empire as the King of Spaynes."[34]

Bargrave's admiration for royal sovereignty, however, by no means lessened his reverence for the planter's office. It was in explaining how the planter and the king could be conjoined to "keep in subjeccion to England a [Virginian] State" that Bargrave developed his elaborate arrangements for the colony's government. The sheer dizzying intricacy of his scheme reflected his almost zealous conviction in the power of a commonwealth headed by an imperial king to provide all the raw materials necessary for holding its members to their respective duties. A quick survey of some of the key elements of Bargrave's proposal captures his eagerness to make that bond between king and planter work. His polity would consist most importantly of five ranks of planters whose relative statuses were based on the numbers

---

Company, IV, 409, 413, Bargrave to [Lionel Cranfield], the Lord Treasurer Middlesex, June 9 (?), 1623, IV, 223–224. For Bargrave's view that Edwin Sandys's leniency toward Brownists and separatists went hand-in-hand with his desire to build an overly popular "free state in Virginia," see [Sir Nathaniel Rich], "Note Which I Presently Took of Captain John Bargrave's Discourse to Me concerning Sir Edwin Sardys," May 16, 1623, IV, 194.

34. [Rich], "Note Which I Presently Took of Captain John Bargrave's Discourse," May 16, 1623, IV, 194, Bargrave to [Cranfield], the Lord Treasurer Middlesex, early December 1623, IV, 437.

of people they brought over. Clearly, for Bargrave, the office of planting involved above all the actual act of planting people in their new home. Allowing those persons to labor hard at their callings would make commonwealth in America possible. Planters for Bargrave were "citizens," their centrality to the polity manifested in his eagerness for them to play an active role at various levels of the colony's government that accorded with their ranks. Not everyone in Bargrave's commonwealth would enjoy this privileged position. Below the planters in Virginia's hierarchy would be a semifree group of tenants and freed servants who were permitted to work the land and participate in trade but not to contribute to government. At the very bottom were mere servants, or as he called these most unfree persons "the planted." Perhaps because his own father was a comparatively humble yeoman whose tannery business had prospered, Bargrave allowed for a significant amount of social mobility among these differentiated orders on the grounds that divine favor sometimes endows worthiness on even the unlikeliest of instruments. He asserted that "the meanest servaunt" could become a "lord patriot," the highest order of planter in Bargrave's commonwealth, as long as, "God soe blesseing him and his endeavours," he attained a sufficiently wealthy estate to fund the requisite number of men that the lord patriot needed to plant to earn such an office. Bargrave even suggested that making such social ascension possible was one of the planters' key responsibilities toward their less privileged counterparts. Servants and tenants were to be "soe cherished that they may prove planters themselves." In general, however, the rewards of membership were reserved for the planters; their exertions under their king were the duties that Bargrave was most concerned to uphold.[35]

Calling the government of king and planter a "contract of this our marriage," Bargrave made clear he envisioned the bond between these two key constituents in much the same rich terms as his fellow writers on the planter commonwealth, even if few of them went quite as far as he did in their devotion to the king's imperium. Bargrave's royalism was always in service to the Christian humanist concern of enlivening all of God's people in their duties. He noted with awe the weight of the king's own divinely conferred responsibility to sanction the legal arrangements under which his people lived: "This

---

35. Bargrave to [Cranfield], the Lord Treasurer Middlesex, early December 1623, in Kingsbury, ed., *Records of the Virginia Company*, IV, 437, Bargrave, "Forme of Polisie," before Dec. 7, 1623, IV, 408, 411, 414, 415, 417. On Bargrave's humble beginnings and his rise through marriage to the daughter of the prosperous London armigerous family of the haberdasher Giles Crouch, see Bann, *Under the Sign*, 28–45.

giveing life to lawes is one of the highest poyntes of our soveraignetye given us from God to benefitte not to destroye our subjectes." Likewise, in one especially lush phrase that he again expressed as though in the monarch's own words, Bargrave captured the marriage between king and planters as a perfect reciprocity of benefits and duties that quietly evoked the redeeming ties of Christ's mystical body: *"Layeing aside force and our coactive power,* wee may *by our justice and bountie* marrye and combinde those our provinces to us and our soveraignetye in naturall love and obedience." The statement suggested why Bargrave felt such frustration with any intermediary like the company that interfered in the relations between monarch and people. Only in the integrity of the sovereign-subject relationship were planters themselves truly free to perform their callings.[36]

In stressing the reciprocal nature of the bond between king and planters, Bargrave made clear how closely he had been attending to the moral reasoning of projectors like Middlesex. Although the treasurer's arguments on behalf of his revenue schemes turned on the dark image of self-interested planters who neglected the king's own needs, Bargrave suggested that this moral imbalance was easily remedied. All that was required was for the polity's form, or constitutional arrangements, to be organized in such a way as to bring those potentially clashing interests into reliable, long-term alignment. The planters were "free subjects to the kinge," who was himself free in the sense of enjoying ample scope for the exercise of his own office. That basic concept of mutual freedom in the pursuit of respective divine callings provided for Bargrave the one desideratum to which every one of Virginia's constituents should be able to subscribe. The familiar Pauline conception of a commonwealth as a composite of persons whose diverse wills are cheerfully and harmoniously turned toward lawful living under God was the glittering aim toward which Bargrave's scheme was pointed. Meanwhile, the only reliable means toward that desired object was a suitable "sett forme of government both heare and in Virginia framed to the attaineing of our end."[37]

All of the intricate provisions of Bargrave's "Forme of Polisie" were di-

---

36. Bargrave, "Forme of Polisie," before Dec. 7, 1623, in Kingsbury, ed., *Records of the Virginia Company,* IV, 408, 411, 414.

37. Ibid., 409. For scholarship that stresses the rootedness of sixteenth- and seventeenth-century English conceptions of liberty in the offices, or realms of duty, required by a godly commonwealth, see Conal Condren, *Argument and Authority in Early Modern England: The Presuppositions of Oaths and Offices* (Cambridge, 2006), 88–94; Keechang Kim, *Aliens in Medieval Law: The Origins of Modern Citizenship* (Cambridge, 2000), 192–196, 208–210.

rected at ensuring that both king and planter enjoyed the expansive liberty they needed to perform their particular offices while also preventing that sinful licentiousness, or abuse of office, that was an offense to God and virtuous humans alike. Bargrave was emphatic that he regarded the planters as capable of the most dreadful misconduct; he blamed many of the colony's woes on the Smythe government's alleged rapaciousness in pursuing quick riches "because from it the planters have learned their inhumanitie and injustice which they nowe use, both against the new comers and adventurers, offeringe the same measure which hath bene measured before to them." Bargrave was also determined to uphold the planters' dignity to preserve their moral, martial, and political capacities. The principal form of punishment in Bargrave's commonwealth would be a downgrade in rank, for "by this meanes we maie avoyde all corporall punishement for freemen except it bee where the case deserves death, and this will breede in the planters the more noble spirittes." Spurred by a sense of honor rather than fear, the planters would serve as the fierce defenders, industrious workers, and powerful magistrates of the king's American dominion, arrayed into various "soveraigne forces" with civil as well as martial responsibilities. Meanwhile, the colony's governmental form would prevent that ferocious freedom from going too far. Because planters would only be able to choose their governors out of the highest ranks, the polity would beneficially "suppresse popular libertie and keepe the soveraigne faculties and the commaund of the forces aloft in these feoffees handes," ensuring that the king's sovereignty would remain at the level of the two highest ranks, called patriots and governors. At the same time, allowing the planters to elect their own governors, "which all free subjectes doe naturally desire," would so gratify them as to serve in itself as a means of holding them to their duties. Pleased by the government that so benefited them, they would feel such "content that they will all strive to maintaine it in the same forme wee shall now settle it." Bargrave's "Forme of Polisie" offered a constitutional order designed to be not only mutually beneficial to planters and the king but also self-sustaining through the ages.[38]

Not surprisingly, then, Bargrave devoted particular attention to the colony's public. He was quick to establish in one letter to Middlesex that this essential element of the polity would be no rival to the king's power. As he

38. Bargrave to [Cranfield], the Lord Treasurer Middlesex, June 9 (?), 1623, in Kingsbury, ed., *Records of the Virginia Company*, IV, 223, Bargrave, "Forme of Polisie," before Dec. 7, 1623, 416–419, 422.

put it, "Under the name of the publique (w[hi]ch is the Kings in right of his Sov[er]aintie) all the benifit of the publique lands and servants will returne unto him though he be no more seene in the buisines then form[er]lie he hath beene." Even Bargrave, despite his pronounced royalism, believed that the public was a thing apart, hallowed in relation to all private interests, including the king's. Virginia would provide a steady flow to the royal coffers, but the public was to benefit the commonwealth as a whole, not any one of its constituents. In addition to the crops and livestock tended by servants on lands set aside for the public, revenues would be raised from fines collected whenever anyone "abused the governement" through such crimes as mutinies, seditions, murders, and lesser misdemeanors. A special syndic staffed by three persons from each of the five orders of citizens would determine these violations, punishing anyone "found guiltie of oppression or the encroacheing farther uppon our soveraigne power" than was permissible. Responsibility over the public treasury would fall to two councils of state, one to meet on each side of the ocean. Bargrave called them collectively the "soveraigne councell of union." A lesser assembly that Bargrave termed the "provinciall councell" would share some further oversight, though its charge seems to have been largely reserved to the executive one of enforcing the laws.[39]

By making the superior council of union a transatlantic body, Bargrave neatly reserved a distinguished place in Virginia's emerging commonwealth even for stay-at-home planters like himself. He underscored the point by requiring the patriots and governors to keep personal estates on both sides of the ocean. By placing care over the Treasury in the hands of these high-ranking councillors with interests in England as well as Virginia, Bargrave clearly sought to cordon off the "publique groweing stocke," safeguarding this vital reservoir of funds at the heart of his polity from all poachers. Undoubtedly Middlesex himself figured among the persons whose grasping fingers Bargrave wanted kept at arm's length. Notably, when he got around to spelling out how the king himself would benefit from these arrangements, Bargrave emphasized only the traditional customs and imposts. Virginia's public might be the king's in name, but in reality it belonged to the commonwealth as a whole. Such prioritization of the public weal over any private interest was a formula for a godly commonwealth that placed Bar-

---

39. Bargrave to [Cranfield], the Lord Treasurer Middlesex, early December 1623, in Kingsbury, ed., *Records of the Virginia Company*, IV, 438, Bargrave, "Forme of Polisie," before Dec. 7, 1623, IV, 418, 421, 422, 428, 432, 433.

grave in plenty of good company. Indeed, it was a premise fundamental to how planters in the colony itself defended their polity.[40]

The view of the colony that Virginia's own planters presented in these years was simpler than Bargrave's yet not altogether different from his in its shared emphasis on the mutuality of the bond between king and planters. Beginning in 1624 and continuing into the early 1630s, the colony's assemblies responded to repeated efforts by first James I and then Charles I to secure a lucrative tobacco contract with the planters by making a highly consistent appeal that centered on several related issues. Most fundamental was the harmfulness of contracts and the corresponding argument that, as a commonwealth, Virginia needed to be treated as a body of persons whose duties came from God and whose divinely commanded role was the forging of a civil polity. Accompanying these points was a sharply revisionist view of the colony's earliest years. In the carefully crafted histories Virginia assemblies produced in the mid-1620s, one subject predominated: Sir Thomas Smythe and his fellow merchants were singleminded pursuers of gain whose resulting tyrannical government so disheartened planters that they neither labored willingly nor desired even to remain in the colony. According to this narrative, only the 1618 reforms that created the General Assembly and the subsequent rise of Sir Edwin Sandys to the treasurership the following year relieved the colony from its original commercial-minded rulers. This polemical rather than straightforwardly historical account of Smythe's regime ignored entirely the earlier paeans to Smythe as a merchant who always placed God's profits above man's. Instead, it took aim against the very real possibility that the colony might be placed in the hands of a governing commission of merchants and other projectors by painting a horrifying portrait of the moral turpitude of a society narrowly centered on the profit making of a few.[41]

---

40. Bargrave, "Forme of Polisie," before Dec. 7, 1623, in Kingsbury, ed., *Records of the Virginia Company*, IV, 432. For Bargrave's provision that patriots and governors keep estates in both Virginia and England, see ibid., 416. For Bargrave's allowance of customs and imposts to the king, see ibid., 432.

41. The Virginia assembly's regular reiterations of this appeal for a planter commonwealth from 1624 through the 1630s can be followed in McIlwaine, ed., *Journals of the House of Burgesses of Virginia, 1619–1658/59*, 21–65. For an example of the earlier rhetoric that cast Smythe as seeking divine over temporal gain, see the dedicatory poem to Smythe at the beginning of William Strachey, *For the Colony in Virginea Britannia: Lawes Divine, Morall, and Martiall, etc.* (London, 1612), n.p.

Writing in 1624, the planters claimed that conditions under Smythe's treasurership had been so bleak that "the happyest day that ever some of them hoped to see" was when, some Indians having killed a mare for their supper, the settlers entertained dreams "whilst she was boylinge that Sir *Tho: Smith* was uppon her backe in the kettle." The assemblymen were obviously making bald rhetorical use of Smythe's regime, treating it as if it readily stood in for anyone who mistook the colony for a mere exploitable field of wealth. Likewise, the 1618 reforms that ended martial law, instituted the General Assembly, and confirmed planters' land title were presented as a turning point that laid the groundwork for the eventual transformation of the colony's fortunes. By reassuring colonists that Virginia was recognized in England as a genuine polity, the 1618 reforms brought about just the harmony of rightly turned wills necessary "for the better establishinge of a Commonwealth heere," the assemblymen argued. In one fell swoop were removed "all those grievances which formerly were suffred" — cruel laws, a limitation on landholding, restraints on trade, a lack of consent in matters pertaining to lives and goods. The creation of the General Assembly in particular had an "effect" that was as instantaneous as it was marvelous, giving "such incouragement to every person heere that all of them followed their perticular labours with singular alacrity and industry, soe that, through the blessinge of God uppon our willinge labors, within the space of three yeares, our countrye flourished." Simple in its lessons, this parable mirrored the ideal of the commonwealth as a concatenation of cheerfully inclined wills that Christian humanists had theorized since the sixteenth century. If the king called off his projectors and submitted to rule Virginia as he would any of his kingdoms, then the labor he most sought from his colonists would be forthcoming. Otherwise, the colony would give way to its earlier wretched state of idleness and discontent, angering God. This message became the Virginians' mantra, a regularly reiterated insistence that commonwealth formation required obligations on the part of the king no less than from his faraway subjects, and only in the mutuality of those duties did the colony win God's blessings.[42]

The writings of the 1620s thus all sought to ground Virginia's polity in a richer vision of the colony's possibilities than the narrowly commercial "forme of Subscription" had prescribed. Whether in the hands of a fierce

---

42. "The Answere of the General Assembly in Virginia to a Declaration of the State of the Colonie," n.d., in McIlwaine, ed., *Journals of the House of Burgesses of Virginia, 1619–1658/59*, 21, "Briefe Declaration of the Plantation of Virginia," n.d., 36.

antipapal writer like Purchas or a Hispanophile like Bargrave, these writings invariably drew on the Christian humanist ideal of commonwealth, emphasizing the reciprocal moral ties that bound planters to their king and both of those earthly actors to their Maker. The ideal of Virginia as a future godly kingdom remained resonant, even if Salisbury's first efforts to tie American commonwealth formation to England's ascendancy as a potent state were rapidly becoming a distant memory. The problem of defending the colony's civil integrity, however, had become newly complicated, and the Treasury's relentless quest for a tobacco contract was only part of the difficulty. These years also witnessed repeated attacks on the planters' own morality, a politics of desacralization that arose precisely because of the outsized claims planters were making for themselves as appropriate guides in directing the king's sovereignty in his American affairs. As a result, the planter was defined in this period as much in relation to his critics as in response to the king and his revenue schemes.

The Planter and His Critics

Theorized as a calling that explained how all polities had come about, planting naturally became enmeshed in the era's confessional debates. Robert Johnson had argued in *Nova Britannia* (1609) that the "papists," whether "professed or Recusant," should be barred from becoming planters. He urged the colonists, if they found one in their midst, to "weede him out, and ship him home for England, for they will ever bee plotting and conspiring, to root you out if they can, howsoever they sweare, flatter, and equivocate." If Catholics made for bad planters, nonconforming Protestants were almost worse, especially if they went so far as to reject the established church entirely as unlawful. William Crashawe, preaching in 1608 on the eve of becoming one of the Virginia Company's most ardent supporters, expressed his own contempt for those sectaries "such as be now tearmed *of the separation,* formerly and usually called *Brownists;* who forsake our Church and cut off themselves from our congregations, and separate themselves to a faction, and fashion, or as they call it, into *a covenant and communion* of their owne devising." Chiding these holier-than-thou Christians for refusing to fight alongside their fellow Protestants against the papal Antichrist, Crashawe mocked them for scurrying into "your corners and conventicles, where you are your own carvers, your owne Judges, your own approvers, but have not one Church in Christendome to approove you." These kinds of swipes at papists and separatists were typical in planter discourse because of the providential view that planting was an activity set in motion by God, a mindset that practically demanded fending off religious adversaries. But such rhetoric also reflected the confessionally based criticism directed at planters themselves. Puritans charged Virginia's planters with worldliness, while Catholics accused them of wielding illicit power. Even as the colonizers sought to insulate Virginia's commonwealth against the king's tobacco contracts, they were also compelled to preserve their own reputation against various critics who denounced them precisely on the grounds that they lacked the moral capacity that commonwealth building required.[43]

As planters of all stripes came under the glare of hostile and often deeply moralistic critics, there was a palpable sense that colonization itself was taking the form of a stage, an arena peculiarly sensitive to the providential question of who was or was not doing God's will. John Winthrop famously referred to the new Massachusetts plantation in 1630 as a "City upon a Hill," a landmark in the Puritan origins of New England. Yet, he could just as easily have been speaking to Virginia's Anglicans in warning that the "eies of all people are uppon us" and "that if wee shall deale falsely with our god in this worke wee have undertaken and soe cause him to withdrawe his present help from us, wee shall be made a story and a by-word through the world." During the three decades following the founding of Jamestown in 1607, the apprehension that Virginia was persistently under scrutiny gave a theatrical quality to the politics of commonwealth formation. This state of affairs reached its dramatic denouement in the highly performative showdown with Governor Harvey in 1635. The episode even featured pregnant references to William Shakespeare's play *Richard the Third* as well as a scene so reminiscent of Charles's contentious parliament of 1629 as to strongly suggest that the Virginians were deliberately invoking it in order to frame their own political action as a parallel act in standing firm against a recalcitrant state. For this, finally, was the essence of the colonists' many stout responses to their critics. Their message was that they were indeed the lawful build-

---

43. R[obert] J[ohnson], *Nova Britannia: Offering Most Excellent Fruites by Planting in Virginia* . . . (London, 1609), D2r; W[illiam] Crasha[we], *The Sermon Preached at the Crosse, Feb. xiiij. 1607; . . . Justified by the Authour, Both against Papist, and Brownist, to Be the Truth: Wherein, This Point Is Principally Followed; Namely, That the Religion of Rome, as Now It Stands Established, Is Worse Then Ever It Was* (London, [1608]), 26, 32.

ers of a godly commonwealth, including when that constellation of rightly performed duties ran up against a state that risked losing sight of its moral actors.⁴⁴

Zealous Protestants made their criticism of Virginia felt early on because they numbered among the first planters journeying to Jamestown. The 1609 requirement that all planters subscribe to the Oaths of Allegiance and Supremacy barred Catholics more than sectarians, albeit the latter could prove just as disruptive in their questioning of the colony's legality. William Strachey described the separatist Protestants who joined Sir Thomas Gates's voyage that year on the *Sea Venture* with a degree of suspicion bordering on paranoia. Nonconformists like the man from Essex who was a "sectary in points of Religion" or the carpenter who "made much profession of Scripture" but was really a "dissembling Impostor" were, in Strachey's estimation, ineluctably drawn to mutiny because of the individualism in judgment and contempt for order that inevitably accompanied such separatism. They were superficially "devout" but not "drawne to the publique," making the hideous Brownist error of confusing their own view of righteous behavior for the real thing.⁴⁵

He was especially outraged by one Stephen Hopkins, who a decade later would accompany the Pilgrims on the *Mayflower*. After the *Sea Venture* became stranded in Bermuda, Hopkins made what Strachey called "substantiall arguments, both civill and divine." In other words, Hopkins pronounced his own casuistry, seeking to determine the shipwreck's providential lessons on the basis of his own analysis. His verdict was basically that Virginia's leaders threatened to bring planters into an unlawful bond. They endangered both their lives and souls by insisting that the colonists leave Bermuda's God-given fecundity and continue the journey to Virginia, where possibly for "their whole life" they would be forced "to serve the turnes of the Adventurers, with their travailes and labours." Hopkins was undoubtedly alluding to the frequent concern by the godly that England's colonizers were simply following in the same worldly footsteps as the Spaniards, brutally treating natives and English subjects alike in their quest for riches. The shipwreck had liberated the colonists from the burden of following their leaders into such an impious course. "It was no breach of honesty, conscience, nor Religion,"

---

44. John Winthrop, "A Modell of Christian Charity," Massachusetts Historical Society, *Collections*, 3d Ser., VII (Boston, 1838), 47.

45. William Strach[e]y, "A True Reportory of the Wracke, and Redemption of Sir Thomas Gates Knight . . . ," July 15, 1610, in Purchas, *Hakluytus Posthumus*, XIX, 29–32.

Hopkins argued, "to decline from the obedience of the Governour, or refuse to goe any further, led by his authority (except it so pleased themselves) since the authority ceased when the wracke was committed, and with it, they were all then freed from the government of any man." Moreover, as a "matter of Conscience, it was not unknowne to the meanest, how much we were therein bound each one to provide for himselfe, and his owne family" over and above the dictates of company and colony. In other words, Bermuda had revealed itself to be the true Promised Land, Virginia standing in contrast as a miserable carnal substitute. Strachey was horrified by such reasoning, which he blamed on "the Scripture falsly quoted." Yet, rather than flinch in the face of Hopkins's separatist reassessments of the planter's office, he scoffed at them, relieved that Gates still had the authority to suppress such "divellish disquiets."[46]

In tussles over rightful conduct like the one at Bermuda, Virginia and the planter became intimately bound up in the era's perennial question about how to determine the line between worldliness and godliness. For Crashawe, the issue was almost hopelessly confused by the separatists' own starting premise that they were God's elected saints and therefore, as he put it, already "healed" from sin while all other English subjects were "deadly wounded." If "they are as good as they pretend to be, and wee as ill as they would make us," he wrote in mock seriousness, then surely, instead of fleeing the realm and turning back only to "call us *Babylon, Antichristian, and the synagogue of the wicked*," they should remain among their still-stricken brethren to "shew us our wounds, and apply the means to heale us." For the separatists themselves, the problem of discriminating between virtue and sin was not so clearcut, though they did increasingly identify one standard for judging worldliness. Virginia, they argued, exemplified a carnal wickedness rivalled only by Holland. The colony's increasingly central role in Puritan polemic was not lost on Strachey. In 1612, he observed that only two types of people were "offended" by Virginia, the "meere ignorant" who knew no better and the "meere Opposite in *scientia Conscientiae*, [that is,] in Religion." Evidently Catholics figured in the latter category because Strachey associated the conscionable objectors in part with the papist view that the Spanish king had a "primer Interest" in the country. But Puritans were undoubtedly among a second set of objectors who argued that Virginia had been "injurious to the Naturalls" and thus clearly aimed at "no other" end

---

46. Ibid., 30–32. For Hopkins's transition from Virginia planter to Plymouth Pilgrim, see Karen Ordahl Kupperman, *The Jamestown Project* (Cambridge, Mass., 2007), 248–249.

than "flat Impiety" that was "displeasing before god." In failing to steer the natives properly to their lawful offices, the colonists had proven themselves hypocrites whose godly rhetoric masked worldly intentions.[47]

This motif of Virginian carnality became especially prominent in the saints' discourse as growing numbers of Puritans, separating and nonseparating alike, began to eye American colonization as a refuge from the creeping sinfulness of societies closer to home. The Pilgrims, for instance, finding their self-imposed exile in the Netherlands too worldly for their liking, appealed in 1617 and 1618 to the Council of Virginia and made further inquiries to Sir Edwin Sandys and the merchant Sir John Wolstenholme for permission to settle in the colony's northern regions as a "distinct body" under the "general Government of Virginia." The negotiations were hung up for a while on close ecclesiastical questions concerning just how far their separatism went. Surely the pope was at least right in holding to the existence of the Trinity! Wolstenholme exclaimed at one point in response to the saints' rigidness on Catholic error. But, once they arrived at Plymouth, the Pilgrims were free not only to leave the Church of England behind but also to turn their backs on Virginia's planters.[48]

In a sermon on December 9, 1621, Robert Cushman offered Virginia as a prime example of the "danger of selfe-love" and the spurning of "true friendship." Cushman's more general theme was commonwealth as glossed by way of Paul's teaching in 1 Corinthians 10:24: "Let no man seeke his owne, But every man anothers wealth." Colonization threatened this ordinance of liberality by making even the "wise and religious" man unusually vulnerable to the moral slippage involved in "carnall love of himselfe." In the case of Virginia, humanity's tendency to revert to their earlier corrupted state had evidently proven an overmatch for the settlers' otherwise sturdy English civility. Cushman had heard that there were "many men gone to that other Plantation in *Virginia*" who, while "they lived in England, seemed very religious, zealous, and conscionable" but "have now lost even the sap of grace, and edge to all goodnesse; and are become meere worldlings." In particular, these planters' concerns were focused on an excessive regard for enhancing their material well-being and elevating their worldly status. Propelled by

---

47. Crasha[we], *Sermon Preached at the Crosse, Feb. xiiij. 1607*, 30–31; William Strachey, *The Historie of Travell into Virginia Britania (1612) . . .* , ed. Louis B. Wright and Virginia Freund (London, 1953), 8–9.

48. William Bradford, *Of Plymouth Plantation, 1620–1647*, ed. Samuel Eliot Morison (New York, 1952), 29 (Wolstenholme's question about the Trinity appears on 355).

"disco[n]tentment, in regard of their estates in England; and ayming at great matters heere, affecting it to be Gentlemen, landed men, or hoping for office, place, dignitie, or fleshly [that is, worldly, as opposed to spiritual] liberty," they had clearly become consumed by the "spaune of selfe-love." Cushman's distaste for the Virginians did not rule out his acknowledgment that sometimes a person may indeed lawfully "gather wealth, and grow rich," but he was confident that "a godly and sincere Christian will see when this time is, and will not ho[a]rd up when he seeth others of his brethren and associates to want." His charge of Virginians' worldliness was less a stark argument about the immorality of riches and more a subtle distinction about the relative godliness of planters. The Virginians had crossed a line into the ambiguous territory of self-love that Cushman was certain amounted to unforgivable sin, and he wanted to ensure that Plymouth's planters did not similarly take that erroneous path.[49]

The Virginians responded to such charges of corruption by arguing that worldliness, if not taken too far, was consistent with rather than antithetical to a holy commonwealth. Their rationalization of the inevitability of a certain degree of sinfulness in the polity was a version of Anglican apologetics, a matter of weighing in on the fundamental question of how fallen man satisfies God. Strachey held to a highly voluntarist view of human will that he evidently derived in part from William of Ockham, the medieval Schoolman. On the knotty Christian question of how to reconcile Paul's various emphases on faith and works, Strachey wrote that "good workes, albeyt they be not *concausae* [causes] yet are they *consectaria* [consequences] (as the Sholeman sayes) of our faith: though not *causa regnandi* [first causes], yet are they *via ad regnum* [ways to the kingdom]; though they justefye not before God, yet they doe glorefye god in his Servants." To some of the more severe of the godly, this endorsement of virtuous action would have veered dangerously in the direction of heretical exaltation of man's will over God's. But for Strachey it was simply a compelling explanation of the "generall office of Mankynd." Humans had a basic calling "not only to wish good, but to bring

---

49. Robert Cushman. *A Sermon Preached at Plimmoth in New-England December 9. 1621; in an Assemblie of His Majesties Faithfull Subjects, There Inhabiting; Wherein Is Shewed the Danger of Selfe-Love, and the Sweetnesse of True Friendship* ... (London, 1622), 1, 5, 10, 11 12. For an example of a conforming Puritan making a similar argument about colonization's tendency toward worldliness, see John Brinsley, *A Consolation for Our Grammar Schooles; or, A Faithfull and Most Comfortable Incouragement, for Laying of a Sure Foundation of All Good Learning in Our Schooles, and for Prosperous Building Thereupon* ... (London, 1622), A2v–A3r.

that to passe, for one of the like creation." Strachey applied this rule of liberal earthly conduct to the planters' particular role in bringing civility and Christianity to native Americans, but he seems to have embraced it more broadly as a more or less apt description of the doctrine of England's established church.[50]

To the Puritans' charge that Virginia was injurious to the natives, Strachey argued that "temporall endes" and "divine Motives" were so intertwined toward these persons' benefit that there was very little use in distinguishing between them; "even common Trade, and hope of proffit" contributed to the "lawfull worke" of planting the gospel abroad. Strachey's confidence that such worldly pursuits were legitimate centered on his humanist conviction that peoples who had arrived at an advanced civilized condition owed this achievement not only to God's blessing but also to their own industrious striving in areas they had good reason to regard as lawful. England's "comonweale" basked in "the supernall light," but it was also "governed with the well-ordered Powers of Philosophie, and all naturall knowledges." Accordingly, the English knew they could rely safely on "the Law of Nations (which is the lawe of god and man)," and this divine and civil guide to proper behavior "admits that lawfull, to trade with any manner of People." Strachey gave a sly twist to this reasoning that made the *ius gentium*'s allowance for trade a minimum basis for upright conduct that rendered any more pious motives simply icing on the cake: "yf traffique be thus justefyable which intendes nothing but transitory proffitt, and increase of temporall, and worldly goodes, shall not planting the Christian faith be much more?" True godliness, Strachey suggested, combined earthly as well as divine motives, and planters could rest assured in walking a path that pursued them both.[51]

Justifying the planter's worldliness involved also denying the saints' claim to know the real route to righteousness. Thomas Scott, probably the same Protestant polemicist who would write *Vox Populi; or, Newes from Spayne* (1620), took a characteristic Anglican stab at the separatists' unrealistic principles in his satire *Philomythie; or, Philomythologie* (which went through two

---

50. Strachey, *Historie of Travell into Virginia Britania*, ed. Wright and Freund, 18, 19. On Ockham, see *Oxford Dictionary of National Biography*, online ed., s.v. "Ockham, William (c.1287–1347)," by W. J. Courtenay, accessed Mar. 20, 2015, http://www.oxforddnb.com/view/article/20493.

51. Strachey, *Historie of Travell into Virginia Britania*, ed. Wright and Freund, 17, 20–21, 22, 23.

editions in 1616 and a third in 1622). Repeating a familiar conformist refrain about the fancifulness of the separatists' vision of a purely godly commonwealth, Scott said of this otherworldly saint: "He lives by the ayre, and there builds Castles and Churches: None on the earth will please him: He would be of the triumphant and glorious Church, but not of the terrene militant Church, which is subject to stormes, deformities, and many violences and alterations of time: he must finde out Sir *Thomas Mores Utopia,* or rather *Platoes* Community, and be an *Elder* there." Virginia's defenders, too, held to Scott's implicit anti-utopian take on the polity, a matter of rejecting the separatists' unreasonable idealism for an acceptance of humanity's obligation to make do on an imperfect Earth. Still not fully reunited with God but in need of the order and obedience necessary for doing battle with Christ's enemies, the commonwealth must necessarily rest its constitutive bonds in part on people's remaining responsiveness to worldly interests.[52]

Articulating this Anglican conception of comingling earthly and godly pursuits in his *New Life of Virginea* (1612), Robert Johnson had urged the colony's magistrates to govern planters with an eye toward not only their capacity for goodness but also the reality of their persistent weakness for material things. "Discourage them not in growing religious, nor in gathering riches, two especiall bonds (whether severed or conjoyned) to keepe them in obedience, the one for conscience sake, the other for feare of losing what they have gotten," he had written. "Without the first they are prophane, without the second desperate, and apt for every factious plot to bee instruments of mischiefe." Captain John Smith similarly argued that temporal interests were inescapable factors in bringing imperfect humans to their civil and religious duties. In defending his planned New England colony in 1616, he wrote, "I am not so simple, to thinke, that ever any other motive then wealth, will ever erect there a Commonweale; or draw companie from their ease and humours at home, to stay in New England to effect my purposes." Smith distinguished this tempered self-love from unrestrained "private covetousness," an illiberal greed whose "excesse of vanity" and "prodigalitie" he associated with the "devouring Turke." His conception of the commonwealth was rather one in which the wealthy did "not grudge to lend some proportion" to those "that have little," while the humblest planter took delight in tending honestly to his own modest plot of earth. Smith described

---

52. Tho[mas] Scot[t], *Philomythie or Philomythologie; Wherein Outlandish Birds, Beasts, and Fishes, Are Taught to Speake True English Plainely* (London, 1616), 48–49.

the latter image lovingly, as though it summed up his Anglican faith that even the smallest amount of virtue in a person was enough to bring out the dutifulness and industriousness needed for civil polity:

> Who can desire more content, that hath small meanes; or but only his merit to advance his fortune, then to tread, and plant that ground hee hath purchased by the hazard of his life? If he have but the taste of virtue, and magnanimitie, what to such a minde can bee more pleasant, then planting and building a foundation for his Posteritie, gotte from the rude earth, by Gods blessing and his owne industrie, without prejudice to any?

In this portrait of the striving, yet not overly ambitious colonist who works hard on his own piece of ground without overturning the larger hierarchical order, one is reminded of Smith's repeated view that the first planters were Adam and Eve. Their innocence rested in simple labor in the earth in accordance with God's wishes. For Smith, much of the allure of the idea of the planter clearly lay in a similarly straightforward morality that stood comfortably at odds with the sectarians' overly lofty idealism.[53]

If Virginia's planter commonwealth rested in part on a self-conscious defense of worldliness, it stood as well on a brusque assertiveness in favor of strong authority. Hopkins's charge that the colony was a miserable scene of hard work overseen by cruel taskmasters was the sort of Puritan complaint that tended to attract scornful replies rather than meek apologies from Virginia leaders who were convinced that turning erring members around through often-severe justice was consistent with a commonwealth still burdened by sin. Objections to the *Lawes Divine, Morall, and Martiall*

---

53. R[obert] J[ohnson], *The New Life of Virginea: Declaring the Former Successe and Present Estate of That Plantation, Being the Second Part of Nova Britannia; Published by the Authoritie of His Majesties Counsell of Virginea* (London, 1612), E3r; John Smith, *A Description of New England; or, The Observations, and Discoveries, of Captain John Smith* . . . (London, 1616), in Barbour, ed., *Complete Works of Captain John Smith*, I, 343, 345, 346. Smith's view that colonists could lawfully "gaine wealth sufficient" was mindful of differences in the planters' callings. The "Carpenter, Mason, Gardiner, Taylor, Smith, Sailer, Forgers, or what other" could expect a profit appropriate to their common station in life, while "Gentlemen" would receive, in turn, "a Captains pay" — again a variegated distribution of wealth that rested on the conventional assumption that a primary duty of the gentleman's office was generosity to others for the sake of drawing those naturally flawed mortals to their own societal obligations (I, 347–348).

had elicited just such a dismissive response. Strachey compared the disorder in Virginia that the *Lawes* sought to correct to the civil conflagration in the German palatinate city of Magonza (present-day Mainz) when in 1461–1462 it became engulfed in religious conflict. All "Lawes, literature, and Vertue" might have perished there, he wrote, "had not the force of piety and sacred reason remaining in the bosomes of some few [lawmakers], opposed itselfe against the fury of so great a calamity." Johnson similarly expressed little remorse about the toughness of the colony's early legal regime. Responding to those objectors who complained that imposing such harsh laws at this time was an unfeeling reaction to a community wracked by hunger and thus understandably desperate and disorderly, Johnson insisted that the company was entirely sympathetic to the deafness to authority imposed by dire straits: "If wholesome lodging, cloathing for the backe and bodilie foode be wanting, the bellie pincht with hunger cannot heare, though your charme be otherwise never so sweet." With the casuist's telltale eye to circumstance, he argued that such reasoning did not apply in this case. Governor Gates had arrived with ample supplies and yet still failed to win the colony's obedience. Full bellies that continued to be deaf to the "charme" of their governors did not just permit severe governance but required it.[54]

Virginia's leaders defended firm authority on the grounds that it was a necessary concomitant of the civilizing process and essential for any commonwealth, especially one just beginning to coalesce around the reciprocal duties of its members. This was Strachey's reasoning, for instance, when he exclaimed in response to the disorders at Bermuda, "Loe, what are our affections and passions, if not rightly squared? how irreligious, and irregular they express us?" Smith voiced this same admiration for the taming power of governance when he observed that Virginia's natives possessed a glimmer of virtue that was visible simply in their impressive adherence to the mutual bond between rulers and ruled: "Although the countrie people be very barbarous, yet have they amongst them such governement, as that their Magistrats for good commanding, and their people for du subjection, and obeying, excell many places that would be counted very civill." In the far more common occurrence in which Smith was unimpressed by the natives' civility, he "curbed their insolencies" with methods that included taking "some childe for hostage" as protection whenever a village seemed recalcitrant toward its

54. Strachey, *For the Colony in Virginea Britannia*, [A3]r; J[ohnson], *New Life of Virginea*, D[1]v.

new English overlords. But Smith's real obsession, like Strachey's, was bringing his fellow planters to heel.[55]

When defending his brief presidency of the colony's council that began on September 10, 1608, Smith and his band of close supporters lauded nothing more than his strictness in turning idle men into industrious workers while more generally reforming viciousness. At one point, he set thirty planters to felling trees, including two "proper gentlemen" whose "tender fingers" were unaccustomed to the brute labor of hewing timber into clapboard. Whenever these axe wielders sinfully swore from the pain of their newly formed blisters, he poured a bracing can of water down their sleeves for every wayward oath. At another time, he lectured the planters against their "idlenesse and sloth" by referencing Paul's second letter to the Thessalonians. The letter was an important source for the Christian humanist ethos of work that so clearly motivated Virginia's early leaders. In it, Paul and other apostles spoke of their own "labour and travaile night and day." Such tireless work not only freed them from encroaching on the resources of the people they were trying to save but also served an instructional purpose, intending "to make our selves an ensample unto you to follow us." Smith's supporters would later stress his role as a responsible leader of planters by describing how, "by his owne example, good words, and faire promises," he "set some to mow, others to binde thatch, some to build houses, others to thatch them, himselfe alwayes bearing the greatest taske for his owne share, so that in short time, he provided most of them lodgings, neglecting any for himselfe." But, in his speech on 2 Thessalonians, Smith emphasized instead a far more austere lesson: the apostles' command to their still sinful brethren that "if any would not worke, neither should he eate."[56]

---

55. Strach[e]y, "True Reportory of the Wracke," July 15, 1610, in Purchas, *Hakluytus Posthumus*, XIX, 28; John Smith, *A Map of Virginia; With a Description of the Countrey, the Commodities, People, Government, and Religion* (Oxford, England, 1612), in Barbour, ed., *Complete Works of Captain John Smith*, I, 173, [Smith], *The Proceedings of the English Colonie in Virginia Since Their First Beginning from England in the Yeare of Our Lord 1606* . . . (Oxford, England, 1612), I, 228.

56. [Smith], *Proceedings of the English Colonie in Virginia* (1612), in Barbour, ed., *Complete Works of Captain John Smith*, I, 238, 259; 2 Thessalonians, 3:8–10, *The Holy Bible, Conteyning the Old Testament, and the New: Newly Translated Out of the Originall Tongues: And With the Former Translations Diligently Compared and Revised, by His Majesties Speciall Co[m]mandement* (London, 1611); Smith, *Generall Historie* (1624), in Barbour, ed., *Complete Works of Captain John Smith*, II, 144.

Smith's tactics were not all draconian. He experimented as well on this occasion with a table of merits and demerits as a "publike memoriall" to "encourage the good, and with shame to spurre on the rest to amendment." However, he also concluded that "more by severe punishment performed their businesse." Later, he warned that anyone who did not work for himself while also contributing some of his harvest to the sick would be banished to the far side of the James River, to "live there or starve." Although "many murmured" that this order "was very cruell," Smith measured its worth on the basis of its effectiveness in preserving the young colony, observing that "it caused the most part so well [to] bestir themselves, that of 200 men (except they were drowned) there died not past 7 or 8." Creating the conditions that motivated planters to perform their duties for the good of the whole far outweighed whatever misgivings the errant individual might feel about finding himself thrust out of the fort.[57]

By the late 1620s and early 1630s, defenses of Virginia's worldliness had hardened into a conviction that any precisionist caviling about them was a sign in itself of a dangerously irreligious stubbornness of will. This was once again an instance of sly Anglican polemic, for Puritans leveled much the same charge of obstinacy against overly worldly leaders like the pope, such as when Cushman warned his brethren that it was to be "Prince-like, or rather Papall, that their very will and word is become a law, and if they have said it, it must be so." To Smith, it was the "wilfulnesse" of unyielding saints like the "Brownists of Leyden and Amsterdam at New-Plimoth" that truly stood at odds with the commonwealth's larger concert of wills. He expressed this antiseparatist conviction in his *Advertisements for the Unexperienced Planters of New England, or Any Where; or, The Path-way to Experience to Erect a Plantation* . . . (1631). By this time, the newly founded Massachusetts colony had also become a magnet for the most zealous of the godly. Smith took a swipe at the "factious Humorists" with whom Governor John Winthrop, himself a "worthy Gentleman both in estate and esteeme," had to contend. These discontented and overly righteous persons, unworthy of the name planter, exhibited an overbearing holiness that had the effect of breaking down bonds of commonwealth rather than forging them:

> Some could not endure the name of a Bishop, others not the sight of a Crosse nor Surplesse, others by no meanes the booke of common

57. [Smith], *Proceedings of the English Colonie in Virginia* (1612), in Barbour, ed., *Complete Works of Captain John Smith*, I, 259–265.

Prayer. This absolute crue, only of the Elect, holding all (but such as themselves) reprobates and cast-awaies, now make more haste to returne to Babel, as they tearmed England, than stay to enjoy the land they called Canaan.

For Smith, such unsteadiness in the enterprise of planting was characteristic of those who took the absolute line of confusing their own holiness with everyone else's sinfulness. Only planters who took a more capacious and down-to-earth view on virtue, a group Smith called "good Catholike Protestants according to the reformed Church of England," were likely to forge a commonwealth capable of persisting through the ages.[58]

If Protestant separatists forced the planters to defend themselves from one direction, Catholics increasingly leaned on them from another. When Secretary of State George Calvert decided to relocate his colony from frigid Newfoundland to the warm Chesapeake, he inserted the specter of papalism abruptly into Virginia politics. Calvert had announced his own Catholicism shortly after Charles I's accession, emblematizing the realm's new openness to popery. Although Calvert was forced to give up his secretaryship once his commitment to the Old Faith became public knowledge, Charles offered him the palliative of a noble title, the first Baron Baltimore of Ireland. Arriving in Virginia in late September 1629 to scout out the new location for his colony, Baltimore immediately received a stern rebuff from Virginia's government. Four Virginian leaders, including interim governor Dr. John Pott, Samuel Mathews (the onetime commissioner), Roger Smith, and Captain William Claiborne, confronted him and his party and promptly ordered them to take the Oaths of Allegiance and Supremacy. "Making profession

---

58. Cushman, *Sermon Preached at Plimmoth in New-England December 9. 1621*, 7; John Smith, *Advertisements for the Unexperienced Planters of New-England, or Any Where; or, The Path-Way to Experience to Erect a Plantation* . . . (London, 1631), in Barbour, ed., *Complete Works of Captain John Smith*, III, 270, 271, 292–293. George Donne, who arrived in Virginia in 1637, similarly wrote of the separatists: "So heartily they hate conformity that they detest order, Ambitious of a new creation of ridiculous novelty and most ridiculous Schisme by Separacion. They are in A Manner desperate E[n]thusiasticks for whereas all Men are moved (as A heathen [Cicero] noted) by Religion, the perswasion whereof is the cheif in policy. . . . These Fanaticks Choose rather without pollicy or religion to bee misled by their lay Elders then bee guided by the true Pastors of their selves or governed by their naturall Soveraigne." See T. H. Breen, "George Donne's 'Virginia Reviewed': A 1638 Plan to Reform Colonial Society," *William and Mary Quarterly*, XXX (1973), 464.

of the Romishe Religion," Baltimore balked and offered to take an oath of his own devising. But the Virginians refused to allow it, explaining in a letter to the Privy Council that James's own writings in defense of the oaths convinced them that no such latitude from the prescribed form was permissible. Flouting Baltimore's high rank, they told him that "they durst not admit any man into their society which would not acknowledge all preeminences belonging to his majesty; and so prayed him to provide himself for the next ship, wherein they have shipped him home." The rude send-off was characteristic of the boldness with which the Virginians would challenge Baltimore's patent in the coming years, especially as Charles's support for the Maryland colony came to seem troublingly bound up with his equally vigorous quest for a tobacco contract.[59]

As a result of such Virginia aggression, the Marylanders developed a Catholic polemic about Virginia that was every bit as vehement as the Puritan argument of Virginia's worldliness. The Catholic claim was that Virginia's leaders were maliciously opposed to popery and vested with a dangerous amount of authority that they inevitably abused for their own advantage. Powerful councillors like Pott, Mathews, Smith, and Claiborne were the bogeymen in this Catholic account, the men whose "spleene and malice" against papists so fanned their hostility to Maryland that they could be counted on to be its most vicious adversaries. Lord Baltimore was sufficiently worried about these figures that he included explicit instructions to his first colonists not to stop at Jamestown except under the greatest duress

---

59. John Pott et al. to Privy Council, Nov. 30, 1629, in William Hand Browne et al., eds., *Archives of Maryland*, III, *Preceedings of the Council of Maryland, 1636–1667* (Baltimore, 1885), 17; Rev. Joseph Mead to Sir Martin Stuteville, Jan. 23, 1629–1630, in [Thomas Birch, ed.], *The Court and Times of Charles the First* . . . (London, 1848), II, 53. For the circumstances behind Baltimore's colonization efforts and his securing of the Maryland grant, see John D. Krugler, *English and Catholic: The Lords Baltimore in the Seventeenth Century* (Baltimore, 2004), 76–128. In light of the Virginians' stated familiarity with James's published defenses of the Oaths of Supremacy and Allegiance, it is interesting to note that John Pory rendered into Italian for the Venetian ambassador, Sir Paul Pindar, the king's *Declaration . . . pour le droit des rois et independance de leurs couronnes, contre laa harangue de l'illustrissime Cardinal du Perron* . . . (London, 1615), one version of James's apologia for the oaths. Pory's translation of the work underscores how intimately the colonial world overlapped with the broader confessional politics of sovereign kingship, whether in Europe or in the New World. On Pory's translation, see *Oxford Dictionary of National Biography*, online ed., s.v. "Pory, John (*bap.* 1572, *d.* 1633)," by Charlotte Fell-Smith, rev. David R. Ransome, accessed Mar. 20, 2015, http://www.oxforddnb.com/view/article/22591?docPos=2.

and always to communicate with Virginia's political leaders via messengers who were "conformable to the Church of England" so as to avoid needless confrontation. Sir John Harvey was one of the few Virginia politicians exempted from this portrait of a group of colonial leaders implacably opposed to their new Catholic neighbors. Appointed governor on March 26, 1628, and probably knighted at that time to enhance his authority, Harvey early on perceived his duty to his king as necessitating a circumspect approach to the colony's councillors.[60]

Charles I's instructions to assist the Marylanders ensured that he would be at odds with these assertive men, for they regarded the Maryland patent as a miscarriage of the king's sovereignty that particularly endangered Virginia, especially with regard to the provisions of Baltimore's charter. This was especially true of Charles's grant of remarkable privileges to Baltimore himself. The Virginians called Baltimore's outsized authority his "Royall and Imperiall Power," and they fretted that Maryland's independence from Virginia threatened to introduce a status differential between the colonies "by exalting the One and decreasing the other." Far from crowing about their own authority vis-à-vis Maryland, they feared yet another hit to Virginia's civil integrity, "the Lord Baltimore's Colonie haveinge power in themselves to manage their Affaires free from all dependancy on others." In other words, the Virginians worried as much about Baltimore's unnatural power as he worried about theirs, a mutual suspicion that set them at loggerheads from the beginning. The Jesuit priest Andrew White exclaimed that his party was so unhopeful of receiving a warm reception from the Virginians that "we expected little from them but blows." "Although we carried the kings letters to their Governour, and the governour himselfe much esteemed and loved my L[o]rd, yet wee feared he could or would doe us little good being overawed by his councell," White wrote. Convinced that the "Councells will" was dead set against Maryland, White was unsurprised when William Claiborne, one of the chief belligerents, informed them that local Indians had armed themselves against the Marylanders on hearing that "6 Spanish ships were a comeing to destroy them all." Far from shocking him, the rumor simply confirmed White's suspicions that Claiborne himself had spread it.[61]

60. "Instructions to the Colonists by Lord Baltimore," 1633, in Clayton Colman Hall, ed., *Narratives of Early Maryland, 1633–1684* [New York, 1953], 15, 17, 18, 21.

61. "Considerations upon the Patent to the Lord Baltimore," June 20, [1632], in Browne et al. eds., *Archives of Maryland*, III, 19; "A Briefe Relation of the Voyage unto Maryland, by Father

Other Catholic writers reinforced this view of the Virginians' intransigence. Agreeing that Claiborne was a relentless foe, they pointed especially to his confrontational claim to Kent Island, a territory within Baltimore's jurisdiction, as a particularly cunning strategy for forcing the question of the patent's validity into the king's courts. But Claiborne was hardly alone in his animosity. As the Baltimore sympathizer Captain Thomas Yong explained in a letter to the crypto-papist Sir Toby Matthew, "Some others also of the principall Councellors of Virginia might justly be suspected to have animated Cleyborne to his foule practises." Yong was at least popishly inclined if not a Catholic himself. In addition to being part of the papist Matthew's circle, he was also uncle to the Virginia surveyor general Robert Evelyn, whom the Virginians accused of being a recusant when he represented Harvey against the councillors before Star Chamber in 1638. In Yong's view, Claiborne's "private friends" Captain Samuel Mathews and Captain John Utie were just as determined as he was to make themselves "Lords of that Country." Mathews especially was the "person on whom the strength and sinewes of this faction depends," Yong observed. An "ancient planter heere," Mathews was a "man of a bold spiritt, turbulent and strong" among "the more refractory sort of the countrey." Yong's description of Mathews and his like-minded councillors as a faction that was "soe fast linked and united" that they could only be reduced if the governor received "some new power from England" was perfectly in keeping with the emerging Catholic view of the Virginia leaders as a colonial oligarchy. But what made them particularly menacing, suggesting that their influence rested on more than a mere concentration of ill-gotten power, was their considerable sway over other planters, both great and small.[62]

Andrew White," 1634, in Hall, ed., *Narratives of Early Maryland*, 33–34, 39. For Charles's instructions to the Virginians to assist Maryland, see The king to the governor and Council of Virginia, July 12, 1633, in Browne et al. eds., *Archives of Maryland*, III, 22–23. On White, see *Oxford Dictionary of National Biography*, online ed., s.v., "White, Andrew (1579–1656)," by Thompson Cooper, rev. Thomas M. McCoog, accessed Mar. 9, 2015, http://www.oxforddnb.com/view/article/29236.

62. "Extract from a Letter of Captain Thomas Yong to Sir Toby Matthew," 1634, in Hall, ed., *Narratives of Early Maryland*, 56, 57, 58, 59. On Yong and his probable Catholicism, see also Mark L. Thompson, "'The Predicament of Ubi': Locating Authority and National Identity in the Seventeenth-Century English Atlantic," in Elizabeth Mancke and Carole Shammas, eds., *The Creation of the British Atlantic World* (Baltimore, 2005), 71–92. On Sir Toby Matthew, see *Oxford Dictionary of National Biography*, online ed., s.v. "Matthew, Sir Toby [Tobie] (1577–1655)," by A. J.

Maryland's Catholics could not deny that Mathews was widely esteemed among local planters and that he was noted especially as a spokesman for the colony's civil integrity, standing forcefully on the colonists' side when new impositions in the name of the state threatened to eclipse Virginia's commonwealth. Yong shuddered at Mathews's authority as "a great opposer and interpreter of all letters and commands that come from the King and state of England" and marveled at his ability "to possesse and preoccupate the judgments of the rest of his fellow councellors" about their true meaning. In particular, these other officials accepted when Mathews told them "letters from the King and from the Lords are surreptitiously gotten and that the obedience to them may and ought to be suspended till they be warranted by second commands from England." Mathews's philosophy for Virginia's government evidently boiled down to an argument about the trust the king needed to have in his leading planters given the sheer distance imposed by the ocean—a view not unlike the one Bargrave had articulated when he wrote that the "perfection and happinesse of a commonwealth, lyeth not soe much in the spaciousnesse of it but first and principally in the government, consisteing in the mutuall duties of commandeing and obeyeing, next in possessing thinges plentifully, necessarie for the life of man." Mathews similarly viewed the colony's essence as lying in this tie between sovereign and planter, and he was prepared to safeguard that bond even against the king's own shortsightedness or poor counsel.[63]

On the grounds that the king's Privy Councillors were never "sufficiently instructed in the necessities and conveniencies of this Government heere," Mathews was able to persuade the council that their decisions mattered and should inform how England itself approached the colony. Or, as Yong contemptuously described Mathews's sway over his fellow councillors, he succeeded in "making them beleeve that evry kind of disobedience doe oftentimes become gratefull to the State." Mathews's great influence at the council table gave him inordinate power because "heere in this place all things are

---

Loomie, accessed Oct. 16, 2016, http://www.oxforddnb.com/view/article/18343. For the accusation of Robert Evelyn's recusancy, see "Proceedings upon a Petition of the Defendants in a Suit in the Star Chamber of the Attorney-General versus John West, Samuel Mathew, William Tucker, Esquire, and Others, to the Lord Keeper," Bankes MSS, 13/27, Oxford, Bodleian Library (copy at Alderman Library, University of Virginia, Charlottesville, Va.).

63. "Extract from a Letter of Captain Thomas Yong to Sir Toby Matthew," 1634, in Hall, ed., *Narratives of Early Maryland*, 58, 59, 60–61; Bargrave, "Forme of Polisie," before Dec. 7, 1623, in Kingsbury, ed., *Records of the Virginia Company*, IV, 411.

carried by the most voyces of the Councell," and the councillors' deliberations were especially directed against Harvey's own sycophantic vote. "It is hard for the Governors to determine or order any thing heere contrary to their dreaming," Yong complained, "for they come all hither preoccupated and resolved to follow and concurr with the votes of their leaders."[64]

But Mathews's command over the colony's affections also extended well beyond the council chamber. Ordinary planters also placed their trust in him. Indeed, they heeded him and his allies to the point of accepting their view of what did or did not constitute loyal behavior to the king. Infuriatingly, Virginia's councillors succeeded even in convincing planters that Maryland was itself so contrary to the king's interests as to forbid assistance to it. "They have so exasperated and incensed all the English Colony of Virginia as heere it is accounted a crime almost as heynous as treason to favor, nay allmost to speak well of that Colony of my Lords." Virginia's leaders had a ready answer for the Catholic critique that they were unnaturally powerful. Their response consisted in the sheer effectiveness of their authority. However much Baltimore's own Catholic allies preferred to denigrate that conciliar governance as illicit and abusive, Mathews and his companions gathered strength from its broad-based popular consent.[65]

Of course, adversaries were quick to criticize this consensual support as a questionable bid for popularity, a politics centered tumultuously on the multitude that invited parallels with Anabaptist anarchism. The councillors emphasized their valuable position between the king and his planter population, a vantage point from which they could coax all uncompromising wills into the congruence necessary for commonwealth. Yet, to the king's treasurers, this vigorous conciliar presence in the colony was a vexing obstacle to their efforts to reorganize Virginia in ways that profited the king

64. "Extract from a Letter of Captain Thomas Yong to Sir Toby Matthew," 1634, in Hall, ed., *Narratives of Early Maryland*, 58, 59, 60–61.

65. Ibid., 58. For an alternative view that stresses the opposition between the councillors and planters on a number of issues, including the councillors' preference that goods be transported on the ships of their London merchant allies rather than cheaper Dutch traders, see Robert Brenner, *Merchants and Revolution: Commercial Change, Political Conflict, and London's Overseas Traders, 1550–1653* (Princeton, 1993), 125–148. The interpretation advanced here does not deny Brenner's finding that councillors and smaller planters sometimes divided over certain economic issues, but it does suggest that those economic concerns were overshadowed by broader fears about the integrity of Virginia's commonwealth and church, a prioritizing of values that was natural in the still intensely providential context of the early seventeenth century.

rather than simply the colony's leading planters. One of the most dramatic attempts at reforming the colony's government in these years sought to reduce the council to a shadow of its former self. On October 8, 1623, a commission headed by Henry Montagu, Lord Mandeville, announced its design for the colony before a group of Virginia Company adventurers who were reportedly so "amazed" by the proposal that "no man spake thereunto for a longe time." Mandeville, who had preceded Middlesex as lord high treasurer before becoming lord president of the council, explained the scheme. In place of the bloated Virginia Company and the once-powerful Virginia Council, a new streamlined group composed of a "Governor and Twelve Assistants" would oversee the colony's affairs from England. A subordinate version of the same body, also to be called the "Governor and Assistants," would meet in Virginia, replacing the Council of State and General Assembly. This radically reduced Virginia government would have "Dependance" on its English counterpart, which in turn would be answerable to Mandeville's board. The only carrot offered the planters and adventurers for this governmental overhaul was a reassurance that their "private interests" would be preserved, including land titles, special franchises like the particular plantations, and other undefined benefits. But, for planters, including the headstrong councillors, private interests had little substance if they stood apart from commonwealth: it was within that moral community that the colonists' robust liberties and duties had meaning. The Mandeville commission's plan, which was undoubtedly the object of the open-ended "forme of Subscription" that Harvey and his fellow commissioners brought to Virginia in 1624, was hardly an encouraging offer in this regard.[66]

Recognizing that Mandeville's proposal was simply an effort to yoke planters more securely to the royal prerogative while abandoning any real vision of the colony's future as a godly kingdom and commonwealth, the 1624 assembly responded with a stream of appeals that lashed out at the prospect of merchant leadership and insisted that God's blessings were reserved for the reciprocal tie between king and planters. In their letters home, the assemblymen pleaded with the Privy Council to continue the General Assembly and

---

66. "At a Court Held for Virginia on Wedensday in the Afternoone the 15 of Oct: 1623," in Kingsbury, ed., *Records of the Virginia Company*, II, 469–470; Francis Wyatt et al. to the Privy Council, February 1623 [1624], in McIlwaine, ed., *Journal of the House of Burgesses of Virginia, 1619–1658/59*, 27. For the Mandeville committee members, see "At a Court Held for Virginia on Wedensday in the Afternoone the 22th of October 1623," in Kingsbury, ed., *Records of the Virginia Company*, II, 476.

to ensure that governors like those envisioned by the Mandeville commission not enjoy "absolute authoritye, but may be restrayned as formerly by the consent of this Counsell, w[hi]ch tytle we desire may be retayned to the honor of this Plantation, and not converted to the name of assistantes." Determined to retain the dignity of their office, Mathews and his fellows clung to their conciliar role not only as a safeguard of Virginia's planter commonwealth but also to hold the line against popery. After all, Mandeville's commission unmistakably wore the face not only of the Treasury but also of English Catholicism In addition to Middlesex and Lord Keeper Williams, the commission also included Secretary Calvert, soon to declare himself openly Catholic as well as a direct adversary of Virginia in its claims to its ancient jurisdiction. No wonder Virginia's councillors responded so forcefully against Baltimore's plantation. They regarded it and the designs of the Treasury as frighteningly interwoven, a combination of forces that threatened the integrity of Virginia's commonwealth just as papists and projectors enjoyed growing influence in the English realm itself.[67]

Not surpisingly then, the planters' defense of their commonwealth also put them in the good graces of a great many powerful Protestant supporters on the other side of the ocean who readily saw the colonists' cause as affiliated with their own. Charles's 1628 and 1629 parliaments were filled with a high-pitched rhetoric similar to the planters' in its shared concerns with Charles's innovatory economic policies, continuing openness to Catholicism, and enhanced willingness to justify such measures on the basis of state necessity. Suggestive of how these issues overlapped and brought Virginia and England into close orbit was the anger directed on both sides of the ocean against yet another deeply resented treasurer, Sir Richard Weston. Middlesex's protégé entered office after Middlesex's inexperienced successor James Ley, first earl of Marlborough, stepped down from the office, Middlesex having been impeached by Parliament in 1624 as a result of his pro-Spanish, antiwar policies. Like his mentor, Weston was similarly a Hispanophile and sympathetic to Catholicism. Soon to be created earl of Portland, he would attract Sir John Elliot's criticism in the 1629 parliament as the person in whom "is contracted all the evill, that we doe suffer" whether concerning "religion, or policye." These were strong words for a treasurer who shared the same devotion to the king's prerogative as many of Charles's other advisers in these years, but Elliot's condemnation of Weston captured the way

---

67. Wyatt et al. to the Privy Council, February 1623 [1624], in McIlwaine, ed., *Journal of the House of Burgesses of Virginia, 1619-1658/59*, 27.

the king's extra-parliamentary methods for raising funds continued to intersect with worrying signs of a church and commonwealth losing their way. Virginians recognized Weston's undue influence on their own polity when the assembly identified him as one of the individuals whom a commission of Virginia delegates headed by Sir Francis Wyatt were to visit personally in England. The assembly instructed Wyatt's group to appeal to Weston, then still chancellor of the exchequer, to "establish a sure and certaine meanes of our subsistance, that wee may noe longer bee alwaies subject to ruine upon the uncertainty of the noyse of any contract." As a result of these parallels in political experience across the Atlantic, Virginia's planters found many friends in England, from powerful merchants and parliamentarians to Privy Councillors and church officials. Above all, they were connected with influential English politicians who shared their fear of Spanish and Catholic inroads in the polity.[68]

The anti-Spanish, prowar coalition that the then-prince Charles and George Villiers, duke of Buckingham, had organized in 1623 after the collapse of the Spanish match was undoubtedly an important foundation for this extensive community of Virginia supporters. At that early moment when militant Protestants still regarded Charles and Buckingham as their best hope for pressuring James into a more aggressive stance against Catholic forces on the continent, even powerful Virginia Company leaders like Sir Edwin Sandys, Southampton, and Philip Herbert, fourth earl of Pembroke, had entered into the prince's patriot coalition despite the oddity of allying with the much-resented royal favorite Buckingham. Other supporters of the colony had ties to this prowar group. Edward Sackville, the fourth earl of Dorset, a onetime ally of Charles and Buckingham, was one person the assembly effusively thanked for helping them to annul a tobacco contract. Dorset in 1631 had been placed in charge of a new commission responsible for overseeing Virginia affairs, and his fellow commissioners included a number of friends of the councillors like Wolstenholme, Wyatt, Sir John Zouche, Nicholas Ferrar, and George Sandys. Zouche would visit the colony in November 1634, joining his Virginia-based son and daughters. His

---

68. Wallace Notestein and Frances Helen Relf, eds., *Commons Debates for 1629* . . . (Minneapolis, Minn., 1921), 259; "The Gen[e]rall Assembly Their Comission to S[i]r *Francis Wyatt* Kn[igh]t, Mr *Edward Bennett*, and Mr *Michaell Marshart*," Mar. 29, 1628, in McIlwaine, ed., *Journals of the House of Burgesses of Virginia, 1619–1658/59,* 50. On Weston, see *Oxford Dictionary of National Biography*, online ed., s.v. "Weston, Richard, first earl of Portland (*bap.* 1577, *d.* 1635)," by Brian Quintrell, accessed Mar. 24, 2015, http://www.oxforddnb.com/view/article/29126.

cousin was the powerful warden of the cinque ports Lord Zouche, a onetime protégé of the Cecils who had been allied with Archbishop Abbot against the pro-Spanish party in James's Privy Council. Both Zouches had long been involved as major adventurers in the Virginia enterprise, and their support stemmed as much from their anti-Spanish sentiments as from their desire to profit from the venture. Governor Harvey would later refer to Sir John Zouche as "of the Puritan Sect," a reference that probably alluded more to his fervent anti-Catholicism than to his particular confessional loyalties. The Zouches were also linked with the Lords De La Warr, whose family had provided two of the most active of the Virginia politicians in this period in the persons of John West and Francis West, the younger brothers of Virginia's first governor, Thomas West, the third Baron De La Warr. As for Samuel Mathews, he enjoyed connections to the powerful merchant Wolstenholme and was linked by marriage to the parliamentarian Sir Thomas Hinton. One of Hinton's sons was a gentleman of the king's privy chamber and, according to Yong, a hopeful to replace Harvey as governor. Similarly, Claiborne, who also possessed important merchant contacts, likewise had the ear of Sir John Coke who had become one of the principal secretaries of state through Buckingham's influence and was also a member of the Dorset commission. What connected all of these persons was a broad militant Anglican concern to keep the Spanish and Catholic threats at bay. Virginia's battles with Lord Baltimore, far from being a liability, were instead a major factor in preserving the support of these powerful Protestant friends at home.[69]

69. "Virginia Gleanings in England," in *VMHB*, XII (1904), 89. On the prowar "patriot" coalition that organized around Prince Charles and Buckingham, see Cogswell, *Blessed Revolution*, 77–105. On the letter to Dorset, see Edward D. Neill, *Virginia Carolorum: The Colony under the Rule of Charles the First and Second A.D. 1625–A.D. 1685* . . . (Albany, N.Y., 1886), 56. For the members of the Dorset commission, see "Commissioners for Virginia (Abstract)," May 24, 1631, *VMHB*, VIII (1900), 29. On Zouche, see Martha W. McCartney, *Virginia Immigrants and Adventurers, 1607–1635: A Biographical Dictionary* (Baltimore, 2007), 68. Sir John Zouche's interest in Virginia even preceded the Virginia Company, for his father contracted with George Waymouth to lead a venture as early as 1605; see "Articles of Agreement," Oct. 30, [1605], in Alexander Brown, ed., *Genesis of the United States: A Narrative of the Movement in England, 1605–1616* . . . , 2 vols. (Boston, 1890), I, 33–34. An updated scholarly biography of Samuel Mathews is needed; in the meantime, see Lyon Gardiner Tyler, *Encyclopedia of Virginia Biography* (New York, 1915), I, 48–49 (though note that the entry occasionally confuses Mathews with his son by the same name). For William Claiborne, see *Encyclopedia Virginia*, s.v. "William Claiborne (1600–1679)," by Warren M. Billings and the *Dictionary of Virginia Biography*, accessed Apr. 8, 2015, http://www.encyclopediavirginia.org/Claiborne_William_1600-1679.

Among the colony's friends in London was one group that was significant especially in linking the Virginians to the parliamentary conflicts with Charles in the late 1620s. This was the body of antiquarians who met in Sir Robert Bruce Cotton's library and who provided much of the evidentiary basis for Parliament's claims at this time about its ancient privileges vis-à-vis the king, including those delineated in the Petition of Right of 1628. Around this time, Cotton played an active part in bringing *The True Travels, Adventures, and Observations of Captaine John Smith* (1630) to publication. He probably regarded a record of Smith's accomplishments as a planter as functioning much like documents that elucidated the historic foundations of English law. In both cases, godly duties and civil bonds were preserved against the erosions of misguided worldly innovations. Especially suggestive of the overlap Cotton seems to have seen between Virginia and England's contemporaneous situations was a manuscript he circulated that concerned England's own ancient commonwealth bonds. Just as Virginians worried about their threatened civil integrity, Cotton warned that England itself might become one of the "Pettie States" brought under the Spaniards' "absolute power" if Charles did not assert his own power more effectively. Far from wanting Charles's own authority weakened, Cotton insisted that the king's capacity to stand up against the Spanish menace was predicated on ruling his subjects in accordance with those historical laws and customs by which the English people judged whether or not they were walking in their vocations lawfully. Hearts turned on the pivot of a clear conscience were the resource that Charles could not afford to squander. And the only reliable guide to those assured affections was the complex of customs and laws that had already been sanctioned by time, the so-called ancient constitution. Cotton's apologia for England's ancient constitution overlapped closely with the Virginians' arguments that only a loving harmony of wills between king and planter would realize Virginia's promise as a strong kingdom capable of rivaling Spanish dominion in the New World. In effect, both the antiquarians and the planters were voicing what had become the era's dominant response to an early Stuart casuistry that distressingly equated potent kingship with the diminished wills of the people. Cotton had a succinct answer to this troubling statism: "Win hearts and you have their hands and purses." It was a formulation that clearly also resounded in Virginia.[70]

70. [Sir Robert Cotton], *The Danger Wherein the Kingdome Now Standeth, and the Remedie* ([London], 1628), 1, 7–8. For Smith's crediting of Cotton with encouraging the writing of the book, see John Smith, *The True Travels, Adventures, and Observations of Captaine John Smith*

Enjoying allies who shared their comparatively worldly Protestantism as well as their righteous indignation at Catholics and Spaniards, the colony's planters were well insulated against the separatists' charge of worldliness as well as papal accusations of exerting illegitimate political power. The more formidable threat came from the statist argument that they selfishly tended to their own political and material wants without satisfying the broader needs of king and commonwealth. John Donne had once warned the planters against such excesses of self-governance and self-sufficiency, preaching that these sins were tantamount to confusing their office with that of the king. "If those that governe there, would establish such a government, as should not depend upon this, or if those that goe thither, propose to themselves an exemption from Lawes, to live at their libertie, this is to be *Kings*, to devest *Allegeance*, to bee under no man," Donne asserted. This logic of the colonists' excessive moral autonomy, already familiar from Middlesex's financial schemes in James's reign, also underlay the continuing pursuit of tobacco contracts under Charles. William Anys, the projector of a tobacco contract in 1626, put the point baldly. When a Privy Councillor asked "if the Inhabitants of Virginia may neither bring hither all they plant nor send it elsewhere, what case will they be in," Anys responded coolly that "they will be by this meanes in the power of the State." It was Marlborough, however, who brought an experienced lawyer's ear for casuistry to the question and captured the denigrating view of planters that lay behind such statist reasoning. Condemning the planters' selfishness, he wrote, "He sawe their intention was . . . to draw all the benefite to themselves and bring none to his Majestie." These remarks captured the charge of sinful independence that hung dangerously over the planters, posing an especially grave risk because it struck directly at the Anglican ideals of natural obedience and reciprocal ties on which the planters' own commonwealth was meant to rest. The Virginians had learned to anticipate this sort of reasoning by stressing that their conduct was conscionably tied to God and king, regardless of how their adversaries twisted it. They had explained to the Privy Council the year before that mere rumors of a "pernitious Contract" had persuaded many of them "to have goune for *Englande*" to petition the king directly for their "redresse

---

(London, 1630), in Barbour, ed., *Complete Works of Captain John Smith*, III, 141. In the book, Smith wrote admiringly of Mathews, Claiborne, and Virginia's other councillors (III, 215). For an illuminating study of the antiquarians' interest in Smith, see David S. Shields, "The Genius of Ancient Britain," in Peter C. Mancall, ed., *The Atlantic World and Virginia, 1550–1624* (Chapel Hill, N.C., 2007), 489–509.

and protection." Insisting that their earnings were "not sufficient to cover our nakednes," they proclaimed that their collective "consciences" spoke to the colony's welfare more truly than the "vindicative mallice" of their enemies. On the eve of the planters' clash with Governor Harvey, Virginia's commonwealth had arrived at a juncture in which everyone could agree that the colony's problems lay in the untoward wills that anger God. What was less clear was whose stubborn wills were most to blame.[71]

The Arrest of Governor Harvey as an Act of Commonwealth

In April 1635, the tensions of Virginia's strained commonwealth boiled over into a dramatic confrontation between the colony's councillors and Governor Harvey in which both sides accused the other of treason. Such a mutual charge of betraying king and commonwealth suggests the critical point at which the colony had found itself. The more-than-a-decade long fears of projectors and Catholic encroachers on Virginia's civil polity fed this first major political test of the colony's young polity. Yet, the conflict arose as well from a brief renewal of optimism about the colony's prospects. This short-lived surge of hopefulness owed a great deal to Charles's succession. Given that many of the colony's supporters had first coalesced at the end of James's reign around the hope that his son would prove a more militant and righteous king, it was natural for them to see Charles as the Virginian emperor they had for so long anticipated. As if boldly affirming this desire for a more belligerent sovereign, Charles had issued in March 1625 *A Proclamation for Setling the Plantation of Virginia* in which he declared assertively what Elizabeth and James had never shown any intention of pronouncing, namely that Virginia as well as the Somers Islands and New England constituted "a part of Our Royall Empire." To that end, he continued, "We hold Our selfe, as

---

71. John Donne, *A Sermon Preached to the Honourable Company of the Virginian Plantation* . . . (London 1622), in George R. Potter and Evelyn M. Simpson, eds., *The Sermons of John Donne* (Berkeley, Calif., 1959), IV, 269; "A Journall Booke of the Proceedings of His Majesties Commissioners for the Lessening of His Majesties Charge and Increase of the Revenew," University of London Library, MS 195, II, fo. 42, quoted in Thomas Cogswell, "'In the Power of the State': Mr Anys's Project and the Tobacco Colonies, 1626–1628," *English Historical Review*, CXXIII (2008), 38, ("if the Inhabitants"), and "Journall Booke," MS 195, I, fos. 21v–22v, 44 ("He saw"); [Petition from the Convention of 1625], in McIlwaine, ed., *Journals of the House of Burgesses of Virginia, 1619–1658/59*, 43.

well bound by Our Regal office, to protect, maintaine, and support the same, and are so resolved to doe, as any other part of Our Dominions."⁷²

This encouraging sign that the king perceived his imperial duties as situated no less across the Atlantic than in his British kingdoms received further reinforcement in the reassuring strides quickly taken by the Dorset commission. By November 1631, Dorset believed the king himself was prepared to endorse a set of reforms that included preserving Virginia's Council of State and General Assembly while also retaining the colony's "Ancient territories . . . in as ample manner as the same were bounded and granted unto the late Company." Given that this latter measure implicitly contested the jurisdiction claimed by the new Maryland colony, the Dorset reforms also prudently provided for a body of officials to meet on a regular basis with the king's attorney general in England "for the reconciling and perfecting" of all such knotty legal conflicts across the Atlantic. A revived Virginia Company was also included in the proposal, a measure that promised not only to facilitate the colony's continuing English commercial connections but also to cement the political influence of such Dorset commissioners as Wolstenholme, Nicholas and John Ferrar, Sir Dudley Digges, and Sir John Zouche— to a man, all ardent foes of popery.⁷³

Five years into Charles's so-called Personal Rule, this original burst of heartening activity on behalf of Virginia colonization had taken a dispiriting turn. The 1629 parliament marked the last time the king called the political nation into assembly to consult on the laws or approve supply. Especially alarming to many Protestant subjects, the king not only had opted to disregard the counsel of his godly people but was also substituting it with far more worrying advice that carried the tinge of Catholicism. The Dorset commission was replaced by a body headed by the new archbishop of Canterbury, William Laud, whose Arminianism seemed downright Romish in the eyes of many former Elizabethan and Jacobean churchmen like Abbot. Another of the leading members of the Laud commission was none other than Lord High Treasurer Weston, now the earl of Portland, the very embodiment of the king's hated revenue schemes. Similarly, Secretary of State Sir Francis Windebank, another concerning member, had long looked to Secre-

72. [Charles I], *A Proclamation for Setling the Plantation of Virginia* (London, 1625), n.p.

73. "Virginia Commissioners to the King," [1631], in "Virginia in 1631," *VMHB*, VIII (1900), 38, 39. For the initial hopefulness of Edward Sackville, the fourth earl of Dorset, that the king embraced the 1631 reforms, see "King's Order as to Virginia Company," Nov. 25, 1631, in "Virginia in 1631," *VMHB*, VIII (1900) 39–40.

tary Calvert as a patron and was an ally, as well, of Weston in his pro-Spanish policies. By this time the Privy Council had already dug in its heels on the question of Maryland's legality, deciding on July 3, 1633, that Virginians and Marylanders should resolve their differences "in such manner as becometh fellow subjects and members of the same State," a remark that was unmistakable in its dismissiveness of Virginia's commonwealth integrity. The clearest signal that the king was under the thrall of dangerous advisers emerged in September 1634 when Charles wrote to the colony indicating his continuing desire for a contract that would give him "the sole pre-emption of all the Tobacco issuing from hence." The abrupt reaction of the Virginians to this news startled even the wary Harvey. As recently as early 1632, the planters had been in a state of euphoric expectation, writing to Dorset and his fellow Privy Councillors of the "happie newes of his Ma[jes]ties gratious Intentions toward this Colony grauntinge his royall Com[m]ission to yo[u]r honors who have beene pleased to undertake the same and patronage thereof, after soe long and languishing a consumption." By December 1634, the alarmed Harvey was conscious of the "secret and unlawfull meetings" that had sprung up in the colony, certain that the councillors were behind them, and already speculating darkly on their "mutinous" intentions.[74]

A symbol-laden reconciliation ceremony that Harvey and the councillors had performed three years earlier captures the commonwealth ideal that continued to resonate and that set the terms by which both sides viewed the other's transgression. Evidently a precondition for the Dorset group's proposed reforms, the reconciliation occurred on December 20, 1631, and took the form of an elaborately formal peace filled with scriptural undertones. In the written description the governor and councillors provided of the rite, it involved pointed references to Psalm 122, in which the Israelites under

---

74. "Orders of Privy Council in Regard to Virginia and Maryland," July [3], 1633, in "Virginia in 1632-33-34," *VMHB*, VIII (1900), 152, 159; Richard Kemp to undisclosed recipient, May 17, 1635, in "Virginia in 1635," *VMHB*, VIII (1901), 302; [Petition of the House of Burgesses to the Privy Council Drawn up at the 1631/32 Session], Mar. 6, 1631, in McIlwaine, ed., *Journals of the House of Burgesses of Virginia, 1619–1658/59*, 55; "Declaration of Sir John Harvey," [1635], *VMHB*, I (1894), 425, 426. For William Laud's commission, see "Appointment of Commissioners for Virginia," Apr. 28, 1634, in "Virginia in 1632-33-34," *VMHB*, VIII (1900), 156. On Laud, see *Oxford Dictionary of National Biography*, online ed., s.v. "Laud, William (1573–1645)," by Anthony Milton, accessed Mar. 25, 2015, http://www.oxforddnb.com/view/article/16112, on Windebank, see s.v. "Windebank, Sir Francis (*bap.* 1582, *d.* 1646)," by Brian Quintrell, accessed Mar. 14, 2015, http://www.oxforddnb.com/view/article/29715.

King David go into the "house of the LORD" where they become "compact together" in bonds of love. The Virginians explained their own understanding of their newfound amity as a matter of silencing willful members: "If there shall be found any unwilling or turbulent spirit amongst us or any other enemy to peace we desire he may be cast out of all good society and accompted as a firebrand to kindle those flames of dissentions." Undoubtedly an acknowledgment of the Anglican critique of the planters as too headstrong in their pursuit of their own interests, the statement also functioned as a reminder to the king and his governor not to confuse their own wills with the commonwealth as a whole. The colonists' denunciation of willfulness in Virginia took the form of an extended meditation on the mystical body of Christ:

> Let us prepare ourselves with that Psalmest to goe into the house of God and after due consideration and contrition for our sinns, seale and deliver this our concord, peace and love, with the seale of that most blessed sacrament of the body and blood of our Saviour who hath called us to the Union of our fayth and made us members of his body that living together in peace in this world, wee may live with him in eternall peace in the world to come.

Such a lush depiction of the bonds of the colony's polity captured the sense of optimism the Dorset commission's reforms had stimulated. At the same time, it also conveyed the planters' expectation that the king's own obliging membership in Virginia's redeemed body politic would itself be forthcoming.[75]

The years surrounding the beginning of Charles's Personal Rule offered considerable proof that the king's complaisance was far from assured. For instance, Harvey clearly had received encouragement to view his gubernatorial station in newly exalted terms as the "King's Lieftenant." The latter designation was one that the colony's secretary of state Richard Kemp would use for him in 1635, and it evidently captured how Harvey perceived his own office. Certainly the label corresponded with his continual frustration that the colony's councillors did not obey him as unconditionally as he considered appropriate. In a revealing letter to Secretary of State Dudley Carleton, the first Viscount Dorchester, in April 1631, Harvey wrote of his fellow colo-

---

75. Psalms 122:1 and 3, *Holy Bible* (London, 1611); "Agreement of the Governor and Council," Dec. 20, 1631, in "Virginia in 1631," *VMHB*, VIII (1900), 45.

nial leaders in a way that leaves little doubt that he adhered to the Mandeville commission's urging that the council serve as obedient aids rather than as the governor's stern moral guides. "Instead of givinge me assistance, they stand contesting and disputinge my authoritie, averringe that I can doe nothinge but what they shall advise me, and that my power extendeth noe further then a bare castinge voice," he complained. But Harvey's eagerness to see his authority as elevated far above that of the colony's leading planters mirrored on a small scale the even more troubling phenomenon of a king who equated his own conscience with the commonwealth as a whole. Charles not only embraced the era's new statism that placed unusual emphasis on the king's interest. He also solicited an equally novel casuistry to show that his royal commandments on behalf of the state properly superseded the laws or consent of his people.[76]

The clergymen Robert Sibthorpe and Roger Maynwaring introduced this severe casuistry in printed sermons in defense of the Forced Loan, insisting on the absolute obedience subjects owed a divinely appointed king. Conspicuously missing in this formulation was the usual corresponding stress on what Ben Jonson had once characterized as the reciprocal love that transforms a sinful king and people alike. The vitriolic reaction by other leading churchmen to this hyper-sanctified understanding of the king's office underscored how far it had moved beyond the conventional Christian humanist insistence on the mutuality of wills in any redeemed polity. Archbishop Abbot was one of these outspoken critics, and he was temporarily banished to Kent for his brashness. Captain Smith implicitly threw his own support behind Abbot's bold move by dedicating his *Advertisements for the Unexperienced Planters of New-England; or, Any Where* (1631) to the prelate. In addition, Smith also dedicated the work to Samuel Harsnett, archbishop of York, who had similarly stood up against Charles's unrestrained will by helping to advance the Petition of Right. Given that Smith's book condemned the disruptive influence of the "absolute crue" of separatists, he was undoubtedly suggesting that a godly commonwealth could not abide absolute wills of any kind, especially when the sovereign's truculence was the corrosive force in question.[77]

76. Richard Kemp, "Account of the Mutiny, etc., of the Virginians," in "Virginia in 1635," *VMHB*, VIII (1901), 304; Sir John Harvey to [Dudley Carleton], [first] Viscount Dorchester, Apr. 2, 1631, in "Virginia in 1631," *VMHB*, VIII (1901), 30.

77. John Smith, *Advertisements for the Unexperienced Planters of New-England* (London,

Virginia's councillors, too, targeted untoward wills in their reaction to the king's tobacco contract. They identified the dangerous obstinacy in question as Harvey's, not the king's. But, the councillors left little doubt that they saw their attack on the governor as part of the broader politics concerned with Charles's worrying prioritization of his own conscience over the upright activities of his subjects. They viewed that conflict as less against absolute power, which they continued to regard as an immensely desirable attribute of a divinely favored sovereign, than against absolute assuredness, the unbending will that refuses to accord with others. An assembly was called for February 20, 1635. Although no records remain of the session, it was probably there that the councillors and burgesses submitted a formal letter to Harvey that rejected the contract amid columns of ordinary planters' signatures and marks as proof of the commonwealth's collectivity of wills. Harvey was so incensed by the document that he retained the original. Explaining this brash move later, he wrote that it arose from his concern not only that the letter would anger the king in its own right, "it being in effect a deniall of his Majesties proposition," but also that the "manner" of it was offensive, the colonists having made the document "a popular business, by subscribing a multitude of hands thereto, as thinking thereby to give it countenance." As a result of Harvey's retention of the letter, the assembly's agents Zouche and Captain William Button were allowed only "bare copies, such as the Secretary would give without either his or the clarkes hand," omissions that lessened the document's validity and raised concerns about Zouche and Button's safety in carrying such a sensitive letter home. Still concerned to legitimize their proceedings, the councillors again turned to the broader populace. At another round of meetings, planters signed petitions attesting that "theyre lives and estats" were in jeopardy, requested a new assembly to express their grievances, and appealed to the council to "call the Governor to account for not sending theyre late answere to the King's letter by theyre

---

1631), in Barbour, ed., *Complete Works of Captain John Smith*, III, 292–293 (for the dedication to Abbot and Harsnett, see ibid., 263). On Abbot, see *Oxford Dictionary of National Biography*, online ed., s.v. "Abbot, George (1562–1633)," by Kenneth Fincham, accessed Mar. 23, 2015, http://oxforddnb.com/view/article/4, on Harsnett, see s.v. "Harsnett, Samuel (*bap.* 1561, *d.* 1631)," by Nicholas W. S. Cranfield, accessed Mar. 11, 2015, http://oxforddnb.com/view/article/12466. For the political significance of Smith's dedication in relation to Mayrwaring and Sibthorpe's sermons, see also Shields, "Genius of Ancient Britain," in Mancall, ed., *Atlantic World and Virginia*, 489–509.

agents." Grudgingly, Harvey summoned a new assembly to begin May 7, but he also kept a close eye on the meetings taking place in the counties.[78]

Toward the end of April, Harvey ordered the councillors to arrest three of the organizers, including the York County burgesses and justices William English and Captain Nicholas Martiau as well as John Pott's brother Francis Pott. According to the governor's informants, the three men had met with ordinary planters at a nighttime gathering at one William Warren's house and held forth on Harvey's misgovernment, saying "noe justice was done" and he "would bring a second massacre among them." Secretary Kemp surmised that such rhetoric was used to "perswade the people to subscribe" to a petition condemning Harvey's abuses, and he noted that planters were also swayed by the news that "some of the Counsell had a hand in it." When Harvey summoned the councillors to meet with him at his house on April 28 to discuss what to do with the arrested men, Mathews and his associates came prepared, evidently having convinced a number of planters to take an especially threatening posture. While the councillors and the governor conducted a tense meeting inside, forty musketeers stood at the ready to emerge in a show of force as soon as John Pott made the agreed-on hand signal.[79]

The message that the councillors sent back to England was not that they were the instruments behind an armed uprising but rather that the latent violence on display that day welled up understandably from the planters' own accumulated sense of grievance. Such a buildup of despair could hardly help but transform even godly people into creatures of incapacitating fury. Insisting that they stood at a remove from such rage-filled planters and so were in a position to counsel the king on how best to preserve their affections without encouraging their licentiousness, the councillors portrayed themselves as the colony's most responsible guardians of commonwealth. For instance, Zouche's son wrote to his father in England using an anec-

---

78. "The Humble Declaration of Sir John Harvey His Majesties Lieutenant Governor of Virginia touching the Mutinous Proceedings of the Councell There and Their Confederates with the Causes Thereof," in "Declaration of Sir John Harvey," *VMHB*, I (1894), 428; Sam[ue]l Mathews to undisclosed recipient, May 25, 1635, in "The Mutiny in Virginia, 1635," *VMHB*, I (1894), 416; Richard Kemp, "Account of the Mutiny, etc., of the Virginians," May 17, 1635, in "Virginia in 1635," *VMHB*, VIII (1901), 303. The February 20 assembly is mentioned in W. Noël Sainsbury, ed., *Calendar of State Papers, Colonial Series, 1574–1660* (London, 1860), 195.

79. Kemp, "Account of the Mutiny, etc., of the Virginians," May 17, 1635, in "Virginia in 1635," *VMHB*, VIII (1901), 303.

dote about the Virginia councillor George Menefie to suggest the agonizing questions of conscience that the councillors faced in taking an action against Harvey that inevitably reflected on the king's own office. According to Zouche, Menefie engaged in his own casuistic meditation, pondering the rightful path at such a perplexing juncture. Unsure whether it was "fit to deale soe with his Ma[jes]ties substitute," Menefie went "to the back river where hee debated w[i]th himselfe, desiring of God to confirme his resolucon or abolish it, but the losse of the Country sticking in his stomacke at least hee came, resolved as the rest," Zouche wrote. Likewise, Claiborne, who was not at the council meeting but who sent a letter to Secretary Sir John Coke on May 23 in defense of his fellow councillors, similarly depicted the proceedings against Harvey as an effort to restore the colony to its original divine order. "Undoubtedly God will make a way for his glory, through the injustice of men, and the end will be an establishment of this long languishing Colony," Claiborne exclaimed. These reflections framed the councillors' arrest of Harvey and their subsequent shipment of him home to England as acts of faith and loyalty.[80]

Mathews claimed similarly that Harvey's recalcitrance had converted the commonwealth's loving bonds into a cacophony of desperate members. According to Mathews, "The Gcvenor usurped the whole power, in all causes without any respect to the votes of the councell, whereby justice was now done but soe farr as suited with his will to the great losse of Many Mens estates." Harvey's gubernatorial abuses generated "a generall feare in all" and gave the council little choice but to intervene to preserve the loving ties that held the planters to their duties. As Mathews put it, "Wee much doubted least the Inhabitants would not be kept in due obedience if the Governor continued as formerly." Mathews's careful emphasis on the colonists' "due" obedience, as opposed to the absolute sort the king and governor were demanding, spoke volumes. It reinforced the longstanding Christian humanist view that commonwealths that sat right under God required a free interplay of wills, the liberty of office that allowed all persons, no matter the modesty of their vocations, to perform their part in a divinely centered polity. Of course, the councillors invoked this enduring ideal of Virginia's godly commonwealth in full awareness that the governor and his supporters were painting them as the real obstacles to order. But by simply reiterating the idea of Virginia as a moral confluence of rightly turned consciences, these

---

80. [John Zouche to Sir John Zouche], n.d., in Neill, *Virginia Carolorum*, 119, W[illiam] Clayborne to [Sir John Coke], May 23, 1635, 122.

leading planters gave their proceedings a commonwealth logic that was recognizable as such on both sides of the ocean.[81]

What especially ensured a transatlantic audience for the councillors' actions, however, were their several allusions to Charles's climactic 1629 parliament. Mathews and his allies drew on emblematic moments of the last of Charles's parliaments before the inauguration of his Personal Rule with unmistakable self-consciousness. Evidently, they sought to give their maneuvers against Harvey a broader set of connotations centered on the era's staunchest defenses of the commonwealth against Charles's troubling statism. In the 1629 parliament, several members of the Commons, fearing that the king would prematurely adjourn the session, followed the lead of the assertive M.P. Sir John Elliot in forcibly holding speaker of the house Sir John Finch in his chair after he weepingly explained that he could not "sin against the express command of his Sovereign" even if the "good of his country" depended on it. Much as the Commoners had restrained Speaker Finch, the Virginia councillors symbolized their commonwealth sympathies with their own firm embrace of Harvey during their April meeting. Mathews claimed that he grasped the governor and "tooke him in my armes" and forced him into his "chayre" when Harvey seemed blinded by "rage" and unable to hear the people's grievances. That rationale was almost identical to the one the Commons had expressed when they kept Finch in his chair to prevent him from adjourning the session. There, too, the speaker was "held in by the Armes" and gripped "with a strong hand" until the "honor and justice of the Kingdome" could be fully addressed, for the members were confident that the king had heard only misrepresentations of their true intentions. As they explained this reasoning, they sought not to question Charles's sovereign office that was "highest under God" but only to consult "the miserable condicion this Kingdome is in." That concern to ensure the king's rightful sovereignty comported with his commonwealth obligations naturally generated a profusion of speeches in the House about the need to act on conscience. Only true hearts could bring everyone to his or her proper duties. Again closely mirroring their fellow parliamentarians across the ocean, Virginia's councillors similarly cast their proceedings as hinging on obligations of conscience that overrode all other considerations.[82]

---

81. Mathews to undisclosed recipient, May 25, 1635, in "The Mutiny in Virginia, 1635," *VMHB*, I (1894), 416, 420.

82. Notestein and Relf, eds., *Commons Debates for 1629*, 105, 253, 259; H. R. McIlwaine, ed., *Minutes of the Council and General Court of Colonial Virginia*, 2d ed. (Richmond, Va., 1979), 480,

It was in stressing such rightly turned hearts that Mathews made yet another pregnant reference, one that underscored the councillors' boldness in criticizing Harvey for sins that had also become discernible in the king. This was Mathews's striking invocation of Shakespeare's *Richard the Third*. One of Shakespeare's early plays, *Richard the Third* was probably written in the early 1590s and was deeply casuistic in focus. It explored in particular the theme of sinful consciences that are willfully disobedient to God, a violation of divine law nowhere more hideously displayed than in Richard's own tyranny. "Conscience is a word that cowards use," Richard declares to his marauding army, "Devis'd at first to keepe the strong in awe: / Our strong armes be our Conscience, Swords our Law." In his own description of Harvey's threat to arrest the councillors for treason, Mathews went so far as to suggest that Harvey used virtually the same words that Richard, still at this point duke of Gloucester, uttered against William Hastings, first Baron Hastings, a councillor originally seduced by Richard's treachery but ultimately responsive to his own good conscience, before arbitrarily calling for his execution. Richard's line, "I pray you all, tell me what they deserve / That doe conspire my death with divellish Plots," became in Mathews's characterization of Harvey's speech, "What do you think they deserve that have gone about to persuade the people from their obedience to his Majestie's substitute?" The line, in Mathews's narrative, as in the play, was an invitation to otherwise innocent councillors to condemn themselves in the worst possible way, by speaking their consciences. In *Richard the Third*, Hastings

---

481; Mathews to undisclosed recipient, May 25, 1635, in "The Mutiny in Virginia, 1635," *VMHB*, I (1894), 420. For Finch's participation on the General Court with his fellow councillors and his dismissal, see McIlwaine, ed., *Minutes of the Council and General Court*, 201, 480-481; see also, McCartney, *Virginia Immigrants and Adventurers*, 297. Virginia's councillors were likely unusually alert to this symbolic political gesture on the commonwealth's behalf because on October 29, 1630, Speaker Finch's own brother Henry Finch became one of the colony's councillors and secretary of state. But, his tenure as secretary would prove short; anti-Catholic forces on both sides of the ocean probably lay behind his abrupt removal from the office only three years after his arrival. Kemp, himself a devoted servant of the crown, was appointed to the secretaryship the following February; however, he, too, quickly faced an outspoken challenge when a Protestant minister Anthony Panton abused him by "calling him *Jackanapes*" and accused him of succumbing to "pride" in wearing his hair done up with a ribbon "as old as *Pauls*." Panton said of Kemp that "the King was misinformed of him that he was unfit for his place [and] wou'd be shortly turn'd out as the other secr[etar]y was.' The attack on Kemp indicated the Virginians' belligerence against any official who seemed too zealous in his adherence to the king's commands (McIlwaine, ed., *Minutes of the Council and General Court*, 201, 480-481).

is left vulnerable when, despite his pronouncements of "love" to his master, he is nevertheless unwilling to accept unreservedly Richard's tyrannical pronouncement against his enemies. Acknowledging the possibility of the innocence of the accused, Hastings uses the conditional statement "If they have done this deed." Richard, however, is heedless of Hastings's tender conscience and responds, "Talk'st to me of Ifs: Thou art a Traytor: / Off with his Head." In Mathews's description, Harvey's own unyielding insistence that his councillors condemn themselves was tantamount to the same tyrannical dealing.[83]

When Harvey demanded that each councillor answer his question about the appropriate punishment due to anyone who sought to "persuade the people from their obedience to his Majestie's substitute," the implication was clear. The answers given would then be forwarded to the king's courts as damning evidence of treasonable intent. Mathews responded that such was "a strange kind of proceeding" and that "there was no Presedent for such a command." Such intimidation of counsel through the threat of treason, Mathews explained, was "by a Tyrant," a phrase he clarified by referring to "that passage of Richard the third against the Lord Hastings." Undoubtedly, Mathews made this rich literary reference in part simply to capture the depth of Harvey's misconduct as compellingly as possible. Yet, his reference to Shakespeare's play was also downright audacious in its potential to be read as a subtle critique of Charles himself. Charles, not Harvey, bore the greatest likeness to the prince turned king depicted in Shakespeare's play. Lurking in Mathews's seemingly offhand remark about the tyrannical Richard, then, was the unmistakable insinuation that Charles was similarly abusing his sovereign office.[84]

The strain between planters and their king had reached a climax, so much so that many contemporaries must have wondered if the commonwealth and state were inevitably adversarial. Certainly both sides in the 1635 conflict clung to their own sense of righteousness and gave little ground to their opponent. Although the councillors never acknowledged the king's own wayward will as the ultimate target of their campaign, Mathews gestured

---

83. William Shakespeare, "The Life and Death of Richard the Third," in *Mr. William Shakespeares Comedies, Histories, and Tragedies; Published According to the True Originall Copies* (London, 1623), 189, 203; Mathews to undisclosed recipient, May 25, 1635, in "The Mutiny in Virginia, 1635," *VMHB*, I (1894), 418–419.

84. Mathews to undisclosed recipient, May 25, 1635, in "The Mutiny in Virginia, 1635," *VMHB*, I (1894), 418–419.

tellingly to that conclusion when he framed his complaint against Harvey as an appeal only secondarily to Charles and first to God. As he wrote in a letter to an unidentified addressee, perhaps Wolstenholme, in 1635, "I beseech God to direct his Majestie in appointing of some worthy religious gentleman, for to take charge of this his colony, and I doubt not by God's assistance and the industry of the people, but Virginia in few yeares will flourish." Over the next few years, the conflict did gradually wind down, though not because a clear resolution had been reached but rather as an outgrowth of the sheer incommensurability of the two views of Virginia that had formed by this time. The planters' insistence that their colony was a genuine commonwealth that aspired to the status enjoyed by Britain's more ancient kingdoms was simply too far removed from the king's outlook. Charles believed his interests were rightly served by approaching the colony almost wholly in its function as a contributor to his revenue, and any resistance to that expectation bordered on sinful disobedience to his authority. In the Privy Council's deliberations on December 11 regarding the colonists' action against Harvey, Charles argued that it was "an assumption of regal power to send hither the Governor," a perspective that echoed Donne's earlier warning to the colonists not to assume so much independence as to mistake themselves for kings. To restore the planters to their rightful obedience, Charles continued, it was "necessary to send the Governor back, though he stay but a day." Although Harvey remained in office until 1638, his role as governor was now mainly a symbol of the king's resentment at the planters who had defied him. The colony's first political test ended in a particularly troubling way, with the king and the commonwealth locked in distrustful opposition.[85]

A decade later, when England itself was immersed in civil war, the possibility that king and commonwealth might become wholly disjoined was realized with sickening finality when on January 30, 1649, Charles was beheaded on the grounds that he had proven himself an implacable adversary of the "public interest," sinfully devoted only to the "personal interest of will, power, and pretended prerogative to himself and his family." Shortly before the king's death, John Ferrar wrote a favorable outlook on Virginia and its leading planters that, given the profound turmoil of the moment, could only be read as a polemic on responsible kingship. He offered this view in the same 1648 pamphlet in which he made the famous accusation that

---

85. Ibid., 424; John Bruce, ed., *Calendar of State Papers, Domestic Series, of the Reign of Charles I, 1635* . . . (London, 1865), 551; "Notes of Proceedings of the Privy Council on Virginia Affairs," Dec. 11, 1635, in *VMHB*, VIII (1901), 404.

James I dissolved the Virginia Company on the accusation of the Spanish ambassador Diego Sarmiento de Acuña, count of Gondomar, that it was a "Seminarie to a Seditious Parliament." Such a charge echoed the colonizers' persistent fears that only seduction by Catholic Spain could fully explain the English kings' sudden coarse treatment of Virginia. By pointing to that Spanish influence, Ferrar hinted that Charles's own Catholic leanings similarly explained not only why Virginia continued to "lack Publick and State encouragements" but also, more generally, why the English commonwealth now found itself horribly at war with its sovereign.[86]

As England's erupting civil war fractured all the commonwealths that claimed Charles as their king, Ferrar's continuing encouragement for Virginia subtly implied that the colony itself was a small ray of hope in a period otherwise engulfed in the shadow of religious and civil warfare. It is striking that within this gloom Ferrar singled out "Worthy Captaine *Matthews*" for commendation. Describing this fiercest of Virginia's councillors as "an old Planter of above thirty yeers standing" and "one of the Counsell," Ferrar also praised him as "a most deserving Common-wealths-man." What qualified Mathews for such distinction? According to Ferrar, one moral trait stood out in particular: Mathews's "industry." In invoking the greatest of Christian humanist virtues, Ferrar did not mean only that Mathews worked but more broadly that he set in motion all the callings of a self-sufficient commonwealth. At his "fine house" that functioned as a busy compound of multifaceted activity, he kept "Weavers," caused hemp and flax "to be spun," put other people to labor at his "Tan-house," ordered his leather "to be dressed," and "employed" eight shoemakers "in their trade." Mathews even directed "forty *Negroe* servants" in various "Trades in his house," an outgrowth of the humanists' own stern willingness to impose the Christian obligation to work on other peoples—through force, if need be. His cattle provisioned ships, his wheat brought in four shillings a bushel, his cows maintained a "brave Dairy," and his pigs and poultry offered sustenance. Here was a distinctly Renaissance vision of the moral underpinnings of commonwealth,

---

86. "The Sentence of the High Court of Justice upon the King," [Jan. 27, 1648–1649], in Samuel Rawson Gardiner, ed., *The Constitutional Documents of the Puritan Revolution, 1625–1660* (Oxford, 1906), 378; [John Ferrar], *A Perfect Description of Virginia: Being, a Full and True Relation of the Present State of the Plantation*... (London, 1649 [that is, 1648]), 5, 9. For the 1648 publication date for Ferrar's pamphlet, see the description of the work in *Early English Books Online*. For Ferrar's authorship of the work as established by David L. Ransome, see Warren M. Billings, *Sir William Berkeley and the Forging of Colonial Virginia* (Baton Rouge, La., 2004), 69n.

all persons held to strenuous work at their offices, not an idle hand in sight. It was a vision that the planters themselves had repeatedly insisted could tie the commonwealth and the state into one, elevating planters and their king simultaneously.[87]

At about this same time, however, another, even more far-reaching argument was being formulated about the unitary nature of the state. Hobbes's *Leviathan* would appear in 1651, providing a radically different answer to the question of how to prevent the sovereign and commonwealth from ever again becoming undone. This viewpoint was also informed by the rhetoric surrounding the Virginia venture. As he developed his dramatic new definition of the properly understood commonwealth, Hobbes quite clearly had one eye on the English colonizing experience in America. But Hobbes's argument would set colonization in such a new light as to constitute a revolutionary break from the Tudor and Stuart planting endeavors. Against Ferrar's continuing Renaissance hopefulness to see a genuine commonwealth realized in Virginia, Hobbes's theory of state sovereignty would question whether a colony could be a commonwealth at all.

87. [Ferrar], *Perfect Description of Virginia*, 15.

[5]
SIR WILLIAM BERKELEY, THE HOBBISTS, AND THE END OF RENAISSANCE-ERA COLONIZATION

Renaissance-era colonization in the English Atlantic ended with the ascendancy of an argument, or, more accurately, with the denial of an argument that had not previously been significantly questioned. The premise that colonization was a continuation of the divinely ordained act of planting new states had gone largely unchallenged through the late sixteenth and early seventeenth centuries. Moreover, because that view seemed to rest on solid casuistic grounds, it had resulted by the 1640s in a constellation of young colonies all of which, to one degree or another, had followed Virginia's own providentially tested pathway in taking their commonwealth status to be a natural, even divinely approved, starting point for understanding their essence as polities. The growing statism that emerged under James I and Charles I, however, exposed the vulnerability of this presumed civil robustness. In associating their own interests with the state's necessities, the early Stuarts came a long way in emphasizing the colonies' commercial potential over their qualities as new kingdoms.

Recognizing this troubling tendency to treat colonies as mere commercial props to the state as early as 1624, Richard Eburne had conceded in his *Plaine Path-way to Plantations* that the king need not regard his colonies as standing at the same exalted level of his other kingdoms. "If the name of a Kingdome shall bee thought too high and excellent, too great and glorious for Countries so vaste and wast, so remote, and obscure as those of our Plantations yet are," he wrote, "let them bee vouchsafed the name but of Dukedomes, . . . or Lordships, as Ireland for a long time was, or by whatsoever other titles, parts or members of a kingdome, hee shall be pleased to stile and nominate them." Yet, Eburne was adamant that the fundamental aim of colonization remained the fostering of an "uprising common wealth." For

Eburne, the commonwealth still meant, as it had for generations of English colonizers, a community that enjoyed fundamental moral and political integrity despite the lingering presence of sin. It attained this objective because of its success in holding its diverse members to their respective callings, an end achievable only through man-made laws that were compatible with, rather than repugnant to, the laws of God and nature.[1]

This familiar Christian humanist view also animated Virginia's newest governor, Sir William Berkeley. In the years immediately following his arrival in the colony in 1642, he referred to Virginia unapologetically as a "Common Wealth." Berkeley was evidently also prepared to see colonies as entities that were inferior in status to kingdoms, a term he rarely used in relation to Virginia. But, even short of the dignity of a kingdom, a colony still needed the civil wholeness and moral coherence of a true body politic. For Berkeley, Virginia was comparable to "all States and republicks" in its need for "good and wholesome Laws" as well as sufficient strength to relieve "disorders and grievances." He invoked the colony's commonwealth condition with a clear eye to its forcefulness in suggesting Virginia's considerable substance as a political community. His use of such language in these early years was directed especially at fending off efforts in England to revive the Virginia Company. By treating the colony as a commonwealth in its own right, he boldly countered the Puritan-led claim that Virginia was so sinful and frail as to require that London-based body's governance. Even at this late date, then, the ideal of the colony as a commonwealth evoked the righteous image of a polity that was new and yet complete, fully realized in particular in the bonds that tied it to God and king and ensured the hard work and well-being of its inhabitants. It was a matter of profound, even era-changing, significance when that long-standing Renaissance ideal of the colonial commonwealth became not only a subject of philosophical dispute but also an error allegedly so great that, by some writers' accounts, it needed to be corrected for the sake of the state's own civil and godly integrity.[2]

---

1. Richard Eburne, *A Plaine Path-Way to Plantations; That Is, a Discourse in Generall, concerning the Plantation of Our English People in Other Countries* . . . ([London], 1624), 36–37, 62. Although Eburne's background remains somewhat obscure, his moderate Anglicanism or at least nonseparating Puritanism can be deduced from his 1609 petition dedicated to the Calvinist Anglican James Montagu; see Eburne, *The Maintenance of the Ministrie* . . . (London, 1609).

2. "Declaration against the Virginia Company," in Warren M. Billings, ed., with Maria Kimberly, *The Papers of Sir William Berkeley, 1605–1677* (Richmond, Va., 2007), 42, "Remonstrance of the General Assembly," 49. Berkeley's 1642 "Declaration" also appears as The Declaration against

The author who was most influential in advancing the view that colonies were qualitatively different than states and developing it in such a way as to attract imitators was Thomas Hobbes. Beginning with his *Elements of Law*, which he circulated widely in manuscript after completing it in May 1640, and continuing in his later Civil War-era writings, Hobbes made a consistent and even central theme out of the idea that groups pursuing enterprises for the commonwealth's behalf were not in themselves commonwealths. In *Elements* (1650) and *De Cive* (the latter work issued in small numbers in 1642 before being published broadly in 1647), he touched on the subject right alongside his main definition of the commonwealth, just after his initial extended discussions of man and the state of nature. By the time he wrote *Leviathan* (1651), he evidently regarded his rather summary treatments of the topic in the earlier books as insufficient; therefore, he elaborated further on the theme, including in *Leviathan*, among other things, a more explicit discussion of colonies. This treatment appeared in the book's twenty-fourth chapter entitled "Of the Nutrition, and Procreation of a Common-wealth." In a single forceful paragraph, he considered explicitly what he called the "Right of Colonies," by which he meant the power and dignity that remained to colonists after having given up the substantive liberty that all subjects necessarily yielded in return for the protection of their sovereign. He examined specifically the conditions in which plantations should be con-

---

the Company to Be Entered as the Twenty First Act, Apr. 1, 1642, in William Waller Hening, *The Statutes at Large; Being a Collection of All the Laws of Virginia . . .* , 13 vols. (New York, 1819–1823), I, 230–236. One of the few instances when Berkeley referred to Virginia indirectly as a kingdom was in an offhand remark to Thomas Ludwell in 1676. There, Berkeley explained that he and the assembly had passed a "severe" law prohibiting Virginians from exporting provisions to war-torn New England on the grounds that "want of provision does impoverish kingdomes and states (of al nations) more then seaven yeares of Luxury" (William Berkeley to Thomas Ludwell, Apr. 1, 1676, in Billings, ed., *Papers of Sir William Berkeley*, 507). In more generally hesitating to call Virginia a kingdom, Berkeley mirrored the sentiment of George Sandys, who in a 1638 dedication to Charles I referred to him as the "King of Great-Britaine, France, and Ireland" but only as the "Lord of the Foure Seas; of Virginia, the Vast Territories Adjoyning, and Dispersed Islands of the Westerne Ocean" (George Sandys, *A Paraphrase upon the Divine Poems* [London, 1638], [*1]v). One of the few explicit references to Virginia as a kingdom in these years came from Charles II. Perhaps in an attempt to flatter the colonists at a moment when he wanted them to engage in vigorous town building, the king remarked in his 1662 instructions to Berkeley that the "Councellors of that Our Kingdom" were to be encouraged to build houses at proposed town seats ("Instructions from Charles II," Sept. 12, 1662, in Billings, ed., *Papers of Sir William Berkeley*, 178).

sidered "a Common-wealth of themselves" or, alternatively, "no Commonwealths themselves, but Provinces, and parts of the Common-wealth that sent them." His answer was in line with his more general strong emphases on the sovereign's fundamental lawmaking capacity and the indivisibility of that colossal power. Only the supreme ruler's letters patent could determine colonies' status because only by freeing them entirely from his authority could they become commonwealths "of themselves." Otherwise, they were merely provinces of the broader commonwealth over which he reigned. As Hobbes's chapter title made clear, he regarded the function of colonies as primarily nutritive, confined largely to the role of adding to those "*Materials* conducing to Life" that their "Metropolis, or Mother" could not produce on her own.[3]

In Hobbes's one simple formulation was an understanding not only of colonies but also of their relationship to the state that brusquely challenged more than a century of colonial discourse. In the emergence of that argument and in its subsequent adoption by first the Puritan Commonwealth government that rose to power during the English Civil War followed by Charles II's Restoration regime, Renaissance-era colonization would come to a quiet, if indeterminate, close. The status of colonies would enter into an entirely new phase of ambiguity, and their subsequent history would depend to a great extent on how midcentury leaders like Berkeley, who had thus far set their compass by colonization's Christian humanist past, navigated what had every appearance of being a significantly different future.

In Berkeley, Virginia obtained a governor who was unusually aware of the rise of Hobbes's arguments and thus uniquely alert to the challenge they posed to Virginia's commonwealth. Although there is no evidence that the two men knew each other, their lives in England had nevertheless intersected in various ways. Both men had connections to Virginia colonization. Berkeley's father, Sir Maurice Berkeley, had been an early investor in the colony, and other Berkeley relations had traveled there as planters long before Sir William's connections at the Caroline court helped him to secure the governor's post in 1641. Hobbes, seventeen years Berkeley's senior, had been a

3. Thomas Hobbes, *Leviathan*, ed. Richard Tuck, Cambridge Texts in the History of Political Thought (Cambridge, 1996), 170, 175, 491; Hobbes, *The Elements of Law, Natural and Politic, Edited with a Preface and Critical Notes by Ferdinand Tönnies, to Which Are Subjoined Selected Extracts from Unprinted Mss. of Thomas Hobbes* (London 1889), 104; Hobbes, *On the Citizen*, ed. and trans. Tuck and Michael Silverthorne, Cambridge Texts in the History of Political Thought (Cambridge, 1998), 73.

member of the Virginia Company and a frequent attendee of its meetings beginning on June 19, 1622, when William Cavendish, later second earl of Devonshire, a major company shareholder whom Hobbes served as tutor and secretary, bought him the single share required for admission, perhaps to attain an extra vote in the company's headcounts. It was not in relation to the colony, however, but in connection with the royal court and the intellectual circles that surrounded it that the two men's lives most significantly converged. In 1632, Berkeley became a gentleman of the privy chamber, a post in which he enjoyed the friendship and patronage of the prominent politician Edward Hyde, later first earl of Clarendon, whom Berkeley had met as a fellow law student at the Middle Temple, and Lucius Cary, Viscount Falkland, a courtier known for his considerable erudition in classical literature and scripture. Both men were acquainted with Hobbes, and their carefully staked out constitutional royalist position on a number of major issues confronting the Caroline regime in the late 1630s and early 1640s was often in deliberate and tense dialogue with Hobbes's own emerging theories. As a minor playwright at court, Berkeley was also loosely connected with the coterie of writers and theologians known as the Great Tew circle that met at Falkland's great estate, a group in which Hobbes was also an occasional participant. That affiliation reinforced both Berkeley's and Hobbes's shared adherence to a strand of skepticism that the Great Tew coterie helped to nurture: a doubtfulness about humanity's capacity always to know God's will with certainty, which had roots in ancient Greek Pyrrhonian philosophy, the Elizabethan Richard Hooker's establishmentarian ecclesiology, and the natural jurisprudence of Hugo Grotius. Although Hobbes would take that skeptical outlook much farther than Berkeley or some of his Great Tew friends like Hyde were prepared to go, it was a point of common ground that made their political and philosophical differences all the more glaring.[4]

4. Warren M. Billings, *Sir William Berkeley and the Forging of Colonial Virginia* (Baton Rouge, La., 2004), 6, 9, 11–28, 32; Noel Malcolm, "Hobbes, Sandys, and the Virginia Company," in Malcolm, *Aspects of Hobbes* (Oxford, 2002), 54–55, "A Summary Biography of Hobbes," 10–11. On the Great Tew circle, see J. C. Hayward, "New Directions in Studies of the Falkland Circle," *The Seventeenth Century*, II (1987), 19–48; Hugh Trevor-Roper, "The Great Tew Circle," in Trevor-Roper, *Catholics, Anglicans, and Puritans: Seventeenth Century Essays* (London, 1987), 166–231. Scholars now accept that Hobbes's involvement in Great Tew's discussions was at most occasional, a view that probably also characterizes Berkeley's level of participation. On Hobbes's involvement in the group, see Perez Zagorin, "Clarendon and Hobbes," *Journal of Modern History*, LVII (1985), 596–599. For a useful discussion of the Great Tew circle that focuses on one

Skepticism was a natural, albeit controversial, outgrowth of the same worldly currents that had all along made up a vibrant part of Renaissance divinity. As early as 1591, the anti-Puritan satirist Thomas Nashe was aware of a portion of Sextus Empiricus's *Outlines of Pyrrhonism* circulating in manuscript in English. The book, which had first made its way to England in Latin editions published in Geneva in the 1560s, offered an authoritative introduction to ancient Greek epistemological skepticism. "The Sceptick" (as the English remnant of the text was called) questioned whether any truth could be known with assuredness given the "great difference amongst living creatures" and the resulting "great diversity in their fantasy and conceit." After all, did not dogs rival and in some cases even "excel man in sense," smelling and hearing far better than humans? And did not dogs and other creatures show signs of basic reasoning, for instance engaging in at least rudimentary calculations of justice in defending their homes from intruders and in revenging themselves on their attackers? "Why then should I condemn their conceit and fantasy concerning any thing more than they may mine?" the author asked. "They may be in the truth and I in error, as well as I in the truth and they err." Choosing to suspend judgment in light of such ambiguities, the Pyrrhonian skeptic rejected not only the rigid certainty of the dogmatist but also the other philosophical extreme: the absolute denial of the accessibility of the truth except to the enlightened, a position associated with the second main school of ancient skepticism, the Platonic Academy. Unlike the Platonist or the dogmatist, the Pyrrhonist sought simply a modest basis for assurance. He took comfort in even a probable cause for confidence in his moral path, recognizing that definitive proof was rarely forthcoming. Since "our opinion . . . gives the name of good or ill to every thing," as Nashe summarized Sextus Empiricus's argument, then conclusions about the lawful order required a broad foundation of evidence that was more substantive than opinion alone but not so daunting that it deterred all freely willed, virtuous action.[5]

---

prominent early Virginian's involvement in it, see James Ellison, *George Sandys: Travel, Colonialism, and Tolerance in the Seventeenth Century* (Cambridge, 2002), 161–174, 212–246.

5. William M. Hamlin, "A Lost Translation Found? An Edition of 'The Sceptick' (c. 1590) Based on Extant Manuscripts [With Text]," *English Literary Renaissance*, XXXI (2001), 42, 45, 47; Ronald B. McKerrow, ed., *The Works of Thomas Nashe* (London, 1904–1910; rpt. with corrections and supplemental notes by F. P. Wilson, Oxford, 1958), III, 332; *Sir Walter Raleigh's Sceptick; or, Speculations . . .* (London, 1651). The classic study of early modern skepticism remains Richard H. Popkin, *The History of Scepticism from Savonarola to Bayle*, rev. and expanded ed.

Unsurprisingly, given this earthward orientation, Pyrrhonian skepticism especially attracted those establishmentarian Protestants who looked to familiar man-made institutions like monarchy, public assemblies, the church, and the state as more reliable anchors of the lawful order than either the lofty prophetical claims of would-be saints or the transcendent assertions of universal imperium purported by the papacy or its Spanish-Habsburg partners. Indeed, when "The Sceptick" finally appeared in print in 1651, the translation was credited to none other than Sir Walter Ralegh, the longtime foe of Spanish sovereign overreach who had also set himself against Anabaptist fervor. Although the attribution remains uncertain, it is nonetheless telling that the author of *The History of the World* (1614), with its overriding focus on how human laws could eventually correspond with God's will despite the corruptions of the Fall, would also have been associated with a skepticism that pointed similarly to the sanctity of civil institutions. In other words, skepticism strongly reinforced the establishmentarian ethos that had long made up one important strand of Christian humanism and that had been such a significant factor in shaping the Virginia colony's own civil arrangements.[6]

A more or less direct line can be traced between the growth of skepticism in England and the particular constellation of personalities and interests that had converged in the Virginia enterprise. For instance, Sir Edwin Sandys and his brother George had been instrumental in promoting the teachings of Hooker, who had benefited from the patronage of their father. Edwin Sandys had personally taken in hand the publication of the first four books of Hooker's *Lawes of Ecclesiasticall Politie* (1593), and Hooker's influence runs through both of the Sandys brothers' writings. Likewise, the reception of Grotius's ideas in England seems to have originated in the same political milieu that had centered on secretary of state Robert Cecil, earl of Salisbury, and that had been so instrumental in reviving Virginia colonization after its disappointing Elizabethan career. On the eve of his death, Salisbury had been involved in the negotiations between English and Dutch East India merchants that ultimately led to Grotius's brief visit to the kingdom in 1613 as a Dutch delegate, and it was Richard Hakluyt the clergyman who, almost

---

(Oxford, 2003); see also, J. H. Burns, ed., with Mark Goldie, *The Cambridge History of Political Thought, 1450–1700* (Cambridge, 1991), 494–498, 606–610.

6. For doubts that Sir Walter Ralegh authored "The Sceptick," see Hamlin, "A Lost Translation Found?" *English Literary Renaissance*, XXXI (2001), 35; Pierre Lefranc, *Sir Walter Ralegh Éscrivain: L'oeuvre et les idées* (Paris, 1968), 48–49, 66–67, 427.

certainly at Salisbury's direction, translated Grotius's 1609 pamphlet *Mare Liberum (The Free Sea)* into English. The Great Tew circle would function as a major locus for scholarly engagement with Hooker's and Grotius's writings, and Falkland and Hyde, in addition to their involvement at Great Tew, would serve as two of Berkeley's key signatories (the third being his brother George) when he petitioned for the Virginia governorship. In short, in a number of ways, both large and small, the Virginia venture intersected with the new skepticism. Even Hobbes's own fleeting involvement in the Virginia Company highlights the striking congruence in this era between persons actively working through the philosophical implications of Pyrrhonian epistemology and colonizers who looked to Virginia as an important undertaking. It is scarcely surprising, therefore, that the colony became one of the arenas in which skeptical philosophy as it related to new understandings of the state aroused tensions and conflicts. Nor is it remarkable, particularly against the backdrop of a civil war era in which questions of God's intentions were as multifarious as they were urgent, that these divisions splintered in several directions at once.[7]

7. On Richard Hooker's skepticism, see Melissa M. Caldwell, "Skepticism and Post-Reformation Ethics: Richard Hooker's Galen," *Studies in Philology*, CIX (2005), 581–608. For Edwin and George Sandys's relationship with Hooker, see Theodore K. Rabb, *Jacobean Gentleman: Sir Edwin Sandys, 1561–1629* (Princeton, 1998), 6, 10, 11, 13, 14–16, 17, 21, 24, 31, 36, 45, 47, 48, 54, 57, 109, 307, 309, 394, 395, 397; Ellison, *George Sandys*, 3, 6, 17, 21–36, 41, 45–46, 49, 57, 70, 74, 112, 185, 187, 222, 246–247. On the involvement of Robert Cecil, earl of Salisbury, in the East Indies imbroglio that brought Hugo Grotius to England, see G. N[orman] Clark, "Grotius's East Indies Mission to England," *Transactions of the Grotius Society*, XX (1934), 45–84. See also, Hugo Grotius, *The Free Sea, Trans. Richard Hakluyt, with William Welwod's Critique and Grotius's Reply*, ed. David Armitage (Indianapolis, Ind., 2004). Among other Jacobean writers who had some association with Virginia colonization, John Donne experimented with Pyrrhonian skepticism warily, Francis Bacon addressed it with an eye toward how his empirical method would confront its epistemological challenges, and Ben Jonson seems to have relished its worldly implications. On Donne, see Takashi Yoshinaka, *Marvell's Ambivalence: Religion and the Politics of Imagination in Mid-Seventeenth-Century England* (Cambridge, 2011), 56; and Itrat-Husain, *The Mystical Element in the Metaphysical Poets of the Seventeenth Century* (New York, 1948), 52–56; on Bacon, see Silvia Manzo, "Probability, Certainty, and Facts in Francis Bacon's Natural Histories: A Double Attitude Towards Skepticism," in José R. Maia Neto, Gianni Paganini, and John Christian Laursen, eds., *Skepticism in the Modern Age: Building on the Work of Richard Popkin* (Leiden, The Netherlands, 2009), 123–138; on Jonson, see Mathew R. Martin, *Between Theater and Philosophy: Skepticism in the Major City Comedies of Ben Jonson and Thomas Middleton* (Newark, Del., 2001), 13, 14, 18, 23–28, 58–78, 95–114, 133–153.

On the one hand, establishmentarians like Berkeley set themselves fiercely against Protestant dissenters as their period's most disruptive dogmatists. Compared with their late-sixteenth- and early-seventeenth-century counterparts who criticized nonconformists for their unrealistic utopianism as well as their tendency toward separatism, Berkeley's generation of Anglicans viewed Puritanism through a more distinctively skeptical lens. Ruing the saints' stubborn assuredness in their beliefs, they identified this righteousness as a malady akin to madness. This view appeared in Robert Burton's *Anatomy of Melancholy* (1621), a much reprinted study of melancholia that drew heavily on ancient and medieval sources while also giving new attention to despair's possible origins in moral confusion. Burton's own exposure to the era's skepticism explains why he gave so much weight to "terror of conscience" or "horror of conscience" as a major source of melancholia. A common worry for skeptics at this time concerned the likelihood that casuistry's relentless pursuit of the truth in the face of God's elusive plan could itself foster a morally incapacitating feeling of anguish, thereby leading people away from their callings rather than toward greater fidelity to their Maker. Hooker placed this skeptical concern right at the heart of his magisterial defense of established churches in *Lawes of Ecclesiasticall Politie*. If Christians accepted that "all things lawful to be done are comprehended in the scripture," Hooker asked, then what would the Bible become "but a snare and a torment to weake consciences, filling them with infinite perplexities, scrupulosities, doubts insoluble, and extreme despaires?" Probably with Hooker's arguments in mind, Burton reflected regularly in his book on the limitations of human knowledge, and he devoted special attention to "Religiousmadnesse" as the peculiar ailment of his age. "Is not this *Mundus furiosus*, a mad world?" he asked, expressing an alarmist view of the fragility of the civil order that largely defined how skeptical Anglicans viewed the threat posed by nonconformity in these years. Treating religious melancholy as a category of madness unto itself, Burton deemed it a condition closely related to the melancholy of love because of how easily the greatest of all longings, adoration for God, gave way to imaginative excesses and political unrest.[8]

8. [Robert Burton], *The Anatomy of Melancholy, What It Is; With All the Kindes, Causes, Symptomes, Prognostickes, and Severall Cures of It* (Oxford, 1621), 27, 29, 773, 779; Richard Hooker, *The Folger Library Edition of the Works of Richard Hooker: Of the Laws of Ecclesiastical Polity*, ed. Georges Edelen and W. Speed Hill, 6 vols. (Cambridge, Mass., 1977–1993), I, 190. On the significance of Robert Burton's theory in this era, see Angus Gowland, *The Worlds of Renaissance Melancholy: Robert Burton in Context* (Cambridge, 2006).

The Great Tew participants continued to build on this idea that religious yearning fed a destructive providentialism that perversely endangered commonwealths already well on the way to redemption. The Church of England clergyman and Great Tew theologian Henry Hammond, for instance, wrote *Of Resisting the Lawfull Magistrate upon Colour of Religion* (1643) as a stern refutation of the mistaken righteousness of the king's enemies in the opening years of the Civil War. The Scottish Presbyterians and their English supporters proceeded as if they were the godly when in fact they had set themselves up against a government that already enjoyed divine sanction. To take up arms and "fight for a Religion distant or contrary to that which is established by Law," he wrote, was not only to risk the "dissolution of any government" but to do so on the basis of a peculiar loss of reason. Surely it was an instance of "Enthusiasme," or a fanciful "dreame of the dreamers," to imagine that God's truths could be pulled down from the heavens more reliably than they could be found in long-instituted political arrangements. Although Hammond did not deny "that the thousand yeeres for the Saints to reigne on earth are now at hand," his millenarianism, like that of most of his fellow Great Tew discussants, was of a quietist variety that emphasized "patience" and "enduring" in the face of God's continuing mysteries instead of the "fighting, destroying, resisting, [and] rebelling" that he identified as proof in its own right that the king's enemies had succumbed to frenzied delusion.[9]

Berkeley would similarly treat the Puritans as given over to a groundless confidence in their providential knowledge. Their certainty, he argued, left them blind to the hazards to their souls they incurred by disobeying and eventually killing the king. Criticizing the Commonwealth regime for its "Oraculous assurance," Berkeley wrote that, far from prescient, the regicides could not even grasp fully their crimes, being too "short sighted in such subtle matters." He leveled a similar critique at the new communities of Quakers who settled in Virginia beginning in the 1650s. In a 1660 law ordering the Quakers' immediate suppression and banishment, Berkeley and the General Assembly argued that such harsh punishment was justified in the case of a sect that was so "unreasonable and turbulent." The Quakers' "lies, miracles, false visions, prophecies and doctrines" were particularly dangerous because of the aggressiveness with which they taught and published such untruths. To tolerate the Quakers would be "to destroy religion, lawes, co-

9. [Henry Hammond], *Of Resisting the Lawfull Magistrate upon Colour of Religion* (London, 1643), 1, 2, 16, 17.

munities and all bonds of civil societie, leaveing it arbitrarie to everie vaine and vitious person whether men shall be safe, lawes established, offenders punished, and Governours rule," the Berkeley administration warned. When Berkeley's ally Edmund Scarburgh approached some of the new conventicles on the Eastern Shore and read aloud the assembly's act with what he called a "becoming Reverence," the Quakers openly "scoft" at it and pontificated about their own godliness even though, as Scarburgh disdainfully put it, they were filled with little more than the "Spirit of Nonsence." No wonder then that Berkeley did not just persecute the Quakers but also encouraged the planter population's own greater skepticism by alerting them to the liars in their midst.[10]

On the other hand, skepticism itself could be taken too far. Burton had warned of this possibility, noting that the terrorized consciences of the zealous might not be as bad as the "cauterised consciences" of the overly worldly. Tellingly, given Hobbes's later self-conscious identification of his project as one of philosophy rather than theology, Burton counted among these "professed Atheists" many of "our great Philosophers" on the grounds that "too much learning makes them mad." The alleged wickedness of Hobbes's own principles and the view that he was a "good Philosopher" before he was a "good Christian" would similarly become central to how the Great Tew circle judged his works. They were particularly sensitive to the exotic uses to which he put the idea of natural law. Michel de Montaigne, one of the great popularizers of Pyrrhonism, recognized the appeal that the laws of nature held for his fellow skeptics, especially as a way to explain how a civil order that pleased God could arise despite humans' fundamental ignorance of his will. "To allow the Lawes some certainetie," he observed, these writers averred the existence of "some firme, perpetuall and immoveable, which they call naturall" and which "by the condition of their proper essence, are imprinted in mankind." Montaigne himself was doubtful that the laws of nature could adequately provide such a basis, for he noted that different nations disagreed even on the question of what was natural. But the Great Tew participants were more accepting of this line of reasoning, and their faith in it was due in large part to their admiration for Hooker and Grotius. Hooker's focus on natural laws to help settle the established church and Grotius's turn to them

10. "Declaration of the General Assembly," Mar. 17, 1651, in Billings, ed., *Papers of Sir William Berkeley*, 98, 99; An Act for the Suppressing the Quakers, Mar. 13, 1659/60, in Hening, *Statutes at Large*, I, 532; Edmund Scarburgh to William Berkeley, [November 1663], in Billings, ed., *Papers of Sir William Berkeley*, 214.

to counter Iberian pretensions in intensely contested arenas of trade and colonization like the East Indies provided the men who gathered at Great Tew with a sophisticated blend of the old humanism and the new skepticism with which to approach their unusually complicated political terrain. Such a synthesis satisfied their view that Puritans and other enemies of the established government acted on the basis of an ill-founded zealotry; at the same time, it reassured them that their own confidence in the instituted church and state rested on solid Christian grounds. The thin line that Hooker and Grotius themselves had walked in avoiding some of skepticism's more troubling implications, however, also left these men sharply aware of how easily that line could be crossed. As a result, they lost no time in perceiving the novel dimensions of Hobbes's natural jurisprudence, and they were especially quick to see that the familiar elements they treasured in Hooker's and Grotius's accounts were precisely those that Hobbes had abandoned.[11]

Where Hobbes's theories most conspicuously parted ways with the ideals of the constitutional royalists was in relation to the bonds that had long been envisioned as incorporating the commonwealth's diverse members into a single redeeming body. Men like Hyde and Berkeley remained highly attached to the traditional view that the tie between ruler and people mirrored the covenant between God and the faithful in its sanctifying purpose. To a considerable extent, their thinking in this regard still harked back, however dimly, to Sir John Fortescue's iteration of the concept of the *corpus mysticum* more than a century earlier. Indeed, an English version of Fortescue's *De Laudibus Legum Angliae* that had appeared in 1616 and that would return to print in 1660 had come from the pen of the antiquarian John Selden who was himself a much-admired author at Great Tew. Hyde's view that virtuous kings should voluntarily limit their own power was consistent with Fortescue's idea that monarchs had historically moderated their ferocious imperium in response to their subjects' growing civility. Hooker made a very similar argument, commending English kings for ruling in accordance with the laws of the realm but also acknowledging that, as "*Godes Liuetenantes,*"

---

11. [Burton], *Anatomy of Melancholy*, 765, 766, 768; Edward [Hyde], earl of Clarendon, *A Brief View and Survey of the Dangerous and Pernicious Errors to Church and State, in Mr. Hobbes's Book, Entitled Leviathan* (Oxon [Oxfordshire], 1676), 4; Michel Eyquem de Montaigne, *Essays*, ed. L. C. Harmer, trans. John Florio (London, 1965), II, 297. On the rise of the new skepticism in relation to humanism, see Richard Tuck, *Philosophy and Government, 1572–1651* (Cambridge, 1993), xiii, xvi, 6, 11, 14, 19, 23–24, 35–64, 78, 82, 83, 97, 108, 110, 111, 113, 127, 172–175, 196, 210, 214, 215, 217, 279, 285, 287–290, 292, 294, 296, 298, 304, 306, 316, 346–347.

they performed a momentous calling and thus had a right at any time to "exact at the handes of their Subjectes generall obedience in whatsoever affayres their power may serve to command." These affirmations of the ideal of a mutual bond between ruler and people that held them both to their respective callings also had the effect of reinforcing the conventional assumption of sovereignty and commonwealth as distinct divine gifts, each with its own part to play in coaxing the world away from sin. Berkeley so strongly took for granted the distinguishability of the king's sovereignty and the integrity of the commonwealths over which he ruled that after the Restoration he thought nothing of drawing a distinction between Charles II's "growing Empire" in America, meaning his increasing strength there, and the "publiques," or discrete and reliable reservoirs of resources and legal privileges, on which each colony relied for its well-being.[12]

A new rich vocabulary had begun to reenvision the bonds between colonies and their monarch in the language of contract. Natural law theory had evolved in the hands of late Renaissance civil lawyers like Grotius whose engagements in overseas commerce were encumbered by far fewer moral doubts than had been true for their late-sixteenth and early-seventeenth-century predecessors. As a result, the political discourse of colonization acquired a fresh layer of references to promise keeping, wages, debts, and consensual and nonconsensual parties, leaving the image of a royal marriage compact like the one once employed by Captain John Bargrave sounding increasingly quaint. But the terminology of contract was not in itself corrosive of older Christian humanist ideals, for it could as readily be used to buttress traditional concepts as to challenge them. Grotius entertained the idea that God, though bound by no law, was nevertheless the archetypal promise keeper purely as a result of his nature as the world's only utterly unchangeable judge. Likewise, in 1676 Hyde, long since ennobled as earl of Clarendon, would attack Hobbes's idea of absolute sovereignty on the grounds that a prince who did not keep his word was like a dishonest employer; he left his subjects with none of that assurance about the future that kept their own

---

12. John Fortescue, *De Laudibus Legum Angliae Writen by Sir John Fortescue L. Ch. Justice, and after L. Chancellor to K. Henry VI* . . . (London, 1616); Fortescue, *De Laudibus Legum Angliae Written by Sir John Fortescue . . . Hereto Are Added the Two Sums of Sir Ralph de Hengham . . . with Notes Both on Fortescue and Hengham by . . . John Selden* . . . (London, 1660); Hooker, *Folger Library Edition of the Works of Richard Hooker,* ed. Edelen and Hill, III, 336; William Berkeley to Edward Hyde, earl of Clarendon, Mar. 30, 1663, in Billings, eds., *Papers of Sir William Berkeley,* 190.

wills animated. Notably, given the important role that such a notion of a contractual bond between king and people would play across the Atlantic, Clarendon's critique of Hobbes's theory in this regard extended to his new definition of colonies in *Leviathan:*

> Since he reckons the sending out Colonies, and erecting Plantations, the encouraging all manner of Arts, as Navigation, Agriculture, Fishing, and all manner of Manufactures, to be of the Policy and Office of a Soveraign, it will not be in his power to deny, that his Soveraign is obliged to perform all those promises, and to make good all those concessions and priviledges which he hath made and granted, to those who have bin thereby induc'd to expose their Fortunes and their Industry to those Adventures.

Perhaps Clarendon was echoing what he came to see as the best retort available for preserving the commonwealth status of the colonies. After all, his friend Berkeley had by this time, in his own attempts to insulate Virginia against the Hobbists, used a very similar argument about the weighty obligations entailed whenever a sovereign made promises.[13]

Probably drawing directly on Grotius, Berkeley relied on that contractual terminology with no assumption whatsoever that it implied a turning away from a conception of the colony as a moral community that stood resolutely under God and king. On the contrary, Berkeley had little trouble reconciling the language of contract with the more familiar Pauline rhetoric of the commonwealth's affective bonds. His impulse was to synthesize these discourses so that the loving ties that held Virginians to their duties were also lushly entwined with their commercial pursuits. It was by redefining the colony as a commonwealth centered on the interplay between royal promises and the corresponding risks undertaken by planters that Berkeley sought to safeguard Virginia's polity in this newly uncertain age.

Hobbes, however, had come to see the very idea of a covenant with God or a contract with a king as a logical absurdity. His own attempt to develop skeptical accounts of commonwealth like Grotius's into a more comprehensive philosophical system had led him to take the remarkable step of denying altogether that the law derived meaning from the bonds that had emerged

---

13. *The Illustrious Hugo Grotius of the Law of Warre and Peace . . .* (London, 1654), 224–225; Clarendon, *Brief View and Survey*, 183. For John Bargrave's view of Virginia as a reciprocally binding marriage contract between planters and their king, see Chapter Four, above.

over time between polities and kings, or from those that had formed across the ages between Christians and God. This was a stunning departure from humanist arguments, and it caught the attention of constitutional royalists with particular force because of how much faith they continued to place in those particular reciprocal linkages. In Hobbes's revolutionary theory, the only bond that could truly withstand the test of skeptical scrutiny was not a covenant with an unknowable God. Nor was it a contract with a grace-filled ruler, for how could sinners who were blind to their own ignorance grasp such virtue? Rather, the only bond that humans were really equipped to establish was the set of basic agreements of mutual safety that they formed with one another as they sought to insulate themselves from the warlike individualism of the state of nature. The notion of state unity that would underpin Hobbes's insistence that colonies relinquish their commonwealth status was not just incidental to his dramatic new focus on the people's own contractual arrangements. Rather, it was the key idea that gave that concept philosophical resonance. Hobbes had cleverly reimagined the moral mechanism that made commonwealth possible. No longer did it rely on the cheerful interchange of rightly turned wills among the polity's diverse members. Instead, it involved a transformative displacement of wills, as the people entering the bonds of commonwealth surrendered the free wills and independence of judgment that had propelled their savagery in the state of nature and yielded to the frightful authority of an "Artificiall" sovereign to which they themselves gave substance as the very incarnation of their collective wills.[14]

Hobbes was fully aware how much his overall theory of commonwealth relied on this one unusual turn of logic that effectively abandoned the old idea of the polity's consensual and loving bonds in favor of a fundamental notion of unity. He now thought of the wills of the people as actively generating the *"Mortall God"* who ruled them rather than intersecting with his own independent will. Describing this novel conception of unitary wills in *Leviathan,* he wrote:

> This is more than Consent, or Concord; it is a reall Unitie of them all, in one and the same Person, made by Covenant of every man with every man, in such manner, as if every man should say to every man, *I Authorize and give up my Right of Governing my selfe, to this Man, or to this Assembly of men, on this condition, that thou give up thy Right to him, and Authorise all his Actions in like Manner.*

14. Hobbes, *Leviathan,* ed. Tuck, 120.

Given the importance of this doctrine of unity in Hobbes's more general natural jurisprudence, it is no wonder he flatly denied the capacity of colonies to be commonwealths. To have conceded on that point would have been to allow that not all members of the polity were similarly obliged to the sovereign to which they had jointly given rise.[15]

Hobbes's theory of state unity was not, however, merely an ingenious philosophical abstraction, for the intense divisions of the Civil War years quickly transformed it into a tangible political force. Hobbes first distributed *Elements* in the spring of 1640, during the closing weeks of the Short Parliament, at the insistence of his then-patron William Cavendish, earl of Newcastle. As a Privy Councillor to Charles I and governor to the prince of Wales, Newcastle was undoubtedly eager for Hobbes to share the theories they had discussed in their private conversations with a broader audience. In particular, he wanted to correct the waywardness of moderate royalists like Hyde and Falkland who had demonstrated in that fractious parliament a troubling willingness to maneuver between defending the king's prerogative and denouncing his policies as an immoral instance of statism. As Hobbes later explained, he wrote the book to "set forth and demonstrate, that the said power and rights were inseparably annexed to the sovereignty; which sovereignty they did not then deny to be in the King; but it seems understood not, or would not understand that inseparability." But Hobbes's ideas did not remain the preserve of the ultraroyalists for long. The Puritan parliamentarians who dominated first the Short Parliament and then the Long Parliament that convened in November quickly grasped the utility of his theories for justifying their own actions against the king.[16]

As early as Henry Parker's 1642 apologia *Observations upon Some of His Majesties Late Answers and Expresses,* the parliamentarians began invoking certain recognizable Hobbesian themes. How were the English to know what was the law in their current circumstances? Parker asked. "It can be nothing else amongst Christians but the Pactions and agreements of such and such politique corporations," that is, of the people themselves assembled in commonwealth. This Hobbesian emphasis on an original contract naturally went hand in hand with the corresponding Hobbesian axiom that obedience was only finally owed to the government capable of protecting its citizens. "Since all naturall power is in those which obay," Parker wrote, "they

---

15. Ibid.
16. Thomas Hobbes, *The English Works of Thomas Hobbes of Malmesbury,* ed. William Molesworth (London, 1840), IV, 414.

which contract to obay to their owne ruine, or having so contracted, they which esteeme such a contract before their owne preservation are felonious to themselves, and rebellious to nature." Hyde had little doubt about where such incendiary ideas had originated. He furiously shared his thoughts on the matter with Berkeley's older brother Sir John Berkeley in 1646, bristling at "the new Maxime, that proteccon and subjection are Relatives and cease together, w[hi]ch I presume was neither divinity nor Law 7 yeares since." Over the next decade, Hobbism became a guide to parliamentary and Commonwealth policies, as figures like Parker and other admirers of Hobbes like Benjamin Worsley and Thomas Povey rose to positions of prominence on advisory councils, including the new committees of trade and plantations.[17]

Yet, Hobbes's theories did not run their course with the collapse of the Commonwealth. The Restoration ushered in new respect for his vision of a unitary state, especially among the factions in Charles II's so-called Cabal ministry that opposed Clarendon. One of the last books Clarendon wrote before his death in 1674, a work he completed while in exile in France after efforts to impeach him, was a lengthy chapter-by-chapter refutation of *Leviathan,* a book he regarded as promulgating some of the most dangerous principles of his era. Berkeley left behind few statements that point as explicitly to his own concerns about Hobbism. Nevertheless, his reactions and written responses to the efforts by the Commonwealth and Restoration governments to realize a unified state leave little doubt that he, too, had come to see one of the period's greatest political challenges as navigating an English Atlantic suddenly intoxicated by dangerous new ideas.[18]

The rise of Hobbism, even more than the vicissitudes of Puritanism, shaped Berkeley's long governorship and influenced in particular the ways he sought to safeguard Virginia's commonwealth from the forces newly aligned against it. Not all his attempts in this regard were successful. His fear of the new philosophy would eventually bring about his downfall, when to his horror he realized that Hobbism had come to Virginia in the form of his wife's younger cousin Nathaniel Bacon, Jr. One of the youthful believers in the still-novel idea that obedience was owed only to a government that

---

17. [Henry Parker], *Observations upon Some of His Majesties Late Answers and Expresses* [London, 1642], 1, 8; Edward Hyde, earl of Clarendon, to Sir John Berkeley, November 1646, quoted in Jon Parkin, *Taming the Leviathan: The Reception of the Political and Religious Ideas of Thomas Hobbes in England, 1640–1700* (Cambridge, 2007), 53.

18. Clarendon, *Brief View and Survey.*

adequately protects its people, Bacon arrived in the colony in 1674 just as a number of disparate circumstances were converging to give that theory special relevance. Not only were the clouds of an impending war with local native peoples gathering, but so, too, was the colony buffeted by new Hobbist initiatives emerging from the Cabal ministry's plantation councils. No other combination of circumstances could have more potently signaled the anxious last chapter of Virginia's Renaissance origins than Bacon's Rebellion. The crisis reverberated with providential terrors about the ferocious violence suddenly erupting on the colony's frontiers while at the same time it resounded with strange and confusing ideas about when a people could or could not properly sever the bonds that had previously secured them. Yet, the storm generated more short-term apprehension than lasting damage. Indeed, as a testament to the Virginia polity's resilience, Bacon's Rebellion was not only Berkeley's undoing but also his greatest triumph, for it was a moment when the planters themselves would ultimately choose to turn away from the dramatic new Hobbesian worldview that Bacon held out for them and stand behind the established order that had been Berkeley's own lifelong passion. The Renaissance era of colonization would leave its most lasting impression on the uncertain age to come in the embrace of the commonwealth by the rebellion's key constituents. That legacy, in turn, owed a great deal to Virginia's longest-serving governor. Berkeley's worldly Christianity and his skepticism both of outsized truth claims and unyielding philosophies made him a highly effective ruler in an unusually perplexing time.

*Berkeley's Moderate Skepticism and the
Problem of Godly Assuredness*

A good example of the role that skepticism played in Berkeley's political outlook appears in a letter he wrote late in his life to Richard Nicolls, the royalist governor of New York. The year was 1668, and England seemed frighteningly once more in the grip of dogmatists. Nonconformists had garnered enough power in Charles II's reign that they had managed to replace the Act of Uniformity with a lenient comprehension law, and rumors crossed the ocean that Presbyterian voices were among those calling for harsh measures against Clarendon in the impeachment proceedings. For Berkeley, this news of Puritan ascendancy brought back dreadful memories of a very particular moment three decades earlier: the National Covenant when Scottish Presbyterians composed and circulated an oath pledging the brethren's commitment to a "General Band" in response to Archbishop William Laud's efforts to bring the Scottish Kirk into line with the Church of England. As Berkeley wistfully described the present state of the kingdom to Nicolls, "You wil find the condition of it in 68 not much from what it was in thirty eight when the Scots first declared those resolutions with the English of their opinions." The National Covenant had been a key precipitant to the civil wars that soon engulfed Charles I's multiple kingdoms. Berkeley's belief that the Scots' challenge to the king's ecclesiastical authority rested on little more than their opinions of what God wanted from them suggests powerfully how his skepticism helped shape his understanding of the resulting conflagration. For Berkeley, the great challenge of his age boiled down in large part to the problem of preserving holy commonwealths from the overwrought imaginations of the godly.[19]

Berkeley's skepticism gave his politics a distrusting edge while leaving his Christian humanist inclinations supple and intact. On the one hand, he was part of a rising generation of establishmentarians who took their faith in the sanctified nature of existing institutions to new heights. The Covenant served for them as an especially charged symbol of godly extremism despite its own traditional elements. The oath was hardly a fiery call for reforms. It stopped short of openly defying Charles I, instead arguing that the innovations from which the Scots and their king had a fundamental obligation to defend themselves were the handiwork of Satan and the Roman Antichrist, implicitly carried out by their minions Laud and his fellow bishops. In effect, the Covenanters claimed to incorporate the king into their own conscionable community for the sake of bending his momentarily distracted will back to God and Scotland's moral polity. The logic of the Covenant was thus little different from that which underlay England's 1584 Bond of Association or, for that matter, the 1587 bond of the "Cittie of Ralegh." But the rise of skepticism had given such sheltering under the sanctifying mantle of commonwealth in opposition to the king's commands a new tinge of illegitimacy. For Berkeley, the state now possessed an integrity that it simply had not enjoyed half a century earlier.[20]

19. John Rushworth, *Historical Collections of Private Passages of State* . . . (London, 1659), II, 739; William Berkeley to Richard Nicolls, Apr. 26, 1668, in Billings, ed., *Papers of Sir William Berkeley*, 339.

20. "Grant of Arms for the CITY OF RALEIGH in Virginia, and for Its Governor and Assistants," [Jan. 7, 1587], in David Beers Quinn, ed., *The Roanoke Voyages, 1584–1590; Documents to*

Yet, Berkeley's contempt for the Covenant was a far cry from Hobbes's. In a passage from *Leviathan* that heaped withering scorn either on the Scottish Covenanters or their English sympathizers who subscribed to their own Solemn League and Covenant, Hobbes made clear just how illicit he regarded any such presumed divine bond to be:

> Some men have pretended for their disobedience to their Soveraign, a new Covenant, made, not with men, but with God; this ... is unjust: for there is no Covenant with God, but by mediation of some body that representeth Gods Person: which none doth but Gods Lieutenant, who hath the Soveraignty under God. But this pretence of Covenant with God, is so evident a lye, even in the pretenders own consciences, that it is not onely an act of an unjust, but also of a vile, and unmanly disposition.

Later, Clarendon would single out this passage as evidence that Hobbes's arguments had gone so far in discrediting humanity's continuing relationship with God that they were "destructive of our Religion, and against the express sense of Scripture." Such a view that skepticism should be approached with wariness and, in particular, with great care that it did not slip into an irreligious materialism also characterized Berkeley's moderate establishmentarianism, a stance that clung to older norms while at the same time contributing to Renaissance divinity's gradual decline.[21]

For most of the Great Tew members, Providence was still a potent force, but its mysterious ways were now directed mainly at upholding civil states and punishing disturbers of the public peace. As English Puritans began taking up arms with their Scottish brethren, Hyde warned characteristically that God's wrath was singularly harsh against those persons who committed treason against "Kings and other supreme Magistrates, his Vicegerents, and

---

Illustrate the English Voyages to North America under the Patent Granted to Walter Raleigh in 1584, Works Issued by the Hakluyt Society, 2d Ser., no. [105] (London, 1955), II, 508.

21. Hobbes, *Leviathan*, ed. Tuck, 122; Clarendon, *Brief View and Survey*, 50. On Hobbes's skeptical beliefs, see Shirley Letwin, "Skepticism and Toleration in Hobbes' Political Thought," in Alan Levine, ed., *Early Modern Skepticism and the Origins of Toleration* (Lanham, Md., 1999), 165–178; Tuck, *Philosophy and Government*, 279, 285, 293, 294, 296, 304, 306, 316, 346; Tuck, "The Civil Religion of Thomas Hobbes," in Nicholas Phillipson and Quentin Skinner, eds., *Political Discourse in Early Modern Britain* (Cambridge, 1993), 120–138.

Deputies here on earth." He even offered his own eschatological prediction as a counterpoint to the millenarianism of the king's Puritan adversaries. In a 1645 pamphlet, he cited the New Testament (2 Timothy 3:1, 2, 4, 5) and proposed that the millennium might be signaled, not by the Saints' triumphs, but by their disorders: "In the last daies, perilous times shall come, for men shall be lovers of their own selves, covetous, boasters, Proud, Blaspheamers, Disobedient to Parents, Traitors, Heady, High-minded, Lovers of Pleasure more then Lovers of God; Having a forme of Godlinesse but denying the power thereof." Berkeley shared this view of a Providence oriented especially against rebels. The fire that destroyed London in 1666, for instance, was for him a "judgment" against the regicides. Likewise, when Bacon died a year into his rebellion in Virginia, Berkeley was confident "that God has brought this most Atheistical man to his deserved end." Conversely, God actively aided rulers who sought to return the people to their rightful loyalties. Berkeley rallied Virginians to his side against the "mutinous and rebellious persons" who had taken up with Bacon with a bold assertion of his own righteousness, "not doubting but God Almighty, who hath commanded obedience to authority, will give me success, in my so just resolutions and determinations." The colonizers' long-standing argument that their resolute actions were needed to enact God's will across the ocean had become, in Berkeley's hands, an apologia for defending the commonwealths that colonization had wrought.[22]

Shared admiration for Hooker and Grotius provided the constitutional royalists like Berkeley with a common intellectual foundation. Hooker's Elizabethan defense of the established church was an important touchstone at Great Tew, helping to explain why some of Berkeley's own first legislative efforts in Virginia on behalf of its "weale publique" centered on strengthening the colony's ecclesiastical structures and ensuring that its "littargie" conformed to England's. Even more suggestive of Berkeley's Hookerite outlook was his more general faith in the wisdom of public assemblies over the dis-

---

22. [Edward Hyde, earl of Clarendon], *Transcendent and Multiplied Rebellion and Treason, Discovered, by the Lawes of the Land* ([Oxford], 1645), 1, 26; William Berkeley to Richard Nicolls, May 4, 1667, in Billings, ed., *Papers of Sir William Berkeley,* 309, Berkeley to Henry Coventry, Feb. 2, 1676/77, 573, "Proclamation Suspending Nathaniel Bacon from Office," May 10, 1676, 518. For the widespread tendency by Restoration Anglicans to associate providentialism with the maintenance of civil order and punishment of rebellion, see John Spurr, "'Virtue, Religion, and Government': The Anglican Uses of Providence," in Tim Harris, Paul Seaward, and Mark Goldie, eds., *The Politics of Religion in Restoration England* (Oxford, 1990), 29–47.

ruptive influence of private opinion. Hooker's view that human reason and civil establishments allowed for substantial points of connection with Providence had encouraged him to see the Protestant Reformation as a corrective to Rome's corruptions, not a continuous project of destabilizing reform. To help give the Reformation an endpoint, he distinguished sharply between the true judgment that holds human institutions to God's will and the vulgar opinions that threaten to tear them apart. In his preface to *Lawes of Ecclesiasticall Politie,* Hooker explicitly addressed those Puritans who nervously sought further reforms for fear that the church was still overly worldly. To soothe their disquiet, he offered a quote by the fourth-century Trinitarian Gregory of Nazianzus: "God is not a God of sedition and confusion but of order and peace." Hooker noted that Gregory uttered this axiom at a moment when he was "offended at the peoples too great presumption in controlling the judgement of them to whom in such cases they should have rather submitted their owne." As that knowing reference to difficult moral cases suggests, Hooker wrote his *Lawes* in a distinctly casuistic vein. He sought to draw anxious Puritans who were filled with doubts about the Elizabethan settlement to a conscionable acceptance of it, just as Gregory had urged fretful early Christians to turn to those civil and church authorities best equipped to guide them. A distinctive Neoplatonic element in Hooker's writings informed this concern for the fears and sorrow that accosted a confused soul. That same Christian Platonism encouraged Hooker's rich emphasis on civil and cosmic hierarchy maintained by a supreme ruler who stood as an intermediary between humans and the angels, allowing "the lowest things to be led back to the highest by those that are intermediate" — an image that still reverberated, albeit faintly, in Hobbes's more worldly notion of the sovereign as an earthly mediator who represented God. For Hooker and his followers, the notion of political and religious establishments as naturally taking a hierarchical form that permitted a people's greater accordance with reason explained how states and churches could rest assured in their lawfulness even without knowing God's will with certainty.[23]

A similar skepticism characterized Grotius's works. An admirer of Hooker, Grotius also sought to identify the grounds on which established

23. Hening, *Statutes,* I, 240–241; Hooker, *Folger Library Edition of the Works of Richard Hooker,* ed. Edelen and Hill, I, 13, 14, III, 494. For Hooker's reliance on Platonic philosophy, see W. J. Torrance Kirby, *Richard Hooker, Reformer and Platonist* (Bodmin, Cornwall, U.K., 2005); Kirby, "Grace and Hierarchy: Richard Hooker's Two Platonisms," in Kirby, ed., *Richard Hooker and the English Reformation* (Dordrecht, The Netherlands, 2003), 25–40.

churches and states could rest their claims of lawfulness despite the ambiguities of God's will. Grotius's writings had become another staple of Great Tew interest by the 1630s. In 1639, George Sandys wrote an English translation of Grotius's *Christus patiens,* to which Falkland contributed a commendatory poem. Clarendon, who studied Grotius in the 1640s in preparation for writing his *History* of the Civil War, would write of "the great Grotius, who may justly be esteemed as good if not the best scholar that age brought out." By the early 1640s, Tew-affiliated writers like Hammond and William Chillingworth built on his Arminian theology, while others like Falkland, John Colepeper, and Dudley Digges exploited his insights on political obligation. Such divergent interests reflected the ambitious scope of Grotius's own scholarly agenda.[24]

Concerned by Christendom's political and religious divisions, Grotius was also determined to justify the Dutch states' resistance to Spanish rule. In writings intimately connected to Dutch political and commercial endeavors, he pursued a moral philosophy by which justice and peace could be restored in terms on which all rational Christians could agree. Like Hooker, Grotius viewed reason as a God-given capacity that had permitted humans since the Fall to move toward greater obedience to God. In seeking the basis on which sense alone might have steered otherwise morally imperfect people toward virtue, he posited self-preservation as just such a foundational principle. The impulse to save life and limb brought people into society; meanwhile, those persons' recognition of their shared desire for safety also spurred them to make laws to prevent undue harm to others, thereby creating the civil foundations for commonwealth. His language for describing this two-part instinct was familiar in its humanistic anti-utopianism. The urge for safety, he argued, arose from "divinely inspired self-love," a species of adoration that he theorized God had planted in all his creatures to help carry out his will. Meanwhile, "love for others" prompted humans to hold their selfishness in

---

24. [Hugo Grotius], *Christs Passion; A Tragedie; with Annotations,* trans. George Sandys (London, 1640) (the date September 17, 1639, presumably indicating when the work was completed, appears after Falkland's poem); Edward Hyde, earl of Clarendon, *An Essay on an Active and Contemplative Life: And, Why the One Should Be Preferred before the Other* (Glasgow, 1765), 43. On Grotius's popularity at Great Tew, see Tuck, *Philosophy and Government,* 272–274, 277, 305; Marco Barducci, "Clement Barksdale, Translator of Grotius: Erastianism and Episcopacy in the English Church, 1651–1658," *Seventeenth Century,* XXV (2010), 265–280; Ellison, *George Sandys,* 220; Edward Hyde, earl of Clarendon, *The History of the Rebellion: A New Selection,* ed. Paul Seaward (Oxford, 2009), xv.

check so that it did not devolve into "immoderate self-interest." Early Virginia colonizers like Captain John Smith and Captain John Bargrave would have perceived their own values reflected closely in this kind of reasoning.[25]

Focusing more on fallen humans' worldly and prudential considerations than their clear understanding of what is right and wrong, Grotius's skeptical theory of commonwealth formation found the impulse for civil society not in "any special Command from GOD" but simply in people's "free Will" and their basic rational "Sense of the Inability of separate Families to repel Violence" on their own. In keeping with his Arminian emphasis on free volition, Grotius identified the "Civil Powers" that resulted from this social coalescence as a purely human innovation, though one that enjoyed unquestionable legitimacy "because GOD approved of this wholesome Institution of Men." By thus tracing law's origins from man's instinct for self-preservation to his forging of sovereign polities that satisfied God, Grotius provided a skeptical explanation for reasonable claims to lawful conduct that stopped well short of Hobbes's additional step of making the sovereign effectively the ultimate casuist, the lawgiver whose determinations of right and wrong superseded all others'. Later, Berkeley would defend Virginia's civil integrity in distinctly Grotian rather than Hobbesian terms. In response to the Commonwealth's insistence that the colony had proven itself rebellious to lawful authority by resisting the Puritans' rule, he maintained that Virginians were "simple men" rather than overreaching saints and thus would choose instead "to follow the perspicuous and plaine pathes of God and our lawes." That statement breathed, not of Leviathan-like absolutism, but rather of the law's more straightforward origins in the choices made historically by communities in their public deliberations.[26]

Berkeley's only extant play, *The Lost Lady: A Tragy-Comedy* (1638), provides a window into his own early experimentation with skeptical insights. He wrote the play in the summer of 1637, and it was performed before Charles and Henrietta Maria that Christmas season. The following year, the piece was staged at Blackfriars and the Cockpit, when it also appeared in print. A rather convoluted tale of court romances and political intrigue be-

25. Hugo Grotius, *De Jure Praedae Commentarius, Commentary on the Law of Prize and Booty*, I, *A Translation of the Original Manuscript of 1604*, trans. Gwladys L. Williams with Walter H. Zeydel (Oxford, 1950), 9, 11.

26. Hugo Grotius, *The Rights of War and Peace, Edited and with an Introduction by Richard Tuck, from the Edition by Jean Barbeyrace* (Indianapolis, Ind., 2005), I, 358; "Declaration of the General Assembly," Mar. 17, 1650/51, in Billings, ed., *Papers of Sir William Berkeley*, 98–99.

tween the ancient Greek polities of Thessaly and Sparta, the play featured two especially prominent themes: the often confusing obscurity of providence and the resulting need for constancy in one's faith and toward one's offices on Earth. Rioting in response to Laud's new prayer book had begun in Scotland as early as July 1637, so the question of constancy pressed with particular urgency at this moment. Additionally, Berkeley made a number of references that appear to have been directed at the Scots' English friends, especially those Puritan aristocrats whose own Platonism was far less worldly than Hooker's. Platonism figured prominently at the Caroline court but took different forms, and Berkeley was evidently especially eager to repudiate Puritans drawn to the philosophy for its implications that God's truth could be accessed directly rather than through the intermediary of established institutions.[27]

In his play, Berkeley placed the most strenuous denunciation of the possibility for clear-eyed understandings of divine will in the mouth of the one character assumed by the others to be a seer, the mysterious Egyptian Moor Acanthe. Berkeley's decision to give Acanthe an Egyptian heritage appears to have centered mainly on his eagerness to take a gentle parodic stab at the Neoplatonic belief in the ancient theology. According to this doctrine, enlightened Egyptians had passed the principles of true religiosity to the Greeks, explaining why Plato, despite his paganism, so profoundly anticipated Christ's teachings. By Acanthe's explanation, she learned her divining skills from her Egyptian mother who had married a wealthy Greek merchant, thus offering a recognizable ancient theological pedigree for her alleged prophetical gifts. Among the Puritan neoplatonists toward whom Berkeley might have directed this joking reference, one possibility is Robert Greville, second Baron Brooke. A Puritan nobleman who viewed the rise of skepticism and Arminianism in these years as a horrifying sign that atheism and popery were gaining ground, Brooke experimented with the Platonic idea that the elect, whether born high or low, might be peculiarly suscep-

---

27. On the production and performance of Berkeley's play, see *The Lost Lady: A Tragi-Comedy*, in Billings, ed., *Papers of Sir William Berkeley*, 8–15. On the 1637 phase of the Scottish troubles, see Kevin Sharpe, *The Personal Rule of Charles I* (New Haven, Conn., 1992), 788–792. On Platonism at the Caroline Court, see R. Malcolm Smuts, *Court Culture and the Origins of a Royalist Tradition in Early Stuart England* (Philadelphia, 1987), 9, 92, 107, 154–155, 165, 167–168, 171, 176, 253–258. The phenomenon of Puritan Platonism receives attention in Jonathan Scott, *Commonwealth Principles: Republican Writing of the English Revolution* (Cambridge, 2004), 47.

tible to a "spiritual ray of heavenly light" that was capable of overcoming the earth's most sinful errors. Berkeley made clear Acanthe was no Brookite oracle. Reputed to know the "Mystery of devination," she explained that her readings of the heavens were "but conjectured, for our Stars encline, / Not force us in our actions." In effect, she was expressing the not only skeptical but also broadly Arminian view that prophecies are inefficacious and that moral activity must then inevitably rest on human choices made on the basis of faith as well as earthbound considerations.[28]

In one of the play's more labored conceits, Berkeley continued to explore the themes of Providential uncertainty and divine truth. Acanthe turned out at the end of the drama to be the lead character Prince Lysicles's long-lost love Milesia, hitherto obscured by black Moorish features but now miraculously restored to her original whiteness. Acanthe's transformation from a dark-skinned African to a fair European was undoubtedly an indirect allusion to the rapidly quickening Atlantic slave trade. During his subsequent years in Virginia, Berkeley would follow the example of leading planters like Samuel Mathews by purchasing and keeping enslaved men and women on his Virginia plantation. Perhaps his focus on Acanthe's transformation signaled his already coalescing view that black complexion implied a hardened will against obedience that only an effective Christian master could properly subdue. But Acanthe's metamorphosis also intersected with such Hookerite and Grotian themes as the virtue of patience in the face of Providential fears as well as the need to preserve the bonds that already constituted a Christian polity. Given Berkeley's well-known association with the group of poets and playwrights known as the Wits who took inspiration from Ben Jonson, it seems plausible that his experimentation with the traditional idea of the unwashed Moor was a matter of borrowing from Jonson's use of the same trope in the first part of *The Queenes Masques* entitled the masque of *"Blacknesse"* (performed in 1605 and published as part of Jonson's works in 1616). There, Jonson identified Britain's own king-led Christian church as sending forth beams capable of blanching an Ethiopian white. Berkeley's message was likewise that the constancy of the affective bond between Lysicles and his true

---

28. Robert Greville, *The Nature of Truth Its Union and Unity with the Soule, Which Is One in Its Essence, Faculties, Acts; One with Truth* (London, 1641), 80; [William Berkeley], *The Lost Lady A Tragy-Comedy* (London, 1638), 14–15, 19. On the concept of ancient theology, see D. P. Walker, *The Ancient Theology: Studies in Christian Platonism from the Fifteenth to the Eighteenth Century* (London, 1972).

love, a tie analogous to the similarly earthbound allegiance between king and subject, was the firmest foundation for godliness. Any quest for saving light beyond such earthly ties was inevitably obscuring.[29]

In his characters' repeated emphasis on the importance of unwavering resolution, Berkeley averred that morality rested not only on choice but supremely on decisions that tended to the preservation of already-established promises and obligations. In one instance that must have seemed to some audience members like a direct answer to the Covenanters, Berkeley addressed whether heavenly petitions should override such earthly arrangements. Hermione, a lady at the Thessalonian court, responded to her uncertainty in being pulled in different directions away from her true love, the exiled Eugenio, by declaring that she "will submit to all but breach of faith," in effect appealing to the Greek gods to lead her through her current perplexity. Acanthe, however, quickly corrected her: "They will not heare us Madam, unlesse we / Contribute to their aide our best endeavours." In other words, humans needed to act decisively at moral crossroads that threatened to sway them from the myriad earthly bonds that rightfully held them and correctly steered them in their moral behavior. To assuage Hermione's concern that her faith necessarily trumped terrestrial obligations, Acanthe went on to explain that the gods were not immediate intercessors who made a practice of violating those commonwealth ties. Instead, they were quiet champions of those civil attachments, reserving their fury for those who failed to adhere to them resolutely:

> They seldome let us know clearly what is to come,
> That we may still implore their aide to helpe us:
> Yet something I can tell, if hope or force,
> Shall make you deviate from your resolves,
> You are the subject of their hate.

Here was about as clear a warning as Berkeley could make that civil rebellion was also a rebellion against God. Voicing a similar caution, a friend of Hermione asked, "What Law, what faith can binde us to remove / Love of ourselves, and Reverence to our Parents?" By suggesting that faith was not

---

29. Ben Jonson, *The Queenes Masques; The First, of Blacknesse: Personated at the Court, at White-Hall, on the Twelv'th Night* (1605), in *The Workes of Benjamin Jonson* (London, 1616), 898. For Berkeley's ownership of slaves, see Billings, *Sir William Berkeley and the Forging of Colonial Virginia*, 74. On Berkeley's association with the Wits, see ibid., 17–18, 20, 136, 137.

the only unimpeachable bond, Berkeley again implied that reciprocal ties on Earth were sacred and that these bonds were themselves reliable guides to righteous conduct.[30]

Berkeley's emphasis was not, however, on blind devotion to authority but rather on the constancy needed even when a ruler momentarily lost sight of his own proper commitments to his people and God. In *The Lost Lady*, obedience was scarcely a simple act; it was an exceedingly demanding one that involved not only a great deal of patience but also numerous difficult choices about what course of action was acceptable in a given circumstance. Hooker's compassion for the anguished soul uncertain about how to determine conscionable behavior mirrored Berkeley's own almost obsessive regard for the role of lawful agreements in steering people away from vicious conduct and toward virtue. Hence his preoccupation with promises, vows, and oaths, which were almost characters in their own right in the play given how insistently he discussed them. Over and over again, Berkeley stressed the binding and reciprocal nature of oaths as well as the complexities that they entailed. Duties were indeed difficult to maintain stringently because obligations were themselves knotty. Sometimes they worked at cross-purposes with other demands on our conscience; other times they were required in such an uncompromising way that the will to comply was itself compromised, leaving otherwise dutiful people too disheartened to feel the pull of obligation.

These sentiments had special purchase in an increasingly war-torn age, but they also marked out Berkeley's particular politics. It was on the basis of this kind of sympathy for the dilemmas faced by moral actors that his constitutional royalism rested, as was true for his similarly inclined patrons, Hyde, Falkland, and Berkeley's cousin Sir Thomas Roe. To these men, the king's more severe policies that tended to alienate the people's affections were just as dangerous to the polity's constitutive bonds as more flagrant rebellions. In both cases, the true lawful ties of commonwealth were horrifically undone, every individual thrown into the confusing ordeal of having to sort out right from wrong paths of action on their own without the authority of sound judgment. Good governance was meant to allay such doubts of conscience, not enflame them.[31]

Berkeley held to the idea at the heart of Burton's *Anatomy of Melancholy* that melancholy was the natural state of a soul that was locked in this con-

---

30. [Berkeley], *Lost Lady*, 16, 26, 27.

31. On Roe's constitutional royalism, see Michael Strachan, *Sir Thomas Roe, 1581–1644: A Life* (Salisbury, U. K., 1989), 193, 245, 255, 263–264, 266, 268, 270, 273–274.

dition of moral uncertainty. Paralyzed by doubts about how to proceed in the absence of his lost love Milesia, Berkeley's lead character Prince Lysicles was engulfed by "deepe Melancholy" that continually tests his constancy. Berkeley had different characters offer what amounted to mistaken routes out of that melancholy, again on the basis of his broadly Arminian view that morality was a choice. One of these routes was the path that Hermione proposes and that Acanthe rejects: to place one's faith solely in God, as the Covenanters were doing. Significantly, another path that was similarly cautioned against was favored by absolutist councillors to the king like Laud: unqualified obedience to the royal will. Hermione's heavy-handed father, Lord Pindarus, privately reevaluates his own obstinacy after he insists that his daughter marry another suitor against her wishes, saying, "Though I doe / Put on a fathers strictnesse in my daughters presence, / I cannot force her to an act whereon / Forever will depend her happinesse." For Berkeley, the notion that consent was the proper basis for obedience had not lost its earlier Christian humanist connotations of the conditions by which souls naturally and enduringly incline toward harmony and dutifulness. Nor was he prepared to see the state's necessity as a legitimate rationale for abandoning that moral logic. This point he put in the mouth of the jesting and unsavory courtier Phormio, who quips: "Women are Common-wealths, / And are oblig'd to their faiths no farther / Than the safetie and honour of the State is / Concern'd." Even framed as a laugh-grabbing barb against women, Berkeley's criticism must have seemed a delicate subject given how prominently the idea of state necessity had figured in the king's politics both before and during his Personal Rule. But statism was a political sin that particularly worried the constitutional royalists, and they had become adept at blaming such reason of state argumentation on the king's servants rather than the king himself. For Berkeley, as for his patrons, the state was truly a moral community only if it allowed for the lawful fulfillment of promises that enabled any commonwealth to prosper. Only then would dreaded melancholia be avoided.[32]

By the time he left for Virginia in late 1641, Berkeley possessed a well-developed philosophy of commonwealth, one that was certain to feel relevant in a colonial political environment that had from the outset similarly fixated on the problems of satisfying God's will and holding the polity's members to their respective duties. Anxious colonists were initially suspicious of this new governor freshly arrived from Charles I's court. The Reverend

32. [Berkeley], *Lost Lady*, 13, 14, 24.

Anthony Panton even hinted darkly that Berkeley had been hand selected by Richard Kemp to follow in Sir John Harvey's tyrannical footsteps. But, just as the constitutional royalists took a dim view of royal servants who pulled the king in despotic directions, so, too, did Berkeley apparently see Harvey as deserving of his rough treatment at his councillors' hands. It is significant that, although Berkeley almost never mentioned Harvey in his writings, nevertheless one of the political myths that outlived Berkeley's administration was that Harvey's onetime tyrannous government gave way to Berkeley's own just one and that this transition was nowhere more palpably demonstrated than in the people's growth of affections Robert Beverley, Jr., whose father Robert Beverley was one of Berkeley's close allies in the Virginia gentry, placed this story at the heart of his *History and Present State of Virginia* (1705). Probably relating a tale he had heard rehearsed many times before, Beverley wrote that, although Harvey's "arbitrary" rule and "Oppressions" dampened the people's spirits, the planters became newly animated in their duties under Berkeley "who had been almost the Idol of the People" and thus threw themselves into the country's improvements. The narrative clearly took its logic from Berkeley's idealist belief that loving bonds made possible the proper performance of earthly offices. Yet, the same ideal also fanned his antagonism toward godly men and women who threatened to dissolve those bonds on the basis of their own ill-founded opinions. From Berkeley's perspective, the early 1640s was a time when both sides of the Atlantic came under the grip of precisely those rebels against commonwealth that he had viewed so disdainfully in 1637–1638. He turned naturally to his establishmentarian beliefs in two of his most important early initiatives as governor: his fight against efforts to renew the Virginia Company and the oath of loyalty he imposed aggressively on the colony's planters when the godly parliamentarians tried to lure them away from their true allegiances.[33]

Berkeley knew to see the Puritans behind the revived interest in the Virginia Company. To be sure, George Sandys, acting as the colony's agent, probably brought the petition for a restored company before the House of Commons in innocence, undoubtedly imagining that firmer ties to England could help bring legal certainty to the colony after its bruising battles with

33. R[obert Beverley], *The History and Present State of Virginia, in Four Parts . . . by a Native and Inhabitant of the Place* (London, 1705), 50, 74. Anthony Panton's allegation of Richard Kemp's involvement in Berkeley's nomination is discussed in Billings, *Sir William Berkeley and the Forging of Colonial Virginia*, 35. On Berkeley's active cultivation of the loyalties of Virginia's most powerful men, see ibid., 79–112.

Charles over the tobacco contract. Berkeley, however, knew that Parliament now wore a new, more menacing face. Very likely it was early on in his first assembly that he emphasized that the House was now frighteningly in the hands of the Puritan John Pym and his powerful noble patrons, such as Lord Brooke and William Fiennes, first Viscount Saye and Sele. The assembly proceeded to debate vigorously the question of how to respond to Sandys's petition, different sides "arguing for as against a Company and looking back into the times under the Company as also upon the present State of the Colony under his Majesty's Government." But Berkeley's arguments prevailed. Perhaps he won the assemblymen over by portraying Pym and his patrons as men who were rashly turning the realm upside down in their millenarian view of the king and his servants as aligned with Antichrist. Probably, too, he stressed that these powerful Puritans already had a grasping arm fully outstretched into the Atlantic. As the founders of the Providence Island Company, they had planted the Puritan Providence Island colony in the 1630s off the coast of present-day Nicaragua, right at the heart of the Spanish king's dominions. Trusting more to their own godly leadership than the moral capacities of their planters, they ruled them as tenants at half, semifree men who owned their lands only at the company's pleasure, while denying them a general assembly. On April 1, 1642, Berkeley and the assembly issued their Declaration against the Company as a forceful rejection of company rule. Although the document never explicitly identified sectarians as the ominous persons who sought to bring Virginia into "conformity to their wills," there can be little doubt that they were the London-based enemy who "by reason of their Power and Interest in great men there" allegedly presented the colony with its greatest current political threat.[34]

Accordingly, the declaration was a masterly application of establishmentarian philosophy to the problem of upholding Virginia's polity, a full-throated retort to adversaries who would attempt to sever the rightful bonds that constituted the colony's moral community. Passed as the

---

34. "Declaration against the Virginia Company," in Billings, ed., *Papers of Sir William Berkeley*, 40–41, 42, 43. George Sandys's petition appears as "Upon an Humble Representation and Petition Heretofore Made by the Commissioners for the Plantation of Virginia Authorised by a Commission of the 27th of June Anno . . . ," in W. L. Grant and James Munro, eds., *Acts of the Privy Council of England: Colonial Series*, I, *A.D. 1613–1680* (Hereford, England, 1908), 238–240. On the Providence Island Company and its tense relationship with Providence Island's planters, see Karen Ordahl Kupperman, *Providence Island, 1630–1641: The Other Puritan Colony* (Cambridge, 1993).

colony's twenty-first act to indicate its perceived importance in articulating the makeup of Virginia's commonwealth, the declaration identified Virginia's ties to its king as fundamental and transcendent. Citing the "unnatural . . . distance . . . a Company will Interpose between his Majesty and us his Subjects from whose immediate protection we have received so many Royal favours and Gracious blessings," the assembly asserted that to admit such a distance would be to "degenerate from the Condition of our birth naturaliz'd under a Monarchical Government and not a popular and tumultuary Government." The latter reference was a contemptuous look back at the company's practice of determining planters' circumstances on the basis of simply "the greatest Number of Votes of Persons of Several humours and dispositions." But it served also as Berkeley's warning about the dangers of committing the property and well-being of planters to would-be stewards who not only had proven themselves the king's enemies but also were likely to treat Virginia's colonists as little more than profit makers for their own topsy-turvy Puritan state.[35]

The declaration vigorously defended the colony's already-existing institutions. These included "the freedom of our Trade (which is the Life and Blood of a Common Wealth)." They included as well the planters' firm title to "our Estates," those properties that allowed for "the Livelyhood of our Selves Wives and Children." Likewise, the declaration invoked "the freedom of yearly Assemblies warranted to us by his Majesty's gracious Instructions" as well as planters' right to jury trials in qualifying civil and criminal cases. But the crux of the declaration was not only that these benefits were best protected if planters remained true to their original allegiance. It was also that their bond with the king was truly binding. It would be a "breach of natural duty and religion" for the planters to give up the benefits they enjoyed by the king's grace, Berkeley wrote, for "besides our Births our Possessions enjoin us as a fealty without a Salva fide aliis Dominis." That is, the colonists' confidence in the sanctity of their property was itself a spur to their consciences, holding them to their bond to the king while excusing them from faith to other lords.[36]

---

35. "Declaration against the Virginia Company," in Billings, ed., *Papers of Sir William Berkeley*, 42.

36. Ibid., 41, 42; The Declaration against the Company to Be Entered as the Twenty First Act, Apr. 1, 1642, Hening, *Statutes at Large*, I, 233. The line "breach of natural duty and religion" appears somewhat differently in Billings's transcription: "the Natural Breach of Duty and Religion." I have opted to use the Henings transcription simply because it seems more logical.

Berkeley drew on his legal education to frame allegiance in especially resonant terms. In his report on the famous *Calvin's Case* (1608), Lord Chief Justice Sir Edward Coke had used just such language (derived from the twelfth-century justiciar Glanville) to argue that those "that are born under the obedience, power, faith, ligealty, or ligeance of the king, are natural subjects, and no aliens." Such natural subjects are within the "ligeance," and, because this condition does indeed suggest an act of "faith" analogous to one's relationship with God, it was filled with connotations of both rightful conduct and the proper enjoyment of benefits. In calling that robust understanding of allegiance to mind, Berkeley injected a visceral sense of Christian toughness into his definition of the colony centered on the planters' "most faithful and loyal Obedience to his Sacred Majesty our dread Sovereign." In that faith-like obedience, planters were free because they could proceed in their endeavors without scruple, a liberty of conscience that would be lost to them if they took up with the Puritans.[37]

If Berkeley's 1642 Declaration was one early instance in which he brought his Hookerite establishmentarianism to bear on Virginia's politics, another was his effort in 1644 to compel planters to swear to an oath renouncing

---

37. T. B. Howell, comp., *Cobbett's Complete Collection of State Trials and Proceedings for High Treason and Other Crimes and Misdemeanors*... (London, 1809), II, 615; "Declaration against the Virginia Company," in Billings, ed., *Papers of Sir William Berkeley*, 43. In response to the Declaration, Charles I wrote to the General Assembly that he had no intention of supporting "all such as shall so go about to alienate you from Our immediate Protection." In endorsing the assembly's assertion, he wrote, "These are to signify that ... Your so earnest desire to continue under our immediate Protection is very acceptable to Us; And that as Wee had not before the least intention to consent to the Introduction of any Company over that Our Colony, So wee are by it much confirmed in our former resolutions as thinking it unfitt to change a forme of Government wherein (besides many other reasons given and to be given) Our Subjects there (having had so long experience of it) receive so much contentment and satisfaction." See Charles I to the governor, council, and burgesses, July 5, 1642, in Billings, ed., *Papers of Sir William Berkeley*, 52. For a brilliant analysis of the role of *Calvin's Case* in contributing to a shift in understandings of personal status whereby subjecthood became the key determinant of whether one was entitled to civil as well as ecclesiastical benefits, see Keechang Kim, *Aliens in Medieval Law: The Origins of Modern Citizenship* (Cambridge, 2000), 176–199. See also Paul D. Halliday, *Habeas Corpus: From England to Empire* (Cambridge, Mass., 2010). *Calvin's Case* had concerned itself particularly with the question of whether James I's Scottish subjects could have land rights in England now that his sovereignty extended over both realms. The doctrine of allegiance that Coke and other jurists cited in the case suggested that the question should turn, not on where a person resided, but rather on whether he was within, or without, the allegiance itself.

Puritan leadership and confirming their royal allegiance. Charles had similarly tendered an oath in Scotland as a countermeasure to the Covenanters, and it is possible that Berkeley had this precedent in mind when he inaugurated his own subscription campaign. When his oath was first imposed is difficult to determine precisely, though the assembly issued an order on June 3 requiring that all county court justices assist in administering the pledge on the grounds that such an affirmation of loyalty was of "noe meane Consequence in these dangerous tymes." The danger to which the assemblymen referred was most immediately the renewal of warfare with neighboring Indian peoples, which had commenced with a massive assault on April 18 led by Opechancanough with a combined group of Nansemonds, Chickahominies, and Weyanocks. But another, subtler threat was the preliminary outreach by English Puritans to win over supporters in Virginia.[38]

In early January, the royalist newsbook *Mercurius Aulicus* reported that the king's godly enemies in Parliament had begun wooing "*their Brethren in other Countries.*" One key strategy in this campaign of persuasion involved abating duties on Virginia tobacco. For Berkeley, this was a sinister tactic because it threatened to seduce the colony's committed Puritans and weak-willed Anglicans alike. In the former camp were resolute godly men like the upper Norfolk county resident William Durand, who in 1642 complained to the Reverend John Davenport in the New Haven colony about the "chaynes of darkenesse" in this "desolate place." Durand, however, was hardly downtrodden, stressing instead that he and his fellow Virginian Puritans would "hold fast against all opposition" to their righteous pathway, "the Lord by his grace strengthening and upholding us thereto." His antagonistic attitude was much like that of the anonymous writer to the Puritan newsbook *Mercurius Civicus* who condemned Berkeley's oath as a pledge that the people took "more for feare then affection." His fellow spiritualists were so disgruntled by the oath, he wrote, that "if the Indians had but forborne for a month longer, they had found us in such a combustion among our selves that they might with ease have cut of[f] every man if once we had spent that

---

38. Orders Passed at the 1643 / 1644 Session, in H. R. McIlwaine, ed., *Journals of the House of Burgesses of Virginia, 1619–1658/59* (Richmond, Va., 1915), 71. On Charles I's use of an oath to counter the Scottish National Covenant as well as its English sympathizers, see Edward Vallance, *Revolutionary England and the National Covenant: State Oaths, Protestantism, and the Political Nation, 1553–1682* (Woodbridge, U.K., 2005), 47–48. The best treatment of the colonies' encounters with the Commonwealth government and the English Civil War generally is Carla Gardina Pestana, *The English Atlantic in an Age of Revolution, 1640–1661* (Cambridge, Mass., 2004).

little powder and shot that we had among our selves." Berkeley knew to expect such belligerence from the Puritans. More unpredictable were the many outwardly conforming planters who might nevertheless be swayed to the parliamentary side, especially because of their intense anti-popery.[39]

Richard Kemp was so conscious that Puritans and Anglicans "all alike hated" their papist Maryland neighbors that he feared an almost instantaneous shifting of loyalties away from the king when Leonard Calvert wrote in early 1645 to report Charles's recent command to seize London ships and confiscate Londoners' estates in the colonies. Sure enough, Kemp discovered, "Whisperings and Rumours were spread among the people that the King had sent a Papist to be Governor (reflectinge upon the person of the Governor of Maryland)." The planters' gossip in turn reinforced "Monstrous inferences . . . of the Kings disaffection to Religion" so "that now they gave Creditt to the Pamphletts which declared his Majesties addiction that way." This fragile loyalty was exactly what Berkeley's oath sought to confront. In his view, the planters' continuing attachment to the king was the only way to preserve the commonwealth as a whole.[40]

Berkeley's government in Virginia began with an aggressive determination to safeguard the established order against the strident voices of the godly. Such an impulse flowed naturally from the new governor's Pyrrhonist inclination to see existing laws and hierarchies as a surer guide to God's truths than any private judgments, no matter how revelatory they might appear to be. Throughout his administration, Berkeley regarded himself first and foremost as the champion of not the colony per se but rather the civil bonds that more generally tied persons to their duties to their Maker, their king, and their fellow inhabitants. It was just such commonwealth bonds that the colony's laws helped to articulate and define. Defending those ties required holding firm against alternative truth claims that might define the contours of lawfulness in Virginia differently. The politics of insulating the polity from rival visions of its relationship to God, however, were about to become much more complicated. Although few persons had previously questioned whether a colony could be a commonwealth in the first place,

---

39. *Mercurius Aulicus* (Oxford), Jan. 3, 1643[/4], 757; William Durand to John Davenport, July 15, 1642, in John Butler, ed., "Two 1642 Letters from Virginia Puritans," Massachusetts Historical Society, *Proceedings*, 3d Ser., LXXXIV (1972), 107–109; *Mercurius Civicus* (London), 104 (May 15–22, 1645), 929.

40. Richard Kemp to William Berkeley, Feb. 27, 1644/5, in Billings, ed., *Papers of Sir William Berkeley*, 63, 64.

the introduction of that Hobbesian question would prove especially troubling for Berkeley because it first came bundled within Puritan legislation. Evidently, Puritans themselves had become the forceful advocates for the unitary state. This startling political development would, in turn, force establishmentarians like Berkeley to refine their arguments about why colonial commonwealths were lawful even in an age of sovereign states.

Confronting the New Ideal of the Metropolitan "Centre"

In early 1647, the English parliament issued a pair of laws that indicated in their respective concerns how rapidly the Hobbesian ideal of a unitary state and Puritan assuredness were already becoming entwined. The first law, passed on January 23, was entitled An Ordinance for Encouragement of Adventurers to the Several Plantations of Virginia, Barbados, and Other Places of America. Its provisions made clear that the adventurers who were most likely to be encouraged by the law were those Puritan merchants who both cheered the saints' political ascendancy as well as longed for unfettered access to colonial goods. Parliament had imprisoned Charles I more than a year before, and the ordinance was explicit in its premise of resting only on the authority of the Lords and Commons. There was a distinctly Hobbesian logic in this assumption that sovereignty was a quality attached, not to the king's own person, but rather to the state, or, as the ordinance put it, the "Kingdom." The 1647 law depended on this view that any state possesses an identifiable supreme power located somewhere within itself and that power resided unequivocally in Parliament. The colonies were, in the meantime, described as little more than England's commercial appendages, and the statute made little secret that it sought mainly to subdue the resistant royalist colonies to create a transatlantic trade emporium centered on London. Duty-free shipping would be made available to the colonies as long as they agreed to cease commercial interaction with all nations other than the mother country while permitting the free entrance of servants sent to America to "advance the Trade there." The vision was undoubtedly that of streams of Puritan apprentices pouring into onetime royalist Anglican strongholds in order to realize the dream of a single godly state fed by American commodities.[41]

---

41. An Ordinance for Encouragement of Adventurers to the Several Plantations of Virginia, Bermudas, Barbados, and Other Places of America, [Jan. 23, 1646/7] in C. H. Firth and R. S. Rait, eds., *Acts and Ordinances of the Interregnum, 1642–1660* [London, 1911], I, 912.

The second law, passed on February 4, focused on furthering this political and economic consolidation by rooting out specifically epistemological divisions. The ordinance outlawed all "Errors, Heresies, and Blasphemies" while calling for a day of public humiliation to seek God's "direction and assistance for the suppression and preventing the same." Although "Popery" was identified as one predictable source of such error, the language of the law focused more intently on uncertainty itself. In other words, skepticism was the heresy that the Puritans were most eager to extricate with their newfound sovereignty. As the ordinance's authors put it, "We are resolved to imploy and improve the utmost of Our Power that nothing be said or done against the Truth, but [only said or done] for the Truth." The day of humiliation was accordingly called for so that the "whole Kingdome may be deeply humbled before the Lord for that great reproach and contempt which hath been cast upon his name and Saving Truths." With that, the Hobbesian state announced itself, though it spoke in a voice of prophetical certainty that Hobbes would have regarded as philosophically opposed to his own system.[42]

Shortly after Parliament assumed the authority of the king and Privy Council in 1643, Puritan Hobbism began to intrude itself on colonial governance. Parliament turned almost right away, on November 24, to the task of appointing an eighteen-member committee for administering plantation affairs. Headed by Robert Rich, earl of Warwick, the committee included a number of committed Puritans like Lord Saye and Sele, Pym, Sir Arthur Hesilrige, Sir Henry Vane the younger, and Oliver Cromwell. These were zealous men who clung to the eschatological view that America had a vital part to play in the End Time. Their eagerness to assert Parliament's sovereignty was inseparable from their desire to inject into the American endeavor the godly resolution it had for so long lacked. At the same time, they received a powerful burst of philosophical encouragement that they were the right persons for that sovereign role in the form of Parker's *Observations*. Parker was Lord Saye and Sele's nephew and only one of several talented apologists for the parliamentary regime in these years, including such formidable writers as John Milton, Francis Rous, Antony Ascham, and Marchamont Nedham. Even in this illustrious group, Parker was distinctive in seeing early on how the Hobbesian ideal of state unity might be exploited. The theory figured conspicuously in his argument for Parliament's lawful power. As he put it in

---

42. An Ordinance concerning the Growth and Spreading of Errors, Heresies, and Blasphemies, and for Setting Apart a Day of Publike Humiliation, to Seeke Gods Assistance for the Suppressing and Preventing the Same, [Feb. 4, 1646/7], ibid., I, 913–914.

his *Observations:* "There is an Arbitrary power in every State somewhere.... If the State intrusts this to one man, or few, there may be danger in it; but the Parliament is neither one nor few, it is indeed the State it self." Likewise, he had insisted in *The True Grounds of Ecclesiastical Regiment* (1641) that "Supream power ought to be intire and undivided, and cannot else be sufficient for the protection of all, if it doe no extend overall: without any other equall power to controll, or diminish it." Parker recognized this distinctively Hobbesian doctrine had implications not only for the saints in their conflict with the king but also for government in the outward dominions.[43]

Parker first explored the connotations of Hobbes's doctrine in relation to Ireland. In a work published in 1642, Parker renewed the long-standing dream of compacting the three British kingdoms into a single monarchy. At the heart of his plan was the view that, whereas Scotland and England were highly dignified kingdoms that deserved to be treated as such in any union that bound them, Ireland was a different matter. Through a combination of historical conquests and consensual arrangements, it was an inferior polity that already formed "one *Body*" with England. Not only connected by a common sovereign head, Ireland and England were also "inseparably knit" together and "reduced to a perfect Unity of Dominion." Parker made little secret that he was responding to the Irish Rebellion of 1641, which for many English Puritans was filled with the same tinge of treachery and illicitness that Anglicans associated with the Scottish National Covenant. In the Irish uprising, the Catholic gentry, fearing invasion from a combined force of Scottish Covenanters and English Puritans, had asserted their independence from England while pledging their continuing loyalty to Charles I. Refuting this view, Parker insisted that "the independance of *Ireland*" had been "taken away" in the same manner as Wales and Cornwall, so that "the Kingdom of *Ireland* is indeed but an *Integrall* member of the Kingdom of *England*." Here, he anticipated, if he did not in fact help to inform, Hobbes's own later view in *Leviathan* that, short of being freed by a sovereign, a civilly incomplete polity like a colony could amount only to a part of the state to which it was attached.[44]

---

43. Charles M. Andrews, *British Committees, Commissions, and Councils of Trade and Plantations, 1622–1675* (Baltimore, 1908) 21; [Henry Parker], *Observations upon Some of His Majesties Late Answers and Expresses* [London, 1642], 34; [Parker], *The True Grounds of Ecclesiastical Regiment* . . . (London, 1641), 8.

44. H[enry] Parker, *The Generall Junto; or, The Councell of Union, Chosen Equally out of England, Scotland, and Ireland, for the Better Compacting of Three Nations into One Monarchy,*

Nevertheless, Parker was not prepared to go as far as those most severe Puritans who wanted to diminish the Irish rebels to a "meer *servile dependence.*" Instead, he argued that Ireland was better seen as "annexed" to, rather than dependent on, England. In a clever Protestant allusion, he called this semi-incorporated status "consubstantiated," as if to suggest that Ireland maintained some of its original integrity in the same way that some Protestants argued that the bread and wine in the Eucharist retained their substance and thus coexisted with, rather than became, the body and blood of Christ. But, Parker was definitive that Ireland's relationship to England was to be seen as far more subordinate than Scotland's. In characterizing this lesser political condition, he wrote, "Though the King be Owner of *England* and *Scotland,* yet he is not Owner of *England, quatenùs* [that is, insofar as he is] Owner of *Scotland,* or Owner of *Scotland, quatenùs* Owner of *England,* but he is Owner of *Ireland quatenùs* of *England.*" In other words, unlike Scotland, Ireland had little or no political meaning apart from its membership in the English state. That same rationale that some dominions were lesser than others and properly subordinated to the broader state also underlay Parliament's 1647 ordinance, which if not directly derived from Parker's plan for Ireland at least operated in much the same spirit.[45]

The ideal of the unitary state would gather even greater momentum in relation to the colonies after the king's execution in 1649 and the subsequent founding of the Commonwealth. Among the most influential voices shaping policies involving the plantations at this time were two additional admirers of Hobbes's theories, Benjamin Worsley and Thomas Povey. Worsley was linked to the parliamentary leadership through his involvement in Samuel Hartlib's circle of scientifically inclined and Puritan-oriented projectors, a group whose zeal in pursuing various so-called improvements, or social and economic reforms, in preparation for Judgment Day enjoyed the support of powerful patrons like Pym and, before his death in 1643, Lord Brooke. As secretary of the newly established Council of Trade, Worsley was one of a number of Commonwealth-affiliated writers, including most notably James Harrington, who approached Hobbes's theories critically while also absorbing his ideal of state unity into their own broadly Neoplatonist view of a divinely ordered and harmonious cosmos. Povey, too, would climb the rungs of Commonwealth administration while mingling Hobbesian theo-

---

etc. (London, 1642), 12, 13. On the Irish Rebellion of 1641, see Nicholas Canny, *Making Ireland British, 1580–1650* (Oxford, 2003), 461–550.

45. Parker, *Generall Junto,* 13.

ries and Puritan agendas. In 1654, he helped Cromwell, recently named the Commonwealth's lord protector, pursue his millenarian dream of defeating the Antichrist once and for all in the so-called Western Design, a massive naval attack on the Spanish West Indies. The expedition would end in humiliating failure, adding to already mounting anxieties that Cromwell's rule was displeasing to God after all. Yet, Povey would survive the fiasco and go on to become a member of the Council of Trade (1655) and eventual secretary and chairman of the Council of America (1657). In those capacities, he was instrumental in promoting Hobbes's conception of colonies as provinces, a view that he approached self-consciously as part of the greater goal of realizing a godly state.[46]

In the hands of the Puritans, Hobbes's ideas took on spiritualist overtones that he neither could have anticipated nor would have endorsed. Worsley, for instance, brought an unapologetic Brookite Neoplatonism to his conception of how God's truth operates in the world. Ridiculing the Pyrrhonists in a letter of 1657 that was possibly meant for Hartlib, he listed a number of their familiar arguments in order to dismiss them out of hand. Must people compare themselves with "Beasts rather then men?" he asked. Should they fear that the "abstruse Web of metaphysicall subtility or unintelligible curiosity" led inevitably to "some species of Melancholy" or seek solid ground in the "Prevalency and Authority of Custome?" Rejecting such Pyrrhonist uncertainty, he wrote that only error is "finite, weake, inconstant, temporary," while "truth is infinite, powerfull, strong, constant, before all time, and the production of necessity[,] unity[,] light." In effect, he was turning on its head Hobbes's derogatory view that the zealous seeker of God's truths is unmanly and vile. For Worsley, the skeptic, not the assured believer, was the frail waverer. Yet, Worsley was very clearly attracted to Hobbes's concep-

---

46. On Samuel Hartlib's circle, see Charles Webster, *The Great Instauration: Science, Medicine, and Reform, 1626–1660* (London, 1975); on their connection to the Puritan leadership, see ibid., 41–44. For Benjamin Worsley and Thomas Povey, see Thomas Leng, *Benjamin Worsley (1618–1677): Trade, Interest, and the Spirit in Revolutionary England* (Rochester, N.Y., 2008); *Oxford Dictionary of National Biography*, online ed., s.v. "Povey, Thomas (b. 1613/14, d. in or before 1705)," by Barbara C. Murison, accessed Aug. 13, 2015, http://www.oxforddnb.com/view/article/22640. On the contemporary ideal of improvements, see Paul Slack, *From Reformation to Improvement: Public Welfare in Early Modern England*, The Ford Lectures, Delivered in the University of Oxford, 1994–1995 (Oxford, 1998), 80–81, 99–100, 102–105. On Cromwell's providentialism, see Blair Worden, "Providence and Politics in Cromwellian England," *Past and Present*, no. 109 (November 1985), 55–99.

tion of state unity. In Worsley's proposals in relation to Virginia, he argued explicitly that a colony did not deserve to be seen as a commonwealth. As he put it: "They of Virginia are no more then an English Colony./ They are no State/, or politick Body/." The likelihood that Worsley was consciously echoing Hobbes's own early iterations on this theme receives some support in the several copies of Hobbes's *Elements, De Cive,* and *Leviathan* in various editions that appeared in Worsley's well-stocked library at his death.[47]

Worsley's mystical spirituality and heady millenarianism made for a strange fit with Hobbes's unrelenting materialism. By the 1650s if not earlier, Worsley was experimenting with a range of spiritualist beliefs, mingling a Puritan Neoplatonism not unlike Lord Brooke's with an interest in alchemy and a conviction in the imminence of the Eschaton, which he dated to 1666. Worsley might have regarded Hobbes's preoccupation with the state's wholeness, however, as connecting naturally with his own elaborate religious views regarding the fundamental unity of all bodies in the universe. In 1658, he conveyed to Hartlib this theory of terrestrial and heavenly oneness, which was filled with not only Neoplatonic but also Newtonian dimensions. The world, he argued, was a series of distinct but parallel "Centres" that oriented all rightly turned earthly beings toward God with a pull that Worsley identified as the equivalent of gravity. Such a cosmic system demanded unity, for "noe Body Spirit or Soull... can stand or be one mom[en]t of time solitary, or by its selfe; but that all things both are in Consortship, and [made] in a dependence with, and upon some other things." Like the state and the human body, the universe, too, abhorred division.[48]

Moving between the ideal of the unitary state and a vision of the harmonized universe was not altogether unusual, for it resembled another work in these years that similarly addressed the subordination of colonies, James Harrington's *The Commonwealth of Oceana* (1656). A learned prescription for stabilizing England's now-kingless government, Harrington's work respectfully criticized Hobbes's theories while adopting his ideal of state unity. In particular, Harrington urged a return to the "ancient prudence" he perceived in the institutions and governments of the Israelites,

---

47. Benjamin Worsley to Samuel Hartlib(?) Oct. 14, 1657, Hartlib Papers 42/1/7B-8A, http://www.hrionline.ac.uk/hartlib, [Worsley], "Further Animadversions about Virginia," circa 1650, Hartlib Papers 61/6/1A; John Dunmore and Richard Chiswell, *Catalogus librorum... Doctoris Benjaminis Worsley... Maii 13. 1678* ([London], 1678), 39, 55, 71, 100, 112, 129, 130, 143.

48. Leng, *Benjamin Worsley*, 120–137; Benjamin Worsley to Samuel Hartlib, Sept. 8, 1658, Hartlib Papers 62/10/1A, 2A, Hartlib Papers, http://www.hrionline.ac.uk/hartlib.

Egyptians, Greeks, and Romans. A similar Neoplatonic streak ran through Harrington's view of the "spherical" nature of earthly and cosmic motions and the need for all such orbits to have their "proper centre." This center, he clarified, was in the case of all governments the "fundamental laws" that guided them. That term would later reappear in the Fundamental Constitutions of Carolina of 1669 that was one of the early efforts, based at least in part on Harrington's theories, to define a provincial colony rather than one that perceived itself as a commonwealth. Harrington found his own model for provincial colonial government in the ancient Roman republic, which he believed proceeded correctly in giving strength to its sovereignty by refusing to plant colonies outside the "bounds of Italy." By preserving colonies within the state rather than treating them as "foreign parts," Rome achieved several ends that ensured its durability in the face of worldly vacillations. It enlarged liberty and empire together, reduced the likelihood of colonial rebellion, enhanced the citizenry by removing the poor to the provinces, gave veterans a provincial dignity that offset their tendency toward sedition, and acquired to itself the "reverence of the common parent" who "from time to time became the mother of new-born cities." By retaining its integrity as a unitary state even while planting colonies, Harrington's republic acquired strength even without a conquering king.[49]

Worsley's measures were similarly bent on showing that the colonies, like Harrington's republic, were effectively already within the bounds of England. As one of his correspondents put it, Worsley's proposals sought "to effect an inclination in all the Plantations to depend upon this State." In judging whether Parliament's right to govern Virginia was "lawfull or Religious," Worsley advanced three claims that were strongly reminiscent of Hobbes's view that sovereignty and the commonwealth were inseparable: first, the colonies properly redounded to the trade and "Interest ... of England"; second, the king's sovereignty had ended at his death and yet "supreame Authority.... must devolve upon some body"; and, third, anywhere the state stood to gain or lose, the "Interest of many good men" was also concerned. In these rationales, Worsley's guiding assumptions were clear. The state already existed in its enlarged transatlantic form in theory if not in fact, and to make this unity real the colonies simply needed to recognize that

---

49. J. G. A. Pocock, ed., *Harrington: The Commonwealth of Oceana and a System of Politics* (Cambridge, 1992), 8, 100, 223; The Fundamental Constitutions of Carolina, Mar. 1, 1669, The Avalon Project: Documents in Law, History, and Diplomacy, Yale Law School, Lillian Goldman Law Library, http://avalon.law.yale.edu/17th_century/nc05.asp.

their interests were naturally entwined with, not separate from, the greater interest of the state.⁵⁰

Povey's approach to the plantations was likewise focused on this ideal of the mutuality of state and colonial interests. In a memorandum written before August 1657 entitled "Overtures touching the West Indies," he, too, argued that the colonies needed to be persuaded of their provincial status. The goal of such persuasive efforts, as he put it, was that "hereafter they may be considered as one embodied Commonwealth whose head and centre is here." Povey's statement might have been the first outright articulation of the idea that England was properly seen as the colonies' imperial center. In his notion of a single embodied commonwealth, Povey captured the ideal of civil unity as a moral end that enabled justice. If the colonies were consolidated, "all of them being as it were made up into one Commonwealth," Povey argued, then they "may be regulated accordingly upon comon and equal Principles." By this logic, the state was a coordinator of multiple, potentially conflicting interests. Such an ideal mirrored closely Hobbes's own view that justice, a prime law of nature, was best realized, not in the barbarous conditions of nature itself, but only under the security of an awe-inspiring sovereign who enabled the promises that underlay covenants to be kept. Povey was similarly certain that incorporating the colonies more fully into the state was a way of "rendering these Dominions useful to England, and England helpful to them" and thus of contributing more generally to civil government and the equal "distribution of Publick Justice." The sovereign state would be beneficial to all its constituent parts—as long as they recognized that they were indeed the parts of a whole and not individual commonwealths.⁵¹

Berkeley, who lost little time in recognizing the Hobbesian logic behind Parliament's laws, had probably known about Hobbes's ideas even before he left for Virginia. As early as September or October 1640, Hyde had acquired a manuscript copy of *Elements* and made annotations in it, perhaps as an aid for discussion of the book at Great Tew. Hyde's notes focused on two themes in particular: the absolutism of Hobbes's sovereign and the ample room Hobbes seemed to allow in his theory for a people to dissolve their commonwealth bonds if the state failed to secure their protection. One passage that Hyde marked in the book seems to have epitomized how he and his Great Tew friends viewed a people who no longer enjoyed the free inter-

---

50. John Dury[?] to Benjamin Worsley[?], Aug. 17, 1649, Hartlib Papers 1/2/11A, Worsley to Samuel Hartlib[?], Aug. 13, 1649, Hartlib Papers 33/2/1B.

51. Andrews, *British Committees*, 58–60.

change of wills between a loving monarch and industrious subjects: The "subjection of them who institute a commonwealth amongst themselves is no less absolute, than the subjection of servants." Hobbes's well-known interest in America sometimes invited nervous jokes that his controversial ideas were best tested on the far side of the Atlantic. In his *Catching of Leviathan* (1657), Bishop John Bramhall would quip that perhaps "T.H. should have sole privilege of setting up his form of government in America ... and if it prosper there, then to have the liberty to transplant it hither." Not that the Americans would welcome their new master for long, Bramhall scoffed, for, as soon as they recognized his awesome power, they would "tear their 'mortal God' in pieces with their teeth, and entomb his sovereignty in their bowels." The frightening possibility that the Hobbesian state would render subjects into servants resonated equally in the colonies as well as England.[52]

Approaching Leviathan from a different tack, one of the moderate royalists Dudley Digges tried the rather less straightforward move of adapting Hobbes's ideas to his own constitutionalist purposes. Digges had already joined Falkland and Sir John Colepeper in penning Charles I's *Answer to the XIX Propositions* (1642), a highly politic effort at assuaging the kingdom's dangerous divisions that attributed to the king a more limited view of his sovereign power than he himself accepted. Berkeley perhaps also knew Digges as someone with connections to Virginia; his father Sir Dudley Digges had been a Virginia Company member, and his younger brother Edward Digges would in 1650 immigrate to the colony, where his experiments in sericulture would interest Berkeley and the Hartlib circle alike. In *The Unlawfulnesse of Subjects Taking up Armes against Their Soveraigne* (1643), Digges employed Hobbes's arguments especially to refute the even more frightening implications of Parker's claim in *Observations* that the people were justified in going to war with their king. Hobbes's argument of corporate wholeness figured in Digges's account in a section on "civill unitie." Using the concept to suggest the inviolability of political ties, Digges argued that the individualism of the state of nature was so dreadful in and of itself that nobody could make a plausible case for dissolving the bonds of commonwealth once they had been forged. As Digges put it, state unity was a remedy to a divisiveness

---

52. Hobbes, *Elements*, 134; *The Works of the Most Reverend Father in God, John Bramhall, D. D., Sometime Lord Archbishop of Armagh, Primate and Metropolitan of All Ireland ...*, ed. John Henry Parker (Oxford, 1844), IV, 597. On Hyde's annotations in Hobbes's *Elements*, see Martin Dzelzainis, "Edward Hyde and Thomas Hobbes's Elements of Law, Natural and Politic," *Historical Journal*, XXXII (1985), 303–317.

whose horrors only humans recently escaped from the barbarous atomism of nature could appreciate fully: "The ready cure was to make themselves... into a civill unitie, by placing over them one head, and by making his will the will of them all, to the end there might be no gap left open by schisme to returne to their former confusion." This recognizably Hobbesian notion of the polity's fully united wills was particularly useful for Digges for denying one of Parker's most important philosophical assumptions: his view of the continuing viability of the natural law argument that the people retain the right of self-preservation. That right, Digges suggested, lost legitimacy on the act of political incorporation. "It ceases to be lawfull, after we have made our selves sociable parts in one body," he argued, "because we voluntarily and upon agreement restrained our selves from making use of this native right." Digges drew freely on Hobbes without taking the additional Hobbesian step of insisting that such a contractual relinquishing of rights also rendered the sovereign's power complete and incapable of being moderated or limited. Rather, Digges was explicit in his continuing view that sovereignty should always be "restrained by positive constitutions wherein a Prince hath limited himselfe by promise or oath, not to exercise full power."[53]

Berkeley's milieu on the eve of his voyage to Virginia was filled with lively talk about Hobbes's theories. Whether holding those ideas at arm's length, as Hyde and Bramhall were inclined to do, or attempting to harness them to a more familiar Christian humanist framework à la Digges, the establishmentarian circles to which Berkeley was attached had wrestled with Hobbes's philosophy early on. As a result, Berkeley not only saw clearly the novel ideals that lay behind Parliament's new laws, but he also turned deliberately to a political discourse that fit more closely his more traditional outlook: namely, the contractual language of Grotius.

In his own writings, Grotius did not insist on the state's unitary nature but rather defended the bonds formed over time between rulers and peoples, even when those ties established multiple polities that looked to the same sovereign. He offered such a justification of the composite polity as a means of bolstering the Dutch states against Spanish claims to universal monarchy.

---

53. [Dudley Digges], *The Unlawfulnesse of Subjects Taking up Armes against Their Soveraigne*... ([Oxford], 1643), 4, 5, 68. On Dudley Digges, see *Oxford Dictionary of National Biography*, online ed., s.v. "Digges, Dudley (1613–1643)," by David Stoker, accessed Apr. 24, 2016, http://www.oxforddnb.com/view/article/7636. On Edward Digges, see *Encyclopedia Virginia*, s.v. "Edward Digges (1621–1675)," by Brent Tarter and the *Dictionary of Virginia Biography*, accessed Apr. 24, 2016, http://www.encyclopediavirginia.org/digges_edward_1621-1675.

One of his earliest apologias along these lines appeared in *De Indis* (later known as *De jure praedae*), a manuscript commissioned by the Dutch East India Company in 1604 that might plausibly have reached the English court, given the work's diplomatic purpose of rallying support behind privateering attacks on Iberian shipping. He invoked the Spaniards' own casuist Francisco de Vitoria to observe that even Spain had suffered little loss in legitimacy from the divided nature of its monarchy. Although "the Kingdom of Aragon forms a state that is distinct from the Kingdom of Castile," he wrote, nevertheless "both kingdoms are subject to one and the same prince" and together they form a "perfect community" that "is (so to speak) a true state." Such civil perfection was, for Grotius, a function, not of the Spanish kingdom's unbroken unity, but rather of the binding promises and agreements that had formed over time as the inhabitants of the various Spanish realms had settled on the laws by which they could live together in peace. He applied the same logic to the Dutch states. Their lawfulness was not contingent on their unity. Instead, it lay in the ancient "covenants handed down by our forebears and consecrated by the oaths of princes." These covenants, he went on, "gave continuity to our sovereign form of government, lest, through the violation of those sacred pacts which had served for many centuries as the basic safeguard of our state, the latter should be made subject, after the fashion of a province, to the greedy caprice of the Spaniards." Clearly, here was a view of the political substance of the Dutch republics certain to resonate for colonies that were sensitive to the possibility of being transformed into subjugated provinces.[54]

Grotius developed this theme of the divisibility of empire further in his masterwork *De jure belli ac pacis* (originally published in Paris in 1625). He composed the treatise as the Dutch states' long-standing revolt against the Spanish monarchy merged with the new tensions of the Thirty Years War. In this tumultuous religious environment, Grotius once again argued that the confederated makeup of a polity was no bar to its enjoyment of the civil status of a true state. "It so happens sometimes," he wrote, "that divers People have one and the same Head, and yet each of those People make a compleat Society." For Grotius, civil completeness, or, as he also put it, perfection, was the ultimate quality of a state. Under such circumstances, the people

---

54. Grotius, *De Jure Praedae*, trans. Williams, I, 283, 287. On the circumstances behind the production of *De Indis*, see Martine Julia van Ittersum, *Profit and Principle: Hugo Grotius, Natural Rights Theories, and the Rise of Dutch Power in the East Indies, 1595–1615* (Leiden, The Netherlands, 2006), 20–28.

and sovereign each had the freedom of will to perform their duties. "The State is a compleat Body of free Persons," he wrote, "associated together to enjoy peaceably their Rights, and for their common Benefit." Given such an emphasis on the mutuality of the bond of allegiance, he saw no reason why it could not tie a single sovereign to multiple bodies politic. Drawing on Aristotle and the Greek philosopher and geographer Strabo, he wrote that "it may also happen, that several States may be linked together in a most strict Alliance, and make a Compound, as *Strabo* more than once calls it; and yet each of them continue to be a perfect State, which is observed both by others, and by *Aristotle* in several Places." Such a league enjoyed a greater coherence but without impinging on whatever historical agreements had defined the political essence of each of its constituent parts.[55]

In developing his own case for Virginia's civil integrity, Berkeley eagerly applied a Grotian framework to the English plantations. For instance, his declaration against the 1647 ordinance responded forcefully against the parliamentarians' presumption that colonial rule fell under their jurisdiction simply because the king no longer effectively wielded power. Rather than a conveyance of authority outward from a centrally located metropolis to distant provinces, Berkeley's portrait of colonial law fixated on the moral give-and-take associated with promises, both in the making of such sacred pledges and in acting on their alluring provisions. His argument in this regard was not altogether different from the one he had offered in 1642, when he fended off efforts to revive the Virginia Company on the grounds that the possessions that planters enjoyed by the king's permission held them indefeasibly to their allegiance. This time, however, his emphasis lay less on the binding nature of that bond than on the free exercise of wills that underlay it.[56]

He posited the reciprocal bond between king and people against the absolutist connotations he perceived behind Parliament's assertions of sovereignty. In his declaration, he feigned incredulity that "the most honorable houses of Parliament" would take away the planters' "right and priviledge" of trading with any nation in amity with Charles I, "especially without hearing of the parties principally interested." Those parties were plainly the king and Virginia's inhabitants, for the colony's right in this case had been "granted us by ancient Charter," specifically James I's original 1606 letters patent. To underscore the moral weight of such authorization, Berkeley compared it to

---

55. Grotius, *Rights of War and Peace*, I, 162, 259–260.

56. Berkeley, "Declaration concerning the Dutch Trade," Apr. 5, 1647, in Billings, ed., *Papers of Sir William Berkeley*, 75–77.

the sanctity that is properly attached to the payment proffered to a worker for his services. As Berkeley put it, "The rights, immunities and priviledges of our Charter [are] by as due a Clayme belongeinge to us, as is the wages of an hirelinge that hath laboured for it, for they onely [and no other incentive] gave us Invitation and were the Conditionall reward and guerdon propounded for our Undertakings in those rugged paths of Plantation." This analogy of the liberal compensation offered for extraordinary service to king and country clearly rested on a still-resonant Christian humanist concern with the conditions by which corrupted human wills are turned favorably toward duties. It thus helped to justify Berkeley's ringing conclusion about the colony's most basic "libertye." As he put it, "Noe lawe should bee established within the kingdome of England concerninge us, without the consent of a grand Assembly here." Calling this liberty of assent "a right of deare esteeme to free borne persons," Berkeley gave a new contractual spin to the old idea of Virginia as a *corpus mysticum* that married the wills of king and people into a mutually redeeming concordance.[57]

Unsurprisingly, Berkeley's vision of a contractual bond defined Virginia as a polity distinct from England's own "kingdome." Grotius's notion of civil perfection undoubtedly informed this view of Virginia's relative autonomy. Almost as if acknowledging this intellectual debt, Berkeley concluded his piece by invoking Grotius's telltale principle of self-preservation. If Parliament resisted the colony's lawful right to trade with other friendly nations, he wrote, then "wee must like Creatures even of sence provide for our owne safeties and subsistence." With its telling nod to Sextus Empiricus's skepticism, that Grotian statement clenched Berkeley's case that Virginians could conscionably disregard Parliament's ordinance as an illicit violation of their common weal.[58]

Berkeley brought the same Grotian sensibility to the tricky politics of Virginia's surrender to the Commonwealth. By August 1649, Worsley had turned his attention to Virginia after a number of Puritans from the colony asked him to use his political connections to remove Berkeley from office and put in his place a governor amenable to their godly designs. Offended by Berkeley's opposition to their declarations against the prayer book and episcopacy and contemptuous of his oath "obtruded on them" to secure their allegiance to the king, these men insisted that Parliament not only had a right to take the government into their own hands now that the king was

57. Ibid., 76.
58. Ibid.

dead but also faced a providential "opportunity" that should not be lost. The governor was weak, having no substantial fort or arms magazine to rely on, and he had a number of the "Cheifest and most Potent" colonists against him. The latter reference might have been to gentleman supporters of the Lower Norfolk County minister Thomas Harrison whom Berkeley had banished from the colony for his dissidence. Some of the older Virginian councillors like Richard Bennett and William Claiborne were also evidently at least partially alienated by Berkeley's fierce anti-Puritanism. Worsley had enough confidence in both men in 1651 to appoint them to a commission for "reducing al the Plantations within the Bay of Chisapiack, to their due obedience to the Commonwealth of England." Berkeley was not as enfeebled as the Puritans made out, however, for he was forceful in issuing a number of appeals concerning Virginia's right to resist the new English government. One such apologia extended well beyond Virginia's borders when Berkeley had it printed in The Hague. This robust turn to Europe spoke vividly to Berkeley's desire to have Virginia's stand against the Puritan Commonwealth acknowledged in a broader milieu.[59]

Hoping to reach other traditional establishmentarians who were as horrified by godly rebels as he was, Berkeley published a pamphlet containing two documents: a speech he had delivered to the General Assembly on March 17 and a declaration to which the assembly consented on the same day that probably also came from Berkeley's pen. The immediate context for both works was a parliamentary statute entitled An Act for Prohibiting Trade with the Barbadoes, Virginia, Bermuda and Antego (1650), a law that Worsley had helped draft as a founding member of the newly formed Council of Trade. Decrying the very idea of sovereignty that underlay this latest effort by the parliamentarians to bar the colonies from foreign trade, Berkeley argued that the "whole Current of their reasoning" was as "ridiculous" as it was dangerous. "The strength of their argument runs onely thus," he scoffed, "we have laid violent hands on your Land-Lord, possess'd his Manner house where you used to pay your rents, therefore now tender your respects to the same house

---

59. Benjamin Worsley to Walter Strickland, n.d. [August / September 1649], Hartlib Papers 61/8/1A–2A; Edward L. Bond, *Damned Souls in a Tobacco Colony: Religion in Seventeenth-Century Virginia* (Macon, Ga., 2000), 152–155; "Surrender of Virginia to the Parliamentary Commissioners," March 1651–1652, *Virginia Magazine of History and Biography*, XI (1903), 32. On Berkeley's publication of his speech and the subsequent declaration of the General Assembly at The Hague, see Berkeley, "Speech to the General Assembly," Mar. 17, 1650/51, in Billings, ed., *Papers of Sir William Berkeley*, 97, description of source.

you once reverenced." Berkeley perceived that the parliamentarians were indeed treating sovereignty as simply part of the architecture of the state.[60]

In response to such a manor-house conception of licit rule, Berkeley held up Virginia's own legal arrangements as grounded on the surer basis of the agreements colonists had historically made with their monarchs. Such commonwealth ties were the planters' proper moral "guides," he wrote, for "these lawes onely in such times of tumults, stormes, and tempests, can humanely prevent our ruines." Postulating a by now familiar view of Virginia as a concatenation of wills linking God, king, and people, Berkeley argued that Virginians could only be truly free if they held to those originating bonds. Warning the assembly against "any cowardly falling of[f] from the[ir] former resolutions," he urged the colony to take seriously its obligations at this particular moral crossroads, not simply giving in to Virginia's would-be masters but holding fast to their own dignity as a free people. In the colony's most important provision in the Articles of Surrender, signed on March 12, 1652 the government's "submission" to Parliament was to "be acknowledged a Voluntary Act not forced nor constrained (by a Conquest) upon the Country." That assertion of voluntary action suggested a people still possessed of a political will and thus capable when the time came of returning to their true sovereign.[61]

Virginia's Uncertain Restoration and the Troubling Persistence of Hobbism

Forced into temporary retirement by the colony's surrender to the Commonwealth, Berkeley must have watched nervously as the colony's Interregnum

---

60. Berkeley, "Speech to the General Assembly," Mar. 17, 1650/51, in Billings, ed., *Papers of Sir William Berkeley*, 96; An Act for Prohibiting Trade with the Barbadoes, Virginia, Bermuda, and Antego, [Oct. 3, 1650], in Firth and Rait, eds., *Acts and Ordinances of the Interregnum*, II, 425–429; "Articles of Surrender of the General Assembly," Mar. 12, 1651, in Billings, ed., *Papers of Sir William Berkeley*, 104. Berkeley's manor house analogy for the Hobbesian view of sovereignty fit well with Worsley's own conception that the "vacancy of the present Government" left by the king's death legitimized Parliament's exercise of rule in the colonies; see Worsley to Hartlib[?], Aug. 13, 1649, Hartlib Papers 33/2/1A.

61. "Declaration of the General Assembly," Mar. 17, 1650/51, in Billings, ed., *Papers of Sir William Berkeley*, 98, Berkeley, "Speech to the General Assembly," Mar. 17, 1650/51, 96, 'Articles of Surrender of the General Assembly," Mar. 12, 1651, 104.

leaders experimented with some of the language of popular sovereignty introduced by writers like Parker. Yet, the men who served as Virginia's governors in these years, Bennett, Edward Digges, and Colonel Samuel Mathews (son of the former councillor), all shared Berkeley's establishmentarian values as well as his devotion to Virginia's commonwealth. Their turn to the language of the parliamentarians appears to have been largely tactical, for Parker's doctrine that power originates in the people was readily adaptable to the problem of insulating the colony against outside directives. Thus, after "long and serious debate and advice taken for the settleing and governing of Virginia," the colony's assemblymen agreed on May 5, 1652, to identify all political offices in the colony, including the governor's, as properly chosen by the burgesses. Such a change was justified on the grounds that that body was the true "representative of the people." This clever formulation built on the legitimating discourse of the Puritan Commonwealth while quietly disregarding Parliament's own claim to embody the English people as a whole regardless of which side of the ocean they inhabited. A similar logic seems to have underlain the second such alteration, this time in relation to Virginia's church. In March 1658, the assembly ordered that all ecclesiastical issues in the colony were to be handled by local vestries, again on the grounds that "the people" should "have the disposal" of such matters. Once more, such a measure sounded a familiar Puritan theme but had the effect of keeping oversight over Virginia's commonwealth affairs centered on the American side of the Atlantic. Such maneuvers would have been risky if Puritan sentiment in the colony had been widespread and if it had resulted in intensive reforms designed once and for all to rid Virginia of its carnal arrangements. But few planters shared the zeal of one William Hatcher who in 1654 was brought before the assembly and ordered to apologize on his knees for calling the new speaker of the house Colonel Edward Hill an "atheist," "blasphemer," and "Devil." Instead, no Puritan majority emerged, and the colonists seem mainly to have bided their time until the confusions of the moment passed. On news of the death in 1658 of Lord Protector Cromwell and the subsequent passing in January 1660 of Governor Mathews, the assembly's leaders appealed to Berkeley to return to his former office.[62]

Although the Stuart monarchy would regain power in 1660, too many new ideas of polity had come into circulation in the previous two decades

62. At The Grand Assembly, James Citty, Apr. 30, 1652–May 5, 1652, in Hening, *Statutes*, I, 371, 372, Publique Orders of Assembly, Nov. 20, 1654, 387, Church Government Settled, Mar. 13, 1657/8, 433.

for the Restoration to be a true return to the status quo ante. The rightful path forward was obscure, as Berkeley expressed reflectively in the several speeches he gave to the burgesses in March. With feeling as well as a pragmatic eye toward justifying the planters' move in electing him when the king was not yet restored to the throne, he spoke to the difficulty that he and his fellow Virginians inevitably experienced in performing their duty of allegiance in such inconstant times. He was prepared to "live most submissively obedient to any power God shall set over me, as the experience of eight yeares have shewed I have done," he explained. Yet, he lacked "the Spirit of Prophecy to offitiate to me what this Supreame power in time may bee." What he longed for most of all was to return to a ruler truly anointed by God rather than one simply permitted by him as a scourge for the "sins of our nation." He recognized the hazard of taking on a gubernatorial authority that was only his king's to give. This was a burden "so volatile, slippery, and heavy, that I may justly feare it will breake my Limbes in the discent of it." Until the king was officially recognized and once again enjoyed a "naturall politique Capacity of being a Supreame power," Berkeley insisted that he possessed only one choice: namely, "to assume a power under a Spirituall Supreame power, without his assent." Clearly such a one-sided bond offended Berkeley's Grotian sensibilities. But strange times demanded unusual measures, and the puzzling nature of the Restoration would become even more pronounced in the months and years to come. By the late 1660s and early 1670s, Berkeley would have good reason to see Charles II's reign, not as a lifeline back to a familiar Christian humanist past, but rather as a troubling drift through newly uncertain Hobbesian waters.[63]

The Restoration began reassuringly for the constitutional royalists. Hyde, acting as lord chancellor and elevated to earl of Clarendon in 1661, initially enjoyed favor as Charles II's chief minister. Berkeley eagerly interpreted Clarendon's great "sukcesse" in exerting his tempering policies in England as a political and moral triumph that would undoubtedly also redound to Virginia's benefit. Buoyed by that promise, Berkeley initiated a number of ambitious reforms in the years immediately following Charles II's return to the throne in the spring of 1660. He encouraged a revision of the colony's laws in 1661–1662, launched the building of a statehouse, began an urban renewal project at Jamestown, prompted a number of statutory changes in the county courts and church, pursued economic diversification to wean planters

---

63. "Berkeley's Speech to the House of Burgesses," Mar. 13, 1659/60, in Billings, ed., *Papers of Sir William Berkeley*, 114, 115, Berkeley, "To the House of Burgesses," Mar. 19, 1659/60, 116, 117.

off their dependence on tobacco, and prepared for westward excursions in search of mines and the East Indian Ocean. All of these projects were in the spirit of the "improvements" that the newly established Council for Foreign Plantations encouraged in its December 1660 instructions to governors. If Berkeley recognized the continuing resonance of Hartlib's reform program in that state-directed quest for civil improvements, he probably was not overly alarmed. After all, his own interests inclined toward some of the same social, scientific, and economic pursuits that animated Hartlib's circle. Moreover, he was himself one of the forty-eight persons appointed to the council, a welcome sign that colonial voices of a sober moderate Anglican tenor would be among those contributing to its deliberations. Even the council's stated aim of bringing all the colonies into "one viewe and management here" so they "may be regulated and ordered upon common and equall ground and Principles" likely struck Berkeley as more felicitous than menacing. That centralizing agenda might very well have come from Povey's pen, for he was one of the Commonwealth policymakers who navigated the transition to the Restoration successfully and who brought Hobbes's ideals along with them into the new regime. Yet, as Digges's *Unlawfulnesse of Subjects Taking up Armes against Their Soveraigne* had made clear, constitutional royalists were not strictly opposed to state unification as long as it took place in ways that did not disrupt traditional ideas of the bonds among God, king, and people.[64]

Berkeley himself often expressed a desire for greater homogeneity in colonial governance. He pushed for such conformity in his several efforts to secure other colonies' compliance to trade regulations that he favored, such as occasional universal stints on tobacco production to relieve gluts in the market. Likewise, he supported uniformity when it came to the Cavalier Parliament's early efforts to root out religious nonconformity. One such statute, the Act for the Well Governing and Regulating of Corporations (1661), sought to purge legally incorporated communities of their still-recalcitrant members by placing them under the oversight of persons "well affected to His Majesty and the established Government," a fitting description of how Berkeley saw his own leadership. Residents were to swear new oaths declaring that no "pretence whatsoever" could justify lawfully taking up arms

64. William Berkeley to Edward Hyde, earl of Clarendon, July 20, 1666, in Billings, ed., *Papers of Sir William Berkeley*, 291; Sister Joan de Lourdes Leonard, "Operation Checkmate: The Birth and Death of a Virginia Blueprint for Progress, 1660–1676," *William and Mary Quarterly*, 3d Ser., XXIV (1967), 44–74; Andrews, *British Committees*, 67–68; "Instructions for the Council for Foreign Plantations," Dec. 1, 1660, in Billings, ed., *Papers of Sir William Berkeley*, 143.

against the king and that the Solemn League and Covenant had been an "unlawfull Oath" maliciously imposed on the king's subjects. The Act for the Uniformity of Publique Prayers and Administration of Sacraments (1662) was similarly a punitive statute directed against sectarians. Although Berkeley generally shared Clarendon's aversion to vindictive measures that might re-enflame civil passions, he nevertheless also regarded regularity of worship and a fortified established church as among the hopeful outcomes of a Restoration directed by establishmentarians like himself.[65]

Berkeley's perception that the time was ripe for stabilizing reforms also underlay one of his most dramatic political actions in these years — his decision, after calling an assembly on March 23, 1661, to prorogue it and return it to order repeatedly for seventeen consecutive sessions. He would not dissolve the assembly for fifteen years, only doing so in 1676 when Bacon's Rebellion gave rise to complaints about the expense of the burgesses' frequent sitting and cries that the colony's government had grown too unaccountable to tax-paying planters and too secretive in its actions. Given that Charles II would institute a similar long parliament, it seems likely that Clarendon stood behind this policy and that he saw it as a way of concentrating loyal and wise voices around the Restoration governments while avoiding the imputation of absolutism that Charles I's Personal Rule had invited. For Berkeley, keeping the colony's assembly intact was highly in keeping with his Hookerite belief that public institutions were steadying and that they achieved their settling role in large part because of their effectiveness in nurturing in officials a level of expertise that was unattainable to the great majority of persons. Hooker himself had argued that, whether in divinity or in law, there were some matters that were "more obscure, more intricate and hard to be judged of." "Therefore," he continued, "God hath appointed some to spende their whole time principally in the studie" of such issues "to the end that in these more doubtfull cases their understanding might be a light to direct others." Lawmaking was one such arena that far exceeded the capacities of most ordinary men: "For in the Civil state more insight, and in those affaires more experience a great deale must needs be granted them, then in this they can possibly have." To Berkeley, the need for superior judgment in public office was a given, but it also posed a problem in the comparatively egalitarian setting of a colonial society.[66]

65. Charles II, 1661: An Act for the Well Governing and Regulating of Corporations, in John Raithby, ed., *Statutes of the Realm . . .* , V, *[1628–80]* (n.p., 1819), 321, 322.

66. Billings, *Sir William Berkeley and the Forging of Colonial Virginia*, 131–135; Annabel

One of Berkeley's allies, the Virginia clergyman Roger Green, articulated concerns regarding the lack of Virginia planters fit for office in a 1662 pamphlet that sought to encourage Church of England officials to take more seriously Virginia's clerical wants. As an explanation for why the colony's ecclesiastical arrangements remained woefully undeveloped, Green wrote that the colony's burgesses were "usually such as went over Servants thither, and though by time and industry, they may have attained competent Estates; yet by reason of their poor and mean education they are unskilful in judging of a good Estate either of Church or Common-wealth, or of the means of procuring it." For Berkeley, the burgesses' obvious need to be sheltered from the disruption of frequent turnover to improve their own abilities left him perplexed when planters expressed anger at such repeated sitting. In his call for new elections in 1676, he wrote:

> When I considder that the more experienced men are in any Act Profession or Practice the more exact and perfect they are in that Profession or Practice[,] it cannot but seeme somewhat strange to mee that the Inhabitants of this Country should bee dissatisfied with those Gentlemen as their Burgesses of the Grand Assembly who were by themselves freely elected and chosen to that great Task for no other reason but because they have soe often mett and consulted the great affaires of the Country in that quallity.

His exasperation reflects how outmoded some of his traditional humanist views had begun to seem in a late Restoration era that had grown ever more nervous about the mysterious dealings of powerful governing cliques. Especially in the years after Clarendon's fall, distrusting English subjects often looked on Charles II's machinations as enabled by his ministry, a group, it was observed, whose individual names began with letters that ominously spelled CABAL. In such a cabal-wary political climate, a government that met for too long behind closed doors naturally invited suspicions of abusing its power. But these were anxieties that Berkeley could not have anticipated in the early 1660s. In those early Clarendonian years, his outlook remained

---

Patterson, *The Long Parliament of Charles II* (New Haven, Conn., 2008), 38–62; Hooker, *Folger Library Edition of the Works of Richard Hooker*, ed. Edelen and Hill, I, 13–15. For complaints about the expense of Berkeley's long assembly, see "The Counties' Grievances," in Michael Leroy Oberg, ed., *Samuel Wiseman's "Book of Record": The Official Account of Bacon's Rebellion in Virginia* (Lanham, Md., 2005), 209, 218, 220, 225, 233, 240, 243, 248.

optimistically trained on the problem of overcoming the nation's recent political and moral confusion. This challenge, in turn, centered on his perception that Virginia, despite its faults, had proven itself admirably unwavering in its loyalty.[67]

Berkeley's view of Virginia's constancy in the face of the era's violent revolutions became key to his belief that the colony now had a duty to provide moral leadership to other, less resolute souls. In trumpeting Virginia's status as the king's "most experimented conspicuously Loyall Country," he was not suggesting its lack of divisions. On the contrary, he was adamant that the truly "Loyal party" in Virginia was a distinct and righteous minority. He and his supporters faced, on the one hand, sectarians who were impishly "inclined to change." On the other side were a great many other planters who were "indifferent," possessed of such base and vacillating consciences that they might easily be swayed from their duties. On the basis of this same understanding of the hierarchy of virtue that prevailed in the colony, the burgesses in October 1660 identified Virginia's recent "Apostacy" as a terrible declension that the current government could nevertheless repair. Asserting that Berkeley's "signall Constancie and loyalltie to his sacred Majestie" made him the appropriate person to seek a royal pardon, they called him their "Immaculate Mediator." The term was rich in Hookerite connotations of the role that leaders should play as moral guides to their people. In a preamble justifying their revision of the laws in 1661–1662, the assemblymen similarly explained that their obligations toward "God, the king and the country" compelled them to bring order to the colony because "the late unhappy distractions" had left the people uncertain "what to obey." The recent "licentiousness of the laws" under "frequent changes in the government" not only encouraged disobedience but also hurt that "just freedome" that came from obeying the right masters. Berkeley committed the revision of the laws to another constitutional royalist in the colony, Francis Moryson, Lord Falkland's brother-in-law. In his dedicatory epistle to Berkeley in the London edition of the revised laws, Moryson explained that his purpose was to purge the "vitious Excrescencies [that] had grown in the body of them, by the corrupt humor of the times . . . that we might not any where leave unrazed the memory of our enforc'd Defection from his Sacred Majesty." Giving Berkeley special credit for having "retein'd us in an inviolated obe-

---

67. R[oger] G[reen], *Virginia's Cure; or, An Advisive Narrative concerning Virginia; Discovering the True Ground of That Churches Unhappiness, and the Only True Remedy* . . . (London, 1662), 18; Election writ, May 10, 1676, in Billings, ed., *Papers of Sir William Berkeley*, 520.

dience to his Majesty," Moryson echoed the governor's own sentiment that whatever success the colony had enjoyed in remaining on a true pathway had resulted primarily from unwavering leaders like himself.[68]

Berkeley also turned this self-assurance outward, exulting in the hope that Virginia would now be recognized in England as the undeniable heart of the American dominions. Writing to Clarendon in 1663, he boasted of subtle indications that the other colonies had begun "to center" on Virginia. Letters arrived "continually" from Barbadian families expressing an interest in relocating to the colony, other West Indian plantations looked to Virginia for leadership, and two hundred New England families had recently settled nearby. In short, centralization in the Restoration era had every appearance of being a favorable process — as long, that is, as it took place under the robust command of morally fit leaders like Berkeley and accorded with an established order that had already proven its lawfulness under God.[69]

The Restoration that Berkeley longed to see never materialized. Instead, expectations of government had shifted with sufficient force as to leave traditionalists like him and Clarendon off-balance, scrambling to maintain their imperfect control over the rapidly changing direction of events. One example of Berkeley's slowness in adjusting to the altered political terrain was his persistent frustration concerning the mysterious new ways in which the Dutch and French figured in English policymakers' imaginations. Attuned to the ideal of state unity and a growing conception of commerce as vital to a polity's well-being, the new generation of English statesmen under the Commonwealth and Restoration governments came to view the aggressive trade tactics of the Netherlands and France as even more relevant to the world of sovereign competition than the onetime specter of Spanish hegemony. Worsley would articulate this novel perspective in a pamphlet

---

68. Petition to Charles II, [circa November 1665], in Billings, ed., *Papers of Sir William Berkeley*, 270, William Berkeley to Charles II, in Billings, ed., *Papers of Sir William Berkeley*, 106; Jon Kukla, "Some Acts Not in Hening's 'Statutes': The Acts of Assembly, October 1660," *VMHB*, LXXXIII (1975), 87; At a Grand Assembly Held at James City, Mar. 23, 1661/2, in Henings, *Statutes at Large*, II, 41–42; *The Lawes of Virginia Now in Force: Collected out of the Assembly Records and Digested into One Volume*... (London, 1662), B[1]r–B[1]v.

69. Berkeley to Clarendon, Mar. 30, 1663, in Billings, ed., *Papers of Sir William Berkeley*, 190. By 1663, Berkeley was writing regularly to Clarendon urging his "Assistance" and "Patronage" on the colony's behalf and his personal "protection" anytime complaints about Berkeley's conduct in office arose that he could not address before the king himself; see Berkeley to Clarendon, Mar. 28, 1663, ibid., 188, Mar. 30, 1663, 190, Apr. 18, 1663, 192.

entitled *The Advocate* (1651), a defense of the Navigation Act of that year that was itself an effort to yoke trade policy more effectively to the exercise of state power. "It hath been a thing for many years generally received," he wrote, "that the Design of *Spain* . . . is, to get the Universal Monarchie of Christendom." Meanwhile, the Dutch had busily laid "a foundation to themselvs for ingrossing the Universal Trade, not onely of Christendom, but indeed, of the greater part of the known world." The English could not afford to ignore this quieter form of conquest, Worsley argued, for it was through their commercial dominion that the Hollanders had reached the point where they "might poiz the Affairs of any other State about them." By 1668, Worsley had taken note also of French aggressions in relation to West Indian trade. Thus, he added the assertive France of Louis XIV and his brilliant minister of finance Jean-Baptiste Colbert to his evolving theory of the relationship between commerce and state politics. He argued that the French were erstwhile friends who "doe actually make warr with us" through restrictive tariffs on English imports and that it was "farr better, to have noe trade at all and to be at open Warr with a nation; Then to have such an unequal peace or Comerce." Berkeley could never quite grasp, let alone accept, England's newly belligerent approach to the Netherlands, but he found even more alarming the increasingly close orbit between Charles II's monarchy and Louis XIV's court.[70]

England's intimacy with France became a concern for Berkeley by about the time of the Second Anglo-Dutch War (1665–1667). In 1668, he confided to Nicolls that he distrusted the French because of their recent conquest of the English Caribbean island Saint Christopher. He deemed them "the worst masters in the world" and feared they had their sights set on other English dominions in America. The previous year, he had written another letter to Nicolls in which he brought up a moment that he regarded as particularly shameful for the English king. This was the instance during the Commonwealth when Louis XIV heeded Cromwell's request and banished Charles II's exiled court from France. Would the king "revenge the

---

70. [Benjamin Worsley], *The Advocate* (London, 1651), 1; [Benjamin] Worsley to [Anthony] Ashley [Cooper, first earl of Shaftesbury], memorandum, Aug. 14, 1668, The National Archives, London, 30/24/49, fols. 225v–226r, quoted in Leng, *Benjamin Worsley*, 159–160. For discussions of the era's discourse of trade that are sensitive to the importance of the context of the Dutch and French ascendancy, see Blair Hoxby, *Mammon's Music: Literature and Economics in the Age of Milton* (New Haven Conn., 2002); Steve Pincus, *Protestantism and Patriotism: Ideologies and the Making of English Foreign Policy, 1650–1668* (Cambridge, 1996)

base affront" given him at that time? Berkeley asked. Even posed as a rhetorical question, this was a remarkably sensitive issue to raise at a time when Charles II was suspected of cultivating unnaturally close relations with the latest pretender to universal monarchy. Yet, for Berkeley, the king's maneuvers were largely inexplicable except as a peculiar sign of his weakness of will. This was an analysis of the period that Berkeley also applied more or less unqualifiedly to the Restoration regime's laxity toward sectarians, indifference toward the colonies, and ambivalence toward Clarendon — all areas in which the Restoration proved distressingly to be guided by principles that evoked Hobbes more than Grotius.[71]

No other event highlighted the strange new political environment in which the traditional humanists had found themselves more than Clarendon's impeachment. For Berkeley, that momentous political upheaval was undoubtedly the nadir of his governorship before he, too, lost his office in a rebellion that bore many of the same hallmarks as Clarendon's fall. By November 1667, Berkeley had heard news that "the lord Chancellor is prisoner in the Tower with divers other Lords spirituall and Temporall." Horrifically, Cromwell's old confidante Lord General Christopher Monck was reportedly Clarendon's chief prosecutor, adding a sickening tinge of zealous Protestantism to his undoing. But the "most monstrous and portentious" rumor of all was that the trial might have been brought about secretly by none other than James, duke of York, Clarendon's own father-in-law. Although Berkeley was skeptical that the latter machination could possibly be true, he took it seriously enough to bemoan to Nicolls that he could think of no political betrayal more calamitous for "a kingdom so weakened and distracted as England now is." Berkeley did not say explicitly, but he probably perceived this assault on Clarendon's steadying constitutionalism as at least an indirect result of the sinister influence of Hobbes's philosophy on the Restoration monarchy.[72]

A cloud of innuendo hung over Charles II's government that tended to link Hobbes's friendly relationship with the new regime to its own drift toward a Francophilic foreign policy and attraction to absolutist theories of governance. Clarendon himself would recall that Hobbes "came frequently to the Court, where he had too many Disciples." Stifling Hobbes's ideas

---

71. Berkeley to Nicolls, May 4, 1667, in Billings, ed., *Papers of Sir William Berkeley*, 310, Berkeley to Nicolls, May 20, 1666, 280.

72. William Berkeley to Richard Nicolls, Nov. 14, 1667, in Billings, ed., *Papers of Sir William Berkeley*, 335.

would become one of Clarendon's major political agendas. Shortly after reading *Leviathan*, he confessed that he "could not enough wonder" that a man who "had so great a reverence for Civil Government, that he resolv'd all Wisdom and Religion it self into a simple obedience and submission to it, should publish a Book, for which, by the constitution of any Government now establish'd in Europe . . . the Author must be punish'd in the highest degree, and with the most severe penalties." Even while Charles II's court was still in exile in Paris, Hyde and his allies in the Anglican clergy had branded Hobbes an atheist and a dispenser of heterodox ideas and had succeeded in temporarily excluding him from the king's presence. The Cavalier Parliament took up much the same cause by treating Hobbes's works, not as royalist philosophy, but as dangerous heresy, leading Hobbes to worry that the bishops would order him burned for that most egregious of crimes. When the fire of London generated widespread apprehensions that the conflagration was God's punishment for England's apostasy, a House of Commons committee ordered *Leviathan* considered for public burning. The only other work the committee recommended for this punishment was a book by Thomas White who in the 1650s had drawn on *Leviathan* in defending Cromwell's government.[73]

Although Clarendon's fall from grace in 1667 would be blamed on his poor handling of the Second Anglo-Dutch War, his most conspicuous enemy in the affair would be one of Hobbes's principal patrons, Henry Bennet, earl of Arlington. As secretary of state, Arlington courted a French alliance, supported toleration as long as it promised greater freedoms for Catholics, and sought to enhance England's commercial might. His patronage of Hobbes no doubt related closely to these policies, which he pursued as one of the principal leaders of the Cabal ministry after Clarendon's eclipse from power. Hobbes dedicated two of his works to the lord in the late 1660s, and Arlington's secretary Sir Joseph Williamson was also in close contact with the philosopher. Too much mystery surrounds Clarendon's impeachment to say with any confidence that Hobbism had brought about his downfall. Yet, Clarendon evidently was convinced of its malicious role in the politics of his day. After going into exile, he would devote himself to writing a more than three-hundred-page warning to Charles II entitled "Brief View and Survey of the Dangerous and Pernicious Errors to Church and State,

---

73. Clarendon, *Brief View and Survey*, 8, 9; Philip Milton, "Hobbes, Heresy, and Lord Arlington," *History of Political Thought*, XIV (1993), 503, 515; Parkin, *Taming the Leviathan*, 104–105, 228.

in Mr. Hobbes's Book, Entitled Leviathan." Not published until 1676, the work was completed in 1670, and it seems likely that even if friends like Berkeley were unaware of the volume at that time they could scarcely have missed Clarendon's more general preoccupation with Hobbes's "monstrous Principles."[74]

Berkeley's own oft-stated distrust of rigidly held doctrines suggests that he, like Clarendon, had come to see Hobbism as one of the post-Civil War era's most formidable challenges. While still lord chancellor, Clarendon had aggressively banned the publication of Hobbes's works in the hope that suppressing his doctrines would allow them to die of their own accord. Berkeley's awareness of Clarendon's reliance on censorship to strangle Hobbes's theories surely accounts for his own famous disparaging remark about not only printing but also schools, which Hobbes had identified as the primary means for his principles to trickle down through society. Answering a set of inquiries sent by the Council for Foreign Plantations in 1671, Berkeley commented wryly, "I thanke God there are noe free schooles no[r] printing and I hope Wee shall not have these hundred yeares for learning has brought disobedience and heresye and sects into the world and printing hath divulged them, and libells against the best Government." Given the reputation for heresy that had stuck to Hobbes by this time, Berkeley's remark no doubt reflected his awareness of the growing influence of Hobbesian ideas on Restoration policy. The newly organized Council for Foreign Plantations, now under Secretary of State Arlington's oversight, had been reduced to ten members, and it leaned heavily on the advice of Hobbists like Worsley. His outlook appeared prominently in instructions for the council that were issued in 1670 in Arlington's name. Asserting that the colonies were unquestionably England's "Soveraigne Posessions," the instructions sketched out a vision of state unity in which a strong metropolitan government took whatever steps it needed to ensure that colonial commerce flourished and benefited the broader commonweal. The council was to "Order, Governe, and Regulate the Trade of our whole Plantations, that they may be most serviceable one unto another, and as the whole unto these our Kingdomes so these our kingdomes unto them," he wrote. An additional set of provisions related to governors like Berkeley. Rather than partners in the grand project of extending English rule to America, colonial administrators were now to be suspected as the likeliest obstacles to the state's aims, scrutinized

---

74. Clarendon, *Brief View and Survey*, 310; Parkin, *Taming the Leviathan*, 241, 247, 312–322, 335–336, 366, 376.

in particular for their "abuse of our Authority." No wonder Berkeley took the opportunity of the council's questionnaire to direct a barb at Hobbism. Hobbes's ideas were once again at the forefront of the metropole's approach to the plantations.[75]

Clarendon's overthrow unsurprisingly also began the gradual decline of Berkeley's governorship, and he spent these waning years at Virginia's helm largely preoccupied by the problem of insulating the colony against its new Hobbesian backdrop. Three new state imperatives that unmistakably hailed from Hobbes's theories now dominated directives out of England: the better protection of subjects, the regulation of colonial trade, and the disabusing of local rulers of their inflated view of their own power. As early as February 1666, Arlington had made clear that he and not Clarendon would steer Virginia through the changes of the Restoration era. He ordered the colonists at that time to build a fort at Point Comfort as a defense against marauding ships during the Second Anglo-Dutch War, and he called for greater output in colonial commodities. Both measures angered Berkeley and reinforced his sense that the new ministry was worryingly deaf to the colony's needs. In a letter to Arlington in July, he wrote that a fort located at such a distance from Virginia's own "Center and H[e]art" at Jamestown would be useless. Moreover, the time was hardly right for stepped-up production of colonial crops when his administration was in the midst of setting in place the inevitably unpopular measure of a one-year cessation of tobacco growing to boost prices and encourage planters to pursue other, more reliable commodities. Clearly a rift had begun to emerge between Berkeley and his English superiors over just where Virginia's sovereign center truly lay, with Berkeley clinging to the Grotian idea that the bond between king and people formed a perfect society in its own right, whereas Arlington pursued the Hobbesian ideal of a state whose authority was singular, unbroken, and located indisputably in the metropolis.[76]

---

75. Parkin, *Taming the Leviathan*, 228 (for Hobbes's Anglican and Presbyterian opponents' awareness of his eagerness to reform the universities, see esp. 145–153); Hobbes, *Leviathan*, ed. Tuck, 236, 462, 491; "Answers to the Inquiries from the Council for Foreign Plantations," June 20, 1671, in Billings, ed., *Papers of Sir William Berkeley*, 397; "Instructions for the Council for Foreign Plantations, 1670–1672," July 30, 1670, in Andrews, *British Committees*, 117, 121 On the Cabal ministry and the colonies, see Robert Bliss, *Revolution and Empire: English Politics and the American Colonies in the Seventeenth Century* (New York, 1990), 103–218.

76. William Berkeley to Henry Bennet, earl of Arlington, July 13, 1666, in Billings, ed., *Papers of Sir William Berkeley*, 289.

For local leaders who had long felt excluded from Berkeley's narrow governing circle, this transatlantic disagreement was a useful wedge to exploit. William Drummond was one such alienated politician. A onetime tenant on Berkeley's lands, Drummond was a Scot who had done well in colonial trade, and he was probably a Presbyterian. In 1664, Berkeley had recommended Drummond for the governor's post at the new settlement on Albemarle Sound, a forerunner to the later North Carolina colony. The appointment was very likely an effort to encourage sectarian outmigration to that southern region, thereby reserving Virginia itself for the king's most dutiful and conforming subjects. As Berkeley explained his position on Scottish colonists to Arlington in 1666, he recognized "that in thes dangerous times they have been very useful to us" and so deserved support in those instances when it was not "prejudicial to his Majesties service." Presumably, serving as buffers for Virginia's southern frontier was one way zealous Scots could satisfy this prescription of being useful to the commonwealth without being prejudicial to the king. Drummond, however, was not satisfied with this marginal role, and he made no secret of his readiness to join instead with the Hobbists to topple Berkeley's regime. As he confided to an unidentified royal official, he knew of an "abundance of people that are weary of Sir Williams Government." The remark resembled closely the claim of weak colonial authority that sectarians had often pressed when they perceived that rulers in England were better disposed to their cause than that of their Anglican adversaries. Berkeley himself was conscious that a dramatic reordering of power in Virginia was likely, a threat made all the greater by the toll the continuing struggle with the Dutch was taking on a colonial populace already exhausted by war.[77]

To fend off critics at this delicate juncture, Berkeley and his supporters repeatedly invoked the familiar Grotian image of the loving bonds needed to preserve civil order. In July 1673, during the Third Anglo-Dutch War (1672–1674), he and his council identified the people's well-turned hearts as the only inducement leading them to take up their arms to defend English merchant ships from Dutch attackers. Unhappy with the stingy English merchants, the planters would not have "appeare[d]" on their behalf at all were it not for the "Motive" of "the affections" they "have to the Gentleness and Justice of the Government they have Soe long lived under." Later that same year, out of concern that "ill affected Persons" would take advantage

---

77. William Berkeley to Henry Bennet, earl of Arlington, Dec. 3, 1666, in Billings, ed., *Papers of Sir William Berkeley,* 303, William Drummond to [?], Sept. 3, 1666, 294.

of the Berkeley government's repeated failures to protect merchant ships from Dutch fleets to "unjustly asperse his Fame" and give the king "ill Impressions of him," the council wrote to England again to express the same message. Berkeley "hath for nere Thirty yeares Governed this Collony with that Prudence and Justice which hath gained him both Love and reverence from all the Inhabitants here," the councillors wrote. "Wee looke on" that love, they continued, "as our greatest Strength, for in this Very Conjucture had the People Distaste of All Governors they Would have hazarded the losse of this Countrey." These statements expressed a continuing confidence in Berkeley's government as well as a lingering attachment to the humanist ideal of the reciprocal ties that hold leaders and subjects alike to their duties. Yet, the council also conveyed a newfound sense of doubt, a fear in particular that the rules by which politics operated were changing and that the question of where a colony derived its strength now encouraged two very different answers: one by the traditionalists and one by the Hobbists.[78]

The first tremors of the Hobbesian revolution in Virginia began in the fall of 1664. On September 20, Berkeley and the council wrote directly to Charles II in a pronounced state of panic. Local leaders and planters had become so "mightyly disturbed," they wrote, that "wee cannott but feare the utter distruction of our selves and this whole Collony." The circumstances behind this latest crisis were profound. As the Third Anglo-Dutch War wound down, news broke in England that Charles II in 1670 had followed Arlington's advice to sign the Dover Treaty, a secret alliance with the French king that committed both kingdoms to the vanquishing of the Dutch on terms that would strike many Englishmen as greatly favoring the French. By January 28, 1673, Arlington had obtained a copy of a pamphlet that exposed his involvement in the Dover Treaty in intricate detail. Entitled *Englands Appeal from the Private Cabal at White-Hall to the Great Council of the Nation,* the anonymous tract warned that Arlington's ministry sought nothing less than to "turn *England* into a *French* Province." Only a few weeks later, on February 25, the king offered Arlington what amounted to liberal compensation for quietly taking the fall for the political debacle by giving up his secretary's post. The gift was stunning in its generosity, though also highly symbolic of Arlington's role in promoting the Hobbesian view of colonies as fundamentally obliged to the sovereign's will. In one fell swoop, Charles II

---

78. Berkeley and the Virginia Council to Charles II and the Privy Council, July 1673, in Billings, ed., *Papers of Sir William Berkeley,* 424, The Virginia Council to the king and Privy Council, October 1673, 430.

gave the entire Virginia colony as a present to Arlington and Thomas Colepeper, second Baron Colepeper of Thoresway, for thirty-one years. Colepeper was included in the grant because of a previous, more limited gift to his father. In 1649, before going into exile, Charles II had awarded John Colepeper, the onetime coauthor of Charles I's *Answer to the XIX Propositions,* and six other proprietors ownership of Virginia's Northern Neck as a reward for their loyalty. But the familiar move of paring off a portion of Virginia as a show of royal benevolence to certain favored proprietors was a far cry from treating the entire colony as dispensable. Few acts could have been more dismissive of Virginia's commonwealth integrity, and a decade later the colony's legislators still staggered at the grant's "evill Consequences." By "divesting the Gover[n]m[en]t of those Just powers, and Authorities by w[hi]ch this Colony had hitherto been kept in peace and tranquility and all mens Rights and properties duely Administred and preserved unto them," the king in a single stroke had rendered questionable the colony's very political essence."[79]

But the troubles had only just begun, for a new arrival in the colony, the customs collector Giles Bland, epitomized the Cabal ministry's determination to reduce local governments that flaunted their own civil wholeness. Bland was none other than Thomas Povey's son-in-law, and he shared his relation's firm commitment to state unity. Responsible for levying the new one-shilling export duty on tobacco instituted by the Plantation Duty Act (1673), Bland answered to Lord Treasurer Thomas Osborne, earl of Danby, Arlington's successor to the management of colonial affairs and a Hobbist in his own right. Danby had employed Marchamont Nedham, the onetime apologist for the Commonwealth, to present the new government's policies in a favorable light, and Nedham hardly refrained from trumpeting his new master's Hobbism. The withering view of incorporated communities that he placed in Danby's mouth, for instance, was more or less identical to Hobbes's theory of colonies in *Leviathan:*

79. Berkeley and the Virginia Council to Charles II, Sept. 20, 1674, in Billings, ed., *Papers of Sir William Berkeley,* 448; Violet Barbour, *Henry Bennet, Earl of Arlington, Secretary of State to Charles II* (Baltimore, 1915), 211n; *England's Appeal from the Private Cabal at White-Hall to the Great Council of the Nation* (n.p., 1673), 30; Grant to Lords Arlington and Culpeper, in Hening, *Statutes at Large,* II, 569–578; The Humble Reply of the House of Burgesses to the Speech of Governor Lord Howard of Effingham, May 20, 1684, in H. R. McIlwaine, ed., *Journal of the House of Burgesses, 1659/60–1693* (Richmond, Va., 1914), 237.

If such considerable Corporated parcels of the *Body Politick*, shall by degrees be corrupted with Men, who by contracting particular Interests, shall march counter to the publick Interest of Government, and imploy the Interests and Credit of their Corporations against it; then, of course, *Princes* and *Parliaments* are constrained, whether they will or no, to provide for a securing the publick Interest by some extraordinary course.

Bland was effectively the embodiment of that "extraordinary course," an enforcer brought in to overcome the private interests of local leaders in favor of the more public interest of the state.[80]

After landing in Virginia, Bland almost immediately became caught up in a conflict with one of Berkeley's most trusted advisors, the colony's secretary of state Thomas Ludwell. Superficially, the quarrel had to do with Ludwell's decision in a legal case in which Bland was involved, but the colony's leaders recognized immediately that his outrageous dealings with the secretary were in fact calculated slights against the entire government. When Bland posted a challenge on the statehouse door declaring for all Virginians to see that Ludwell was "a Sonn of a Whore[,] mechannick ffellow[,] puppy[,] and a Coward," the assemblymen were quick to decry his disrespectful act as a deliberate assault on the honor of the "whole Assembly." Likewise, they denounced Bland's complaints about Ludwell's inferiority in dispensing justice as an insult directed at the "Whole Court." They even perceived Bland as the busy whisperer behind a sinister rumor that Ludwell had himself been complicit in bringing about the Arlington grant. Berkeley's administration was in the midst of preparing a group of agents for a voyage to England to challenge the grant's legitimacy, and now these men, who included Berkeley's trusted allies Ludwell and Moryson, received an additional mission. They

---

80. *Encyclopedia Virginia*, s.v. "Giles Bland (bap. 1647–1677)," by Warren M. Billings and the *Dictionary of Virginia Biography*, accessed on Apr. 21, 2016, http://www.encyclopediavirginia.org/Bland_Giles_bap_1647-1677; [Marchamont Nedham], *A Pacquet of Advices and Animadversions, Sent from London to the Men of Shaftsbury... Occasioned by a Seditious Phamphlet, Intituled, A Letter from a Person of Quality to His Friend in the Country* (London, 1676), 17. On Danby's commissioning of Nedham to write *A Pacquet of Advices*, see Blair Worden, "'Wit in a Roundhead': The Dilemma of Marchamont Nedham," in Susan D. Amussen and Mark A. Kishlansky, eds., *Political Culture and Cultural Politics in Early Modern England: Essays Presented to David Underdown* (Manchester, U.K., 1995), 303.

were to approach Lord Treasurer Danby and impress on him that Bland's disdainful "Carriage" tended "to mutiny and contempt of the Government." The message conveyed clearly the Berkeley administration's acute awareness that Bland's strange conduct derived from his Cabal superiors, and it offers a glimpse as well of the siege mentality that had begun to take hold in Virginia's government.[81]

The threat of a Hobbist reorientation of colonial politics had begun to press in on all sides. It was against this backdrop of already intensified anxiety about a fundamental realignment of power that Berkeley and his supporters were suddenly confronted by another problem: an Indian war of seemingly massive proportions that practically invited the Hobbesian premise that the government that protects the people is the one that deserves their obedience.

The violence that broke out between Virginia frontiersmen and local Doegs and Susquehannocks in the summer and fall of 1675 inspired fears on all sides of a spiritual world suddenly off-kilter. The Susquehannocks, according to one settler, considered themselves to be tormented by the "wandering ghosts" of their slain fellows, and only the murders of dozens of frontier families could satisfy the provoking spirits. For their part, panic-stricken planters, deserting entire frontier counties and calling "both to God and man for releife," gave in to their own vengeful impulses. The bloodshed began with a double murder in Stafford County, one of the most remote parts of English settlement on the Northern Neck. Years later, planters would still recall that the deaths of a Virginia herdsman named Robert Hen and a native man, probably one of the Doegs whom Hen implicated before he died, occurred on a Sabbath day, a detail that fed colonists' already heightened expectation that they were becoming swept up in a major providential event. Frightening reports had arrived from the northern colonies that native Americans had joined forces in a catastrophic attack on New England. That conflict, later known as King Philip's War, encouraged planters to see the Stafford County killings as a link in a broader chain of cosmic occurrences. Berkeley was confident the Puritans were simply getting their just deserts for killing Charles I, and he blamed the war as well on the saints' hubris, not only in "covet[ing] more Land than they are safely able to hold from those they have disposest of it" but also in explaining this "uncharitable expulsion" on the hypocritical grounds that "God had given" them such contested territo-

---

81. H. R. McIlwaine, ed., *Minutes of the Council and General Court of Colonial Virginia*, 2d ed. (Richmond, Va., 1979), 399; William Berkeley to Thomas Ludwell, Francis Moryson, and Robert Smith, circa December 1674, in Billings, ed., *Papers of Sir William Berkeley*, 465.

ries. To Berkeley, the Stafford County inhabitants who responded to Hen's killing by leading an indiscriminate, fury-filled vigilante campaign against neighboring Indians were driven by a blinding zeal that was not much less loathsome than the Puritans'.[82]

Berkeley's establishmentarian instincts led him to approach the escalating chaos far more cautiously than many frontier planters desired. Rather than give in to their vigilantism, he sought to temper the settlers' own enthusiasm while also managing the growing Indian war. However, his discretion invited suspicions of indifference, leaving planters increasingly frustrated with their governor and eager for a leader who was more receptive to their anxieties. When Berkeley's newest councillor, the young Nathaniel Bacon, Jr., made clear that he was prepared to step forward as their longed-for guardian, the crisis suddenly entered into a wholly new phase. What had begun as a frontier struggle filled with providential connotations had now become the ultimate testing ground for Hobbes's theory of sovereignty as little more than an expression of humanity's desire for self-preservation.

Bacon fit well the heroic persona that both planters and the Hobbesian regime in England sought. Like the Puritan Hobbists of the Commonwealth, he leaned toward nonconformist Protestantism as well as Platonism. He described his spiritualism at one point as a matter of taking delight in "solitude and mistique imployments." In the 1660s, he had supplemented

---

82. "The History of Bacon's and Ingram's Rebellion," [1676], in Charles M. Andrews, ed., *Narratives of the Insurrections, 1675–1690* (New York, 1915), 49, 50, T[homas] M[athew], "The Beginning, Progress, and Conclusion of Bacon's Rebellion in Virginia in the Years 1675 and 1676," 16; William Berkeley to [Sir Joseph Williamson?], Apr. 1, 1676, in Billings, ed., *Papers of Sir William Berkeley*, 509. For helpful analyses of Bacon's Rebellion, see Stephen Saunders Webb, *1676: The End of American Independence* (Syracuse, N.Y., 1995); Wilcomb E. Washburn, *The Governor and the Rebel: A History of Bacon's Rebellion in Virginia* (Chapel Hill, N.C., 1957), 30–31; James D. Rice, *Tales from a Revolution: Bacon's Rebellion and the Transformation of Early America* (Oxford, 2012); Billings, *Sir William Berkeley and the Forging of Colonial Virginia*, 210–266; Warren M. Billings, "The Causes of Bacon's Rebellion: Some Suggestions," *VMHB*, LXXVIII (1970), 409–435; Brent Tarter, "Bacon's Rebellion, the Grievances of the People, and the Political Culture of Seventeenth-Century Virginia," *VMHB*, CXIX (2011), 2–41; Peter Thompson, "The Thief, the Householder, and the Commons: Languages of Class in Seventeenth-Century Virginia," *WMQ*, 3d Ser., LXIII (2006), 253–280; Edmund S. Morgan, *American Slavery, American Freedom: The Ordeal of Colonial Virginia* (New York, 1975), 215–292; Kathleen M. Brown, *Good Wives, Nasty Wenches, and Anxious Patriarchs: Gender, Race, and Power in Colonial Virginia* (Chapel Hill, N.C., 1996), 137–186; Thomas Jefferson Wertenbaker, *Torchbearer of the Revolution: The Story of Bacon's Rebellion and Its Leader* (Princeton, 1940).

his Cambridge studies by touring Europe with his tutor John Ray, a natural philosopher and theologian who gravitated toward the so-called Cambridge Platonists like Henry More and Ralph Cudworth. Given this background, Bacon's reference to mystical employments suggests a deliberate distancing of himself from Hobbes's materialism while accepting some of his broader jurisprudence, a position similar to the Cambridge Platonists' own mixed reception of Hobbes. To judge from his various speeches, letters, and declarations, Bacon approached Hobbes's political ideas by a very particular route: through theories that had been developed by his kinsman and namesake, the Suffolk lawyer Nathaniel Bacon. One of the apologists for the parliamentary side in the English Civil War, the senior Bacon had written a learned treatise entitled *An Historicall Discourse of the Uniformity of the Government of England* (1647) that defended the popular basis of sovereignty in England from a Presbyterian perspective. Undoubtedly drawing on either Hobbes or Parker, Bacon had embraced fully the doctrine of state unity. As he put it, "The utmost perfection of this nether worlds best government consists in the upholding of a due proportion of severall interests compounded into one temperature."[83]

Grounding this theory of state unity in history, Bacon found the basis for both Presbyterian ecclesiastical structure and Parliament's supremacy in England's Saxon past. The Saxons, he argued, had benefited from the Romans when the latter brought religion and the state into "one uniform government" and elevated that rule into a "vast body" on the basis of a true understanding of "Imperiall power." Through the Romans, the Saxons had learned that sovereignty and commonwealth were indistinguishable. Both of these elements of the polity rested on the power inherent in the people. Accepting that monarchy when "rightly ordered" was effective in spreading the true faith, the Saxons had nevertheless regarded "the publique weale" as the true object of the people's allegiance. Monarchs, in contrast, were simply intended to "mannage" the state and could be deposed if they failed in that

---

83. Nathaniel Bacon to William Berkeley, circa May 1676, in Billings, ed., *Papers of Sir William Berkeley*, 530; *Encyclopedia Virginia*, s.v. "Nathaniel Bacon (1647–1676)," by Brent Tarter and the *Dictionary of Virginia Biography*, accessed Apr. 24, 2016, http://www.encyclopediavirginia.org/bacon_nathaniel_1647-1676; *Oxford Dictionary of National Biography*, online ed., s.v. "Ray, John (1627–1705)," by Scott Mandelbrote, accessed Aug. 13, 2015, http://www.oxforddnb.com/view/article/23203, s.v. "Bacon, Nathaniel (bap. 1593, d. 1660)," by Janelle Greenberg, accessed Aug. 13, 2015, http://www.oxforddnb.com/view/article/1000; Nath[aniel] Bacon, *An Historicall Discourse of the Uniformity of the Government of England* (London, 1647), [A4]v.

duty. The Saxon people's freedom lay in part in their consensual participation in making laws in their assembly called the Wittagenmot, or Folkmot. But their liberty lay equally in their active contributions to the "strength and wealth of the Kingdom" through trade and especially military service. The importance of economic exchange to the well-being of the polity meant that the largest commercial towns deserved to be seen as "the very limbs of the Kingdome." Meanwhile, warriors needed to be free men who nevertheless obeyed the authority of higher-ranking military commanders, the so-called Decenners. This combination of commoner freedom and gentry supervision resulted in an orderly collectivity of households and local militias that for Bacon was the very essence of the "Saxon Commonweale": "By their armies gathered, not by promiscuous flocking of people, but by ordered concurrance of families, kindreds, and Decenners, all choosing their own leaders ... honour, love, and trust conspired together to leave no mans life in danger, nor death unrevenged." Once bound together in this mutual fellowship for their collective safety, the Saxons swore oaths manifesting, not their loyalty to the king, but their "tender regard of the publique above all." Protection was the ultimate responsibility of the Saxons' popular state, and that duty was properly in the hands of the entire "brethren." Only the "brotherhood" as a whole could satisfactorily preserve its own safety.[84]

The younger Bacon readily applied these ideas to Virginia's mounting frontier war. He would later explain that he felt compelled to lead an unauthorized band of armed colonists against the natives at the end of April 1676 because the "cryes of his Bretherens blood ... alarm'd and awakened him to this Publike Revenge." Like his senior Presbyterian relation, Bacon warmed to the idea of an imperiled brotherhood, and he repeatedly invoked the political imperative of the people's protection. His actions were conscionable, he argued, because they were directed at the "Countrys safety" and "the defence of our Brethren." By holding up Virginians as a populace whose security was forever endangered by a "most inveterate Enemy," Bacon justified the position that he declared openly among throngs of frightened planters: namely, that Indian peoples were "all alike" and that the colonists were therefore entitled to treat them universally as adversaries. Bacon was equally assertive in his contempt for Berkeley's horrified insistence that the treaties that the colony had historically established with particular Indian nations were sacred. For the governor and his circle of supporters, these alliances constituted ties of mutual promises that meaningfully recognized some natives as

---

84. Bacon, *Historicall Discourse*, 6, 49, 81, 82, 112, 117.

amicable neighbors who were united with the colony against common enemies. However, such Grotian reasoning fell flat for Bacon, who scoffed that this contrast between friendly and unfriendly native polities was a "fatall undistinguishable distinction." Bacon's own blend of Hobbesian and spiritualist logic reassured him that "the Principles of morality goodness and Justice" were on his side in seeking "to ruine and extirpate all Indians in Generall."[85]

On May 10, Berkeley declared Bacon a rebel on the grounds that he engaged in "unlawfull practices" while drawing others to his mistaken cause through "his specious pretences." The same day, Berkeley called for new elections, conceding that if planters regarded him as their "greatest Greviance" he would happily join them in petitioning the king for a new governor as long as they respected the General Assembly as the proper forum for consulting "for the Glory of God[,] the honor of his Majestie[,] and the publique Weale of this Country." These were the actions of a politician who perceived the winds of change as suddenly blowing at gale force. Eager to find safe harbor for a polity that he still regarded as filled with divine as well as political significance, Berkeley had good reason to see his young adversary as endangering in a few short months a long history of arduous commonwealth formation, or what Richard Kemp, in the rather different context of the 1640s, had called "a worke which had bene perfecting upwards of forty yeares att the expense of much blood and many millions of money." As would soon become apparent, Bacon was prepared not only to ally with other Hobbists against Berkeley's government but also to contemplate a previously unimaginable possibility: a Virginia body politic that had emancipated itself fully from its English sovereign. That extreme idea would prove to be a step too far. Although planters' awareness of the full scope of Bacon's doctrines would dawn only slowly, their basic commitment to the colony's

---

85. "A Narrative of the Rise, Progresse, and Cessation of the Late Rebellion in Virginia by His Majesties Commissioners," in Oberg, ed., *Samuel Wiseman's "Book of Record,"* 153; Nathaniel Bacon to William Berkeley, Apr. 27, 1676, in Billings, ed., *Papers of Sir William Berkeley*, 517; Nathaniel Bacon, Jr., "Manifesto," in Warren M. Billings, ed., *The Old Dominion in the Seventeenth Century: A Documentary History of Virginia, 1606-1700*, rev. ed. (Chapel Hill, N.C., 2007), 343, 345; "Mr. Bacon's Acct of Their Troubles in Virginia by ye Indians, June ye 18th, 1676," *WMQ*, 3d Ser., IX (1900), 6, 9. Bacon had plenty of company in his ferocious attitude toward Virginia's native neighbors. Some of his supporters were planters who had been petitioning Berkeley since the 1660s to give them a freer hand against the Indians; see John Catlett, Thomas Goodrich, John Weir, and Humphrey Booth to Berkeley, circa June 22, 1666, in Billings, ed., *Papers of Sir William Berkeley*, 284.

already established constitutional arrangements would serve as a powerful counterpoint to his exotic principles.[86]

Berkeley might very well have been the first person in the colony to grasp the Hobbesian drift of Bacon's thought. When the royal commissioners who were ultimately sent to investigate the rebellion described Bacon as possessing "an ominous pensive melancoly aspect" and as guilty of expressing "a Pestilent and prevalent Logicall discourse tendinge to Atheisme," they adopted a perception of Bacon that Berkeley had already intuited at a very early stage. Berkeley corresponded a number of times with his newest councillor toward the end of 1675 and beginning of 1676, and his letters convey a growing sense of frustration that Bacon showed him no "defference" and instead operated by his own judgment. This independent streak became a matter of particular concern for Berkeley as Bacon's belligerence toward Indians threatened to aggravate a rapidly worsening frontier conflict. Bacon's continuing stubbornness in this regard seems to have hardened Berkeley's growing conviction that his relation harbored worrying ideas, and his language suggests an emerging suspicion that Bacon was one of the youthful disciples of Hobbes that Clarendon had feared would inevitably arise in a Restoration that did too little to suppress Hobbes's books.[87]

In an appeal to the people on May 29, 1676, Berkeley urged Virginians to see Bacon as so attached to his erroneous ways that he amounted to a philosophical dogmatist. "I am of opinion it is only for Divels to be incorrigeable and men of Principles [are] like the worst of Divels," Berkeley wrote, "and thise he has if truth be reported to me of divers of his Expressions of Atheisme, tending to take away al religion and lawes." Among the reports to which Berkeley was alluding, one was undoubtedly a May 24 letter from his trusted councillor Abraham Wood. A justice of the peace and major general of forces in his region, Wood was a longtime planter who had arrived in Virginia around 1620. As a member of Berkeley's own generation of humanistic planters, he was similarly suspicious of the newfangled idea that the people's safety was enough on its own to determine the bounds of lawful power. On May 24, Wood wrote to the governor to report that Bacon and his party had

---

86. "Proclamation Suspending Nathaniel Bacon from Office," May 10, 1676, in Billings, ed., *Papers of Sir William Berkeley*, 519, Election Writ, May 10, 1676, 520, Richard Kemp to William Berkeley, Feb. 27, 1644/5, 63.

87. "Narrative of the Rise, Progresse, and Cessation of the Late Rebellion in Virginia by His Majesties Commissioners," in Oberg, ed., *Samuel Wiseman's "Book of Record,"* 146; William Berkeley to Nathaniel Bacon, Sept. 14, 1675, in Billings, ed., *Papers of Sir William Berkeley*, 487.

stopped by his home in Charles City County, demanding that he release into their custody an incarcerated Indian named Jack Nessom. When Wood resisted in the "Kings Majesties name" and asserted that Nessom was "my prisoner," Bacon's men cited a different authority, saying, "The Country would not bee soe sattisfyed." As if simply conveying the Hobbesian logic that both he and Berkeley knew lay behind this bold brandishing of the people's sovereignty, Wood provided a chilling description of Bacon's own role in the confrontation. In Wood's depiction, Bacon was nothing less than Leviathan incarnate: "Hee standing upon the Hill right against mee said I suppose the Major General hath power and I have some power to[o], I suppose hee meant the power of the sword." Wood's reference here was to Hobbes's own antihumanist view that civil bonds were meaningless apart from their guarantee of protection. As Hobbes had put it in *Leviathan*, "Covenants, without the Sword, are but Words, and of no strength to secure a man at all." If Berkeley's circle was increasingly convinced that it faced a distinctively Hobbist revolution, it was in part because the Baconites themselves were sometimes open in deploying Hobbes's theories, albeit in ways that Hobbes himself would have abhorred.[88]

One of Bacon's followers Anthony Arnold would later invoke Hobbes's sword-wielding sovereign in a remarkably bold challenge to the legitimacy of monarchy itself. Arnold reportedly asserted that "hee had noe kindnesse for Kings, and that they had noe Right but what they gott by Conquest and the Sword, and hee that could by Force of the Sword deprive them thereof had as good and just a Title to it as the King himselfe." Constitutional royalists like Clarendon had long feared precisely this kind of manipulation of Hobbes's starkly materialistic natural jurisprudence, and so it is unsurprising that Berkeley also picked up quickly on its familiar refrains.[89]

Berkeley and his followers were alert to signs that Bacon's movement was attracting other likeminded leaders, a coalescence of Hobbesian forces that affected Berkeley deeply. By July 1, Berkeley was conscious that Giles Bland had "openly and Insultingly declared himselfe of Mr. Bacons Party," a relationship that Berkeley apparently regarded as natural, if sickening, given that the Baconites' evident desire to "absolutely governe" in the colony mirrored

---

88. "Declaration and Remonstrance," May 29, 1676, in Billings, ed., *Papers of Sir William Berkeley*, 527, Abraham Wood to William Berkeley, May 24, 1676, 522; Hobbes, *Leviathan*, ed. Tuck, 117.

89. "From the Commissioners to Mr. Secretary Williamson," Mar. 27, 1677, in Oberg, ed., *Samuel Wiseman's "Book of Record,"* 104.

the Hobbist intentions of English officials like Danby. By September, he was aware that Bacon also enjoyed a close alliance with Drummond as well as with another coleader named Richard Lawrence. An Oxford-educated man who kept a tavern at Jamestown and sometimes served as its burgess, Lawrence soon earned a reputation as "Mr. Bacons Principall Consultant." Evidently sharing Bacon's philosophical leanings, he was endowed, according to one writer, with "such learning . . . that inables a Man for the management of more then ordnary imployments." The latter reference was to the baleful rumor that circulated shortly after the uprising that Lawrence was the rebel who eventually set fire to his own house in order to burn Jamestown to the ground. Predictably, given this cavalier disrespect for the established order, Lawrence became known among the Berkeleyites simply as "that Athisticall and scandalous p[er]son," another Hobbist among the Hobbists.[90]

For Berkeley, the convergence of all these proponents of Hobbes's dark philosophy on his government was almost too much to bear. His rapidly growing anxiety about the "seditious sperits amongst our selves" explains why he responded to Bacon and his followers so ferociously, to the point where his own anger greatly exacerbated the chaos and fearfulness of an already perplexing moment. Blinded by his rage and overzealous in his determination to snuff out the Hobbists, he alienated planters at the very moment he most needed their support. Yet, his personal incapacities as Virginia's leader at the end of his governorship helps to underscore the political achievement of his earlier years. Rather than giving way to the Hobbists, Virginia's commonwealth held firm against the forces suddenly arrayed against it. Perhaps the greatest testament to Berkeley's success in buttressing the colony's polity on solid humanist foundations during his quarter century in office was that, ultimately, it was not his leadership but rather the tenacity of the planters themselves that secured Virginia's established order.[91]

The planters were slower to gather the strangeness of Bacon's ideas but

90. William Berkeley to Thomas Ludwell, July 1, 1676, in Billings, ed., *Papers of Sir William Berkeley*, 538, "Proclamation Pardoning Rebels," circa Sept. 7, 1676, 543; T[homas] M[athew], "The Beginning, Progress, and Conclusion of Bacon's Rebellion, 1675–1676," in Andrews, *Narratives of the Insurrections*, 30, "The History of Bacon's and Ingram's Rebellion," [1676], 96; [William Sherwood], "Virginias Deploured Condition: Or an Impartiall Narrative of the Murders Comitted by the Indians There, and of the Sufferings of His Ma[jes]ties Loyall Subjects under the Rebellious Outrages of M[iste]r Nathaniell Bacon Jun[io]r to the Tenth Day of August A[nn]o Dom[ini] 1676," in Massachusetts Historical Society, *Collections*, 4th Ser., IX (1871), 170.

91. Berkeley to Ludwell, Apr. 1, 1676, Billings, ed., *Papers of Sir William Berkeley*, 508.

also sensitive to any change that too greatly violated their sense of conscionable action. They initially saw Bacon, according to the royal commissioners' report, as "the only Patron of the Country and Preserver of their lives and fortunes," a savior who understood the people's plight. Their favorable impression of him also rested on his political stature. Bacon's membership in the Council of State helped to endorse his conduct even when he openly defied the governor's commands. Berkeley's recognition of the luster that Bacon received from his conciliar seat explains the hastiness with which he suspended Bacon as soon as he turned to the population at large. Just as planters in the 1630s had been prepared to follow Samuel Mathews and his fellow councillors against Governor Harvey, the inhabitants likewise looked to the council for leadership amid their current confusions. Their uncertainty about how to judge the legitimacy of Bacon's actions only increased after Berkeley tried to reach an accord with him that led to his official pardon and reinstatement on the council as a "Penitent Sinner." When Berkeley balked in authorizing further violence against the native American population, however, Bacon, still eager for an unrestrained war, turned once again to armed planters to exact a commission by force.[92]

Although news that the governor had declared Bacon a rebel and was mounting a militia against him and his followers dramatically transformed Bacon's movement from a questionable military expedition into an outright civil war, Bacon's supporters still had good grounds to see his conduct as licit. As many planters asserted after the uprising, they misunderstood the circumstances behind his newly appointed office as Virginia's general, "not Knowing his Commission to be violently extorted." His invocation of the natural law of self-preservation in arguing that colonists had no choice but "to turne our Swords to our own defence" was familiar enough rhetoric, not unlike that which the colony had used against the Puritan Commonwealth years earlier. Likewise, his condemnations of Berkeley for attacking planters while "his Majesties Country here lyes in blood" rang with a similarly reassuring focus on the sanctity of the bond between king and people that had long defined Virginia's commonwealth.[93]

Bacon's efforts to solicit the support of the colony's gentry population and propertied planters also confirmed his upright conduct. A relation written by Mary Horsmanden Filmer Byrd, William Byrd's wife, around June

---

92. "Narrative of the Rise, Progresse, and Cessation of the Late Rebellion in Virginia by His Majesties Commissioners," in Oberg, ed., *Samuel Wiseman's "Book of Record,"* 147, 150.

93. Ibid., 154, 251.

sought to affirm the licit nature of Bacon's campaign for an unidentified group of English readers. Officials like Danby could be expected to see the former sister-in-law of the ultra-royalist Robert Filmer as a credible witness of the events unfolding on the other side of the ocean. "The most of th[e]m w[i]th Mr. Bacon," she penned, "were substantiall housekeepers who bore their own charges in this warre against the Indians." Such a portrait of Bacon's followers as heads of households countered the Berkeleyites' claim that the rabble alone had been seduced away from their allegiance. It also conveyed many Baconites' own preferred view of themselves: namely, as the indisputable embodiment of the Virginian polity, a suffering populace who now anticipated their king's protection. Given their self-image as loyal subjects, many of Bacon's followers must have taken comfort in his repeated insistence that his intention in leading them against Berkeley and his government was simply to "represent our sad and heavy grievances to his most sacred Majesty as our Refuge and Sanctuary," a statement that would later appear to have been more a salve to the planters' own anxieties about betraying their allegiance than a true reflection of Bacon's own royalism. The planters' confidence in Bacon, however, did not last long, and the rock on which it foundered was unsurprisingly the often-treacherous one of oaths, those critical tests of loyalty that demanded that subscribers weigh solemnly whether the pathways they were walking were truly lawful.[94]

Bacon imposed a number of oaths on his followers that progressively alienated their support, each new demand on their scruples revealing just how great the chasm was between their sense of the moral order and the one by which Bacon directed his own actions. The frontiersmen who first agreed to follow him without Berkeley's commission signed a paper "Circular wise" and agreed to "stick fast together" in a crude brandy- and rum-filled ritualization of their band of brothers. A more formal swearing ceremony took place on July 15 during Bacon's "Generall Rendezvous" at the falls of the James River shortly after he intimidated Berkeley into appointing him general. He personally took the Oaths of Allegiance and Supremacy as a show of "his Loyallty to his Prince," encouraging the armed planters who had joined him to do the same. In addition, he required his soldiers to declare an oath of

---

94. "Mrs. Byrd's Relation, Who Lived Nigh Mr. Bacon in Virginia and Came from There July Last for Feare of the Indians," [n.d.], *WMQ*, 3d Ser., IX (1900–1901), 10; Bacon, "Manifesto," in Billings, ed., *Old Dominion*, 346. On Mrs. Byrd, see *Encyclopedia Virginia*, s.v. "William Byrd (ca. 1652–1704)," by Martin H. Quitt and the *Dictionary of Virginia Biography*, accessed Apr. 22, 2016, http://www.encyclopediavirginia.org/byrd_william_ca_1652-1704.

fidelity, one of whose provisions was to alert him to any "Plott or conspiracy" against his leadership. The real turning point in the conflict occurred on August 3 at yet another engagement convention, a gathering at Middle Plantation that attracted "most of the prime Gent[le]men in these parts," including several members of the Council of State. A "long debate pro and con" took place over the terms by which planters were to engage to Bacon's authority.⁹⁵

The planters found Bacon's views expressed at the Middle Plantation conference shocking in their divergence from conventional Christian humanism. Planters were also amazed by his "sophisticall dixterety," a great "many of those counted the wisest men in the Countrey" left so stunned by his "subtill pretences" that "at length there was litle said, by any, against the same." The arguments he put forward proved heedless of "all reasoning to the contrary." One attendee noted Bacon's mystifying insistence on the "harmlesness of the Oath, as he would have it to be." Evidently the leader to whom planters were looking as their "Gardian Angle" did not take their bond with God very seriously at all. Likewise, he justified the colonists' opposition against Berkeley's government on the bare foundation of "necessity," an imperative that Hobbes had placed right at the heart of his philosophy of rightful action but that seemed more "specious" to those Middle Plantation participants whose humanism inclined more to the idea of the ethical gravity of all volitional conduct. It was the oath's provisions, however, that most revealed the exotic way forward that Bacon was offering the planters. Not only were they to swear to the illicitness of Berkeley and his Council of State in their dealings with him, thereby testifying that his proceedings were lawful. More horrifically, they were to swear their loyalty to him even against the king's forces if the latter should arrive before Bacon had an opportunity to communicate the people's grievances clearly to royal officials. This shocking requirement sent a wave of panic through the assembled inhabitants, who saw their very capacity to safely challenge Berkeley's authority as resting on their continuing loyalty to the king. To assuage their distress, many of the planters swore to the oath under certain qualifications. Bacon himself assured them that, "if there was any thing in the same of such dangerous consequence that might ta[i]nt the subscribers Alegence, that then they should stand absalved from all and every part of the s[ai]d oath." Such mental exemptions and equivo-

---

95. "Narrative of the Rise, Progresse and Cessation of the Late Rebellion in Virginia by His Majesties Commissioners," in Oberg, ed., *Samuel Wiseman's "Book of Record,"* 147, 153, 156; "The History of Bacon's and Ingram's Rebellion," [1676], in Andrews, *Narratives of the Insurrections*, 60.

cations had often figured in the politics of oath taking during the Civil War years, and here they served similarly to ease the thorny questions of conscience raised by measures that might throw into doubt one's bond to rightful rulers. The sense that Bacon was seducing the people into swearing an "Illegal Oath" became a nagging concern that would build quickly over the next few weeks. By the time of Bacon's death on October 26, his movement had already bled many followers.[96]

Although the rebellion would limp along for several more months under the new leadership of one Joseph Ingram, the uprising had lost much of its original legitimacy. Virginia's planters neither fully accepted Bacon's Hobbist reasoning nor were willing to relinquish civil arrangements that still carried for them powerful connotations of divine approval. Disagreeing that self-preservation alone determined the nature of their polity, they continued to see their commonwealth as a body politic that bound them together with their king and God in reciprocal ties that could not simply be relinquished at will.

In Bacon's Rebellion, Virginia's commonwealth confronted the era's Hobbism in a direct and forceful way and yet survived the encounter. The royal commissioners hinted at a haunted feeling when they described Bacon's death not only as brought about by "providence" but also as leaving forever obscure the full nature of the young rebel's "designes, which none but the eye of Omniscience could penetrate." One writer conveyed how powerfully Bacon's Middle Plantation oath in particular had left planters anguished and divided. Some cursed it, he observed, as aiding in their "approcheing destruction"; others wished for Bacon's "presence, as there onely Rock of safety"; while others "look'd upon him as the onely quick sands ordained to swollow up and sinke the ship that should set them on shore, or keep them from drownding in the whirle poole of confuseion." There was a profound sense in the colony of having approached uncomfortably close to the edge of a frightening abyss.[97]

Troubling hints of the lengths to which Bacon had been prepared to take his rebellious activities appeared in testimony that emerged after his death.

---

96. "The History of Bacon's and Ingram's Rebellion," [1676], in Andrews, *Narratives of the Insurrections,* 52, 62–64, 70. On mental reservations and the politics of oaths in the English Civil War, see Vallance, *Revolutionary England and the National Covenant,* xx.

97. "Narrative of the Rise, Progresse and Cessation of the Late Rebellion in Virginia by His Majesties Commissioners," in Oberg, ed., *Samuel Wiseman's "Book of Record,"* 171; "The History of Bacon's and Ingram's Rebellion," [1676], in Andrews, *Narratives of the Insurrections,* 66.

One glimpse into his fearsome imagination came in the form of a transcript of a conversation that had taken place in early September between Bacon and John Goode, a Henrico County planter. Byrd, who directed Goode to record the account for the royal commissioners, no doubt saw it as his own penitential offering in exchange for the king's pardon, for the document was remarkable in casting light on Bacon's principles. According to Goode, Bacon shared freely with him his belief that "the mind of this Country, and of Maryland, and Carolina alsoe" was "to cast of[f] their Governours" and set up for themselves. When Goode expressed alarm that Bacon seemed to desire a "total defection from Majestie and our native Country," Bacon coolly answered, "Have not many princes lost their dominions soe?" Goode's further protest that the planters would not easily sustain themselves without their connection to their sovereign prompted yet another unconcerned reply. Like any independent people in the emerging commercial Atlantic, Bacon said, they could rely on trade with "the King of France, or the States of Holland." Goode's relation was startling but also believable, for Bacon's followers sometimes voiced similar sentiments. Berkeley's ally William Sherwood, for instance, had heard some of the Baconites boast of "throwing off all allegiance to his most sacred Majesty and the Crowne of England, and dareingly say they will have the dutch to trade thither, with such like expressions." These kinds of statements highlighted how readily Hobbes's ideas could have been twisted and spread to render Virginia's historical commonwealth bonds well nigh meaningless. Nevertheless, those ties had withstood their most revolutionary moment. In the end, Virginia's planter community had reached an exceedingly vexed moral crossroads and had made a choice. True to Berkeley's establishmentarianism, they had opted to preserve their polity, holding on to it as a robust act of faith in its lawfulness.[98]

The colony entered the late seventeenth century still committed to its original civil integrity while at the same time conscious of the challenging new political landscape that it confronted in facing the future. This complicated environment was epitomized in the differing philosophies of the three royal commissioners sent to inquire into the causes of Bacon's Rebellion and oversee Virginia's return to order. As Berkeley quickly recognized, the future of the colony lay poised between the central Hobbist state envisioned by one faction and the contractual government posed by the other.

98. John Goode to William Berkeley, Jan. 30, 1676/7, in Billings, ed., *Papers of Sir William Berkeley*, 566, 567; Sherwood, "Virginias Deploured Condition," in Massachusetts Historical Society, *Collections*, 4th Ser., IX (1871), 176.

Two of the officials, Colonel Herbert Jeffreys and Sir John Berry, were career military officers attached to the household of James, duke of York. They gravitated toward the duke's absolutist vision of the Hobbesian state. Their anticontractualist outlook received expression in the words of Jeffrey's onetime lieutenant Sir Richard Bulstrode, who wrote that there was "nothing more irreconcileable and contradictory, than a Contract by which our Kings are made judicially accountable to their People, or censurable for Miscarriages in their Government," for "by the Constitution of the *English* Government, the King is singly Sovereign, and no Power on Earth co-ordinate with him." Perceiving that such unapologetic Hobbists were effectively the military counterparts of Bland's new breed of treasury agents, Berkeley opposed them from the outset and even at one point directed a calculated insult against them that was highly reminiscent of the campaign of humiliation that Bland had launched against his own government. Sending a coach to receive them as a faux-ceremonial gesture, he quietly replaced its postilion with an enslaved black man who was also the common hangman. The affronted officials immediately condemned this "High Indignitie," no doubt seeing clearly that Berkeley was making a crude reference to the political slavery and civil death that the colony could expect if it fell under such absolutist rule.[99]

The third commissioner, in contrast, was a contractualist through and through, for he was none other than Berkeley's old ally Francis Moryson. Since 1663, Moryson had been in England as the colony's London-based agent, and, during his time there, he seems to have aligned himself with the faction in the Cabal ministry that centered on Anthony Ashley Cooper, first earl of Shaftesbury, his secretary John Locke, and their mutual friend the secretary of state for the Northern Department Henry Coventry. Adherents of Hobbes's theory of the unitary state, especially as a solution to the dangers of civil war, these men sought to reconcile his ideal of a unity of wills between sovereign and people with a conception of limited as opposed to absolute monarchy. Shaftesbury became president of the Council of Trade and Foreign Plantations in September 1672, and Locke served as the assistant to the ubiquitous plantation advisor Worsley, now employed as the council's

99. Sir Richard Bulstrode, *Memoirs and Reflections upon the Reign and Government of K. Charles the Ist and K. Charles the IId* (London, 1721), 66–67; John Berry, Herbert Jeffreys, and Francis Moryson to William Berkeley, Apr. 23, 1677, in Billings, ed., *Papers of Sir William Berkeley*, 608. On Bulstrode's connection to Jeffreys, see Stephen Saunders Webb, *The Governors-General: The English Army and the Definition of the Empire, 1569–1681* (Chapel Hill, N.C., 1987), 123–124.

secretary. The project of these men was the familiar one of bringing the colonies into closer orbit around a perceived metropolitan center. As Locke put it in explaining why Jamaica's council of state should be appointed in England rather than by the governor, "The Government would thereby more immediately depend upon his Majesty," a sentiment more or less the same as Worsley's and Povey's position over the years. In keeping with these ideas, Moryson remained true to his constitutional royalist principles while nevertheless moving toward a Hobbesian conception of colonies as provinces.[100]

Berkeley had no question that a gulf separated Moryson's politics from that of his fellow commissioners. As Berkeley wrote bluntly to Jeffreys in April 1677, Moryson had, "besides other advantages," a knowledge of, and respect for, "the Lawes[,] Customes[,] and Nature of the people [in Virginia] with all which you are as yett utterly unacquainted." The remark captured succinctly Berkeley's instinctual grasp of where colonial politics were headed at the outset of the Enlightenment age. As the sovereign state evolved from being a bold proposition to an accepted reality, the question would not be the simple one of whether such an entity could rule licitly over the communities that continued to look to it for legitimacy. It would rather be the more complicated issue of whether those communities could be governed effectively without acknowledging that they, too, had laws, histories, and identities of their own. Given the long Renaissance era of colonization, those factors in turn were almost unthinkable except in the moral terms by which Christian humanists had historically defined their commonwealths.[101]

---

100. John Locke to Lord Arlington, Jan. 6, 1674, TNA, CO 1/3, fol. 4r, quoted in Thomas Leng, "Shaftesbury's Aristocratic Empire," in John Spurr, ed., *Anthony Ashley Cooper, First Earl of Shaftesbury, 1621–1683* (Surrey, U.K., 2011), 118–119. Leng's article provides a good analysis of Shaftesbury's imperial politics and especially the tensions he perceived between the colonies' political integrity and the need for central state authority.

101. William Berkeley to Herbert Jeffreys, Apr. 28, 1677, in Billings, ed., *Papers of Sir William Berkeley*, 610.

EPILOGUE

In the 1750s and 1760s, Richard Bland, a Virginia planter, lawyer, and veteran lawmaker with an abiding antiquarian interest in the colonies' legal and constitutional origins, cast back over a hundred years to a Renaissance period that he was confident possessed the key to understanding the political nature of the British American empire. Working his way through such sixteenth- and seventeenth-century texts as the royal charters that Elizabeth I issued to Sir Walter Ralegh and that James I granted to the Virginia Company as well as the numerous other remonstrances, declarations, and proclamations that had crisscrossed the Atlantic in the colony's earliest decades, he developed a sophisticated theory of the relationship between the plantations and their mother country that owed as much to his investigations of Virginia's past as to his intensive readings in natural philosophy, international law, belles lettres, and scripture. Putting his historical knowledge to work, he wrote several tracts in response to such midcentury controversies as the Pistole Fee dispute and the Stamp Act crisis. He argued that the empire had been, from its beginning, a confederation of individual polities that he called "states." Each state centered vitally on the intimate and mutually benefiting bond formed between the "people" of that particular dominion and the English king. This bond was one that both parties, people as well as monarch, had entered freely (Bland's view of the "people" quietly excluded slaves) and whose terms they both played a role in working out over a period of time, with particular vigor, in Virginia's case, in the decades leading up to the Restoration. The "Compact" formed those many years ago, Bland reasoned, still stood. It created "civil Rights" that no sovereign could willfully violate, for the "Rights of the Subjects are so secured by Law that they cannot be deprived of the least part of their property without their own consent." Indeed, Bland wrote, the law of the community stood as a bulwark against even the greatest "Leviathan of Power." This creature, he made clear, became truly monstrous when it disregarded the constitutional bounds that rightly contained it. Condemning the "Iniquity of every measure which has the least tendency to break through the legal Forms of government," Bland gave his jurisprudence a rich moral quality that carried distinct echoes of the Tudor-Stuart age from which the colony had arisen.[1]

Fittingly, in the months before his death on October 26, 1776, Bland was present at the Virginia constitutional convention where delegates for the newly independent state agreed to call their polity a "Commonwealth." Oaths, commission, seals, and writs that had once referenced the king were now to run "in the name of the Commonwealth of Virginia," and indictments were to specify that malefactors had violated "the peace and dignity of the Commonwealth." Although made without fanfare, the decision to name the polity a commonwealth nevertheless imparted conviction, for the term became an enduring designation. Years later, the word would still capture succinctly the sense of Virginia as a community forged by reciprocal ties of obligation that benefited the polity as a whole. Few symbols could have more vividly underscored the persistence of Renaissance principles in an Enlightenment era that had otherwise veered in new directions.[2]

Bland's grounding of Virginia's history in the colony's Renaissance origins provides a glimpse of both the staying power of those earlier Christian humanist ideals as well as their subtle transformation amid the changing circumstances and evolving values of eighteenth-century Anglo-American life. As a devoted antiquarian, Bland was highly alert to the nuances of the past. He spent so much time studying the colony's founding documents that one commentator quipped his complexion was as "staunch and tough as whitleather," having "something of the look of [the] musty old Parchen'ts w'ch he handleth and studieth much." Yet, he was no naïf on the subject of the sovereign state. As befitted the great grandson of Richard Bennett and distant cousin to Giles Bland, he was, on the contrary, a keen student of the theory. His own intellectual touchstones included such latter-day inter-

---

1. Richard Bland, *An Inquiry into the Rights of the British Colonies, Intended as an Answer to the Regulations Lately Made concerning the Colonies, and the Taxes Imposed upon Them Considered...* (Williamsburg, Va., 1766), 14, 23, 26; Richard Bland, *A Fragment on the Pistole Fee, Claimed by the Governor of Virginia, 1753*, ed. Worthington Chauncey Ford (Brooklyn, N.Y., 1891), 37, 38.

2. The Constitution or Form of Government, Agreed to and Resolved upon by the Delegates and Representatives of the Several Counties and Corporations of Virginia, in *Ordinances Passed at a General Convention, of Delegates and Representatives, from the Several Counties and Corporations of Virginia, Held at the Capitol, in the City of Williamsburg, on Monday, the 6th of May, Anno. Dom. 1776* (Richmond, Va., 1816), 6.

preters and critics of Thomas Hobbes as John Locke, Emer de Vattel, and William Wollaston. Indeed, the premise of the unitary state was so fundamental to Bland's outlook as to help dictate his categories of political and historical analysis. Rather than seeing the sixteenth and seventeenth centuries straightforwardly on their terms, he struggled to reconcile their logic with his own. His treatment of Virginia's commonwealth origins was a complex synthesis of Renaissance and Enlightenment ideas. In reconstructing Virginia's pre-Restoration history, he gave voice to the lingering attraction of the notion of the colonial commonwealth while also welcoming in the resonant new concept of state sovereignty.[3]

Bland wrote against a political-philosophical backdrop filled with change, perhaps in no respect more dynamic than in the sustained efforts by imperial officials to realize the ideal of state unity. The Restoration regimes of Charles II and James II had continued that Hobbesian project in a way that Hobbes himself would have considered appropriate. Not only did they challenge charters that no longer satisfied the sovereign will but they also attacked the language by which the colonies had originally justified themselves. In 1665, commissioners authorized by Charles II to investigate the Massachusetts Bay colony took particular umbrage at words like "publick" and "commonwealth" found in the colony's *Booke of Generall Lawes and Liberties*. These terms were to be forcefully expunged on the grounds that they conveyed an inflated sense of the colony's status and, in particular, an independence from the king's sovereignty. "If there be any other undecent

---

3. Roger Atkinson to Samuel Pleasants, Oct. 1, 1774, in A. J. Morrison, ed., "The Letters of Roger Atkinson, 1769–1776," *Virginia Magazine of History and Biography*, XV (1908), 356. On Bland and his significance to the constitutional debates of the imperial crisis, see Jack P. Greene, *The Constitutional Origins of the American Revolution*, enlarged ed. (New York, 2011), 75, 76, 78, 80, 81–82, 83, 88–89, 92, 129; Greene, *Peripheries and Center: Constitutional Development in the Extended Polities of the British Empire and the United States, 1607–1788* (Athens, Ga., 1986), 86, 87, 88–89, 90, 94–96, 112, 121; Bernard Bailyn, *The Ideological Origins of the American Revolution* (Cambridge, Mass., 1992), 5, 8, 11, 15, 32, 58, 64, 81, 82, 168, 176, 181, 210–211, 212, 235, 252–253, 254, 258, 307, 308; J. G. A. Pocock, "Empire, State, and Confederation: The War of American Independence as a Crisis in Multiple Monarchy," in Pocock, *The Discovery of Islands: Essays in British History* (Cambridge, 2005), 134–163; Craig Yirush, *Settlers, Liberty, and Empire: The Roots of Early American Political Theory, 1675–1770* (New York, 2011), 24, 158, 162–163, 172–179, 183, 229–233, 248, 261; Clinton Rossiter, *Seedtime of the Republic: The Origin of the American Tradition of Political Liberty* (New York, 1953), 247–280; Rossiter, "Richard Bland: The Whig in America," *William and Mary Quarterly*, 3d Ser., X (1953), 33–79.

expressions and repetitions of the word, 'commonwealth,' 'state,' and the like, in other pages," they said, "wee desire they may be changed." To the new generation of post-Hobbesian statists, any hint that a colony aspired to a state-like condition was clear evidence of seditious intent. Writing to the Lords of Trade in 1676, the customs agent Edward Randolph warned that settlers in Massachusetts had "formed themselves into a Common Wealth, denying any Appeals to England, and contrary to other Plantations doe not take the Oath of Allegiance."[4]

James II's most extreme experiment with concentrating colonial government was his short-lived attempt to reduce the northern plantations into a single Dominion of New England. A dramatic attempt to centralize authority, it sought to "join[,] annex[,] and unite" colonies that had previously been woefully separate into a single whole. James's stated rationale for this change, which followed directly on the heels of his annulment of the Massachusetts charter in 1684, was that it was "necessary for our service and for the better protection and security of our subjects." Massachusetts inhabitants would ultimately rebel against an arrangement that placed them under a New York-based governor who was under no obligation to govern by local laws or in consultation with local assemblies. Arguing that "the Hedge which kept us from the wild Beasts of Field" had been "effectually broken down," they could think of no other explanation for this assault on their polity than that "the great Scarlet Whore" lay behind it. Yet, the later Stuarts' attacks on the colonies' commonwealth integrity were not directed at the saints alone. Virginia, in the aftermath of Bacon's Rebellion, was also the subject of new inquiries into its original legitimating discourse.[5]

In the mid-1680s, Governor Lord Howard of Effingham scrutinized the language of the colony's laws and found a telltale offender in the word "publique." Such "a name," Effingham complained to the colony's assembly, was

---

4. "To the Generall Court of His Majesties Colony of the Massachusetts," May 24, 1665, in Nathaniel B. Shurtleff, ed., *Records of the Governor and Company of the Massachusetts Bay in New England...*, IV, Part 2, *1661–1674* (Boston, 1854), 211, 213; "Representation of the Affaires of N: England by Mr. Randolph," in Robert Noxon Toppan, ed., *Edward Randolph; Including His Letters and Official Papers...* (Boston, 1898–1899), II, 266.

5. "Commission of Sir Edmund Andros for the Dominion of New England," Apr. 7, 1688, The Avalon Project, Yale Law School, Lillian Goldman Law Library, http://avalon.law.yale.edu/17th_century/mass06.asp; "The Boston Declaration of Grievances," April 18, 1689, in Michael G. Hall, Lawrence H. Leder, and Michael Kammen, eds., *The Glorious Revolution in America: Documents on the Colonial Crisis of 1689* (Chapel Hill, N.C., 1964), 42.

"certainely most odious under a Regal Government and that which doth in name, soe in consequence, but little differ from that detestable one (Republick)." In a speech before the colony's burgesses, he announced his chosen remedy for three generations of laws that lamentably placed at the very heart of the Virginia polity the conceit of "the publique" — "as then so termed," he dourly acknowledged. Reassuring the burgesses how "very much persuaded" he was that the king's loyal Virginia subjects "really abhorre[d]" a kingless republic, he insisted that they promptly redraft all of the colony's laws to make fees appropriated, not to the public, but "to his Majesties use for the benefit of this his Majesties Dominion." No wonder the Virginians of Bland's day would so eagerly reclaim the designation commonwealth. By the Hobbesian reasoning that drove these Restoration-era language campaigns, the very words by which the colonies had justified themselves now amounted to an offense against the state.[6]

In disabusing the colonies of their commonwealth status, late-seventeenth-century officials assuredly attributed to colonists a far greater longing for autonomy than had in fact characterized their Renaissance political experience. Determined to redefine the state as a polity with a single sovereign center, royal agents like Randolph and Effingham used the accusation of the planters' antimonarchical leanings and disdain for lawful authority as a blunt intimidation tactic, a stick intended to cow the colonies into accepting their new inferior identity as provinces. Lost in such a rebranding of colonists as would-be revolutionaries was the colonizers' own long history of political maneuvers to steer monarchs toward a greater commitment to their American dominions. In effect, the era's statists were turning the original logic of Renaissance colonization on its head. Rather than transatlantic polities meant to overcome the moral distance imposed by the ocean by tying planters firmly to God and king, the colonial commonwealths now acquired a reputation for independent mindedness and antiauthoritarianism, a rebellious persona instantiated especially in their evident failure to give the state the respect to which it was now due.

Francis Burghill, the onetime governor of Calshot Castle who angled in these years for a gubernatorial post on one of the Atlantic or Caribbean islands, reinforced just such an unflattering portrait of the colonies as rebel-

---

6. H. R. McIlwaine, ed., *Legislative Journals of the Council of Colonial Virginia* (Richmond, Va., 1918), I, 66; Journal of the House of Burgesses, Nov. 9, 1685, Effingham Papers, 5, Library of Congress, Washington, D.C. See also, McIlwaine, ed., *Journals of the House of Burgesses of Virginia, 1659/60–1693* (Richmond, Va., 1914), 223.

lious provinces when he argued that Bermudans' desire for greater control over their judiciary was simply out of step with the Hobbesian imperatives of the moment. "Is it reasonable," he asked "to thinke the Kinge willbe Setting up Comon welthes in any of his Dominions at this tyme of Day?" In a similar slight aimed at plantations that failed to comply with their provincial condition, Christopher Codrington in Nevis complained in 1689 that the West Indian colony's assembly took on a "high and mighty" style as if it were a parliament on the order of England's own Parliament, and "some here have almost the vanity . . . to fancy these Colonys Independent States." Robert Quarry, in Virginia, likewise accused planters of acting on the basis of "Commonwealth Principles." The allegation hinted that any effort on the colonists' part to insist on their membership in a commonwealth that held king and people alike to their godly responsibilities would be met with unreserved suspicion as evidence of republican sentiments. Such a logic placed planters in the position of having to choose between surrendering their customary understanding of their polities and risking the displeasure of monarchs who took Hobbes's framework as a significant reinforcement to their own absolutist theory of royal sovereignty.[7]

Even the ascendancy of the Whigs after the Glorious Revolution did little to stop the subtle recalibrating of the meaning of the state that rendered the very idea of colonial commonwealths harder and harder to sustain. Hobbes's ideas experienced considerable adaptation in the late seventeenth and eighteenth century as the era's constitutionalists made the concept of state unity their own. In accepting the premise that sovereignty and commonwealth were fully united rather than merely consensually joined, Whigs of various stripes also embraced the logic that divisions in the state's singular integrity interfered with the careful balancing of interests that only a recognized governing center could manage. As a result, a palpable tinge of metropolitan contempt worked its way into officials' criticisms of the colonists' persistence in clinging to their plantations' civil stature. Caleb Heathcote, survey general of customs, snidely mocked settlers in 1719 for their gripes and groans

7. [Francis] Burghill to Samuel Trott, Dec. 31, 1681, Rawlinson Mss, D 764, fol. 35, Bodleian Library, cited in Owen Stanwood, *The Empire Reformed: English America in the Age of the Glorious Revolution* (Philadelphia, 2011), 42; Christopher Codrington to the Committee on Trade and Plantations, Nov. 8, 1689, CO 153/4/194 197, 199–200, National Archives, Kew, cited in Stanwood, *Empire Reformed*, 173; Resolutions of the House of Burgesses, Apr. 24, 1705, in H. R. McIlwaine, ed., *Journals of the House of Burgesses, 1702/3–1705, 1705–1706, 1710–1712* (Richmond, Va., 1912), 93.

over "the growth and prosperity of their little commonwealths." How could it be "imagined," asked members of the Board of Trade in the late 1740s, "that this happy regulated Monarchy, should ever intend to establish such little independent Commonwealths"? By the 1760s, George Grenville's ministry was prepared to see the Stamp Act, whatever its flaws, as useful at least for exposing continuing colonial confusions that would undoubtedly prove detrimental to the British state.[8]

In *The Regulations Lately Made concerning the Colonies, and the Taxes Imposed upon Them Considered* (1765), the Grenville ministry's answer to colonial complaints about the anticipated law, Thomas Whately cut right to the heart of concerns regarding the proper relationship between the crown and her colonies. He called attention to the confederated rather than consolidated notion of polity that seemed implicit in the planters' outcry against the new taxes. If the colonies thought of themselves as states, and their assemblies as versions of Parliament, he warned, "Their Connexion would otherwise be an Alliance, not an Union." "They would be no longer one State, but a Confederacy of many." The entire notion of the British state would be rendered meaningless.[9]

Hans Stanley, whose support for Grenville had at one point put him in the running for one of the lordships of the Treasury, similarly denounced the colonists' reasoning as leading inexorably toward an enfeebling British fissiparousness. During the debates over the Stamp Act in the House of Commons in February 1766, he sounded an alarmist note: "The danger is not approaching but already begun. They have begun a Federal Union." This political reality, which he saw signaled especially in the colonists' willingness to meet in an unauthorized Stamp Act Congress, called for resolute action on the part of Parliament. Although he was in favor of "the most moderate measures, provided they do not prove fatal to our authority," he worried aloud that "if we do not mix firmness with our lenity, they [that is, the colo-

---

8. Caleb Heathcote to the Board of Trade, Sept. 7, 1719, quoted in Dixon Ryan Fox, *Caleb Heathcote, Gentleman Colonist: The Story of a Career in the Province of New York, 1692–1721* (New York, 1926), 188; "Some Considerations Relating to the Present Condition of the Plantations; with Proposals for a Better Regulation of Them," n.d., Colonial Office Papers, Class 5, Public Record Office, London, V, fols. 313–318, reprinted in Jack P. Greene, ed., *Great Britain and the American Colonies, 1606–1763* (Columbia, S.C., 1970), 269 (Greene suggests that the document was probably prepared in 1748 or 1749).

9. [Thomas Whately], *The Regulations Lately Made concerning the Colonies, and the Taxes Imposed upon Them, Considered* (London, 1765), 38.

nists] will become more useful allies to France and Spain than to this country." Clearly the tense international environment after the Treaty of Paris of 1763 was part of what had aroused Stanley's distress. But, so, too, was his awareness that Hobbes's theories lent themselves not only to the strengthening of governments but also to their dissolution. Observing fretfully that certain unnamed commentators "have reasoned as if the first Planters had recovered their State of Nature," he insisted, "this Doctrine [would be] mischievous to the Colonies." "No British Subject can renounce his Allegiance," he concluded. Given his language elsewhere in the debates of impending "civil war," there can be no doubt what he feared. A little more than a century after *Leviathan*'s original publication, Stanley, like Whately, perceived nothing less than the onset of a Hobbesian crisis. Britain's commonwealth, lurching under the resistance of its provincial American members, careened once again toward the terrible political splintering that awaited any such unnatural strain on the state's unity of wills.[10]

From his own vantage point across the Atlantic, Bland observed bitterly the recurring metropolitan efforts to give the state greater substance at the colonies' expense, and he took particular offense at what he recognized as the Grenville ministry's newfound determination to bring the realm's restless provinces to heel. He wrote his *Inquiry into the Rights of the British Colonies* (1766) as a trenchant reply to Whately's published justification of the Stamp Act, striking out at the insidious "Principles of Colony Government" that he perceived as lying behind that legislation. He saw the new regime's distrusting approach to the planters as mirrored in the civil lawyer William Strahan's preface to his English translation of Jean Domat's *Les lois civiles dans leur ordre naturel*. Strahan advocated the utility of harsh Roman laws in governing the English colonies "for no better Reason than because the *Spanish* Colonies, as he says, are governed by those Laws." In Whately's own writing, Bland found similar signs of a settled assumption that planters were potential enemies rather than ready friends. "*Divide et impera* is your Maxim in Colony Administration," Bland wrote ruefully, "lest 'an Alliance should be formed dangerous to the Mother Country.'" "Ungenerous Insinuation! detestable Thought!" he fumed. But nowhere were the oppressive machinations toward the plantations laid more bare than in the writings of Thomas

10. Lawrence Henry Gipson, "The Great Debate in the Committee of the Whole House of Commons on the Stamp Act, 1766, as Reported by Nathaniel Ryder," *Pennsylvania Magazine of History and Biography*, LXXXVI (1962), 15–16; "Debates on the Declaratory Act and the Repeal of the Stamp Act, 1766," *American Historical Review*, XVII (October 1911–July 1912), 566–567.

Pownall, governor of Massachusetts from 1758 to 1760 and a British member of Parliament.[11]

In Pownall, Bland perceived another writer of Whatley's sensibilities and, in particular, someone who was similarly "fond of his new System of placing *Great Britain* as the Centre of Attraction to the Colonies." Pownall, however, was even more explicit in calling for the colonies' political subordination. Quoting Pownall at length on his view that the colonies "must be guarded against having or forming any Principle of Coherence with each other above that whereby they cohere in the Centre," Bland asked rhetorically how this severe "System of Administration" was to be established. Did Pownall envision a "military Force, quartered upon private Families?" Or perhaps the enlarged jurisdiction of admiralty courts, "thereby depriving the Colonists of legal Trials in the Courts of common Law?" Or maybe a swarm of "overbearing Taxgatherers" who would think little of "ruining Men" by dragging them far from their homes to stand before "Prerogative Judges, exercising a despotick Sway in Inquisitorial Courts?" For Bland, the "Leviathan of Power" was not just unconstrained but actively breaking through the constitutional arrangements that preserved planters in their lives and property.[12]

Yet, Bland was no opponent of the unitary state. On the contrary, he took for granted the indivisibility of sovereignty, and he attributed to that supreme power a vital moral as well as political function. Unsurprisingly for someone whose writings often concerned the health of Virginia's ecclesiastical establishment, he judged the state's worth in large part in relation to its effectiveness in preserving a delicate equipoise among people of different faiths while also allowing for the unhindered argumentation that permits the truth to conquer error. Bland held closely to his era's latitudinarian response to the religious divisions of the past century, keeping an ever prudential eye on the danger of reinvigorating passions better left undisturbed. Despite his evidently strong commitment to his Anglican Church as a lay reader, he opposed efforts to establish an American bishopric. As well, he unhesitatingly defended orthodoxy against Quaker confusion. His latitudinarian Anglicanism merged readily with his natural law, Whig sensibilities. In civil government as in matters of the church, he regarded a mild approach to dis-

---

11. Bland, *Inquiry*, 4, 13, 27–28. Jean Domat's book was published in 1689; William Strahan's English rendering, *The Civil Law in Its Natural Order: Together with the Publick Law*, appeared in 1722.

12. Bland, *Inquiry*, 28–29; Bland, *Fragment on the Pistole Fee*, ed. Ford, 38. The first edition of Thomas Pownall's *Administration of the Colonies* was published in London in 1764.

agreements and misconceptions as a far more effective regulator of humans' always-imperfect conduct than an uncompromising severity. Lenity and unity, however, were not opposites, and Bland had no doubt that a single supreme power that governed benevolently without undue challenges to its authority was necessary for civil governance.[13]

A controversy over the ambiguity of the colony's ecclesiastical constitution allowed Bland to articulate his view on why unitary sovereignty was essential. Bland explicitly defended undivided sovereignty as a precondition for clear understandings of virtuous conduct in a 1773 address entitled *To the Clergy of Virginia*. The question at hand centered on whether the colony's governor enjoyed lawful visitorial power over Virginian clergy, or whether that authority, as Bland believed, the king's alone to delegate and historically granted only to the bishop of London and, by extension, his Virginia-based commissary. Comparing the jostle between competing sovereign centers to the irreconcilable opposition between wickedness and goodness that Augustine of Hippo associated with the Roman deities known as the Manes, Bland wrote, "The establishment of two distinct jurisdictions, with equal judicial authority, would be a strange solecism in political government, and could have no other effect than (like the good and evil principles in the religion of Manes) to counteract and destroy the authority of each other." Bland accepted the basic Hobbist premise that only a single sovereign who represents the will of the people as a whole deserves to be regarded as truly a sovereign. Where Bland disagreed with the Grenville ministry, then, was not in the merits of a unitary polity but rather on the question of whether the colonies had ever made up part of the British state in the first place — or at least whether it had done so on the terms that figures like Whately, Stanley, and Pownall had suggested.[14]

Bland outlined his own argument about the nature of the British empire most fully in his earlier counterpoint to Whately's apologia for the Stamp Act. Whately's pamphlet had justified the new legislation in part on the grounds that it was in fact a quite late attempt to make good on Parliament's longstanding sovereignty over the colonies. He developed this idea in an especially pointed way by providing a brief history of the empire's foundation that was carefully calculated to suggest that the state had been in exis-

---

13. Bland's religious views remain underexplored, but, for general remarks, see Rossiter, "Richard Bland: The Whig in America," *WMQ*, X (1953), 48–50, 73.

14. Richard Bland, *To the Clergy of Virginia; Gentlemen, at the Desire of Several of Your Reverend Body, I Take the Liberty* ... (Williamsburg, Va., [1773?]), 3.

tence since the mid-seventeenth century. Arguing that the colonies' original inhabitants were "but a few unhappy Fugitives, who had wandered thither to enjoy their civil and religious Liberties, which they were deprived of at home," he implied that the settlers' migration across the ocean left them deplorably outside any civil community whatsoever. Little more than congeries of individuals tending to their own wants, they were "separate, weak, necessitous, and truly infant Colonies, nursed by perpetual Supplies from the Mother Country, exposed to every Hazard, sustained with Difficulty, and only beginning to give Hopes that they might hereafter be what they now are." The hero who finally stepped into this starkly individualistic scene, saving settlers from their own primitive isolationism, was Parliament, and its instrument of salvation was the law. By passing the Navigation Act of 1651, Whately wrote, Parliament transformed the colonies' "Dependance" into genuine "Connection," their rudeness into true civil bonds. By this account, a Parliament-led English state was intimately interwoven in the colonists' early history and "nearly co-aeval with their Existence as a People."[15]

In response to Whately's shrewd tale of the colonists' stateless beginnings, Bland offered his own history of early settlement. Focusing specifically on Virginia, his account appeared right at the heart of his *Inquiry* and took di-

15. [Whately], *Regulations Lately Made concerning the Colonies*, 88–89. One wonders in contemplating Whately's arresting notion of settlers as "a few un[h]appy Fugitives" if he himself derived the image from Edward Johnson's *History of New-England*, published in 1653 in London. The work not only would have served Whately's general purposes by offering a plausible account of the colonies on the very eve of the Navigation Act of 1651 but it also made much of the New Englanders' uncertain beginnings as a "few ... Fugitives." Of course, Johnson's casuistical purposes were a far cry from Whately's own eighteenth-century polemics. Writing at a moment when the lawfulness of New England settlement was denounced especially by the godly in England — one set of Reformed Protestants denouncing the others for shirking their duties in helping to realize England's promise as the New Jerusalem — Johnson sought to show that the New Englanders' very success in incorporating themselves into a godly and moral polity proved their congruence with God's will. As he put it, only the "wonderful providence of the most high God toward these his new-planted Churches" could explain why, in a mere "ten or twelve years planting, there should be such wonderful alteration, a Nation to be born in a day, a Commonwealth orderly brought forth from a few Fugitives." If Whately did draw the notion of settlers as 'Fugitives" from Johnson's account, what for the seventeenth-century author could only be achieved by God, the incorporating of a woeful collection of individuals into a genuinely orderly "Commonwealth," had become for the eighteenth-century writer a decidedly secular achievement accomplished most plausibly by the regulatory powers of Parliament. See [Edward Johnson], *A History of New-England; from the English Planting in the Yeere 1628. untill the Yeere 1652* ... (London, 1654 [1653]), 172–173.

rect aim at Whately's allegation that the colonists were in flight from their legitimate ruler, stranded on a lawless frontier, and in need of political salvation. Even if what Whately had claimed about the planters' early circumstances were true, Bland wrote, the colonists would not have needed Parliament's assistance. "When Subjects are deprived of their civil Rights," he reasoned, "they have a natural Right to quit the Society of which they are Members, ... retire into another Country ... and form themselves into a political Society." He drew explicitly from the natural law theories of Vattel, Locke, and Wollaston to amplify the speciousness of Whately's reasoning. But the bulk of Bland's attention was devoted to showing that Whately's account of the colonies' early decades was not good history. Bland was scathing in his contempt for Whately's mischaracterizations. "You have been guilty of a gross Anachronism in your Chronology, and a great Errour in your Account of the first Settlement of the Colonies in *North America*," he wrote. Bland insisted that only a correct political history of the colonies could give rise to a genuine understanding of the empire's lawful arrangements.[16]

The history Bland recounted in lieu of Whately's was in many respects faithful to the Renaissance experiences and Christian humanist logic of Virginia's settlement. At a basic level, his narrative amounted to little less, or more, than a chronicle of the "sacred Band of Union" that had linked the planters directly to their sovereign rulers since the earliest years of colonization. Reflective of the significance that colonizers had historically attributed to that tie as a link that mirrored their redeeming relationship to God, Bland treated it as the very foundation of the colony's body politic. He identified this bond as manifested in the royal charters by which colonists were originally authorized to travel across the Atlantic. Important, too, to his story were certain provisions included in those patents such as permission to "establish a civil Government." His depiction of the planters centered on the familiar idea of their freedom and loyalty as political actors. They "came over voluntarily" but also safely "within the Allegiance of the Crown of *England*" — an image of dutiful free agency that evoked the faith-like obedience that earlier leaders like Sir William Berkeley had similarly invoked. Likewise, Bland described the planters as commonwealth builders. According to his narrative, they erected a polity in the face of "immense Difficulties" and "without receiving the least Assistance from the *English* Government." Struggling toward the condition of civil wholeness, or perfection, that Hugo Grotius and others had identified as the very essence of state-

16. Bland, *Inquiry*, 14, 15.

hood, they busied themselves with the project of laying the foundation for a future commonwealth.[17]

Although he got the date slightly wrong, Bland hailed the inauguration of the General Assembly in 1619 with much the same reverence as his early-seventeenth-century predecessors, holding to their own view that the creation of such a body allowed for a genuine mutuality of wills between king and planters. As he put it, the colony had "attained to such a Degree of Perfection that in the Year 1621 a General Assembly, or legislative Authority, was established in the Governour, Council, and House of Burgesses . . . and they have continued from that Time to exercise the Power of Legislation over the Colony." On a soberer note, his discussion of the colony under James I and Charles I acknowledged that their reigns were an uncertain time characterized by "much Confusion" as well as "Disquietude and Dissatisfaction." This dreary detail, however, permitted him to underscore allegiance's mutual nature and especially to highlight the humanist theme that a reciprocal performance of duties provides the ultimate antidote to alienated and despondent wills. He described the planters as becoming so "reconciled" to Charles I at one point that "their Affection for the Royal Government grew almost to Enthusiasm." Thus inclined, they "began again to exert themselves in the Improvement of the Colony" — a redemptive moment that still echoed with the Pauline ideal of the power of agape-like love in drawing people to their callings.[18]

Once Bland reached Virginians' refusal to surrender to the Puritan Commonwealth except on their own terms, he punctuated the significance of the event in a way that Berkeley himself would have appreciated. Pausing in his narrative to provide a lengthy abstract of the treaty of surrender, he explained that he did so because he did not think its articles were "commonly known" and because they "reflect[ed] no small Honour upon this Infant Colony." Over and over again, Bland's eye was drawn to those aspects of the colony's history that sixteenth- and seventeenth-century actors themselves might have underscored. He highlighted those areas that most spoke to Virginia's success in realizing itself as a recognizable polity.[19]

Where Bland apparently struggled in making sense of the colony's Renaissance past was in grasping, or even imagining, an age before the rise of the concept of the unitary state. From his Enlightenment perspective, state

17. Ibid., 15–19, 20–21.
18. Ibid., 17–18.
19. Ibid., 19.

sovereignty was not really a theory at all but rather a truism, or a fulfillment of natural laws. As a result, his account strained in a couple of instances as he encountered oddities that did not fully align with his eighteenth-century assumptions.

In the first place, Bland was evidently puzzled by the ease with which English monarchs had set commonwealth formation in America in motion without Parliament's consent. An uncharacteristically speculative tone entered into his analysis when, having acknowledged that Parliament was "without Doubt supreme within the Body of the Kingdom," he then pondered more conjecturally how it could have been that earlier rulers had simply sidestepped consultations with English parliaments in an endeavor as momentous as the creation of a new kingdom: "May not the King have Prerogatives which he has a Right to exercise without the Consent of Parliament?" he asked rhetorically. He answered his own question in an equally suppositional manner: "If he has, perhaps that of granting License to his Subjects to remove into a *new* Country, and to settle therein upon particular Conditions, may be one." Bland's hesitation evinced a sense of unease about the strange conditions that could have allowed the monarch's will to act on its own. He could not quite fathom a time when sovereignty and commonwealth were sufficiently distinct that the one could act independently of the other.[20]

The second instance in which Bland's history ran up against the limits of his interpretive categories concerned the stark way that the theory of state sovereignty hinged on the difference between true states and nonstates while rendering more or less obsolete the wider spectrum of petty commonwealths and grand kingdoms that had once entertained Renaissance European imaginations. Because his narrative turned on the colonies' own complete civil integrity, he had little choice but to identify Virginia as a "sovereign State, independent of the State from which they separated." This designation could feel extreme. John Dickinson, in his "Letters from a Farmer in Pennsylvania," would respond to such language of colonial statehood in a way that suggests strongly that he was remarking directly on Bland's use of the term. "He who considers these provinces as states distinct from the *British Empire*, has very slender notions of *justice*, or of their *interests*," Dickinson wrote. "We are but parts of a *whole*; and therefore there must exist a power somewhere, to preside, and preserve the connection in due order." That power, Dickinson insisted, was "lodged in the parliament," and the colonies were "as much dependent on *Great Britain*, as a perfectly free people can be on another."

20. Ibid., 21.

Bland, though, evidently saw little value in a vague distinction between perfect freedom and independent statehood like the one Dickinson envisioned. For his analytical purposes, Virginia could scarcely be anything short of a genuine sovereign state.[21]

Bland's effort to reconcile Virginia's sovereignty with its membership in a broader empire led him to build on a concept that had originated in the same late Renaissance moment where his history left off. This was the idea that natural law can be separated into internal as well as external spheres of obligation. He capped off his discussion of Virginia's early history by dramatically brandishing this idea of internal and external polities, as though it offered the vital solution to the dissonance he had encountered between his Enlightenment values and the colonies' Renaissance realities. In terms meant to provide a final rebuttal to Whately's argument, he stated that, even before the Navigation Act, planters and their king were "respected as a distinct State, independent, as to their *internal* Government, of the original Kingdom, but united with her, as to their *external* Polity, in the closest and most intimate LEAGUE AND AMITY, under the same Allegiance, and enjoying the Benefits of a reciprocal Intercourse." The distinction between internal and external government had a long history by this time. Unsurprisingly it arose from the same skeptical milieu and natural law tradition that had generated the theory of sovereign statehood in the first place.[22]

In positing that civil society emerges from the human instinct for self-preservation, writers had experimented with the idea that a higher-level sense of duty was also possible alongside humanity's more utilitarian calculations when seeking a bare minimum of peace in their interactions. Grotius was an early expositor of the idea. In his *Rights of War and Peace,* he had spoken of internal justice as going beyond merely what external laws allow or prohibit. Whereas external laws are concerned with the basic safety of persons and things in their encounters with one another, internal justice touches on the deeper level of duty, honesty, honor, and equity. Hobbes had similarly identified the laws of nature as obliging either "in foro interno" or "in foro externo," the first implying what "should take place" as a moral duty and the latter only what may take place in practical consideration of "Security." Vattel, in his *Law of Nations,* would sum up such principles as

---

21. Ibid., 14; Forrest McDonald, ed., *Empire and Nation: Letters from a Farmer in Pennsylvania, John Dickinson; Letters from the Federal Farmer, Richard Henry Lee,* 2d ed. (Indianapolis, Ind., 1999), 7–8.

22. Bland, *Inquiry,* 20.

they had evolved in the writings of James Harrington, Samuel von Pufendorf, and Jean Jacques Burlamaqui and their elaborations on Grotius and Hobbes. Vattel designated an *"internal law of nations"* that was "obligatory to nations in point of conscience," and an external one that concerned itself more narrowly with what was allowable. One example he provided of the relationship between the two concerned the master of a particular piece of territory. This ruler enjoyed an indisputable external right to forbid access to his lands to strangers, but when it came to his internal rights he could not conscionably refuse passage to "a stranger who comes with the hopes of recovering his health in the country, or to acquire instructions in the schools and academies." Even a "difference in religion is not a sufficient reason to exclude him, provided he abstains from disputation" and thereby keeps the peace, Vattel wrote. Vattel also applied this framework to colonization. He observed, "Every man has a right to quit his country, in order to settle in any other, when by that step he does not expose the welfare of his country." But this external right quickly ran up against the moral quandaries associated with such a departure, for "quitting our associates upon slight pretences, after having drawn considerable advantages from them" affected scruples. As a result, "a good citizen will never resolve to do it without necessity, or without very strong reasons." External laws might permit it, but the stronger tug of conscience that gave meaning to that person's status as a "good citizen" would not.[23]

It is easy to see why Bland would have been attracted to the idea of a two-part order to the empire, with the colonies' internal polities functioning as genuine moral communities while the external sphere of imperial exchange existed solely to maintain a modicum of peace and civility in those states' commercial and other interactions with one another and the British state. Such a view of the colonies' relationship to the mother country nicely preserved the idea of colonial commonwealths without disregarding entirely their historical relationship with Britain. A pleasing patina of Enlightenment moral philosophy rested over such a vision while keeping alive those Renaissance humanist principles that had given meaning to the colony's commonwealths in the first place.

---

23. Hugo Grotius, *The Rights of War and Peace, Edited and with an Introduction by Richard Tuck, from the Edition by Jean Barbeyrace* (Indianapolis, Ind., 2005), III, 1411–1420; Thomas Hobbes, *Leviathan*, ed. Richard Tuck, Cambridge Texts in the History of Political Thought (Cambridge, 1996), 110; Emer de Vattel, *The Law of Nations; or, Principles of the Law of Nature: Applied to the Conduct and Affairs of Nations and Sovereigns* (London, 1760), 2, 94, 164.

INDEX

Aaron, 226
Abbot, George, 54–55, 219–220, 222, 227, 255, 259, 262
Abraham, 10n, 20, 85
Absolute power, 12–14, 19, 44, 51–52, 146, 217; and absolute wills, 210, 246, 253, 256, 262–263, 265, 325; and Hobbes's theory of sovereignty, 284–285, 295, 300, 314–315, 318, 330, 344, 351, 358. *See also Potestas absoluta*
Act in Restraint of Appeals, 12, 72–73, 88
Act of Uniformity, 289, 325
Adam and Eve, 9, 20, 83, 88, 221, 242
Adventure (verb), 38, 42, 133, 138, 144, 153n, 162, 175, 285
Adventurers, 72–73, 112, 169, 171–172, 186, 211, 220–221, 226, 230, 236, 252, 255, 307
Agape, 71, 365. *See also* Consent; Love
Agricola, Gnaeus Julius, 41
Albemarle Sound, 334
Alexander the Great, 86
Alexander VI (pope), 47–48; and the Bulls of Donation, 47–48, 52, 65, 110, 137
Allen, William, 29n, 109–111, 114, 123
Amalekites, 49
America: and English monarchical duties, 1, 11, 16, 65–66, 86, 88–89, 92–93, 129–130, 159, 202, 357; providential import of, 18, 34–38, 41–44, 46–55; as scene of competing godly and worldly impulses, 21, 238–246, 307–308; as focus of rival European sovereign and confessional claims, 28, 31, 47–48, 50, 108–111, 114, 137, 189, 212, 216, 329; as royal frontier, 67–68, 85, 189, 194; as licentious, 126–127, 134–135, 192; Hobbes's interest in, 285, 315
American Revolution, 22–23, 360
Anabaptists, 15, 251, 278
Anael (the angel of Venus), 65
Ancient theology, 296, 312–313
Anglo-Dutch Wars: Second, 329, 331, 333; Third, 334–335
Antichrist, 53, 63, 223, 234, 237, 290, 302, 311
Antinomianism, 41
Antiseparatism, 15, 108–109, 126, 210, 226–227, 234–238, 240–241, 245–246, 257, 262, 275n, 280. *See also* Antiutopianism
Anti-utopianism, 240–242, 280, 294–295
Anys, William, 257
Apostles, 45, 48, 69–70, 79, 244. *See also* Paul (apostle); Peter (apostle)
Aquinas, Saint Thomas, 31, 39, 41
Aristides, 29–30
Aristotle, 5, 318
Arlington, Henry Bennet, first earl of, 331–337
Arnold, Anthony, 344

Aróstegui, Antonio de, 183–184
Arthur (legendary king of Britain), 53–54, 65–66, 85–86, 103
Ascham, Antony, 308
Assemblies, 18, 75, 144–145, 147, 155–157, 177–178, 231, 259, 278, 286, 292–293, 302, 325–326, 341, 358–359. *See also* Virginia: General Assembly of
Aucher, William, 119
Augustine of Hippo, 47, 362
Austria, 200, 212
Avilés, Pedro Menéndez de, 29n
Aylmer, John, 108
Azores, 48, 143

Bacon, Francis, Viscount Saint Alban, 10, 14, 17, 74–77, 156–158, 186n, 191, 218–219, 279n
Bacon, Nathaniel (Suffolk lawyer), 340–341
Bacon, Nathaniel, Jr., 37, 288–289, 292, 339–350
Bacon's Rebellion, 21, 36–37, 288–289, 292, 325, 338–350, 356
Baffin Island, 53
Balboa, Vasco Núñez de, 116
Baltimore, George Calvert, first Baron, 193–194, 220, 246–249, 251, 253, 255, 260
Barak, 95–96, 98
Barbados, 307, 320, 328
Bargrave, George, 224, 225n
Bargrave, Isaac, 225
Bargrave, John, 224–232, 234, 250, 284, 295
Bargrave, Thomas, 224
Bennett, Richard, 320, 322, 354
Berkeley, George, 279
Berkeley, Sir John, 288
Berkeley, Sir Maurice, 275
Berkeley, Sir William, 17, 36–37, 90, 273, 275–285, 288–292, 295–307, 314–316, 318–330, 332–335, 337–339, 341–348, 350–352, 364–365
Bermuda, 35, 176, 181–182, 206, 224, 236–237, 243, 258, 307n, 320, 358. *See also* Somers Island Company
Berry, Sir John, 351
Best, George, 42–43
Beverley, Robert, 301
Beverley, Robert, Jr., 301
Bible, 3, 6, 13, 20, 33, 51, 69–70, 96, 222, 236–237, 276, 280, 291, 353; Old Testament, 6; Hebrew, 6, 47, 49, 69–70, 95, 220–221, 260–261; King James, 69–70; Latin Vulgate, 70; Wycliffite, 70; New Testament, 74, 79
Black Legend, 49, 51
Bland, Giles, 336–338, 344, 351, 354
Bland, Richard, 353–355, 357, 360–368
Bodin, Jean, 17, 19, 69, 141–142, 146, 155, 160, 167, 224. *See also* Statecraft literature
Boethius, 39–40
Bohemia, 193n, 212
Bond of Association, 111–112, 123, 290
Bonds: as inalienable, 5, 13, 302–304, 315, 321; and Civil War, 21, 289, 342; rhetorical basis of, 23, 41–42; and civility, 41–42, 243, 363; of commonwealth, 43n, 70–81, 121–124, 131–132, 146, 153, 162, 188, 197–198, 205, 209, 212–234, 241, 245, 250, 256, 273, 282–285, 297–299, 306, 316–319, 321, 324, 333, 346, 350, 364–365; between God and the faithful, 69–70, 77–79, 348; as analogs of Christian love, 71–72, 261, 265, 301, 334–335; of allegiance, 87, 103, 297–298, 304, 323, 349; and the "CITTIE OF RALEGH," 121–125, 290; sinister, 132, 210–211, 236; as contractual, 284–285, 316–319, 353; as insignificant

to state unity, 285–287, 291, 344; as provisional, 289, 314; and the National Covenant, 289–290. *See also* Bond of Association
Botero, Giovanni, 141, 146–149, 160, 188, 217, 224. *See also* Statecraft literature
Brooke, Robert Greville, second Baron, 296–297, 302, 310, 312
Brownists, 15, 108, 109n, 227, 234, 236, 245
Brutus, 12–14, 77n
Buck, Richard, 197
Buckingham, George Villiers, duke of, 191–192, 207n, 254–255
Bulstrode, Sir Richard, 351
Bunny, Edmund, 6, 96–97
Burghill, Francis, 357–358
Burghley, William Cecil, first Baron, 26, 28, 34–35, 58, 109–112, 128, 139–141, 151, 156, 159, 165n, 255
Burlamaqui, Jean Jacques, 368
Burton, Robert, 280, 282, 299
Button, William, 263
Byrd, Mary Horsmanden Filmer, 346–347
Byrd, William, 346, 350

Cabot, John, 46, 54, 92–93
Cabot, Sebastian, 46, 89, 92–93, 98
Caesar, Augustus, 13n
Caesar, Julius, 85–86, 103
Caesar, Sir Julius, 221–222, 225
Calahorra, Diego Ortúñez de, 133
Callings. *See* Offices
Calvert, Leonard, 306
Calvin, Jean, 40
Calvinism, 22n, 38, 40–41, 62, 89, 190, 200, 273n
Calvin's Case, 77n, 304
Cambridge Platonists, 340
Campion, Edmund, 109, 137

Canaan, 4, 7, 19, 21, 49, 67, 95–98, 116, 175, 183, 188, 246
Canaanites, 49, 95, 175, 188
Captains: moral persona of, 3–4, 84–91, 209; biblical precedent for, 4, 7, 19; and female sovereignty, 86–87, 89–90, 103–106; and godly resolution over birth, 88–89, 91; failures of, 90–91, 124–128, 130–135, 138, 141, 143–149, 161, 163–164; as divinely favored conquerors, 92–106; as "private men," 106–107, 112–122, 124
Carolina, 313, 334, 350
Castile, 31, 51, 65, 317
Casuistry: and law, 4, 37; Protestant adaptation of, 7; and colonization, 7, 56–66, 83–84, 97, 115–117, 134–135, 156, 173–175, 198, 215n, 236–237, 243, 272, 363n; and conventional morality, 20–21, 49–50, 92n, 102–106, 265; as a defining feature of Renaissance culture, 30, 33, 46, 56, 159, 223; and projects, 57–59; and callings, 59–61; and the Spanish-Habsburg monarchy, 94, 317; and sovereign vacillation, 107, 125; and Reformation politics, 108–112, 123; and statism, 117, 138, 203, 256–257, 262; and sophistry, 203; in Shakespeare's *Richard the Third*, 267–268; and melancholy, 280; and establishmentarianism, 293; and Hobbes's sovereign, 295
Catholic Counter-Reformation, 5, 28, 32, 109–112, 137–138, 143, 146, 167, 171–172, 200, 212, 223, 227, 254, 317
Catholics, 7, 15, 17, 26, 27n, 52–53, 61, 63–66, 109–110, 123–126, 151, 162, 188, 190, 209, 213–214, 216, 227, 234–238, 246–255, 257–259, 267n, 270, 309, 331. *See also* Catholic Counter-Reformation

Chapman, George, 125, 127–136
Charlemagne, 86
Charles I (king of England), 18, 73, 190, 207n, 209–210, 212, 216, 225, 232, 235, 246–274, 287, 290, 292, 295, 299–310, 313, 315, 318–320, 325, 336, 338, 365
Charles II (king of England), 275, 284, 288–289, 323, 325–331, 334–336, 355
Charles V (Holy Roman Emperor and Spanish-Habsburg king), 50–52, 56n, 63, 65, 167, 217, 227
Cheswell, Joseph, 137–138
Chickahominies, 187, 305
China, 53, 66–67
Chowanocs, 120
Christian humanism: optimism of, in aligning worldly arrangements with providential order, 2–3, 8, 29–30, 33, 38–42, 59n, 64, 91, 278, 294; as basis for Renaissance colonizing discourse, 2, 9, 57, 61, 275, 354, 364, 368; and commonwealth, 5, 13–14, 17, 19, 78, 93, 131, 217, 233–234, 262, 265, 273, 284, 300, 335, 365; and imperium, 5, 13–14, 30–31; influence on, by Reformation biblicism, 6–7, 32, 70; and role of states in satisfying God's will, 11; and insecure sovereigns, 11, 14–15; and vigor needed for world's redemption, 13–14, 76–77, 91–92; rhetorical focus of, 23–24; and civilizing process, 41–42; and industry at callings, 42, 93, 228, 240, 244, 270, 319; and skepticism, 283, 290; and Hobbism, 286, 316, 323, 326, 330, 343–345, 348, 352
Church of England, 15, 18, 30, 38, 40, 63, 78–79, 107–112, 119–120, 123, 125, 128, 213–214, 223–227, 234, 238–242, 245–246, 248, 254–255, 257, 259, 261–262, 273n, 280–283, 290–293, 297–298, 305–307, 309, 324–326, 331–334, 361–362
Churchyard, Thomas, 88–89, 103–106
Claiborne, William, 90, 246–249, 255, 257n, 265, 320
Clare, Richard fitz Gilbert de (called Strongbow), second earl of Pembroke (earl of Chepstow), 116
Clare College, Cambridge, 225
Clarendon, Edward Hyde, first earl of, 276, 279, 283–285, 287–289, 291–292, 294, 299, 314–316, 323, 325–326, 328, 330–333, 343–344
Codrington, Christopher, 358
Cogan, Thomas, 54
Coke, Sir Edward, 213, 304
Coke, Sir John, 212–213, 255, 265
Colbert, Jean-Baptiste, 329
Colepeper, John, first Baron Colepeper of Thoresway, 294, 336
Colepeper, Thomas, second Baron Colepeper of Thoresway, 336
Colonies: as commonwealths, 9, 11, 16–19, 21–22, 74–75, 78–81, 101, 120, 185, 269, 272–273, 313, 322, 336, 349, 355–359, 364–366, 368; as churches, 9, 15–17, 30, 80–81, 119–120, 182, 197, 221, 223, 226, 322–323, 363n; as kingdoms, 10–11, 16, 65, 114, 119, 168, 177, 188–189, 199–200, 206, 216–217, 219, 221–234, 252, 256, 259, 269, 272–273, 366; as provinces, 16, 19, 22–23, 101, 229, 231, 275, 311, 313–314, 317–318, 352, 357–358, 360, 366; as branches of the state, 148, 151, 208; as nurseries for the state, 148, 188; as sovereign states, 366–367
Colonization: as first instantiated at Canaan, 7, 19, 97; as securing earthly dominion, 9–10, 103; as a calling, 9–10,

46, 52; as commonwealth formation, 9–11, 16–17, 101–103, 207, 271–273, 357; as centered on metropolitan interests, 16, 194, 200, 271, 357; as a private enterprise, 106–125; as a Protestant plot, 110–111, 171; as a context for deliberating over sovereign power, 114; as an excessively worldly undertaking, 124–125, 134–135, 238–239; as a state-led endeavor, 138–158; as a stage showcasing God's will, 235–236

"Colony": as unfamiliar word, 9n

Columbus, Christopher, 13, 37, 46–55, 114

Columbus, Ferdinand, 48–49, 54n, 65n

Commerce, 44, 54, 165–166, 220, 259, 283, 288, 297, 310–311, 320, 334; evolving theories of, 3n, 24n, 38–39, 42–43, 100–102, 107n, 147n, 151–158, 160, 162–163, 178–179, 191–194, 200, 202–209, 211, 214–234, 238–240, 251–252, 270–272, 284–285, 294–295, 303, 307, 313–314, 319, 324, 328–329, 331–333, 341, 350–352, 368

Commonwealth: as archetypal community centered on divine callings, 1, 6–7, 9–10, 16, 33, 37–38, 41, 60, 64, 69–70, 87; reciprocal bonds of, 5, 77–81; Israel as prime exemplar of, 6–7, 69–70, 97, 188; reform impulse toward, 58, 93; legitimating weight of, 69; and incorporation, 70–73; binding nature of, 71–72, 80, 224, 303, 315–316, 349; distinguishability of, from sovereignty, 73–77, 284; reenvisioning of, as the unitary state, 271, 286–288, 309–314, 340–341; as guide to lawful living, 321

Companies: trading, 154–158, 208–209; and commonwealth, 121–124, 155; joint-stock, versus regulated, 157–158.

See also Corporations; *Corpus mysticum*, Monopoly; *individual companies*

Company of Merchant Adventurers, 151

Condren, Conal 61

Conscience, 7, 20, 28, 45, 47, 61, 63, 64n, 72, 79–80, 104–107, 110, 134–135, 150, 159, 173, 176, 194, 198, 202, 213, 215, 237, 241, 256, 258, 262–263, 265–268, 280, 282, 291, 299, 303–304, 327, 349, 368. *See also* Casuistry

Consent, 29, 71–72, 121–122, 158–160, 180, 194, 206, 233, 251, 253, 262, 283–287, 300, 304, 319, 353, 366. *See also* Agape; Love

Constantine I (Roman emperor), 48

Contracts, 72, 204, 212, 228, 284–286, 316, 319, 337, 350–351; tobacco, 204–207, 209, 232, 234–235, 247, 254, 257, 260, 263, 302; "forme of Subscription" (1624), 210–211, 252; original, 287–288. *See also* Great Contract

Conversatione, 70, 77–78

Cope, Sir Anthony, 167

Cope, Sir Walter, 140, 167, 186

Copernicus, 38n

Copland, Patrick 174

Copper, 58, 93, 120–121

Cornwall, 118, 309

Cornwallis, Sir Charles, 153n

Corporations, 72–73, 79n, 81, 120, 137, 147, 150, 155–157, 166, 174–177, 183, 195, 287, 315, 324, 336–337. *See also* Companies; *Corpus mysticum*

Corpus mysticum, 14n, 69, 71n, 80–81, 196–198, 229, 261, 283, 319

Correr, Marc'Antonio, 170

Cortés, Hernán, 99–100, 114, 116

Cotton, Sir Robert Bruce, 213–214, 256

Council of the Indies, 167

Coventry, Henry, 351

Crakanthorpe, Richard, 172, 174–175
Crashawe, William, 7, 14, 174–177, 234–235
Creation, 1, 9, 43
Cromwell, Oliver, 37, 308, 311, 322, 329–331
Cromwell, Thomas, 12
Cudworth, Ralph, 340
Cushman, Robert, 238–239, 245

d'Ailly, Pierre, 47
Dale, Sir Thomas, 96, 182–183, 187
Danby, Thomas Osborne, earl of, 336–338, 344, 347
Daniel, 96
Daniel, Samuel, 186
Dante, 5–6, 50
Davenport, John, 305
David, 86, 260–261
Deborah, 95–96, 98
Dee, John, 53–54, 61, 63–67, 74–76, 85–86, 103, 117, 154–155
De La Warr, Thomas West, third Baron, 171, 175, 182, 255
Denmark, 161
Devon, 118
Devonshire, William Cavendish, second earl of, 276
Dickinson, John, 366–367
Digby, Sir John, 183–184
Digges, Dudley, 294, 315–316, 324
Digges, Sir Dudley, 259, 315
Digges, Edward, 315, 322
Doddridge, John, 140, 167
Doegs, 37, 338
Domat, Jean, 360
Dominion of New England, 356
Donne, George, 246n
Donne, John, 7, 14, 36, 60–61, 78–81, 174, 257, 269, 279n

Dorchester, Dudley Carleton, first Viscount, 184, 261
Dorset, Edward Sackville, fourth earl of, 214, 254–255, 259–261
Douai, 109
Dover Treaty, 335
Drake, Sir Francis, 82, 127, 135
Drayton, Michael, 212
Drummond, William, 334, 345
Durand, William, 305
Dutch East India Company, 317
Duties. *See* Offices

East India Company, 139n, 143
Eburne, Richard, 57, 219–220, 272–273
Eden, Richard, 9n, 17, 52–53, 85, 88–89, 94–95, 98, 101, 103
Edward VI (king of England), 51
Effingham, Francis Howard, fifth Baron, 356–357
Election, 78–79, 237, 246, 296–297
Elizabeth I (queen of England), 3, 11, 14, 18, 25–26, 28–30, 51, 54, 61–67, 83–84, 86–87, 89–91, 95–96, 98–99, 103–104, 106–130, 133n, 136, 139, 141, 143–144, 147, 149–153, 156–157, 160–161, 164, 166, 168, 171, 180, 209, 220, 258–259, 276, 278, 292–293, 353
Elizabethan cult, 222–223
Elizabeth Stuart (queen of Bohemia), 129, 216
Ellesmere, Thomas Egerton, Baron, 171
Elliot, Sir John, 253–254, 266
Empire. *See* Sovereignty
End Time, 4, 8n, 47, 50, 52, 65, 105, 308. *See also* Eschatology
England: Parliament of, 12, 18–19, 62n, 71–72, 82, 117–118, 128, 150n, 152, 155–165, 171, 180, 190–194, 206, 208, 216, 235, 253–256, 259, 266, 270, 287–288,

301–302, 305–310, 313–314, 316, 318–322, 324–325, 331, 337, 340, 358–359, 362–364, 366; Privy Council of, 12, 26, 58, 109–110, 114, 122, 171, 199–200, 205, 217, 221, 247, 250, 252–255, 257, 260, 269, 287, 308 Commonwealth of, 73, 275, 281, 288, 295, 310–311, 319–322, 324, 328–329, 336, 339, 346, 365; Treasury of, 190–192, 203, 206, 208, 212, 229, 234, 251–254, 259, 336, 338, 351, 359. *See also* Church of England; English Civil War
— colonial councils and commissions of: New England Council, 43, 75n; Council of Virginia, 43, 81, 102, 166–169, 171, 172n, 174, 181–182, 187, 238, 252; Mandeville commission, 252–253; Dorset commission, 254–255; Council of America, 311; Council of Trade, 311, 320; Parliamentary commissioners, 320; Council for Foreign Plantations, 324, 332–333; royal commissioners (Bacon's Rebellion), 343, 346, 349–352; Council of Trade and Foreign Plantations, 351–352; royal commissioners (Massachusetts Bay), 355; Lords of Trade, 356; Board of Trade, 359
— counties of: Cumberland, 67, 189; Northumberland, 67, 189; Westmoreland, 68, 189
— ministries of: Cabal, 288–289, 326, 331, 333, 335–336, 351; Grenville, 359–360, 362
English, William, 264
English Civil War, 16, 21, 36–37, 269–270, 274–275, 279, 281, 287, 290, 294, 332, 340, 349
English College, Rome, 137
Enthusiasm, 15, 281, 339, 365

Eschatology, 3–4, 8n, 32, 45–47, 52–53, 55, 63–66, 74, 80–81, 214, 281, 292, 302, 308, 311–312. *See also* End Time
Essex, Robert Devereux, second earl of, 90–91, 96, 143–145, 165n, 171, 188
Essex, Walter Devereux, first earl of, 90, 112–113
Essex (county in England), 236
Essex's Rebellion, 96
Establishmentarianism, 2–3, 15, 18, 40, 46, 108, 142, 225–227, 234–235, 239–240, 276, 278, 280–283, 289–307, 314, 316–322, 324–325, 328, 331, 339, 341–343, 345, 350, 361–362. *See also* Anti-utopianism; Worldliness
Evelyn, Robert, 249
Eyanoco, 121

Falkland, Lucius Cary, second Viscount of, 276, 279, 287, 294, 299, 315, 327
Fall, the, 1–4, 9–11, 19–20, 38–39, 41, 45, 60, 69–70, 77, 85, 91, 103, 129, 141–142, 146, 155, 188, 239, 278, 294–295
Familists, 15
Faroe Islands, 53
Ferdinand of Aragon (king of Spain), 46–48, 50, 85, 89, 101, 103
Ferrar, John, 259, 269–271
Ferrar, Nicholas, 194, 254, 259
Filmer, Robert, 347
Finch, Henry, 267n
Finch, Sir John, 266
Forced Loan, 210, 262
Form of policy, 145–146, 224, 229–230, 304n, 317, 354n
Fornari, Baliano de, 48–49
Forset, Edward, 141, 180–181
Fortescue, Sir John, 5, 12–13, 17, 20, 76, 283
France, 7n, 13n, 62n, 84, 137, 153, 162,

274n, 288, 328–329, 331, 335, 350, 360; and Huguenots, 28, 100–101, 350
Francis (duke of Anjou), 62, 107
Frederick V (elector Palatine of the Rhine), 129, 190, 193n, 200, 216
Frobisher, Sir Martin, 42, 61, 87, 93, 114

Galileo, 38n
Garden of Eden, 9
Gascoigne, George, 87
Gates, Sir Thomas, 90, 93, 96, 171, 176, 182, 187, 236–237, 243
Gentry, 28, 56, 60, 79, 88, 156, 172n, 178, 194, 202, 239, 242n, 244–245, 269, 276, 320, 326
Gilbert, Sir Humphrey, 25–31, 35, 58, 61, 64–65, 83–84, 86–87, 89–90, 103–106, 115, 119–120, 134, 159
Gilbert, Sir John, 119
Glanville, 304
Glorious Revolution, 358
God: providential plan of, 1, 3, 6, 9–11, 13, 27, 29–30, 38, 49–50; and worldliness, 2–3, 6–7, 21, 49, 51–52, 135, 237, 239–242, 291–295, 298, 325, 306, 328; and law, 2–3, 8, 18, 37, 43–46, 57, 76–77, 79–81, 83, 146; willful disobedience toward, 3, 49, 267; restored earthly kingdom of, 3–4, 32, 79; and callings, 4, 6, 27, 39–42, 50–51, 60, 283–284, 299; elusive will of, 4, 18, 20–21, 28, 35–37, 45, 56–59, 106–108, 110, 112, 186, 236, 265, 276, 278–282, 285–286, 290–291; moral autonomy of, 5, 284; as the primary will behind American colonization, 9, 19–20, 43–44, 46–47, 52–55, 65–66, 78–82, 96–97, 114, 116, 174, 179, 188, 196, 199, 205, 235, 338; as the giver of imperium, 12, 14, 30, 32, 67, 71, 119, 126, 128–130, 213, 229, 266, 323; and commonwealth, 12, 69–70, 78, 123, 154, 197–198, 200, 229, 232, 261, 265, 269, 273, 283, 285, 290, 321, 327, 342, 348, 357, 363n; and female sovereignty, 14, 62–64, 89, 95–96; anger of, 25–26, 34, 48, 94, 141, 162, 169, 182–183, 233, 258, 311, 331; and wealth, 35, 42–43, 203, 233; constancy of, 38, 89, 144–145, 284; and human equality and inequality, 61; and the state, 74–76, 141–142, 147–148, 151, 155, 159–160, 175–176; and reciprocal moral bonds, 77–78, 304, 349, 364; and the persona of the captain, 84–86, 88–91, 97–106, 113; and civility, 93; and the persona of the planter, 201–202, 211, 215–216, 219, 222–224, 228, 230, 252, 257; and Puritan assuredness, 296, 300, 308, 311–312
Godfrey of Bouillon, 86
Gold, 2n, 42–43, 51, 95, 114, 119, 129, 131, 134, 166
Gómara, Francisco López de, 99
Gondomar, Diego Sarmiento de Acuña, first count of, 51, 190, 193, 270
Goode, John, 350
Gorges, Sir Ferdinando, 74–76, 194
Gorricio, Gaspar, 47n
Gray, Robert, 57, 174–175
Great Contract, 180, 190, 193, 226n
Great Tew circle, 276, 279, 281–283, 291–292, 294, 314–315
Green, Roger, 326
Greenland, 53
Gregory of Nazianzus, 293
Gregory XIII (pope), 28
Grenville, George, 359–360, 362
Grenville, Sir Richard, 82, 118
Grindal, Edmund, 108
Grotius, Hugo, 276, 278–279, 282–285, 292–295, 316–319, 330, 364, 367–368

Guiana, 1, 2n, 43, 85, 90
Gunpowder Plot, 171, 185

Hague, The, 320
Hakewill, George, 38
Hakluyt, Richard (clergyman), 26, 35n, 53, 58–59, 96, 98–102, 108–109, 115–118, 121n, 134, 136, 140, 151, 153, 220, 221n, 223, 278
Hakluyt, Richard (lawyer), 26, 34–35, 102–103
Hall, Joseph, 124–128, 136
Hammond, Henry, 281, 294
Hamor, Ralph, 187–189
Harrington, James, 310, 312–313, 368
Harrison, Thomas, 320
Harsnett, Samuel, 262
Hartlib, Samuel, 310, 312, 315, 324
Harvey, Gabriel, 142n
Harvey, Sir John, 199, 210, 235, 248–249, 251–252, 255, 258, 260–269, 301, 346
Hatcher, William, 322
Hatton, Sir Christopher, 62–63, 108
Hawkes, Henry, 34–35
Hayes, Edward, 25–27, 29–30, 31, 58, 156, 159–162
Hayes, Thomas, 159–162
Healey, John, 169
Heathcote, Caleb, 358–359
Hebraism, 6–7, 32, 70
Hector, 86
Hen, Robert, 338
Henrietta Maria (queen of England), 295
Henry VII (king of England), 46, 92–93, 115n
Henry VIII (king of England), 7n, 8n, 12, 51, 72, 88–89, 91, 93, 98, 103
Hesilrige, Sir Arthur, 308
Hill, Edward, 322
Hinton, Sir Thomas, 255
Hobbes, Thomas: and colonies' civil inferiority to the state, 16, 19, 200, 274–275, 306–307, 309, 311–314; skeptical materialism of, 22, 31–32, 33n, 282, 285, 291, 293, 308, 340, 344; colonial experience of, 22, 275–276, 279; eschatology of, 32; and the doctrine of state unity, 68n, 73–74, 77, 271, 286–287, 307–315, 333, 340, 351–352; and sovereign state theory, 69, 75–76, 307, 339, 342; and rift with constitutional royalists, 276, 283–285, 295, 314–316, 330–332; absolutism of, 284, 314–315, 330, 344, 351; on the sovereign as casuist, 295; on internal and external obligations, 368
Hobbism, 287–289, 307–316, 330–362
Holland. See Netherlands
Hooker, John, 82–89, 96, 103
Hooker, Richard, 276, 278–280, 282–284, 292–294, 296–297, 299, 304, 325, 327
Hopkins, Stephen, 236–237, 242
Hore, Robert, 34
Humanism. See Christian humanism

Imperium. See Sovereignty
Improvements, 301, 310, 323–328, 365
Incorporation, 13, 58, 70–73, 76, 103, 120, 145, 170, 177, 187, 200, 214, 283, 290, 310, 314, 316, 363n
India, 54, 116, 216, 279n, 283, 324
Industry, 9, 38, 42–43, 54, 58, 87, 93, 101–102, 108, 131, 147, 153, 160–162, 178, 181, 189, 195, 201–202, 221, 223, 228, 230, 232–233, 240–242, 244, 269–271, 273, 285, 315, 326. See also Offices
Ingram, Sir Arthur, 202, 206
Ingram, Joseph, 349
Interest, 73, 132, 144, 152, 157, 163, 169, 177, 201, 203–204, 208–209, 211, 215, 229, 231–232, 237, 241, 251–252, 261–

262, 269, 272, 295, 302, 313–314, 318, 337, 340, 358, 366
Internal and external obligations, 367–368
Ireland, 44, 82, 85–86, 89n, 90, 96, 106, 111–113, 116, 132, 171, 206, 211–212, 246, 272, 274n, 309–310
Isabela of Castille (queen of Spain), 46–47, 50, 55, 89
Isaiah, 47
Ishmael, 10n
Israel, 1, 3n, 6–7, 21, 69–70, 77, 79, 85, 95–98, 116, 177, 183, 187–188, 211, 222, 260–261, 312–313
Ius commune, 31
Ius gentium, 31, 44–45n, 161, 240

Jacob, 96–97
Jacob, Abraham, 202, 204–206
Jamaica, 352
James I and VI (king of England and Scotland): as insecure sovereign, 3, 19, 143, 150; and colonial letters patent, 11, 158–159, 166, 169, 318, 353; persuasive efforts on, by Spaniards and Catholics, 51, 111, 137–138, 176–177; and view of Virginia as a royal frontier, 67–68, 158, 189, 194, 219; coronation pageant of, 71–72; and Anglo-Scottish union, 77n, 141, 165, 304n; attack of, on the lotteries, 78, 193–194, 202; succession of, 125, 139, 185; praise for, as male emperor, 126, 128–130; and Anglo-Spanish peace, 149, 152; and distrust of popularity, 150, 159; and view of Virginia as royal revenue source, 150, 190–192, 194, 211; persuasive efforts on, by colonizers and Protestants, 161–165, 170–171, 173–174, 216–234, 254; and the Council of Virginia, 168; and view of Virginia Company as private undertaking, 170; revenue problems of, 180, 190; growing involvement of, in Virginia project, 184, 191–195, 202–205, 210–211; opposition of, to universal monarchy, 189; statism of, 193, 200, 202–205, 214–215, 272, 365; and the dissolution of the Virginia Company, 195, 207, 270; and the Palatinate crisis, 207n, 216, 254; and eased restrictions on Catholics, 213–214; and tobacco contracts, 232; writings of, in defense of the Oaths of Allegiance and Supremacy, 247
James II (king of England): as duke of York, 330, 351–352; and Hobbist approach to colonies, 355–356
Japan, 66
Jeffreys, Herbert, 351–352
Jesus Christ, 3, 13, 15, 48, 53, 59–60, 69–71, 80–81, 197, 221, 229, 241, 261, 294, 296, 310
Johnson, Edward, 363n
Johnson, Francis, 109n
Johnson, Richard, 139n, 186
Johnson, Robert, 139–140, 143–149, 158, 166, 171n, 174, 182, 187, 195, 207, 234, 241, 243
Johnson, Robert (archdeacon of Leicester), 139n
Johnson, Sir Robert, 139n
Johnson, Dr. Samuel, 68n
Jones, Sir William, 217–218
Jonson, Ben, 72, 125, 127–136, 202, 279n, 297
Joseph, 96, 175
Josephus, Titus Flavius, 4n, 7, 85, 97, 211
Joshua, 4, 7, 86, 96, 116, 175
Judah Maccabee, 86
Judgment Day, 3, 5–6, 21, 32, 47, 50, 63, 65, 310. *See also* Eschatology
Justinian (Roman emperor), 31, 45n

Kant, Immanuel, 59, 84n
Kemp, Richard, 37n, 251, 264, 267n, 301, 306, 342
Kent (county in England), 262
Kent Island, 249
King Philip's War, 338–339
King's Bench, 195
Knolles, Richard, 39n, 69
Knox, John, 62, 89

Labor. *See* Industry
Lane, Ralph, 35, 82, 118
Las Casas, Bartolomé de, 20, 49, 94
Latitudinarianism, 361–362
Laud, William, 259, 290, 296, 300
Laudonnière, René Goulaine de, 29n, 100, 102, 116
Law: and the American colonizing endeavor, 2, 8, 14, 16, 25, 28, 30, 43–44, 46, 61–66, 82, 99, 103–106, 110–111, 138–139, 152, 164–165, 173–177, 216, 222, 235–236; and human invention, 2–3, 18, 142, 295; providential basis of, 2–4, 8, 31–32, 34–35, 39, 42–45, 51–52, 328; as conscionable pathways, 2–4, 45–46, 52–55, 57–58, 83, 148, 347; as reliant on casuistry, 4, 33, 56–66, 97, 103–108, 135, 174; natural, 4n, 13, 74, 76, 273, 282–284, 314, 316, 346, 361, 364, 366–367; civil (Roman), 7n, 13, 30–31, 44, 57, 62n, 82, 161, 225, 240, 360; and commonwealth, 11, 69, 73, 75, 80–81, 101, 121–124, 145–146, 167, 213, 229, 262, 300, 317–318, 321, 341, 352–354; divine, 13, 74, 130, 267, 273; as potentially superseded by God's will, 13–14, 20–21; in Virginia, 28, 96, 182–183, 196, 198, 226, 229, 231, 236–238, 240, 257, 273, 281–282, 319, 323–325, 327–328, 356–357; as reimagined in sovereign state theory, 32, 275, 285–288, 307–308, 313–314, 316, 342–344, 356, 363; and skepticism, 36, 277–281, 293–295, 298–299, 306, 325; and antinomianism, 41; common, 76, 213, 256, 361; martial, 96, 182, 213, 233, 242–243; of equity, 213
Lawrence, Richard, 345
Leicester, Robert Dudley, first earl of, 58, 63–64, 113, 116
LeRoy, Louis, 141–142, 145–146, 150n, 203n, 224. *See also* Statecraft literature
Letters patent: for colonization, 5, 11, 14, 30, 62, 72, 78, 92, 106, 115, 117–119, 144, 150, 158–159, 161, 166, 169–171, 173–174, 178, 187, 193, 196–198, 204–205, 221, 226, 247–249, 275, 318–319, 353, 355–356, 364; for monopolies, 58, 156, 191, 204; for corporations, 72, 156
Levant Company, 151
Liberty: of office, 13–14, 230, 265, 317–318; as contingent on commonwealth bonds, 20, 78, 229, 321, 327, 364; and free will, 40–41; as opposed to sinful licentiousness, 41, 230, 239; and unitary statehood, 274, 313; of consent, 303, 319, 341; of trade, 303, 341; of conscience, 304, 331; and military protection, 341
Lincoln's Inn, 225
Lipsius, Justus, 141, 145–146, 188. *See also* Statecraft literature
Locke, John, 351–352, 355, 364
Lodge, Thomas, 7, 97–98, 211
Lok, Michael, 114
London, 34, 37n, 71–72, 78–79, 114, 127, 131, 133, 135, 137, 139–140, 165–168, 178, 182, 191, 220, 228n, 251n, 256, 273, 302, 306–307, 327, 351, 362, 363n; Great Fire of, 292, 331
Louis XIV (king of France), 329–330
Love, 69, 71–72, 82, 99, 102–103, 123,

131–132, 134, 144, 154–155, 177, 179–180, 229, 238–239, 241, 243, 248, 256, 261–262, 264, 266–268, 280, 292, 294, 297–299, 300–301, 305, 334–335, 341, 365. *See also* Agape; Consent
Low Countries. *See* Netherlands
Ludwell, Thomas, 274n, 337

Machiavelli, Niccolò, 148
Madoc (also Madog) ap Owen Gwynedd (Welsh prince), 53–54
Mair, John, 5, 13
Mandeville, Henry Montagu, Viscount, 252–253, 262
Manes, the, 362
Marches (England), 67–68, 166, 189
Maria Anna (infanta of Spain), 190, 216
Marlborough, James Ley, first earl of, 253, 257
Marston, John, 125, 127–136
Martiau, Nicholas, 264
Martin, John, 221–222, 224, 226n
Martyr, Peter, 52, 98
Mary, Queen of Scots (Mary Stuart), 8n, 112
Mary I (queen of England), 14, 51–52, 62, 64, 89, 95
Maryland, 208, 246–251, 253, 259–260, 306, 350
Massachusetts Bay colony, 17n, 21, 61, 235, 245, 355–356, 361
Mathews, Colonel Samuel, 322
Mathews, Samuel, 90, 199, 246, 249–251, 253, 255, 257n, 264–271, 297, 346
Matthew, Sir Toby, 249
Maximilian I (Holy Roman emperor and king of the Romans), 65
Maximilian II (Holy Roman emperor and king of Hungary), 63
Mayflower (ship), 236

Maynwaring, Roger, 262
Mede, Joseph, 55
Mendoza, Don Bernardino de, 28, 112n
Menefie, George, 265
Mercator, Gerard, 66
Merchants, 28, 34, 79, 100, 114, 115n, 139, 144, 151–155, 163, 165, 172, 176, 178–179, 191, 194–195, 200, 202, 207, 209, 219–220, 232, 238, 251n, 252, 254–255, 278, 296, 307, 334–335
Merivale, Herman, 17n
Middlesex, Lionel Cranfield, first earl of, 191–194, 202–206, 208, 211–212, 215, 218, 225, 227, 229–231, 252–253, 257
Milan, 146
Millenarianism. *See* Eschatology
Milton, John, 308
Monck, Christopher, 330
Monopoly, 58, 150, 153–160, 191, 193–194, 205
Montagu, James, 273n
Montaigne, Michel de, 282
Moors, 85, 116, 129, 212, 296–297
More, Henry, 340
More, Thomas, 93, 126, 241
Moryson, Francis, 327–328, 337, 351–352
Moses, 4–5, 7, 76, 97–98, 183, 226
Muscovy Company, 62n, 151, 166

Nansemonds, 305
Nashe, Thomas, 277
National Covenant, 289–291, 298, 300, 305, 309; and Solemn League and Covenant, 291, 325
Native Americans: European abuse of, criticized, 20, 35, 49, 94, 134, 182, 236–238; as still-fallen persons in need of reform, 20, 49, 93, 101, 108, 240, 243–244; violence of, as manifesting God's anger, 25, 36–37, 289, 338–339; illness

of, as evidence of the colonizers' legitimacy, 44; and righteous Christian violence, 52–53; as instantiating moral archetypes, 60; as rebels against their true sovereigns, 101–102, 202, 220; on the Thames, 127–128; and treaties with the colony, 187–188, 341–342; as sinful originators of tobacco, 192; resistance of, as evidence of planters' enlarged liberty, 215–216; debates concerning the extirpation of, 215, 222, 341–342, 346. *See also individual nations*

Natural obedience, 71, 77–78, 224, 227, 229, 257, 300, 303–304, 365

Nedham, Marchamont, 308, 336–337

Nero, 226

Nessom, Jack, 344

Netherlands, 13n, 50–51, 61–63, 102, 106, 112n, 113, 137, 171, 225, 238, 251n, 278, 294, 316–318, 328–329, 331, 333–335, 350

Nevis, 358

Newcastle upon Tyne, William Cavendish, earl of, 287

New England, 9, 21, 22n, 34n, 43–44, 74–75, 191, 194, 217, 224, 235, 241, 245, 258, 262, 274n, 328, 338, 356, 363n. *See also* Massachusetts Bay colony

Newfoundland, 25, 30, 34, 58, 90, 220, 246

New Haven colony, 305

Newport, Christopher, 165–166, 188n

New York, 289, 356

Nicholas, Thomas, 100

Nicolls, Richard, 289–290, 329–330

Noah, 7, 9, 97, 221

Nobility, 28, 60, 84, 88, 105, 116, 127, 130, 133, 135, 144, 147, 175, 185, 200, 246, 284, 296, 302

Northampton, Henry Howard, earl of, 2n, 190

Northumberland, Henry Percy, ninth earl of, 185

Northwest Passage, 42, 66–67, 161

Oaths: of Supremacy, 171, 197, 236; of Allegiance and Supremacy, 246–247, 347, 356; and establishmentarianism, 299, 301, 304–306, 316–319, 324–325; Saxons', 341; Bacon's, 347–349; to post-Revolutionary Virginia's Commonwealth, 354. *See also* Bond of Association; National Covenant

Ockham, William of, 239

Oedipus, 177

Offices, 4, 24n, 32n, 33, 38–39, 49, 59–61, 70–72, 77, 80–81, 83, 101, 107n, 113, 146n, 183, 188n, 212–213, 239–240, 271, 296, 301. God's, 5; sovereign's, 11, 14, 46, 48, 51, 61–67, 95, 187, 189, 193, 226, 229, 259, 262, 265–266, 268, 285; earth's, 44; liberty of, 56, 265; captain's, 85–91, 119; patriarch's, 104; bishop's, 108; statesman's, 142–143, 181; planter's, 201–202, 210–211, 215, 227–228, 230, 237–238, 257; gentleman's, 242n; governor's, 261. *See also* Industry

Opechancanough, 36, 78, 214–216, 222–223, 305

Palatinate, 129, 190, 193n, 200, 207n, 212, 216, 217n, 223; Magonza (Mainz), 243

Panton, Anthony, 267n, 300–301

Papacy, 12, 21, 28, 29n, 31, 44, 47–48, 52, 62n, 65n, 73n, 111, 137, 143, 189, 190n, 207, 210, 212, 214, 223, 227, 234, 238, 245–246, 257, 278

Parker, Henry, 287–288, 308–310, 315–316, 322, 340

Patawomeck, 187
Patriarchs, 1, 19, 211, 221. *See also* Abraham; Jacob; Noah
Patriot prowar coalition, 207n, 216–217, 227, 254
Paul (apostle), 45, 48, 69–71, 78, 197, 229, 238–239, 244, 267n, 285, 365
Paul's Cross, 172, 175
Pearls, 119, 212
Peckham, George, 28–30, 33, 54, 83, 115–116
Peckham, Sir George, 28n, 119
Pembroke, Philip Herbert, fourth earl of, 254
Pembroke, William Herbert, third earl of, 140, 186
Percy, George, 185
Perkins, William, 7, 41n, 56, 60
Persians, 1, 53, 116
Persons, Robert, 137
Peter (apostle), 48
Petition of Right, 212–213, 256, 262
Philip II (king of Spain), 28, 34, 44, 50–51, 62n, 63, 85, 89, 94–95, 112n, 113, 227
Philip III (king of Spain), 137, 149, 165, 171–172, 183
Philip IV (king of Spain), 212
Piercy, Abraham, 199
Pilgrims, 227, 236, 238–239
Piracy, 26, 69, 115, 152–153
Pistole Fee dispute, 353
Planters: as divine calling, 9–10, 20, 211–212; and Virginia's commonwealth, 18–19, 79–81, 196–198, 201–203, 207–210, 214, 216–234, 260–271, 282, 285, 289, 297, 301, 303–304, 334–335, 357–361, 364–367; as abusing office, 20, 49, 82, 214–215; in Virginia's patent, 72–73, 171; in Ireland, 82; at Roanoke, 120–122, 124; and bonds with native Americans, 188–189; as defined by sovereign state theory, 200; liberty of, 210, 215–216, 303–304, 318–323, 325–327; and Stuart statism, 210–211; as defined in confessional terms, 234–235; Puritan critique of, 236–239; worldliness of, defended, 239–246; Catholic critique of, 246–253; support of, by English prowar Anglicans, 253–256; and accusations of undue independence, 257–258, 261; at Providence Island colony, 302; and Bacon's Rebellion, 338–352
Platonic Academy, 277
Platonism, 39, 277, 293, 296–297, 310–313, 339–340
Plymouth (England), 166
Plymouth colony, 21, 237n, 238–239
Pocahontas, 188–189
Popham, Sir Francis, 167
Popham, Sir John, 140, 166–167, 186
Popularity, 150, 251
Portland, Richard Weston, earl of, 253–254, 259–260
Portugal, 31, 46, 62n, 115n, 116, 133, 147, 148n, 153, 216
Pory, John, 196–199, 247n
Potestas absoluta, 12–13
Pott, Francis, 264
Pott, John, 246–247, 264
Povey, Thomas, 288, 310–311, 314, 324, 336, 352
Powhatan, 188
Powhatan people, 36, 120, 187, 198
Pownall, Thomas, 360–362
Presbyterians, 281, 289–290, 333–334, 340–341
Price, Daniel, 174–175
Prince Henry (Henry Frederick, Prince of Wales): as "Protector of Virginia," 1, 3, 33, 74, 137, 170, 183, 186–187, 189

Princess Anne (infanta of Spain), 137
Print culture, 7, 23, 32–33
Projects, 16, 23, 45, 57–59, 61, 65, 83, 102, 124–125, 139n, 140, 143, 147, 152, 153n, 158–164, 168, 173, 176–177, 179, 186, 191–192, 200, 202–209, 219, 229, 232–233, 253, 257–258, 282, 310, 323–324, 352, 365
Prophesyings, 107–108
Protestant Reformation, 5–8, 11, 15, 20, 32–33, 41, 73n, 90n, 109, 293; and sectarianism, 15, 21, 36, 125–126, 209, 226, 236, 242, 302, 325, 327, 330, 334; and separatism, 15, 108, 126, 210, 226–227, 234–238, 240–241, 245–246, 257, 262, 273n, 280; and anti-popery, 21, 43, 227, 234, 247–248, 253, 255, 259, 267n, 306, 308. *See also* Catholic Counter-Reformation
Providence: as prime mover in earthly affairs, 1; as working in concert with human invention and free will, 2–3, 39–41; as necessitating human resolution and industriousness, 3, 39, 42–43; and storms, 25, 34–35, 135; and attacks by native peoples, 25, 36–37, 214, 289, 338–339; as fundamental source of truth, 29–30; and American mysteries, 34–36; and God's earthly instruments, 39; as demanding casuistic interpretation, 56–66; and sovereignty's role in a still-fallen world, 67–68; and the lawfulness of commonwealth, 69–70; and sovereignty and commonwealth's mutual importance, 70–81; and the persona of the captain, 91–106; and the state as steadying agent, 141–149, 151–164, 196–198; and opportunity, 148–149, 162, 320; and Jamestown's ordeal, 168–169, 176–186; and the planter's persona, 201–202, 209–210, 214–216, 235. *See also* Fall, the; God; Offices
Providence Island Company, 302
Providentialism: as intensified in post-Reformation culture, 5, 7–8, 32; and skepticism, 21, 36, 281; and interpreting Columbus's discovery, 46–55; as encouraging interest in colonizing narratives, 96–98; perceived dangers of, 281; as modified by establishmentarians, 291–300, 339; and the Western Design, 311
Public, the: as cognate of republic and commonwealth, 17; inviolability of, 19; in Virginia laws, 19n; in English Civil War, 73, 269; and private men, 107n, 112; and statism, 142, 146, 204; and the Virginia Company, 150–165, 168–170, 173, 196; and Virginia's polity, 198, 208, 217, 230–232, 236, 270, 284, 292, 342; and Pyrrhonian establishmentarianism, 278, 291–293, 295, 325; and the Hobbesian state, 314, 337, 340–341, 355–357
Pufendorf, Samuel von, 368
Purchas, Samuel, 54, 57, 174, 188n, 219, 222–224, 227, 234
Puritans, 36, 37n, 61, 108–109, 128, 131, 216, 235–242, 245–247, 255, 273, 275, 280–281, 283, 287–293, 296, 298, 301–314, 319–322, 338–341, 346, 365
Pym, John, 302, 308, 310
Pyrrhonism, 276–279, 282, 306, 311

Quakers, 281–282, 361
Quarry, Robert, 358
Quicksilver (mercury), 35, 58

Ralegh, Sir Walter, 1–4, 6n, 7–19, 27n, 33, 35, 38, 43, 49, 58–59, 67, 72, 74–77, 82–87, 89–91, 96, 98–100, 102, 108,

109n, 116–125, 127–128, 134, 136, 141–143, 146, 148–149, 168, 180, 185, 211, 223, 278, 290, 353
Randolph, Edward, 356–357
Rastell, John, 92–93
Ratcliffe, John, 177n
Ravis, Thomas, 140, 172
Ray, John, 340
Res nullius, 44
Rex est imperator in regno suo: doctrine of, 12
Rhetoric, 5, 23, 33, 41–42
Ribault, John, 100, 102n
Rich, Sir Nathaniel, 207
Richard (ship), 152, 165
Roanoke, 35, 90, 120–125, 127n, 134, 148–149, 161, 168, 186n, 290
Roe, Sir Thomas, 299
Rolfe, John, 188–189
Romans, 1, 5, 7, 15, 31, 32n, 41, 44, 57, 74, 101, 177, 218, 220n, 226, 293, 313, 340, 360, 362
Rous, Francis, 308
Royal frontier, 67, 69, 85, 92, 95, 112, 161, 166, 194, 219

Saint Christopher, 329
Saint John's College, Cambridge, 7
Saint Paul's Cathedral, 7, 36
Saint Paul's Churchyard, 28, 30, 57, 175
Salamanca School, 57
Salisbury, Robert Cecil, earl of, 26, 128, 139–145, 149–153, 156, 158–170, 172, 174, 177n, 180–181, 183–196, 203, 208–209, 221, 226n, 234, 255, 278–279
Sandford, James, 62–63
Sandys, Sir Edwin, 140, 187, 193–195, 205–208, 212, 215, 217, 226–227, 232, 238, 254, 278

Sandys, George, 212, 254, 274n, 276n, 278, 294, 301–302
Satan, 176, 194, 203, 214, 290, 322
Saxons, 340–341
Saye and Sele, William Fiennes, first Viscount, 302, 308
Scarburgh, Edmund, 282
Scholasticism, 5–6, 8, 11–13, 14n, 17, 20, 30, 32, 39–42, 76–78, 239
Scotland, 5–6, 8n, 12, 14n, 41, 44, 77n, 111–112, 125, 127, 132, 141, 189, 224, 281, 289–291, 296, 304n, 305, 309–310, 334
Scott, Thomas, 240–241
Sea Venture (ship), 35, 176, 181, 236
Selden, John, 6, 213–214, 283
Seneca, 47, 97
Sextus Empiricus, 277, 319
Shaftesbury, Anthony Ashley Cooper, first earl of, 351–352
Shakespeare, William, 35, 235, 267–268
Sherwood, William, 350
Sibthorpe, Robert, 262
Sidney, Philip, 113, 115–117
Silver, 42–43, 51, 119, 129
Sins: schism, 15, 108, 126, 210, 226–227, 235–238, 240–241, 245–246, 257, 262, 280; pride, 26, 50–51, 114, 130–131, 145, 267n, 292; greed, 34, 51, 72, 125, 132, 149, 241, 292, 317, 338; idleness, 44, 93, 102, 126, 148, 161, 181–182, 220, 233, 244, 271; gluttony, 126; usury, 131–133, 203; blasphemy, 244, 292, 308, 322; self-love, 292, 294
Skepticism, 21, 36, 276–283, 285–286, 289–300, 306–308, 311, 319, 323, 343, 367–368. *See also* Platonism; Pyrrhonism
Slavery, 60, 129, 134, 215, 270, 297, 351, 353

Smith, Adam, 17n
Smith, John, 9–10, 14, 44, 90, 93, 169, 181, 187, 191, 217–218, 221, 241–246, 256, 262, 295
Smith, Roger, 246–247
Smith, Sir Thomas, 58, 122
Smythe, Sir Thomas, 139n, 143n, 165–166, 187, 195, 200–201, 206–207, 230, 232–233
Solomon, 147, 177, 223
Somers, Sir George, 35
Somers Island Company, 206
Somers Islands. *See* Bermuda
Song of Solomon, 221
Southampton, Henry Wriothesley, earl of, 140, 187, 193–195, 207, 215, 254
Sovereignty: as special God-given monarchical power, 5–6, 9, 16, 32, 39–40, 64–66, 71–72, 78–79, 99, 128, 130, 153, 159, 187, 210, 227–228, 259; Spanish claims to, 5–6, 48, 50–51, 137, 216, 227; and universal monarchy, 5, 50–51, 278; assertion of, in England, 11–12, 14, 72, 88, 107–108; English claims to, in America, 11–12, 25, 28, 30–31, 53–55, 63–68, 97, 99, 137; as transcending local law and norms, 13–14, 139, 189, 194; as sin-vanquishing puissance, 14, 64, 69, 76–77, 88–89, 91, 103, 128–129, 283; and insecure monarchs, 14–15, 107, 112–125, 150, 165; as a quality of the state, 16, 22, 271, 274–275, 284–285, 307–315, 320–321, 333, 339–341, 344, 351–352, 354–362, 365–367; as distinguishable from the commonwealth, 17, 73–77, 282; as potentially abused power, 51–52, 72, 114, 145, 248, 268, 278; and reliance on casuistry, 56, 61, 107–108; and female rule, 62, 89, 95–96, 98–99,
103, 125–128; and tie of obligation to the public, 161, 180, 196, 224, 229, 250, 285–287, 304, 316–318, 321, 333, 352–353, 364–365; and absolute wills, 213, 262–263; popular, 322, 340, 344; and Dutch and French ascendancy, 328–329, 350
Spanish Armada, 124
Spanish-Habsburg monarchy, 5, 50–51, 65, 129, 167, 200, 217, 227–278, 278
Spanish match, the, 190, 207n, 213, 216, 254
Spenser, Edmund, 142n
Stamp Act, 353, 359–360, 362
Stamp Act Congress, 359
Stanley, Hans, 359–360, 362
Star Chamber, 249
Statecraft literature, 141–142, 145–149, 150n, 155, 158, 167, 170, 188, 217, 224. *See also* Bodin, Jean; Botero, Giovanni; LeRoy, Louis; Lipsius, Justus
States: as vital steadying agents in the providential order, 11, 13, 20, 51, 74–75, 104, 117, 138–139, 141–148, 151–153, 160, 164, 167, 173, 180–181, 188–189, 270–272, 278, 283, 291, 293–294, 317–318, 325; medieval, 13; sovereign (or unitary), 16, 22–23, 30, 68n, 75–76, 271, 273–275, 286–288, 307–316, 328–329, 332–333, 336–337, 340–341, 350–352, 354–355, 357–368; as status applied to colonies, 17, 151, 157, 177, 179, 181, 183, 185, 196, 199, 208, 216, 218, 227, 273, 333, 356; petty, 38, 256; reason (or interest) of, as moral rationale, 200, 202–206, 212–215, 227, 236, 250, 253, 257, 260, 262, 268, 272, 300
Statism, 139n, 142–143, 179–181, 187–188, 191, 202–203, 212–213, 227, 256–258, 262, 266, 272, 287, 300, 356–357

Strabo, 318
Strachey, William, 20–21, 41, 54, 96, 181–182, 185–187, 191, 232n, 236–240, 243–244
Strahan, William, 360
Suffolk, Thomas Howard, first earl of, 140
Susquehannocks, 37, 338
Sutcliffe, Matthew, 43–44
Swallowfield, 122–123
Symonds, William, 20, 34, 174

Taxes, 19n, 154, 162–163, 192–193, 200–202, 204–205, 213, 231, 325, 336, 359, 361
Thirty Years War, 200, 207n, 212, 216, 223, 317
Three Estates of Christendom, 91
Throckmorton plot, 111
Tobacco, 192, 194–195, 200, 202–206, 209, 211, 232, 234–235, 247, 254, 257, 260, 263, 302, 305, 324, 333, 336. *See also* Contracts
Treaties, 187–188; Anglo-Spanish (1604), 143, 149, 152, 165, 188; native American, 215, 341–342; Virginia's Articles of Surrender (1652), 321, 365; Dover (1670), 335; Paris (1763), 360
Trithemius, Johannes, 65
Turks, 15, 39, 46, 53, 116, 241
Tuscaroras, 120
Twisse, William, 55

Universal history, 1–5, 7, 33
Universal monarchy, 5–6, 15, 44, 50–51, 101, 146, 189, 227, 278, 316, 329–330
Utie, John, 249

Vane, Sir Henry, the younger, 308
Vattel, Emer de, 355, 364, 367–368
Venice, 170, 184, 225, 247n

Virginia: church of, 15–16, 80–81, 182, 197, 235, 251n, 260–261, 305–307, 322–323, 326, 361–362; General Assembly of, 17–18, 196–201, 210, 232–233, 252–254, 259, 263–264, 274n, 281–282, 302–303, 305, 319–322, 325–327, 337, 342, 356, 365; governor of, 72, 90, 96, 119–122, 170–171, 178, 181, 196–197, 200, 248–249, 251–253, 255, 260–266, 269, 275, 279, 288–289, 300–301, 319–320, 322, 324, 330, 332–333, 335, 339, 342, 345–346, 362; Council of State of, 166, 168–170, 178, 221, 244, 247–254, 258–271, 301, 320, 322, 334–335, 339, 343, 346, 348, 365
Virginia Company (also London Company of Virginia): and attempts to anchor colonization to Parliament, 18–19, 158–164, 193; incorporation of, 72–73, 170; and vision of Virginia as a commonwealth-in-the-making, 78–81, 179–183, 196–198, 206, 216, 218, 223–224, 227–232; debates within, concerning justifying colonization, 138–139, 173–174; as the state in microcosm, 139, 147, 151–152, 155–158, 160–164, 174–178; Robert Cecil, earl of Salisbury's leadership of, 139–140, 165–166; and the ignominy of private colonization, 140–141, 143–145, 151–153, 157, 160–161; and Salisbury's death, 150, 183–189; as a source of royal revenue, 150, 163, 165, 190–195; as distinct from trading companies, 151; as a body poised between king and Parliament, 159, 161–162; as a means of encouraging greater sovereign commitment to Virginia, 164–165; criticism of, 176–177; lottery for, 178–179, 193, 200, 202, 206; quo warranto proceedings against, 195, 199, 270; and

tobacco, 203-207; and Virginia's public, 208-209, 230-232; and the moral persona of the planter, 214-232; and defense of strict authority, 242-245; and the Mandeville commission's plan to overhaul, 252; and anti-Spanish, prowar coalition, 254-255; planned revival of, by the Dorset commission, 259; attempted revival of, by Puritan parliamentarians, 273, 301-304, 318

Vitoria, Francisco de, 20, 56-57, 317

Waad, Sir William, 167
Wales, 53, 116, 192, 287, 309
Walsingham, Sir Francis, 26, 28, 34-35, 61, 100, 109-111, 113, 151, 156
Warren, William, 264
Warwick, Robert Rich, second earl of, 207, 308
Waterhouse, Edward, 214-217, 222-223
Waymouth, George, 67, 255n
Wedderburn, Robert, 8n
West, Francis, 255
West, John, 255
Western Design, 311
Weyanocks, 305
Whately, Thomas, 359-360, 362-364, 367
Whigs, 358-359, 361
Whitaker, Alexander, 174
White, Andrew, 248
White, John, 120-124, 127n
White, Thomas, 331
Whitgift, John, 108
William, prince of Orange (William the Silent), 51, 111
Williams, John, 213-214, 225, 227, 253
Williamson, Sir Joseph, 331
Wilson, Thomas, 41-42, 92
Windebank, Sir Francis, 259-260

Winthrop, John, 61, 235, 245
Wits, the, 297
Wollaston, William, 355, 364
Wolstenholme, Sir John, 238, 254-255, 259, 269
Wood, Abraham, 343-344
World: redemption of, 2-3, 10, 19, 39, 42, 70, 77, 129, 261, 284; as alive with providential signs, 3; sinful mutability of, 3, 38, 45, 74, 84, 91, 103, 123, 129, 139, 145-146, 284, 313; as approaching Judgment Day, 4, 47, 63, 65, 104-105, 312; as composed of ethereal and elemental spheres, 38-39, 42-43, 58; as propelled by callings, 56, 60; Platonic view of, 293, 312
Worldliness: as congruent with Providence, 2-8, 21, 33, 70, 107, 142; as sinfulness, 15, 40, 45, 52, 69, 104, 110-111, 144, 202-203, 216, 256, 282; Puritan critique of, 108, 235-239, 293; Anglican defenses of, 239-246, 257, 292-293; and skepticism, 277-278, 282, 295
Worsley, Benjamin, 288, 310-314, 319-320, 321n, 328-329, 332, 351-352
Wotton, Sir Henry, 184n, 225
Wyatt, Sir Francis, 201-202, 221
Wyatt, George, 221
Wycliffe, John, 70

Yeardley, Sir George, 196-197, 225n
Yelverton, Sir Henry, 204-205
Yong, Thomas, 249-251, 255

Zouche, Edward la, eleventh Baron Zouche, 214, 224, 255
Zouche, John, 264-265
Zouche, Sir John, 254-255, 259, 263-264
Zúñiga, Don Pedro de, 2n, 137-138, 164-167, 170-172, 174, 189

www.ingramcontent.com/pod-product-compliance
Lightning Source LLC
Chambersburg PA
CBHW031413230426
43668CB00007B/294